To Chelsea Ted

[signature]

25/11/10

omantic Ballet in Paris

The Romantic Ballet in Paris

Marie Taglioni and Paul Taglioni in *La Sylphide*. Oil-painting by G. Lepaulle, 1832.

The Romantic Ballet in Paris

Ivor Guest

DANCE BOOKS

First published in 2008 by Dance Books Ltd
The Old Bakery
4 Lenten Street
Alton
Hampshire GU34 1HG

Copyright © 2008 Ivor Guest
ISBN: 978 1 85273 119 9

A CIP catalogue record is available for this book from the British Library

Printed and bound in Great Britain by The Charlesworth Group

Contents

Illustrations

Frontispiece: Marie Taglioni and Paul Taglioni in *La Sylphide.* Oil-painting by
   G. Lepaulle, 1832. (Musée des Arts Décoratifs, Paris; Photo Laurent-
   Sully Jaulmes; tous droits réservés.)

Foreword

Some forty years have passed since I completed the original typescript of *The Romantic Ballet in Paris*, which was published in 1966. A second edition followed in 1980, but this contained only a few very minor corrections. At that point I had no intention of investigating in depth the half-century that preceded the starting-point of that book (1820), for I had become so absorbed in the Romantic period that I indulged myself by investigating more fully, and writing up, the life histories of some of the great dance personalities of that period. I had in fact already written biographies of two such figures – Fanny Cerrito, for long the darling of London, and a tragically fated and lesser-known English dancer, Clara Webster And no sooner were they disposed of when two more important figures of the ballet of that time were to claim my attention: Fanny Elssler, the first top-flight ballerina to conquer the Americans; and a little later, Jules Perrot, the master-choreographer of the Romantic ballet and the predominant creator of that classic of the Romantic ballet, *Giselle*.

Then, at the suggestion of my publisher, David Leonard, I took on the task of editing the dance writings of the great French poet and novelist, Théophile Gautier, a work that was to be published first in English in my translation, and then in French, using, of course, Gautier's own text, along with my introduction and commentary. Following this, I took a breather to write a book that had nothing to do with the dance, and it was during the five years I spent on this task that the idea took root in my mind that I should take my detailed study of the ballet of the Paris Opéra back another half-century to the historic moment when the ballet had begun to separate itself from the opera, telling the story of its development from 1770, which for historical reasons offered a tidy starting-point, to 1820, when the story had already been taken up in the earlier editions of this book.

Returning to my roots, as one might say, I discovered to my delight that the archival material on the Paris Opéra for the period on which I was now to embark was rich beyond my expectations, as, too, were many of the contemporary reviews of the ballets presented at the Opéra. It soon became clear that two volumes, not one as I had originally envisaged, would be needed not only to do justice to the subject, but also to give the study of those years a balance when placed alongside the already published studies on the Romantic period and the Second Empire. *The Ballet of the Enlightenment* and *Ballet under Napoleon* were respectively published in 1996 and 2002, and no sooner had I handed the manuscript of the latter work to my publisher than I began working on a revised edition of *The Romantic Ballet in Paris*. During the forty years that had passed since I had put the finishing touches to that book, I had from time to time enriched my knowledge of that period by further reading and research, notably in stumbling upon the archives of the Royal Household under Louis XVIII and Charles X, and by expanding my coverage of the press of that time. In consequence, the text that follows has been enriched by a wealth of new material that cried out to be shared with my readers.

The task still remains for me to revise what will be the last volume of the series, although it was, in fact, the first to be written and published: *The Ballet of the Second Empire*. This, too, needs expanding on account of later research, and will contain a considerable amount of new material arising from my own research. I find that I have embarked on this task with no diminution of the enthusiasm that gripped me in my younger days, and even perhaps with an increased awareness of the historical period that has come with a lifetime of reading and research.

I have, of course, many people to thank for assisting me in various ways during the course of the preparation of this new edition of *The Romantic Ballet in Paris*. In particular I owe a great debt of gratitude to the librarians and staff of the Bibliothèque-Musée de l'Opéra, the Bibliothèque Nationale de France, the Bibliothèque Nationale (Musique), the Bibliothèque de l'Arsenal and the Archives Nationales in Paris, and those of the British Museum and the London Library, in whose peaceful reading rooms I have spent so many happy and productive hours throughout more than half a century to conduct the research that lies behind this volume and its companions. Among the many individuals who have assisted me in various ways during the course of the very thorough revision this book has undergone, I have to thank in particular Marie-Françoise Christout, who has answered so many queries over the years, Jean-Louis Tamvaco (editor of that jewel of scandal and behind-the-scenes activities at the Opéra in the late-1830s, *Les Cancans de l'Opéra*), Dr Richard Ralph, who read the type-script with his customary exemplary care and expertise, and my editor Dr Rod Cuff who lent his skilled eye and computer expertise in preparing the text for publication. And, most warmly of all, I have to thank my wife Ann, who has borne with me through all the travail that this book has entailed in the course of its three editions, listening to each chapter being read and saving me from many a gaffe.

Introductions to the first edition

By Dame Ninette De Valois, D.B.E.

A lively gallery of dancers and an exciting museum of ballets fill the pages of this book. France and the Romantic ballet: it is soon made clear that here lay the core of the whole matter – in the heart of Paris.

We are shown the development from the pure classicism of the eighteenth century; we see it with the French school in full command of the situation. Although the changes can be felt and the various new influences at work are stressed, yet every now and then great masters of the preceding period, such as Auguste Vestris, appear for brief moments, and this reminds us of their busy background work in the school.

Humbly – through what we read about here – we take this opportunity to pay our homage to the great school of French ballet, lest we forget that it stands as the undisputed fountain-head of ballet history.

Such enchanting Gautier moments! A particularly good one occurs when he was confronted, after the dancer's absence for a period of time, once more with the return of his much admired Taglioni. She returns to dance a role that – alas! – a lady of not such great distinction had just performed, and who had nevertheless captured the heart, head and pen of the poet-critic. (However, wherever Gautier and Taglioni may be, they are no doubt aware that critics do not change.)

I would like to read more of the wit that sprang from the pen of a critic named Albéric Second. His description of Grahn: "a genius for diplomacy in its most subtle, intangible and ethereal form. She is Metternich and Talleyrand in one: she is the whole Congress of Vienna in petticoats."

Taglioni is dealt with brilliantly. Her character, her dancing and her life appear to be aloof – altogether on another plane from the rest of her profession. Again the wisdom of Saint-Léon's remarks about her, some thirty years after her first triumph, tally with much that has been said today about certain great stars of the immediate past.

Time is even found (lively time) for Lola Montez. She moves swiftly and violently through a few pages, just as swiftly and violently as she lived through the whole of her astonishing life. This stormy, vulgar and impetuous creature was "born in the army barracks at Limerick, where her father was serving as a junior officer". That little streak of illumination conjures up a possible Spanish–Irish background, and there were many of such racial mixtures in the South of Ireland at that time. Such a combination could indeed account for Lola Montez. "From what country does she really come? That is the question," murmurs the puzzled, perturbed Gautier.

Interesting again is the disclosure that the popularity of the male dancer was suffering an eclipse, both with the public and with the critics. I have a suspicion, though, that the critics were the more to blame. Yet the book historically proves that the actual development of the ballet was in the hands of the male dancers. Jules Perrot is a male dancer and choreographer of particular interest in this book: a *demi-caractère* dancer who actually suffered the displeasure of Taglioni for daring to be the recipient of the greater ovation.

Paris of those days, with its rich heritage of the ballet to give to the world, could be (and was) extremely generous when dealing with the question of guest artists. Nor did the great French artists of the preceding classical era remain as sulky recluses in their classrooms among their pupils, shaking their heads in disapproval of what was happening in the theatre. Touching is the account of the great Auguste Vestris as an old man standing in the wings watching Lucile Grahn's performance of *La Sylphide* – and at the end murmuring, as he embraced her, "You are an angel". Yet how far removed was the Romantic ballet from the days of his own and his father's triumphs. Again it is as well to remember that Auguste gave a pupil, the young Bournonville, to Denmark for the full flowering of the Royal Danish Ballet.

If I appear to reflect on the lighter side of this work, it is only to emphasise one important and pleasant fact: here is a book of historical interest and immense research that always manages to entertain as well as instruct.

Humour abounds: in the light of today could any inclusion be more amusing, yet terse and subtle than the following?

Her name was Caroline Forster, and she possessed a quality that the novelist Taxile Delord thought so unusual for a dancer that he included the following dialogue in one of his stories, *La Lune de miel:*

"I prefer Forster. Do you know Forster?"

"What is Forster?"

"She is a *coryphée* at the Opéra, an Englishwoman who can dance. It is extraordinary."

It is indeed extraordinary that today Paris expects, as a matter of course, a stout bevy of Forsters on the other side of the Channel.

The notes on *Giselle* are of immense interest. It would seem that some particularly apt passages of both mime and story have been lost of a period of a hundred and twenty-five years. We should note that the very first

Bathilde was the English "Miss Forster" and that in this particular role Gautier honoured her with a poem in which he sang her praises.

It is a convention to mourn the slow fade-out of this wonderful period of French ballet, yet in so doing I feel that what followed was underestimated. Seen in proper perspective the immediate advent of Delibes, with the scores of *La Source, Coppélia* and *Sylvia,* marked a milestone in the development of music for the ballet. Not long afterwards Tchaikowsky was writing for the ballet in Russia – Tchaikowsky who regarded Delibes with reverence and admiration.

Grateful should we be for this monumental work, for it allows us to search according to taste and inclination. The appendix dealing with the names of all principal dancers at the Paris Opéra between 1820 and 1847, and the full list of ballets first performed between the same dates paints a comprehensive picture of the Paris Opéra's immense contribution to the Romantic era of ballet: some research into the music scores of forgotten ballet *divertissements* is surely indicated.

Perhaps one day Mr Guest will find time to single out Webster,[1] Forster, Plunkett and Smithson[2] – sturdy English names that, with the exception of the first, managed to make an impression in Paris during the years when that city was the Mecca of the ballet world. A little book on the lives of our modest nineteenth-century pioneers deserves someone's attention. Again, what about the why and the wherefore of Louise and Nathalie Fijan, two ladies of the Paris Opéra corps who took the resounding Scottish name of Fitzjames?

NOTES

1. I had in fact already written a biography of Clara Webster some years before, under the title of *Victorian Ballet-girl* (London, 1957).
2. I think Dame Ninette must be referring to the actress, Harriet Smithson, who was the great love of Berlioz.

By Lillian Moore (for the American edition)

The magic of the Romantic ballet is timeless. Its essential spirit transcends the limits of any one particular and place. Its symbol, in dancing, is flight: the aerial flight of the ballerina as sylphide, or dryad, or wili: the ballerina as a supernatural being, the visible incarnation of man's idealism and aspiration. In the midst of our materialistic civilisation, the Romantic spirit is alive. It lies at the heart of our current cultural explosion.

The Romantic Movement, as Ivor Guest so clearly points out, was a revolutionary one, an escape from the constricting bonds of classicism in all the arts. In dancing, it found its most typical expression in the *ballet blanc*, in the winged, weightless, enchanted creatures of the "white ballet" which, after more than a century, can still hypnotise an audience and transport it to a very different and less grimly terrifying world. It was the Swedish–Italian ballerina Marie Taglioni, the embodiment of diaphanous lightness and grace, who personified this spiritual aspect of Romantic ballet. She transmuted the arduous technique of the classical dance into a poetic language. When she soared across the stage in an endless arc, or rose effortlessly on the tips of her toes, she created an image which lingered in the air with the compelling power of a dream.

The explosive vitality of this nineteenth-century artistic revolution was responsible for another aspect of Romantic ballet, diametrically opposed to Taglioni's ethereality: the exotic, vigorous, warmly human style exemplified by Fanny Elssler. Her art, too, provided an escape from everyday reality, for it transported her spectators to distant, more glamorous localities. She brought them the languor of the east, the exhilarating rhythms of Slavic peoples, and above all, the colour and passion of Spain. Taglioni's dancing lifted the spirit; Elssler's dazzled the eyes and intoxicated the senses.

It was Paris which saw the birth of the Romantic ballet, on a chilly March night in 1832, when Taglioni first danced *La Sylphide*. Although its triumph was unprecedented and it was to mark an epoch in the history of theatrical dancing, this ballet did not come as a sudden revelation. Rather, it was the culmination of a long period of restless preparation, the crystallisation, in nearly flawless form, of influences which had been in the air for more than a decade. Before *La Sylphide*, with its setting in the Scottish highlands, there had been other ballets, such as the *Tyrolienne* in Rossini's opera *Guillaume Tell*, which exploited local colour; there had even been other ballets which had evoked the mystery of the supernatural, such as the haunting scene of the renegade nuns in Meyerbeer's *Robert le Diable*. Other dancers had risen on their toes, but none had done it with consummate artistry as Taglioni; no one had made *pointe* work an integral part of the choreographic drama instead of a meaningless acrobatic feat.

It was Paris which first saw Elssler's glorious *Cachucha*, the single dance which contained the concentrated essence of all that was brilliant, voluptuous and enticing in the dancing of the time. Introduced at the Opéra in the divertissement of Jean Coralli's ballet *Le Diable boiteux* in 1836, the *Cachucha* became Elssler's personal trademark. With this ravishing dance she not only conquered the discriminating balletomanes of Paris, she not only subjugated audiences from Rome to Moscow to New Orleans, but she paved the way for a whole succession of character ballets (*La Tarentule*, *La Gitana*, *Napoli* and *Flower Festival in Genzano*, to name a few) which were among the highest achievements of the Romantic ballet.

It was Paris which saw the première of *Giselle*, the work which united in the finest balance the two contrasted aspects of Romanticism. If *La Sylphide* was the prototype, *Giselle* was the epitome of the Romantic ballet, and it has survived into our time, not as a quaint museum piece, but as the very touchstone of the dancer's art. The theme of *Giselle* was inspired by one poet, Heinrich Heine, and adapted to the stage by another, Théophile Gautier. No matter that its final form was planned by Henri Vernoy de Saint-Georges, who was little more than an able craftsman: the poetic germ flowered and is still bearing its fruit.

In Carlotta Grisi, the first Giselle, were united the aerial fragility of Taglioni and the theatrical flair of Elssler. Ever since 1841, when Grisi created the part, ballerinas have attempted to emulate her in encompassing the widest possible range of classical dancing, from the delicately lyrical to the intensely dramatic. In artists like Margot Fonteyn, Alicia Alonso and Galina Ulanova, Giselle lives and breathes and dances today.

La Sylphide, *Le Diable boiteux*, *Giselle* – all of them live in their original freshness and excitement in the pages of this book. The story of this richly creative period has never before been told in all its depth and complexity. It has been touched upon with tantalising brevity (and often with considerable inaccuracy) in various histories of theatrical dancing, but it has not previously been described and analysed with the profound knowledge and fervent understanding Mr Guest has brought to his very congenial subject. With the imaginative persistence of a detective, and the meticulous accuracy of a mathematician, he has ferreted out the tiniest forgotten details and fitted them together like a gigantic jig-saw puzzle, to give us a clear, panoramic picture of the times.

This is not only the story of great collaborations and history-making events. Mr Guest gives us the human side of ballet while he describes its artistic course. With the deft touch of an artist, he shows us how a handful of sensitive, daring, determined, capricious, inspired people shaped the trends. He takes us behind the scenes to work and suffer with the dancers, to glimpse their struggles and disappointments as well as their public successes.

We "assist", in the French sense of the term, at the final performances of the great pre-Romantic dancer-mime Emilie Bigottini. Old Auguste Vestris, spry survivor of an earlier time, leaves his imprint on the new era. Jules Perrot, almost the only conqueror of the ridiculous prejudice against male dancers which was prevalent then, bounces through this chronicle with the lively resilience of a rubber-ball. The wild little American, Augusta Maywood, flashes across its pages like a fiery meteor.

From the initial stirrings of the Romantic impulse, Mr Guest traces the nineteenth-century ballet through its gradual development to the time of its greatest glory. There, before the commencement of its inevitable corruption and decline, he closes this book. (The later, sadder history has already been told in his *Ballet of the Second Empire*.) This is a story of exploration, of discovery, of creation and fulfilment, in an art which returns for enrichment to this period of fertility and abundance.

1

The Triumph of Romanticism

On the evening of 23 July 1827, a young dancer stepped on to the gas-lit stage of the Paris Opéra to confront a French audience for the first time. Her name was Marie Taglioni, and the sensation she created was so immediate that if any moment can be selected to mark the beginning of the golden age of Romantic ballet, it must be this.

To her contemporaries her coming was nothing less than a revelation. For, as a critic of the time explained, before her momentous appearance

> the sceptre of the dance was entrusted to the hands, or rather to the legs, of Messieurs Paul and Albert. Theirs was a dance of the springboard and the public square, and the daughters of Terpsichore (old style) were fashioned in their image. No elegance, no taste; frightful pirouettes, horrible efforts of muscle and calf, legs ungracefully stretched, stiff and raised to the level of the eyes or the chin the whole evening long; *tours de force*, the *grand écart*, the perilous leap. All the male dancers were brought up in this school and built on this model, and the female dancers dislocated themselves by imitating those muscular and semaphoric exercises. Then Marie Taglioni appeared and started a revolution against the dominance of the pirouette, but it was a revolution gently accomplished through the irresistible power of grace, perfection and beauty in the art. Marie Taglioni loosened the legs, softened the muscles, gradually changed by her example the tasteless routine and unstylish attitudes, revealed the art of seductive poses and correct and harmonious lines, and established the dual kingdom of grace and strength, that most beautiful and most pleasing and rarest of kingdoms. Marie Taglioni dethroned Albert and Paul, and opened the door for Perrot and his school. And if male dancing no longer charms and attracts today – [this critic is writing in 1840] – it is because there is no sylphide, no magic-winged fairy capable of performing a similar miracle and doing something that is supportable in a male dancer. As for the *danseuses*, they take pride in following in the footsteps of Taglioni and gathering up some of the grace and lightness that [she] has let drop. [1]

While this passage conveys the suddenness of the impact created by Taglioni's first appearance in Paris, the renaissance of ballet that was to follow cannot be explained so simply. Romantic ballet did not flourish in isolation. It was in fact only one facet of a burgeoning movement of revival, which breathed new life into every form of art in the early part of the nineteenth century. The spirit of Romanticism that animated this revival was a symptom of a world caught in a process of violent change. Its roots were to be found in the previous century, when voices of discontent and doubt were raised to question principles that had long been accepted in many branches of human activity; but it was the turmoil of the French Revolution and the Napoleonic Wars that prepared the soil for it to flourish. That vast cataclysm and the Industrial Revolution, which began almost simultaneously, wrought so radical a change in human society that there could be no return to the past. The social and political structure had been brutally and irreparably overturned; new social concepts of liberty and equality were gaining acceptance; and consolidating its new wealth and power was a growing middle class that belonged to the modern world of the nineteenth century, a class brought up with ideas and values very different from those which the aristocratic ruling class of the old régime had professed.

Romanticism was essentially a revolutionary movement. It gave rise to new conceptions of art in opposition to the rigid observance of form demanded by the academic schools that had dominated artistic activity in the eighteenth century. That had been the Age of Reason, when artists had tended to look outwards and to concentrate on achieving a classical perfection in their works, often at the expense of feeling and inner meaning. The clarion call of the Romantics was liberation: liberation from the bonds of classical restraint. In an outburst of revolt a new generation of artists, most of whom had come to maturity in an unstable world beset by revolution and war, turned inwards on themselves; they sought more personal means of expression and allowed their imagination and their inspiration to soar freely into the headiest heights of lyricism. They did not discard form, but they bent it to a more subservient rôle: in their hands it became the artist's servant, not his master.

In its origins Romanticism was a literary movement, and every art form it touched was to be strongly influenced, in one way or another, by literary sources. Its first stirrings were felt in Germany, and it was to describe the personal writing found in Northern literature, as opposed to the objective approach of the classical school which then dominated the literature of France, that Madame de Staël in 1810 used the term 'Romanticism' in her book *De l'Allemagne*. Early in the nineteenth century, works of German and English literature were becoming increasingly popular in France. The writings of Shakespeare, Byron, Goethe and Schiller made a strong impression on younger artists, who were becoming ever more dissatisfied with threadbare conventions and were seeking new and freer forms of expression. They revealed sources of inspiration that in a few years were to impregnate Romantic art in all its forms. Among these were the occult and the supernatural, which held a special appeal for the Romantics, who were fascinated by the mysterious dark corners of the mind. These proved to be a wonderfully fertile source, inspiring the dream-worlds conjured up by Hoffmann and La Motte Fouqué in their *märchen* and Charles Nodier in his fantasies. More particularly, they inspired the theme that was to recur over and over again in Romantic ballet – from *La Sylphide* to *Swan Lake* – of man's pursuit of the unattainable, the infinite, exemplified in the hopeless love of a mortal for a spirit. Complementary to this element of mystery that became such a dominant feature of Romantic art was a preoccupation with the exotic. The early meaning of the word 'romantic' – conveying an emotional response to a scene of wild natural beauty – foreshadowed the Romantic artists' obsession with local colour, their evocation of strange landscapes and the customs and manners of distant peoples, and, at a further remove, their interest in the past. The vogue for Gothic art and the advances made in oriental studies were also significant by-products of Romanticism.

At the heart of the Romantic revival was a heightened sensitivity that imbued the works of the new school with added warmth and emotional impact. Working at a fever pitch of enthusiasm, the Romantics were excitedly aware of the momentous significance of the movement they were initiating. This was how it appeared to Théophile Gautier, one of the most militant of their number:

> It was a movement akin to the Renaissance. A sap of new life was circulating with impetuous force. Everything was sprouting, blossoming, bursting out all at once... The air was intoxicating. We were mad with lyricism and art. It seemed as if the great lost secret had been discovered, as indeed was true, for we had discovered a long-lost poetry. [2]

In France, Romanticism triumphed in the twenty years following the end of the Napoleonic Wars in 1815. Its victory embraced every form of art, and hardly a year passed without the appearance of some masterwork that in one way or another advanced its cause. In 1819 Géricault's great picture *The Raft of the Medusa* was hailed for the intense energy with which the artist had conveyed the exhaustion and agony of the shipwrecked sailors. The following year Lamartine's *Méditations* revealed a style of poetry that spoke, lyrically and seemingly artlessly, from the heart. In 1826 Victor Hugo launched his violent manifesto of Romantic drama in his Preface to *Cromwell*, condemning the absurdities of classical tragedy, which still monopolised the stage of the Théâtre Français. *Cromwell* was never performed, but Hugo's triumph came in 1830, when his drama *Hernani* was produced. The 'battle of *Hernani*' was to become the most glorious memory of the Romantics. Several hundred fervent admirers turned up to applaud the work of their acknowledged leader and to drown the hissing of the champions of the old classical order. Conspicuous in their midst was Gautier himself, wearing his hair to his shoulders and resplendent in a rose-coloured waistcoat. The same year also witnessed the first public hearing of Berlioz's *Symphonie fantastique*, a full-blooded expression of the composer's anguished passion for the English actress Harriet Smithson, and a year later Meyerbeer's opera *Robert le Diable* was produced, a study in the Gothic and the ghostly that was directly to affect the development of ballet. All these works had one feature in common: their creators had disregarded meaningless conventions and produced works that throbbed with energy and vitality and spoke directly to the senses of the spectator, the listener or the reader.

It was in this stimulating climate that ballet, too, was to be revitalised. For some four decades the ballet of the Opéra had prospered under the inspired and firm leadership of Pierre Gardel, who himself contributed the greater part of the repertory, most notably with a series of highly successful ballets based on classical legend. Even before he retired, the vogue for neo-classicism was on the wane, and not long after his retirement in 1827 the time became ripe for the revolution that was to launch ballet – not only in Paris, but wherever it had taken root – on a new course, stimulated by the ideas and sources of Romanticism.

A factor of no small importance in the evolution of ballet at this time was the change that had taken place in the make-up of the theatre-going public. One effect of the Revolution had been to attract to the theatre more and more people from the poorer classes. Filling the cheaper parts of the houses in ever-increasing numbers were clerks and shop assistants, soldiers and workers, who lacked artistic pretensions and cultural background, and were unimpressed by academic conventions and classical allusions. Entertainment was what they demanded, and their staple fare was provided by the melodramas and vaudevilles staged at the popular theatres of the boulevards such as the Porte-Saint-Martin. Elements of Romanticism, albeit crudely realised, such as historical settings, local colour, ghosts and spirits were a common feature of these spectacularly mounted productions some time before they infiltrated into ballet. Also, several of these theatres supported ballet companies of their own, that of the Porte-Saint-Martin in particular attaining quite a reputable standard. Indeed, a number of dancers and choreographers who were to play a part in shaping the Romantic ballet worked on these popular stages, where the light comedy ballet which Jean Dauberval and Jean-Baptiste Blache had made their speciality retained its popularity. Here there were no traditional conventions to be observed, no effects to be scorned as being below the dignity of art; here a more broadly based public demanded to be entertained and amused. Though the Romantic ballet flowered most brilliantly at the Opéra, some of its most productive seeds were sown at the Porte-Saint Martin.

In 1830 the Revolution of the 'Three Glorious Days' swept away the Bourbon monarchy that had been restored after the defeat of Napoleon, and one of the consequences was the removal of the Opéra from Court control. The appointment of an independent Director accelerated the process of reform in an institution that had become noted for its inertia. Already Marie Taglioni had shown how a freer, more graceful style enhanced the meaning of the dance, a revelation that in itself was an innovation in the Romantic spirit. After 1830, however, ballet was to be completely transformed by Romanticism. Responding to the taste of a public that was becoming increasingly middle-class in its composition, choreographers, composers, scenarists and designers all submitted to the influence of Romantic ideas. In one way or another they sought their inspiration from Romantic sources and brought to their work that warmth and inner depth which, in parallel spheres, illumined the poetry of Byron and Hugo, the music of Berlioz and Liszt, and the canvases of Delacroix and Martin. Ballet thus found itself almost ideally suited to express the moods of Romanticism, its mystery and its magic, its exoticism and its colour – an awareness that received a most significant recognition when Théophile Gautier, one of the leading poets of the Romantic school, turned to writing ballet scenarios.

In its consequences, Filippo Taglioni's ballet *La Sylphide* (1832) was as momentous a landmark in the chronicles of Romantic art as '*The Raft of the Medusa*' and *Hernani*. The prototype of the *ballet blanc*, it pointed to the new direction that ballet was to take under the impulse of Romanticism. Much of Romantic art was inspired by Northern sources, and ballet was to be no exception. The fusion of a technique and discipline, which were fundamentally Latin, with the moonlit mysticism and the poignant sadness of German Romanticism – the formula so triumphantly applied in *La Sylphide* – produced the most exalted form of Romantic ballet. One need not take too seriously the charges of plagiarism made against Filippo Taglioni, even the accusation that the theme of *La Sylphide* was borrowed from an earlier ballet. The significance of *La Sylphide* was more than a matter of theme; it was to be found in its scenic atmosphere and dance style, and in the rapport between the choreographer and the ballerina, who on occasion came to be regarded as much an author of a ballet as the choreographer and the composer. The vision of Marie Taglioni as the Sylphide has haunted choreographers ever since. Hers was truly a creative triumph, for she was the first to show how the *pointes* could be used to further an artistic end, to convey an illusion of weightlessness and impalpability, and to express an ethereal spirituality that was essentially Romantic. This formula, with variations, was repeated so effectively that the gods and heroes of antiquity, so favoured by Gardel and his generation, found themselves virtually banished from the ballet stage and their place taken by sylphides, peris, naiads, wilis and other wraiths of fairy tale and folklore. No one understood the Romantic revelation better than Gautier, and the most successful application of this formula was undoubtedly *Giselle* (1841), which marked his first essay as a ballet scenarist, and for which he drew his inspiration from Slavonic legend.

This, the shaded mysterious aspect of Romantic ballet, was to be complemented by a sunlit side, the brilliance of which was as sharp as the moonlight was muted. Local colour, in which Romantic artists indulged their yearning for the exotic, became a common feature of ballet almost simultaneously with the discovery of the formula of *La Sylphide,* and reached its peak in the astonishing triumph of Fanny Elssler's *Cachucha.* In the imagination of the ballet-going public, Elssler personified this passionate, earthy aspect of Romanticism just as Taglioni stood for its spiritual side. Few rival ballerinas have been more dissimilar in physique, temperament and style than these two, the sylphide and the cachucha dancer, or, to use Gautier's brilliantly apt metaphor, the Christian dancer and the pagan. This contrast underlined the dualism that underlay so much of Romantic art and was to be found in a most marked form in Romantic ballet.

The energy of Romantic ballet was to spend itself all too quickly. Its most fertile period barely lasted beyond the mid-century, but its legacy has endured not only in the few ballets from that period that have been handed down to this day, but in the added poetic dimension and the new aesthetic foundation, which were the lasting benefits that Romanticism brought to the art of ballet.

* * * * * * *

Ballet was still young, and a somewhat minor art, in 1820, when this chronicle begins. In that year one of the Opera's oldest *habitués* could be heard boasting how his father had almost swooned with excitement when Camargo had performed an *entrechat six* and, on another occasion, had wanted to clasp Marie Sallé in his arms as she darted into the wings breathless from a ravishing *passacaille.* The son had been born too late to see these two rival ballerinas, whose complementary talents Voltaire had paused to describe in a poem, but his own experience extended back for sixty years. He had seen the majesty of Gaétan Vestris and the brilliance of his son Auguste; he had applauded the Gardel brothers, Dauberval, Madeleine Guimard and Anne Heinel when their talents were at their peak; and he had witnessed the demise of the old opera-ballet, with its loosely connected *entrées* concocted half of dancing and half of singing, and the introduction on the Opéra stage of the *ballet d'action*.

The development of the *ballet d'action* in the latter half of the eighteenth century ended the subservience of ballet to opera and established it as an independent theatre art. Jean-Georges Noverre, the great champion of the *ballet d'action,* was engaged at the Opéra for only a short period, but his ideas quickly gained general acceptance, although it would fall to others to continue his work. After his departure, the ballet of the Paris Opéra came under the domination of the Gardels. Maximilien, the elder brother, died young at the outset of a brilliant career, but Pierre, who succeeded him, was to impose his rule throughout the years of revolution and war. His most successful productions – *Télémaque* and *Psyché,* both created in 1790 – were founded on legends of antiquity and were very popular during the reign of Napoleon, who encouraged a revival of classical art to emphasise the analogy between the new French Empire and Augustan Rome.

With the fall of Napoleon, the mythological ballet went rapidly out of favour. Gardel was then growing old, and although he was still to produce several more ballets and innumerable opera *divertissements,* it was the second *maître de ballet,* Louis Milon, who reflected the changing tastes more accurately. Milon was particularly adept at devising ballets on sentimental themes. His most popular work was *Nina* (1813), which gave Emilie Bigottini, the Opéra's brilliant dramatic ballerina, one of her most touching rôles.

The adoption of sentimental themes and the dramatic genius of Bigottini gave ballet a greater expressiveness some time before it became affected with the spirit of Romanticism, but this expressiveness did not go very deep. Few would then have seriously claimed ballet to be more than a mimed representation of something that could be better accomplished with the use of words, interspersed with charming dances. When the golden age came, not many years later, ballet acquired a prestige and a dignity that it had not known before. It discovered how to fulfil a public need by revealing the unattainable for which people craved as an escape from a world grey with their cares and anxieties. Ballet offered a beguiling form of illusion that was quite novel, a development that was achieved in each of its component parts – dramatic content, music, scenic design, and above all choreography and dance style – with a cumulative effect that transformed it into a potent expression of the Romantic ideal.

The appearance of the scenarist as one of a ballet's authors was a significant development. It occurred for the first time, so far as Paris was concerned, in 1827, shortly after Marie Taglioni's début at the Opéra, when the dramatist Eugène Scribe anonymously contributed the scenario of *La Somnambule*. Before then the choreographer himself had been responsible, at least outwardly, for working out the action, sometimes taking a play, novel or *opéra-comique* and translating it more or less literally into a ballet. Of the ten new ballets presented between 1820 and the middle of 1827, no fewer than eight were directly derived from a literary source: *Les Pages du duc de Vendôme* (1820), *Le Page inconstant* (1823) and *Le Sicilien* (1827) from plays; *Clari* (1820) and *Aline* (1823) from novels; and *Cendrillon* (1823), *Zémire et Azor* (1824) and *Astolphe et Joconde* (1827) from *opéras-comiques*.

With the appearance of the scenarist as a co-author in his own right – and in most ballets from 1827 onwards, the functions of scenarist and choreographer were separated – this literary derivation became much less direct, and the source often provided an inspiration rather than a model to be slavishly imitated. Only a vague similarity, for instance, can be discerned between the plots of *La Sylphide* (1832) and the work that inspired it, Charles Nodier's novel *Trilby*, while other ballets were only indebted to their literary source for an idea: thus, Shakespeare provided the germ for *La Tempête* (1834), La Fontaine for *La Volière* (1838), Cervantes for *La Gipsy* (1839), Cazotte for *Le Diable amoureux* (1840), and Heine for *Giselle* (1841). Examples of a more direct adaptation were much rarer after the arrival of the scenarist, only about a fifth of the ballets produced during the twenty years between *La Somnambule* (1827) and *Ozaï* (1847) – in fact six out of twenty-nine – being so derived: *Manon Lescaut* (1830) and *Le Diable boiteux* (1836), which were based on novels; *L'Orgie* (1831), which was adapted from a comic opera; and *La Jolie Fille de Gand* (1842), *Le Diable à quatre* (1845) and *Betty* (1846), which were versions of plays.

The men of letters who devoted their talents to writing scenarios made significant contributions to the development of Romantic ballet. Scribe and Saint-Georges displayed the craft of the professional dramatist, while Gautier brought the infinitely more precious gift of a poet's vision. Scribe had already gained the reputation of being the most successful and prolific playwright in Paris when he wrote his first ballet. Most of this experience had been gained in writing for the middle-class audiences of the boulevard theatres, and just as he understood and catered for the tastes of this public, so he was quick to appraise the audiences of the Opéra. His ballets formed only a very small part of his vast output, but to him is due the credit for establishing the scenarist as one of the authors of a ballet. His colleague, Saint-Georges, was a lesser figure, but he too knew how to hold the attention of the public of his time. Gautier, however, was in a class apart. He was a poet, and a Romantic poet at that, with an imagination that soared freely in the realms of fantasy; yet he was at the same time a working journalist, who, through his experience as a dramatic critic, acquired a profound understanding of ballet.

The scenarios that these writers produced were full of situations, settings and ideas that reflected the Romantic outlook of the time. A sharpened sense of the historical past, a feeling for local colour, and the creation of an atmosphere of mystery and reverie were novel developments in ballet, and while choreographer, musician and designer all made important contributions to the general illusion on the stage, it was the scenarist with his literary background who usually initiated the process. The emotions of the spectators were stirred, their eyes dazzled and enchanted as never before, as ballet in the Romantic period under the guidance of the scenarists drew on an unparalleled proliferation of sources and a wide variety of settings.

A sense of history was a highly developed trait in Romantic art and literature. In *Alfred le Grand* (1822) Aumer had chosen a historical setting – indeed, one that was typically Romantic in its choice of period – some years before the appearance of the literary scenarist. But it was only when Scribe evoked the old-world graces of the eighteenth century in *Manon Lescaut* (1830) that any serious attempt was made to recreate the historical past in a ballet at the Opéra. Later there came a whole series of productions that transported the audience not only into times long past but to other lands: *La Révolte au sérail* (1833) to Spain during the Moorish wars, *La Gipsy* (1839) to Edinburgh in the reign of Charles II, *Lady Henriette* (1844) to the England of Queen Anne, *Paquita* (1846) to Spain during the Peninsular War, *Betty* (1846) to England again, this time under Charles I, and *Ozaï* (1847) to France and the South Seas in the reign of Louis XVI.

Often, when the past was not evoked, scenarists would inject local colour by dictating an exotic setting, which the designer would realise in his sets and the choreographer reflect by composing national or pseudo-national dances. From the 1830s Spanish dances were highly popular in Paris, and Spain was the setting of *L'Orgie* (1831) and *Le Diable boiteux* (1836). *Nathalie* (1832) unfolded against a Swiss background, *La Tarentule* (1839) was an Italian tale, *La Jolie Fille de Gand* (1842) was set in the Netherlands, and the action of *Le Diable à quatre* (1845) took place in Poland. Farther afield, primitive America was evoked in *Les Mohicans* (1837), China in *La Chatte métamorphosée en femme* (1837), San Domingo in *La Volière* (1838), and Egypt in *La Péri* (1843).

Historical and local colour made up only one side of the Romantic ballet. Infinitely more far-reaching in its consequences was the influence on ballet of German Romanticism, which introduced the supernatural element and inspired the theme of mortal man's quest for the unattainable, personified by a fairy spirit such as a sylphide, wili or peri. With the improved technique of stage lighting, it was perhaps inevitable that the element of moonlit mystery that imbued the paintings of Casper David Friedrich and other Romantic artists from beyond the Rhine should sooner or later find its way into the ballet – but few could have foreseen the vast development that was to stem from *La Sylphide* (1832). The moonlit forest of its second act owed much to the eerie scene that Henri Duponchel and the designer Ciceri had between them devised for the episode of the spectral nuns in Meyerbeer's opera *Robert le Diable* the year before. The crux of the formula, however, which was to be repeated in *Giselle* (1841) and many other ballets produced outside the Paris Opéra, lay in the theme, which was ideally suited to the genius of Marie Taglioni, whose style became a model and an inspiration for so many ballerinas of the Romantic period.

Moonlight was the outward symbol of the atmosphere of poetic mystery, conjured up in plot, choreography, design and music, that was the great discovery of Romantic ballet. As Gautier put it, with a certain exaggeration, in an article written in 1844:

> *La Sylphide* opened the door to a whole new era in choreography, and through it Romanticism entered the realm of Terpsichore. After *La Sylphide, Les Filets de Vulcain* and *Flore et Zéphire* were no longer possible. The Opéra was given over to gnomes, ondines, salamanders, elves, nixes, wilis, peris, and all such strange, mysterious creatures who lend themselves so wonderfully to the fantasies of the ballet-master. The twelve mansions of marble and gold of the Olympians were relegated to the dust of the scenery store, and artists were commissioned to produce only romantic forests and valleys lit by that pretty German moon of Heinrich Heine's ballads. Pink tights remained pink, for there can be no choreography without tights, and all that was changed was the satin ballet slipper for the Greek *cothurna*. This new genre brought in its wake a great abuse of white gauze, tulle and tarlatan, and colours that dissolved into mist by means of transparent skirts. White became almost the only colour to be used. [3]

As Romanticism began to exert its beguiling magic on the developing art of ballet, the musical content was to be affected no less than the choice of theme, the décor and costumes, and the dance style itself. Although composers had written for the dance since the distant time of the court ballets, the introduction of the *ballet d'action* as a discrete theatrical form, in which passages of mimed action and dance alternated, presented composers with a new challenge. Such productions usually required an hour and more of music, the composition and arranging of which presented a different kind of challenge to that set by an opera libretto. For while the composer of an opera was recognised as the prime creator of his work, the musician commissioned to provide the score for a ballet played a more modest role, being subservient to the choreographer. It was from the choreographer that he received the synopsis of the action to which the score had to be adjusted, and the choreographer who would be in charge of the production. The relationship between the two was thus not an equal partnership, although it was eased somewhat by the fact that the choreographer was himself generally well versed in music: Gardel, in particular, was a violinist of concert standard, who had even appeared on stage to play the violin to accompany a minuet in his ballet, *La Dansomanie*.

This difference in the musician's status was partly accounted for by the ballet-master being regarded as the primary author of the ballet; for until the appearance of the literary scenarist in the late 1820s, he was the author of the scenario as well as being the choreographer of the dances and the producer of the stage action. This was in strong contrast to the situation in opera, where the composer enjoyed the status of primary author. When Cherubini agreed to compose the score for Gardel's major ballet, *Achille à Scyros*, it may well have been Gardel who required that he insert a number of passages from other composers, including two from the symphonies of Haydn. Nevertheless, as well as Cherubini, several other distinguished composers – Méhul, Catel, Kreutzer and Persuis – were happy to write for Gardel, although none of them considered such an assignment to be anything more than a minor commission.

Among the requirements made of them were likely to be demands to introduce at certain points in the action a borrowed theme from some well-known aria or song to illustrate a passage of mime that might otherwise mystify the spectator – usually because of the inherent inability of mime to convey information that could be explained by spoken or sung words, such as an event that had taken place in the past. Such interpolations, known as *airs parlants*, would be selected by the choreographer from familiar operatic arias or popular songs, the words of which, it was hoped, would come to the spectator's mind and help to illuminate the direction that the action had taken.

This aid to understanding had certainly come into use in the early years of the century, if not before then, although it does not seem to have been noticed in reviews until the latter part of Gardel's long reign as ballet-master. An early example, but almost certainly not the first, was the use of a song or aria entitled *Daignez écouter* in Louis Duport's *Figaro* (1806), and later examples of *airs parlants* were heard in Venua's score for Didelot's *Flore et Zéphire* (1815) and Schneitzhoeffer's score for Albert's *Le Séducteur du village*

(1818). These were specific examples, but many scores of the early years of the century contained passages borrowed from other composers. [4]

It has to be borne in mind that the division between dance and mime was much more clear-cut than it would later become. For the most part, the dances were an adjunct to the narrative, usually being interspersed at relevant points in the action – for example, a festivity that could logically be fitted into the action – or else to close the ballet with a final *divertissement.*

It was, therefore, perhaps not surprising that this rather minor category in the art of composition attracted little comment from musicians, and in fact the first illuminating account of it appeared as late as 1822, from the pen of Castil-Blaze, writing under his pseudonym of X.X.X. after seeing Aumer's ballet, *Alfred le Grand:*

> A ballet with a score that is original – that is to say composed specially for it – is generally not remarkable from the musical point of view. A few more or less trivial *contredanses*, some resounding marches without design or taste, and a sort of orchestrated 'tum-ti-tum' to accompany the mime that is all too often no more than a succession of nonsensical accompaniments – such are the elements that go to make up a ballet score. True, the composer is allowed to introduce his work with a fine overture, but he must take care not to exceed the licence thus granted him.
>
> There are several reasons for ballet music not being good music. The first is the uniformity of the groups, tempi and movements. A musician can compose three or four excellent *contredanses* in succession, but to produce forty, each distinguishable from the others, with well-chosen and novel motifs and a quality that is original and fresh is beyond even the most prolific. For since dancers are always doing the same thing, they require the music to be always cut to the same measure. So we are presented with pieces in 2/4 and 6/8, either graceful or strongly rhythmed, very symmetrically constructed, with rests on the dominant and their faithful minors, mighty chords for the mighty *entrechats*, and a final *crescendo* for a rush down to the footlights. The musician is the first to yield to the dread influence of uniformity, his melodies betraying his boredom and his anxiety to get his score finished.
>
> It may be pointed out that skilled composers have written music for the ballet, which consequently must be as good as their operas. Certainly Méhul and Cherubini, who worked for Gardel and Milon, were able to produce good work. That is undoubtedly true, but such fine work was lost on the ballets that inspired them. The composer has found a naive and simple formula, a pompous or naive motif, a phrase of generous melancholy, a martial passage, proud and marked – all such motifs being

remarkable for their elegance and originality. But do you really believe that a composer will pay such little regard for his reputation to squander the fruits of his genius... in a choreographic jumble? No, he will reserve all his riches for opera scores, where they will be put to better advantage, and he will serve the dancer with his second-best ideas and commonplace things that a musician can toss off at any time without invoking Apollo... Every ballet is preceded by an overture, but has any of these been performed in concert? And have the dance melodies in ballets ever been regarded on the same level as melodies in operas?

Our old ballets such as *Le Jugement de Pâris*, *Psyché* and *Persée et Andromède* were composed on well-known melodies. The composer, who could choose from the rich repertoires of symphonists and dramatic composers, selected only what was excellent. For where else can one find more elegant *contredanses* than in the andantes and finales of Haydn and the rondos of Steibelt and Viotti, or action music more dramatic and strongly conceived than the overture to *Démophon*, the magnificent *agitato* in F minor from a violin duet by Viotti, the air from *Ariodant*, which Méhul himself placed in *Persée et Andromède*, and countless other examples I could cite? If the audience grew tired of the insipid monotony of the dancing, the orchestra was there to console them and counsel patience by letting them listen to some very good music admirably performed. A ballet was a concert full of interest in which all the musical genres combined to please by a seductive variety. Lovers of the new style applauded Mozart and Beethoven. Those who retained their veneration for our old melodies sometimes discovered them anew, but in an embellished form, presented in a richer harmony and with better taste. I leave it to the reader to imagine the effect that would be produced by certain pieces by Rossini should they ever be artistically woven into our ballets. Furthermore, operatic arias, even when shorn of their words, make a valuable impression on the memory that can clarify the enigmatic language of mime, while a new and unoriginal score will not stir the imagination enough for its meaning to be felt, and so its meaning, if it had any, is lost on the bemused listener.

Let me give just one example of the power of well-known melodies and the clarification that they bring to the mute exchanges of pantomime.

[In *Le Jugement de Pâris*,] Paris, when joining in the gambolling of the shepherds on Mount Ida, dances a *pas* to the melody, *Enfant chéri des dames*. This *pas*, the most brilliant of his rôle, must be committed to [the spectator's] memory, and the melody, fashioned as a rondo and repeated twice, makes an impression. In the second act, Discord casts the fatal apple, to which each of the three goddesses lays claim. To put an end to their rivalry, Jupiter... conceives the idea of making them appear before a simple mortal, who will present the apple to the most beautiful, in his eyes, of the three. In a ballet no one speaks. Nothing is easier to express in gesture than love, hatred or despair, but how does one convey that the adjudicator chosen by the Overlord of the Gods is none other than the shepherd of Mount Ida? Mime is of no avail, and a written banner, the usual resource of the boulevard theatres, would be hissed at the Opéra. But the melody of a song played on a single instrument triumphs over every obstacle. The flautist has only to play a passage from the melody of *Enfant chéri des dames*, and everything becomes clear. Paris comes into one's mind, and one remembers having seen him before, dancing among the shepherds.[5]

* * * * * * *

The appearance of the scenarist in the person of Eugène Scribe towards the end of the 1820s presaged a general improvement in the quality of ballet music, largely because the younger generation of composers was beginning to regard writing for the ballet as an area of expertise, but the use of the *air parlant* continued until the late 1840s. The arrival of the scenarist as an additional contributor to a ballet's gestation also gave rise to a new vision of ballet as the joint product of a team made up of choreographer, scenarist and composer, who between them produced a unified *oeuvre*. The choreographer may have remained *primus inter pares*, but the composer was now gaining respect as a specialist in the genre of writing for the dance, and no longer a musical drudge.

The earliest of the Romantic school of French ballet composers was the convivial Jean-Madeleine Schneitzhoeffer, or, as he was familiarly known at the Opéra, 'Chênecerf,' which was jokingly said to be the closest that a Parisian tongue could get to pronouncing his name. He laughed at this as much as anyone, and was said to have had his visiting cards printed, 'Schneitzhoeffer, pronounced Bertrand'. Schneitzhoeffer had shown great promise in his youth but lacked the application to make the most of his opportunities. His father was an oboe player, and his mother, before her marriage, had been engaged to an obscure young soldier called Bernadotte, who later was to become one of Napoleon's Marshals and King of Sweden. Their son obtained the post of one of the second chorus-masters at the Opéra, where he discovered his avocation, composing the scores for six ballets – *Proserpine* (1818), *Le Séducteur du village* (1818), *Zémire et Azor* (1824), *Mars et Vénus* (1826), *La Sylphide* (1832) and *La Tempête* (1834) – and collaborated in a seventh, *Le Sicilien* (1827). His claim to fame rested largely on his score for *La Sylphide*, which showed a feeling for atmosphere that made a positive contribution towards the effect of the whole work, and, musically, was the precursor of Adam's score for *Giselle*. Ill health cut short his career, and he composed no more ballet music in the last eighteen years of his life, which sadly closed, in 1852, in an asylum in Montmartre.

Schneitzhoeffer's superior at the Opéra was for a time Ferdinand Hérold, a brilliant young musician who had studied under Méhul, Kreutzer and Louis Adam and won the Prix de Rome in 1812. His family and the Adams were closely linked: both were of Alsatian origin, and Louis Adam, the father of Adolphe Adam, was godfather to young Hérold. It was Hérold's abiding ambition to compose opera, and just before he became chorus-master at the Opéra, his comic opera *Marie* had been successfully performed at the Opéra-Comique. His hopes of being commissioned to write a grand opera, however, were never to be fulfilled – his compositions for the Opéra being limited to ballet scores: *Astolphe et Joconde* (1827), *La Somnambule* (1827), *Lydie* (1828), a thorough reworking of *La Fille mal gardée* (1828), and *La Belle au bois dormant* (1829). In these scores he revealed not only an elegant style of composition and a varied use of rhythm, but also an unusual understanding of dramatic action. It was his conscious aim to make his music echo the sentiments being expressed on the stage. The 'German melancholy' that was noticed in his scores was appropriately Romantic in spirit, but he could also enliven his music with passages of Italian brilliance that were particularly effective in comic scenes. He devoted great care to his ballet music, reducing the insertion of borrowed airs in order to make a score that was essentially original. How much he scorned the old practice of accompanying mime passages with well-known melodies can be gleaned from a remark he made to a friend: 'Here's a theme that M. — wants me to use. I have already given it as much time as it takes to write a whole act of a ballet, and I still have not finished it.'[9] Hérold died of consumption early in 1833, at the age of 42, and while he never achieved his life's ambition to write a grand opera, he was to be remembered for three very successful *opéras-comiques* – *Marie*, *Zampa* and *Le Pré-aux-clercs* – and for his contribution to the development of ballet music. 'In this type of music,' acknowledged no less an authority than Adolphe Adam, 'Hérold had no rival. All those who write music for the dance will seek to do it as well as he. But none will be able to do it better.'[6]

Jacques Halévy and Ambroise Thomas, who were to make their names as two of the great operatic composers of the century, both composed ballets for the Opéra in the early years of their careers. Halévy was chorus-master at the Opéra from 1829 to 1840, and at the outset of his engagement, some five years before the production of his grand opera *La Juive*, he wrote an outstanding score for Aumer's *Manon Lescaut* (1830). Ambroise Thomas composed part of the music for one of Fanny Elssler's triumphs, *La Gipsy* (1839), and shortly afterwards wrote a complete ballet score for *Betty*

(1846). These early compositions did not exhaust Thomas's interest in ballet; over forty years later, in 1889, by which time his operas *Hamlet* and *Mignon* had been acknowledged as masterpieces, he turned his attention once more to the dance and composed the music for Joseph Hansen's *La Tempête*.

Halévy and Thomas were both brilliant young musicians who passed from ballet to higher spheres of composition, but there were other composers in the 1830s and 1840s who were content to specialise in the field of ballet. The most prolific were Adolphe Adam and Casimir Gide, who, by a coincidence, had collaborated in writing the music for an English pantomime, *La Chatte blanche*, produced at the Nouveautés on the eve of the 1830 Revolution.

The lesser of these composers was Gide, whose music was first heard at the Opéra in 1835, when he wrote the ballet music for *La Tentation*. This he followed with four ballets – *Le Diable boiteux* (1836), *La Volière* (1838), *La Tarentule* (1839), and *Ozaï* (1847) – before abandoning his musical career to take over the family bookselling business.

It was in the work of Adolphe Adam that Romantic ballet music reached its peak. The scores that he wrote for the Opéra span two decades and represent about two-thirds of his total ballet compositions: *La Fille du Danube* (1836), *Les Mohicans* (1837), *Giselle* (1841), *La Jolie Fille de Gand* (1842), *Le Diable à quatre* (1845), *Griseldis* (1848), the lion's share in *La Filleule des fées* (1849), *Orfa* (1852) and *Le Corsaire* (1856). For him, composing for the dance was a labour of love, with ideas coming into his head so fast that he could produce a fine score in an astonishingly short time. He also wrote several successful *opéras-comiques*, including *Si j'étais roi* and *Le Postillon de Longjumeau*, but it was as a ballet composer that he achieved, in the words of the critic Fiorentino,

> a complete, dazzling and unchallengeable supremacy. There he was the absolute master, and it can be said that he knew no rivals. It was in the ballet most particularly that he revealed his great poetic feeling, and the delightful scores of *Giselle* and *La Fille du Danube* are there to prove it. Moreover, he brought to this type of music all the flexibility of writing and all the diversity of style that he had shown elsewhere. The score of *Orfa* has a character of real grandeur, that of *Le Corsaire* is powerfully dramatic, while *Le Diable à quatre* contains the vivacity of comedy and, if I can put it this way, that amusing loquaciousness which explains the success of several of his comic operas. [7]

* * * * * *

At the same time that scenarists were introducing Romantic themes and situations and composers were making ballet music more colourful and more descriptive, the stage designer was adding a contribution of prime importance. The trend towards greater scenic illusion and spectacle that was such a marked feature of the Romantic theatre had first made itself felt, not at the Opéra, but in the more popular theatres such as the Porte-Saint-Martin, where melodramas were staged with a multiplicity of sets and effects. New techniques of scenery construction, involving greater use of *praticables*, or 'built pieces', the introduction of effects produced by the recently invented diorama by lighting partly translucent cloths from front and back, and the introduction of gas-lighting, which made possible the gradual variation of illumination and did not soil the scenery, all made possible effects of breathtaking illusion which would have been inconceivable a generation before. Not only was no expense spared on the spectacle at these boulevard theatres, but the melodramas provided designers with countless opportunities to indulge in Romantic fancies. Gothic ruins set in wild mysterious landscapes, thick forests, storms and heavy seas, and reasonably faithful reconstructions of distant lands were commonplace on these stages in the 1820s. At last the Opéra could ignore this trend no longer, and in April 1827 a special committee was established to supervise the scenic department. The dominant figure on this committee was Henri Duponchel, a man who, for his wide knowledge of architecture and his appreciation of the value of spectacle, was to be hailed as 'the Alexander of the *mise en scène'*.

Duponchel's influence was felt for more than twenty years. He supervised the scenic department throughout the managements of Emile Lubbert and Dr Véron, whom he succeeded as Director in 1835. After relinquishing that position in 1840, he remained attached to the Opéra in an administrative capacity until 1843, and then, after a gap of four years, became Director again, this time in partnership with Nestor Roqueplan, from 1847 to 1849. Outworn traditions were never allowed to stand in his way, and one of these he lost no time in discarding. Before 1829 it was customary at the Opéra to lower the great curtain only once during a performance, between the opera and the ballet, and never between the acts. The scenery, in those days, whether representing an exterior or an interior, was lightly constructed on a relatively simple plan, with a series of wings on either side converging on each other as they neared the backcloth to give an illusion of perspective. Scene changes were mostly carried out in full view of the audience. The lack of natural effect was apparently accepted as a convention at the Opéra, despite the reforms that had taken place in the popular theatres. In 1829, when Rossini's opera *Guillaume Tell* went into production, Duponchel authorised the designer Ciceri to construct his sets in a more complex, though still mobile, manner, and from then on the curtain was lowered between each act. In this manner the vogue was launched for elaborate, realistic scenery that became the accepted style for French grand opera and ballet throughout the rest of the century and beyond.

The scene designer in Romantic times was an artist-craftsman working primarily and almost exclusively for the theatre. His craft was essentially his profession, and, as the century wore on, many of the busiest scene designers went into partnership and founded thriving firms. Scene designing and construction then became an organised profession, with studios such as those of Séchan and Diéterle, Philastre and Cambon, Despléchin and Lavastre providing the French theatre for several generations with impressive, realistic scenery, even if by the end of the century their style had degenerated into a conventional naturalism.

The great master of French scene design in the early nineteenth century was Pierre Ciceri. He was engaged at the Opéra in 1809 as 'painter of landscape scenery', and the following year succeeded his father-in-law Jean-Baptiste Isabey as *décorateur-en-chef* at the age of 28. Working also for the popular theatres, he transformed the art of stage decoration by making it an integral and important part of a production. He was soon introducing Romantic ideas into the scenery he designed for the Opéra, most notably in *Alfred le Grand* (1822), but it was not until Duponchel began to supervise new productions that he was given full scope to exercise his imagination. One of Duponchel's first acts was to send Ciceri to Milan in 1828 to study Italian techniques and seek ideas for the volcano scene that was to be the climax of *La Muette de Portici.* Ciceri's greatest triumph came three years later, with the cloister scene in *Robert le Diable.* Although it was Duponchel who conceived the original idea for this historic set, it was Ciceri who realised it. Its effect was shattering. 'It is perhaps a blasphemy,' wrote Gautier, 'but for us the nuns' cloister in *Robert le Diable,* with its magic, its effectiveness, and its vague tremor of the unknown, was on an equal level with the music, which was enhanced by the mysterious depth of its arcades.' [8] This Romantic air of mystery was to be captured again by Ciceri in the last acts of *La Sylphide* and *Giselle. La Sylphide* was in fact directly inspired by *Robert le Diable,* and its magnificent forest scene had not lost its power twenty years later when Fiorentino declared that it should be preserved for posterity in a museum.

The reforms that Ciceri initiated in the art of stage design were not confined to scenes such as these, but were evident also in the wide range of settings he was called upon to produce for works evoking historical and local colour. Playwrights, opera librettists and ballet scenarists were all setting works in past epochs and far-off lands, and Ciceri and his disciples such as Séchan, Cambon and Despléchin took up the challenge, reproducing these periods and settings on the stage with a more scrupulous attention to historical and geographical detail.

Most intimately connected with the dancers in this world of illusion were the costume designers, and under them the band of seamstresses and cobblers who prepared the costumes and footwear in which the dancers transformed themselves into their fanciful characters to the delight of the public. These anonymous workers dutifully gave form to the designers' sketches, making them up with no less care than that which Ciceri lavished on his sets. In the hierarchy of those who contributed behind the scenes to the operas and ballets, the costume designer occupied a modest position. While the scenery designers were now honoured with a mention on the bills and in the printed scenarios, the costume designers were the anonymous poor relations. But their work was no less essential a part of the whole moving picture that was presented for the delight of the public. Only a century later were they to be given a belated recognition in Carlos Fischer's monumental study of the costumes of the Opéra, and it is only right that their names should be recorded here: Auguste Garnerey (1819–24), who owed his engagement to the Duchesse de Berry; Alexandre Fragonard (1824–25), a nephew of the famous painter in the rococo style; Hippolyte Lecomte (1825–30); Eugène Lami, who worked only casually, contributing little more than designs of military uniforms and a number of authentic-looking Scottish costumes for *La Sylphide*; and Paul Lormier (1832–55), a less original artist perhaps, but one who contributed his vision to the great spectacles of opera and ballet in the heyday of Romanticism.

NOTES

1. *Constitutionnel*, 27 July 1840. The review was signed 'A'.
2. Gautier, *Histoire du Romanticisme*, 2.
3. *Presse*, 1 July 1844 (Guest, *Gautier*, 142).
4. Guest, *Ballet under Napoleon*, 216, 411, 457.
5. *Journal des débats*, 28 September 1822.
6. Pougin, *Hérold*, 78.
7. *Moniteur*, 11 May 1856.
8. Quoted in Séchan, *Souvenirs*, 8.

2

The Dancers' World

However cataclysmic the invasion of Romanticism was in the fields of literature, music and the graphic arts, the resurgence of ballet under its beguiling influence might never have been possible had not choreographers, teachers and dancers coincidentally been themselves swept along by new influences to shape their art afresh. In the first two decades of the century there had been a remarkable strengthening of technique, including the introduction of a rudimentary form of *pointe* work. In previous years many dancers were probably unaware of the clash of ideas that was beginning to resonate in the wider world of culture, but by 1830 this struggle was to come belligerently into the open at the Comédie Française on the first night of Victor Hugo's drama *Hernani*, when rival factions in the audience even came to blows.

Change was in the air, but where the dance would fit into this revolution of ideas was still uncertain. Indeed, how was the dance to react to the movement that was inspiring a new era not only in drama, but in the broader field of literature and the pictorial arts? The art of stage design was already being affected, even at the Opéra, with injections of *couleur locale* in the scenery; but how was the art of the classical dance to respond, and indeed could it respond, to the heady new philosophy that was taking root in the wider artistic world? And precisely how was the art of ballet to align itself with this strange new philosophy, when it was by definition classical? It was becoming increasingly evident that somehow the dance had to follow the Romantic banner if the art was to survive, and there was already an awareness that the answer might lie in remoulding the style of the dancers. At first, however, there was some resistance to early attempts at departing from the strict classical pattern, as the following brief comment, made more than eight years before the Battle of *Hernani*, reveals:

> Classical methods are still in force at the Opéra. The most correct *enchaînements* still express love, and *entrechats* are reserved for passages of eloquence. The Romantic aerial style has made its appearance there now and then, but if the public has forgiven certain legs of genius their few errors, it usually applauds, as hitherto, only purity of method and correctness of style.[1]

In fact, much was already being done within the Opéra to prepare the ground. Gradually, improved methods of teaching were setting new standards by honing and expanding the technique and, what was more significant, glossing it with a new, poetic style. According to Léopold Adice, Albert and Filippo Taglioni were to devise a syllabus, which preserved much of the old methods that clearly remained fundamental, but introduced new *enchaînements* of gruelling length which progressively developed the lungs, gave the legs a new-found mastery, and prepared the body for movements of a difficulty and complexity that to an earlier generation would have been considered impossible.

In 1820 Carlo Blasis, a young Italian dancer who had made a successful début at the Opéra three years earlier, brought out a remarkable book called the *Traité élémentaire, théorique et pratique de l'art de la danse*, in which he codified the technique of ballet as it then existed and laid the foundations of many of the great teaching methods of later times. During the half-century that preceded the full flowering of the Romantic ballet in the 1830s and 1840s, great advances were made in technique. As Blasis himself wrote:

> Among our ancient artists, those beautiful *tems* [*sic*] of perpendicularity and equilibrium, those elegant attitudes and enchanting arabesques were unknown. That energetic execution, that multiplicity of steps, that variety of *enchaînements* and pirouettes were not then in practice; and the rising art, unadorned with those complicated embellishments, encircled the performer in the narrow limits of simplicity. [2]

The great innovation around the turn of the century was the pirouette. According to Blasis, pirouettes were 'unknown to Noverre and all our old masters, who thought it impossible to go beyond the three turns on the instep'; [3] but they were probably performed in the more popular theatres while not admitted to the opera house. Giovan Battista Grimaldi, grandfather of the great English clown and an intrepid dancer popularly known as *Jambe de fer* (iron leg), [4] was supposed to have performed multiple pirouettes at the Opéra-Comique in the Foire Saint-Germain early in the eighteenth century, and such feats may well have been part of the technique of Italian dancers of that period. Blasis, however, who was concerned only with the main stream of classical technique in the opera house, credited Pierre Gardel and Auguste Vestris with the invention of pirouettes, and claimed that it was the latter – and later the ebullient Louis Duport – who, by perfecting them and varying them, brought them into vogue.

As early as 1804, protests were being made about the excessive use of pirouettes. A dancing master from Versailles, M. Papillon, tactfully reproached his friend Gardel for overlooking the dangers of pandering to the public's desire to be dazzled by virtuosity. [5] The temptation to display the latest technical development, however, was too strong to be resisted, and for many years choreographers packed their *pas* with pirouettes that often had no apparent purpose: in 1823 Castil-Blaze boldly commented on the 'sheer absurdity' of Paul's pirouettes in *Aline.* [6]

Some of the older followers of ballet were disturbed to see the female dancers trying to emulate their male colleagues in these feats. But already the first signs had appeared of a technical revolution that was to initiate an enormous expansion of the ballerina's vocabulary, giving her a supremacy over her male counterpart that would remain unchallenged in Western Europe until Nijinsky burst upon Paris in 1909. The discovery and subsequent exploitation of *pointe* work was one of the outstanding features of the Romantic ballet; as the nineteenth century drew to a close, feats of ever-greater difficulty were being performed as a result of the development of the blocked shoe, which was introduced in a primitive form around 1880. Marie Taglioni was not the first ballerina to dance on her *pointes*, but it was she who revealed the artistic possibilities inherent in this new development. The date of its origin may never be precisely ascertained, but it was not an unknown feat well before 1820. When Taglioni made her début at the Opera, her dancing reminded the Paris audience of Geneviève Gosselin, who had died at the height of her fame in 1818. Gosselin's extraordinary ability to perform feats on the very tips of her toes had been specifically noticed in 1813, two years before she created the rôle of Flora in Didelot's revised version of *Flore et Zéphire* – and it may be significant that some of the early evidence of the use of *pointes*, whether descriptive or pictorial, relates to that ballet. There are prints, dated 1821, showing Fanny Bias and Angélique Mées (daughter of a Paris Opéra dancer of the late eighteenth century called Saint-Romain) in the rôle of Flora, both quite clearly on point. *Pointe* work, then in its rudimentary stage, was to develop gradually. The earliest achievements can have been no more than momentarily held poses on the tips of the toes to give an illusion of extra lightness. By the 1820s ballerinas such as Amalia Brugnoli and Élise Vaque-Moulin were expanding the vocabulary of this technical novelty, but their efforts, astonishing though they were to the audiences of their day, were still little more than *tours de force.*

To Taglioni is due the credit for weaving the use of the *pointes* into the fabric of dance technique so that it became a means of expression. As practised by her, the *pointes* brought a new poetry to the dance, reinforcing the added illusion that was being achieved by developments in scene design and the stronger atmospheric qualities being introduced into ballet music. It gave the ballerina a fairy-like quality to appear so lightly attached to the ground. It was exactly what was required for the interpretation of an aerial spirit, and it found its most sublime expression in those scenes of Romantic mystery, the Ballet of the Nuns in *Robert le Diable* and the second acts of *La Sylphide* and *Giselle*, in which the ballerina became transformed into a vision of the Romantic ideal, remote and imponderable.

With the 'taglionisation' of ballet – the verb *taglioniser* was commonly used in the early years of the ballerina's appearance in Paris – the art took on a new meaning, and its very structure before her arrival became outmoded overnight. The disappearance of the *genres*, those three categories, *noble*, *demi-caractère* and *comique*, in which the dancers of the Opéra had been classified for longer than any living person could remember, was as much a Romantic victory as was the successful assault by the Romantic dramatists on the three unities of classical tragedy.

The *genres* had in fact long been an anachronism, and in supporting their retention until well into the 1820s, Gardel and Milon were fighting a hopeless battle against progress. In 1817 an attempt was made to restore order to the classification, it being explained that 'the distinct *genres* have for too long been confused, and this abuse, which arises as a result of the laxity of the *maître de ballet*, encourages the dancers to dance, for preference, in the *demi-caractère*, without regard for their talent and appearance'. [7] The three *genres* were therefore redefined, and it was laid down that the establishment was to consist of one *premier sujet* for each of the *noble* and *comique* categories, and two for the *demi-caractère*. Five years later Gardel and Milon were still struggling to preserve this classification, and although they were forced to admit that 'choreographers [had] to some extent dissolved the difference between the *noble* and *demi-caractère* categories', they made a further attempt to impose the classification. [8]

Fundamentally, Gardel and Milon were men of the eighteenth century, who had grown too old to discard long-held conceptions and adapt themselves to the changes that had to come. They were not, however, reactionary without a reason. When, for example, they recommended that male pupils should wear breeches instead of trousers, it was for the purpose of enabling the teachers to observe the articulation of the knee; and again, when they advised that the study of the *grande passacaille, chaconne* and *passepied* should be restored to the syllabus, it was with the hope that the great days of the male dancer associated with the names of Vestris and Gardel might be revived.

In 1820 the dancers who practised the *genre noble* were headed by Albert and Mme Anatole, sister of the mourned Geneviève Gosselin. In physique, the essential requirements of a *danseur* or *danseuse noble* were a tall stature, a perfectly proportioned figure, shapely legs, a well-formed instep, and flexibility about the hips. Dancers considered the *genre noble* to be the most difficult of the three *genres*, for it required the utmost precision and correct execution in those majestic adagios which, when correctly performed, were regarded by Blasis as the touchstone of the dancer's art. An air of majesty was the keynote of this *genre*. The solemn elegance of his movements, and the gracefulness of his attitudes and arabesques, were the prerequisites of the *danseur noble*, who acquired added nobility by slow deliberate preparations and the required touch of majesty in the developments of the arms and legs. In the 1820s a *danseur noble* had also to perform such feats as 'the finest pirouettes in the second position, in attitude, or on the instep, *entrechats*, and every other *temps d'élévation*',[9] which not only greatly broadened his technical vocabulary but also began the breaking down of the dividing line between him and the *danseur de demi-caractère.*

The ideal *danseur de demi-caractère* was of medium height, slender and elegantly built. His dancing was a mixture of all three *genres*, and exploited all the technical resources that in those days were at a dancer's command. Nobility and elegance were demanded in his execution, and even the most brilliant and intrepid movements had to be performed with a certain restraint. But the *grands temps* that were the secret of the majesty of the *danseur noble* were not to be found in the performance of the *danseur de demi-caractère*, the representatives in 1820 of that *genre* being Paul, known as '*l'aérien*', Emilie Bigottini and Fanny Bias.

Finally, those dancers who were short of stature and tended to be thickset were classified in the third of the *genres*, the *genre comique*. National dances such as the bolero, the tarantella and the allemande came within their province, while, according to Blasis, 'the *pas Chinois*, the *pas de Sabotiers*, *l'Anglais*, steps of caricature',[10] belonged to the lower *comique* style. This *genre* was considered the least important of the three, and one of its last exponents was Pauline Montessu, sister of the dancer Antoine Paul.[11]

Even in 1820 the boundaries defining these *genres* had become artificial and vague. As *Le Miroir* commented in 1822:

> Since the success of Albert and Paul, every dancer feels obliged to follow in their footsteps and wants to copy the superiority of those masters. All the *genres* are now becoming blurred, and are converging, so to speak, towards a single style. Monotonous execution leads to monotonous choreography... This blurring of the *genres* is such a danger to dancers' talent that it is occasionally having an adverse effect on the two leading artists, MM. Albert and Paul, the latter finding it impossible to wear tunic and plumes, while Albert is too solemn in the gay *genre*.[12]

But despite a strong attempt that same year by Gardel, Milon and Aumer, the three *maîtres de ballet* of the Opéra, to re-establish the *genres* in the interests of order, they had become virtually extinct by 1830.

To all intents and purposes the *genre de demi-caractère* was left alone in the field; the *genre noble* had quite disappeared, its old-fashioned graces no longer acceptable to audiences of 1830. Certainly, in its latter days it had appealed to a very limited segment of the public. As Blasis had noticed in 1830, it could be appreciated only by connoisseurs and persons of refined taste. To the increasing numbers from the middle classes who were beginning to frequent the Opéra, it was incomprehensible unless overlaid with the *tours de force* of the *demi-caractère* dancer. It even came to be scorned by the dancers themselves. 'Away with so-called *pas nobles* which make our second-rate dancers look like tight-rope walkers,' wrote a critic in 1830, 'away with ever-lasting pirouettes and the ridiculous elastic *entrechat* which is known backstage as the *entrechat du pal egyptien* (Egyptian torture) and *entrechat du clyssoir* (enema). Those ridiculous names, bestowed by the dancers themselves, only go to show that the dance, which has become a task of patience and suffering ... must be restored to its former state, which required natural grace and lightness.'[13]

The virtual disappearance of the *genre noble* in its purest form, in which male dancers specially excelled, foreshadowed the declining importance of the male element in ballet. French ballet in the Romantic period produced only one truly great male dancer who could compete with the ballerinas on terms of equality – Jules Perrot, 'the very model of the *danseur de demi-caractère*, [who] instinctively danced *terre à terre*, feats of strength and *grand ballon* with equal perfection',[14] but he was forced by injury to curtail his dancing activity at the height of his powers and thereafter devoted himself to choreography. There were, indeed, a number of very talented male dancers who appeared in Paris in Romantic times, notably Lucien Petipa (elder brother of Marius Petipa), Antonio Guerra and August Bournonville – but as time went on, the male contribution in ballet was eventually reduced to acting parts and, in the dance itself, modestly supporting the ballerina.

By the 1840s such a revulsion against male dancers had set in that they were excluded from the *corps de ballet* whenever there was an excuse. The charms of the *danseuse en travesti* were then discovered, and the female hussars in *Paquita* and the ship-boys and sailors, whose true sex was not concealed, in *Betty* (both 1846) were the forerunners of the travesty hero who made an occasional appearance in the 1860s and 1870s.

How strong this prejudice had become by 1840 can be judged from a passage written by Jules Janin:

As you may already know, we are hardly a supporter of what are called the *grands danseurs*. To us the *grand danseur* seems so sad and heavy! He is, at the same time, so unhappy yet so pleased with himself! He fills no purpose; he does not represent anything, he is a non-entity. But speak to us about a pretty dancing girl, displaying the grace of her features and the elegance of her figure, and revealing so fleetingly all the treasures of her beauty, and thank God, we understand everything perfectly. We know what this lovely creature is saying to us, and we would willingly follow her wherever she pleases into the sweet realm of love. But a man, a frightful man, as ugly as you or I, a wretched fellow leaping about without knowing the reason why, a creature whom nature has fashioned to carry a musket and a sword and wear a uniform – can you really expect such a fellow to dance like a woman? It is impossible! That this bewhiskered individual, a pillar of the community, an elector, a municipal councillor, a man whose business it is to make and above all unmake laws, should appear in our presence in a sky-blue satin tunic, wearing a hat with a plume amorously caressing his cheek, that this frightful *danseuse* in male clothing should turn up and pirouette in the foreground while the pretty ballet girls stand respectfully at a distance – this is surely out of the question and not to be tolerated, and we have done well to remove such great artists from our pleasures. Today, thanks to this revolution that we have effected, woman is the queen of ballet. She breathes and dances there at her ease. No longer is she forced to sacrifice half her silk to clothe her neighbour. Nowadays the male dancer is tolerated merely as a useful accessory; he is the green hedge surrounding the flowers in the flowerbed; he is the shading of the picture, the obligatory foil. [15]

This revulsion naturally had its effect on the general standard of male dancing, for fewer men adopted dancing as a career, and those that did lacked encouragement to spur them to greater endeavour. In 1847 there were only twelve boys among the ninety pupils in the Opéra's School of Dance. Adice, who taught the male dancers at the Opéra between 1848 and 1863, was in despair at the ruin of the *noble* style of dancing. 'As performed today,' he wrote in 1859, 'this style, instead of appearing noble, is trivial and meaningless, whereas the *danseur noble*, regarded purely as a dancing machine, should be perfection itself from his walk down to the minutest details of his execution. Our so-called *danseurs nobles* have no allure and therefore have no idea how to present themselves to their audience. Their noble style consists merely of *ronds de jambe* and *entrechats* – in short, *tours de force* worthy of the Arabs – without giving any thought to their body, arms, legs, knees, feet or toes, and always performing the same steps and the same *enchaînements*.' [16]

* * * * * * *

This chronicle opens some seven years before Marie Taglioni made her sensational début in Paris – on the evening in February 1820 when the Duc de Berry was assassinated outside the Opéra. That dark deed does not, of course, mark the beginning of the Romantic ballet, for the opening of a period of art history cannot be attached to a fixed instant like the opening or closing of a sovereign's reign, but has here been chosen as a suitable point from which to recount the story of the Romantic revival of French ballet.

In 1820 the Opéra was a royal institution, subsidised mainly from the Civil List of the King and partly by a tax imposed on the receipts of the minor theatres of Paris. Ultimately responsible for its administration was the Minister of the King's Household, between whom and the Director, who managed the theatre, was yet another official, the Intendant of the Royal Theatres. Generally the men who held these posts left little or no mark on the ballet, but one, the Vicomte Sosthène de La Rochefoucauld, who assumed the duties of Intendant in 1824, was long remembered with amusement for his well-intentioned order that the dancers' skirts be lengthened so that carnal thoughts should not be aroused in the gentlemen who sat close to the stage! To do him justice, however, complaints had been appearing in the theatrical press before he took over responsibility for the Opéra. [17]

After the Revolution of 1830 the organisation of the Opéra underwent a drastic change. From being a direct charge on the State, it became a private enterprise, with a fixed subsidy from public funds. The Director was granted the privilege of exploiting the theatre for a specified period on certain conditions, which governed, among other matters, the number of artists to be employed, the number of new works to be presented, and the maintenance of the building and the contents – all of which were set forth in a document known as the *Cahier des charges.* Supervision was exercised by a Committee appointed by the Minister of the Interior. Under this arrangement, which continued until Napoleon III turned the Opéra back into a State institution in 1854, Dr Véron made a fortune, but his successors, Henri Duponchel, Léon Pillet, then Duponchel and Nestor Roqueplan in partnership, and finally Roqueplan alone, all discarded their burden, leaving a heavy deficit behind them.

It was during the private exploitation of the Opéra that the organisation of the ballet company became more flexible. The golden age of the Romantic ballet was in this respect a period of transition, for the classification of the company into the three *genres* and the division of the *sujets* into the ranks of *premier sujet, remplaçant* and *double* was no longer strictly adhered to after 1830, while the modern hierarchy, based on a system of promotion through regular examinations, did not make its appearance until 1860.

From its very early times the Opéra needed a regular supply of proficient dancers for the danced insertions in the operas, and later in the ballet-pantomimes that came into favour in the 1770s. To meet that need, its School of Dance had been founded by Louis XIV and placed under the overall authority of the principal ballet-master. In about 1821, after a somewhat peripatetic period, it found a settled home in the building formerly occupied by the recently abolished Menus-Plaisirs in the Rue Richer, where the Opéra stored its scenery. At that time it was served by two teachers: Georges Maze, who was responsible for the senior class, and Romain, who was in charge of the younger children. Alternate days of the week were set aside for the two classes, each of which consisted of up to thirty pupils. In addition to the teachers, there was an assistant teacher (Paul) and a general dogsbody. For exceptionally gifted senior pupils, there were the perfection classes, given by Jean-François Coulon and Auguste Vestris, with the purpose of preparing them for débuts, which, if successful, would enable them to join the company as junior soloists rather than having to pass through the *corps de ballet*. These classes, however, were generally given elsewhere, either in the teacher's own studio or sometimes in the theatre. There was also a mime class, given by Milon until his retirement in 1826.

When a report on the School was placed before La Rochefoucauld, he proposed that daily classes should be given for each class; but Gardel and Milon were against this, not only because it would double the expense by requiring two studios instead of one, but also because the senior students, who were regularly required to take part in performances and to attend rehearsals, would be exhausted. The proposal would also impose an impossible burden on the teachers. In order not to appear too negative, the ballet-masters suggested that the seniors might be retained until the age of eighteen instead of sixteen, that regular examinations should be held to monitor progress, and that a teacher who produced an exceptional student might be rewarded with a bonus. [18]

The continuity of the school was not broken when the Opéra became a private enterprise, although there were several changes in the staff after 1830. Maze and Charles Petit alone continued as teachers. The former retired after a few years, but Petit remained until 1848 – long enough for his portrait to be drawn by Gavarni for one of the illustrations to Albéric Second's book on backstage life, *Les Petits Mystères de l'Opéra*. In 1832 Dr Véron engaged Jean-Baptiste Barrez, who remained as principal teacher until 1844, when he left to take up the post of ballet-master in Madrid. Other teachers were Varin (1843–48), Georges Elie (1846–48), and Antoine-Louis Coulon, the son of the celebrated teacher of former days, who was engaged in 1845 to improve the discipline of the *corps de ballet*.

Paradoxically there was a marked decline in the efficiency of the School of

Dance at the height of the Romantic ballet. Pupils received only three lessons a week, mime was not restored to the syllabus, and there was no adequate supervision. The institution was progressively reduced for a number of years until, by 1841, the year of *Giselle,* pupils were paying the teachers out of their own pockets for additional classes. This was not through any rapacity on the part of the teachers, for they received little enough from the Opéra: there were still only two of them to service between sixty and eighty pupils. Jean-Baptiste Barrez, who took the senior class, was paid 1500 francs a year, and Petit, the teacher of the junior class, only 800 francs. For the more able and ambitious pupils this entailed a heavy sacrifice. Those in Petit's class had to pay him 12 francs a month each for additional classes, while Barrez charged 25 francs a month. The girls who studied with Coulon were charged 30 francs, and *coryphées* who attended Albert's class, 50 francs a month. [19]

When Albéric Second was making his survey of the Opéra in 1843, he found there were four classes for the company. Joseph Mazilier taught the *premiers sujets* in the Foyer de la Danse, the accompaniment being provided, as was customary, by a solo violin; he charged his pupils 60 francs a month. Barrez, apart from his duties at the school, taught a few of the leading dancers, including Carlotta Grisi and Maria, and Lucien Petipa, in the Foyer des Choeurs. Albert, who had preserved his youth so well that he seemed thirty years younger than his true age, gave his classes at his home at No.15 Rue des Moulins, providing the violin accompaniment himself, while Jean Coralli's classes were held in his first-floor, well-heated apartment within the premises of the Opéra on the side abutting the Rue Grange-Batelière. [20]

The costumes of the students were simple and practical:

> The girls are bareheaded and *décolletées*. Their arms are bare, and their waists confined in tight bodices. A very short, very bouffant skirt made of net or striped muslin reaches to the knees. Their thighs are chastely concealed beneath large calico knickers, which are as impenetrable as a State secret. The men, open-necked and without neckties, wear short white piqué jackets and breeches reaching half-way down the leg and held at the waist by a leather belt. [21]

Gautier was likewise fascinated by the appearance of dancers in class. In an essay on the *rat*, his description of their costume contains a detailed examination of the slipper in use at that time:

> Having arrived in the classroom, the child undresses from tip to toe and puts on her dancing clothes, which are not unattractive. These consist of a short skirt of white muslin or black satin, a piqué bodice, white silk stockings, and knee-length cambric knickers that replaced tights, which are worn only on the stage. The white or flesh-coloured slippers, in

technical language called *chaussons*, merit a special description. The sole, which is pinched in at the centre, does not extend to the tip of the foot, but ends squarely, leaving projecting about two finger-breadths of material. The purpose of this is to enable the dancer to perform *pointe* work by giving her a sort of jointed point of support, but as the whole weight of the body is borne on this part of the shoe, which would inevitably break, the dancer has to strengthen it by darning, almost as old-clothes menders do to the heels of stockings to make them last. The inside of the shoe is lined with strong canvas and, at the very end, a strip of leather and cardboard, the thickness of which depends on the lightness of the wearer. The rest of the shoe is chevronned on the outside by a network of ribbons firmly sewn on, and there is also stitching on the quarter, which can be adjusted by means of a little tag of ribbon in the Andalusian manner. [22]

Before 1830 the progress of a dancer from the day she joined the *corps de ballet* was very strictly regulated. To emerge from the *corps de ballet*, it was necessary to make a début. Permission for this was granted by the Minister, following a successful audition before a panel. The *débutante* was then presented to the public on six occasions, appearing twice in each of three different parts: a rôle and a *pas* chosen by herself, and a third part or dance chosen by the Director. She automatically ceased to be a member of the *corps de ballet* and, if successful, was engaged by the Opéra as a *double* for a term of 15 years, terminable by either party at 6 months' notice. To remain in the company, she had to be promoted to the next grade of *remplaçant* within 5 years, and, once promoted to that grade, the power of terminating her engagement ceased.

A dancer's emoluments were divided into the basic salary and bonuses, or *feux*, which were payable for each appearance. From this, two deductions had to be made: 5 per cent for the pension fund and a further 5 per cent for the savings fund, which was invested in government stock, the interest being capitalised. Other deductions might be made for breaches of discipline, because the Regulations laid down a table of fines ranging from a day and a half's salary for arriving late at rehearsal to a month's salary for missing a performance.

After 1830 those artists who were already in receipt of pensions, or whose contracts entitled them to pensions on retirement, were assured of their rights by the government. Véron and his successors until 1854 were relieved of this liability, being given complete freedom to enter into contracts on whatever terms they desired, and in consequence dancers newly engaged between 1831 and 1856 had no pension rights. [22]

A dancer's life was hard in those days. They came, almost without exception, from the poorest families. As one of them told Albéric Second:

Most of us first saw the light of day in a concierge's lodge ... If you only knew the courage, patience, resignation and hard work that was needed, the frightful tortures to be endured, the silent tears to be forced back, before a young girl could become even a mediocre dancer, you would be shocked and horrified. I was barely seven when I was sent to M. Barrez's class in the Rue Richer. I left home in the morning fortified only by a cup of so-called coffee. I had neither clogs for my feet, nor a shawl for my shoulders, and more often than not my poor cotton dress was full of holes. I arrived shivering and often starving. Then began the daily suffering, a suffering of which my description, however exact, cannot give you a real idea ... Every morning my teacher imprisoned my feet in a grooved box. There, heel to heel, with knees pointing outwards, my martyred feet became used to remaining in parallel by themselves. This is called 'turning out'. After half an hour in the box, I had to endure another form of torture. This time I had to place my foot on a *barre*, which I had to hold with the opposite hand to the foot in exercise. This was called 'breaking in'. When this toil was over, you might think I was allowed to rest. Rest! Does a dancer ever rest? We were just poor wandering Jews at whom M. Barrez was incessantly shouting, 'Dance! Dance!' After being turned out and broken in, we were forced, under pain of our teacher's reprimands and maternal corrections, to study assiduously *assemblés, jetés, balancés, pirouettes sur le cou-de-pied, sauts de basque, pas de bourrée* and finally *entrechats quatre, six* and *huit*. Such are the delightful elements of which the art of dance is composed. And do not imagine that such brutal fatigues last only for a short time. They must continue forever and be continually renewed. For only on that condition can a dancer maintain her suppleness and lightness. A week's rest has to be paid for with two months of double work without any respite. The dancer personifies the fable of Sisyphus and his rock. She is like a racehorse that sacrifices repose, weight and freedom for the rapid victories of Chantilly and the Champ de Mars. [23]

* * * * * * *

In the reign of Louis-Philippe, ballet acquired a glamour that not only stirred the public's enthusiasm for the great ballerinas of the day, but also aroused curiosity about all that went on in the mysterious, enclosed world beyond the curtain. Every little detail had its interest, from the private lives of the stars down to the struggles of the poorly paid, poorly fed and poorly clad children who trudged to the School of Dance to prepare for their future careers. These were the *petits rats*, and the golden age of the Romantic ballet is, in a sense, as much their age as Taglioni's; for if they could never aspire to the individual fame of the prima ballerina, they were seen, for the first time – albeit a little sentimentally, for it was a sentimental age – as human beings with an existence of their own.

The term *petit rat* was undoubtedly in use among the dancers and the habitués of the Opéra long before it came into general usage in the 1830s. Its origin lies concealed in a cloak of mystery such as often shrouds slang expressions. Littré, in his dictionary, defined the term *rat* as meaning 'a kept woman', because in former times people used to invite dancers of the Opéra to small parties, referring to them merely by the last syllable of the word Opéra. If there is any truth in this suggestion, the term must at some time have ceased to apply to adult dancers and come to signify child dancers, as it did in Romantic times and has done ever since. The explanation hazarded by Nestor Roqueplan seems more credible:

> The *rat* is a pupil of the School of Dance, and it is perhaps because she is a child of the building, because she lives there, and nibbles, chatters and plays there, and gnaws and scratches the scenery, frays and makes holes in the costumes, and causes untold damage and creates a lot of hidden, nocturnal mischief that she has received this somewhat unbelievable name of *rat* ... The real *rat* ... is a little girl of between six and fourteen, a ballet pupil, who wears cast-off shoes, faded shawls and soot-coloured hats, who warms herself over smoky oil lamps, has bread sticking out from her pockets, and begs for ten *sous* to buy sweets. The *rat* makes holes in the scenery to watch the performance, rushes about madly behind the backcloths, and plays puss-in-the-corner in the wings. She is supposed to earn twenty *sous* a night, but, with the enormous fines that her pranks entail, she receives only 8 to 10 francs a month and thirty kicks from her mother. The *rat* remains a *rat* until the age when she assumes the title of artist, until the age when she no longer demands sweets but receives bouquets. [25]

Several dancers of the Opéra – Tullia, Florentine, Marie Godeschal – appear in the novels of Honoré de Balzac, who tells of their rise to fame through the influence of their noble protectors and the support of venal journalists; [26] but the finest and most complete account of all the goings-on backstage comes from the pen of the journalist, Albéric Second. His book, *Les Petits Mystères de l'Opéra*, contains an unromanticised description of that small world, which is indeed not so very different in its essentials from what it is today. Apart from being an informative guide, Second had at his fingertips all the backstage gossip with which the Opéra buzzed, and it is a wonder he was not visited with a plague of libel actions after his book was published. Happily for him, most of the people whose faults he pitilessly recorded chose to ignore what he had written, but two dancers – Caroline Forster, the Englishwoman who created the rôle of Bathilde in *Giselle,* and her friend Elina Roland – had the temerity to summon him before the Police Court for defamation, for which he was fined 100 francs. [27]

Second opens his book by imagining himself waking one evening in the darkened auditorium of the Opéra, having dropped off to sleep during the performance. Stumbling into the orchestra pit, he is groping his way backstage when he meets the shade of Poinsinet, [27] the Opéra's friendly ghost, who initiates him into the mysteries of the building. At the stage door he is introduced to Madame Crosnier, an almost legendary figure who, like Cerberus, scrutinises all comers from her concierge's lodge, turning away those with no right to enter. This old woman, whose stepson was to become Director of the Opéra during the Second Empire, was a great personality. Her turban, which she was seldom seen without, and her pretentious airs were sources of endless amusement. It was said that only the all-powerful Rosina Stoltz, the favourite of the Director, Léon Pillet, dared address her in familiar terms. Living in her little lodge with an adored but insignificant husband and an ancient, half-paralysed poodle, she was the trusted recipient of messages from the host of swains loitering outside the stage door, and many a half-starved *petit rat* blessed her for being invited into the warmth of her room and given a hot supper. [28]

Penetrating into the skein of dark and narrow corridors and steep staircases, Second eventually finds himself in the Foyer de la Danse, a large room, rather poorly lit, situated just behind the stage. Apart from a semi-circular bench and a bust of Guimard on a wooden pedestal, the room was unfurnished, but the *barres* attached to the walls and the large mirrors revealed its true function. It was here that the dancers gathered during the hour before the ballet, entering with their little watering-cans, their legs and feet covered in canvas gaiters to protect their tights and shoes. Before the Revolution of 1830, when few strangers were admitted backstage and guards and lacqueys in royal livery were stationed to ward off intruders, the Foyer de la Danse served merely as a room in which the dancers could gather and limber up before going on to the stage. But all that was changed by Dr Véron, who transformed the bare working room into a glittering centre of social life. This was an adroit move, which made the Opéra fashionable overnight. The dancers were then joined by a select band, consisting of the *corps diplomatique,* the more important *abonnés* and other distinguished men, who found in this hour an added source of pleasure in the evening's entertainment.

Many of the men-about-town, who were for the most part members of the Jockey Club, acquired the habit of looking on the *coulisses* of the Opéra as a sort of private seraglio. The most fashionable of these watched the performances from the proscenium boxes that abutted on the stage and were known as the *loges infernales.* 'The Opéra,' it was explained, 'provides them with their amorous pleasures, in much the same way that the Pompadour stud-farm provides them with their equestrian pleasures; they look on it as a stable for remounts and nothing more.' But the real nature of its back stage, in the words of a more perceptive dancer, was

> bourgeois, which is the worst of all natures. No one is too virtuous there, for that would be stupid, but no one is too sinful either, because that becomes wearisome. The backstage area of the Opéra is, above all, boring. It suffers from the spleen, like a fat English millionaire, and it would be difficult for it to be otherwise. A large proportion of the *abonnés* have frequented the Opéra for years. To them the *coulisses* no longer possess any mystery, savour, novelty or poetry. As for the others, the newcomers, they do nothing but look on, not being rich enough to touch. [29]

Second's attention was not entirely absorbed by the Foyer de la Danse. He also stood in wonder before the bustle of scene changing, and was shown a stout, bespectacled man directing operations with a whistle. This, he was told, was the chief machinist, Contant – *'Contant-de-lui-même'*, as he was maliciously nicknamed – who was said to line his pockets by making economies in his department. Second also noticed, sitting apart at the black wooden table in the Foyer de la Danse, a man with a sallow, bloated countenance, the untidiness of his dress contrasting sharply with the studied elegance of the gentlemen around him. This was the *régisseur de la danse,* Desplaces *père,* the sergeant-major of the ballet who was responsible to the *maîtres de ballet* for discipline.

But it was the dancers themselves who fascinated Second above all else, from the *petits rats,* who plagued the good-natured *sujets* with their prattle, to Carlotta Grisi herself, who passed him by the stage door as she paused to ask after Mme Crosnier's health in 'her adorable little Franco-Italian patois'. [30] Nor did he fail to observe the presence of the dancers' mothers bustling about their offspring like a brood of old hens. He described the tasteful decoration of the dressing room of a *premier sujet,* and in a dressing room shared by ten girls he noticed a number of amusing caricatures on the wall: an impossibly skinny Louise Fitzjames, Sophie Dumilâtre, her face drawn without a vestige of a nose, and Louis Frémolle breaking into a smile that stretched from ear to ear. Here he watched the dancers make up with astonishing speed:

> While their hair was being dressed with a plait added here and a false ringlet there, and the dressers were buttoning up their bodices, fixing their veils, and fastening their wings and headdresses, [the dancers] were

painting their faces, whitening their arms and darkening their eyebrows. Some of them were sticking horrid little taffeta patches on their cheeks and at the sides of their mouths, while others were making their eyes appear larger by the stroke of a brush skilfully applied at the corner of their eyelids, which magnified their fascinating brilliance. [31]

Coming to the front of the house, he was initiated into the mystery of the *claque*, which was then commanded by the formidable Auguste, who would assemble his men before the performance in a low *estaminet* in the Rue Favart to give them their orders. His army of applauders numbered sixty, a third being paid, another third giving their services for the privilege of free admission, and the remainder paying half-price for a 4-franc seat. In the auditorium they were scattered about the pit, where it was their duty to applaud at a tap of Auguste's cane. Auguste grew very rich, for many artists paid him to assure themselves of a good ovation and others gave him the free seats to which they were entitled. He died in 1844, the owner of a house in Paris and another in the country, and his income was said to be not far short of that of a Marshal of France.

Finally there was the public – journalists and actors, deputies, stockbrokers, lawyers, foreign millionaires, the Court and high society, who gathered at the Opéra of an evening to take part in what was a social ritual as well as an entertainment. They formed a virtual cross-section of Parisian life, from the clerks who filled the upper boxes to the duchesses and marquises, the elegant actresses, and the *demi-mondaines* such as Marie Duplessis, the ravishing Lady of the Camellias, who glided into their carriages with a rustle of rich silks, leaving a haunting aroma of perfume behind them in the theatre where, but a few minutes before, Taglioni, or Elssler, or Carlotta Grisi had held an audience spellbound.

NOTES

1. *Journal des théâtres*, 7 October 1821.
2. Blasis, *Code of Terpsichore*, p.82.
3. Blasis, *Code of Terpsichore*, 83.
4. Grimaldi danced at the Opéra-Comique in the Foire-Saint-Germain in 1742 in the *divertissement, Le Prix de Cythère* by Favart. It was there that the following incident is said to have taken place. Having laid a wager with his comrades that he would astonish the Turkish ambassador, Mehemet Effendi, by jumping as high as the chandelier, he had the misfortune to strike it too violently. One of the crystal pieces broke off and struck the face of the Turkish envoy, who was so furious that he had the dancer beaten and exacted a public apology.
5. Papillon, *Examen impartial sur la danse actuel de l'Opéra en forme de lettre* (Paris n.d.).
6. *Journal des débats*, 3 October 1823.
7. Bibl.-Mus. de l'Opéra. Order of the Comte de Pradel, Minister of the King's Household, 27 December 1817; order of the Marquis de Lauriston, Minister of the King's Household, 29 May 1822.

8. Arch. Nat., AJ[13] 113. Report by Gardel and Milon on the Ecole de Danse, 18 February 1822.

9. Blasis, *Code of Terpsichore*, 90.

10. Blasis, *Code of Terpsichore*, 92.

11. Bibl.-Mus. de l'Opéra. An order of the Comte de Pradel, 29 December 1817, embodying the definitions of Gardel and Milon, listed the movements and characters applicable to each of the three *genres* as follows:

> For the *genre noble:*
> La Sarabande; la Passacaille; l'Adagio à 3 et 4 tems; la Loure; le Menuet noble; la Chaconne à 2 et 3 tems; l'Air marqué à 2 tems, tel que Marche, etc.; Gigue lourée, la Gavotte noble, qui approche du mouvement de la Chaconne à 2 tems; et généralement tous les grands caractères tels que Faune, Tartares, Polonais, Furies, etc. etc.

> For the *genre de demi-caractère:*
> La Romance; la Sicilienne; la Musette galante; le Menuet gracieux; l'Andante; la Pastorale agréable; le 6/8 idem; la Gigue ordinaire; le 2/4 plus ou moins allegro; la Gavotte; le Passe-pied; et généralement tous les caractères de Zéphires, Sylphes. Troubadours, Bergers français, Grecs, Romains, etc. etc.

> For the *genre comique:*
> La Musette champêtre et montagnarde; le Menuet de genre, et comique, et grotesque; le 4 temps louré; le 3/8, 6/8 et 12/8; le Tambourin; et généralement tous les Airs de Pâtre, Contredanses françaises, Allemandes, et les caractères comiques ou de genre, tels que le Chinois, le Lapon, l'Anglaise, la Cossaque, les Furies, les Sauvages, etc. etc.

12. *Miroir,* 9 October 1822.

13. *Corsaire,* 25 December 1830.

14. Adice, 108.

15. *Journal des débats,* 2 March 1840.

16. Adice, 108. Adice was in charge of the boys' elementary class at the Opéra from 1863 to 1867, when he was retired.

17. On the indecent appearance of garters, see *Le Pandore* (30 November 1823) and *Almanach des spectacles* (4th year), the latter of which expressed shock that garters 'indicated precisely that part of the body where the legs begin'. La Rochefoucault may have been responsible for giving the order for lengthening of the skirts by 6 inches, but the *Courrier des spectacles,* after reporting the order (13 September 1826) came round to the view that longer skirts could be dangerous, citing near-falls by Julia and Amélie Perceval (3 December 1826).

18. Arch. Nat., O³ 1672.

19. In 1840 a wealthy balletomane, Nicolas Guillaume, offered to found an *Ecole Speciale Conservatoire de la Danse,* for which he was prepared to purchase a building and have it converted for use as a dance school at his own expense, and to assume responsibility for the maintenance and education of a hundred pupils in exchange for a rent of 9600 francs a year and 36,000 francs a year subsidy. He further proposed that the school be organised on the same lines as the Imperial and Royal Academy of Dance attached to La Scala, Milan, and a copy of the regulations of that Academy was submitted to the Minister of the Interior in 1842. Albert was proposed as Director of the school at a salary of 5000 fr.; in addition to himself, there were to be three other teachers, Perrot being suggested as chief of these, and also a teacher of mime. Guillaume's offer seems to have been treated in an off-hand fashion. Eighteen months passed before it was even submitted to the Minister of the Interior, and it was then overlooked and forgotten. (Bibl.-Mus. de l'Opéra, formerly 2028[III])

20. Tamvaco, 28, 1148.

21. Second, 180-01.

22. Gautier, *La Peau de tigre,* 335–6.

23. Dancers' pensions were to be re-established by a decree of 14 May 1856.

24. Second, 149–51.

25. Roqueplan, 44–6. The tradition that Roqueplan himself invented the term is without foundation. Most of the passage quoted here was originally written for *Nouvelles à la main* (issue of 20 December 1840), but the term is considerably older than that. It appears in an article by Jules Vernières entitled '*Les Coulisses de l'Opéra*', in the *Revue de Paris* in 1836.

26. See *'Les Comédiens de la Comédie Humaine'* by Maurice Descotes *(Revue d'Histoire du Théâtre,* 1956, IV, 290-291).
27. The passage in Second's 'infamous article', with its 'monstrous insinuations', can be read in *Le Monde musical* of 26 October 1843 (the work was originally serialised in that periodical between 11 May 1843 and 13 March 1844). It described 'the veritable and unique wonder of the Opéra ... – a sight no less touching than outdated, that of two ... dancers whose hearts are entwined in the firmest and sincerest friendship ... See what a pretty picture Mlle Forster and Mlle Roland make together. There they are, arm in arm, hand in hand, cherished companions gazing at one another with looks of chaste and pure friendship. Never did two sisters ... love one another so entirely, so completely, so exclusively. These ladies carry friendship to the point of living in the same street – the Rue Bourdaloue – in the same house, in the same apartment, and often, when the weather is very cold, in the same bed.' When the work was published in book form in 1844, the offending passage was deleted, but in a postscript, Second took relish in recording that 'Mme Roland and Mlle Forster, dancers of an aggregate age of eighty-three, had been expelled from the Opéra.'
28. Poinsinet was the ghost of the librettist of the opera *Ernelinde,* produced in 1767. This character, who was drowned in the Guadalquivir at the age of thirty-four as a result of going swimming too soon after a heavy meal, was the butt of many practical jokes in his lifetime. The saying 'as stupid as Poinsinet' was proverbial at the Opéra. Mme Crosnier retired in 1855 and died in 1857.
29. Second, 217.
30. Second, 126.
31. Second, 204–5.

3

The Opéra Dispossessed

When the King's nephew, the Duc de Berry, was fatally stabbed outside the Opéra on the night of 13 February 1820, a disrespectful wit remarked that he had perished on the field of honour. During the five years between the decisive defeat of Napoleon and the restoration of Louis XVIII, the Opéra had been one of this amorous prince's favourite hunting grounds, where he freely indulged his predilection for young dancers. His liaison with the beautiful but not particularly talented Mlle Virginie was common knowledge,[1] and she was by no means the sole object of his philandering.

At the instance of the Archbishop of Paris, the theatre in the Rue de Richelieu was never again used for public performances after that fateful evening and was soon being demolished, with the pious intention of replacing it with an expiatory chapel in the Duke's memory. The irony of erecting such a monument on the scene of its object's extramarital peccadilloes apparently never occurred to those worthy people who subscribed to its cost, nor to the municipality which contributed too – but Louis XVIII sensibly refused to sanction the project. His successor, Charles X, the last reigning King of France of the Legitimist line and father of the victim, was not so wise, and ordered the building to proceed. Providence, however, was to have the last word, for the Revolution of 1830 supervened before the works were completed, and the chapel was demolished in its turn some five years later, when the present Place Louvois was laid out on the site.

With no further performances possible in the Salle Richelieu, as the old building was called, temporary quarters had to be found for the large company of singers and dancers while a new opera house was designed and built. The choice fell first on the Théâtre Favart, which was little more than half the size of the former opera-house, both in audience capacity and in stage area.[2] Although a more permanent theatre for the Opéra was not expected to become available for at least a year, very few retrenchments were made in the personnel, Anatole being the only dancer in the upper ranks unlucky to be prematurely retired.[3] Time was needed to organise the move, and it was not until 10 April that, in these very restricted conditions, the Opéra reopened its doors to the public, offering a programme that included one of the favourite ballets in the repertory, Milon's *Nina*, with Emilie Bigottini in the title-rôle.

Emilie Bigottini had long been the queen of the Paris ballet. In 1820 she was thirty-six, a tall, slender woman with black hair framing expressive features which, if not strictly beautiful, were illumined by fine dark eyes and given piquancy by the mischievous smile that would play on her lips. In her temperament were combined the petulance of a Gascon and a Roman's *morbidezza*, qualities that derived from her lineage. The Bigottini family were, by tradition, theatre-folk, and had migrated to France from Rome during the eighteenth century. Emilie's father, Francesco Bigottini, had been a celebrated Harlequin, and her half-sister Louise, who was nearly twenty-eight years her elder, had danced in secondary rôles at the Opéra before the Revolution and was now married to the ballet-master Louis Milon.

Emilie, a child of her father's second marriage to a Frenchwoman from Languedoc, was born in Toulouse on 16 April 1784. There was probably never any question of her taking up any other vocation than the theatre, and on her showing an early aptitude for the dance there was providentially an excellent teacher at hand in the person of her brother-in-law Milon, who in 1799 was appointed a *maître de ballet* at the Opéra. She gained her first experience of the stage at the age of fourteen or fifteen, at the Ambigu-Comique, a small theatre on the Boulevard du Temple, in her brother-in-law's ballet *Pygmalion*.[4] When her début at the Opéra followed in 1801, she made an immediate impression not only by her dancing but, even more, by the piquancy of her miming.

Her gift of expression must have been inherited from her Harlequin father, but Milon's careful teaching had borne wonderful fruit and, to crown everything, she possessed a driving ambition and a profound sense of vocation. After her successful début at the Opéra she was offered an engagement as a *double*, and, feeling that this was not a just recognition of her talents, she boldly applied to the Minister of the Interior to be given the higher rank of *remplaçant*. 'I belong to a family,' she told him,

> whose irreproachable standards would have prevented me from going on the stage had they not held the arts in such high esteem as to consider they could offer an honourable career to one of upright character and talent. My talent will be my dowry. I have no desire to live at the expense of my honour. I wish to make myself worthy of my parents and of him to whom my talent is due, my brother-in-law, Citizen Milon.[5]

These sentiments did not imply that she was cold by nature or that she sternly held her passions in check, for in the course of her career she won the devotion of several men of high distinction. Her liaisons with Napoleon's stepson, Eugène de Beauharnais, and Duroc, the Grand Marshal of the Palace, were both lasting and serious attachments, and by the latter she had a son and a daughter. Although she herself may not have thought it so, many considered it a far greater triumph – for it was, in a sense, a double victory – when she enticed the wealthy Count de Fuentes, son of the Spanish ambassador in Paris, from one of the senior ballerinas of the Opéra, Mlle Clotilde. Another daughter, born in 1807, resulted from this association, and nine years later she gave birth to her fourth child, a son, whose father some guessed to be the Duc de Berry and others an Austrian archduke. Her name was also romantically linked with that of the dancer Albert.

Even Napoleon admired her, on one occasion commanding Fontanes, an eminent man of letters, to present her with a gift on his behalf. Fontanes, who was unfamiliar with dancers' tastes, sent her a collection of richly bound French classics. Some months later Napoleon inquired whether she had been pleased with his gift.

'*Ma foi*, sire,' she answered, 'not very much.'

'And why not?'

'He paid me in *livres*,' she explained, 'and I would rather have had *francs*.'

The Austrian Emperor Franz I was another of her admirers, and it would be at his personal wish that she came to dance in Vienna while the Congress was in progress. Pleasure went hand in hand with weighty discussions at the conference table, and one evening when the British Foreign Secretary, Lord Castlereagh, arrived to dine with his French counterpart, Talleyrand, he was delighted to discover that instead of a tedious company of fellow statesmen, with whom he had been engaged all day long in reshaping the map of Europe, there was only one other guest present, Emilie Bigottini.

Bigottini achieved her successes on the stage honourably, through her artistry, and the admiration of her friends was reflected in the devotion not only of the public, but also of nearly all her fellow dancers, who were disarmed by her gentle nature. As early as 1804, when Mme Gardel was granted leave of absence to take part in Napoleon's coronation festivities, she took over all of that ballerina's rôles; and two years later, in 1806, she was given her first important creation, the part of Marie, the black slave-girl, in Gardel's *Paul et Virginie*.[6] It was at this stage in her career that Noverre, who was living out his last years at Saint-Germain-en-Laye, within easy reach of Paris and the Opéra, wrote a critical appraisal of her talent. She was, he considered,

> well made, with a slender figure and interesting features. She follows, although still far behind, in the brilliant and light footsteps of [Mme Gardel], but comes unstuck whenever she loses the thread. The public encourages her by its applause, but lovers of the ballet would like her to pay more attention to her head, arms and shoulders, which she could use to better advantage. They would also like her to acquire a larger degree of turn-out that would add brilliance to her *entrechats*.

He also criticised her for not following the measure of the music sufficiently closely, and for her long absences from the stage that resulted from the demands of her private life.[7]

Bigottini lacked the attack and strength of some of her companions, and did not try to astonish the public with *tours de force*. Hers was, rather, a style that relied on elegance and grace, and which might not have carried her to the top of her profession had she not also excelled in the portrayal of sentimental heroines. Her greatest achievement was unquestionably the title-rôle in her brother-in-law's ballet *Nina*,[8] which she had created in 1813, the year after her promotion to *premier sujet*, and only six months after her lover Duroc had been killed in battle.

Her interpretation of this rôle was one of the highlights of pre-Romantic French ballet, and its inclusion in the programme for the opening performance at the Théâtre Favart was an obvious choice. It seemed impossible not to be moved, whatever the surroundings, by her touching portrayal of the heroine, who at one moment loses her reason in the belief that she will never see her lover again. Yet on this occasion the ballet, taken as a whole, somehow lost much of its illusion and effect. The dancers were obviously cramped, particularly the bounding Paul, who, as one observer remarked, was 'obliged to hold himself in check so as not to land in the middle of the orchestra pit'.[9]

There was no question of shelving new works that were already planned or in course of rehearsal, provided that they could be adapted to the restricted dimensions available, and the new ballet on which Louis Milon had been working met this criterion. Entitled *Clari, ou la Promesse de mariage*, with characters drawn from everyday life, its scenario was based on a novel by Baculard d'Arnaud, published in 1768, called *Clary, ou le Retour à la vertu récompensée*, a sentimental story of repentance with an English setting. In the ballet, the villainous Lord Mévil of the novel is transformed into the Duke of Mevilla (Albert), who has persuaded the young peasant girl, Clari (Bigottini), to leave her parents' home for his castle on the strength of a promise of marriage, which he has no intention of honouring. However, all the jewels that he presses on her cannot banish her feeling of shame as she contemplates her peasant costume. The Duke engages some strolling players to amuse her, but being called away in the course of their performance, does not witness the dramatic scene that is presented by the actors. For their piece contains an incident that reflects Clari's own situation, and as the actor playing the heroine's father is giving vent to his despair, Clari, imagining she is seeing her own father before her, rushes forward and swoons at his feet. On the Duke's return, she implores him to fulfil his promise to marry her, but he refuses. In desperation she tries to snatch his sword, then runs out of the room. The maidservant Betti (Courtin), who is charged to watch over her that night, drops off to sleep. Clari then quietly puts on her peasant costume and, leaving the jewels and the Duke's written promise behind on the table, makes her escape through the window. She finds her way to her native village, where a wedding celebration is in progress. But she finds her elderly parents still grieving over her lapse. Her mother receives her kindly, but her father (Milon) bids her to be gone. At that moment the Duke arrives in search of her. Clari's father draws his sword, but is disarmed. The Duke then shows him the promise of marriage and declares his intention to honour it.

In adapting the novel, Milon had made only one important concession to the taste of the time. The Duke's change of heart in the last act, an incident that does not occur in the book, made him a passably acceptable hero, but the effect of Clari's plight was thereby diminished, and the moral of the story – that true repentance finds its own reward – was much weakened. Several incidents in the novel had to be sacrificed, and one critic regretted that Milon had not been daring enough to include an adventure that takes place between her escape and her arrival at her parents' village, in which Clari is rescued from the clutches of a lascivious priest by a young man, who refuses to declare his love for her because he is betrothed to another.

In its final form, as presented on 19 June 1820 to a necessarily reduced audience at the Salle Louvois (the Opéra having meanwhile moved to another temporary home, only slightly larger than the Favart), *Clari* came under the scrutiny of the Comte de Pradel, the Minister of the King's Household, within whose purview the affairs of the Opéra then fell. Pradel, in common with many others who had served the King in exile, was particularly sensitive to the delights of the Opéra ballet. 'I am very satisfied with the way in which every aspect of the ballet *Clari* has been carried out,' he wrote next day to the Director, 'and am increasingly coming to the conclusion that a few new works staged with similar care would not fail to attract the public to the Opéra and would at least alleviate many of the miseries of exile.' He did, however, have some reservations:

The first act seems to be open to criticism as being a little long, particularly at the beginning. Would it not be possible to cut some of the mime that fills the action at this point, or interlace it with a little dancing? I feel that the dance should not be too long delayed in making its appearance in a ballet at the Opéra, particularly so as to counteract any impression that it is a purely pantomime piece such as is seen at other theatres.

Then, at the beginning of Act Two, I find the dancing lesson or rehearsal a little too long, and the part of the dancing master too fussy and too boisterous. Furthermore, this piece of pantomime will only make sense to

a very few spectators who know from experience what a ballet-master has
to do at a rehearsal.[10]

The main criticism levelled at this ballet was that its dances seemed to
have very little connection with the action, and prolonged it to an
unwarranted length. Castil-Blaze thought it should have been condensed
from three acts into two, but the need to make full use of the company, who
had been under-employed for several months, had been deemed necessary
for the state of their morale: this accounted for the lengthy *divertissements*
that inflated each act.

As in all Milon's ballets, the plot was clearly conveyed by the mime. In
preparing the score for such scenes, the composer, Kreutzer, had had to
follow the accepted practice of introducing familiar themes, or *airs parlants*,
to emphasise the purport of certain key points in the mimed action. Clari's
inner conflict between her feeling of shame at having wronged her parents
and her affection for the Duke, for example, was emphasised by a familiar
melody from Grétry's *Le Sylvain*, 'Je puis braver les coups du sort'. While her
hopes were being revived by the Duke's gifts, the orchestra played the
familiar chorus from Salieri's *Les Danaïdes*, 'Descends, du Ciel, doux Hymenée',
and the duet 'Ne doutez jamais de ma flamme; de ce doute cruel mon amour est
blessé' from Gluck's *Iphigénie en Aulide*. Another instance of this accepted
practice accompanied an amusing mime scene between Ferdinand and
Fanny Bias in the first act, when one of the strolling players, a dancer,
mistakes the Duke's valet for his master and, to the melody of the duet 'Je
brûlerai d'une ardeur éternelle' from Grétry's *Le Tableau parlant*, demonstrates
how she can portray every emotion.[11]

There could be no doubt that the ballet owed its success primarily to Emilie
Bigottini's outstanding interpretation of the role of Clari, which would be
equalled by no other ballerina during the eleven years that it remained in the
repertory.[12] The power of her acting in the players' scene was tremendous.
'In an analysis that must necessarily be cold and colourless,' wrote Castil-
Blaze,

> I can only give a very imperfect idea of the effect produced by this scene,
> which was brought to life by the affecting acting of Mlle Bigottini. But
> what I can say is that in no other rôle, not even Nina, has she shown
> herself to be a more profound or more skilful actress. Her astonishment at
> recognising the similarity between the play and her own situation was
> very natural. Her first feeling of unease gave way to a much deeper
> emotion, and then to the most passionate and frenzied disorder by degrees
> that were very skilfully managed; and her effort to control her feelings and
> ward off the disturbing curiosity of those around her was expressed with

great artistry. In short, she was so perfectly tragic that it is hard to conceive what words could have added to the force and clarity of the situation. Mlle Bigottini reveals to us all those marvels that the classical authors tell us about the mimes of their day, and the singular tribute of Cassiodorus might well be applied to her: 'She expresses herself with her hands, she has a tongue on the tips of her fingers, there is eloquence in her silence, and her speech has no need of words'.[13]

* * * * * * *

'She dances like a well-bred little urchin.'[14] Such was the impression which Pauline Paul made on one spectator at her début at the Opéra on 17 July 1820.

This was no ordinary début, for the young dancer's appearance had been awaited with more than usual interest, not only because she was the sister of the amazing Paul, whose awesome elevation had earned him the epithet of '*l'aérien*' but also because she had already given some tantalising glimpses of her own very extraordinary talent. As a child prodigy of seven, she had first danced in public at Lyons, partnered by her brother. She had then accompanied him to Paris and, not long after her sensational début at the Opéra, had been entered as a pupil of the School of Dance. In 1818 she had been seen on the Opéra stage in *La Servante justifiée*,[15] but this fleeting appearance had not ranked as a début.[16] The public's curiosity had only been really awakened when reports filtered through to the capital of the triumphant tour that she and her brother were making in the provinces towards the end of 1819. At Bordeaux, it was reported that they attracted larger houses than either Talma or Mlle Mars, and the fourteen-year-old Pauline enjoyed a true *succès de vogue*.

She astonished the Parisians no less when she made her début at the Opéra. Her style, they found, was quite novel. She had the boldness of execution and the lightness of her brother, but softened by a very feminine grace and a childlike air that was very appealing. Her vitality was infectious. 'Her lively and capricious dancing,' wrote one who was there, 'seems to reflect her character. She is like a butterfly, which the eye can hardly follow and which escapes just when you think you have caught it.'[17]

Her début and the performances that followed gained her much popularity, which perhaps encouraged her to exert herself a little too consciously, for she was advised by one critic not to model herself too closely on her brother. The style that he had created for himself, the *Journal des théâtres* pointed out, was 'quite eccentric', with constant infringements of the rules and much play of strength, and, unless drastically adapted, was not suitable for a ballerina.[18]

She was truly *une fille mal gardée,* and in more ways than one. The Opéra was to make good use of such an original dancer in the years to come, and the public was to be fascinated by stories of her frailty. In 1822 she married the dancer François Montessu, but did little more, it was said, than to take his name. The number of her lovers showed little diminution, and Léonard de Géréon was to sum up her character in these words: 'Good-hearted and generous, talented and pleasure-loving, this charming dancer combines the qualities and faults of the true artist.'[19]

* * * * * * *

Under Gardel and Milon the ballet of the Opéra had enjoyed an exceptionally long period of stability. The former had become first ballet-master after the death of his elder brother Maximilien in 1787, and Milon had joined him as assistant ballet-master in 1799. Between them they had endowed the Opéra with a rich and varied repertory, and the ballet had enjoyed a popularity that had at times raised it to a level equal, if not superior, to that of the opera. But as the 1820s approached, the need for a new direction had been increasingly felt. Gardel's three masterpieces based on classical mythology – *Télémaque, Psyché* and *Le Jugement de Pâris* – had between them notched up more than a thousand performances since their creation in the early 1790s. His comedy ballet, *La Dansomanie,* still seemed as fresh as it was at its creation, although his more recent works had proved less lasting. Tastes were changing; now in his sixties, Gardel was probably too set in his ways to absorb the enthusiasms of the younger generation. The productions of his associate, Milon, were less affected by such changes, for he worked in the more approachable genres of comedy and sentiment. The Opéra was vastly indebted to these two distinguished and devoted masters, but for some years the need to secure the future had become increasingly felt.

In 1817 negotiations had been opened with Jean-Louis Aumer, who was at that time ballet-master at the Court Opera in Vienna; but owing to an unfortunate lapse in their correspondence, the discussions had languished. Aumer then had no choice but to renew his contract with Vienna, but he had the foresight to insist on a provision that it could be terminated if his services were required in Paris.

Born of humble parentage at Strasbourg on 21 April 1774, Aumer was a full generation younger than Gardel. Being one of a large family subsisting on the meagre wages of their father, he had received only a modest education before having to start earning his own living. He must have taken a theatrical job, for at some point in his early youth he attracted the notice of the celebrated ballet-master Dauberval, who was so taken by his quick intelligence and his promise as a dancer that he took him under his wing. To young Aumer this was a stroke of great good fortune, and he made the most of it. Exactly how old he then was, history does not relate, but it was early enough for him to acquire an excellent grounding for the career that was then opening up before him. He became one of Dauberval's favourite pupils, and his enthusiasm and gratitude were to be shown not only in his growing prowess as a dancer, but also in his earnest endeavours to assimilate his master's choreographic method and, with it, a sound knowledge of music and the fine arts. In 1791 he accompanied his master to London for his first professional engagement. He was then still sixteen but had already progressed to the point of being named among the principal dancers of the company at the London opera-house. And while he was there, he probably danced in the first London production of his master's comedy ballet, *La Fille mal gardée.*

It may have been on Dauberval's recommendation that he secured an engagement as a dancer at the Paris Opéra in 1797. There he was never to rise above the modest rank of *double*, but his above-average height was an advantage in his becoming a very useful mime, in which capacity he understudied Milon himself. His ambition, however, lay in the field of choreography, and when the recently opened Porte-Saint-Martin began to include ballets in its programmes, the Opéra turned a blind eye to his producing a number of ballets there between 1804 and 1806. Apart from presenting several of Dauberval's works, no doubt with his blessing, Aumer staged a number of ballets of his own composition, which were well received. However, the last of his productions there, *Les Deux Créoles,* involved him in a clash with Gardel, who was simultaneously preparing a ballet for the Opéra based on the same source, the well-known novel of *Paul et Virginie.* Aumer's success prompted the Opéra to demand that he cease working for the Porte-Saint-Martin on pain of being dismissed, but Aumer was cunning enough to persuade the Opéra, as a *quid pro quo* for his sacrifice of a lucrative source of income, to agree to his staging a major ballet.

The success of this ballet, *Les Amours d'Antoine et de Cléopâtre,* had led to an engagement in Kassel, then the capital of the newly formed Kingdom of Westphalia, ruled by Napoleon's brother, Jérôme. From there, in 1814, after a brief spell in Lyons, he secured the prestigious post of ballet-master at the Court Opera in Vienna, where, over the next six years, he gained an impressive reputation by staging a string of successful ballets.

It was hardly to be wondered at that the Opéra had turned its attention to him when the need arose to engage a younger ballet-master in reserve.

Discussions were resumed early in 1819, and the point was reached when all that remained to be decided was the date at which he would be available. In the course of this correspondence Aumer suggested that he might first stage *Aline*, which had been the most successful of all the ballets he had staged in Vienna. There was a suggestion that an objection might be made by the Opéra-Comique, where Berton's *opéra-comique* on the same subject had been performed seventeen years before; but this was discounted when it was realised that the subject had originally been used for a work at the Opéra many years before that.

In November 1819, learning that Ciceri had already started to work on the scenery for *Aline*, Aumer began to feel he was being pressured. He was concerned because he had become aware that a major new opera, *Olympie*, was in preparation; since Milon was to arrange the dances in it, it seemed unlikely that he would be able to start rehearsing his ballet until March at the earliest. He was also worried that his ballet might suffer if it were to follow two major opera creations.

At the same time he was under pressure in Vienna to defer his departure by six months. His recent restaging there of a Dauberval ballet, *Le Page inconstant*, had been a triumph, and the Court Opera now wanted him to follow it up with a grand historical ballet based on an incident in the life of Alfred the Great, for which Count von Gallenberg was on the point of completing the score. To this the Opéra readily agreed, and Aumer was to remain in Vienna to produce two more ballets: *Emma* (a reworking of his earlier Porte-Saint-Martin success, *Jenny*) in February, and two months later, *Alfred der Grosse*, the success of which augured well for his forthcoming engagement in Paris.[20]

Whatever the reaction might have been to this last-minute request for a postponement, circumstances were to intervene that more than justified the Opéra's acceptance of his request. In February the Duc de Berry was assassinated. When Aumer eventually arrived in Paris in the summer, he found the Opéra still in crisis, with its former theatre in the Rue de Richelieu permanently closed and performances only recently resumed on a stage totally inadequate for a ballet on the scale of *Alfred*. These circumstances inevitably necessitated a change of plan, and Aumer had no choice but to substitute a minor work if he was not to risk losing the opportunity of working in Paris. Wise enough to recognise the impossibility of mounting a major ballet in the restricted surroundings of the Salle Favart, he agreed to produce a smaller-scale work, *Les Pages du duc de Vendôme*, but on the strict condition that either *Aline* or *Alfred le Grand* would be staged for the opening of the new theatre. 'If my demand cannot be accepted,' he wrote to the

Director, 'I beg you to be good enough to obtain the cancellation of my contract from the authorities.'[21]

On this basis, agreement was reached, and *Les Pages du duc de Vendôme* was presented at the Théâtre Favart on 18 October 1820. It was danced to the score composed for the Viennese production by Adalbert Gyrowetz, who twelve years previously had written the music for a one-act operetta on the same subject and with the same title.[22] Thanks to the charm of its plot and the economical scale of its production, this unpretentious piece was to retain a place in the repertory until 1830. Such durability could hardly have been foreseen in the light of its cool reception from the critics after its first Paris performance on 18 October 1820. The *Journal des théâtres* called it 'a little piece of nonsense, a feeble composition... hardly worthy of the Porte-Saint-Martin'.[23] Its main criticism was directed at the dances, which were bunched together in two seemingly interminable *divertissements* that had little bearing on the action and indeed disrupted it. In particular, the dances were criticised for a lack of local colour, which required a greater contrast between the French and Spanish *pas*.

However, the choice of *Les Pages du duc de Vendôme* had one merit: the plot was already familiar to Paris theatre-goers, for the action was taken from a comedy of the same name given at the Théâtre du Vaudeville in 1807.[24] The Duc de Vendôme (Aumer), who is campaigning in Spain, has found time to choose a husband, the Comte de Muret (Milon), for his ward Elise (Bias). Elise, however, is in love with one of the Duke's pages, Victor (Bigottini). Victor persuades the pages to erect their tent close to the house so that when night falls he can climb up to Elise's balcony. The Duke interrupts this escapade, but fails to recognise which of his pages is the culprit. So he goes into the darkened tent where they sleep and removes the aiguillettes from the uniform of the page whose heart is pounding most strongly so that he can identify him in the morning. Victor, however, tricks him by removing the aiguillettes of all his companions. Next morning, after Elise has refused Muret's proposal, the lovers beg the Duke to forgive them, and finally, at Muret's intervention, he relents and gives them his blessing.

In his review Castil-Blaze observed that if theatrical dancing was to be considered seriously, it must be governed by the same principles as other stage arts, and that there was no place in a ballet for anything redundant:

Appling these observations to M. Aumer's ballet, everyone enjoyed the scene in the first *divertissement* in which the pages are discovered chasing and teasing the village girls, and trying to steal kisses with all the petulance of youth and the liberty allowed them by their uniform. This lively little scene, which is entirely in character, is followed by a grotesque peasant dance by Ferdinand and Mme Aimée, offering a natural contrast that is not ineffective. Then comes the bolero danced by Victor and his sweetheart, which, even if it had not been done with the perfection that Mlles Bigottini and Fanny Bias always bring to their acting and their dancing, would have indicated quite plainly that the two principal characters had discovered their attraction for one another in a *pas de deux*. So far, so good, and nothing out of place with the ballet's subject, but we are far from finished. It is necessary to bring on Albert and the choreographer's daughter, which is fair enough; and so there has to be a new *entrée* for Albert and Julie Aumer. And would the proceedings be complete if Paul did not make an appearance with his sister? So now room must be found for Mlle Paul, her brother and Fanny Bias. Is that all? No! All the pages and the entire *corps de ballet* must then dance an interminable tarantella. After the tarantella, the action is resumed, but only to be interrupted again by a *pas* for Mlle Hullin, another for Coulon and Mlle Marinette, and a second appearance for Paul, this time as the indispensable partner of Mlle Noblet and the condescending cavalier of Mlle Julie Aumer.[25]

Perhaps Castil-Blaze was exaggerating a little to press his point when he said that this ballet was composed of one part of pleasure to four of boredom, being the ratio of action to dancing, but few would have cavilled at his statement that of the pleasurable portion Bigottini's talent counted for a good half. Indeed, a new facet of this versatile talent was revealed in her lively, natural miming as the mischievous and lovable page Victor. To her, more than anyone else, was due the success that this little work achieved.

* * * * * * *

Throughout the winter and into the following spring, the singers and dancers of the Opera continued to struggle against odds in their cramped temporary quarters. Early in 1821 Gardel's *Vénus et Adonis* and *Paul et Virginie* were revived, and the same choreographer's *La Dansomanie* took on a new lease of life. Albert gained a special triumph in this last ballet. 'I have seen the finest days of Vestris,' wrote one critic, 'and I have no hesitation in saying that Albert is very much superior to him, even as a mime. Albert, whose art is classical, disputes the favour of the public with Paul: the former is the Virgil of the dance, the latter the Ariosto of the dance.'[26] But the styles of these two dancers were so different that no comparison was possible: 'it would be equally ridiculous to compare Isabey and David,' commented another observer.[27] Here already, a distinction was being drawn between the classical style of dancing and a freer, Romantic style. *Le Carnaval de Venise*, another popular work, with choreography by Milon, which had been performed at the old Salle Richelieu on the night of the assassination, was also included in the final programme at the Salle Favart on 11 May 1821.[28]

The new opera-house was not yet completed, and another temporary move followed, to the Salle Louvois, where four performances were given in May and June. At the last of these, on 15 June, Aumer presented a *divertissement* under the title of *La Fête hongroise*. This was no doubt a reworking of a little work he had staged in Vienna six years before under the title *Das ländliche Fest im Wäldchen bei Kis-Bér* (The Peasant Festival in the little wood at Kis-Bér).[29] Presumably Joseph Kinsky's score for the Viennese production formed the basis of the music for the Paris revival, which was attributed to the Viennese composer Adalbert Gyrowetz. It was not particularly memorable, but one critic recognised a Hungarian dance tune he had heard at one of Prince von Schwarzemberg's balls and an unidentified borrowing from Rossini. It was a work of little consequence, and was not considered for revival when the new opera-house opened; indeed it never had another performance in Paris. It consisted of no more than a series of dances performed before a Hungarian count (Aumer) by his vassals, with an incident thrown in of a town dandy (Ragaine) who is infatuated with a peasant girl and is tossed in a blanket by the villagers. It was all very unpretentious, but the dances were lively enough, even if there could have been more variety in their composition: a Cossack dance by Joséphine Hullin and Capelle was found rather monotonous, but the imposing figure of Simon Mérante made up for that with an amusing grotesque dance. It could perhaps be claimed that this introduction of local colour advanced the cause of Romanticism by a tiny step, and it was at least encouraging to see how strong the company was, even in such pitifully limited surroundings and during a season of the year when a number of dancers were on leave fulfilling lucrative engagements in London.

NOTES

1. Virginie Oreille (1795–1875) was the daughter of a wig-maker of the Comédie-Française. Before her liaison with the Duc de Berry she had been the mistress of Marshal Bessières, who was killed in 1813. She had two sons by the Duc de Berry, the second born eight months after the assassination. For a full account, see Guest, *Ballet under Napoleon*, ch. 34.
2. It occupied the site on which the Opéra-Comique stands today.
3. Arch. Nat., AJ[13] 119.
4. *Pygmalion*, ballet-pantomime in one act, choreography by Milon, music arranged by Lefebvre, f.p. Ambigu-Comique, 8 May 1799, and revived at the Opéra, 20 August 1800, in a two-act version.
5. Arch. Nat., AJ[13] 79. Letter dated 10 nivôse an X (31 December 1801).
6. *Paul et Virginie*, ballet-pantomime in three acts, choreography by P. Gardel, music by Kreutzer, f.p. Paris Opéra, 24 June 1806.
7. Noverre, *Lettres sur les arts imitateurs*, II, 162–3.

8. *Nina, ou la Folle par amour,* ballet-pantomime in two acts, choreography by Milon, music by Persuis after Dalayrac, f.p. Paris Opéra, 23 November 1813.

9. *Constitutionnel,* 21 April 1820.

10. Arch. Nat., AJ[13] 111. Pradel to Viotti, 20 June 1820.

11. All these operas had been in the repertory for many years, *Le Tableau parlant* since 1769 and *Le Sylvain* since 1770 at the Opéra-Comique, and *Iphigénie en Aulide* since 1774 and *Les Danaïdes* since 1784 at the Opéra.

12. The rôle of Clari was later played by Amélie Legallois (6 September 1822), Lise Noblet (19 November 1824) and Evelina Fleurot (15 May 1825).

13. *Journal des débats,* 22 June 1820.

14. *Almanach des spectacles* (4th year), 60.

15. *La Servante justifiée,* ballet *villageoise* in one act, choreography by P. Gardel, music by Kreutzer, f.p. Paris Opéra, 30 September 1818.

16. Castil-Blaze is incorrect in saying (*Académie,* II, 153) that she danced on 6 June 1817 in *La Caravane.* It was her future husband, François Montessu, who made his début on that occasion.

17. Géréon, 34.

18. *Journal des théâtres,* 12 April 1821.

19. Géréon, 35.

20. Arch. Nat., AJ[13] 125. Aumer to Courtin, 13 November 1819.

21. Arch. Nat., AJ[13] 125. Aumer to Viotti, 4 September 1820.

22. First performed at the Court Opera, Vienna, on 5 August 1808.

23. *Journal des théâtres,* 20 October 1820.

24. *Les Pages du duc de Vendôme,* comedy in one act with vaudevilles by Dieulafoy and Gersin, f.p. Th. du Vaudeville, 17 July 1807. Aumer's ballet had been presented at the Court Opera, Vienna, on 16 October 1808.

25. *Journal des débats,* 20 October 1820.

26. *Journal des théâtres,* 5 February 1821. On 8 November 1822 this critic again commented on Albert's superiority to Auguste Vestris as a mime when the former appeared as Azaël in a revival of Gardel's *L'Enfant prodigue.*

27. *Journal de Paris,* 12 May 1822.

28. *Vénus et Adonis* (1808), *Paul et Virginie* (1806), *La Dansomanie* (1800) and *L'Enfant prodigue* (1812) were all ballets by Gardel; *Le Carnaval de Venise* (1816) was a ballet by Milon. For further details of these ballets, see Guest, *Ballet under Napoleon.*

29. First performed at the Court Opera, Vienna, on 29 November 1815, it remained in the repertory there for five and a half years, achieving a total of 54 performances.

4

Aumer Strikes his Claim

The condition imposed by the Archbishop of Paris for permitting the last rites to be administered to the Duc de Berry within its walls – that the opera-house in the Rue de Richelieu should never again be used as a place of entertainment – set in motion an urgent search for an alternative site. Little time was lost: within a few weeks a proposal to erect an opera-house on the site of the Bourse was under discussion, but this was quickly discarded on the grounds of expense when it was realised that the project would involve not only tearing down an existing theatre, the Feydeau, but also considerable demolitions in the surrounding area. In May attention was turned to another possible site, that of the Hôtel de Choiseul, and this choice was formally ratified in August by a Royal Ordinance authorising a credit of 900,000 francs. Meanwhile, the former opera-house was to be sold by public auction after the removal of 'such wooden fixtures and fittings, machinery and scenery as could be used'.

Work on the new theatre was quickly under way. The eastern end of the Hôtel de Choiseul, with its entrance on the Rue Drouot, was preserved for administrative offices, the theatre itself being constructed in the grounds behind, with its façade fronting the Rue Le Peletier. Its northern wall abutted the Rue Pinon, later to be renamed the Rue Rossini, while along the southern edge ran a passage in which would be installed the Café de l'Opéra. From this, in 1824, two more passages were opened up at right angles leading from the original passage southward to the Boulevard des Italiens. The theatre itself, built for only about half the cost of an entirely new opera-house designed to be a landmark in the city, was envisaged as no more than a temporary home for the Opéra until more prosperous times returned; but in the event it was honourably to serve its purpose for more than 50 years before being burnt to the ground in October 1873.

Having taken only a year or so to build, the new opera-house in the Rue Le Peletier was inaugurated on 16 August 1821. Whether the opening had been insufficiently publicised – no newspapers having been published that day (the day after the Feast of the Assumption) – or whether people feared discomfort in the August heat from the smell of newly painted plaster, the anticipated rush for seats did not materialise and tickets were still available up to half an hour after the box office had opened. That the audience found themselves quite at home when they entered and looked around was not surprising, since much of the material of the previous building had been incorporated into the new. The auditorium, however, had been given a more pronounced horseshoe form, which harmonised better with the domed ceiling and provided more accommodation for the audience; and without decreasing the number of boxes the architect had even managed to make them more spacious. The performers were also given more space, the proscenium being slightly wider and the stage area considerably larger than in the former house.

The programme that evening opened with the royalist anthem 'Vive Henri IV', with variations by Paër.[1] There followed Catel's opera Les Bayadères, and finally Gardel's ballet Le Retour de Zéphire,[2] in which Mlle Aimée appeared as a rather thickset Flora, prompting a comment in the Journal des théâtres that it seemed

> amazing to find that Floras and Hebes should be selected by order of seniority. Generally speaking, many of the danseuses have put on too much flesh since we saw them last, and yet these girls have more opportunity than most to keep up their activity. Come, ladies, take some exercise! It is a remedy you will find easy, pleasant and profitable.[3]

Before the end of 1821, on 1 November, Viotti was retired as Director of the Opéra. The problems of the past 18 months had deprived him of all pleasure in the post and had had a devastating effect on his health. In 1823 he left France to spend the last few months of his life in London. His successor was another distinguished violinist, François Habeneck, who had succeeded Rodolphe Kreutzer as first violin and conductor of the orchestra in 1819. When he was appointed, the routine of theatre life was well under way in the new building, and the ballet company had been brought up to full strength by the return from London of Lise Noblet. For her the season there had been a most profitable one, for she had subjugated a rich nobleman, Earl Fife, who was an influential figure in London's operatic world. Throughout that summer, rumours had been circulating in Paris that His Lordship had settled £500 a year on her and was even contemplating marrying her – and the first of these rumours seemed to be given some credence by the elegant carriage she brought back with her from England.

It was soon clear that she had returned to Paris much better provided with the luxuries of life, for she appeared before the public one evening wearing in her hair such a splendid diamond-studded comb that a gasp of admiration went up from every side. Unfortunately it was not too firmly secured, and during a brilliant passage of turns it flew off and would have been trampled underfoot had not her partner, Paul, without for a moment disturbing the flow of his movement, deftly gathered it up and dropped it into the hands of one of the *corps de ballet*. Somebody was heard to murmur, 'She has lost her diamonds', and from one box, it was reported, there came 'an exclamation that was not French'.[4]

Lord Fife also had a ward, a lovely Spanish girl called Maria Mercandotti, who had come to his notice as a child dancing in a theatre in Cadiz. The Peninsular War, in which he was serving, was then at its height; but in the summer of 1814, after Napoleon's abdication, he had brought her to England, given her a good education and placed her in charge of Armand Vestris, from whom she took classes before making a single appearance at the King's Theatre in London. Apart from dancing a few times at Brighton before Queen Charlotte, she did not appear in public again until her début at the Opéra in December 1821, which was planned as a prelude to her participating in the London season of 1822, for which she was engaged at a salary of £800 – a considerable figure for a *débutante*. Lord Fife's influence in the operatic world was not confined to London, where he was on the Governing Committee of the King's Theatre, but extended also to Paris, where he shared with ambassadors and great functionaries of state the most exclusive privilege of entry into the Foyer de la Danse. Consequently he had little difficulty in arranging for his protégée to be prepared for her début at the Opéra by Jean-François Coulon, and he left nothing undone to ensure that her success should be as brilliant as it could be. If anything, indeed, he erred in being excessively enthusiastic in his efforts on her behalf.

Maria's first appearance at the Opéra took place on 10 December 1821, when she danced in a *pas de deux* with Antoine Coulon, her teacher's son, in the opera *La Caravane du Caïre*, followed later in the evening by a *pas de trois* with Paul and Mme Anatole in *Nina*. Strategically scattered among the audience was a strong English contingent; it was said that Fife had spent 1500 francs on hiring boxes for his friends, and to judge from their enthusiasm they certainly earned His Lordship's generosity. A loud cheer went up as soon as Maria was first seen, and the resulting pause gave the audience time to take stock of her. Maria, who was then about twenty, was in the full bloom of her remarkable beauty. The sobriquet, 'the Andalusian Venus', which an English admirer applied to her, seemed entirely appropriate. Her black hair had the sheen of sable, her features were delicate and regular, and on the rare occasions when she smiled – for on this auspicious evening she was very frightened – her dark eyes seemed to sparkle beneath her finely arched brows and her expression to glow with a sudden radiance. Her figure was trim and supple, her legs shapely and her feet dainty, and if her arms were perhaps a trifle thin, the general effect of her appearance was one of striking and unspoilt loveliness.

No sooner had she begun to dance than an English contingent in the audience broke out into shouts of *'Bravo! Bravo! Ah! Ah! Bravissimo!'* – a demonstration that understandably prejudiced some critics against her. Castil-Blaze, who was later to call her the prettiest woman he had ever seen on the stage, was shocked and disgusted by this blatant demonstration, which seemed to take no account of false steps, badly finished pirouettes, unsteady poses and a grimacing expression, and he was pained to observe the audience's neglect of Pauline Paul, whom he thought very much more deserving.[5]   Maria, however, triumphed over the excessive zeal of her guardian's compatriots and succeeded in creating a favourable impression. The grace of her movements and her lightness made up for her deficiencies. One critic praised her for not attempting a display of *tours de force*; 'those convulsive whirlings, which people want to make fashionable,' he said, 'are more like a fakir's enthusiasm or a juggler's delight than the cadenced steps of a dancing girl'.[6] Another went so far as to say that she was 'almost a Demoiselle Noblet',[7] a remark that the more raffish of Lord Fife's friends might have taken in two ways.

At her second appearance exactly a week later, the vociferous English element was less in evidence and Maria herself had lost much of her nervousness. Castil-Blaze revised his unfavourable first impression, and recognised that 'she invested her steps with as much precision and correctness as before she had shown feebleness and unsteadiness. The characteristics of Mlle Maria's talent,' he went on,

> are grace and nobility, and this talent, although formed in a different school, has many points of affinity with that of Mlle Noblet ... There is not the polish and delicacy of Fanny Bias's steps, nor yet the fine set of the head and the bold movements of Mme Anatole, but there is suppleness combined with dignity and decency. It is a style midway between the sudden and somewhat disordered flashes of character dancing and the cold and grave monotony of the minuet.[8]

By the time Maria gave her last performance, dancing a Spanish *pas de caractère*, the *Guaracha*, on 4 January 1822, Castil-Blaze, like nearly everyone else, was completely under her spell.

Many theatre-goers must have looked forward to the pleasure of Maria's return to the Opéra. Some had even sensed a budding romance with Paul, which might in time have drawn her back; but their hopes, and perhaps Paul's as well, were dashed by the intervention of another suitor, a wealthy Englishman by the name of Edward Ball-Hughes, who enjoyed Lord Fife's friendship and, after persistent wooing, persuaded the beautiful young Spaniard to marry him. This marriage cut short what promised to be a distinguished career, and – sad to relate – was to end in divorce. Castil-Blaze retained an interest in her, and in his history of the Opéra recorded that in later years she became Mme Dufresne, which is the last known fact about the Andalusian Venus.

* * * * * * *

With the new opera-house now in operation, spectacular ventures could be launched once again, and the first creation to be presented, on 6 February 1822, exploited the theatre's modern scenic resources to the full. Neither musically nor dramatically was the faery opera *Aladin* a work of any great moment, but the spectacle, on which no less than 170,000 francs had been expended, was unforgettable, and it would be performed more than fifty times before the end of the year. 'There is no doubt,' wrote the *Moniteur* after the first performance, 'that yesterday the Opéra was, more than ever before, a temple of magic and the most brilliant theatrical illusions.' [9] The magician was Louis-Jacques Daguerre, from whose designs the scenery had been constructed under the masterly direction of Ciceri, the Opéra's *décorateur-en-chef*. A man of fertile and practical imagination, Daguerre was to be best known as the inventor of the diorama and the daguerreotype, but his genius as a stage designer was no less remarkable. His designs were said to surpass in splendour those of his predecessor and master Degotti, and some of his admirers were even bold enough to compare him with the Bibienas. Stage lighting held a particular fascination for him, and in *Aladin* he made history by using gas lighting for the first time to light the stage.

The vast concentration of effort on this massive production left little opportunity for Aumer to undertake any useful work, and apparently no objection was made to his entering into short-term engagements elsewhere. From December 1821 to March 1822 he was at La Scala, Milan, staging several ballets that he had originally created in Paris or Vienna. On his return to Paris, rather than remaining inactive, he produced a series of ballets at one of the minor theatres on the Boulevard du Temple, the Panorama-Dramatique. That struggling little playhouse had bravely assembled a small company of dancers headed by a Mlle Chéza, and there Aumer passed some of his time between March and June 1822 reviving an early work of his own, *Jenny*, as well as three ballets by Dauberval: *Le Déserteur, Annette et Lubin* and *La Fille mal gardeé.* [10]

The Opéra had assured Aumer that either *Aline* or *Alfred le Grand* would be produced as soon as the new opera-house was ready, and the choice fell on the latter work, which had already proved successful in both Vienna and Milan. [11] This decision was made in the spring of 1821, when Aumer undertook to take account of French taste and the talent at his disposal, and give his work what he called 'an entirely novel appearance, from both the choreographic and the musical points of view'.[12] In October 1821 the scenario was submitted to the reading jury, who made a few comments, not on the choreography but on the action, recommending that the public should be made aware, when Alfred made his first appearance in disguise, that this was the King, and that Act Two might be enlivened with more incident, perhaps by 'exposing Alfred to frequent dangers'.[13] The composer of the score, Count Robert von Gallenberg, joined Aumer in Paris 'to direct and revise the ballet as necessary to make it worthy of the Opéra',[14] but it was not until the beginning of June 1822 that the stage became available for rehearsals.

The cause of the delay was another major opera production, Manuel Garcia's *Florestan*, for the final rehearsal of which both Gardel and Milon required use of the stage and the presence of the dancers. Only when that opera had been presented was Aumer able to make a serious start on *Alfred*. Ciceri was then set to work on the scenery, while Aumer took some two months to reshape the ballet for a French audience. At last all was ready, and on 18 September 1822 it was given its first performance.

It was a truly epic work inspired by the struggle between King Alfred of Saxon England and the Danish invaders. Earl Edelbert (Milon) and his daughter Alswith (Mme Anatole) are preparing for a village festival when Alfred (Albert) and his page Oliver (Bigottini) arrive in disguise. They are given shelter by an old farmer, Denulf (Aumer), to whom, when they are alone, Alfred confides his identity. Denulf's daughter Bertha (Julie Aumer) is chosen as the queen of the festival, for whose hand the villagers compete by shooting at a hawk. In this contest Alfred is the winner and asks Denulf to give his blessing to Bertha's betrothal to her sweetheart (A. Coulon). The festivities are then interrupted when a band of Danish soldiers are sighted on the hillside, carrying away the Earl as their prisoner. Alswith comes running into the village to seek help, and with Alfred at their head the men set off to the rescue.

After freeing the Earl, Alfred, still in disguise, returns to the castle where, alone with his page, he confesses that he has fallen in love with Alswith. Believing Alfred to have fallen asleep, Alswith dances before him, expressing her sadness that she can never marry a man of such lowly status. Odun (Montjoie), the Saxon chief who is betrothed to her, then returns from battle and becomes jealous of Alfred, who declares his intention to leave the castle. But Alswith persuades him to stay, and when, during the celebrations of Odun's victory in the Hall of Knights, news is brought that the Danes have set fire to the village, Alfred rises in anger and is recognised as the King. After swearing fealty, the warriors depart, leaving the women offering up prayers for their victory and safe return.

A clash with the Danes has already taken place when the third act opens, and the Earl and Alswith are brought into the tent of Gothrun, the Danish chief (S. Mérante), as prisoners. Denulf, disguised as a Danish soldier, then comes to tell Gothrun that Alfred is dead, and in the resulting confusion the prisoners make their escape. Alfred's ruse has succeeded. Disguised as a blind musician, he enters the Danish camp and surveys the ground, to return shortly afterwards at the head of the Saxon army and rout the carousing enemy. The ballet closes with Alfred magnanimously pardoning Gothrun and crowning Alswith as his queen.

Aumer's claim to novelty was not without foundation. His treatment of the subject and his respect for the historical background not only had no precedent in French ballet, but also offered evidence of what could be seen as a Romantic approach. The choreography, however, did not of itself strike out in any new direction. The attempt to cover such a large canvas with its contrasting scenes of village festivities, sentimental exchanges and battles resulted in the central theme becoming somewhat overloaded with subsidiary themes – which not only deprived the work of clarity but detracted from the development of the characters. Here Aumer was forgetting some of the lessons he should have learnt from his master, Dauberval, and the *Constitutionnel* made some pertinent remarks about the complexity of the action:

> This would be a defect in any dramatic work, for it not only reveals a kind of sterility of imagination, but a great variety of resources has to be employed to make up for it. Ballets in the heroic style such as *Alfred* belong to a type that uses the dance as such merely as an ornament or an accessory to the choreographic action, something which, if necessary, could easily be dispensed with. Dauberval adopted a different method, for he knew how to weave the dance into the action. If the danced portion of one of his productions were to be removed, there would no longer be any action, for there would be nothing left. But if modern ballets were deprived of the brilliant *pas* and the pageantry with which they are adorned, all that would remain would be uninterrupted action, a mass of uninteresting mime... Dauberval, in his delightful productions and his own brilliant performances, succeeded in fusing his art with the drama. The modern method, on the other hand, tends to ignore this honourable relationship. M. Aumer may be an able ballet-master, but Dauberval was in the true sense of the word a dramatic author.[15]

The critics found little fault with the first act. It certainly contained nothing redundant, and the manner in which Aumer linked the dancing with the action was specially praised, particularly the situation in which Alfred joins in the village dances without revealing his identity. In the second act, the episode of Alswith dancing before the King while the latter is pretending to be asleep might smack of improbability, although the dance itself was a delight – 'a veritable picture by Albano',[16] as one critic put it. The *divertissement* in the Hall of Knights was generally considered too long, but this scene was remarkable on other counts: it marked the first appearance on the stage of the Opéra of a military band, thirty-one strong, while Ciceri's lofty Gothic hall with its distant perspectives was indisputably Romantic in atmosphere and owed not a little of its illusion to lighting effects inspired by the diorama. The last act, both scenically and choreographically, was the least successful: the action was slowed down by an over-long and uninteresting *pas des amazones*, while to some the staged combats seemed somewhat tame by comparison with the fights that brought many a melodrama to a close in the boulevard theatres.

   Alfred le Grand was to be the last ballet produced at the Opéra for more than a hundred years in which the principal character was a male hero played by a male dancer.[17] Albert was an ideal choice for the part of Alfred, for his natural dignity gave him a kingly air even when in disguise, and his convincing and expressive acting was matched by the classical perfection of his dancing. It was very much Albert's ballet, although Bigottini gave a spirited performance as the page and Mme Anatole appeared as a noble, if a trifle colourless, Alswith; and there were, of course, plenty of opportunities for the other members of the company to shine in the *divertissements.*

   The score for the original Viennese production of *Alfred le Grand* was composed by Count Robert von Gallenberg, an Austrian nobleman who had married Beethoven's early passion, Giulietta Guicciardi, and acquired a reputation as a prolific composer of ballet music. Writing to Viotti in May 1821, Aumer had spoken of Gallenberg's plan to come to Paris to make such adjustments to the score as might be necessary;[18] but when the time came for the ballet to be staged, he was faced with such criticism of Gallenberg's 'Italianate' music that he had to agree to a French composer, Gustave Dugazon, being brought in to make the musical adjustments required. According to the *Journal des théâtres*, these difficulties may have been inspired more by a desire to exclude a foreign composer than by any real objections to the standard of his composition.[19] In fact, the score attracted more attention than was usually given to the music of a ballet. Obvious to every knowledgeable listener was the influence of Rossini, which was particularly remarked in the use made of the resources of the orchestra. It was, of course, the work of a lesser composer, and one critic found the orchestration in places monotonous. And while there was a 'happy abundance of pleasing melodies' admirably suitable for dancing, the critic of the *Journal des débats* complained that the composer had been excessively original in not following the practice of inserting recognisable melodies to assist the audience to follow the action.[20] With all its shortcomings, it was to a certain extent a forward-looking score not unworthy of the dramatic, almost melodramatic, ballet it accompanied.

* * * * * * *

Albert was not only a naturally gifted dancer, but also a man of unusual intelligence who possessed an absorbing passion for his art. This he had studied with great thoroughness. His extensive library of dance manuals in several languages, the tapestries of Greek and Oriental dances that decorated the walls of his apartment in the Rue des Moulins, his knowledge of music, and his ability to converse on many different subjects all testified to his scholarship.[21] So, too, in a different way, did his style of dancing, which was based on the traditions of the *genre noble* as practised in former times by Dupré and the elder Vestris. When he was in his prime, he commanded general admiration and respect, although there were some even then who found his dancing a little cold; but as the audiences at the Opéra became less exclusively aristocratic, his style began to appear something of an anachronism alongside the warm realistic miming of his colleague Ferdinand and the brilliant dancing of some of his companions. Feats of virtuosity, such as those that had made Paul famous, were not for him. 'Albert does not jump,' wrote a contemporary, 'for he prefers the God of Grace to the God of Entrechats.'[22] In spite of the changing taste of the public, however, he maintained his position at the Opéra – for there still remained many old theatre-goers who had been reared in the traditions of the eighteenth century.

Albert's real name was François Decombe, and he was born in Bordeaux in 1787. Strangely enough, his father, a retired cavalry captain, not wishing to risk losing all three of his sons, refused to allow him to follow his two brothers into the navy, and raised no objection to his taking up a theatrical career. At first the boy was not particularly happy, and he was seriously considering whether to abandon dancing altogether when Auguste Vestris happened to visit his native town and kindled his ambition. He lost no time in making his way to Paris, where he obtained an engagement at the Théâtre du Gaîté and took classes with Lefebvre. A second revelation followed when he saw Louis Duport dance at the Opéra, and shortly after this, in 1808, he was himself preparing to make his début on that same stage under the guidance of Jean-François Coulon. It took him only three years to become *premier sujet*, and now, in 1823, at the age of thirty-six, he had no rival as a *danseur noble*, and in addition had proved himself to be a competent choreographer and an inspired teacher. One of his pupils, Félicité Hullin, who made her début at the Opéra on 5 February 1823, was to marry the Spanish guitarist Fernando Sor and become a leading figure in the ballet at the Bolshoi Theatre, Moscow.

Albert's talent as a choreographer had been first revealed in 1818 when he staged a pleasing little ballet at the Opéra, *Le Séducteur au village*.[23] He had continued to produce ballets during engagements at the King's Theatre, London, in 1821 and 1822, and also at Lyons in 1821. In April 1822 the Opéra had recognised this gift by giving him a new contract, not only as a dancer, but also as *maître des ballets adjoint*, for a term of five years at a salary of 20,000 francs a year with a bonus of 40 francs for each appearance.

The most successful of Albert's early ballets was undoubtedly *Cendrillon*, which he had produced in London with Mercandotti as Cinderella in the spring of 1822,[24] and which he revived just under a year later, on 3 March 1823, at the Paris Opéra. Apart from its familiarity as a fairy tale, the story of Cinderella had inspired two operas within recent memory: Isouard's *Cendrillon*, produced at the Opéra-Comique in 1810, and Rossini's *La cenerentola*, which had had its first Paris performance at the Théâtre Italien as recently as June 1822. Albert, however, based his scenario much more faithfully on the tale as told by Charles Perrault and took very little from the libretti of these operas beyond the names for the prince and Cinderella's stepsisters.

In the first act, Cinderella (Bigottini) is sitting forlornly by the fireside while her stepmother (Mme Elie) and her stepsisters (Mme Anatole, Bias) are preparing for the ball. An old beggar-woman to whom Cinderella alone has shown kindness returns when she is alone and transforms herself into the fairy Mélisse (Gaillet). She conjures up a ball gown and a carriage, and Cinderella goes to the ball – the scene of the second act – where the prince (Albert) falls in love with her. But midnight strikes; remembering the fairy's warning, she slips away, leaving one of her slippers behind in her flight. Cinderella, in rags again, is taken to the palace garden by the fairy, but when she puts on the slipper, the prince at first fails to recognise her. He complains to the fairy, who bids him look again, and there before his eyes is Cinderella resplendent once more in her ball dress.

The dance was assuming an increasing importance at the Opéra, where new ballets were being staged with a magnificence and a taste that a few years before would have been undreamed of. Not everyone, however, was satisfied by the rate at which the repertory was being renewed, although those of every shade of opinion welcomed the addition of Albert's *Cendrillon*. While its success with the public was unequivocal, some critics observed a lack of invention in the choreography. But if Albert did not possess such a lively and fertile imagination as Gardel or Milon, his new ballet was arranged with skill and good taste and was full of charming dances. Among the most successful of these was a *pas de douze* for Cinderella's attendants in the ball scene and a *contredanse*, half French and half Spanish in conception, performed by twelve of the prettiest girls in the company.

Despite its surfeit of dances, however, *Cendrillon* had one major shortcoming. Albert had not made the most of his subject dramatically, the situations and the characters seeming insufficiently developed. The vanity of the stepsisters and the proud stupidity of Cinderella's father were not fully brought out in the action, and even the rôle of Cinderella, it was felt, could have been more strongly drawn by making more of her persecution at the hands of her stepmother and stepsisters. As the critic of the *Constitutionnel* pointed out, the fault went to the very heart of the ballet's structure: for Albert, in common with other choreographers of his time, had departed from the close association of mime and dance, which had been the remarkable feature of Dauberval's ballets, some of which, although now thirty years old, were still occasionally performed at the Porte-Saint-Martin. This critic, who had already criticised Aumer for jettisoning some of his own master's principles, now repeated his call for the mime to be more closely interwoven with the dance:

> At the Opéra today, a ballet is accorded the same treatment that the Italian *dilettanti* mete out to the works of their greatest composers. People chatter and walk about during the mime passages and reserve their attention for the dances. This has been brought about by the new method adopted by our choreographers. With a few exceptions, they give little thought to developing the dramatic action, but occupy themselves almost exclusively with arranging *pas* in which the dancers, and particularly the ballerinas, can shine. Also, in most new ballets the dance element is wholly separated from the mimed part, so much so indeed that the one could easily be suppressed without any real harm to the other. Now Dauberval followed a different method. His dances form part of the action, so that to cut a *pas* in one of his works involves suppressing a scene. Plays were made from Dauberval's ballets, whereas today's trend is to look for plays on which to base ballets. Let us hope that M. Albert, who is still at the beginning of his career as a choreographer, will not only profit from the principles of Gardel and Milon, but also remember those of Dauberval.[25]

While the action of *Cendrillon* might have been more effectively presented had the spirit of Dauberval hovered above Albert during the ballet's production, it could hardly have had more suitable interpreters than Bigottini and Albert himself in the leading rôles. On stage almost throughout, Emilie Bigottini conveyed Cinderella's gentleness and simplicity without for a moment forgetting the underlying dignity of the character. To quote one instance from the first act, when Cinderella hears her stepmother and her stepsisters ringing for her at the same time, she appears gauche and embarrassed, but yet graceful enough to avoid giving an impression of stupidity, which a less intelligent mime would have done.

Although the spectacle did not approach the scale of *Alfred le Grand*, some 42,000 francs were spent on this side of the production alone, enabling Ciceri to design some magnificent settings. His first set was in the Gothic style, with a backcloth depicting a fine landscape that was revealed when the castle door opened; but the visual highlight of this scene was the emergence from the chimney of Cinderella's carriage, drawn by two white horses made up to represent unicorns. Another effective piece of stage-magic in this act was the fairy Mélise's costume change, devised by Joseph-Barthélémy Delaistre, a former costumier who then held an administrative post at the *contrôle*. The ballroom scene in the second act was the most splendid of Ciceri's sets for this ballet, full use being made of the stage to accommodate some 200 people; but the garden scene at the end of the ballet, although elegantly designed, was unfortunately encumbered by a large arch, which obstructed not only the vista but the dancers too. The costumes, designed by Albert himself, were praised for their elegance and lightness.

The weakest element in the ballet was undoubtedly the music, which had been composed for the London production of the year before by Fernando Sor, a Spanish musician known more for his skill on the guitar than as a composer. Inevitably his music would face more critical scrutiny in Paris, and Castil-Blaze duly damned it as an inadequate accompaniment to what he described as 'the vast and sublime conceptions of a large-scale, interesting and passionate drama, such being the scale on which Albert conceived his subject'. He also chided the composer for being too proud to borrow useful *airs parlants* from Rossini's *La cenerentola* and Isouard's *Cendrillon*, which would have been familiar to those who frequented the Théâtre Italien and the Opéra-Comique.[26] Sor's music was not entirely unremarkable, however, for two of its numbers – a charming waltz and a march – were both to be published in arrangements that could be played in the intimacy of the home.

Certainly any shortcomings in the score had no effect on the ballet's success. It remained in the repertory until 1831, becoming only the fifteenth ballet to achieve the distinction of a hundred performances at the Opéra.

* * * * * *

Since his post as third ballet-master was supernumerary, Aumer had more latitude in making outside engagements than either Gardel or Milon. However, the three-year term of his contract was approaching its end, and by the spring of 1823 he still did not know whether his engagement would be extended. Towards the end of the previous year he had been given leave to accept the post of ballet-master in London for the first few months of the opera season, for which he staged revivals of *Alfred le Grand* and *Aline*. During his stay in England he learnt that the Opéra was considering proposals from two other outside choreographers, Deshayes and Degville. This did not seem to disturb him unduly, for he could see no immediate prospect of either Gardel or Milon retiring. His leave was due to expire at the end of April 1823, and he agreed to remain in London a little longer to supervise the appearance of Mme Anatole. In his letter to Habeneck, telling him that his return would be a little delayed, he explained his reasons for having taken this step:

> I hope... this short delay will not trouble the administration of the [Opéra], particularly since, to my knowledge, the opera *Virginie* is not yet ready, the stage being in use for the *divertissements,* and since M. Ciceri will not be able to work on the scenery for *Aline* until after that opera has been presented, assuming that that ballet will be accepted and authorised to follow immediately after *Virginie.* Knowing how zealously I work, you can confidently depend on my being ready before the scene-painters. You have my promise that five weeks after my arrival my ballet *Aline* will be completely finished.

> Since there was much talk of a ballet by M. Deshayes, for which, I have even been told, a start has already been made on the scenery, and since, to my knowledge, M. Degville has been requested by you to send you his music, I assumed there would not be any problem in extending my leave of absence; but seeing my hopes dashed, I at least do not wish to suffer a delay of three months, as happened at the time of *Aline.*[27]

It had long been understood that *Aline* would be the next major ballet that Aumer would produce at the Opéra, and an understanding was reached that it would be produced before the end of 1823. Like *Alfred le Grand,* it had been created during Aumer's spell as ballet-master in Vienna. On its first performance there in 1818, it had been an immediate success; and by 1823 it had gained the added distinction of being, at that time, the most frequently performed ballet to have been produced in the Austrian capital.[28] It was based on a novel, which despite its brevity had created a sensation when first published in 1761; five years later it had been adapted as an opera, and in

1803 as an *opéra-comique* by Henri-Montan Berton. The author of the novel, Stanislas-Jean de Boufflers, was regarded as a somewhat romantic figure. He had been brought up in Nancy in the cultured court of the exiled King Stanislaw II of Poland, where his engaging personality and ready wit had caught the fancy of Voltaire. After abandoning an ecclesiastical career, he then became a soldier of fortune and the author of a few elegant novels, of which *Aline, reine de Golconde*, the shortest of them all, was to earn him a modest place in the literature of his time. Whether or not Aumer had read the novel, it was Berton's *opéra-comique*, which was first produced at the time he was staging his first ballets at the Porte-Saint-Martin, that provided the basis for the ballet's scenario.

A major factor in the delay in producing *Aline* at the Opéra was the need to adjust the score. Partly this may have been due to revisions Aumer was making, but more fundamental was the fact that Karl Ludwig Blum's score for the Vienna production was considered, probably by Habeneck, to be unsatisfactory. To deal with this problem, the services of Gustave Dugazon, who had revised Gallenberg's score for *Alfred le Grand*, were called upon once again. His participation no doubt went further than introducing some of Berton's themes as *airs parlants* to accompany passages of mime action, for he was given sole credit as composer.

Castil-Blaze was surprised that greater use had not been made of Berton's music. Dugazon's score was 'easy on the ear and graceful', but he listened almost in vain for an echo of Berton's celebrated romance for Aline in his opera, catching only a bare reference to it in a few bars. However, Dugazon had incorporated Berton's Provençal rondo in the last act, and for this Castil-Blaze complimented him on being appropriately regional.[29]

In common with the librettists both of Monsigny's opera and Berton's *opéra-comique*, Aumer had trivialised Boufflers's original story, which told, simply and without ornamentation, of the three fleeting, passionate meetings between the hero Saint-Phar (in the novel a projection of the author himself) and Aline before they finally find one another in the evening of their lives and discover the state of true contentment that comes with maturity. The adolescent passion of their first meeting was to be engraved in each of their memories. But an unlucky chance had separated them, and twice in later years their paths were briefly to cross. In the ballet, as in both lyric works, the episode of their second meeting was understandably omitted as being too explicit to represent on the stage. For in the novel, after their first encounter, Aline finds herself pregnant and is turned out of her home. Making her way to Paris, she has a series of lovers and eventually marries a rich nobleman for his money. There she and Saint-Phar meet again by chance – appropriately, outside the Opéra – and pass a passionate night together, but he leaves her in a mood of sated disillusionment. The omission in all the stage versions of the novel's final section, in which they finally come together in old age to pass their declining years in the desert, necessitated a readjustment of their preceding encounter in the kingdom of Golconda, which brought all the stage versions to a conventional happy conclusion. To achieve this, Aline had to be made the reigning sovereign, not the consort of the king; and whereas, in the novel, Saint-Phar and Aline are discovered *in flagrante delicto* and Saint-Phar escapes through the window, leaving Aline to be banished, in both theatrical versions Saint-Phar is accepted as the queen's consort.

Aline (Bigottini), a Frenchwoman who has become Queen of Golconda as the widow of the former king, has made an enemy of Sigiskar (Aumer) by rejecting his advances and introducing liberal reforms. She confides in her friend Zélie (Noblet) that she can never forget an early love for a young man whom she met by chance many years before in Provence when she was a simple milkmaid. (At this point in the ballet, at the press of a button, the back of her throne slid aside to reveal the scene of this distant idyll.) The arrival of a new French ambassador to the court of Golconda is then announced. Realising that the ambassador, Saint-Phar (Montjoie), is none other than her first lover, Aline quickly covers her face with a veil. Zélie, to whom Aline has confided the secret of her love, realises the reason for her mistress's disquiet, while Sigiskar's curiosity is aroused by the strange reaction of the queen and her confidante to the new visitors.

The second act takes place in the palace gardens. Aline has asked Zélie to take her place so that she can put Saint-Phar's constancy to the test. However, Saint-Phar remains unmoved by Zélie's allurements, being more attracted to Aline, who has assumed the disguise of a dancing girl. He is then drugged and, on Aline's orders, borne away insensible. Sigiskar, who has witnessed this scene, is shocked that the queen should so demean herself with a foreign envoy, and plots to overthrow her and assassinate Saint-Phar.

Saint-Phar is then conveyed, insensible, to a site that Aline has caused to be transformed so as to resemble the landscape of Provence where first they met. When he awakes to see her crossing the bridge over the stream, dressed as a milkmaid, he believes he must be dreaming of their first encounter so many years before. She shows him the ring he had then given to her, and, observing that he is still wearing her own ring, is certain of his love for her. But then news comes of Sigiskar's rebellion. With the fortuitous aid of Saint-Phar's grenadiers, the revolt is put down and Sigiskar taken prisoner. In the ensuing scene Aline, still veiled, offers Saint-Phar her hand, but he refuses, his mind still obsessed with the memory of the shepherdess of their first meeting. At the sight of Zélie, however, he realises that the queen is none other than Aline, and he begs to be taken to her. The curtains of the royal tent are then drawn back to reveal Aline coming forward to embrace him and invite him to share her kingdom.

The title-rôle gave Bigottini another opportunity to display her flair for characterisation by contrasting the regal authority with which Fate has invested her in a distant land with the simple graces of the Provençal milkmaid that she once was. To act alongside the experienced Bigottini was a stern test. Lise Noblet, having already proved herself as a dancer with a pure style and a strong, precise technique, now had to show in the rôle of Zélie that she could hold her own in the scene in which she impersonates her queen and offers Saint-Phar the draught that will make him believe, when he revives, that he is dreaming of his first encounter with Aline so many years before. Castil-Blaze realised what an awesome task it must be for Lise Noblet to have to impersonate Bigottini in her very presence. 'For half the ballet,' he wrote in his review,

> she had to assume the guise and costume of Bigottini, together with her gestures, her dignity and her mannerisms. To do this it was beholden on her to be, if not quite perfect, then at least very close to being so. The public was as much taken in as was Saint-Phar. I can think of no more flattering praise for Mlle Noblet than this unexpected success. [30]

For her this was an act of justification: for only a few weeks before, the Opéra had submitted to her ultimatum that if she were not promoted to *premier sujet* from the beginning of 1824, she would resign in protest at the advancement of Amélie Legallois to take Bigottini's place on the latter's retirement – a place which, as Noblet reminded the powers-that-be, had been promised to her.

Although *Aline* achieved a respectable tally of 45 performances during the three years it remained in the repertory, it made less of an impression in Paris than it did in Vienna. In his review, Castil-Blaze criticised Aumer for ignoring the precepts of Noverre by sacrificing perfection of illusion to pure spectacle and *divertissements*. Furthermore, however praise-worthy in the eyes of pedants, Aumer's respect for the unities of time, place and action had deprived the plot of much of its interest, and an acquaintance with Boufflers's novel was indispensable to enable the spectator to fill in the gaps and understand what was happening on stage. To some, Aumer seemed to have regarded the plot primarily as a background for the dances, and more than one critic complained of a surfeit of them. 'The profusion of dances,' surmised Castil-Blaze, 'can only be explained as an attempt to conceal the lack of originality and the feebleness of the action. These dances, although excellently performed, are almost continuous, and since nearly all of them are of same voluptuous nature, they become monotonous and wearisome.'[31]

The critic of the *Gazette de France*, Delaforest, also found much to criticise:

The battle in the third act, in which Saint-Phar pits himself against the treacherous Sigiskar, is rendered in mime, and reminds one, as do all Aumer's ballets, of the productions at the Porte-Saint-Martin. This is the main fault of Aumer's compositions, and if the Opéra is not careful, it will soon come to resemble an offshoot of the boulevard theatres. *Alfred le Grand* had much in common with melodrama, and everything Aumer has done in the new ballet is tainted with the bad taste of mimodrama: excessive gestures, false expressions, exaggerated and bizarre effects – in short, all the vulgarity that one sees at the Ambigu and the Gaîté. When Aline, in her disguise as a peasant girl, wishes to approach Saint-Phar, she does so, not with a quick, yet naive and timid, movement – oh no! that would be too simple and lifelike – but by crossing the stage in two or three leaps with her arms outstretched, which is neither natural nor graceful.

The *pas de sept* that brings the ballet to a close is another example of a tasteless obsession with bizarre effects. It is performed by, among others, four girls carrying little mirrors with bells. When struck, these bells give off different notes and form an *obligato* accompaniment to the melody of the dance. This is relying for success on means that are grotesque and inartistic... Aumer does not seem to care whether he hits the nail squarely on the head, as long as he hits it hard. There are two ballets in every single one of his. It offends good taste, but the eyes are dazzled. His latest ballet is like a kaleidoscope: it has everything in it, but only the fantastic parts remain in the memory.

Yet this work was undoubtedly a success, which must be attributed to the charm of its story, the incredible splendour of its spectacle, the freshness of its costumes, and the very fault of the ballet itself. For the shock produced by all the bustle and uproar and the confused comings and goings of the players contribute to its success, even if such ingredients are not to be encouraged.[32]

Aumer, one senses, was now becoming increasingly dissatisfied with his situation at the Opéra. The success of Albert's *Cendrillon* may have come as a reminder that Aumer's eventual succession as ballet-master was not assured, but there now arose another cause for anxiety. His salary at the Opera was modest, a mere 5000 francs a year, and earlier that summer he had been able to augment it by being given leave to accept the post of ballet-master in London for the first half of the season. And such was his success in

that city that there had now come another offer, for the whole of the season
of 1824, at a salary of £1000 (the equivalent of 10,000 francs) for himself
and £600 for his daughter Julie, who had been engaged with him. Aumer
had set his hopes on the Opéra's granting him leave to accept this offer under
an agreement that existed between the two theatres, but London's request to
the Opéra was rejected. Almost in desperation, Aumer wrote to Habeneck,
begging him to intercede on his behalf:

> I am writing in the hope that the request that I am making to you and the
> authorities will be granted.
>
> As a result of Colonel Cook *(sic)* having received a rejection with regard to
> my leave, I find I have no option, since I cannot refuse the advantageous
> terms I have been offered, but to ask you to intervene on my behalf to
> obtain my release.
>
> By this you will be doing me a great favour, for it will enable me to improve
> my position, which at the Académie Royale de Musique is and always will
> be nothing but very precarious.[33]

And so Aumer's connection with the Opéra was amicably terminated, and he
and his daughter departed for London, leaving the Opéra with the succession
to Gardel and Milon still unresolved.

* * * * * * *

Before his departure Aumer had had one obligation to meet, and a most
acceptable one at that. Emilie Bigottini would be retiring at the end of the
year, and he had most willingly agreed to stage a new work as the centrepiece
of the benefit performance that was her due. Any other ballet-master faced
with such a request might have produced an entertaining little work with a
sentimental plot, but Aumer had a more original idea. Bigottini, he realised,
deserved a rôle to be remembered by, one that would seal her reputation as
an actress. And he had just such a part in mind that was very dear to his
heart – not a tragic character, for that would hardly be suitable for the
occasion, but one that would reveal her deft understanding of character, the
natural quality of her acting, and above all her subtle gift for comedy. Casting
his mind back to his youth, his choice had fallen on a ballet by his master and
mentor, Dauberval, *Le Page inconstant*, an adaptation of Beaumarchais's
classic comedy, *Le Mariage de Figaro*, which he had first staged twenty years
before at the Porte-Saint-Martin. And the part reserved for Bigottini would be
that of Figaro's wife, Susanne – the rôle that Dauberval's own wife, Mme

Théodore, had created in Bordeaux thirty-seven years before. What indeed could have been more appropriate to honour Bigottini?

Aumer must have been a boy of about thirteen to have seen a performance of this ballet in Bordeaux, but when he had first staged it in Paris, Dauberval was still alive and active and making periodic visits to the capital to keep in touch with friends in the dance world. If one were to categorise his *Page inconstant*, it would be as a pantomime with dances rather than what was then described as a ballet-pantomime, the distinction being that it did not include a long *divertissement* but introduced dances as its action required. It is possible, therefore, that in 1805 Aumer was free to arrange the dances himself without prejudice to the main structure of the work, yet without the authorship of the work ceasing to be Dauberval's. However, in 1819 Dauberval had been dead for many years and a new factor had emerged, namely that in the world of the lyric theatre the piece was now associated not only with Beaumarchais's comedy, but even more potently with the music that Mozart had written for the operatic version, *Le nozze di Figaro*. So when Aumer had begun to consider a revival for the Hofoper in Vienna, the score that Dauberval had strung together some thirty-seven years before could no longer be regarded as adequate, and Adalbert Gyrowetz had prepared a new score introducing a number of themes from Mozart's opera.[34]

At the time that this new version was being prepared, Aumer was in Vienna, corresponding with the Opéra about the terms of his forthcoming engagement, and he commented on it in passing in one of his letters. Gyrowetz's score, he wrote, was 'charming, and the Mozart tunes in it very well adapted, although, in following the scenario, I have composed the pantomime and the dancing quite differently from what this ballet was like at the Porte-Saint-Martin and in Lyons.'[35]

He no doubt had in his possession copies of both the original score and that of Gyrowetz, and the latter was handed to Habeneck. It had been decided that if it were successful, the work would be taken into the repertory. Habeneck therefore took it upon himself to make such revisions as he deemed necessary to accord with Parisian musical taste, adding the first 125 measures of Beethoven's Fifth Symphony for the opening of Act I and, if the ears of certain critics[36] can be relied upon, a few passages borrowed from Rossini, Boccherini and Haydn.[37]

This new version of the ballet was by now more identifiably Aumer's own work, although he punctiliously required that Dauberval be credited when it was presented at the Opéra at Bigottini's benefit performance on 18 December 1823. There, it was given the place of honour at the end of a generous programme that included Duval's play *La Jeunesse d'Henri V* (in which Mlle Mars appeared and Bigottini made her first and only performance

in a speaking rôle),[38] and the first act of Paër's opera *Agnese* with Giuditta
Pasta. Although prices had been trebled for the occasion, there was not a
vacant seat in the house, and jewellery sparkled in the gaslight all around,
even in the orchestra stalls, where ladies were admitted for just this one
occasion. The Duc and Duchesse d'Orléans were in their box, and the total
receipts approached 25,000 francs. On her first entrance Bigottini received
the warmest of ovations, appearing visibly moved by this demonstration of
affection. Her début as an actress, in the rôle of the page in Duval's comedy,
was a revelation that could only add to the regret at her impending
retirement, and the *Journal de Paris* praised her 'excellent diction and
enchanting voice, even alongside Mlle Mars'.[38]

Le Page inconstant was the final item in the programme. The audience,
being well acquainted with Beaumarchais's comedy, could have had no
difficulty in following the plot. The inconstant page is Cherubino (Marinette),
who infuriates his master Count Almaviva (Montjoie) by his pranks.
Almaviva is attracted to his wife's lady's maid Suzanne (Bigottini), who is
engaged to Figaro (Ferdinand), and after many intrigues is finally cured of
his fickleness.

Dauberval's treatment of this comedy in dance and mime was still, nearly
four decades later, recognised as a model, as the critic of the *Courrier des
spectacles* stressed in his review:

> The action of the ballet, compressed by the simplification necessary in a
> choreographic adaptation, is charmingly interspersed with danced scenes
> that arise naturally out of the subject and often even aid its development.
> The *farandole* at the end of the second act is an example, for nothing could
> be more comical than the enraged Figaro, tormented with jealousy, being
> forced to take part in a *divertissement*, which only adds to his anguish.
> Dauberval did not take this idea from Beaumarchais, but he has woven it
> so cleverly into his work that the 'join' escapes the keenest eye. Dauberval
> was a man of genius.[39]

The *Journal de Paris* added that much of the pungency and vivacity of the
comedy had been retained. The only criticism was that there was a surfeit of
dances in the first two acts.

The ballet was a happy choice for the occasion, and in the five
performances[40] in which Bigottini appeared before retiring at the end of the
year, she left her admirers with an enchanting memory of this last creation.
The *Journal de Paris* observed that 'the grace, delicacy and expressiveness
which animated her every gesture will make it difficult for her successors to
match her in the rôle'.[41] Both that journal and the *Courrier des spectacles*
made special mention of the scene of the quarrel between Suzanne and

Marceline at the beginning of the second act, in which Bigottini surpassed herself in the warmth of her acting.

The curtain rang down half an hour after midnight. There were loud cries for her, and she reappeared surrounded by her companions, who turned towards her, adding their own applause to that of the audience. Then Montjoie stepped forward and placed on her head a crown of flowers, which was accompanied by some lines that the playwright Eugène Scribe had written in her honour:

> *Clari, Nina, toi que Paris adore,*
> *Toi, qui jusqu'à Thalie élevant Terpsichore,*
> *Sus peindre la parole et parler au regard,*
> *Sur notre scène en deuil, où brillèrent tes charmes,*
> *Par ton talent tu fis couler des larmes,*
> *Et plus encor par ton départ.*[42]

Eleven days later, on 29 December, her final appearance took place. As a special tribute the programme was selected so as to include both *Le Page inconstant* and *Nina*. The two rôles she played that evening displayed the extraordinary scope of her talent, for after delighting the public with her sprightly Suzanne, she then tore at their heartstrings with her moving account of Nina's misfortune. It was a fitting end to an evening that had inevitably been tinged with sadness. She was applauded long and loud at the end, and when the curtain descended for the last time and the house fell silent, the audience remained awhile in their places, hoping for one last sight of her. But already her companions were leading her, weeping with emotion, back to her dressing room, which she was to enter for the last time.

For Bigottini, retirement implied a complete break with her career, and only on one occasion was she prevailed upon to emerge from her retreat. Her brother-in-law Louis Milon retired at the end of 1826, and at his benefit performance on 18 April 1827, she reappeared to perform her most famous rôle, Nina.

In the audience that evening was a young woman who was later to become celebrated in literary circles as the Comtesse Dash. It was the only occasion on which she saw Bigottini. 'Never again,' she wrote afterwards,

> did I experience what I felt that day. She made me cry my eyes out, cry at a piece of miming! And I was not the only one who did this ridiculous thing, if ridiculous it was. The whole audience was affected. The play of her features and her gestures were so touching, and so convincingly did she convey her madness, a madness brought on by love, that not a single heart remained unmoved. Never, I believe, has this art been carried so far...

Great was the enthusiasm when she left the stage, but so long as she was in one's sight, one gave no thought of applauding, for one was all eyes and ears. One became identified with a grief that was so heart-rendingly expressed. Let me say again, never since then have I had a similar experience. At the end, when, reunited with her lover, she recovered her reason, her face radiated intelligence and happiness, and the applause broke out like a clap of thunder. But while she was suffering, one kept one's admiration in check, in spite of oneself, out of respect inspired by her despair.[43]

This wonderful close to her long and brilliant career was the occasion for a final expression of admiration and gratitude on the part of both the public and her fellow artists. At the end of the ballet, all who had taken part assembled on the stage, and after verses had been sung in praise of her talents, one of the dancers led her forward and crowned her with a wreath of laurel, while the others grouped themselves around her, bearing garlands and crowns of roses. She was weeping unashamedly when the curtain fell and hid her from view.

Her retirement marked the end of an epoch, and there was much shaking of heads over the future of ballet, for no one could foresee the flowering that was to take place in the years ahead. As a mime Bigottini had been unrivalled, and now, on her retirement, only the most sanguine prophet dared hope that she might ever be adequately replaced. Her power of expression and the simple, natural manner of her acting, whether in scenes requiring a delicate touch or in situations demanding passion, was a gift of extreme rarity. Her every action was touched with grace, and to many she brought the revelation that the art of mime was a significant force in the theatre – an art which, as one critic observed, had also been mastered by the greatest tragedian of the day, Talma.

Emilie Bigottini retired to the peace and quiet of the village of Passy, where she owned a small house built in the then popular neo-Greek style. There she grew with the years into a 'good and very kind little old lady, with an intelligent look and a friendly smile', often to be seen walking, still elegant, erect and graceful, in the shaded alleys of Ranelagh, where Béranger and the ageing Rossini were also wont to wander.[44] She never lost her charm, and around 1900 there was still an old inhabitant of Passy who recalled her with a glow of admiration. 'Ah! Had you but seen her!' he exclaimed to a young inquirer, 'you would have fallen in love with her.'[45] In the intimacy of her home she was an amusing and affable companion, who never mentioned the subject of her past glories unless someone else brought it up. Then, with a very human simplicity, she did not conceal her pride and pleasure.

She was taken ill quite suddenly one day in the early summer of 1858, as she was preparing to leave her Paris apartment, No. 67 Rue de Richelieu, to return to Passy. As she lay on her deathbed, she found satisfaction in recalling the lines that Scribe had written for her farewell. She died as she had lived, quietly, on 28 April, and was laid to rest at Père-Lachaise in the presence of her family and friends beneath a kindly summer sky.

NOTES

1. This melody is still well known to modern ballet-goers, Tchaikowsky having borrowed it for the apotheosis of *The Sleeping Beauty*. It also appears in the original score of Dauberval's *Le Page inconstant*.
2. *La Vallée du Tempé ou le Retour de Zéphire*, a *divertissement* in one act, choreography by P. Gardel, music by Steibelt, f.p. Paris Opéra, 3 March 1802.
3. *Journal des théâtres*, 18 August 1821.
4. *Miroir*, 30 October 1821.
5. *Journal des débats*, 12 December 1821.
6. *Miroir*, 12 December 1821.
7. *Journal des théâtres*, 11 December 1821.
8. *Journal des débats*, 19 December 1821.
9. *Moniteur*, 8 February 1822.
10. *Jenny* had been first produced at the Théâtre de la Porte-Saint-Martin on 20 March 1806.
11. As *Alfred der Grosse* at the Court Opera, Vienna, on 24 April 1820, and as *Alfredo il grande* at La Scala, Milan, on 16 February 1822.
12. Arch. Nat., AJ[13] 125. Aumer to Viotti, 2 May 1821.
13. Bibl.-Musée de l'Opéra. Fonds Aumer, folder 7.
14. Arch. Nat., AJ[13] 125. Aumer to Viotti, 2 May 1821.
15. *Constitutionnel*, 20 September 1822.
16. *Journal de Paris*, 21 September 1822.
17. The male dancer did not come into his own again at the Paris Opéra – leaving aside the short guest seasons of the Diaghilev Ballet – until the Lifar era in the 1930s, when ballets such as *Icare* (1935), *David triomphant* and *Alexandre le Grand* (both 1937) were produced.
18. Arch. Nat., AJ[13] 125. Aumer to Viotti, 3 May 1821.
19. *Journal des théâtres*, 20 September 1822.
20. *Journal des débats*, 28 September 1822.
21. In the Salem Collection at Harvard University is a note written by Albert after his retirement, which lists a number of *objets d'art* he had collected and records the fact that he was the owner of paintings by Van Dyck, Rembrandt, Teniers, Watteau and Boucher.
22. *Petite biographie dramatique*,
23. *Le Séducteur au village, ou Claire et Mectal*, ballet-pantomime in two acts (later reduced to one), choreography by Albert and music by Schneitzhoeffer, f.p. Paris Opéra, 3 June 1818.
24. King's Theatre, 26 March 1822.
25. *Constitutionnel*, 10 March 1823.
26. *Journal des débats*, 10 March 1823.
27. Arch. Nat., AJ[13] 125. Aumer to Habeneck, 26 April 1823.
28. *Aline, Königin von Golkonda*, f.p. Hofoper, Vienna, 18 May 1818. Revived as *Aline, reine de Golconde*, King's Theatre, London, 16 May 1823. Berton's *opéra-comique* was first performed at the Opéra-Comique on 2 September 1803. Boïeldieu composed a new score to the same libretto for a production in St Petersburg in 1804.
29. *Journal des débats*, 3 October 1823.
30. *Journal des débats*, 3 October 1823.

31. *Journal des débats*, 3 October 1823.

32. Delaforest, I, 254–5.

33. Arch. Nat., AJ[13] 125. Aumer to Habeneck, 22 November 1823. Col. Sir Henry Cooke was negotiating with Aumer on behalf of the King's Theatre, of which he was a member of the Committee.

34. *Le Page inconstant* was first produced at the Grand-Théâtre, Bordeaux, on 2 October 1786. Aumer revived it at the Porte-Saint-Martin on 17 July 1805, and, with Gyrowetz's score, as *Die flatternafte Page, oder Figaros Hochzeit*, at the Vienna Hofoper on 10 November 1819.

35. Arch. Nat., AJ[13] 125. Aumer to Courtin, 13 November 1819.

36. Smith, 84–91.

37. *Pandore*, 21 December 1823; *Courrier des théâtres*, 24 December 1823.

38. The *Journal de Paris* of 20 December 1823 spoke of 'the entrancing warmth of her acting'. Bigottini had, in fact, spoken just two words on the stage before, in Dalayrac's one-act comic opera, *Deux Mots*, at the benefit performance of Mme Desbrosses at the Opéra-Comique on 19 April 1823.

39. *Courrier des spectacles*, 24 December 1823.

40. Four of these were at the Opéra, the other at the Théâtre de l'Odéon at the benefit performance of Mlle Petit on 21 December.

41. *Journal de Paris*, 20 December 1823.

42. Clari, Nina, thou whom Paris adores,/ thou who, like Thalia in bringing up Terpsichore,/ could give added colour to words and speak to the eye,/ on our stage, now in mourning, which glittered with your charms,/you moved us to tears by your talent,/ and now, even more, by your departure.

43. Dash, III, 19–20.

44. *Journal des débats*, 10 May 1858. Article by Jules Janin.

45. Félix-Bouvier, 30.

5

An Accident-prone Ballet

Aumer's sudden decision to withdraw must have reawakened hopes in the minds of Gardel and Milon, for both were still active and full of ideas for new works. Gardel's *Méléagre et Atalante*,[1] a major project, had already been accepted by the Reading Committee, and in March 1823 had even been proposed for production, but much to his chagrin it was then to be passed over in favour of another work, André Deshayes's *Zémire et Azor*. The fact that Deshayes had been an émigré throughout the Napoleonic wars must have been a source of great irritation to Gardel, whose disappointment was no doubt only slightly allayed when the Director, Habeneck, proposed that he might prepare a 'little carnival ballet' to amuse the public before Lent. When Gardel put forward a few ideas, Habeneck disclosed that a friend of his had also had some thoughts and suggested that the two should meet. But Carnival came and went before they could make a mutually convenient appointment, and the project was shelved. Eventually they did meet, and on the basis of their exchange of ideas, Gardel fleshed out a slight plot leading into a scene at a masked ball, in which Lise Noblet and Pauline Montessu were to appear as themselves, and perform in the style of their period, dressed up as the two celebrated eighteenth-century ballerinas, Sallé and Camargo. It was an attractive idea, but like *Méléagre et Atalante*, it was to be still-born.[2]

Gardel, looking back to the time of Napoleon and remembering how well he had then been esteemed and rewarded, could not help feeling he was being unfairly rejected by the new régime for political reasons. His colleague Milon, on the other hand, although somewhat similarly affected, seems to have taken a more philosophical attitude in working towards his retirement. Although he too had hopes of producing one more ballet, the project on which he was working when his time came – a major *ballet d'action* about Joan of Arc – would remain unfulfilled.

The year 1823 had been an exceptionally busy year for the ballet, with the production of two major creations, *Cendrillon* and *Aline*, as well as two new operas containing substantial ballet scenes staged by Gardel; and it had closed with Bigottini's retirement, which brought with it the problem of finding someone to take over her rôles. This had been foreseen by the *Journal de Paris* a year before, when its critic had observed how unfortunate it was for the Opéra that

the younger school of dancers has not sought to follow in Bigottini's footsteps. Instead they are concerned with jumping a little higher and beating more complex *entrechats* than their rivals, and they neglect the art of mime. We seek actresses, but all too often we find only dancers.[3]

Bigottini's retirement had left a void that would have been difficult enough to fill in any circumstances. As it was, no dancer in the company came near to matching her in dramatic ability, but, come what may, someone had to be found to succeed her if the repertory was to be preserved. The choice finally rested between Amélie Legallois and Lise Noblet, both of whom were still in their early twenties.

Amélie Legallois, who was the first to be considered, was seldom without friends in high places. She was reputed to have been the mistress of the Duc de Berry at the time of his assassination, and after a decent interval following the tragedy she accepted the protection of the Marquis de Lauriston. Lauriston was a professional soldier who had fought with distinction under Napoleon and received his marshal's baton from Louis XVIII after the Spanish campaign of 1823. However, a far more significant distinction, at least in the eyes of his mistress, was that he held the prestigious post of Minister of the Royal Household, among whose responsibilities was that of supervising the Opéra.

Legallois was a Parisienne, and her parents, who were poor, had decided she should become a dancer in order to begin earning her living at an early age. She entered Coulon's class in 1817, but her progress was retarded by frequent absences. 'Still sick,' Coulon laconically observed in his reports for 1819 and 1820; but in the latter year he remarked on her 'willingness', and Milon, who taught her mime, also found her quick to learn.[4] Her singular beauty and her stage presence particularly suited her for prominent rôles, for she was one of those dancers who make an immediate impact on entering the stage. She had fair hair, dark expressive eyes and an enchanting smile; and her superb carriage showed off her tall, elegant figure to fine advantage. Her début in the title-rôle of *Clari* on 6 September 1822 was hailed by the *Journal des théâtres* as 'a most happy augury',[5] and it soon became apparent that she was being groomed to succeed Bigottini. Even before the latter retired, Legallois was seen in *Nina* and *Cendrillon*, and in the first half of 1824 took over no fewer than four more of the great ballerina's characters – in *Le Page inconstant*, *Aline*, *La Servante justifiée* and *La Dansomanie*.

At first, allowances were made for her inexperience, and the 'hidden protection' that so obviously supported her was overlooked; but after a while such tolerance wore thin. For this her advisers were to blame. No one would have complained if the claque encouraged her a little more warmly than the paying public, but when it displayed such ridiculous partiality as to greet the popular Bigottini on the same evening, as once happened, with a few tepid and condescending claps, many honest spectators began to take a more hardened view of Legallois's talent. Nevertheless, by dint of perseverance and hard work, she developed into a useful, if not outstanding, mime, being particularly suited to rôles requiring a dignified bearing. But no one could be under the illusion that she might satisfactorily replace Bigottini; however hard she tried to emulate her, her miming remained somewhat artificial, studied and lacking in expression. As one critic put it, she made three times as many gestures as Bigottini to achieve only a third of the effect.[6]

By the summer of 1824 she was being judged severely. 'She seems ambitious,' commented the critic of the *Diable boiteux*, 'and up to a point ambition is to be commended in one of her position. But does this love of glory have to be carried so far as to impose a sort of dictatorship in the Court of Terpsichore, exploiting a monopoly of mime rôles in the way that others exploit the monopoly of tobacco?'[7]

Meanwhile, Lise Noblet's claim to share in Bigottini's heritage could not be overlooked, particularly since she had been promoted *premier sujet* in the latter's place at a salary of 8000 francs a year, while Legallois remained only at the lower grade of *remplaçant*. Although the younger of the two by some months, Noblet had several more years of experience behind her, having made her début in 1818. Until now, however, it had been more particularly as a dancer, rather than a mime, that Paris had known and applauded her – her style being distinguished by a voluptuous quality in her movements, great lightness, elegance in her poses, and what one critic termed 'graces that were very French'.[8] Her perfect figure and the vivacious sparkle in her eyes gave the illusion of a greater beauty than she really possessed, and she was courted by a large band of admirers. But she was not to be easily won. An astonished observer exclaimed in 1821:

> A dancer who never makes a false step, who prefers a circle of friends to a crowd of lovers, who comes to the theatre on foot and leaves in the same way! Monsieur D... S... V..., one of the fashionable gallants, who grudges nothing – neither horses, gold, nor vows – for a beautiful woman, has seen his siege artillery prove unavailing before her defences. To a friend who enquired if his homage had been accepted, he replied:
>
> > 'Oui, cette jeune déité,
> > Est tout le portrait de Lucrèce;
> > Elle en conserve la beauté
> > Et, de plus, la sotte sagesse.
> > Landau, cachemire, rubis,
> > Ne peuvent la rendre traitable:
> > Ma foi, si je ne l'ai pas pris,
> > Il faut qu'elle soit imprenable.'[9]

Another admirer, Lord Fife, lavished a fortune on her in London, but she was to reserve her affection for the elderly General Comte Claparède, a hero of the battle of Wagram, who had rallied to the Royalist cause after Napoleon's fall and served on the panel of judges that had passed sentence of death on Marshal Ney. They made a touchingly devoted couple. She was to remain faithful to him until his death in 1842, and whenever they were separated, it was said that at any moment of the day he could tell, to the minute, how long she had been away.

Lise Noblet's ambition was to become Bigottini's successor in every respect, and in the summer of 1824, during an engagement at the King's Theatre, London, she appeared as Suzanne in *Le Page inconstant*, revived for her by Aumer, and met with a most flattering reception: the *Morning Post* declared that her 'archness and significant gestures absolutely spoke the part she meant to represent'.[10] It was the success of the season, and she returned to Paris determined to play that rôle at the Opéra.

In the middle of September Louis XVIII died, and the new king, Charles X, made his ceremonial entry into Paris only a few days before Lise Noblet's reappearance at the Opéra on 1 October. The bills announced that after dancing in the opera *La Caravane*, she would make her début as a mime in *Le Page inconstant*. A welcoming burst of applause broke out when she appeared to dance her *pas* in the opera. This *pas* had been dropped some time before, and its revival on this occasion was happily appropriate, for it was performed to the melody of the royalist song, *Vive Henri IV, vive ce roi vaillant*, the allusion being quickly taken up by the audience, who broke out into loyal cries of '*Vive le roi!*' When the curtain rose on *Le Page inconstant*, the feeling of excitement still persisted. Noblet had chosen her moment well, and, encouraged by the mood of the public, she gave a delightful portrayal of Suzanne. No one expected her to efface the memory of Bigottini, but even at this first attempt, Noblet displayed an unquestioned superiority over Legallois. Her natural sprightliness, her gaiety and her piquant charm contrasted sharply with her rival's rather colourless performance in the same part.

The honours were rather more even when Noblet assumed the title-rôle in *Cendrillon* (30 October), one of Legallois's best interpretations; but in *Clari* (19 November) she again asserted her superiority. By now it was clear that Lise Noblet's claims could not be overlooked, and at the end of the year it was arranged that the two young dancers would henceforth share the rôles in Bigottini's former repertory.

* * * * * * *

Aumer's decision not to renew his engagement as third *maître de ballet* at the end of 1823 had no doubt been prompted by the need to keep busy and earn an income that was commensurate with his standing as a choreographer of international repute. However, this had left the Opéra in a state of uncertainty, given the approaching retirement of Gardel and Milon, for although London engagements were made on a seasonal basis so that it was likely that Aumer would be available at reasonable notice when the time came, the pressing need for new ballets in the meantime would remain. It had to be accepted that Gardel and Milon, who were still active in arranging ballet scenes for new opera productions and revivals and attending to their administrative duties, could no longer be relied upon to keep the ballet repertory replenished with new works. This meant that the Opéra, which had hitherto prided itself on producing its own ballet-masters, would now, as a matter of necessity, have to seek choreographers from elsewhere until such time as a home-grown ballet-master might emerge.

The first of the two outside choreographers who were to stage major ballets at the Opéra in the mid-1820s was almost certainly imposed by higher authority, for it is hard to believe that such an experienced Director as Habeneck would, on his own initiative, have proposed a man with such meagre credentials as André Deshayes, whose experience as a senior ballet-master was restricted to a single season in London in 1821. He had been trained in Paris, at the Opéra's School of Dance, of which his father was then head, and had graduated to become one of the most promising male talents to emerge in the revolutionary decade of the 1790s. But just as he seemed to be mounting the ladder, he was tempted, in a moment of folly, to slip away to Madrid and London. Quickly regretting this escapade, he had returned to the fold to find himself clapped into prison. Freed after a few days through the Opéra's intercession, he had resumed his career, only to suffer a serious injury on stage that put him out of action for more than a year. His return was awaited with impatience. To welcome him back, Gardel flattered him with a new ballet made to his measure, bearing the title *Le Retour de Zéphire* – a unique homage. A brilliant future seemed to be in store for him, but his head had been turned by over-zealous supporters and he deserted his *alma mater* a second time, resigning to leave Paris for the more lucrative fields of Milan and London.

This time there was to be no question of his returning, and with France and England locked in a bitter struggle, he had seen out the war years as principal male dancer in London from 1804 to 1811. Not until after Napoleon's fall did he return to France. By then his dancing days were over, and he had turned to teaching. During his exile he had made useful connections among the royalist émigrés, and in 1816, having returned to France, he was appointed dancing-master to the King's pages and teacher of deportment at the Royal School of Music. However, the Opéra still remained closed to him. In London he had produced a few modest ballets, but none of sufficient worth to sustain a reputation that would satisfy Paris; and his submission of a ballet called *Terpsichore* was rejected by the Opéra's reading panel.

But in 1821 there came a change in his fortunes. The London opera season opened at the King's Theatre under new management, with a strong ballet company recruited largely from Paris for the three-month season. By a helpful coincidence, negotiations for these engagements were conducted through Louis Boisgirard, the second ballet-master, and a friend of Deshayes of long standing. Their relationship had been forged in dramatic circumstances nearly twenty years before, when Boisgirard, then a royalist agent, had abetted the escape of the English naval hero, Captain Sir Sidney Smith, from the Temple in Paris where he was imprisoned. Now, having fulfilled an engagement as principal ballet-master in London at the highly acceptable salary of £930, Deshayes returned to Paris not only with two new ballets to his credit, but also having made some useful friends among the French dancers in the company, notably Lise Noblet, Fanny Bias and Albert. The following year he enhanced his reputation as a man of ideas by a thoughtful little book entitled *Des Idées générales sur l'Académie Royale de Musique et plus spécialement sur la Danse.*

It had long been his ambition to produce a ballet at the Opéra, and he presented a synopsis of a ballet entitled *Terpsichore.* He was to claim that it had been accepted, only to moulder in the Opéra's files, but this not deter him from making another attempt with a synopsis entitled *Zémire et Azor.* This was submitted in March 1823 – at the same time as Gardel's *Méléagre et Atalante* – for the decision of the Minister of the Royal Household, the Marquis de Lauriston, who ruled that, of the two, Deshayes's work was 'the more appropriate'.[11] However, it was not until January 1824 that the first positive steps were taken towards its production. On the basis of the requirements set out in the scenario, the initial estimates for the scene painting, costumes and machinery amounted to some 60,000 francs,[12] and a horrified Lauriston had to remind Habeneck that the budget allowed only 40,000 francs for a work by an unknown author, and that Deshayes must be required to work within that limit. If the Minister hoped that this firm line would be dutifully observed, he was soon to be disillusioned. The ballet's first mention in the press, as *La Belle et la bête,* appeared in the *Courrier des théâtres* on 8 January; and by April it was being mentioned under its eventual title of *Zémire et Azor,* after Grétry's *opéra-comique* of that name on which it was based.[13] Rehearsals began in the summer and were apparently not without problems, to read between the lines of a letter from August Bournonville to his father in August, in which he disclosed that Gardel and Milon were 'not very happy with what [Deshayes] had been allowed to compose'.[14]

In trying to keep expenditure within the budgeted allocation, Habeneck's life was made a misery by the choreographer's constant demands. Finally, when the first performance was only two weeks away, he learnt that Deshayes was about to complain over his head to the Vicomte Sosthène de La Rochefoucauld, who as Director of Fine Arts had recently been given the responsibility of supervising the Opéra. Habeneck's patience now snapped, and he released his pent-up exasperation in a letter to his superior:

> M. Deshayes, a former dancer of repute, but unknown as a choreographer, has been battling continually with the Administration over the expenditure on *Zémire et Azor*, a ballet of his own composition. As far back as May 1824, Marshal de Lauriston, foreseeing the obstacles that would arise with this most difficult artiste, whose talent as a ballet producer offered no guarantee since he had never had anything performed in Paris ... had issued orders, by express letter, that on no account was the sum of 40,000 francs to be exceeded on the production of this work.
>
> This is a positive order, which the Administration must do its utmost to obey.
>
> But M. Deshayes is meticulous to an unprecedented degree: he never sees anything in perspective, but concerns himself with minute details. He demands perfection in every area, and particularly in the costumes, a perfection that is of no use in the theatre, where the eye is satisfied by illusion. And since his demands involve inconceivable expenditure, the Opéra has thought it necessary to refuse him.
>
> And then he complains, loses his temper, and will no doubt take the matter to you, M. le Vicomte, if he has not done so already.
>
> I feel it is my duty to assure you, in advance of any report that he might make to you, that I am more than justified in refusing to meet his repeated demands on the grounds that the cost of his work, whatever savings might be made, will exceed that of our finest ballets – *Cendrillon, Aline, Alfred* etc., etc.
>
> I also beg you not to take any notice of the complaints of the designer, M. Fragonard, who would like to supply all the old works with new costumes and has nothing good to say of either the past or the present. However, in

the designs he has given us up to now, there is nothing sufficiently remarkable to persuade us of' the ignorance of his predecessors.

These details, M. le Vicomte, may seem of little importance, but their purpose is to prevent authors from ruining the Opéra, and to observe economy in expenditure, which is all the more necessary in view of the sorry state in which this establishment finds itself.[15]

Deshayes' letter of complaint landed on the Vicomte's desk that same day:

I am sorry to have to trouble you, but I find myself forced by circumstances to make this approach on the ground that an author is responsible to the public for the faults committed in the preparation of his work. The problem, M. le Vicomte, is this:

On the 7th of this month I went with M. Fragonard, costume designer to the Académie Royale de Musique, to inspect and approve those for my ballet, *Zémire et Azor*. Not only, M. le Vicomte, did we find that the greater part of those costumes had been ridiculously made and were completely inaccurate when compared with the designs, but in addition they were intolerably dirty for a type of work that depends above all on their richness and even magnificence.

I have complained both verbally and in writing to the Administrators of the Opéra, who have probably not made a thorough examination of the way in which those costumes have been made up, since they have neither replied to my complaints nor acknowledged the note I sent them about the costumes in need of repair.

I humbly beg you, M. le Vicomte, to have a look at the costumes for the ballet of *Zémire et Azor* so that you can see for yourself how necessary it is that the said costumes should be inspected. At the same time I must point out to the Administrators that the care taken in staging a production is part of its intrinsic merit.[16]

La Rochefoucauld did not brush Deshayes's letter aside, at least going through the motions of sending someone in whom he had confidence to inspect the costumes in question. This emissary reported that the costumes seemed to him to lack nothing of the richness required, nor were they unfaithful to the designs. Deshayes was duly informed, and must have realised that there was nothing more he could do than trust to luck that all would go well at the first performance, now only a week away.

As events turned out, the unfortunate choreographer had good reason for concern, if not alarm. Few first nights can have been so punctuated with scenic mishaps as that of' *Zémire et Azor* on 21 October 1824.

Its plot would have been familiar to those in the audience who had seen the *opéra-comique*. The hero, Azor (Montjoie), incurs the wrath of the wicked fairy Emirzène (Mme Elie) by refusing to marry her, and for this slight is changed into a beast. However, through the intervention of another fairy, Thaïs (Gaillet), this spell will be broken if, despite his frightening exterior, Azor can win a maiden's true love. Azor then loses the ring that Thaïs has given him, but it is miraculously restored by a magic rosebush, which he orders to be carefully protected and tended. Two other characters, Sander (Milon) and his slave Aly (Godefroy), then make their appearance, seeking shelter in the palace from a storm. To their amazement a table laden with food rises out of the ground. But when Sander plucks a rose from the magic bush to take back to his daughter Zémire, an alarm is sounded. In a furious rage Azor orders Sander to be put to death, but at the sight of Zémire's portrait he softens and agrees to spare him in exchange for his daughter. Aly advises Sander to feign acceptance. As a result Sander is allowed to return home, where Zémire (Legallois) learns what has happened and resolves to go to Azor herself to plead for her father to be forgiven. On their arrival Aly is refused entry into the palace, and Zémire enters alone. At her first sight of Azor she swoons in horror, but gradually his gentle manners reassure her. Learning the cause of her sadness, Azor conjures up a vision of her father grieving at her absence and agrees to let her see him once more if she will promise to return. Azor entrusts her with the magic ring, and she is carried back to her father in a chariot, drawn by two winged dragons. The wicked fairy then tries to prevent her from returning to Azor by stealing the chariot, but Zémire invokes the aid of the magic ring and is carried back on a cloud. The wicked fairy, believing that her plan has succeeded, tells Azor that Zémire will never return and is about to turn Zémire into a monster when the supreme genie Hormixda (Elie) appears as a *deus ex machina*, and the wicked fairy is swallowed up in a burst of flames. The ballet ends with Zémire declaring her love for Azor, who resumes his natural form.

Having sat through an interval of an hour and a quarter after the end of the opera, the audience was not in the best of humour when the ballet began, and was no doubt doubly exasperated by the extraordinary chapter of accidents that followed – the result, one might justifiably suspect, of a concerted intrigue against the unfortunate choreographer. Things began to go wrong almost from the beginning. First of all, the curtain covering the mirror in which the wicked fairy was supposed to be shown the absurdity of her marrying Azor, would not draw. Then Azor's metamorphosis from man to beast failed to work. For this, Montjoie's costume had been designed so that the beast's mask, which was enclosed in a sort of crown on his head, would, at the pull of a string, drop and cover his face. But when Montjoie released it, the whole crown fell on to his shoulders like a halter. The music stopped. Mme Elie, who was playing the wicked fairy, tugged at the string, but to no avail. Finally the unfortunate Montjoie had to run into the wings to have the metamorphosis properly attended to. A few minutes later the mirror was giving trouble again. Its curtain still would not draw. Coulon lent a hand to assist the efforts of the stagehands, but it had well and truly stuck.

In the second act the smooth working of Aly's ejection from the palace on a sliding trap gave hope that the stagehands were at last getting into their stride. Far from it! According to the printed scenario, the magic picture showing Sander grieving at his daughter's absence was to have vanished at Zémire's approach. It did indeed vanish, but the human agency was all too clearly revealed by shouts from the stagehands: 'Here she comes! Heave ho!' The audience dissolved into laughter and hisses, and when, at the end of this act, the winged dragons obstinately refused to leave the ground and had to be pushed manually into the wings, they broke out into exasperated cries of 'Push! Straight on now! Whoa!'

These were only some of the accidents that marred the performance. The scene changing, which took place in sight of the audience, was hopelessly mismanaged, palaces rising only halfway, clouds being lowered at the wrong moment, borders for the forest scene appearing when the stage was being set for an interior scene in Sander's house, all to the accompaniment of full-throated oaths from behind the scenes and laughter from the audience. A break of twenty minutes between the second and third acts tried the audience's patience still further, and all in all poor Deshayes must have felt that it was he, not the hero of his ballet, who was under the spell of a malevolent fairy that evening.

By being first in the field after Bigottini's retirement, Amélie Legallois had sufficient advantage over Lise Noblet to be chosen for the leading part in *Zémire et Azor*, which had gone into rehearsal when Noblet was on leave of absence, dancing in London. It was Legallois's first important creation. She was always a prey to nerves when playing a new rôle, and her ordeal must have been painfully increased by all the disturbing mishaps. Her presence, however, was one of the few pleasures of the first night, and at the second performance, when nearly everything worked perfectly and the reluctant dragons had been replaced by a more easily shifted cloud, she was warmly received. Critical opinion may have been divided on the subject of her miming, but her dancing was a delight in the two *pas* Deshayes had arranged for her – a lively *pas de schal* in the second act and a *pas de deux* with Montjoie in the third act that was full of voluptuous poses inspired by classical sculpture.

   What little applause there had been on the first night was mainly awarded
to the dancers who took part in the *divertissements*. The authors of the ballet
were not even called for at the end, although there were a few ironic shouts
for the machinist. Some of the critics wrote their reviews in a very bad humour, but their strictures contained more than a grain of truth. The action,
over-burdened with redundant details that had been superimposed on the
opera libretto, was in places obscure and tedious. The action did not begin
until after a long *divertissement* featuring the leading dancers of the company, and at the end there was another equally lengthy *divertissement,* which,
being performed by dancers of lesser standing, came as something of an
anticlimax. Nevertheless the production was enlivened by a certain amount
of 'imagination, grace, freshness and often wit',[17] and Deshayes refused to
allow himself to be disheartened, setting to work at once to remedy the ballet's defects. Some judicious cuts were made before the second performance,
and within a few days the *Journal de Paris* announced that 'the stock of *Zémire
et Azor* has risen to a *succès d'estime,* although one may doubt whether it will
rise any higher, since this mimed fairy tale is hardly anything more than a
"translation" of Grétry's opera'.[18]

   Many of Grétry's airs had been preserved in Schneitzhoeffer's score,
which, although lacking homogeneity, contained several excellent passages,
notably a solo for a seven-stringed viola d'amore, played by the violinist
Chrétien Urhan, an oboe solo by Vogt, and in the third act a 'real violin
concerto'[19] with Baillot as the soloist.

   The complicated sequence of effects with which the chief machinist
Gromaire[20] had grappled so incompetently was not accompanied by a corresponding splendour in the *mise en scène.* Ciceri had had to work on a relatively
modest budget and could do no more than touch up a few sets taken from this
work and that. An interesting property, however, was a full-length portrait of
Zémire, seen in the first scene of the second act – the work of Nicolas Gosse,
whose painting of St Vincent de Paul had been much admired in that year's
Salon.

   Despite the many successful ballets that he was to produce in London in
his later years, Deshayes would not be invited to work for the Opéra again.
The failure of *Zémire et Azor* created a lasting prejudice against him in Paris.
His plans for another ballet, *Phaéton,* did not materialise, and when he took
the opportunity of putting in an appearance at the Opéra shortly after the
resignation of Aumer in 1831, the *Courrier des théâtres* made it abundantly
clear that his re-engagement would not be welcomed.[21] As for Lise Noblet,
she did not even trouble to claim her right to share the rôle of Zémire with
Legallois.

   Notwithstanding the grumbles of Gardel and Milon and the untoward

comedy provided by the machinist and the stagehands at the first performance, *Zémire et Azor* was not entirely a failure. However, its tally of 22
performances in two-and-a-half years was modest, and the ballet disappeared without a note of regret. Yet it did leave a mark in the memory of
Filippo Taglioni, who must have seen it during his visit to Paris in the late
summer of 1825 – for among the ballets that he staged that winter in Stuttgart is to be found one bearing the very same title.

* * * * * * *

More than eighteen months separated that luckless work from the next new
ballet to be presented at the Opéra. They were months that held little interest
for followers of ballet beyond a bereavement that touched colleagues and
admirers alike when Fanny Bias died at the age of thirty-six, and an excuse
for nostalgic reminiscence when Auguste Vestris made two appearances in
his sixty-sixth year.

Fanny Bias, who on Bigottini's retirement had become the senior *premier
sujet*, a grade she then shared with Mme Anatole and Lise Noblet, had grown
up and matured as a dancer within the walls of the Opéra. Born in the fateful
year of 1789, she had entered the School of Dance as a child and soon attracted the notice of Gardel, who described her in 1806 as 'a well-made
young person, with a pleasing figure, a pretty face and already a useful talent'.[22] After making her début on 12 May 1807, she rose steadily in the
hierarchy of the company, becoming *double* in 1808, *remplaçant* in 1813 and
premier sujet in the genre of *demi-caractère* in 1818. She owed this progress to
her remarkable precision and aplomb, and above all, her lightness, which an
anonymous poet described in these lines:

> *Fanny rase le sol de ses pieds délicats;*
> *L'abeille est moins légère, et Zéphyr moins agile.*[23]

The speed and neatness of her *terre à terre* work evoked memories of Marie
Gardel, while her extreme flexibility earned her the epithet of '*la désossée*', the
boneless one. Castil-Blaze recorded that 'she was long considered to be one of
the front-rank virtuosos of the dance',[24] and, on the evidence of an English
lithograph of 1821,[25] she was among the first generation of ballerinas to rise
on to her *pointes*.

In the winter of 1823 Fanny Bias had fallen dangerously ill. She seemed to
recover, and reappeared at the Opéra in September of the following year, but
after only a few months had to abandon her career once again. The gravity of
her condition – described as 'one of those illnesses which, by terrible predi-

lection, strike only persons of the gentler sex' – could no longer be doubted, and in the early hours of 6 September 1825 her sufferings were mercifully brought to an end. The *Courrier des théâtres* mourned her as 'the dancer who had most completely inherited the talent of Mme Gardel', and paid tribute to 'her character, her morals, the goodness of her heart, and the eminent merit that enabled her to shine among companions from whom it is so difficult to stand out – qualities that made Mlle Fanny Bias dearly cherished by all who knew her.'[26] The respect in which she was held was displayed by the crowd of mourners who attended the Requiem at the Church of Saint-Roch, where not long before, in an incident that had incurred the wrath of Napoleon, the priest had refused to say Mass for the repose of the soul of another dancer, Louise Chameroy.[27]

Still very spry for his years, Auguste Vestris was a survival from an earlier age. The son of an equally famous father, Gaétan Vestris, he had retired as a dancer in 1816 after a career that stretched back through the Napoleonic and Revolutionary periods into the long-vanished years of the old régime, for he had made his début in 1772. After his retirement, he had devoted his energies to teaching. The year 1826 was to be a memorable one for him, for not only did he present a young pupil, August Bournonville, who was destined to become a legend in his own right, but he himself made two appearances on stage: the first at his benefit performance on 1 February and the second, some four weeks later, at that of the singer, Mme Branchu, on 27 February. At his age he could of course no longer sustain a strenuous dancing rôle, and he therefore chose two character parts – the black slave Domingo in *Paul et Virginie* for his own benefit, and the title-rôle in *La Dansomanie* at Mme Branchu's. As Domingo he revealed such dramatic talent that many regretted he had not carried on his stage career as a mime instead of retiring when he did, while as the 'dansomane' Saint-Léger in Gardel's ever-green ballet he gave an astonishing display of agility for one of his years. His own benefit concluded with a tribute, all the more touching for being spontaneous, when a crown of pink and white flowers was thrown on the stage, and Pauline Montessu ran forward, picked it up and placed it with affectionate reverence on the old dancer's grizzled head.

The début of young August Bournonville, Vestris's most promising pupil, in the spring of 1826, came as a welcome sign that a great tradition was not being allowed to wither. Born in Copenhagen, where his father Antoine Bournonville, himself a pupil of Noverre, had directed the Royal Danish Ballet from 1816 to 1823, young August had unhesitatingly chosen a dancer's career, notwithstanding almost equally precocious talents as an actor and a singer. Being awarded a state grant to study dancing in Paris, he was taken there for the first time in the summer of 1820 by his father, who introduced him to his friends Coulon, Maze and Auguste Vestris. Four years later, after his father had been dismissed from his position in Copenhagen, young August returned, with added determination to make good, to continue his classes with Vestris. After a year's toil, with the prospect of a début at the Opéra coming closer, he was struck down with rheumatic fever. His father's old friend Louis Nivelon invited him to his country home at Neaulles-Saint-Martin in Normandy, where he made a quick recovery. Back in Paris again, he resumed his classes with redoubled determination, taking additional lessons with Baptiste Petit to improve his pirouettes. At last, on 16 March 1826, he was summoned to be examined for a début, and wearing knee breeches and hose and the embroidered shirt in which he had been confirmed, he appeared before the panel of judges. Three weeks later, on 5 April, he made a very promising début, dancing in a *pas de trois* in *Nina*. 'His style of dancing,' wrote the *Courrier des spectacles* approvingly the next day, 'has something of Albert's and something of Paul's, forming a happy medium between the two.'[28] That he also possessed ability as a mime was revealed not long afterwards, on 30 April, when he played Zephyr in *Psyché*. And later that summer came his reward in the form of an engagement as a *double* at 1800 francs a year, to which a further 600 francs were added to enable him to continue his studies under Auguste Vestris.

Young Bournonville was a dedicated and ambitious young man, and when the two-year term of his engagement was nearing its end, he was emboldened to approach Emile Lubbert, the recently appointed Director, with a request to be promoted to the grade of *remplaçant* when his contract was renewed. To his dismay, Lubbert refused and – fearing perhaps that Bournonville might continue to press through influential friends – set out his reasons in a carefully worded report to La Rochefoucauld. In this he explained that it was essential to maintain the numerical strength of the *doubles* to meet calls to replace at short notice senior dancers who had fallen ill or were injured, and furthermore, there were more senior *doubles* who in fairness should have a prior claim to promotion. Such reasons were not necessarily invalid, but it may be that Bournonville had been a little too pressing in advancing his case for promotion. In his letter to his superior, Lubbert commented: 'M. Bournonville has promise, but it is to be feared that his excessive pride might prove damaging to his qualities'.[29]

It was only when Aumer intervened on his behalf a year later that Bournonville's usefulness to the company was recognised. Even then, Lubbert procrastinated, and it was not until a year later that Bournonville was promoted. A three-year contract was then promised, to commence at the beginning of 1830 – but by then events had taken their own course. Bournonville now stood at a crossroads in his remarkable career, the full import of which would not become clear until a century later. For it was in 1830 that he cut his ties with the Opéra and settled in his native Denmark to become, for virtually the rest of his long life, the director and guiding spirit of the Royal Ballet of Copenhagen. In that modest city, later in the century, when in major capitals such as Paris and London the ballet had slipped into decadence, he not only maintained its integrity as a theatre art, but more specifically – on the basis of the training that he had received from Auguste Vestris – preserved the standard and prestige of male dancing.

NOTES

1. The scenario of *Méléagre et Atalante* is preserved in the Archives Nationales (AJ[13] 1023).
2. The scenario, entitled *Le Bal masqué*, together with a note by Gardel in the form of a letter to Habeneck explaining the circumstances of its conception, are preserved in the Archives Nationales (AJ[13] 1023). The scenario is published in full, in an English translation, as an appendix to an article by the author in *Dance Research*, XXI, 2 (Winter 2003), 27–41.
3. *Journal de Paris*, 8 November 1822.
4. Arch. Nat., AJ[13] 111.
5. *Journal des théâtres*, 8 September 1822.
6. *Corsaire*, 2 June 1824.
7. *Diable boiteux*, 19 May 1824.
8. *Journal de Paris*, 5 September 1821.
9. *Un Vieil abonné*, 107–8. Yes indeed, that young goddess,/ Is Lucretia to the life:/ She possesses the latter's beauty,/And, what is more, her tiresome wisdom./ No amount of landaus, cashmeres or rubies/Can make her accommodating:/ Well, if I have not had her,/She must be impregnable.
10. *Morning Post*, 14 June 1824.
11. Arch. Nat., AJ[13] 114. Lauriston to Habeneck, 1 May 1824.
12. Arch. Nat., O[3] 1663.
13. *Zémire et Azor, opera-comique* by Grétry, libretto by Marmontel, f.p. Palais de Fontainebleau, 9 November 1771.
14. Bournonville, *Lettres*, I, 19. Letter dated 10 August 1824.
15. Arch. Nat., O[3] 1663. Habeneck to La Rochefoucauld, 7 October 1824. Alexandre-Evariste Fragonard, son of the celebrated painter, Jean-Honoré Fragonard, had succeeded Garnerey as costume designer of the Opéra in the spring of 1824.
16. Arch. Nat., O[3] 1663. Deshayes to La Rochefoucauld, 7 October 1824.
17. *Courrier des théâtres*, 21 October 1824.
18. *Journal de Paris*, 1 November 1824.
19. *Journal des débats*, 22 October 1824.
20. Gromaire [Jean de la Pommerie] was chief machinist of the Opéra from 1816 to 1832. In 1807 he had been implicated in the scandal following Angélique Aubry's fall on to the stage from a *gloire* during the first performance of Milon's ballet, *Le Retour d'Ulysse*, in the presence of the Empress Josephine (see Guest, *Ballet under Napoleon*, ch. 16). For his unfortunate contribution to *Zémire et Azor*, he was pilloried in a parody entitled *Jérôme Gâcheux, cousin de Cadet Buteux, à la première représentation du ballet de Zémire et Azore (sic), ou la Belle et la Bête*, 'a *pot-pourri* dedicated to the machinist of the Opéra,' attributed by Seymour Travers to Savinien Pointe.
21. *Courrier des théâtres*, 11 August 1831.
22. Arch. Nat., AJ[13] 82.
23. *Almanach des Spectacles* (1819), 45. Fanny skims across the floor with her delicate feet;/ No bee is so light, nor Zephyr so agile.

24. Castil-Blaze, *Académie*, II, 111.
25. Guest, *Romantic Ballet in England*, plate Va.
26. *Courrier des théâtres*, 7 September 1825.
27. Guest, *Ballet under Napoleon*, 119–21.
28. *Courrier des spectacles*, 6 April 1826.
29. Arch. Nat., O³ 1680. Lubbert to La Rochefoucauld, 6 May 1828.

6

Blache's Mars et Vénus

Aumer's somewhat unexpected departure had placed the Opéra in a quandary, for it revived, with even greater urgency, the problem of ensuring the succession to Gardel and Milon. Early in January 1824, the *Courrier des spectacles* reported that Jean Coralli, the ballet-master at the Porte-Saint-Martin, was to be engaged in the same capacity by the Opéra. Although no firm evidence survives to support this report, it may not be wholly without foundation, for three months later the same paper reported that Coralli's first work for the Opéra would be a ballet called *Paul et Rosette.*[1] However, nothing was to come of this proposal, possibly because the very idea of engaging a ballet-master from a boulevard theatre was repugnant.

In the meantime, Habeneck had been directing his attention to the provinces. Having come to the conclusion that a short-term solution would have to be sought to fill the gap until 1826, when Aumer might be tempted back, he had travelled to Bordeaux to seek out an elderly but still active ballet-master whose renown stood high in his profession, despite his never having worked in Paris.

Jean-Baptiste Blache came of a family with a dance tradition, and in the course of a long and productive career had acquired a very considerable reputation that extended throughout the provinces, and most particularly to Bordeaux, where for many years he had held the post of chief ballet-master. It also extended, vicariously, to Paris, where a number of his ballets had been respectfully revived by his eldest son Frédéric. He was now approaching sixty, having been born in 1765, in Berlin of French parents. The family may have even then belonged to the dance fraternity, for the name Blache is occasionally to be found in theatrical records of that time: a Mimi Blache had danced in Madrid and Barcelona in the late 1770s and a Henri Blache at La Scala, Milan, under Gaspare Angiolini in 1782. Even more interesting is that a cast-list of the first performance of Dauberval's *La Fille mal gardée* includes a Mlle Blache, who may have been Jean-Baptiste's sister. Jean-Baptiste himself began his dance training early, and at the age of eleven was showing such promise that his father, concerned at the lack of good teachers in Berlin, took him to Paris and placed him under Jacques-François Deshayes, who was then ballet-master of the Comédie-Française. After a few years Deshayes took over the direction of the Opéra's School of Dance, and young Blache may well have continued his training there.

However, his future was not to lie in Paris, for in about 1786 he left the capital to embark on a career in the provinces. In the small town of Montpelier in 1787, as a budding choreographer of twenty-two, he produced a modest comic ballet called *Les Meuniers*, which was to remain a regular money-spinner throughout his career. Its success came at a most opportune moment, and for many years it was a major source of support, bringing into the family's coffers no less than 60,000 francs. His elder sons, Frédéric and Alexis, were born a few years after he left Paris, and after the death of their mother he remarried, almost certainly more than once, and begat a further brood. And a brood it certainly was, coming surely from more than one other mother if his biographer Saint-Léon got his statistics right in observing that he earned the epithet of 'fecund' in the full meaning of the word, for 'during his second marriage he stole from Cupid's quiver a little battalion of thirty-two children'.[2]

When Habeneck approached Blache with a view to solving the Opéra's immediate problem – of replenishing the repertory before a permanent successor to Gardel and Milon could be found – Blache was comfortably settled as ballet-master in Bordeaux, assisted very ably by his son Alexis. He was even beginning to contemplate retirement, and was initially reluctant to accept what was likely to be a somewhat daunting engagement. He was beginning to feel his age and to suffer aches and pains in his legs, but he still remained actively in charge of the ballet in Bordeaux, for which he was receiving a salary of 12,000 francs a year. Retirement cannot have been far off, but the thought of crowning his career in Paris now caused him to cast prudence to the winds and listen favourably to Habeneck's proposal. There was a small problem over some sort of a commitment he had entered into with the Porte-Saint-Martin in Paris, but through the intervention of his son Frédéric, who was ballet-master there, it was soon disposed of. Habeneck's approach had taken him by surprise, but the opportunity had been too tempting to refuse, particularly when Habeneck offered a two-year contract providing for the production of no fewer than four of his ballets. The first of these was a work very close to his heart: one that he had successfully staged in Bordeaux fourteen years before, *Les Filets de Vulcain.*[3] And for the honour of a Parisian triumph, he was even prepared to sacrifice half of the salary he was receiving in Bordeaux.

Later, when matters did not turn out as smoothly as he had expected, he was to grumble that the Opéra had coaxed him out of retirement; but in fact he had only partially retired, for just a year earlier he had signed a contract with the Grand-Théâtre, Bordeaux, as principal ballet-master with his son Alexis as his assistant. The latter was in fact already very competent, and, as events turned out, would take over very proficiently as ballet-master when his father left for Paris.

Indeed, there had been little let-up in Jean-Baptiste Blache's activity during his final year in Bordeaux. In March 1824 he had produced a ballet called *La Laitière polonaise*, which contained a novel skating scene, for which the dancers wore roller-skates that he himself had ingeniously adapted for stage use. This was an effect that he was looking forward to presenting in Paris, but in this he was to be disappointed – discovering, not without some bitterness, that the dancer who had tested them in Bordeaux had signed a contract for their use at the Cirque Olympique.[4]

Blache's output had been spread over a working life of nearly forty years, and comprised works of many different kinds. Paris had already been shown a selection of these when his son Frédéric had been ballet-master at the Porte-Saint-Martin in 1817–19. A proportion of the Opéra's public would therefore have already had a foretaste of his genius, to which a choreographer of a later generation, Arthur Saint-Léon, was to pay a fulsome tribute:

An excellent musician, who had mastered the difficulties of the violin, [Blache] could also draw admirable sounds from the cello, and this conjugation of talents was naturally a great help to him in composing his ballets, in that it gave him the privilege of following nothing but his own inclination. For without anyone else's assistance he himself arranged the music for nearly all his works, and the cohesion of his scenes and their perfect consistency was entirely a natural consequence of his genius as one who was at the same time both dancer and musician. Like Grétry, who was never more satisfied with his compositions than when hearing them played on a barrel-organ, Blache only felt he had really succeeded when he saw those in the cheaper seats understanding his subject and appreciating his work. All his ballets were thus marked by a great lucidity of conception. Although they gave the appearance of being slight, they revealed an artistry and an imagination that knew no bounds, for such was his skill in arranging scenes of action and *pas* and giving a scene light and shade that he very soon found himself classed among the most celebrated choreographers of his time.[5]

Blache arrived in Paris towards the end of April 1824, no doubt fully expecting to be soon at work preparing the ballet selected for his début. This was an anacreontic work that had been an outstanding success when originally produced in Bordeaux some fifteen years before, under the title of *Les Filets de Vulcain*. The formalities of agreeing the terms of his contract were soon concluded, and he was engaged for a term of two years expiring in April 1826, during which time he would stage four ballets. The Opéra may have been prepared to bind him for a longer term, but on that point he was not to be moved, even though it meant he would have no right to a pension.

If he expected to set to work immediately, he was soon to be disillusioned, for he arrived in Paris to find the dancers already fully occupied in rehearsing Deshayes' *Zémire et Azor*. Not until October was that work presented – by which time five months of Blache's two-year term had already elapsed. Then, in the following month, another blow fell when Habeneck, with whom he had established a comfortable understanding, was replaced as Director of the Opéra by Raphaël Duplantys, an administrator pure and simple with no experience of running a theatre.[6]

Standing by with little to do while Deshayes struggled seemingly interminably with his ill-fated *Zémire et Azor*, Blache began to wonder whether political factors were impeding his progress. Unlike Deshayes, he had not emigrated after the Revolution, preferring to remain in France and keep his political leanings, whatever they were, to himself. Shortly after Napoleon had been banished to St Helena – when a host of *émigrés* returned to France, eager for favours to reward them for loyalty to their monarch – Blache had deemed it wise to provide himself with a number of testimonials to his own loyalty to the Royalist cause. One of them was from a royalist agent from London to whom he had given shelter, another from employees of the theatre in Bordeaux recording that he had purchased lilies for a royalist demonstration; another testified that he had saved the lives of several royalist sympathisers. These he now sent to that good friend of Mlle Noblet, the Marquis de Lauriston, who until recently had been Minister of the Royal Household, begging him to speak in his favour to his successor, the Duc de Doudeauville. He had, he pointed out, 'exposed himself to danger in the King's cause, but had never solicited any favour from His Majesty, although M. de Martignac and other persons of note had encouraged him to make demands, which they were prepared to support in the Council of State'.[7]

In January 1825 it was ominously reported that preparations for *Les Filets de Vulcain* had been discontinued. Happily, this proved to be only a temporary hitch, which Blache managed to overcome; and six weeks later it was announced that his ballet would go into rehearsal as soon as the festivities attending the coronation of Charles X were over. Duplantys was not unhelpful, but there was little he could do now that the dancers were fully committed to a string of operatic productions. In June 1825 Blache made a strong request to La Rochefoucauld, who now had supreme responsibility for the Opéra, that his ballet should be given priority after the revival of Gluck's *Armide*, which was then in preparation. It was only at this point, when he had been kicking his heels for more than a year, that his scenario came before the Reading Committee, which justified its existence by proposing certain modifications that happily were attended to with little delay. His problems, however, were not over yet; finding himself still kicking his heels at the beginning of September, he was driven to make a desperate appeal to La Rochefoucauld:

In consequence of the unhappy events that occurred in 1824, my first ballet was postponed. And now preparations for the operas *Les Deux Salem, La Belle au bois dormant, Pharamond* and *Don Sanche* have delayed the rehearsals still further.

Armide was to have been the final obstacle to my work, as you, Monsieur le Vicomte, were good enough to inform both myself and the gentlemen of the Administration. Furthermore, I thought I could rely on their assurance that I had been authorised by MM. Duplantys and Audry de Janvy[8] to give orders for copying the parts to M. Lefèvre, to whom the score had already been delivered by the composer, M. Schneitzhoeffer.

As soon as the violin rehearsal score was copied, I asked for, and received from M. Dubois, notice of my rehearsals. Two of these I held at the end of September, but the third was cancelled to give way to those for the ballets in *Armide.*

Now from today's papers I learn that the opera *Mahomet II* is to result in an indefinite postponement of the ballet *Les Filets de Vulcain*!

I have had the honour, Monsieur le Vicomte, of informing you both verbally and in writing that the thought of applying to the Opéra had never occurred to me, and that it was M. Habeneck, the administrator of the Académie Royale de Musique, who of his own volition (and by fine promises in writing) had overcome my reluctance. As a result I gave up a salary of 12,000 francs and a three-year engagement in Bordeaux. My son has replaced me there, and I am too much of a father to dispossess him. Consequently I am losing 24,000 francs to my replacement, an enormous loss for a father burdened with a very numerous family! And my engagement at the Opéra will come to an end next April, 1826.

Since I have held a number of special rehearsals with the principal dancers, whose zeal I greatly respect, I cannot in all honesty (in my present state of uncertainty) impose any further on their time, their willingness and their efforts if the ballet is not going to be given; and so, if that is the Administration's decision with regard to this ballet, I am appealing to your sense of justice and humanity, Monsieur le Vicomte, to pay me for the few months left to me and for the deductions that have been made, as compensation for the losses I have suffered by giving up my engagement in Bordeaux, and for the four ballets that the Administration of the Opéra was to have had me stage.

I am venturing to send you, Monsieur le Vicomte, my just and respectful grievances. The complete confidence I have in your justice and probity gives me the assurance that you will be good enough to devote a moment's thought to the painful position in which I find myself.[9]

Matters then began to move, but all too slowly. Early in August the young Danish dancer, August Bournonville, wrote to his father with the latest news: 'M. Blache has had nearly six rehearsals since his ballet has been in preparation, and so many obstacles have been placed in his way that he is ready to give it up, for his engagement is at an end and he will have had 12,000 francs for two years without anything to show for it.'[10] The very next day a news-item in the theatrical press reported a rumour that Blache was leaving,[11] but in fact the old ballet-master was too worldly-wise to take such a precipitate step, preferring to keep up the pressure on La Rochefoucauld, to whom he wrote again in December:

The flattering letter with which Your Excellency has deigned to honour me, including a reassuring postscript in your own hand, has somewhat eased my mind.

The order to proceed with my rehearsals and the scenery was about to be implemented when my work was halted once again – for the ballet, *Paul et Virginie*. Since that work was being given for the benefit of a great artist [Gardel], I need say no more about that. But this hitch was accompanied by another, as I shall now relate. Yesterday I had the honour of seeing M. Duplantys, of whose loyalty I am well aware. The machinist, being occupied with work for the operas *Olympie* and *Mahomet II* and making repairs to the scenery of *Fernand Cortez*, is unable to supply M. Ciceri with anything more for my ballet, and M. Ciceri is complaining that he has not received any of the flats needed by the painters.

M. Duplantys, who has gone to great lengths to sort out this affair, has told me: 'Your ballet will be given, but the machinist is asking for more time!' This would not have worried me, Monsieur le Vicomte, if I had signed a contract for 4 years instead of the 2 which will expire on 1 April 1826 (in three months' time), and on looking at my contract again, I find the following clause: 'In the course of the last year of your engagement, and on being given notice in advance, we will renew [it] either for a fixed term or for an indefinite term, which will thereby bring you into the category of members of the Académie and entitle you to a proportionate pension at the end of ten years'.

Furthermore, Monsieur le Vicomte, if I could be sure that my contract would be extended, I would have the certainty of staging *Les Filets de*

Vulcain as well as the three other works that I ought already to have given. Your Excellency will easily appreciate that, as the father of a numerous family, I could not spend my money in Paris without a salary while waiting for my first ballet to be produced. Two months ago I received an excellent offer, which I turned down on receiving the reassuring letter that Your Excellency was kind enough to write to me.

Monsieur le Vicomte, I have worked for forty years to acquire the reputation I enjoy today, and I am risking losing it for ever without making myself known. With the matter dragging on *ad infinitum* and the end of my engagement no more than three months away, Your Excellency will not be surprised at my alarm. Just a word, a reply, Monsieur le Vicomte, can put my mind at rest as to my future fate.[12]

This desperate appeal had the immediate effect of orders being given for the production to be hastened, but a work on the scale of *Mars et Vénus,* as by then it had been re-entitled, needed several months' preparation, and it was not until 19 May 1826 that it was given its first performance at the Opéra. By the mid-1820s, mythological subjects were going out of fashion, despite the continued presence in the repertory of Gardel's 35-year-old *Psyché.* Bearing in mind this shift in public taste, the brilliant success of Blache's *Mars et Vénus* was a striking proof of his exceptional skill as a choreographer and of the respect that he clearly enjoyed among the dancers and backstage staff. Of the sixty-six new ballets created in the Salle Le Peletier between its opening in 1821 and its destruction in 1873, only *La Sylphide, Giselle,* and *Coppélia* were to achieve a greater number of performances. A crop of parodies in the popular theatres[13] offered further evidence of the sensational success of *Mars et Vénus,* which the *Journal de Paris,* recalling the magnificence of *Aladin,* described as 'a new *Lampe merveilleuse* – and, thank God, without the words'.[14]

The plot of the original production had remained unchanged. Venus (Noblet) is in love with Mars (Albert), but Jupiter (Seuriot) decrees that she must marry Vulcan (S. Mérante). When Mars protests, Jupiter orders him to go and wage war on the Titans. Venus is then confided to the care of Minerva (Lacroix), but Cupid (M. Bertrand) persuades Vulcan to take Minerva to his forge, leaving Venus in the charge of Zephyr and Flora (Paul and Mme Montessu). By this subterfuge Cupid is able to bring the lovers together, but their tryst is observed by Apollo (Gosselin), who is also in love with Venus. Cupid then implores the aid of Zephyr, who calls upon his followers to spirit the lovers away. However, Apollo then intervenes to persuade Vulcan to forge a net to trap Mars and Venus together. Meanwhile Minerva comes upon the lovers as they are about to enter Cupid's temple, and prevails upon them to be sensible. While she is urging Mars to obey Jupiter's command, the Winds drop the net over their heads. Overjoyed at this apparent proof of Venus's innocence, Vulcan begs her to forgive him, and the ballet closes with Hymen uniting Vulcan and Venus, and Zephyr and Flora.

The plot had been made easy to follow by Blache's respect for the unity of time; while the care he had given to every detail of the production had its reward in the smooth running of the first performance, which was marred by no such untoward mishaps as had plagued Deshayes a few months before. Some critics thought there was too much dancing in the first and second acts, but no one disputed Blache's skill in arranging charming and original *pas*. One of the most effective of these was a heavy-footed dance for the Cyclops in Act I; this was interrupted by the entrance of Zephyr and Flora, which formed a strikingly imaginative contrast. The dance of the Three Graces (Marinette, J. Hullin, A Bertrand),[15] who abandon their celestial dances for the simple steps of shepherdesses, was another highlight.

The Opéra had been exceptionally generous in its expenditure on this production, for which Ciceri had painted five new sets, and magnificent costumes had been provided. From the opening of the first act, when the gods and goddesses descend from the heavens or emerge from the waters or from beneath the earth, until the ballet's closing moments, the audience's attention was never allowed to stray. The lovers' aerial exit at the end of the second act, with Zephyr hovering gracefully over them – the first quadruple flight to have been seen at the Opéra – was greeted with gasps of surprise; but even this effect was overshadowed by the scene in Vulcan's forge, which was generally acclaimed as the high-point of the ballet. 'Here,' wrote the *Journal des débats,*

> that fine description of the Cyclops at work, which can be admired in Virgil's Georgics, is realised and rendered into action to delight the eye rather than the ear. The frail boards of the stage sag beneath the weight of the anvils on which the heavy hammers of Vulcan's companions pound in time to the music... The scene glows red with the flames emerging from the heart of the furnace.[16]

In this scene the same critic found Schneitzhoeffer's music perfectly adapted to its subject; but while acknowledging the composer's skill, he considered that the score as a whole lacked grace and variety and that its cohesion was marred by borrowings from Mozart, Haydn and Grétry. Although the ballet was dropped from the repertory in 1837, a march from its score was to gain an unexpected distinction many years later in 1853, when it was chosen to accompany the bridal procession at the wedding of Napoleon III and Eugénie de Montijo in Notre Dame.

The public's interest was soon to be whetted by a change of cast. The honour of creating the rôle of Venus had fallen to Lise Noblet, whose 'piquant graces and expressive mime'[17] had earned her a considerable triumph; but she had been unable to acquire the sole right to play it. Some weeks before the opening night she had made a formal request that no one else should have the right to appear in rôles she herself had created, but on the advice of Gardel, Milon and Albert, this had been rejected. The three ballet-masters took the view that the regulation establishing the right of Noblet and Legallois to share after the tenth performance the rôles that each had created was in the best interests of the public.[18] After the tenth performance, therefore, Amélie Legallois duly claimed her right. There was an immediate outcry. Noblet, in a moment of temper, swore she would never play it again, while Charles Maurice, Legallois's champion, responded with an article in the *Courrier des spectacles* pointing out that Legallois had the right to the part, just as Noblet – had she so wished – could have shared that of Zémire.[19] However, Legallois's assumption of the rôle at the eleventh performance on 23 June 1826 was something of a disaster. Charles Maurice, who staunchly reported that she played it with 'a modest, noble and virginal air'[20] and hinted at the presence of a hostile faction in the house, was almost alone in his opinion. The public received Legallois politely but coolly and found her interpretation wanting: she appeared to have copied many of Noblet's movements but with an affectation that seemed to show that she did not fully understand the character, which, as one critic remarked, she interpreted as if it were Clari or Nina or a repentant Magdalene.[21] Noblet's triumph was complete. Her vow never to dance the part again was forgotten, and after Legallois had played it twice, Noblet resumed it to nearly everyone's delight.

Blache's contract contained a provision for an extension, and since it was likely to have expired a few months before the expected production of *Mars et Vénus*, it had been extended until April 1827. There was no suggestion, however, that Blache might follow this ballet with another work, for by then Aumer had been re-engaged and the Opéra's need for another choreographer had disappeared. Blache's workload must have been considerably reduced, but it seems that both he and the Opéra were content for his contract to run on until its specified end in April 1827. However, a few months before the extension would expire, he received news that his father-in-law, the Chevalier Seguenet, was dying and had requested his presence to attend to certain matters of family business to avoid possible litigation after his death. Blache explained the circumstances to La Rochefoucauld and requested to be released from his contract. These family problems must have been very pressing, for the consequences of cutting short his contract was that his period of service fell below three years, and that thereby he lost his entitlement to a pension. Blache philosophically accepted this sacrifice, but on La Rochefoucauld's instructions he was given an *ex gratia* payment,[22] with which one hopes he was satisfied. Certainly, in *Mars et Vénus* he had left a crowning achievement that was a fitting end to a distinguished career.

That spring he rejoined his wife in Toulouse, where her family was based, and settled down to enjoy what one trusts was a happy retirement. He died there, at the age of sixty-eight, on 24 January 1835.

* * * * * * *

In the last few years of his active career Louis Milon, like Gardel, was still hopefully devising plots for new ballets. Among these was a work entitled *La Française à Ispahan*, which was to be doomed to oblivion in the files of the Opéra,[23] but another came almost within a hair's breadth of being staged. This was a spectacular three-act ballet based on an episode in the life of Joan of Arc. It had been conceived shortly after the death of Louis XVIII, when the prospect arose of his successor's coronation – the first such ceremony since that of Louis's older brother, Louis XVI, half a century before, because Louis XVIII had dated his reign from the death of his brother's infant son (Louis XVII) in captivity during the Revolution. This hallowed ceremony would by long tradition take place in Orléans, where the new king, Charles X, would be anointed with the holy oil which, according to legend, had been brought to St Rémi by a dove from Heaven. A few drops of it had miraculously, so it was believed, been preserved after the phial had been smashed during the Revolution. To Royalists this would be an event of the greatest significance, and it was Milon's fondest desire to add his contribution to the surrounding festivities with a ballet on the theme of Joan of Arc. This would conclude, not with her glorious death in battle, but with the coronation of Charles VII that symbolised the rebirth of France after many decades of humiliating war with England.

Milon's scenario was presented to the Reading Committee shortly before the coronation was to take place, and examined by its members with a minute care such as had seldom before been given to a choreographer's script. Milon's plot had envisaged a closing scene depicting the coronation of Charles VII with Joan of Arc at his side, but perhaps on the ground that no theatrical representation could ever come near to presenting the awesome ceremonial of the actual event, the Committee vetoed the proposed finale, preferring a different *dénouement*. And its members, in their zeal, went even further, suggesting quite radical changes in their report:

This ballet contains nothing relative to topical events apart from the coronation with which it closes, and it was therefore necessary to omit a closing scene of that kind and various episodes that might have been taken as allusions. It is believed that the choreographer intended only to make a ballet about Joan of Arc that would close with the relief of Orléans and the departure for Rheims.

The first act seems well composed. One might only wish that Joan's long monologue, with which the piece opens, be shortened and that the heroine should sleep more deeply. Several members proposed that [St] Geneviève should be substituted for the Archangel Michael in Joan's vision, if this would not offend proprieties.

The confrontation of Sinaldo and Douglas in the second act seemed lacking in taste. It was thought that this act would be improved if it were composed differently. The court of Charles VII was gallant and voluptuous. The courtiers, following the monarch's example, were concerned more with their own pleasures than with the misfortunes of France. The act might open with the preparations for a festivity, which could lead into some charming and varied scenes. Charles would make his appearance and have his monologue as in the fourth scene [of Milon's draft]. Agnès would arrive unexpectedly, and have the same conversation with Charles as in the fifth scene. The courtiers would then enter with the actors for the fête that is being prepared. This festivity would be interrupted by the arrival of Dunois and then by Joan. Sinaldo's plot being cut, Joan, having sufficiently proved her divine mission by the incident in the eighth scene, would in some way give the signal for the departure for Orléans, and at this point the act would end.

The third act would remain as it is, apart from the attack being directed not at the little-known fort of Gergeau, but at Orléans itself, and the episode of the traitors being excised as distressing and having at least as many disadvantages as advantages, since, by giving an opportunity for the King's clemency, it demonstrates the crime of some of his subjects. Once Orléans has been taken, the king would enter the city with the same pomp as the choreographer proposed for his entry into Rheims, and that spectacle would be preserved in its entirety. Such are the ideas that have been put forward, not of course as a formal requirement, but above all in relying on his experience to improve his work, which is considered to be susceptible of interest by the variety of its content, the first act being wholly pastoral, the second displaying the elegant pomp of court life, and the third having a wholly martial aspect.[24]

Milon must then have revised his scenario, for in June 1825 the ballet, under the title of *Jeanne d'Arc*, was reported as in the schedule for production during the coming winter. But alas, this was not to be. For one thing, preparations for Blache's *Mars et Vénus* had at last got under way, while the re-engagement of Aumer as ballet-master to succeed Gardel when he retired meant that a new work by Aumer had to be given priority. By the time these two productions had been given, Milon had retired and the chance of his producing another ballet had vanished.

* * * * * * *

It was ironic that the work that sounded the death knell for Milon's *Jeanne d'Arc* should have been such an insignificant little piece as Aumer's *Astolphe et Joconde*, which was given its first performance on 29 January 1827. Produced at no great expense, it was little more than a slavish imitation of Isouard's popular *opéra-comique* of that name, which had survived in the repertory of the Opéra-Comique since its creation in 1814.[25] As adapted for the ballet, the hero Astolphe (Albert) is smitten with the charms of Edile (Noblet), who is betrothed to his friend Joconde (Paul). Pretending to be unsure of his fiancée Mathilde (Mme Anatole), he suggests that Joconde should put her devotion to the test by paying court to her. But the two women overhear this conversation and decide to teach their lovers a lesson. When the men discover that both their sweethearts appear to be fickle, they leave the palace in despair, ostensibly to fight the infidels in the Holy Land. Disguised as troubadours, they arrive at a village, where they press their attentions on a local beauty, Jeannette (Mme Montessu). She tells them that if they will wait for her after dark, each under a different tree, she will come to the one who takes her fancy. But Jeannette tricks them, going to meet her own sweetheart (Ferdinand) instead, and leaving Astolphe and Joconde each under the impression that the other has been favoured. The bailiff (Aumer), suspecting that they are loitering with evil intent, has them arrested; to add to their discomfiture, Mathilde and Edile, who have turned up disguised as gypsies, warn the bailiff that the two men will claim to be the prince and his friend. Astolphe and Joconde are alarmed to learn that Mathilde plans to visit the village to crown Jeannette as queen of the festival. To their mortification their identity is revealed, but all ends happily with the celebration of Jeannette's betrothal to her sweetheart.

The practice of transposing well-known *opéras-comiques* was perhaps becoming a little too commonplace, and the reception given to *Astolphe et Joconde* was no more than polite. 'Choreographers,' suggested the *Pandore*, 'should not be excused from inventing their own subjects, since it is through their imagination that they have to make their mark.'[26] Aumer had adapted the plot with his usual skill, however, and was praised for the scene in which Astolphe and Joconde, from their respective hiding places on either side of the stage, are each trying to attract the attention of Jeannette by playing on his harp, unwittingly accompanying the steps to which she and her village sweetheart are dancing.

That Aumer was not a product of the school of Gardel and Milon was evident from his treatment of the action, which was far removed from the more restrained approach of those two eminent masters. Furthermore, the critic Delaforest was disturbed to find choreographic ideas that, to him, seemed to smack of the boulevard theatres. 'My God!' he exclaimed,

what a lot of business he has to introduce to express the slightest thing! If one character has to approach another, M. Aumer makes him perform three leaps and four little steps instead of walking up to him like anyone else. If a lady has to tell a swain to keep at a respectful distance and not to overstep certain limits, is this simple thought conveyed with a noble and expressive gesture? Oh no! M. Aumer would think that too ordinary. He prefers to introduce from the wings a maidservant accompanied by two or three children scattering bouquets of roses around the lady, which is supposed to convey to the gentleman, who must be very sharp-witted to understand it, that he must go no further. All M. Aumer's works are filled with little inventions like this, with roguish little gallantries that are meaningless, unnatural and offensive to people of good taste. M. Aumer calls this imagination. And alas, it is indeed imagination, but of the worst kind, inappropriate and excessive. He is distorting the style of ballets and the dance at the Opéra. Whatever he gives the dancers to do lacks dignity and grace because of the strangeness and profusion of ideas and gestures. He strains after effect, unaware that he is missing the mark by such exaggeration.[27]

The dancers playing the leading rôles, however, had no difficulty in making an impression. Showing a hitherto unrevealed vein of comic talent in his portrayal of Joconde, Paul was an admirable foil for the noble and elegant Albert, who took the part of Astolphe. But the outstanding success of the evening was by common consent Pauline Montessu's sparkling performance as Jeannette.

A comparatively small sum had been laid out on the production, most of it on the costumes. The backcloth used for the second act had originally served for the Provençal scene in *Aline*, to which had been added a large property tree that had been designed for the last act of *Clari*.

There were borrowings, too, in the music. Several of the best-known airs from the opera, as well as a rondo by Hummel, had been woven into the score by Ferdinand Hérold, whose own melodies seemed to suffer little from the comparison. The passage that attracted most attention, and indeed was responsible for the only stir the ballet created, was the finale of the *divertissement* in the first act, an arrangement for two trumpets of a melody by Romani. To play this, the Opéra had specially engaged two celebrated soloists, the Gambati brothers, to whose presence the regular trumpet players of the orchestra objected so violently as to be suspended from their duties for a fortnight to teach them a lesson.

* * * * * * *

The year 1827, which was to be a historic one for the ballet of the Paris Opéra, was marked by another change of Director. Duplantys was replaced by Emile Lubbert, who certainly possessed more appropriate qualifications than his predecessor, but was still subordinated to the strait-laced and interfering Vicomte Sosthène de La Rochefoucauld. Lubbert, a man with a sound knowledge of music, was to administer the Opéra with great probity, and at the end of his four-year term of office would leave a solid legacy of achievement to his successor. Three operas by Rossini – *Moïse*, *Le Comte Ory* and *Guillaume Tell* – and Auber's *La Muette de Portici*, all produced while he was Director, were to remain favourites for many years; it was he who accepted *Robert le Diable*, although his successor, Dr Véron, would take credit for it; and in the first summer of his term, Marie Taglioni made her sensational début in Paris.

However, the first ballet to be commissioned by Lubbert offered little promise for the future. Anatole Petit, the husband of Mme Anatole and a choreographer of modest talent, had submitted the scenario of a ballet he had produced in London five years earlier called *Le Petit Chaperon rouge*,[28] but this was rejected in favour of another proposal – a balletic version of Molière's comedy, *Le Sicilien*. In accepting this latter proposal, the management of the Opéra had laid down a strict condition. Every effort was at that time being concentrated on the production of Chélard's new opera, *Macbeth*, and Anatole was told that the preparations for his ballet were not to interfere in any way with the rehearsals of the opera. These instructions were respected to the letter, the ballet being given its first performance on 11 June 1827, apparently just a fortnight after going into rehearsal. Expenditure had been reduced to the barest minimum: only four new costumes had to be made, and those only in consequence of demands from the dancers.

Molière's comedy-ballet was well known both as a classic on its own

account and also for having inspired Beaumarchais's *Le Barbier de Séville;*
and very wisely Anatole Petit had not presumed to alter the plot in its main
outline. Alphonse (Albert) has fallen in love with Léonore (Noblet), who is
vigilantly watched over by her guardian, Don Pèdre (S. Mérante), who plans
to marry her himself. Aided by his valet Diego (Ferdinand), Alphonse
therefore resorts to a stratagem to win her. He assembles a group of singers
and dancers to distract Don Pèdre's attention and enable him to pass a note
to Léonore. He then changes places with an artist who has been engaged to
paint her portrait, and helped by Diego – who, posing as an itinerant carpet
seller, distracts Don Pèdre's attention – manages to divulge his plan to
Léonore. A girl in distress (Julia) then comes running in and implores Don
Pèdre to protect her from her angry lover. The lover himself, none other than
Alphonse under a further disguise, shortly follows her. Don Pèdre calms him
down and, sensing the moment to be ripe for reconciliation, goes to fetch the
girl. Not until too late does he realise that his ward has changed clothes with
her and slipped from his grasp.

To translate Molière's comic wit adequately into mime was a task before
which even the most talented choreographer might have quailed. How, for
example, was one to present the scene when Diego enters Don Pèdre's house
to be greeted with a violent cuff and the cry, 'Who goes there?', and to give in
return a similar blow with the reply, 'Friend!'? However, lacking the
interchange of words, this scene in Anatole's ballet degenerated into a sort of
boxing match, and in the same way, throughout much of the action, the
light spirit of Molière's comedy nearly always eluded the choreographer. A
few passages, however, such as Léonore posing for her portrait, presented
less difficulty and were treated more successfully. In this scene Anatole took
full advantage of Lise Noblet's charms, which were displayed in a series of
voluptuous poses. The *dénouement* of the ballet also presented an easier
problem, since in Molière's comedy this had depended more on the action
than on the dialogue.

Nevertheless, most people found the ballet tedious, despite the efforts of
the dancers. Ferdinand distinguished himself by giving an amusing
portrayal of Diego, which prompted the *Constitutionnel* to compare his
miming to that of Dauberval,[29] but the others made their mark in the dances
rather than in the action. A tarantella by Ferdinand and Pauline Montessu
was the most successful *pas*, while the two *divertissements* enabled the
audience to admire the classical style of Mme Anatole, the precision of Julia,
who reminded many of Fanny Bias, and the budding talent of Lise Noblet's
younger sister Félicité, who had made her début the previous year and had
recently married the singer Alexis Dupont.

Schneitzhoeffer and the guitarist Fernando Sor had between them produced a score for this hurriedly staged work, the former being responsible for the overture and the music for the dances. On the whole, it was a mediocre accompaniment despite the introduction of a few borrowed melodies by Boïeldieu and Pedro Albeñiz. 'If one may be allowed to praise something in it,' caustically remarked Castil-Blaze, 'at least it did not make very much noise!'[30] At the end of the ballet, when the names of the authors were announced from the stage, those of Anatole and Sor were received 'without any marked show of disapproval', but Schneitzhoeffer's contribution was ignored, the pronunciation of his name having perhaps defeated the person charged with that task.

This unpretentious little piece would have quickly slipped into oblivion had it not been for the chance circumstance that in one of its six performances a few weeks later a newly engaged dancer by the name of Marie Taglioni made her Paris début. Across the Channel, where standards in ballet were not so demanding, *Le Sicilien* was to be restaged by its choreographer in the following year with the addition of a sparkling bolero danced by August Bournonville and his first love, Louise Court.

NOTES

1. *Courrier des spectacles*, 31 March 1824. This was a ballet that Coralli had first produced at the Hofoper, Vienna, on 15 January 1811, and had revived there in 1823. He was to produce it again at La Scala, Milan, on 9 April 1825.
2. Saint-Léon, *Portraits*, 33.
3. Arch. Nat., AJ[13] 125. Habeneck to Blache, 25 April 1824. *Les Filets de Vulcain* had been first performed at the Grand-Théâtre, Bordeaux, on 21 June 1809.
4. Arch. Nat., AJ[13] 125. Blache to Habeneck, 20 March 1824.
5. Saint-Léon, *Portraits*, 31–2.
6. Duplantys had been in charge of the workhouse at Villars-Cotterets when La Rochefoucauld chose him to direct the Opéra. He did not enjoy his new task, and was once heard to say pathetically to his master, 'Why did you ever come and seek me out at Villars-Cotterets?'
7. Arch. Nat. O[3] 1708. Blache to Marquis de Lauriston, 7 August 1824. Lauriston had that very day resigned and been succeeded by Doudeauville, the father of Sosthène de La Rochefoucauld.
8. Haudry de Janvry, Secretary to the Director from 1824 to 1828.
9. Arch. Nat., O[3] 1669. Blache to La Rochefoucauld, 1 September 1825.
10. Bournonville, *Lettres*, I, 96.
11. *Courrier des théâtres*, 9 November 1825.
12. Arch. Nat., O[3] 1673. Blache to La Rochefoucauld, 19 December 1825.
13. *Les Filets de Vulcain, ou la Vénus de Neuilly* at the Variétés; *La Pêche de Vulcain, ou l'Ile des fleuves* at the Vaudeville; *Les Filets de Vulcain* at the Porte-Saint-Martin.
14. *Journal de Paris*, 9 June 1826.
15. Adèle and Marinette Bertrand were shortly to leave the Opéra to accept engagements in the Imperial Ballet of St Petersburg. Adèle, who danced in leading rôles from 1827 to 1834, was to marry a French actor called Atrux. Marinette's career was less successful. She had a son, whose father was probably an influential nobleman, for she was most unusually granted a pension. (Information supplied to the author by Vera Krasovskaya.)

16. *Journal des débats*, 1 June 1826.

17. *Journal des débats*, 1 June 1826.

18. Arch. Nat., AJ[13] 118.

19. *Coureur des spectacles*, 23 June 1826.

20. *Coureur des spectacles*, 24 June 1826.

21. *Frondeur*, 24 June 1826.

22. Arch. Nat., AJ[13] 119. Blache to La Rochefoucauld, 24 February 1827.

23. Arch. Nat., AJ[13] 139.

24. Arch. Nat., AJ[13] 115. The scenario, as submitted, was entitled *Charles VII à Rheims*, and is preserved in box AJ[13] 138.

25. *Joconde, ou les Coureurs d'aventures, opéra-comique* in three acts, music by Isouard, libretto by Etienne, f.p. Opéra-Comique, 28 February 1814. It had a long life in the repertory, being given more than 400 times before its last performance in 1876.

26. *Pandore*, 6 February 1827.

27. Delaforest, ii, 281–2.

28. *Le Petit Chaperon rouge*, choreography by Anatole, music by Venua, f.p. King's Theatre, London, 13 June 1822.

29. *Constitutionnel*, 13 June 1827.

30. *Journal des débats*, 15 June 1827.

1. The Façade of the Paris Opéra, Salle Lepelletier, c. 1840.

2. Back-stage at the Opéra in the 1840s.

3. The Foyer de la Danse in the Paris Opéra, Salle Lepelletier, c. 1841. Figures include from the left, Mlle Forster, seated, Halévy and Duponchel behind her; Auber to his left, Maria in dance pose; middle foreground: Musset, Cte de Belmont, Montguyon, Fanny Elssler, Véron, Adèle Dumilâtre; behind her left shoulder Eugène Coralli; Latour-Mézeray leaning against pillar; Célestine Emarot (mother of Emma Livry).

4. Théophile Gautier, dance critic and scenarist.

5. Eugène Scribe, ballet scenarist and playwright.

6. Ferdinand Hérold, composer.

7. Adolphe Adam, composer of *Giselle* and other ballets.

8. Jean Aumer.

9. Albert.

10. Jean-Baptiste Blache.

11. Jean Coralli.

12. Emilia Bigottini in the title-rôle of Aumer's ballet, *Aline*, pictured in her regal robes, with, in the background, an image of the character as a young peasant girl.

13. Emilie Bigottini as Victor in Aumer's ballet, *Les Pages du duc de Vendôme*.

14. *Alfred le Grand,* ballet by Aumer. Act II, Scene II, Hall of the Knights.

15. *Alfred le Grand,* Act III, Scene II, the Danish camp. Lithographs by G. Engelmann from drawings by Schmidt and (for the figures) Weber.

16. Caroline Brocard as the Fairy in *Cendrillon*, ballet by Albert. Water-colour by Le Faget.

17. Albert and Emilia Bigottini in *Cendrillon*. Lithograph by Martinet.

18. Pauline Montessu in the sleep-walking scene in *La Somnambule*, ballet by Aumer.

19. Pauline Montessu as Manon Lescaut in Aumer's ballet of that name. Costume design by H. Lecomte.

20. Pauline Montessu as the Fairy Nabote in Aumer's *La Belle au bois dormant*.

21. Charles Mazurier in *La Neige* (Théâtre de la Porte-Saint-Martin).

22. Lise Noblet as Fenella in Auber's opera, *La Muette de Portici*. Drawing by Dévéria.

23.   Auber's opera, *Le Dieu et la Bayadère*. Adolphe Nourrit and Marie Taglioni.

24.   *Le Dieu et la Bayadère*. Marie Taglioni as Zoloé. Water-colour by Le Faget.

25. Meyerbeer's opera, *Robert le Diable*. The entrance of the Nuns.

26. *Robert le Diable*. Marie Taglioni as Héléna and the tenor, Adolphe Nourrit, as Robert.

27. Pauline Duvernay as Miranda in the opera, *La Tentation*. Lithograph by Benard from a drawing by A. Lacauchie.

28. *La Tentation.* Act V. Lithograph by Benard from a drawing by A.Læderich.

29. Louis Véron.

7

The Coming of Marie Taglioni

The name of Taglioni was not unfamiliar in the dance world of Paris. Towards the end of the previous century, Carlo Taglioni, an Italian ballet-master of modest renown,[1] had brought two of his children, Filippo and Luigia, to Paris to perfect their technique under the celebrated teacher, Coulon. His hopes that they might be engaged at the Opéra were eventually fulfilled after the two young pupils made their début together in 1798. However, they had to wait a year before being given engagements – for times were hard and the Opéra was short of funds. While Luigia was to remain in Paris until 1806, Filippo, the more ambitious, departed four years earlier to fulfil an engagement in Stockholm, and there fell in love with and married the daughter of the celebrated opera singer Cristoffer Karsten, becoming on 23 April 1804 the father of a baby girl who was given the name of Marie. Owing to the exigencies of Filippo's engagements, the growing family had no settled home. After leaving Stockholm they went first to Vienna and then to Kassel, at that time the capital of Jérôme Bonaparte's newly created Kingdom of Westphalia. In 1813 a contract to dance at La Scala, Milan, forced Filippo to leave his family behind in Kassel. Napoleon's armies were then reeling westwards after the disastrous retreat from Moscow, and Kassel was soon to be threatened by the advance of the Cossacks. While a last stand was being made before the city, the Taglionis managed to escape. Making in the direction of France, they reached Mainz, where, by a stroke of good fortune, a friend recognised them and arranged for them to travel on to Paris in the carriage of a wounded French general under the pretence that they were his wife and children.

While Filippo Taglioni pursued his peripatetic career as a dancer in Austria, Bavaria, Sweden, Denmark, Naples and elsewhere, Marie spent the rest of her childhood in Paris with her mother. As soon as she was old enough, she began to take dancing lessons. She could have had no finer teacher than her father's old master, Coulon, and although there were days when she and her friend Evelina Fleurot played truant, she attended his classes in the Rue Montmartre sufficiently regularly to gain a thorough grounding in the rudiments of the art. She was a skinny child with a tendency to stoop, and her fellow pupils used to taunt her by asking, 'How can that little hunchback ever become a dancer?' Coulon, however, recognised her promise, and her mother, perhaps reading more into his encouraging reports than he intended, gave such a glowing account in her letters to her husband that he negotiated an engagement for his daughter as *première danseuse* in Vienna in 1822.

When Coulon became aware of this, he felt bound to explain to Mme Taglioni that her daughter was by no means ready to dance in public. Realising that there could be no question of cancelling Marie's contract, he advised that she should make the most of the six months before she was expected in Vienna: she must be the first to arrive and the last to leave his studio, and furthermore, she was to attend the three classes he gave each week for ladies of high society. This was a most exceptional favour, which Coulon had never bestowed on any other pupil training for a professional career. The experience may well have been a factor in developing Marie's style and endowing her dancing with an aura of gentility that would set her apart from her professional contemporaries. At this stage of her training, however, her potential talent was not generally apparent. Aumer, on one of his visits to Coulon's class in search of dancers to be engaged for the London opera season, even told Mme Taglioni that her daughter would never make a good dancer. On the other hand, Marie Gardel, whose style had been particularly notable for its decency and elegance, found the girl charming, and was so taken with her modesty and grace as to forecast a successful career if she persevered with her training. 'I hope I shall prove a good prophet' were her parting words.[2]

During those last few months in Paris Marie made such good progress that Coulon was sorry to see her go. Her father, however, was very disappointed when she arrived in Vienna, and for five months made her work at a ferocious pitch that few others would have endured. Such means, brutal though they must have appeared, were to be amply justified by the end; for her début on 10 June 1822, in her father's *divertissement*, appropriately entitled *La Réception d'une jeune nymphe à la cour de Terpsichore*, was undeniably successful.

With single-minded determination Filippo Taglioni had set to work to form her style, building upon the foundations that Coulon had laid. Before her début, and for some time after it, he insisted on her practising at least six hours every day – two hours in the morning, two hours before dinner, and two hours last thing at night: a gruelling curriculum which she accepted with a willingness that only those who knew her dedication could understand. At least two hours each day were devoted to a tedious and fatiguing series of exercises, aimed at producing a suppleness that would enable her to overcome the most formidable difficulties: even at the height of her career she never omitted this elementary practice. Another two hours were spent in the study of *adagio*. Under her father's eye she would slowly develop poses on the *demi-pointe*, sometimes holding a difficult position while counting to a hundred in order to perfect it. Then, unsupported, she would make complete turns in various poses until she was fully satisfied with the grace, precision and assurance of her execution. The idea of having a partner to assist her in these poses was abhorrent, and the *adages* of Fanny Elssler, supported by her sister Therese *en travesti*, although much to the liking of the public, seemed to her in bad taste and inartistic. Finally she devoted another two hours to jumping: after performing *pliés* to ensure a soft landing, she began to practise jumps, paying special attention to the use of the knee and the correct manner of alighting through the toes. Here her model was the ballerina Therese Heberle, who was a pupil of Armand Vestris, son of the great Auguste, and was noted for her bird-like lightness. Marie loved to jump and to feel almost unaware of the ground. 'I truly shimmered in the air,' she remembered ecstatically in her old age.[3]

Behind all this gruelling training, the fundamental purpose of combining her various qualities into a cohesive, harmonious style was never lost from view. To achieve grace and spirituality of movement, attention was given to the minutest detail. The way she moved her hands, the avoidance of simpering grimaces, the acquisition of a natural air of happiness as she danced, the carriage of her body: these were only some of the qualities she developed, corrected and perfected during those productive hours of toil.

Soon another influence was to make its mark on her style. On the last day of 1823 an Italian ballerina, Amalia Brugnoli, another pupil of Armand Vestris, made her début in Vienna, causing great astonishment by the 'very extraordinary things'[4] she performed on the *pointes* of her long and very narrow feet. However, the effort that such feats entailed was all too obvious in the way she used her arms to rise on to her toes, but what she did was to open up new vistas of possibility to the far-sighted Filippo Taglioni. So Marie's lessons soon included still more exercises to acquire and perfect this new extension of technique, and above all to give it a veneer of grace to conceal the muscular effort.

Marie was to continue this rigorous training throughout her career, whether or not her father was there to guide and counsel her. Adice recorded that in Paris during the 1830s she always worked at least twice a day, and he attributed her wonderful balance and precision to her conscientiousness at practice; on one occasion he timed her while she performed nothing but *demi-coupés* for twenty-five minutes.[5] Her father was merciless in his demands on her strength, and there were times when Marie was so exhausted at the end of a two-hour class that she would drop to the floor and have to be undressed, sponged and dressed again before she recovered. Sometimes she cried out with fatigue, but the gruelling training went on. Often Marie's mother was moved to tears at the sight of her daughter being so brutally treated, and afterwards would spoil her unstintingly to make up for her ordeal.

After a short visit to Munich in the summer of 1824, Filippo Taglioni decided to take his family to Paris in the hope of arranging an engagement at the Opéra.[6] The Director, Duplantys, received him with a boorish lack of courtesy, and told him that he would see his daughter alone and acquaint him of his decision in due course. Seething with indignation, Taglioni took his leave and left Paris without further ado, determined to have nothing more to do with Duplantys.

He gave the Opéra no further thought until, one evening in the autumn of 1826, an old friend, Baron Laflèche, visited him after seeing Marie dance at Stuttgart. The Baron, who was a friend of the Vicomte Sosthène de La Rochefoucauld, offered to use his influence to enable Marie to make her début at the Opéra, insisting that Paris was the proper setting for her talent. With this, her father was in full agreement, but in making his formal approach to La Rochefoucauld, he attached three conditions: that the customary audition be dispensed with, that he himself should arrange her *pas*, and that Marie be allowed nine début appearances instead of the customary six. Such exceptional treatment was bound to appear presumptuous, and Duplantys, who had clearly discussed the matter with Gardel and Milon, did his best to dissuade La Rochefoucauld from accepting this demand. Why, he asked in his reply to the Superintendant, should an outsider be granted a greater prerogative than was laid down in the Regulations? Did Mlle Taglioni's reputation really warrant such an exception? 'We are rich in female principals,' he pointed out, 'and instead of adding to their number, ought we not to be reducing it?' And in a postscript, he added: 'Mlle Taglioni had talent two years ago, but has her talent increased or diminished in the absence of good models since her departure from Paris? That is the question.'[7]

In the event, compromises were made: the customary audition was waived, the number of début performances would remain at the regulatory six, and for three of these she would appear in a *pas de deux* composed by her father. Nor had Marie been forgotten by the good Baron, who had promised to send her a supply of ballet shoes from Paris – for there now arrived a welcome parcel from the shoemaker Janssen, from whom Marie was to order her shoes from that moment on.

The Taglionis arrived in Paris in the middle of June 1827, some six weeks before the début was scheduled to take place. Marie and her brother Paul lost no time in visiting their old teacher, Coulon, seeking his advice concerning the *pas* that her father had arranged for her. Her old teacher was greatly impressed by its novelty, and at once realised that, if any of the other dancers saw it beforehand, they might do everything in their power to prevent the début. He recommended, therefore, that Marie should attend the rehearsal with the orchestra dressed in her ordinary clothes and merely mark the *pas*; on the day before the début, she should dance it in the presence of the conductor of the orchestra alone to give him an idea of the tempo.

Marie's début was at length billed to take place on 23 July 1827, and her *pas*, which had been arranged to a violin solo composed by Mayseder, was inserted in the ballet *Le Sicilien*. A murmur of interest arose in the house when she and her brother came into view. The audience was at once struck by her tall slender figure, her dignified carriage and her piquant features, which were given a strange attraction by the concentrated expression in her eyes. In the space of the next few minutes the future course of ballet was set. It took no special knowledge of the dance to realise that something very extraordinary was taking place. The air became charged with excitement. Such harmony of movement, suppleness and grace had never before been seen. Her grace was not one to which the Parisians were accustomed; there was something natural, even strangely original, about it that gave her style an extraordinary attraction. Such fluidity of movement, particularly that of her arms, was almost unearthly; as a critic remarked, 'she performed new and difficult things with unbelievable assurance and steadiness'.[8] Among these extraordinary qualities, which had prompted Coulon to counsel Filippo Taglioni to keep the *pas* from being seen by other dancers beforehand, was an ability to 'hold herself on the tips of her toes'.[9]

It took very little time, after the public had recovered from its first shock, for this aspect of her dancing to arouse memories of a favourite dancer from an earlier generation, Geneviève Gosselin, a white hope who had been forced by the onset of tuberculosis to retire prematurely early in 1816 after creating the rôle of Flora in *Flore et Zéphire*, and had died, greatly mourned, little more than two years later. Her unique speciality had been her ability to rise on to the very tips of her toes for longer, and much more firmly, than anyone else before. This was a feat towards which many others had striven, but through an ability that seemed to be hers alone, Mlle Gosselin had aroused extraordinary enthusiasm, not by a momentary effort of which she alone seemed capable, but by showing, if still in a primitive form, how this new-found ability might be incorporated to artistic effect in the fabric of the dance itself. In the wake of the sensation she caused, other dancers had attempted to emulate her, but their efforts were forced and awkward in comparison until, on the evening of her Paris début, Marie Taglioni reawakened this vision.

Pointe work was not, and never would be, Taglioni's principal speciality, even though she was an able exponent of this branch of technique. She presented it rather, not as an eye-catching feat, but as an inseparable part of her style that emphasised the spiritual quality inherent in all her movements. Lady Blessington, who was in the audience, at once recognised the unique merit of her dancing. 'Hers is a totally new style of dancing', she wrote,

> graceful beyond all comparison, wonderful lightness, an absence of all violent effect, or at least the appearance of it, and a modesty as new as it is delightful to witness in her art. She seems to float and bound like a sylph across the stage, never executing those *tours de force* that we know to be difficult and wish were impossible, being always performed at the expense of decorum and grace, and requiring only activity for their achievement ... There is a sentiment in the dancing of this charming votary of Terpsichore that elevates it far beyond the licentious style generally adopted by the ladies of her profession, and which bids fair to accomplish a reformation in it.

Bursts of applause had punctuated her *pas*, but these were nothing compared with the volume of clapping and cheering that burst out at the end. Lady Blessington was enchanted by the 'decent dignity' with which Marie acknowledged this ovation, 'very unlike the leering smiles with which, in general, a *danseuse* thinks it necessary to advance to the front of the proscenium, showing all her teeth, as she lowly *(sic)* curtsies to the audience.'[10]

After Marie and her brother had repeated their *pas* four days later, on the 27th, the *Courrier des théâtres* reported that 'the resurrection of Mlle Gosselin' was attracting great crowds to the Opéra.[11] Such a comparison was not confined to this one observer. 'Marie Taglioni,' wrote the *Réunion*, 'holds herself on the tips of her toes with truly remarkable steadiness. Not since Mlle Gosselin has a nymph of Terpsichore been able to maintain such an attitude for so long.'[12] Another interesting comparison was made by an old habitué whose memories went back to the days of Guimard. He was reminded of Marie's aunt, Louise Taglioni, who 'fresh, affable, and as light as a sylphide' – a prophetic choice of word – had danced at the Opéra in the early years of the century. Marie, he wrote, 'dances like her aunt. I do not venture to say she dances better, but the art has made great strides and technique has been much perfected, especially in *attitudes à la seconde* and *jetés battus*'.[13]

Marie's triumph naturally aroused a great deal of jealous resentment within the company, and certain dancers and their protectors were soon spinning a web of intrigue to place a limit on her success. Little more than a fortnight before her début, there had been a change of Director, Duplantys being replaced by Emile Lubbert, who at least had the advantage of a passion for music. One of his first concerns was to consider a proposal that Marie Taglioni should now be seen in one of the established *pas* of the repertory so that her talent could be properly judged. Filippo Taglioni suspected an ulterior motive behind this new demand, but in all fairness Lubbert could not ignore it, and a sensible compromise was reached whereby she would dance two *pas* – one, a second *pas de deux* with her brother, composed by her father, and the other to be selected from the repertory.

For the latter, it was arranged that Marie should dance the *pas* known as *Le Prix de la danse* in a forthcoming performance of Spontini's opera *La Vestale*. Constance Anatole, *née* Gosselin, who had perhaps been piqued by the comparison with her sister, expected that Marie would be unable to learn it in time for the performance on 3 August, and that she herself would be called upon to replace her and would dance it with such superior style that Marie would surely not hazard an invidious comparison. In this she was far too sanguine, for Filippo Taglioni was alert to such devious ways and not only saw that his daughter was thoroughly and expertly coached, but also made a strong protest to Lubbert to ensure that she danced it.

Although the evening was hot and close, the Opéra was packed to see Marie face this new test. As she emerged from the wings on to the stage, she heard one of the dancers whisper, 'Take care! I do not know what is on the stage, but it is very slippery'. She danced the *pas* brilliantly and without mishap; but afterwards an *habitué*, whose box abutted the stage, drew her father aside and told him that someone had put soap on the stage and that three of the *corps de ballet* had fallen shortly before Marie made her entrance.

No one could now question Marie's triumph, but up to now she had been judged solely as a dancer and had had no opportunity of revealing her powers of expression. In the opinion of the *Journal des débats,* it would only be when she appeared in a mime rôle that one would really be able to judge whether she had inherited the gifts of Genevieve Gosselin, but in the meantime the similarity in technique and style was not to be denied. 'One is reminded of the elder Mlle Gosselin,' wrote the critic of that paper,

> of the astonishing flexibility of her limbs, a muscular power that enabled her to remain suspended for a minute or two *(sic)* on the tips of her toes, her lightness of movement, the elegance of her figure, and such an extraordinary ability to perform difficulties with that air of abandon, naturalness and freedom that is the triumph of art when artistry is no longer discernible... The character of [Taglioni's] dancing has much in common with that of her predecessor. She is almost the same height, and has the same steadiness in her poses and the same suppleness of movement.[14]

When Filippo Taglioni had demanded that Marie should dance in one of his own *pas* after the *pas de deux* from *La Vestale*, Lubbert had ruled that the performance would have to count as two début appearances. Only two more performances, therefore, remained to complete the series. On 6 August she and her brother Paul repeated their first *pas de deux*, and two days later, at what was to have been their last performance, they danced a *pas de schal*. Again the comparison with Mlle Gosselin was made, and 'eight volleys of unending applause' testified to the public's delight.

So great was the enthusiasm that Lubbert could no longer withhold a sixth appearance, and on 10 August she danced, with a charm that no one could resist, in the *pas de deux* from Blache's *Mars et Vénus*, which had been seen a week previously and was now inserted in the ballet *Le Carnaval de Venise*. Henri Duponchel, a future Director of the Opéra, had come to this performance with an enormous crown of white roses, which he intended to give afterwards to Pauline Montessu. But the proposed recipient was ill, and urged by a sudden whim, Duponchel leaned out of his box and threw his tribute on to the stage as Marie hurried into the wings.

In these six brief appearances Marie Taglioni made history, not only by being the first dancer to have flowers thrown to her on the stage of the Opéra, but because her dancing came as a dazzling vision of a new approach. She was 'truly the ideal of the graceful style,' wrote the *Figaro*. 'Her début will open a new epoch. It is Romanticism applied to the dance... There is a vaporous, voluptuous quality in all her movements.' The *Courrier des théâtres* was also aware of the revolutionary, Romantic character of her style. Her talent, it informed its readers,

> differs from those routinely presented on our stage in being a delightful mixture of those graces usually seen in the theatre and the graces required in society. Her dancing is a combination of that of the Opéra with that of the best ballrooms. The result of this fusion, which is as much the result of art as of nature, is that the 'semaphoric' lines disappear. There are no protruding shoulders heaving and thrown forward by ungainly balancing from side to side, no jutting elbows, no broken wrists, no extending of little fingers. In short, there is no hint of professional toil, the artifices of a craft, or anything that might suggest the classroom. Mlle Taglioni presents a general appearance of delightfully rounded curves and lines of admirable purity. She gives the impression of a well-brought-up young person, modest, reserved, gracious without affectation, who dances on the stage as she might dance at a ball in her mother's house, and who knows better than anyone else the importance of bringing to the exercise of her art all the requirements of a calling. To us that seems to explain the mystery of this great success.[15]

Writing nearly thirty years later, Saint-Léon tried to analyse the effect that she had on the ballet of her time. 'Did Mlle Taglioni dance better than her predecessors?' he asked himself.

> Certainly not, but her dancing differed from the style then in favour, being particularly remarkable for its mixture of poetry and simplicity, grace and gentility that made an immediate impression on the public. In a word, it was a model. Sticklers for detail criticised her arms, which, unlike other dancers, she nearly always kept lowered. They also criticised her body, which she held more *en avant* than the school of that time allowed, but it was precisely these happy faults that caused the enormous sensation she made at that time. There is no question that Mlle Taglioni inaugurated a new style, for it is to her that we owe the complete change that has taken place in our dancers and even in the style of choreography.[16]

For some weeks the question of her engagement lay in the balance. 'If we can read anything into backstage intrigues,' prophesied the *Corsaire* a day or two after her last appearance, 'this charming dancer is lost to us. Her success gave rise to too many little passions.'[17] Happily, however, these fears were not realised, and on 6 September 1827 she signed a contract with the Opéra. Her engagement was to commence on 1 April 1828, from which date she would hold the rank of *remplaçant* at an annual salary of 7200 francs with a bonus of 30 francs for each performance. From the beginning of 1829 she was to become a *premier sujet* at 9000 francs a year, with a further increase of 1000 francs to be effective from 1 January 1830. Having learnt from experience, Filippo Taglioni was now emboldened to insist on two stipulations: firstly, that during the first three months of her engagement she would dance only in *pas* composed by him, and secondly, 'so as not to disrupt the normal duties of the dancers of the Opéra', that she should be partnered by her brother, who would give his services to the Opéra without payment. During 1828, while she held the grade of *remplaçant*, she undertook to dance in such *pas* as were allotted to her in ballets and operas and to play three mime rôles, two to be chosen by herself and the other by the management.

During the winter months that followed, the memory of her appearance haunted the Opéra like a phantom. In less than three weeks she had become a model for the other dancers to reshape their own styles. 'Open revolution has broken out at the Opéra,' reported the *Courrier des théâtres* in October 1827. 'Since the latest newcomer appeared, all the dancers have been taglionising.'[18]

NOTES

1. Little is known of the professional career of Carlo Taglioni. A note in Marie Taglioni's hand, preserved in the Bibliothèque de l'Opéra (Fonds Taglioni, R18) records: 'I believe that my grandfather was also an artiste, but memory is very confused about this'. There is also a brief reference to him in the *Court Journal* of 19 June 1830, where he is said to have been 'one of the best burlesques of his day'.
2. Vaillat, 68.
3. Vaillet, 77.
4. Vaillet, 85.
5. Adice, 113.
6. Ehrhard's statement in his biography of Fanny Elssler (p.162) that Taglioni came to Paris in 1824 and made her début at the Théâtre de la Porte-Saint-Martin, where she received a welcome that was far from encouraging, clearly has no foundation in fact.
7. Arch. Nat., O^3 1708. Duplantys to La Rochefoucauld, 15 December 1826.
8. *Courrier des théâtres*, 24 July 1827.
9. *Réunion*, 26 July 1827.
10. Blessington, 83–4.
11. *Courrier des théâtres*, 29 July 1827.
12. *Réunion*, 30 July 1827.
13. *Journal des débats*, 3 August 1827.
14. *Figaro*, 13 August 1827.
15. *Courrier des théâtres*, 17 August 1827.
16. Saint-Léon, *De l'Etat actuel*, 16.
17. *Corsaire*, 12 August 1827.
18. *Courrier des théâtres*, 30 October 1827.

8

The Scenarist to the Rescue

Of the ten new ballets that had been produced at the Opéra since 1820, no fewer than six had been based upon works already seen as plays or operas. Choreographers seemed to be slipping into a lazy habit of working on a ready-made dramatic base. This may have had the advantage of enabling spectators familiar with the original source to follow the mute action more easily, but at the same time it added fuel to the argument that ballet was a derivative art and, however talented the dancers, was not to be seriously considered on an equal level with drama or opera.

A solution to this problem was now proposed by the emergence of the scenarist as a collaborator in his own right. As Castil-Blaze put it in his history of the Opéra, 'a rich capitalist, an opulent financier of liberal views, taking pity on the poverty of invention of [ballet-masters], opens his safe and his jewel case, and in the twinkling of an eye ballet, that mute imitation of the best-known and often most trivial plays, becomes a witty drama, replete with interest and a rare and striking originality'. [1] It was no secret that this benefactor was the most prolific playwright of the age, Eugène Scribe – notwithstanding that his name neither appeared on the printed scenario nor was formally announced from the stage after the first performance of Aumer's ballet *La Somnambule* on 19 September 1827. If Bournonville, who was then still a member of the ballet of the Opéra, is to be believed, Scribe had submitted his scenario as something of a joke, and Aumer had been commissioned only after Albert had refused on principle to produce a ballet based on someone else's plot.[2] It was no secret either within the walls of the Opéra or without that Scribe was the writer concerned; more than a month before, the *Journal de Paris* had reported that he had given a reading of his scenario to the members of the Institut, and prophesied great advantages from the collaboration of dramatist and ballet-master.[3]

Scribe was then the most popular and prolific of French playwrights, and at the age of only thirty-five had more than 130 comedies and fifteen comic operas to his credit. He brought to his vocation not only an exceptional capacity for work, but, what was more to the point, a practical skill, which he applied with remarkable consistency, a preference for depicting the life and vagaries of contemporary society rather than drawing on stock characters, and a predilection for the pathetic mood.

His scenario for *La Somnambule*, which was to be the first of several ballet plots to flow from his pen, was entirely original and bore no resemblance to a comedy of the same name that he had written eight years previously. The action unfolds in a village in Provence. The curtain rises to reveal, on one side, the inn owned by the flighty young widow Gertrude (Legallois), and on the other the farmhouse belonging to Edmond (Ferdinand). It is harvest-time, and the villagers are dancing in their midday break. Edmond is to be married on the following day to his sweetheart Thérèse (Montessu), an orphan who has been adopted by the mill-owner Mme Michaud (Mme Elie). However, Gertrude, who has set her heart on Edmond, cannot forgive him for rejecting her. Two travellers then arrive in the village. One, Saint-Rambert (Montjoie), is the new lord of the manor, on his way to take up residence at the nearby château; the other, his servant Olivier (C. Brocard). Saint-Rambert has decided to rest his weary limbs at the village inn before proceeding further, but his servant disobeys his instructions to keep his identity secret, and in this way Edmond becomes aware of the visitor's identity.

For the second act, the action moves to a room in the inn. Saint-Rambert, who has dined and wined well, is shown in by Gertrude, who dismisses the maidservant and, with a meaningful look, tells him she herself will attend to his wants. Taking this as an invitation, he seizes her shawl and presses her to remain. But they are interrupted by a sound from outside. Gertrude hurriedly hides in a cupboard. To his amazement, Saint-Rambert sees the window open and Thérèse step into the room. At the same moment Gertrude peeps out of the closet, to be shocked by the sight of what she takes to be a prearranged tryst. Quickly and quietly she withdraws into the closet and closes its door.

Saint-Rambert, who has been equally taken aback, now realises that Thérèse is sleepwalking, and, to extract himself from this awkward situation, quietly makes a swift departure through the open window. At that moment Edmond, Mme Michaud and a group of friends come into the room bearing flowers to offer to their new lord. To their astonishment they find Thérèse alone, asleep on the sofa. At this point Gertrude emerges from the closet, convinced that Saint-Rambert has arranged a rendezvous with Thérèse. Distraught, Thérèse runs to Edmond, who, unaware that she is a sleepwalker, angrily pushes her away, declaring that he will have nothing more to do with her. She is carried away in a faint.

The last act is set in the countryside. It is the following day, and preparations are in progress for the wedding. Thérèse is in great distress. Her mother freely accepts her explanation, but points out that it is Edmond she has to convince. But he remains sure she has betrayed him. Saint-Rambert then appears with a bouquet for her. She tells him what has happened and begs him to explain the situation to Edmond. But Edmond refuses to listen, for she seemed wide awake when he arrived on the scene. He announces his intention to go ahead with his marriage, but his bride will now be Gertrude. Distraught, Thérèse is carried back to the mill in a faint.

When Gertrude makes her appearance in a bridal gown, Saint-Rambert cannot conceal a smile, for he is enough of a man of the world to see through her. As the wedding procession is assembling, Mme Michaud produces Gertrude's scarf, which she has found in the bedroom at the inn. All are dumbstruck at this disclosure, but Edmond remains unconvinced. At that moment Saint-Rambert points towards the mill. To everyone's horror Thérèse has emerged, sleepwalking, with a candle in her hand, and is making her way towards the great mill-wheel. Saint-Rambert tells everyone to keep absolutely still and silent, for the shock of coming out of her trance might prove fatal. At this point the orchestra falls silent, save only for a muted roll on a drum. When Therese arrives at the middle of the roof, she turns to face the audience, as if about to place her foot on the great revolving wheel. The shocked onlookers fall to their knees to offer up a prayer for her safety. The suspense is almost unbearable. But, as if in response, Thérèse turns away and, continuing her progress, makes her way to safety.

In the mime scene that follows, she finds herself in the centre of the stage. She listens, thinking she is hearing the church bell chiming for Edmond's wedding. She falls to her knees and prays for him. 'May happiness be his! But alas, there is no happiness in store for me.' [She looks at her hand.] 'My ring! It is no longer there! He has taken it to give to another! But what he cannot take from me is my memory of him. His image is engraved on my heart. And yet...' [She looks about her.] 'Nobody is looking...' [She draws from her bosom the bouquet of roses that Edmond had given her.] 'They are wilted, withered!' [She weeps over it, covering it with her kisses.]

Seeing her thus, Gertrude's animosity vanishes, and Edmond places the ring back on Thérèse's finger. The wedding veil is placed on her brow, and as the village band strikes up she wakes and comes back to reality.

'A more happily chosen subject for a ballet would be difficult to imagine,' wrote the *Moniteur*,[4] a conclusion that was generally shared. The situations were affecting, and the action arranged with great economy and clarity. The *Journal des débats* called it 'no ordinary ballet, but a little drama that is perfect in its entirety and charming in all its details. In it two situations stand out – one lively and bold, and the other moving and perfect – which would have guaranteed the success of a good straight play'.[5] The tables were turned almost at a stroke; for whereas in the past, successful plays and operas had been resuscitated as ballets, Scribe's scenario was to inspire not only a play at the Variétés,[6] but one of the greatest operas of that time, Bellini's *La sonnambula*.[7]

There could be no denying that Scribe's contribution had played a crucial part in this triumph. As a professional dramatist who saw it as his duty to become fully acquainted with whatever theatrical form he chose to adopt, he was particularly conscious of the importance of interweaving mime and dance and making each of them play a part in the development of the action. *La Somnambule* had literally opened with a swing, when the curtain rose to reveal the villagers dancing in the village square – 'a novel effect,' observed Castil-Blaze, 'which caused much pleasure'.[8] After this, the miming of the players was twice interrupted to introduce a passage of dancing: first, a *pas de deux* in which Edmond and Thérèse express their love for one another and he places the ring on her finger and presents her with a bouquet; and, later, a lengthier round of festivities as evening begins to fall, including a game of blind man's bluff, and a more formal *divertissement* to bring the act to a close.

Most critics, however, found the dances in the first act too long, 'a fault,' suggested the *Moniteur*, 'that would not have been noticed had the dances possessed more character, and if all the entrances had been given with the gaiety of a Provençal wedding.'[9] 'Generally speaking, dances are only well placed at the end of a work,' added the *Corsaire*, 'but here they induce tedium and the audience waits impatiently for them to finish so that it can make the acquaintance of the sleepwalker, whose part does not really begin until the second act.'[10]

At this point the relationship between the characters had been skilfully set. The drama was now to come. Arguably, there may have been a certain amount of discussion before Pauline Montessu was cast as Thérèse. Noblet or Legallois would have been a more obvious choice for the part, for Mme Montessu was small in build and so far had revealed no particular aptitude for dramatic expression. However, she had become Lubbert's favourite, and that had turned the scales in her favour. In the event she triumphantly justified the opportunity, surprising many critics by the vivacity, warmth and conviction of her miming.

Although she appeared in the first act, it was not until the sleepwalking scene in the second that her rôle became dramatically interesting. Unfortunately, on the first night, her appearance at the window at the back of the stage failed to produce its full effect because, owing to the presence of candles on the table, the lantern she carried did not throw enough light on her features. When this was put right at the second performance, her entrance, in a simple white nightdress, with one foot bare, produced 'a flurry of alarm.'[11] The sleepwalking scene on the roof of the mill that followed in the third act was a passage of extraordinary tension that had the audience on tenterhooks, the mime scene, which Scribe had described in his scenario in such detail, being rendered with a pathos that brought tears to the eyes of many in the audience. In response to criticisms, the structure of the roof on which Thérèse performs her sleepwalk was adapted for the second performance so as to make the scene even more effective. 'The attic window through which the sleeping girl emerges,' reported the *Courrier des théâtres*,

> is now placed in the middle of the roof instead of at the side, so that it is towards the edge on the audience's right that she is making her way towards a dreadful death. A precipitous drop opens up before her. But it is at the very moment of putting out her foot and holding it suspended over the abyss that Thérèse imagines she hears church bells, and then turns and descends by the ruins on the other side, passing over a mill-wheel much larger than the original one. This moment sends a chill of fear tingling down the spine of the least impressionable spectator.[12]

In Ferdinand Hérold, the musician chosen to compose the score, Scribe found a collaborator who, like himself, had something new to offer to ballet. Being too conscientious to be satisfied with turning out an undistinguished patchwork of borrowed melodies, Hérold applied himself to composing and arranging a score which, allowing for the conventions that applied to writing for the ballet, would have the merit of cohesion. While he was not so bold as to put his ideas into full force, his music for *La Somnambule* was sufficiently original to draw an assessment even from some of the more conservative critics. 'He has indeed made use of some known motifs to express situations,' wrote the critic of the *Moniteur*,

> but he has been too miserly with such a natural and ready means of assisting the spectator's understanding. He has made numerous borrowings from Rossini, and in his own original work the same forms are repeated, which produces a certain monotony that a different approach might have avoided. Generally speaking, one expects from a ballet composer not music, but rather an accompaniment that will translate and comment on the text, which otherwise one might not follow. Take *Psyché*, *Télémaque*, *Le Déserteur*, *Clari*. There, in recognisable motifs the spectator found the words he could not hear. However, although *La Somnambule* suffers from this shortcoming, it was made much less noticeable by the realistic miming of those who played it.[13]

Among the borrowings that Hérold had inserted to stress the message to be conveyed in mime scenes, the most effective was apparently the melody of the aria *Che sarà* from Rossini's *La Cenerentola*,[14] which accompanied Saint-Rambert's shock at the sight of the sleepwalking Thérèse entering the bedroom at the inn. Other borrowings identified by critics were the popular melodies *Dormez, mes chers amours* and *Malbrouck s'en va-t-en guerre*, a duet from Auber's *Le Maçon*,[15] a fragment from Gluck's *Armide*, another extract from *La Cenerentola* (from the sextet), and one from Mercadante's opera, *Elisa e Claudio*.[16]

La Somnambule was to remain in the repertory of the Opéra for eleven years, longer than any other of Aumer's ballets. Of these, only *Les Pages du duc de Vendôme* was more frequently performed – 126 performances to *La Somnambule*'s 120.

* * * * * * *

Not long after *La Somnambule's* first performance, Pauline Montessu interrupted her career to have a baby, and on 30 November 1827 the rôle of Thérèse was taken over by Mimi Dupuis, a promising young dancer who had made her début only sixteen days before, but was to leave the Opéra the following year. Mme Montessu resumed the part in April 1828, and in that same year two other dancers were seen in it: Pauline Leroux, who played it for the first time on 28 May, and Aumer's daughter, Julie Rozier, who chose it for her début on 30 July.

A long and distinguished career, unluckily interrupted by injury, lay before Pauline Leroux, the daughter of an army paymaster who had given his life in the retreat from Moscow. As a child she had caught the eye of the Comte de Luçay, who, learning that her mother had been left very little money to bring up her family, arranged for her to be presented to Gardel. As a result Pauline entered the School of Dance on 23 August 1817, three days after her eighth birthday, as a paying pupil at 12 francs a month. After a short spell in Romain's class she was promoted to the senior class under Maze, whose reports to Gardel spoke glowingly of her progress.[17]

She had her first stage experience of any consequence when she was engaged at the King's Theatre, London, for the season of 1826. There, in the words of the manager, John Ebers, 'she proved a great favourite. Her pretty little sylph-like figure and light laughing eyes were greatly admired.'[18] On her return to Paris, Coulon took her in hand to prepare her for her début at the Opéra, which followed on 20 December 1826. Though clearly terrified by the ordeal, she revealed great promise and had gained greatly in confidence by the time she had completed the six regulation performances. The *Courrier des théâtres* was particularly impressed, commenting on the dignity of her bearing, the piquancy of her expression, her lightness and her assurance, and told its readers that she was 'a brilliant acquisition for the Opéra. Such charm and such talent should be of great value to her in miming, for which few dancers possess the necessary qualities.'[19]

These were prophetic words, as her portrayal of Thérèse in *La Somnambule* was to show. 'She brought to the part,' wrote the *Courrier des théâtres,* 'a courageous ardour doubly served by the example and the advice of our Mme Montessu... Mlle Pauline played this part with gentleness to begin with, and then with quite remarkable feeling and energy, which augur well for the future.'[20]

Within a few months of the creation of *La Somnambule,* Scribe extended his activity into the realm of grand opera by writing the libretto for Auber's *La Muette de Portici.* The germ of this work had been sown some years before, in the spring of 1823, when Auber had confided to Scribe his desire to write a grand opera – if only for the pleasure of confounding his detractors – and had asked for his help in thinking of a suitable subject. Shortly afterwards, they found themselves sitting next to one another at a benefit performance, watching Bigottini playing a rôle in the comic opera, *Deux Mots.* When the curtain fell, Scribe clapped his friend on the shoulder:

'I have found our subject,' he cried. 'The Opéra has no great soprano at the moment, and a mime rôle would create a sensation. What do you think?'[21]

From that moment on, Scribe was obsessed with the idea of writing an opera with a dumb girl as its heroine, but it was some time before he put his pen to paper. When he did, he and his collaborator Delavigne completed their libretto in a week. Auber was fired with enthusiasm when he read the manuscript. Working at fever pitch, he composed the score in three months, being so exhausted at the end that he could not write another note for some time afterwards.

Scribe's hero was the fisherman Masaniello, a historical character who led a revolt against the Spaniards in Naples during the seventeenth century, only to be murdered within a few hours of victory for his cause. The dumb girl of the opera was Masaniello's sister Fenella, whose seduction by the Spanish viceroy's son stirs her brother into action and who, in the final moments, throws herself into a stream of molten lava from Vesuvius.

Bigottini had been in retirement for some time when the question arose of casting the rôle of Fenella, and the choice rested on Lise Noblet, whose power in the Opéra at that time depended on the political fortunes of the Vicomte de Martignac, a close friend of her protector, General Claparède. During the final rehearsals Noblet fell ill and there was talk of replacing her by Amélie Legallois. Noblet, however was determined that no one but she should create the rôle, and, thanks to the recent appointment of Martignac to the Ministry of the Interior, her will prevailed. So strong was this support that Legallois, who had been chosen to take her place if Noblet was not then well enough, had to rehearse in secret, and Aumer, it was said, did not dare to express openly his opinion that Legallois was a better choice for the part. In the event Noblet soon recovered, and on 29 February 1828 created the rôle of Fenella with such success that Scribe might have almost forgotten his regret at Bigottini's retirement. Indeed, the *Moniteur,* in praising the eloquence of her miming, went so far as to say that no more could have been expected from the consummate talent and the great means of expression of Mlle Bigottini.[22]

La Muette de Portici quickly became one of the most popular works in the repertory. It was essentially a work in the Romantic mode, for never before had local colour been reproduced so brilliantly in an opera. The atmosphere of Naples was conveyed with astonishing fidelity, and the effect was heightened by the important part played by the chorus, who took on the appearance of being real people whose very lives were being affected by the stirring events taking place around them. At first, however, the mime rôle was not unanimously accepted. Many critics, including Castil-Blaze, felt that Fenella's silence was a weakness and remarked on the incongruity of one character expressing herself in one medium while the rest did so in another. Aumer's *divertissements,* which were an important feature of the opera, included Spanish and Italian dances, which added to the local colour.

* * * * * * *

Meanwhile, during her absence from Paris that winter to fulfil an engagement in Stuttgart, Marie Taglioni had been forgotten neither by the public nor by the dancers of the Opéra. As spring approached, her legion of admirers were in a fever of expectation, and they were not to be disappointed when she made her reappearance on 30 April 1828 in the *pas de schal* with her brother. If it were possible, she even seemed to have gained in lightness: 'she descends without falling,' remarked old Vestris in amazement.[23] Many of the audience rose from their seats to get a better view of her *pointe* work. Her fellow dancers, of course, were particularly interested in this aspect of her style, which was already revealing how that extension of technique could be assimilated artistically in a dancer's execution. The lesson was not lost on them, and much toil was now being expended on attempts to discover and master the secret that was still hers alone.

'Well might one call Mlle Taglioni a revolutionary dancer,' wrote the *Courrier des théâtres,*

> for since her arrival a real revolution has taken place in the world of the dance. Every dancer wants to mould her talent on the gift that Nature has bestowed upon this reincarnation of Terpsichore. In our opinion not all will succeed in doing this. The really talented will be able to take just what is necessary from this graceful style and study it with discernment, with the result that it will be suggested rather than imitated, but the mediocre will fall into the pitfall of excess... They will imitate, but so clumsily that,

instead of gaining, they will be the losers. This is what usually results from the efforts of the servile herd! Derision and ridicule, which are always ready to pounce upon mistakes, have already struck at those who fail to 'taglionise' well, and whom the wits of the Opéra are calling *'danseuses sur l'ergot'* [dancers on claws]. To rise on their *pointes* is in fact all they manage to do, but they are strangely mistaken if they think this is the only difficulty. Dancers stood on their *pointes* before Mlle Taglioni. It was an achievement of a sort, but one acquired by purely mechanical means and at the expense of grace in certain parts of the body – in the arms, for example, which were thrust skywards and ceased to serve as a gentle accompaniment to the rest of the body. Since the arrival of the charming revolutionary, this fault has been corrected and, if dancers succeed in doing exactly what she does, a thousand qualities will replace it.[24]

A few days earlier the same paper had wondered what new facet of Taglioni's talent would be revealed when she appeared in a mime part. Her début as a mime was then imminent; to mark the importance of the occasion, Aumer was hastily producing a ballet that would be new to Paris, although in fact it was merely a revised version of *La Coquette soumise*, which he had staged in London three years before.[25]

Its new title was *Lydie*, after the name of the heroine, played by Marie Taglioni. Cupid (Marinette) is determined to have his revenge on the shepherdess Lydie for having mocked his statue. While dancing, she finds herself pursued by a faun (Ferdinand), who leads her to the little god's statue to declare his love. She seems on the point of yielding when, on a coquettish impulse, she spurns him. Just as the infuriated faun is about to carry her off forcibly, Cupid, disguised as a nymph, intervenes to rescue her, asking her to acknowledge the God of Love as a mark of her gratitude. She is not, however, to be so easily tricked – for she has recognised Cupid's wings beneath his disguise; laughing in his face, she makes her escape. But Cupid then draws his bow and looses an arrow, which pierces the heart of Amyntas (Albert). Lydie is then discovered, exhausted, by a band of shepherds whom Cupid has sent to look for her. While dancing before them, she plucks a rose, the petals of which open to reveal Cupid, whose arrow this time finds its mark. Lydie falls into the arms of Amyntas, and in a final apotheosis the lovers are entwined with garlands and united by Venus (Julia).

This sorry piece, its theme so much out of touch with the Romantic spirit of the time, was one of the cheapest productions the Opéra has ever staged: the sets and costumes cost no more than 1109 francs. It was first performed on a very warm summer evening, 2 July 1828, but the heat could not be blamed for the public's lack of enthusiasm. 'Mythological, anacreontic,

allegorical and bacchic subjects are no longer in season,' pointed out the
Constitutionnel,

> particularly when given with threadbare sets and old dances performed by
> half a dozen fauns leaping about, we will not say in time, but to the
> harmonious beat of a drum... A few *pas*, which were very well danced by
> Taglioni, Julia, Athalie and other nymphs, are not enough to justify the
> title of ballet. Nothing could have been more poverty-stricken or more
> shabbily staged than this... Since nothing can come out of nothing, Mlle
> Taglioni's début as a mime must be considered as put off to another day.
> The Opéra has made fools both of her and of the public.[26]

Had Taglioni not danced in it, *Lydie* would probably have met with a rowdy
reception; but in the event, it survived for five performances, rescued by the
novelty of Taglioni's style. As one observer put it, she lacked 'that Opéra look,
which anyone can acquire with a little application and coquetry' and also
that 'banal manner of performing something mechanically learnt, such as
we have seen in so many others. Mlle Taglioni is herself, and by being herself
is entirely delightful'. Albert seemed unusually inspired to be dancing with
her, and Julia, it was reported, 'had the good sense to "taglionise"'[27]

Taglioni made little impression in the mime passages, but it was hardly fair
to judge this aspect of her art in such a poor work. The only other criticism of
her was directed at her make-up. 'We should like to advise Mlle Taglioni,'
wrote the *Corsaire*, 'to be aware of the reflection of the footlights and not be
afraid of resorting to the little acts of charlatanism of her fellow dancers. It is
not enough that the complexion should appear white in daylight; it must also
appear white on the stage. Could not Mlle —— show Mlle Taglioni how to
apply white lead and vermilion?'[28]

The new score that Ferdinand Hérold had put together, probably very
hurriedly, was not particularly distinguished. The overture was criticised for
being noisy and monotonous, and the most praised passage was a
borrowing: the drinking song from Weber's opera *Der Freischütz*.

In accordance with her contract, Taglioni assumed two more mime rôles
before the end of the year. On 29 August she played Venus in *Mars et Vénus*,
and on 17 December the title-rôle in *Cendrillon*, but the general opinion
remained that she showed no particular talent for dramatic expression.

* * * * * * *

Thanks in part to Aumer, several of Dauberval's ballets had retained their
popularity in spite of changes in taste and developments of technique since
their creation late in the eighteenth century, and were still occasionally

performed not only in the provinces, but also in Paris itself. The most popular of these was *La Fille mal gardée*, which had first been produced in Bordeaux on the eve of the Revolution in 1789, and had lost none of its freshness with the passing of the years.[29] In the 1820s it was still a popular choice for benefit performances at the Porte-Saint-Martin and other Paris theatres, and even dancers of the Opéra would on occasion give their services to appear in it. Pauline Montessu and Ferdinand had played the two lovers, Lise and Colas, with conspicuous success. 'What fire and vivacity!' the *Courrier des théâtres* had written of the former after seeing her as Lise at the Porte-Saint-Martin in 1825. 'The eye can hardly follow her steps. One's entire attention is gripped by her acting and her dancing.'[30]

When this long-established favourite entered the repertory of the Opéra in the winter of 1828, the casting of the two principal rôles presented no problem, although Ferdinand had to wait until the second performance before playing the part of Colas there. This was because that rôle was to be played, on the first night only, by Marinette Launer, for whose benefit that performance was given.

Marinette Launer had performed the duties of *premier sujet comique* at the Opéra for several years, although ranking only as a *remplaçant*. She was the sister of the actress Jenny Boissière, and a gifted mime. She had succeeded to the rôles of Marie Courtin on the latter's retirement, and had been chosen to play the part of Cherubino when Aumer produced *Le Page inconstant*. Many of her admirers maintained that she would have been a successful actress in soubrette rôles, but no good judge ever claimed her to be a dancer of more than ordinary talents.

Her benefit took place on 17 November 1828, and was one of those marathon performances that were customary on such occasions. It lasted for five-and-a-half hours. Marivaux's comedy, *Le Jeu de l'amour et du hazard*, opened the programme, and was followed by the second act of Rossini's opera *Il barbiere di Siviglia*. After this there came *La Fille mal gardée*, and the programme continued with the comic opera *Deux Mots* with Pauline Montessu as Rose. Finally, the exhausted audience was treated to a mime scene and a battle-scene on horseback produced by the circus proprietor, Adolphe Franconi.

La Fille mal gardée was presented in a revised version by Aumer, with a new score by Ferdinand Hérold that preserved many of the best numbers of the original score, including that for the love scene in the last act, which was based on a once-popular song, *La Jeune et gentille Lisette*, which Haydn also used in his 85th Symphony. Hérold also made other borrowings, including the overture from Martini's opéra-comique, *Le Droit du seigneur,* and four extracts from operas by Rossini – the opening chorus from *Il barbiere di*

Siviglia for the beginning of the first scene, an aria from *La gazzetta*, which probably accompanied the entrance of Colas and the harvesters,[31] the storm music from *La Cenerentola*, and an aria from the second act of *Elisabetta, regina d'Inghilterra* (the last probably used, as it is today in the Royal Ballet version, for Lise's mime in the second act when she daydreams of marrying Colas). To weld his score together, Hérold had composed a certain amount of new music and, of course, modernised the orchestration.[32]

The plot of the ballet was left unchanged, and no doubt much of the traditional business that went back to the original production was retained. Since Aumer had studied under Dauberval, it was almost certainly the master himself who told him how the idea for this ballet had come to him; and one may surmise that Aumer passed the story on to Charles Maurice, who recounted it in his *Courrier des théâtres* a few days after the first performance of this revival:

> Dauberval, the dancer and the ballet composer, like all authors who are unceasingly preoccupied with their productions, was ever on the lookout for subjects wherever his steps led him. In this frame of mind he paused one day to yield to one of those little calls of Nature, which are imposed no less imperiously on man than on animals, and placed himself before a shop window where some wretched pictures were displayed. And there, right in front of his nose, was an engraving that can still be seen in shops and glaziers' windows, showing a young village girl in tears, with her dress somewhat disarrayed, while the seducer, adjusting his clothes, is making his escape from the abuse that the girl's angry mother is hurling at him. That was enough for Dauberval. In the space of a minute he conceived, thought through and sketched out the plan for a new work.[33]

In the ballet, Lise (Montessu) and Colas (Marinette, then Ferdinand) are in love, but Lise's mother Simone (Bernard-Léon, then Mme Elie) plans to marry her to a simpleton called Alain (Klein, then Elie), the son of Thomas (Godefroy), a neighbouring farmer. At a picnic meal during harvest-time, Colas seizes every possible opportunity to be with Lise. Thomas and Alain are annoyed by his behaviour, and Simone is even more determined to keep him apart from her daughter. Unseen by anyone, Colas then steals into Simone's house and conceals himself behind some sheaves of corn. After Simone has gone out and locked Lise in the house, Colas emerges from his hiding place. The lover's tryst is soon interrupted by Simone's return. Colas bounds up the stairs into the old woman's room before she can see him. Suspecting that Colas may be hanging around, Simone orders her daughter upstairs to put her out of mischief's way. Alain and Thomas then arrive with the notary to complete the marriage contract, but when Alain goes to fetch his intended bride the lovers are discovered together. Lise and Colas beg Simone to give them her blessing, and finally the old woman relents, to the great joy of all save Thomas and Alain.

Pauline Montessu repeated her effervescent portrayal of Lise. She was 'full of vivacity and gentleness,' recalled Jules Janin some years later. 'She came and went, and laughed, and was so mischievous that it was a pleasure to see her. In those days we applauded her, admired her, and proclaimed her unique and unrivalled. And indeed she had found something new in her art: she had invented a neat, rapid, vigorous way of dancing, which demands at least as much muscle as intelligence and wit.'[34]

For the first performance, two well-known comedians gave their services to play Simone and Alain. In the rôle of the mother, the jovial, rotund Bernard-Léon was greeted with gusts of laughter every time he rolled his eyes, while the antics of the spindly-legged Klein – the Alain of the piece – were hilariously funny.

At the second performance Ferdinand took over the rôle of Colas, Georges Elie succeeded Klein as Alain, and Louise Elie became the first woman to play the part of Simone. Duenna rôles were the speciality of Louise Elie, who, being the daughter of M. Launer by a previous marriage, was thereby the stepsister of Marinette Launer.[35] Her lack of beauty, which was an asset in playing this particular part, had not hampered her love life. She had been ironically known as 'the seductive Mme Elie' ever since a newspaper, in the days when only princes of the blood, noblemen and dignitaries of the church were allowed backstage, published a report that 'the seductive Mme Elie, who used to belong to Monseigneur the Bishop of Meaux, has gone over to Monseigneur the Bishop of Cambrai'.[36]

Although very little money had been spent on the new production of *La Fille mal gardée*, it became a popular favourite and was to remain in the repertory for many years. This 'ballet from the good old days',[37] as the *Figaro* described it, had lost none of its appeal. The *Courrier des théâtres* called it 'a masterpiece of its kind', and went on:

It reveals an extraordinary freshness and imaginative power, since with a situation that remains constant throughout, both in its moral implication and in the action to which such implications give rise, the celebrated Dauberval has managed to fill three acts with charming and natural details. His genius has given such life to the subject that after the first scene one ceases to notice the similarity of the others, and at the end is as moved and touched as if all these incidents of a little village love affair had been events of the greatest importance.[38]

NOTES

1. Castil-Blaze, *Académie*, II , 205.
2. Bournonville, *Mit Theaterliv*, I, 30.
3. *Journal de Paris*, quoted in the *Moniteur*, 15 August 1827.
4. *Moniteur*, 21 September 1827.
5. *Journal des débats*, 22 September 1827.
6. *Le Villageois somnambule, ou les deux fiancés*, comedy-vaudeville by Dartois and Dupin, f.p. Théâtre des Variétés, 15 October 1827. Two parodies also appeared about this time: *La Somnambule du Pont aux choux* at the Gaîté and *La Petite Somnambule, ou coquetterie et gourmandise* at the Théâtre de M. Comte.
7. *La sonnambula*, opera in three acts, music by Bellini, libretto by Romani, f.p. Teatro Carcano, Milan, 6 March 1831.
8. Castil-Blaze, *Académie*, II, 206.
9. *Moniteur*, 25 September 1827.
10. *Corsaire*, 21 September 1827.
11. *Courrier des théâtres*, 22 September 1827.
12. *Courrier des théâtres*, 3 October 1827.
13. *Moniteur*, 21 September 1827.
14. *La Cenerentola*, created in Rome in 1817, had been first seen in Paris at the Théâtre Italien in June 1822.
15. *Le Maçon*, opéra-comique in three acts, libretto by Scribe and Delavigne, music by Auber, f.p. Opéra-Comique, 3 May 1825, and still being occasionally performed there in 1827.
16. *Elisa e Claudio*, Saverio Mercadente's first great operatic success, f.p. La Scala, Milan, 30 October 1821.
17. Arch. Nat., AJ'[3] 111, 113, 114. Reports of 1819, 1820, 1822, 1824.
18. Ebers, 286.
19. *Courrier des théâtres*, 10 February 1827.
20. *Courrier des théâtres*, 30 May 1828.
21. Mirecourt, *Auber*, 26.
22. *Moniteur*, 2 March 1828.
23. *Constitutionnel*, 5 May 1828.
24. *Courrier des théâtres*, 9 July 1828.
25. *La Coquette soumise*, choreography by Aumer, music selected and composed by R. Lacy, f.p. King's Theatre, London, 12 March 1825.
26. *Constitutionnel*, 7 July 1828.
27. *Courrier des théâtres*, 4 July 1828.
28. *Corsaire*, 4 July 1828.
29. *La Fille mal gardée* was first performed at the Grand-Théâtre, Bordeaux, on 1 July 1789, under the title of *Le Ballet de la Paille*.
30. *Courrier des théâtres*, 24 April 1825.
31. This melody was adapted by John Lanchbery in his arrangement for Frederick Ashton's version for the cock-and-hens dance in the first scene.
32. For a detailed examination of Hérold's score for this ballet, see Lanchbery and Guest, *The Music of 'La Fille mal gardée'*.
33. *Courrier des théâtres*, 1 December 1828. Maurice later recounted the anecdote in an abbreviated form, and with a slight variation of detail due presumably to a lapse of memory, in his *Histoire anecdotique du théâtre*, published in 1856. Maurice's original description exactly fits the Baudouin picture *'Jeune Fille querellée par sa mère'*, the original of which was sold in 1900 under the title of *'La Fille mal gardée'*.
34. *Journal des débats*, 2 January 1837.
35. She had been the wife of a dancer known latterly in his career as Elie *aîné* to distinguish him from a younger dancer bearing the same name. The Archives of the Opéra reveal no evidence to show that they were brothers. The elder Elie died in 1817. Elie *jeune*, whose real name was Georges Roissy, was

then able to discard his suffix, becoming just Elie.

36. Un Vieil abonné, 101, quoting from the *Figaro*.

37. *Figaro*, 19 November 1828.

38. *Courrier des théâtres*, 18 November 1828.

9

The Aumer-Scribe Partnership Continues

Such was the success of *La Somnambule* that its joint authors, the dramatist Scribe and the ballet-master Aumer, were encouraged to try their hands again. In August 1828, within a year of that ballet's creation, the two men were reported to be working together on two contrasting themes, Charles Perrault's fairy tale of the Sleeping Beauty and the Abbé Prévost's provocative novel of Manon Lescaut's fall from grace in eighteenth-century Paris. Aumer had cause to be grateful to Scribe for *La Somnambule,* and their first open collaboration had apparently been marred by no serious disagreements. For their next effort, however, they began to work on an idea that Aumer himself had earlier worked into a draft synopsis, presumably before his acquaintance with Scribe, and possibly during his years in Vienna. Its starting point was Perrault's classic children's story on which Aumer had woven a tale so complex that it would have been understandable if the Viennese authorities had rejected such a proposal.

On being shown this synopsis, Scribe must have realised at once that it would not do. The sub-plot of two fairies, one good and the other wicked, was far too complicated to be clearly conveyed in pantomime, and the dramatist virtually had to start afresh. Perrault's tale remained the basis of the new scenario, but much else had to be rewritten. Scribe retained the malicious fairy, to whom Aumer had given the name Nabote, and also the idea of having two principal male rôles: the knightly character who marries the Princess in the end, and a man of lower rank. But the greater part of Aumer's over-complicated first act was jettisoned and replaced by a narrative that would be somewhat easier to follow. The next act, however, retained Aumer's concept of a dance scene in which ondines, exerting their supernatural wiles, try to deflect the hero from his purpose. Of course, the awakening and the marriage were fundamental; but here again Scribe forcefully intervened to replace Aumer's over-complicated plot with a more straightforward and somewhat lighter narrative, closing with a neatly devised *dénouement.*

So drastic was Scribe's rewriting of Aumer's original draft that one may wonder what arguments took place between the two men in their discussions over the text. However, since they went on to collaborate in a third ballet, it may be assumed that their inevitable differences were amicably resolved in an atmosphere of mutual respect. Aumer had good reason to appreciate the benefit of a collaborator knowledgeable in dramaturgy; while, for his part, Scribe surely welcomed the challenge of writing in what was for him a new genre, in which the action had to be presented entirely visually without recourse to explanatory dialogue.

What the public saw when the ballet reached its final form certainly revealed the advantages to be derived from collaboration with an experienced dramatist – even if, in this case, the final result could not be hailed as perfect. In the form in which the public saw it at its first performance on 27 April 1829, *La Belle au bois dormant* opened with preparations for a banquet to celebrate the engagement of Princess Iseult (Noblet) and Prince Gannelor (Montjoie). The princess's page Arthur (Legallois, in travesty) is in despair, for he has long been in love with his mistress. Iseult's godmother, the fairy Nabote (Mme Montessu), then arrives in a furious temper at being left off the invitation list. Apologies are made and a place laid for her, but she is not to be placated. At a wave of her wand she conjures up fire-eating reptiles to display her malevolent power. Then, when the ball opens, she freezes the dancers in mid-movement, and then amuses herself by releasing them singly to dance with her. She is finally prevailed upon to lift the spell, and the ball comes to a close.

As Iseult leaves for her chamber, Arthur is on the point of following when she gives him a sign to remain. A sympathetic maid of honour (C. Brocard) then helps him to gain access to Iseult's chamber. But they have been overheard by Nabote, who conceals the princess's father and Gannelor so that they will witness the scene that follows, when Iseult and Arthur realise they are in love. At this point Nabote vanishes with a shriek of glee, and an infuriated Gannelor gives orders for Arthur to be put to death. Iseult pleads for mercy, and Gannelor relents, but only so far as to reduce Arthur's sentence to banishment – and that on the condition that Iseult marries Gannelor without further delay. On these terms the marriage is celebrated. Iseult then snatches Gannelor's dagger from his hand with the intention of killing herself, having fulfilled her part of the bargain. Happily the blow is deflected, and she is carried to her chamber still alive, although mortally wounded. Gannelor entreats Nabote to save her, but malicious to the last, the fairy decrees that Iseult shall sleep for a hundred years and that whoever then awakens her must marry her unless he already has a spouse. This doom is spelled out on a transparent cloth lowered in front of the border of clouds that has descended to cover the entrance to the bedchamber. Meanwhile, unseen, Arthur has slipped into a chest, which is then carried into the chamber where Iseult lies asleep, surrounded by her wedding gifts.

When Act II begins, a hundred years have passed. The scene is a simple hut, in which the widowed peasant-woman Mme Bobi (Mme Elie), her son Gombault (Godefroy) and his daughter Marguerite (M. Dupuis) are living in extreme poverty. The old woman recounts the legend of the Sleeping Beauty, and Gombault, feeling that he has nothing to lose, is on the point of going to the castle himself when Gérard (Ferdinand), Marguerite's suitor, appears. He has come to ask for her hand, but Gombault will only listen to his request if he will first go to the castle and come back a rich man. Gérard is on the point of despair when Nabote appears and touches him on the shoulder. Learning the cause of his unhappiness, she gives him a magic horn, the tones of which will dispose of any obstacle he might meet on his journey. Thus his hopes are reawakened, and he bids farewell to Gombault, who expects never to see him again, and to Marguerite, who gives him a token of her love.

The scene changes to a forest, where Gérard is beset by dragons, which he wards off with a blast from his horn. He then finds himself at the edge of a lake, from which the distant walls of the castle can be seen rising above the forest. Finding a boat conveniently moored nearby, Gérard is about to row across the lake when he finds his way barred by a bevy of nymphs and naiads emerging from the water. The leading naiad (Taglioni) attracts him by her voluptuous wiles, and he is on the point of yielding to her seductive charms when the sight of Marguerite's token brings him back to reality. Another sound from his horn causes these seductive charmers to vanish, and he steps into the boat. After a long journey he reaches the far bank.

The third act opens with Gérard entering the chamber where Iseult lies asleep. He moves cautiously towards her, and, as if uncertain what to do next, again sounds his horn. All at once the sleeping figures begin to stir. Iseult is at first confused, wondering where she is. Gérard tells her of her long sleep, and her thoughts turn immediately to Arthur. At this point Mme Bobi, Gombault and Marguerite appear with a group of neighbours, the news of the spell being broken having travelled fast.[1] Gombault's objection to Gérard's marrying his daughter has vanished; but now Nabote appears to remind everyone of the terms of the spell, by which Gérard is beholden to marry Iseult. When Gérard refuses, the fairy threatens to turn him into a toad. Sorrowfully Marguerite tells him they must resign themselves to his fate, and Gérard is led away to be dressed for the wedding. Iseult is also in despair as her memory turns to her beloved Arthur, whom she assumes to have died, along with all the other courtiers. But then, as if by a miracle, the page bursts out of the cupboard where he had taken refuge and, like Iseult, merely slept for all those years. But at Nabote's approach, he slips back into the cupboard.

The time has now come for the wedding formalities. Nabote enters with Gérard and tells him it is his duty to woo Iseult. Both parties are embarrassed, for Iseult now knows that Arthur is both alive and nearby, while, at the same time, Gérard's eye has caught sight of Marguerite hiding behind a statue. The couple persuade Nabote to allow them to exchange their vows in private, and with some reluctance the fairy leaves them alone to attend to this formality. At this point, Arthur and Marguerite come out of hiding, and the two couples are reunited. However, their quandary remains unresolved. Nabote then returns, accompanied by the inhabitants of the castle, for the time has come to celebrate the marriage. An ornate veil, falling to her feet, is then placed on Iseult's head. But just as Nabote is about to pronounce them man and wife, it is discovered that Gérard has no ring. A frantic search for a ring of suitable size then distracts the fairy's attention, and she fails to observe Marguerite taking Iseult's place behind the veil. Gérard does not see this substitution either, and has to be forcibly pushed by Arthur to kneel on the bridegroom's cushion. With a gesture of triumph, Nabote then declares them to be married, only to be confounded when Marguerite discloses that she, not Iseult, is the bride.

As Nabote rises in anger, brandishing her crutch, a peal of thunder announces the appearance of Cupid, who breaks Nabote's wand and takes the two couples under his protection.

Most critics did not share the public's liking for this ballet. 'Long, slow, heavy, deadly dull,' was the judgment of the *Journal des débats*. In the eyes of one critic, only the appearance of Marie Taglioni in the third act relieved the tedium. 'Like Venus,' he wrote,

> she emerged from the bosom of the waves followed by the loveliest retinue: *ducit Cytherea choros.* If we go by paintings of old and modern masters, the costumes of these naiads, with their skirts and petticoats, will seem very singular. But if Neptune can rise out of the sea well curled, surely nymphs such as these can escape from their damp grottoes in ball dresses. This scene produced a delightful effect, and was the only one to be applauded with enthusiasm by the entire audience. Mlle Taglioni bounded about the stage with the lightness of a sylphide and the most perfect grace.[2]

She was in her element as she danced 'the bewitching *pas*'[3] that Aumer had arranged for her and which brought into play all her characteristic qualities, 'her modest elegance, her gentleness, her sparkling lightness.'[4]

Taglioni aside, the ballet's appeal depended to a large extent on its lavish spectacle: Ciceri's fine sets, the richly coloured costumes, and particularly the 'new and ingenious machinery',[5] which produced the magical effects for which the ballet was to be largely remembered. The disastrous chapter of accidents that had marred the first performance of *Zémire et Azor* had rudely awakened the Opéra to the inadequacies in the chief machinist's department. Being reluctant to dismiss Gromaire, who had only a few more years to serve before retiring, the Opéra had been looking around for an eventual successor. The choice was made in favour of an enterprising young machinist, Clément Contant, who was keen to acquire an expertise in developments in his craft that were then taking place in London. Contant was anxious to spend some weeks there to study these developments, and Lubbert had released him in the winter of 1828 on the understanding that he would travel at his own expense, but that his salary would be reviewed when he resumed his duties.[6]

La Belle au bois dormant, for which preparations began shortly after his return to Paris, gave him the opportunity to his show his mettle. In the first act, gasps of surprise greeted the transformation of the dishes and flowers on the banqueting table into reptiles breathing multi-coloured flames at a wave of Nabote's wand; but the most spectacular effect of all was the panorama that Contant had designed for Gérard's journey to the enchanted castle. As Ferdinand stepped into the property boat and began to row, the scenery representing the bank of the river and the landscape beyond began to move. The panorama by which this was achieved was made up of three separate set-pieces, composed of hinged sections, which were slowly moved, one behind the other, from the audience's right to left at varying speeds, giving the illusion of a three-dimensional woodland scene passing by the boat. An imaginative touch of realism was added by the manipulation of the boat itself, which did not remain stationary while the panorama behind it was in motion. Rather, as described by one spectator, the boat was seen to 'advance a little at a time, and recede as if carried back by the current, when the boatman rests on his oars to admire the beauty of the surrounding country; and when he arrives at the enchanted castle the vessel has reached the opposite side of the stage.'[7] The set-pieces were of different lengths – 144 feet, 120 feet and 90 feet – the closest to the audience being the longest; the two larger set-pieces each consisted of twelve hinged sections. They would have been operated manually, each a little more slowly than the one immediately in front, so as to give the illusion of depth. To Castil-Blaze the effect was somewhat marred by the stationary trees forming the wings,[8] but a more generous eyewitness found the scene 'most admirably effective, the laws of optics and perspective being observed to perfection.'[9]

Far less satisfactory was the vehicle designed for Nabote's departure in the second act, 'those so-called clouds,' as the *Journal des débats* described it, 'with cut-out horses in a horizontal gallop. If the Opéra is trying to attract good houses with its ballet, it will have to follow a less beaten track than this.'[10]

The score, which was to be Hérold's last contribution to a ballet, was disappointing. It was a lightweight composition, with few remarkable features. It contained the customary proportion of borrowings, including

the overture from Weber's *Oberon* and a chorus and a cavatina from Rossini's
La pietra del paragone.

As if to underline that it stood at the threshold of a new age, *La Belle au
bois dormant* marked the close of one career and the beginning of another.
The rôle of old Gombault was the last to be created by Godefroy, one of the
Opéra's most forceful mimes, who was to die five months later after a short
illness. A happier association was the introduction to the public, as Cupid in
the apotheosis, of a pretty ten-year-old girl called Nathalie Fitzjames, who
was to become one of the minor luminaries of the Romantic ballet in years to
come. *La Belle au bois dormant*, while not achieving the success that had been
hoped for it, survived in its complete form until 1837, after which three
performances of the second act on its own were given in 1838 and 1840.

* * * * * * *

Perhaps the most significant indication that an old order was passing was the
retirement of Pierre Gardel in 1827. Gardel was a legendary figure, having
entered the Opéra fifty-six years before, in 1771, when Guimard and Heinel
were at the height of their powers. He had succeeded his elder brother
Maximilien as *maître de ballet* on the latter's death in 1787. Since then he had
held the permanent post of first ballet-master for an unbroken forty years, a
record that has not even been approached to the present day. In his prime, he
had steered French ballet through the disturbed and uncertain years of the
Revolution and the Directoire, and under Napoleon had enriched the
repertory with a flow of major works in many different genres, presiding over
a veritable flowering of his art. Being brought up with a classical education,
he had sought inspiration for many of his finest ballets in the legends of
antiquity: *Télémaque*, *Psyché* and *Le Jugement de Pâris*, his early masterpieces
created at the height of the Revolution, retained their places in the repertory
for more than thirty years, and a lighter work with a modern setting, *La
Dansomanie*, was no less popular. He produced no more ballets after 1818,
but retained his position as *premier maître de ballet*, revealing from time to
time, in the numerous *divertissements* he staged in operas up to his
retirement, that his compositional skill was unimpaired.

To mark his retirement he was rewarded with a benefit performance on 23
February 1829, which left him richer by some 25,000 francs. The Duchesse
de Berry and the Duc d'Orléans both attended to honour the veteran
choreographer, whose warrant as ballet-master to the King had been
renewed by Charles X only the year before. After Malibran had sung in the
second act of Zingarelli's opera, *Romeo e Giulietta*, Marie Taglioni appeared
for the first time in the title-rôle of Pierre Gardel's greatest masterpiece,

Psyché, the score of which had been specially rearranged by Schneitzhoeffer for this, its 561st performance on the Opéra stage.[11]

Gardel's ten years and more of retirement were unhappily to be clouded by failing health and bereavement. His wife, who had succeeded Guimard as *premier sujet de demi-caractère* and retired after a distinguished career in 1816, died very suddenly in May 1833. Four years later his elder son, a cavalry major who had survived the retreat from Moscow, succumbed to a lung complaint. Bereft and now suffering from the stone, the old ballet-master lived out his lonely last years under the devoted care of his daughter Rose in Montmartre, where he died, at the age of eighty-two, on 9 November 1840.

The news of his passing stirred many memories. Although the first performance of *Giselle* lay only a few months ahead, the *Courrier des théâtres*, in its obituary notice, put the record straight by speaking fondly of the past as though contemporary ballet was sadly decadent by comparison with the years of his glory. 'His ballets were the pride of the Opéra at a time when the public was more knowledgeable and more exacting than it is today,' recalled its anonymous author.

> One of his sorrows was to see his name no longer on the bills, for he was always passionately devoted to his art. But in due course of time, when there will be a renewed interest in the good things of the past, the finest of Gardel's ballets will be revived and people will be amazed at the imagination, taste, delicacy, skill and versatility of their choreographer. Then the dance will no longer comprise only so-called *pas de caractère*, performed only by women in accordance with the ridiculous notion of excluding male dancers, as if one sex alone could lay claim anywhere to a monopoly in this pleasurable art. We are certainly not advocating a return to tunics *à pluie*, green slippers and bare chests and arms for male dancers: *autre époque, autres idées*. But does an artist correct a painting by destroying it? Because panniers are no longer in fashion on the stage, have actresses been suppressed because they once wore them?...

> Gardel devoted all his efforts to choreography, although he had studied several other arts as well. Older theatregoers will remember how well he played the violin solo in his ballet, *La Dansomanie*. He also played a part in the abolition of the *pochette*.[12]

There was a now a widening breach between the new order and the old. Gardel and Taglioni seemed hardly to belong to the same world; and indeed the former repertory, to which Gardel had so largely contributed, was on the point of disappearing. The Classicism that Gardel had championed was becoming increasingly out of favour, now that Romanticism was beginning to usurp its place as the driving force behind the ballet. This was already becoming apparent in the introduction of local colour, as in the Spanish and Italian dances inserted in *La Muette de Portici*, and again, on 3 August 1829, when Marie Taglioni, in the costume of a Swiss peasant, danced the *Tyrolienne* to an unaccompanied chorus at the first performance of Rossini's opera *Guillaume Tell*.

Taglioni's gentler style was already providing the Parisian public with new standards of criticism, which were now stringently applied to a hopeful young débutante, Angelica Saint-Romain, who appeared before the public of the Opéra on 14 September. For this, the newcomer could only blame her advisers, who had unwisely spread the extravagant claim that she was a more astonishing dancer than Taglioni. Such presumption had created an unfortunate impression; for even after allowing for her nervousness, it was obvious to all that she was not in the same class as Taglioni, with whom indeed she had little in common in matters of style and presentation. She was a *terre à terre* dancer, undeniably musical, rapid and precise in her turns, and proficient in *pointe* work, but she possessed what the *Courrier des théâtres* described as an Italian manner – a certain flamboyance, particularly noticeable in *temps de batterie* and the high level to which she would raise her leg.[13]

Her début drew some pertinent remarks on current trends in style from Castil-Blaze, who foresaw an imminent invasion of Italian dancing, coming in the wake of Italian music. 'The main body of troops is still far off,' he wrote,

> but scouts are advancing to try out the land, and the advantages they are gaining augur well. Mlle Taglioni and Mlle Saint-Romain have nothing in common except that they belong to the same school. I should not really use this term, since our pundits contend that the dancing of these ladies is not classical. Never mind about that! We shall call it romantic... If I were to go to the trouble of consulting the works of classical authors, I would have no difficulty in proving that if any form of dancing on our stages is eminently classical, it is that of Mlles Taglioni and Saint-Romain. These virtuosi owe a great part of their success to the simultaneous action of every part of their bodies, while our own classical form of dancing leaves the torso, arms and head, if not immobile, at least in a very displeasing state of stiffness and inaction.[14]

A closer analogy with Taglioni's style was discerned in the dancing of Albert's daughter, Elisa, who made her début on 28 October. In training her, Albert was reported to have taken as his model the Italian ballerina Amalia

Brugnoli, whose style was not dissimilar to Taglioni's, and with happy results, for as the *Courrier des théâtres* declared, 'she is a dancer of the new school'.[15]

The old school was certainly now out of favour, and Auguste Vestris, seen as a relic of a bygone age, although still usefully active as a teacher, found himself the butt of the *Courrier des théâtres.* Reporting that 'the personification of rococo', as he was scornfully dubbed, was to arrange the *divertissement* in a new opera, this paper's critic wondered what was to be dug out of store – and with a touch of malice asked whether the Opéra might be thinking of reviving *Les Indes galantes.*[16] It was soon to be made clear that Vestris was no choreographer, for his mediocre *divertissement* in Gineste's opera *François Ier à Chambord* was almost immediately heavily cut, and he received no invitation to try his hand again. As a teacher he was criticised no less severely when his pupil, Giovanni Casati, made his début on 9 June 1830. The *Courrier des théâtres* delivered an attack that by implication was aimed against Vestris. The young man's performance, it declared, left much to be desired – 'less movement and more correctness, less strutting and more grace, strength that is not gained at the expense of elegance, and results that are obtained by the cultivation of an art rather than being a mountebank's tricks'.[17] To a growing proportion of the public, the old school was becoming as dead as the minuet.

* * * * * * *

Manon Lescaut, the third ballet that Aumer produced in association with Scribe, had a protracted and frequently interrupted gestation. In a letter to La Rochefoucauld, Lubbert complained of the difficulties he had to face before that ballet finally went into production: 'orders and counter-orders which, one after another, had hustled him into action, stopped him in his tracks, and then pressured him anew'.[18] The problem had arisen because La Rochefoucauld had been negotiating with Filippo Taglioni throughout the greater part of 1829 after the latter had suggested producing a ballet – no doubt with his daughter in mind to play the principal rôle – coupled with a request to be engaged himself as a principal ballet-master in company with Aumer and Albert. When asked for his comments, Lubbert was not averse to Taglioni's being asked to produce a ballet; but, for reasons of expense, did not feel he should be given an official post. However, when La Rochefoucauld replied to Taglioni, he passed over the latter's request without comment, hoping perhaps that it would be dropped.[19]

But Taglioni was not prepared to let that matter drop, and eventually La Rochefoucauld, ignoring Lubbert's reservations, gave in. Filippo Taglioni was offered a contract as joint first ballet-master, backdated to the beginning of 1829, at an annual salary of 3000 francs coupled with a bonus of 2000 francs. That Taglioni had made the most of his daughter's triumph in these negotiations was reflected in the final passage of La Rochefoucauld's letter: 'I am delighted to profit by the brilliant success of your daughter to assure you of the interest I take in a master who has been able to form such a distinguished pupil.'[20]

Discussions then followed on the subject of the ballet itself. Filippo Taglioni submitted a scenario of his own invention entitled *Bianca Capello*, which was provisionally scheduled to go into rehearsal as soon as *La Belle au bois dormant* had been launched, taking precedence over *Manon Lescaut*. However, as time passed, La Rochefoucauld became increasingly uneasy, realising that Taglioni's scenario needed considerable amendment to make it palatable to a Parisian audience. Discussions on these changes eventually reached a point at which neither side was prepared to give way, with Taglioni complaining that the ballet would be changed out of all recognition from his original conception. So the project was abandoned, and early in January 1830 Lubbert was instructed to resume preparations for *Manon Lescaut* with all possible dispatch.

* * * * * * *

Lubbert now found himself under intense pressure to hasten a production that had long been in cold storage, and as a matter of urgency to obtain estimates from the various heads of departments so that the required credits could be applied for. Promptest of all was Ciceri, whose estimate for the scenery was approved at a figure of 23,590 francs. The costumes, however, presented a more difficult problem. These were planned on a most spectacular scale, and the task of overseeing their design had been confided to Henri Duponchel, an influential member of the Opéra's production committee, with a brief to recreate the opulent splendour of Paris society in the time of Louis XV. Not surprisingly, in view of the scorn in which the rococo style was then held in artistic circles, Duponchel could find nothing in the Opéra's costume store that could be reused or even adjusted, and the designing and estimating of these costumes proved a complicated and time-consuming task. For this, more than one designer was employed, most notably Hippolyte Lecomte, who had succeeded the son of the celebrated Fragonard, for the military uniforms, and Eugène Lami, a young artist fulfilling his first commission for the Opéra. It was perhaps hardly surprising that the estimate for the costumes was finally authorised at the exceptional total, for a ballet, of 31,860 francs.

To offset this additional expenditure on costumes, Gromaire's estimate for the scenery had been slashed from his original figure of 16,556 to 3000 francs by the apparently simple expedient of reusing materials from productions no longer in the repertory.[21] And there was another item, which was to be overlooked until some months after the ballet had been presented. This was for the wigs, which were so numerous that the wig-makers had demanded an advance, adding a further 3663 francs to the total cost.[22]

A further cost was for the effect that Contant, now officially designated *premier machiniste adjoint*, had devised for the arrival of the Governor's ship in the last act. This was a *tour de force* of illusion, for the property ship was so constructed as to give the illusion that it was growing in size as it approached the shore. For this eye-catching effect Contant was rewarded with an *ex gratia* payment of 500 francs and a commendation from La Rochefoucauld. 'Like me,' wrote the Vicomte to Lubbert after the first performance, 'you will understand the necessity of giving recognition to the talents of M. Contant, which it is in the management's interest to encourage, since it will be counting on him to bring about the improvements that it is advisable should be introduced by stages in the theatre's machinery department.'[23]

The scenario for *Manon Lescaut* – the third to be written for the Opéra by Eugène Scribe in association with Jean Aumer – was based on the celebrated novel written by the Abbé Prévost nearly a hundred years before, and by now regarded as a classic of its kind. For a ballerina avid for a rôle with dramatic possibilities, that of Manon was worth almost any effort to obtain, and those two rivals, Lise Noblet and Amélie Legallois, were quick to stake their claims. Nor was interest in their rivalry confined to the salons of Paris – for their struggle made news in London too, inspiring a report in the favourite weekly of high society, the *Court Journal:*

> A new ballet has for a long time been in preparation, entitled *Manon de Lescaut* (*sic*), founded on the famous French novel of that name; and it was at first determined that the clever and accomplished new dancer, Mlle Legallois, should perform the chief character, Manon Lescaut – she being considered by the best judges in Paris as alone uniting the various qualities required for giving effect to the part. The rehearsal of the piece has, however, been delayed (without any apparent cause) for a long time; and we now learn that the playing of it is put off altogether, for an indefinite period, solely on account of the cabals and intrigue that have been going on, with a view to procuring the part to be performed by a dancer who has more powerful friends than Legallois, but who must be considered as in some degree *passée*, even in person, not to mention her style being in the same predicament – we allude to Mlle Noblet.[24]

In 1830 the *Courrier des théâtres* made little secret of its bias in favour of Lise Noblet, which presupposed a prejudice against Taglioni. Early that year, Noblet, who was waging a losing struggle to recover her former supremacy, made use of that paper's columns to deny some rumours. She and Albert had not, she declared, insisted on a *pas de deux* being included for them in *Guillaume Tell*, nor had she intrigued to prevent Léontine Fay, an actress with pretensions as a mime, from playing the title-rôle in a revival of *Nina*. Thirdly, she placed on record that the delay in staging *Manon Lescaut* was due to causes for which the management was responsible.[25] This, in fact, was true, for it was only in January, after Filippo Taglioni had refused to modify his ballet *Bianca Capello* to suit the requirements of the Opéra, that La Rochefoucauld instructed Lubbert to proceed forthwith with the production of *Manon Lescaut*.

A firm decision now had to be taken on the casting of the title-rôle, and Lise Noblet was disappointed to be passed over in favour of Lubbert's mistress, Pauline Montessu, whose star was in the ascendant following her successes in *La Somnambule* and *La Fille mal gardée*. The part of the sleepwalking heroine in the former ballet had revealed a remarkable gift for conveying pathos; while in the latter her performance as Lise had been marked by a delicious sparkle that might appropriately enhance the giddy side of Manon's character. And in addition to these considerations, she was then much in favour in royal circles, having recently been presented by Charles X with a gold brooch after dancing at Court.

The first performance of *Manon Lescaut* was originally scheduled for 27 April, but a last-minute problem resulted in a short postponement. Ciceri's set for the last act had not been ready for the general rehearsal on 25 April, and it had been necessary to call another on the 28th. The first performance eventually took place on 3 May.

The Abbé Prévost's novel had not been used for a ballet before. Since it was first published nearly a century before, taste and sensibility had undergone radical changes. Although every educated Frenchman was familiar with the story, Scribe appears to have decided to transform Manon from a scheming charmer into an innocent, naive girl from the provinces – in other words, a victim of an earlier society now held in some contempt – so as to make the stage adaptation acceptable. However, in making this adjustment, much of the spirit and content of the original work would inevitably be lost. In particular, Scribe's decision to ignore the long section of the novel dealing with the later adventures of Manon and Des Grieux in Paris led to the ballet's main weakness, in that the stage action failed to explain how it was that Manon was deported to America in a consignment of common prostitutes.

The ballet opens in the garden of the Palais Royal. Manon (Mme

Montessu) and her cousin Marguerite (Roland) enter and attract the attention of a group of noblemen. Manon's young lover, Des Grieux (Ferdinand), runs to greet her, chiding her for being late. He brings good news – that his father has at last consented to their marriage. To this Manon, distracted by the gaiety of the scene around her, pays scant attention, for the noblemen, attracted by her beauty, are trying to catch her attention. Des Grieux leads her away, but one of the gentlemen, the Marquis de Gerville (Montjoie), boldly comes forward with an offer to show her round the garden. Des Grieux takes offence that Manon seems to have encouraged him, and she begs to be forgiven. To make amends, Des Grieux has the idea of buying her a gift; but although tempted, she refuses, knowing he cannot afford such an extravagance. At that moment a rascally recruiting sergeant (S. Mérante) approaches him with an offer of a loan requiring only a simple receipt. Without a thought Des Grieux accepts, and as soon as he signs what he takes to be the receipt, the money is handed over. Unobserved by Manon and her cousin, Des Grieux slips into a nearby shop to buy a gift for his beloved, emerging with a splendid cloak, which he places on Manon's shoulders. He then proposes they have supper together, and enters a restaurant to make arrangements. Left outside, the two girls are accosted by Gerville and his aristocratic friends, who press Manon to accompany them to the Opéra, which is only just around the corner.[26] The offer is too tempting, and the innocent girl, imagining perhaps that she will be away for only a few moments, follows them. So when Des Grieux emerges from the restaurant, he finds her gone. One misfortune then follows another, for he is seized by the recruiting sergeant, who informs him he has signed up to join the army. Ordered to follow him, Des Grieux breaks away and, in a state of panic, is last seen running into the passage leading to the Opéra.[26]

The scene changes to the interior of the Opéra, showing the stage with benches on either side for courtiers. Gerville leads Manon to one of the side boxes, and the performance begins with a ballet. Danced in the costumes of the time, its subject is the triumph of Cupid, with the supporting dancers dressed as wood spirits, shepherds and shepherdesses. Mlle Camargo (Legallois) enters to dance a solo to an air by Rameau, and this is followed by a gig. Finally the shepherdesses emerge from a temple, where they have been making an offering. But at that point the stage action is interrupted by the sudden appearance of Des Grieux, who leaps upon the stage, only to be apprehended by the pursuing guards and placed under arrest. Manon falls back in a faint as the young man is led away.

The second act is set in an elegant salon, where Gerville is hosting a supper party. Manon is given a lesson by Camargo and Mme Petitpas (Buron), who are among the guests. She then learns that although Des Grieux has been released from arrest, he is now facing a charge of desertion. She implores Gerville to obtain his release, but he cynically points out that Des Grieux is his rival, and he will only do what she asks if she agrees to become his mistress and promises never to see Des Grieux again. Trapped, she tearfully accepts his terms. At that moment a violent storm breaks. Delighted at having had his way, Gerville leaves on other business, instructing his servants to accept Manon as their mistress. Left alone, Manon realises what she has done. She goes to shut the window against the storm, but before she can do so, it blows open to reveal Des Grieux standing before her on the sill. He is amazed to find her there, for he had merely been seeking shelter and evading his pursuers. She silences his reproaches and soon subjugates him to her charms. He begs her to abandon Gerville and flee with him. To this she is only too willing, but they are hungry and she orders the servants to serve them supper. He is shivering with cold, and she presses him to put on one of Gerville's dressing gowns. Supper is then served, but unwisely they linger over it, and are interrupted by a knock on the door. Manon takes no notice, being unaware that there is also a secret entrance to the room. From this Gerville emerges to surprise them together. Des Grieux, who has drawn his pistol, is quickly disarmed, and Manon is ordered to be taken to the Salpêtrière, the whores' prison, to be transported to Louisiana. Gerville, who has been wounded by a shot from Des Grieux's pistol, takes Des Grieux's engagement out of his pocket and, in a gesture of forgiveness, tears it into pieces. Manon and Des Grieux are led away under guard on opposite sides of the stage.

Several months have passed before Act III opens. The scene is the interior of a fort in New Orleans. A group of women clad in rough dresses, Manon among them, are occupied in mending sails, while an Indian girl, Niuka (Taglioni), the slave of the brutal overseer Synelet (Aumer), is weaving a hammock. The bell rings for their work-break, and the blacks and the Indians amuse themselves by dancing. When the time comes to resume work, Niuka is so absorbed in her dancing that she fails to observe Manon signaling her master's approach. Synelet raises his cane, and the Indian girl shrinks to her knees in fear. Manon tries to restrain him, and threatens to complain to the new Governor, whose arrival is expected that very day. Synelet angrily turns on Manon, and is struck for the first time by her beauty. He dismisses Niuka, and is making an approach to Manon when a large ship is sighted on the horizon. At that moment Des Grieux appears, and Manon recognises him; he has followed Manon across the ocean in an earlier vessel. Synelet orders the women to return to their cells, allotting to Manon a cell conveniently accessible for him to make her his mistress. When Synelet leaves, Des Grieux reappears and bribes the turnkey to allow him to speak to her alone. In the few brief moments they have together, he tells her how, after selling all his possessions, he had crossed the ocean to find her. Synelet then returns, and offers Manon her freedom if she will become his mistress. She rejects his advances, while Niuka warns Des Grieux of her danger. Drawing his revolver, Des Grieux backs Synelet into one of the cells and locks him inside. Niuka tells the lovers that they now have no alternative but to flee – not towards the sea, but inland, to the desert.[27] Descending the bastion wall presents a problem, which is solved by the fortuitous discovery of a rope. Manon goes down first, but Des Grieux is spotted by a guard. A shot is fired, as he tumbles over the wall after her. Asked which way the fugitives went, Niuka points towards the sea. Cannons are then heard firing a salute, as the new Governor's ship is seen approaching in full sail.

The scene changes to reveal yet another impressive set, depicting 'a forest and a distant horizon of red sky, a frightening desert of sand and the flashing of distant storms'.[28] The lovers are exhausted, but it does not appear they are being followed. They find themselves alone in a vast wilderness, and Manon is frightened. She wants to hold Des Grieux in her arms, but to her horror, he faints. It is only then that she realises he has been shot. She sprinkles the last drops of their precious water on his wound. He recovers, and insists that they press on. But she is at the end of her strength, and reveals that they are out of water. As Manon begins to lose consciousness, the sound of horses is heard, and a column of men appears, headed by the new Governor. It is Niuka who first sees the lovers. Synelet gives an order for their arrest. Niuka pleads for them, and the Governor intervenes to reproach the overseer for his cruelty and dismisses him. Des Grieux drags himself to the Governor's feet, imploring him to have pity on Manon. Only when he raises his eyes does he realise that the Governor is none other than the Marquis de Gerville. With what little strength he has left, Des Grieux returns to Manon's side and raises her veil. The Governor places his hand on her forehead. 'She is dead,' he says gently, as Des Grieux falls fainting over her body.

Virtually alone among the critics, Hippolyte Prévost of the *Moniteur* questioned how successfully Scribe had conveyed the character of the Abbé Prévost's heroine through the pantomime of Pauline Montessu. His was a valid judgment, in which he pointed out the fundamental flaw that had arisen through Scribe's decision to reduce Manon's infidelity towards her rich protector to just a single incident. The ballet's principal situations, he wrote,

> which the authors have either themselves invented or borrowed from the novelist, offer a happy mixture of gaiety, interest and originality. They might perhaps be open to criticism for having failed to show Manon Lescaut in any of those episodes ... that at least justify the terrible

punishment inflicted upon this woman. How has Des Grieux's beloved deserved to be associated with fallen women, rejected by society and cast upon a distant shore? Was her crime nothing more than being unwilling to yield to the Colonel's desires? So why is she repentant? What is the wrong that she is weeping over so bitterly in New Orleans? This vagueness in the first act casts a chill, particularly in the second act, which is the weakest in the work.[29]

Judged as an adaptation of the novel, the work was certainly flawed. However, while certain critics had reservations, the public found the ballet to their liking, and it became increasingly popular. Over the next few years it was performed forty-six times (not counting a single performance of the Camargo scene given on its own), and was probably dropped only then because of the enormous triumphs of *Robert le Diable*, *La Sylphide* and other new productions, and by its not being a vehicle for Taglioni. Judging by box-office receipts, *Manon Lescaut* was very definitely a success: over the previous decade, only one other ballet, *Mars et Vénus*, had brought in better figures. The principal ingredients of its success were to be found in the spectacular production, the music, and the quaintness, to the public of 1830, of its period setting rather than in the plot, which had been much emasculated in the course of its conversion into a ballet. Perhaps with an eye to the Opéra's public, which would include wives and daughters of the rich and powerful in the lower boxes, Scribe had felt it politic to compress Manon's fall from grace into just a single incident. But this must have left those in the audience who were unfamiliar with the novel quite mystified by Manon's deportation across the Atlantic in a shipload of common prostitutes.

The Opéra had spared no expense in staging *Manon Lescaut*: the original estimate had been exceeded, and it was reliably understood that in the final accounting, the scenery, costumes and machinery had cost considerably more than 70,000 francs. Ciceri's sets – 'exact reproductions of Boucher and Watteau', to quote the *Constitutionnel*[30] – were as superb as they were authentic in their period evocation, while the costumes were dazzling in their rich colours and elegance. In his first major assignment as *premier machiniste adjoint*, Contant made a spectacular contribution to the last act by turning to profit what he had learnt during his visit to London and devising a brilliantly original effect by which the Governor's ship was seen from the audience's point of view to increase in size as it approached the shore.

The score, Jacques Halévy's first work for the ballet, was composed with unusual care, as might have been expected of a talented and ambitious young musician striving to make an impression with his first commission from the Opéra. For its time it was a remarkable composition. It was expressively scored, included numerous allusions to suggest the period setting, and, in a recurring theme for Manon, contained perhaps the earliest example of *leitmotiv* in ballet music. Among the songs of the time that were worked in at appropriate moments were *La Camargo, Dans les Gardes françaises, Avant la Bataille* and *Vive le vin de Ramponneau.* Another borrowing was a duet from Garcia's opera *Il califfo di Bagdad.* It was reported that Halévy had also intended to interpolate the melody, *Où allez-vous, monsieur l'abbé?* to accompany a scene in the second act when an abbé was to be seen creeping back into Manon's room after everyone else had left, but this passage was cut as being too *risqué.*

Meyerbeer, who was a severe critic, was quite favourably impressed when he listened to the first act. It was his opinion that

> this music is somewhat sterile for ballet music. There is very little real thematic invention, and grace is often lacking. On the other hand, the parodying of the music of France as it was in those days (1720) is excellently constructed, and the way in which the great quantity of original songs and dances of that time are interpreted, worked, counterpointed and orchestrated is perfect and reveals an able master. Finally, I have to admit that several of those old French melodies pleased me greatly.[31]

The mid-eighteenth century was not yet remote enough for its style to be appreciated by the general public of 1830. Typical of the scorn in which the modes of the old régime were still held was the *Figaro's* opinion that it was 'the most prominent period of decadence for all the arts in France'.[32] The public was therefore amused rather than enchanted by the first act's evocation of the manners and fashions of their grandfathers' day, which still suffered from the stigma of being ridiculously outmoded. The ballet within the ballet, which was authentically rococo both in theme and in costume, was presented in a spirit of caricature and caused much merriment in its first few minutes. But to some, the joke went on too long. 'Rameau's ballet would now be very boring and very ridiculous,' wrote the *Constitutionnel,* and 'it is hard to see how the public was expected to be amused by a ballet of this kind. Our dancers, who can dance so well, did their best to dance badly.'[33] The old days, however, did not lack a champion. 'Mlles Sallé and Camargo did not dance as awkwardly as that,' Castil-Blaze pointed out in the *Journal des débats.* 'We have with us learned men such as M. Gardel, who have seen dancers of this style performing on the stage, and could furnish accurate particulars on the subject.'[34] But Gardel's word counted for little now he had retired. Aumer, who was only fifteen when the Revolution broke out, had grown to manhood in the more Spartan 1790s.

Although, arguably, not the obvious choice for the rôle of Manon, Pauline

Montessu gave an energetic portrayal. In the last scene she seemed particularly inspired, and it was suggested that she had taken the English style of acting as her model, but without its exaggerated gestures. If this was true, she had probably been influenced by the English company, headed by Edward Kean and Charles Kemble, that had presented a season of Shakespeare in Paris some two years earlier. She was well matched by Ferdinand, who no less energetically mimed the rôle of Des Grieux. The *Courrier des théâtres* thought that his interpretation might have been improved by being toned down a little, but Hippolyte Prévost in the *Moniteur* paid him a compliment that any dancer might have given his soul for: that he acted 'with an expression, a naturalness and an impetus that would have made Dauberval and Vestris weep with emotion and joy'.[35]

Marie Taglioni was for once cast in a secondary rôle, appearing only in the last act as the creole girl Niuka, for which at the first performance she was covered with such dark make-up as to make her almost unrecognisable – a failure promptly put right by an order from the Director 'not to darken her face in future'.[36] By the terms of her contract, the one *pas* she danced in this act had to be arranged by her father, who produced what the *Constitutionnel*, which was very much in the Taglioni camp, praised as the best thing in the ballet. *Figaro*, on the other hand, described it as 'a run-of-the-mill *pas* completely lacking in local colour, and inappropriate' in the setting of the ballet,[37] while the *Courrier des théâtres*, in whose columns Lise Noblet could count on fulsome praise, also complained of its lack of character, describing it as being

> composed of all those *temps de cuisse, pointes* and *ronds de jambe* that, up to now, [her father] has inserted into everything he has done, both in the *genre noble* and in the *genre villageois*. In short, it is an exact repetition of all that Mlle Taglioni has been doing ever since she arrived, and that, you will agree, is either a very skilful or a very ridiculous thing for a mulatto to do. The public is becoming tired of always seeing the same steps, and is now leaving the task of approving them to the claque: the *decrescendo* was noticeable.[38]

Amélie Legallois managed to make something of the small rôle of Camargo, even if, as the *Courrier des théâtres* put it, 'she had to bring all her charm into play in order to look attractive beneath the theatrical paraphernalia of the time of Louis XV'.[39] No doubt her admirers would have preferred to see her as Manon, a part that might have suited her well, for, like Manon, she seemed in her private life quite literally to exercise a fatal attraction over her lovers. After being the mistress of the Duc de Berry, she had accepted the protection of the Marquis de Lauriston, formerly Minister of Louis XVIII's Household, who in June 1828 had the misfortune to suffer a stroke in her apartment that carried him off. Announcing his demise the next day, the *Moniteur* – with a rare touch of humour, unless it was unintended – reported that he had 'died in the arms of religion', and from that moment on, Legallois was jokingly referred to in the little world of the Opéra as 'Mlle Réligion'. Rumour also had it that another of her admirers was killed in a duel, defending her reputation, and that no fewer than three men had committed suicide for her – one of them a young man by the name of Villette whom she found one evening, on returning home after a performance, lying dead on the floor of her apartment with a bullet in his brain.

Manon Lescaut was the last ballet to be produced by Jean Aumer. Reproached by some of his colleagues for accepting the collaboration of a scenarist, he was said to have come to regret this new departure when he found he was no longer allowed to arrange ballets to scenarios of his own choice or devising. Frustration and wounded pride, added to the effort of contending against intrigues, led him to offer his resignation in the spring of 1831, a decision that caused him great distress. He retired to the village of Saint-Martin-en-Bosc in Normandy, where he lived out the few years that were left to him, comforted by the attentions of his family and friends, and sustained by the hope that his services might still be required. But the awaited summons never came, and in July 1833 he died, disappointed, from the effects of a stroke.

NOTES

1. How they arrived almost on the heels of Gérard is not explained in the scenario. This seems a strange lapse for the punctilious Scribe to let pass.
2. *Journal des débats*, 29 April 1829.
3. *Courrier des théâtres*, 29 April 1829.
4. *Courrier des théâtres*, 3 May 1829.
5. *Moniteur*, 28 April 1828.
6. Arch. Nat., O³ 1691. La Rochefoucauld to Comte de La Labouillerie, 21 June 1830. Contant was appointed chief machinist on 1 January 1829.
7. *Morning Post*, 14 February 1833, in a review of Anatole's version of Aumer's ballet given at the Theatre Royal, Drury Lane, the evening before. The critic, who had seen Aumer's production at the Opéra, was disappointed that in London the boat remained stationary.
8. Castil-Blaze, *Académie*, II, 210.
9. *Corsaire*. 28 April 1829.
10. *Journal des débats*, 29 April 1829.
11. It was inaccurately announced as the 905th performance. Last performed on 10 April 1829, *Psyché* was given in all 564 times at the Opéra, a figure that has so far been exceeded only by *Coppélia* and *Giselle*.
12. *Courrier des théâtres*, 10 and 14 November 1840. The *pochette*, or kit as it was known in England, was the miniature violin that was part of a dancing-master's professional equipment in the eighteenth and early nineteenth centuries.

13. *Courrier des théâtres*, 16 September 1829.

14. *Journal des débats*, 6 September 1829.

15. *Courrier des théâtres*, 30 October 1829.

16. *Courrier des théâtres*, 14 February 1830. Rameau's opera-ballet *Les Indes galantes* is a prime example of rococo, a style much out of favour in 1830.

17. *Courrier des théâtres*, 11 June 1830.

18. Arch. Nat., O[3] 1691. Lubbert to La Rochefoucauld, 8 May 1830.

19. Arch. Nat., O[3] 1683. Lubbert to La Rochefoucauld, 14 January 1829: the latter's reply (draft), 17 January 1829.

20. Arch. Nat., O[3] 1683. La Rochefoucauld to Taglioni (draft), 1 April 1829.

21. Arch. Nat., O[3] 1691. Lubbert to La Rochefoucauld, 8 May 1830.

22. Arch. Nat., O[3] 1691. Lubbert to the Royal Household office, 1 November 1830.

23. Arch. Nat., AJ[13] 135. Contant continued to assist Gromaire until February 1832, when he took over as sole chief machinist. He held the post until 1849.

24. *Court Journal*, 16 January 1830.

25. *Courrier des théâtres*, 14 January 1830.

26. In 1733, the year of the novel's first publication, the Opéra was situated in the east wing of the Palais Royal.

27. This is strictly a geographical error, for there is, of course, no desert to the north of New Orleans, but an equally inhospitable stretch of land known as the *bayou*.

28. *Moniteur*, 5 May 1830.

29. *Constitutionnel*, 5 May 1830.

31. Bibl.-Mus.de l'Opéra, 2071[II]. Extract from Meyerbeer's diary, 12 January 1831.

32. *Figaro*, 5 May 1830.

33. *Constitutionnel*, 5 May 1830.

34. *Journal des débats*, 5 May 1830.

35. *Moniteur*, 5 May 1830.

36. Arch. Nat., AJ[13] 1040.

37. *Figaro*, 5 May 1830.

38. *Courrier des théâtres*, 5 May 1830.

39. *Courrier des théâtres*, 5 May 1830.

10

The Porte-Saint-Martin: an Alternative Arena

As the 1820s progressed, the theatre-going public of Paris became increasingly aware of another arena in which the dance held sway: the large unsubsidised theatre on the outer boulevards, known as the Porte-Saint-Martin, after the great triumphal arch erected by Louis XIV just a stone's throw away to mark one of the northern entrances into the city. It had been erected to house the Opéra after its theatre in the Palais Royal was destroyed by fire in 1781, and five of the greatest ballets produced by the Gardel brothers had been created on its stage: Maximilien's *Le Premier Navigateur* and *Le Déserteur*, and Pierre's *Télémaque*, *Psyché* and *Le Jugement de Pâris*. It had remained the Opéra's home until August 1793, when the Committee of Public Safety requisitioned Mme de Montansier's newer and more centrally located theatre in the Rue de Richelieu and assigned it for the Opéra's use.

The Porte-Saint-Martin then reverted to private enterprise, and, after a chequered start during the Napoleonic period, ballet had featured prominently in its programmes, providing a forum for a succession of notable choreographers: Jean Aumer, Louis Duport, Louis Henry, Frédéric Blache and, from 1825, Jean Coralli. By the late 1820s, on the strength of a succession of ballets by Coralli, it might have seemed that the Porte-Saint-Martin was on its way to establishing a considerable reputation in the field of dance, appealing to a wider segment of society than frequented the Opéra.

That, however, was not to be. Shortly before the Revolution of 1830 its ballet company was disbanded. However, the efforts of those years were not to be entirely in vain, for three of the leading lights of its ballet company were to be offered engagements by the Opéra. For each this would mark a turning point in his career. Coralli would be appointed ballet-master, to preside over the ballet at the Opéra until his retirement in 1850 and to stage several master-works, most notably *Le Diable boiteux*, *Giselle* (in association with Perrot) and *La Péri*. Mazilier was given an engagement as principal dancer, but his major legacy would be as the choreographer of such works as *La Gipsy*, *Le Diable amoureux* and *Le Corsaire*. The third and youngest of the trio was Jules Perrot, who within a year was appointed star male dancer but would soon depart to embark on an international career as a choreographer, mainly in London and St Petersburg, but twice returning briefly to the Opéra: first, in 1841, to stage anonymously the greater part of the rôle of Giselle, and again, eight years later, to produce Carlotta Grisi's last Paris creation, *La Filleule des fées*.

The engagement of these three men made up the great windfall that the Opéra gathered in the early 1830s, and effectively laid the foundations of the brilliant revival of the Paris ballet in the age of Romanticism. To this list another name might be added – that of the most prolific playwright of the day, Eugène Scribe, who began his association with the ballet by working with Coralli anonymously at the Porte-Saint-Martin.

* * * * * * *

The story of the Porte-Saint-Martin's contribution to the history of ballet must begin at the beginning. When the Opéra took possession of Mme de Montansier's theatre in the Rue de Richelieu in 1794, the theatre by the Porte-Saint-Martin that it vacated was not immediately disposed of, but was used by the Opéra for some years as a scenery store and workshop. It was eventually sold in 1799, to be reopened three years later as a commercially managed playhouse, only to be closed again in 1807. In that brief period of five years, it established a modest reputation as an alternative venue for the dance by presenting a series of ballets by Dauberval, staged by the master's former pupil, Jean Aumer, who was then one of the principal male dancers of the Opéra. Among these ballets were *La Fille mal gardée* and *Le Page inconstant*, the latter an adaptation in mime and dance of Beaumarchais's comedy, *Le Mariage de Figaro*. While there appears to be no evidence that Dauberval was consulted by Aumer during the staging of these revivals, it is known that he made regular visits to Paris to keep in touch with his professional friends; and since Aumer was the most distinguished of his former pupils, it seems reasonable to assume that his old master would at least have been invited to see and comment upon the revivals.

In 1806 Aumer produced two ballets of his own – *Jenny*, a sentimental drama performed in pantomime, with dances, and *Les Deux Créoles*, a ballet based on the popular novel, *Paul et Virginie*, but given another title to avoid confusion with the ballet Gardel was preparing for the Opéra on the same theme. But now, belatedly, the Opéra, which had been casting a blind eye on Aumer's activities for another theatre, took a more aggressive stance. Faced with making a choice as to which master to serve, Aumer severed his connection with the Porte-Saint-Martin and returned to the Opéra on the understanding that he would produce a major ballet on a tragic historical theme, *Les Amours d'Antoine et de Cléopâtre*. For him this proved a wise choice, for not long afterwards the Porte-Saint-Martin fell victim to Napoleon's draconian reduction in the number of the city's theatres.

Ignoring a brief period from 1810 to 1812, when it was permitted to open for gymnastic displays, the Porte-Saint-Martin remained closed until after

Napoleon's first abdication. It reopened in December 1814 with a *privilège* granted by Louis XVIII, and survived the 'hundred days' of Napoleon's return. A new management under Alexandre de Saint-Romain then restored ballet to its former place in its programming, and a respectable, if small, company of dancers was engaged. By comparison with the Opéra, its ballets were modest productions, the ranks of the dancers being augmented by actors, who played rôles that depended purely on pantomime in order to support the fiction that such works were basically pantomimes, as opposed to *ballets d'action*, which lay within the province of the Opéra. On this basis it presented from the beginning, and without objection, ballets by experienced choreographers, the first of whom was Louis Duport. After producing a modest work entitled *Les Six Ingénues*, he was followed by a ballet-master with a name later to be made famous by his sons: Jean Petipa, who staged a rousing ballet on a Spanish theme, *Les Bergers de la Sierra Morena*. The following year, 1816, Louis Henry – an Opéra-trained dancer-choreographer, who had slipped out of France in disguise to continue his career in Italy – returned with his wife, Marie Quériau, to stage four ballets in eight months, including a ground-breaking, if not entirely successful, adaptation of Shakespeare's *Hamlet* and a ballet on the biblical theme of Samson and Delilah.

To succeed Henry, the Porte-Saint-Martin then engaged a ballet-master with a provincial reputation, Frédéric Blache, who staged a long sequence of ballets composed in Bordeaux by his celebrated father, Jean-Baptiste Blache. These were tried successes, and three of them – *La Chaste Suzanne* (another work with an Old Testament theme), *Almaviva et Rosina* (a version of Beaumarchais's *Le Barbier de Séville*, and not to be confused with Duport's ballet *Figaro*) and *La Fille soldat* – had satisfyingly long runs.

Early in 1822 Blache's relations with the Porte-Saint-Martin were to be soured when he discovered that the management was in negotiation with Louis Henry. In the spring of 1822, Henry had let it be known that he and his wife and muse, Marie Quériau, would be available for a summer season in Paris. The management of the Porte-Saint-Martin, apparently without thought for Blache's feelings, lost no time in coming to terms. Six years had passed since Henry was last in Paris, but the stir then caused by his *Hamlet* was still remembered. This time he looked for inspiration, not to Shakespeare, several of whose plays he had adapted in Italy as ballets,[1] but to a French dramatist, Antoine-Marin Lemierre, whose *La Veuve de Malabar* had long been a pillar of the repertory of the Comédie-Française. The Paris production of *Le Sacrifice indien* – the play's subtitle, which Henry had chosen for his ballet – was not strictly speaking a creation, since it had already been produced at the San Carlo in Naples.[2] While the ballet did not claim to be based on a historical episode, its hero was a character in Portuguese history: Afonso de Albuquerque, the coloniser of Goa and Malacca in the early sixteenth century. Henry's ballet opened with a stirring set-piece battle scene between the Portuguese and the Indians, which was followed by a mime scene in which the Rajah receives Albuquerque to celebrate the cessation of hostilities. To everyone's dismay the Rajah dies from a sudden seizure. According to the Indian tradition of suttee, his widow had to be incinerated alongside her husband, a situation that led into a dramatic mime scene for Marie Quériau as the widow Lanassa that was thus described in Henry's synopsis:

> The Brahmins allow Lanassa a few moments to offer up a prayer so that she will enter the next life worthy of her god's forgiveness. Her handmaidens deck her with precious jewels and crown her with flowers.

> The unfortunate woman tries in vain to stifle her maternal feelings, but they are too strong. She begs to be allowed to see her children, and, clutching them to her breast, cannot bear to be separated from them. But the sight of the Brahmins, who are to accompany her to the pyre, restores her courage, and she consigns the children to their care. The effort triumphs over her maternal feelings, but the spirit of her husband materialises before her, reproving her for want of courage. She begs his forgiveness, pointing to her children, but the stern shade is inexorable; and becoming more and more delirious, she tears herself from the embraces of her offspring in the hope of appeasing the ghostly figure. She then leaves with the Brahmins.

The need for the royal theatres such as the Opéra to be protected against undue competition from the popular, unsubsidised stage was still official policy, and in some circles Henry's arrival at the Porte-Saint-Martin had been seen as a potential threat. No one was now seriously objecting to the Porte-Saint-Martin presenting ballet, but exactly what kinds of ballet were permissible had not been precisely defined. The Opéra had regarded the engagement of Henry with some concern, fearing that advantage might be taken if a ballet were to fall in the no-man's-land between the *ballet d'action*, which the Opéra saw as its sole preserve, and the *pantomime mêlée de danses*, which was accepted as falling within the preserve of the Porte-Saint-Martin. The question was where to draw the line, and rumour had it that drastic last-minute amendments had to be made to the synopsis of *Le Sacrifice indien*. Whether these were very substantial may be doubted; for according to report, they were attended to in the course of a single day.[3]

Happily, Louis Henry was a fast worker, helped by the facts that mime was the predominant element in his ballets and that he and his wife played the leading rôles. In *Le Sacrifice indien* the only rôle of any significance was that of the Rajah, who is disposed of halfway through. This applied also to his second offering, *Agnès et Fitz-Henri*, a sentimental two-act pantomime, newly composed for Paris. In it Henry and Marie Quériau played the two leading rôles of father and daughter, the latter having run away with her lover many years before. After a long interval of separation she now returns to find that her father has lost his mind, and is under the delusion that he has killed her abductor in a duel and that she is dead too. The restoration of his sanity and the eventual family reconciliation provided Henry and his wife with opportunities as father and daughter. The dance scenes were purely incidental: a dream scene at the beginning, in which the father has a vision of the spirit of his long-lost daughter appearing to him through a mist; and later in the piece, a peasant *pas de trois* danced by Télémaque, Louise Pierson and Nanine Nara. This sentimental plot produced no problems with the censor, who 'did not bother to turn the piece inside-out and force the author, as had happened with *Le Sacrifice indien*, to recast three-quarters of the action on the day before the first performance'.[4]

Henry's third offering for the Porte-Saint-Martin that summer was the pantomime *La Fortune vient en dormant*, which included a tournament scene and a colourful masked ball, introducing a variety of brief character sketches and bizarre apparitions such as heads walking with no visible body, a man progressing with his legs in the air, and a spectacular finale – invented by Henry and the machinist, Poulet – showing Fortune in the person of a pretty girl balancing on tip-toe on top of a spinning golden ball.

The Henrys left Paris in October, leaving the Porte-Saint-Martin bereft of a ballet-master – for Frédéric Blache, out of pique, had meanwhile submitted his resignation. Jean-Baptiste Hullin had been approached with a view to taking his place, but, luckily for Blache, had not responded by the time the latter realised he had been hasty and withdrew his resignation. Blache was to remain at the Porte-Saint-Martin until 1825. He produced little in that time that could be described as noteworthy, apart from a pantomime based on a historical theme, *Milon de Crotone*, inspired by a celebrated wrestler of classical times. Much of his later work for the Porte-Saint-Martin was directed towards presenting the extraordinary comic dancer Charles Mazurier, culminating in the dances and antics he devised for the rôle of the monkey Jocko in the melodrama of that name. In 1825, when presumably his contractual term expired, Blache departed, to be succeeded by a choreographer of a very different standing, Jean Coralli.

Coralli was Italian by extraction, but he had been born in Paris in 1779 and brought up there. According to the brief account of his life that he gave to Saint-Léon, he had been a pupil of the Opéra's School of Dance under Jacques-François Deshayes. He and his wife had returned to make a joint début in 1802, but there was apparently no question of their seeking an engagement. According to his account, he had begun his choreographic career as early as 1800 in Vienna, and by the time of his return to Paris in the 1820s he could point to an impressive tally of ballets, produced not only in Vienna, but also in Milan, Lisbon and Marseilles.

On his arrival in Paris, Coralli probably lost no time in submitting two scenarios for consideration by the Opéra's Reading Committee. Both were considered at the same meeting, on 23 April 1823: one, *Lisbell*, being rejected by 10 votes to 4, and the other, *Paul et Rosette*, accepted by a similar majority. Acceptance, however, did not of itself guarantee that it would be produced, and Coralli may have withdrawn the latter scenario when he was engaged at the Porte-Saint-Martin two years later.

At the Porte-Saint-Martin Coralli found an experienced company already installed, headed by several excellent soloists: Zélie Molard, Louise Pierson and Florentine Conard[5] among the women, and in the male ranks, Alexis, who had a fine classical technique, Moëssard and the sensationally double-jointed Charles Mazurier.

There had also been an interesting addition to the male ranks, Joseph Mazilier, whose career was to run parallel to Coralli's own, a talented male dancer with a restrained classical style and a flair for characterisation, who in time would develop a remarkable gift as a choreographer.

Coralli's first production for the Porte-Saint-Martin was a 'pantomime interspersed with dances,' *Lisbell, ou la novelle Claudine*, which he had formerly submitted unsuccessfully to the Reading Jury of the Opéra, and which was now to be created at the Porte-Saint-Martin on 8 September 1825. Its plot was lightly based on *Claudine*, a well-known novel by Florian, which not long before had been turned into a comedy by Pigault-Lebrun and produced at the Porte-Saint-Martin. The ballet's hero, Henri (Mazilier) has long been in love with Lisbell (Volet), whom he has married secretly and by whom, unknown to his family, he now has a son. Meanwhile, Lisbell's mother, also unaware of this, has promised her to a rich farmer's son, Fritz (Mazurier). To his dismay, Henri now learns that his father has plans for him to marry. Lisbell learns of this in such a way as to make her believe she has been rejected. In her frenzy, she is about to throw herself into a river, when a violent storm breaks and the cottage where the child has been placed is struck by lightning. Lisbell takes flight with her child, causing her mother to believe that both have been drowned. Meanwhile, Henri's father has found a rich widow (Zélie Molard) for his son, and Henri, in the belief that he has lost Lisbell, raises no objection. Lisbell, however, then reappears disguised as a boy, seeking employment, and the widow is so touched that she engages her as a servant. However, while perusing Henri's sketchbook, the widow's suspicions are aroused by a portrait of Lisbell; confronting Henri, she learns the whole story. Happily the widow is possessed of such a generous nature that she not only reunites the couple, but effectively intercedes with the father, who forgives his son and accepts Lisbell as his daughter-in-law.

Coralli's first production for the Porte-Saint-Martin had no pretension to being anything more than a lightweight ballet-pantomime, but it was nonetheless appreciated for being carefully and skilfully arranged, notwithstanding a somewhat colourless interpretation of the title-rôle by Mlle Volet. Happily this was counter-balanced by a comic part, introduced for the dancer-acrobat Mazurier, of a suitor for Lisbell's hand who in spectacular fashion falls out of a tree while spying on her tryst with Henri, and later, in his attempt to hide in a cornfield, finds himself battered by flails. Later, he enters the burning cottage in an attempt to rescue Lisbell, only to escape by means of an extraordinary fall such as only he could accomplish without injury, throwing himself into the river to douse the flames.

In its programme policy, the Porte-Saint-Martin was unconcerned with building a repertory, and Coralli was soon at work on a new ballet. For this he had devised a simple plot, which one critic was bold enough to place in the same category as Dauberval's *La Fille mal gardée*. Entitled *Les Ruses espagnoles* and presented on 24 November 1825, its plot centred around two young lovers, Carlos (Mazilier) and Sylva (Florentine), and the latter's mother, who disapproves of her daughter's choice of sweetheart. The mother is in debt to her landlord, whose rascally agent conceives a passion for the daughter and, for his own ends, locks up the lovers in separate cells. However, Carlos manages to escape and frees Sylva, persuading the mother to take her daughter's place. The agent then slips into the cell, expecting Sylva to be there at his mercy, but instead, when Carlos throws open the cell in the presence of the landlord, it is the agent who finds himself caught in a compromising situation with her mother.

It was a slight piece, 'very skilfully filled' with delightful touches of humour, and including a reference to *La Fille mal gardée* in the opening scene when Carlos enters Sylva's home concealed in a sack amid a delivery of corn. Mazilier and Florentine played the lovers, Ciceri contributed a new set for the second act, and the music, composed by a recent graduate of the Ecole Royale de Musique, Alexandre Pâris, gave general pleasure.

Once again Coralli received favourable notices, but he still had to make his mark, for which a challenging opportunity presented itself with his next offering. The choice of a Molière farce, *Monsieur de Pourceaugnac*, as the subject for this new ballet probably originated with the management of the theatre, for its primary motive was undoubtedly to provide a vehicle for the comic genius of Charles Mazurier, who was cast in the title-rôle.

Molière's piece, as presented in the time of Louis XIV, was a comedy with interludes of dancing, for which Lully had composed the music. Coralli's ballet was structured on an anonymous scenario that was acceptably faithful to the original but with Molière's dialogue replaced by pungently expressive pantomime. As described in the very explicit scenario on sale at the theatre, it was remarkably faithful to the original – the misadventures befalling the unfortunate provincial on his arrival in Paris as the heroine's prospective husband, being recounted in some splendid knock-about pantomime. After being delivered to the mercy of doctors and apothecaries, the unwelcome provincial is faced with a string of women claiming he has fathered their children. Finally, to escape from predicaments that his simple mind can barely comprehend, he disguises himself as a woman – with further unwelcome consequences – before all is explained and the lovers are united.

To judge from the critical reception, the transformation of the comedy into a pantomime farce was a complete success. This was borne out by the number of performances it received before being taken off – no fewer than thirty-six, double the number achieved by each of Coralli's preceding ballets.

The critic of the *Courrier des spectacles* devoted two long notices to it on successive days. The first was in the nature of a general appreciation:

> To turn *Pourceaugnac* into a ballet, the plot had to be shortened so as to link the situations more closely, thus making up for what the spectator would be missing by placing greater emphasis on the burlesque and the spectacle. It was also necessary to retain and emphasise the comic aspect of the situations, which play such a powerful part in Molière's work. This M. Coralli has achieved with complete success. By fully understanding his source, he has successfully presented its main outlines, and shown much wit in translating into action what in the original were nothing more than divertissements. The dances are well introduced, and conceived with a variety and originality that reveal a master's touch. The divertissements, composed by the celebrated Lully when *Pourceaugnac* was performed before Louis XIV, and which the Théâtre Français, with a delicacy that is perhaps a trifle arrogant, has disdained to make use of in these saturnalian times, ... have thus been restored.

> The production is most meticulous... The task of setting the interludes of *Pourceaugnac* into dumb-show has been wonderfully carried out by M. Coralli... The brilliance of the spectacle, the period costumes, and Mazurier's antics will surely attract all Paris to see it.[6]

In this, as in Coralli's two earlier productions, the company was still adjusting to its new master, from whose sure touch they were now benefiting. Alexis and Mimi Dupuis, who played the parts of Sbrigani and Nérine, were given a roguish *pas de deux*, and Mazilier and Florentine as the two lovers, Eraste and Julie, with Mlle Volet, danced a *pas de trois* with a precision that would not have gone amiss at the Opéra. Furthermore, the ballet had been charmingly opened by a Mlle Louise, whom Coralli had plucked out of the *corps de ballet*, and who revealed a style that to knowledgeable observers might well have been fashioned in the School of Dance of the Opéra. All in all, it was a production of which the Porte-Saint-Martin could feel justifiably proud.

On the next day, the same critic made some illuminating observations on the production, and particularly on Mazurier's portrayal of Pourceaugnac. When he first came to the notice of the Paris public, this dancer had caused astonishment by 'the extraordinary strength, suppleness and agility of his limbs'. Then, as he took on rôles in such light comedy ballets as *Le Déserteur* and *Les Meuniers*, he had begun to reveal a highly original gift for comedy, and his reputation had soared sensationally when he appeared as the monkey in *Jocko*. Now, with Pourceaugnac, he was given another major comic rôle, in which he had to replace the dialogue of Molière – a challenge that he overcame, in the words of one critic,

> like a true actor, with a gaiety and wit that held the public throughout in a state of delight. Our only criticism was that in some scenes he gave Pourceaugnac a little of the foolishness of the *grand cousin* instead of the ridiculous self-importance of a fool who is rich, over-dressed and inordinately proud of his status as a gentleman.[7]

Mazurier's performance was inimitable, touched by his personal genius. A lesser artist than he might have aroused derision and protests by the antics he introduced, but coming from him, they were accepted by a delighted public that for the most part was disturbed by no thoughts of literary sacrilege. The critic of the theatrical journal, *Le Corsaire*, was unstinting in his praise:

> Molière had already conceived many comic tribulations to befall the Limousin [i.e. Pourceaugnac], providing [Mazurier] with many opportunities to test his skill, but the authors of the pantomime have gone even further than Molière, and if not all the stunts they give to [Pourceaugnac] to perform are in the best of taste, they are justified in the context, and particularly at Carnival time. It was impossible for Mazurier not to arouse laughter as the Limousin, for he had already given proof of his skill... but the task was made doubly difficult in that it could not be

separated from the comedy, and even though translated into pantomime, it still had to be faithful to M. Molière. Mazurier proved himself as an actor, and, while remaining close to the text, he was still recognisable as the clown and the simpleton of the Boulevard. Thanks to the originality of his acting, the pantomime was a complete success, and although a little on the long side, it amused the audience throughout, notwithstanding the proverb that has it that the best jokes are the short ones.[8]

From beginning to end there was never a dull moment. One highlight was a scene in which a band of young student-apothecaries scrambled up from the stage to the second tier of boxes. In the supporting rôle of the doctor, Moëssard put on an air of splendid gravity. And as an after-piece to the ballet – a *bonne-bouche*, one might say – Mazurier and another dancer, Dumas, dressed as athletes to give a hilarious parody of a wrestling act, 'Les Alcides', which had been recently seen at the Porte-Saint-Martin.

Coralli's next assignment, a slight two-act ballet-farce entitled *Gulliver*, first presented on 9 May 1826, was again planned unashamedly as a vehicle for Mazurier's acrobatic genius. Inspired by Jonathan Swift's classic novel, the first act opened with a scene showing the preparations for one of Gulliver's travels, and ended with his ship finally disappearing over the horizon. This was but a prelude to the second act, in which Gulliver and Laboussole land in a storm with a dozen Lilliputians, and realise to their horror that they are in the Land of Giants. While Gulliver goes to scout out the land and seek food, Laboussole has a series of adventures with a family of giants. Terrified by a giant turkey, he hides while the giants set out on their daily toil and their lunch is prepared, only to slip and tumble into a gigantic bowl of soup. After this, he finds himself hoisted up a tree-trunk in a cage, where he is eventually rescued by Gulliver. The giants, however, prove to be peaceful creatures, and the ballet ends with a general dance.

A group of children was used to represent the Lilliputians whom Gulliver has brought with him. He hides them under a gargantuan cabbage to prevent them from being eaten by the giants. Among the concluding dances was a number performed on stilts by Mazurier and two women representing giantesses. The ballet also contained a delightful *pas de trois* that revealed Coralli's talent in the purely classical style.[9] Alexandre Piccini's music was dismissed by one critic as appalling, but the audiences found this inconsequential ballet entertaining enough for it to survive into the following year.

Jean Coralli was now to embark on a new phase of his career, in which his name was to be associated with the most prolific of living playwrights, Eugène Scribe. Seldom did a day go by in Paris without a comedy or vaudeville by Scribe being performed on some stage or other; but so far he had not turned his talents to writing for the opera or the ballet. However, the day was approaching when his mind would begin to turn to these new fields of activity, and his ambition in this direction may have been sparked, in part at least, by Coralli at the Porte-Saint-Martin. For in 1826 Jean Coralli began to prepare a ballet based on one of Scribe's most popular one-act comedies, written for the Théâtre de la Vaudeville eight years before.[10] Since Coralli's ballet was to be presented under the same title, *La Visite à Bedlam*, with the same characters and – in broad outline – the same plot, there can be little doubt that the playwright's consent, if not his active collaboration, was obtained in the process of adapting the piece for a ballet.

The final result was first shown to the public on 19 September 1826. It followed Scribe's comedy closely, with such amendments and dance insertions as were necessary to present the action in pantomime. The scene is set in England, close to the asylum of Bedlam. The Baron de St-Elme (Moëssard), the owner of a nearby property, is planning a fête to cheer the spirits of his niece Amélie (Zélie Paul), who believes she has been deserted by her husband. An eccentric Italian dancing master, Gavottino (Mazurier), has been engaged to produce a ballet for this occasion. Alfred, the husband (Mazilier), then turns up, and the Baron, who has not met him before, conceives the idea of teaching him a lesson by making him believe he is in Bedlam. Amélie plays her part in appearing as an inmate who has lost her reason, and Albert, coming upon her in the moonlight, realises who she is. She, however, pretends not to recognise him, while speaking lovingly of her husband – remembering, among other things, how well he waltzed. Albert eventually realises he is being duped, and, to have his own back, pretends so successfully to be mad himself that Amélie is convinced that he has remained true to her.

The only substantial change in the adaptation of the play into a ballet was to transform Scribe's character of the musician Crescendo into the puffed-up Italian dancing-master, Gavottino. This provided an excuse for a divertissement in the first act. While this seemed a little over-long, it fulfilled its purpose by giving Mazurier time to give a hilarious impression of the English actor Cooke, who was then playing Frankenstein's monster in the melodrama *Le Monstre et le Magicien*.[11] The cast clearly enjoyed themselves in playing at being lunatics. Even the normally restrained Mazilier unwound a little in the final scene, when he had to feign madness himself, while Zélie Paul – the former Mlle Molard, who had married Paul, an actor of the Gymnase – made such an impression as Amélie as to be hailed by the *Corsaire* as 'a choreographic treasure'.[12] With Mazurier's participation, the ballet could not fail to draw the public; but once again its musical accompaniment – by Alexandre Piccini – was found wanting.

Coralli's association with Scribe progressed a stage further with his next ballet for the Porte-Saint-Martin, *Le Mariage de raison*, a straightforward adaptation of a play, *Bertrand et Suzette*, which had been presented at the Gaîté-Dramatique only five months before and was still being performed.[13]

Its plot was therefore already familiar to many in the audience. Suzette (Zélie Paul), the ward of a widowed General, has two admirers: the General's rake of a son, Edouard, and Bernard, a former soldier with a wooden leg, who is now in the General's service. Bernard worships her from afar, but the rakish Edouard is paying court to her. Suzette is so infatuated with Edouard that she hardly pays attention when the worthy Bernard summons up courage to declare his love. He has confided this to his friends, the Pinchons, who are well aware of Edouard's dalliance with women. And, indeed, Edouard still has designs on Suzette's virtue, as his father is quick to perceive. When upbraided, Edouard feigns contrition, but Suzette realises that he will never mend his ways. To avoid trouble, she decides to leave the household. The General, however, will allow none of this, and proposes that she should marry. He is pondering over who might make a suitable husband for her when the Pinchons appear. Mme Pinchon speaks up boldly on Bernard's behalf. To the General this seems a heaven-sent solution; for not only will it prevent Suzanne from leaving and facing an uncertain future, but it might even put an end to his son's philandering. Suzette is at first hesitant, but eventually agrees. The engagement is announced, but it is clear that Edouard has not given up hope of seducing her. The marriage takes place, but Edouard sends her a note seeking a rendezvous, in which he threatens to kill himself if she rejects his advances. At this point Bernard, aware that she does not love him, hands her the key to her bedroom until such time as she willingly gives it back. Edouard continues to press her, and makes one last attempt to persuade her. But he is forced to hide when Mme Pinchon turns up and tells Suzette that Edouard had made similar approaches to her. Edouard, however, now finds himself disgraced for failing to appear at a duel in which he was the challenger, and Suzette, realising at last her husband's true worth, hands him back the key.

The ballet was presented on 3 February 1827, less than four months after the play's première. The critic of *Figaro*, who gave it notices on two consecutive days, called it 'a complete and well-deserved success'[14] – which was praise indeed, seeing that the play must have been familiar to a fair proportion of the audience. Coralli, this critic continued, had omitted none of the original's principal features, including, in particular, the society ball that opened it and the village dance that concluded it. It was, of course, in these two sections that the dances were inserted. As a result, the pantomime element was more or less continuous and afforded excellent opportunities for

Zélie Paul's warm personality to come across in her sympathetic portrayal of Suzette, for Pierson to give a rounded portrayal of Bernard, and for Mimi Dupuis to reveal a remarkable gift for character rôles in the part of the chattering Mme Pinchon. In this way the company as a whole was developing a cohesion and a sense of ensemble that was fast gaining the respect of the public. Both Coralli and the often-denigrated Piccini received a warm round of applause at the close, and the ballet was to continue to entertain the audiences of the Porte-Saint-Martin until the time came for Coralli to present another novelty.

For a change, the plot of Coralli's next offering for the Porte-Saint-Martin was inspired by an *opéra-comique* by Auber, *La Neige*.[15] This was still in the repertory of the Opéra-Comique with more than 60 performances to its credit when Coralli's ballet was first given on 6 October 1827. Although the opera's libretto was clearly the starting point for the adaptation, the plot of the ballet diverged from it considerably. The heroine, Emma (Zélie Paul), marries her sweetheart Edgard (Mazilier) in secret. She is the daughter of the reigning Duc d'Erfeld, who in a recent battle has decisively defeated the Prince de Lynbourg. Hostilities have now ceased, and such goodwill now reigns that the defeated prince requests Emma's hand in marriage. Emma's father, unaware of the secret marriage, is keen to give his consent and plans a great festival to mark the conclusion of peace. The two lovers decide to flee, but a heavy snowstorm results in their plans being discovered. Emma feels forced to reveal the secret of the marriage. At first her father is beside himself with fury, but he eventually comes round to accepting the situation. The union of the young couple is then confirmed, and the ballet closes with general celebrations.

In presenting this story, a generous place had been found to display the extraordinary antics of Mazurier, which to many seemed to approach the very margins of what was humanly possible. For this a sub-plot had been devised to capitalise upon that dancer's comic genius. It was built around Mazurier's rôle of Misko, Edgard's aide-de-camp, who is in love with Emma's lady-in-waiting, Catherine – a rôle deliciously played by the sprightly Mimi Dupuis. Mazurier was thus featured in all three acts, and in his scenario Coralli described in great detail the comic action, which he had undoubtedly worked out with Mazurier himself. In the first act, Misko and Catherine are witnesses at the secret wedding. This is followed by a scene in which he joins in the games of some village children, who ridicule him for his ineptitude in a game of skittles and rouse him to such a pitch of frustration that he overturns a pastry-cook's stand, catches his head in a window frame, and finally has to pay for the damage. In the second act, he suffers further tribulations. He is made to hide inside a grandfather clock, which he then finds he cannot open, and in order to eavesdrop on what is going on around him, he shuffles the clock over to the other side of the room, much to the puzzlement of Catherine when she returns. But the climax was reserved for the last act, which Coralli described in detail, although no words could have adequately described the brilliance of Mazurier's performance:

> Misko enters from the back of the stage, skidding in the wake of a mocking band of children, and in attempting to chase them away, takes a tumble. He gets to his feet, thinking what fun it must be to skate... except that he does not know how. A merchant produces a pair of skates and offers to give him a lesson. He accepts, and is offered a chair while the skates are put on. He raises his leg very high, and a skater, crouching low, passes under it. When his skates are attached, he gets to his feet and tries to keep his balance. But this he cannot manage, and he has to grab hold of a chair as a support. But the chair topples over and he falls; he then finds himself skidding along of his own volition, imitating the actions of a swimmer. The merchant manages to stop him, and puts him back on his feet. Ashamed at having fallen, Misko casts the chair aside to make another attempt to skate, and ends up by performing the most extraordinary feats. Enchanted, he returns to the back of the stage, sets off again, bent double, and in no time reaches the front of the stage. Unable to stop, he tumbles into the prompt box. Ashamed at this mishap, he takes off the skates and throws them at the merchant. The children jeer at him, and the angrier he becomes, the louder they laugh. He pelts them with snowballs, but they respond in kind, and unable to fend off their volleys, he breaks away and climbs into a tree. He is followed, but the branch breaks and he finds himself buried in the snow.[16]

In addition to including Mazurier's antics, the ballet was unusually rich in dances. Early in the first act, while waiting for the arrival of Emma and Edgard, Misko and Catherine perform a clog dance. At the end of that act there was more dancing: a general dance, then a *pas de deux* by Mlle Volet and M. Allard, followed by a Hungarian dance by Mazilier and Zélie Paul, and finally a *galopade* led by Mazurier and Mimi Dupuis. There was more dancing at the end of the third act, which featured a skating *pas de quatre* by four men, who may have worn those specially adapted roller-skates that Jean-Baptiste Blache had so bitterly claimed to be his own invention and which he had learnt had been offered to the Porte-Saint-Martin by a dancer recently engaged there from Bordeaux.[17]

La Neige was to prove the most frequently performed of Coralli's ballets at the Porte-Saint-Martin. There was no concealment of the debt to the authors of the *opéra-comique*, which suggests that the adaptation was done with the express agreement of both Scribe and Auber, whose music for the opera was the main source for the ballet's score, which was attributed to Chautagne and Ferrand.

Shortly before the end of Carnival, on 18 February 1828, Coralli presented an appropriately merry little ballet, *Les Hussards et les jeunes filles*. This was based, not on a play by Scribe, but on a short comedy entitled *Les Petites Pensionnaires*,[18] which had been produced nearly fifteen years before at a dark moment in the country's history, when Napoleon's armies were reeling back towards their homeland after the carnage of the Battle of Leipzig. However, no such melancholy association came to the audience's minds when the tale was recounted in pantomime and dance, for the slight plot was ideally suited to divert the public before the theatres closed for Lent.

It hinged on the predicament faced by a colonel of hussars on discovering that on the very day he had arranged to entertain some of his young officers on his estate, his wife had invited three girls. It has thus become necessary for the Colonel to find a means of keeping the young men away, and he hits upon the pretext of having them placed under arrest. The young men, however, ply their guard with liquor, and make their escape while he is sleeping it off. The ballet then develops into a romp, with much diverting by-play between the girls and the officers, who have come disguised as women. It is brought to a close when the sergeant, having come to his senses, enters to take his charges back to barracks, but the colonel is now in a forgiving mood and all ends happily.

It was a merry, inconsequential piece, ideal for the Carnival season, but entertaining enough to be retained when the theatres reopened. The dancers themselves entered into the jollity of the proceedings, notwithstanding that they were mourning their celebrated comrade, Charles Mazurier, who just two weeks before had succumbed to tuberculosis, for which there was then no known cure. Several of them had no doubt attended his burial, an event marred by the Church's refusal to grant him final absolution.

The precise spot where Mazurier's body was buried can no longer be identified with any precision, for he was interred in the common grave. But short though his career had been – it was little more than four years since his Paris début – he had left indelible memories to those who had performed alongside him. In that short space of time he had developed from being little more than an extraordinarily gifted acrobat into a comic artist of the rarest kind, thanks largely to one rôle, that of the monkey Jocko – a study so convincing and so touching that he had drawn many a tear in the scene of the poor animal's death. He was to prove truly inimitable, for he had no successor. As an admirer had written of him in his prime, 'he displayed such extraordinary agility that his limbs seemed made of elastic. He was particularly applauded for his fearsome splits and astonishing poses that convinced you that he possessed, uniquely, a conformation different from that of ordinary mortals.'[19]

* * * * * * *

Mazurier's death deprived Coralli of a comic dancer of true genius, but at the same time may have enabled him to achieve a truer balance in the presentation of his next ballet by toning down the farcical element. *Léocadie*, which was offered to the public on 9 June 1828, only four months after Mazurier was laid to rest, had the advantage of a stronger plot than any other of Coralli's previous offerings, and in particular presented Joseph Mazilier with a powerful rôle that would shortly stand him in good stead. In his original conception, Coralli may have conceived a part for Mazurier, for one critic noted that 'the author had inserted a comic character who injects much gaiety into the action'.[20]

Léocadie also marked a further stage in Coralli's association with Scribe, even if not yet formally acknowledged; for it was quite openly a balletic version of Auber's *opéra-comique* of the same name, for which Scribe, in collaboration with a colleague, Mélesville, had written the libretto, and which was still in the repertory of the Opéra-Comique.[21]

Whereas, in the opera, the incident on which the plot was based had already taken place when the first act opened and could be vocally described as a past event, in the ballet it was necessary to act it out. When the curtain first rises, therefore, a regiment is about to depart from a Spanish town, where it has been based for some time. During the farewell festivities, a veiled village girl, Léocadie (Zélie Paul), is ravished in a darkened room by one of the officers, Frédéric (Mazilier), who is under the mistaken impression that she is a certain flighty young woman of the town (Virginie Léon). Five years then pass, and Léocadie has become the mother of a child, who has been placed in the care of a foster-mother. The regiment then returns, and is giving a fête to celebrate Frédéric's engagement when the distraught foster-mother comes to seek help because Léocadie's little boy has fallen into the river. Fortunately, the child is rescued, but, to Léocadie's shame, her secret is now out. Her brother, Philippe (Moëssard), is shattered and upbraids her. In explaining her predicament, she shows him the portrait she had snatched from the wall of the darkened room of her dishonour, and he recognises the sitter to be the sister of a fellow officer, Fernand. Assuming Fernand to be the father, Philippe challenges him to a duel. Fernand, who is unaware of the true circumstances, is prepared to fight for the honour of his colonel, but a confrontation is averted when the latter, Frédéric, realises that he must be the father of the child. Filled with remorse, he now offers to make amends by marrying Léocadie, who overcomes her shame and accepts him.

Although somewhat convoluted, it was a neatly constructed plot, into which Coralli had inserted two ballet interludes, the first of which opened with a *pas de trois* featuring a new recruit to the ballet company, the seventeen-year-old Jules Perrot. This dancer's early successes at the Gymnase had been in the acrobatic genre of Mazurier, but now, under the guidance of Auguste Vestris, he was developing into a classical dancer of unusual promise. The ballet achieved success on its intrinsic merits. The *Courrier des théâtres* awarded it particular praise for 'the grace, good taste, and rare perfection of detail in the first act', while 'the interesting and pathetic scenes of the second would have ensured success even had it been announced under a less well-known title.'[22]

The music for this ballet, now long since disappeared, introduced themes from Auber's score for the opera, and was the product of two little-known composers. One of these was P.Q. Béancourt, who had written the score for the melodrama *Faust*, then in preparation at the Porte-Saint-Martin; the other was announced merely as Miller.[23]

The ballet was a triumph for all concerned, and was performed almost every evening until the end of the month. No doubt it would have run for much longer had not the necessity arisen of closing the theatre for several months to enable structural repairs to be carried out. For the dancers in particular, who were to be disbanded, this would result in financial hardship; and the actors of the theatre gave a dinner in honour of Coralli at Goupil's restaurant on the Boulevard du Temple, to which the administrator of the theatre was invited. At an appropriate moment Coralli made a request that the fines recently imposed on the performers be cancelled, to which that gentleman, by then mellow with good food and wine, was pleased to give his consent.

When the Porte-Saint-Martin reopened at the end of October, it was with a new work – a three-act melodrama, *Faust*, featuring Frédérick Lemaître and Marie Dorval. For this, Coralli arranged the ballet insertions, including a *pas des sylphides*, of which, tantalisingly, no detailed account appears to have survived. The ballet also featured Jules Perrot, who danced 'with a precision and strength of which note must be taken'.[24]

In January 1829 the Porte-Saint-Martin presented another full-length melodrama, *Rochester*, for which Coralli contributed an inserted ballet scene. With this task behind him, he turned his mind to preparing a two-act *ballet d'action*, *Les Artistes*. This work was closely based on yet another work by Scribe, a one-act vaudeville called *La Mansarde des artistes*, which had entered the repertory of the Gaîté in 1824 and was still being occasionally performed.

As the term 'vaudeville' implied, the play was interspersed with songs sung by the characters to a selection of melodies that would have been familiar to the audience. In transforming the action for a ballet, however, account had to be taken of the inadequacy of mime to achieve the skilful unravelling of the plot that led to the happy ending. So Coralli, whether or not he had Scribe at his elbow, had to devise a simpler *dénouement* that could be clearly understood by the audience. The vaudeville had told the story of three young bachelors – a painter, a musician and a very recently qualified doctor – who share a garret and find they have no money to clear the arrears of their rent. This predicament is resolved by an extraordinary coincidence, when a patient of the young doctor turns out to be the uncle of the girl with whom all three young men are in love.

In the transition from spoken dialogue to pantomime, one of the three young students – the budding doctor – had been converted into a budding choreographer, Armand (Mazilier). As in the play, the plot hinged on the students' difficulties in finding the money to pay their rent and avoid the pressing danger of being evicted by their landlord. They share their attic with an old soldier, César (Moëssard), who is down on his luck, and his pretty daughter Lucile, (Aimée Gautier), who cooks for them and generally looks after them. The students' dilemma is resolved by the felicitous appearance of the general under whom César had served. The landlord is locked up in a chest and the general has the students' belongings and furniture taken to his mansion, where the landlord is eventually released and the arrears of rent paid by the general.

The music for this ballet was 'arranged', as the title-page of the scenario made clear, by Alexandre Piccini, who may have interpolated some of the themes used for the songs in the play.[25] The ballet closed with a *divertissement* that included a *pas de trois* performed by the astonishing young virtuoso, Jules Perrot, with Florentine and Aimée Gautier; a Cossack dance by Etienne Laurençon[26] and Eulalie Roux; and a finale in which the entire company of dancers took part. In this closing *divertissement*, the song *'Garde à vous'* from Auber's opera *La Fiancée*, was very amusingly introduced.

The ballet was found pleasing in all its parts – even in its music, composed by the often maligned Piccini. A particular point of interest was the introduction, in the rôle of Lucile, of a new ballerina, Aimée Gautier, who was accounted 'a pleasing mime and a dancer of good schooling' and a credit to her celebrated teacher, Jean-Baptiste Barrez. But the laurels were mainly earned by the choreographer, Jean Coralli, who received a warm tribute in the pages of the *Courrier des spectacles*:

Considering the difficulties [involved in basing a ballet on a literary work], we have to recognise its merit. In the face of many obstacles, of which men of letters are unaware, the choreographer's triumph is all the more glorious for the obstacles he had to overcome. Here Coralli has shirked none of these difficulties. Indeed, it can be said that he has overcome them by his skill, both in the arrangement of the pantomime scenes and by his happy choice of melodies. In *Les Artistes* he always says what he has to say with clarity, and the action proceeds with gaiety and wit. This ballet is certainly one of minor importance to a man of such merit, but that is no reason not to recognise the good things in it.[27]

By the end of 1829, the status of ballet at the Porte-Saint-Martin had waned almost to insignificance. Coralli, Mazilier and Perrot had all departed, and in 1830 only a few light ballets – *La Fille mal gardée*, *Les Meuniers* and *Les Six Ingénues* – occasionally found a place on the bills. Not until the 1840s would the Porte-Saint-Martin resume its place as an alternative arena for dance, but it would never regain the prestige it had enjoyed under Coralli. For now it was the Opéra that would profit, not only by the disappearance of a competitive arena for the ballet, but more directly because Mazilier, Perrot and finally Coralli himself – three of the major choreographers of their time – were soon to be gathered under its roof to share in the splendid florescence of ballet that was to come.

NOTES

1. *Otello* (1808), *Romeo e Giulietta* (1814) and *Amleto* (1816). In 1830 he was to add a fourth, *Macbetto*. *Otello* and *Amleto* were created at the San Carlo, Naples; *Romeo* and *Macbetto* at La Scala, Milan. Pugni wrote the music for *Macbetto*, Gallenberg for the other three.
2. As *Il sacrificio indiano*, on 9 November 1819, to music by Carafa, which was presumably used for the Paris production.
3. *Journal des théâtres*, 15 and 23 July 1822.
4. *Journal des théâtres*, 23 July 1822.
5. She was born Florentine Dufour and was briefly in the *corps de ballet* of the Opéra (Arch. Nat., AJ[13] 126, II, 1820).
6. *Courrier des spectacles*, 29 January 1826.
7. *Courrier des théâtres*, 30 January 1826. The '*grand cousin*' was one of the principal characters in *Le Déserteur*, one of the most popular ballets from the end of the eighteenth century.
8. *Corsaire*, 29 January 1826.
9. *Courrier des théâtres*, 10 May 1826.
10. First performed there on 19 September 1826.
11. First performed at the Porte-Saint-Martin, 10 June 1826. Probably the actor was William Cooke. The rôle of Frankenstein's monster was a silent one.
12. *Corsaire*, 4 February 1827.
13. Comédie-vaudeville by Scribe and Varner, first performed on 10 October 1826.
14. *Figaro*, 4 February 1827.

15. *La Neige, ou le nouvel Eginhard*, opera-comique in four acts, music by Auber, libretto by Scribe and G. Delavigne, f.p. Opéra-Comique, 8 October 1823.

16. Coralli, *La Neige*, 16–17.

17. See p.101.

18. *Les Petites Pensionnaires, ou les Jeunes Filles en vacances*, comedy in one act by Merle and Brazier, f.p. Th. des Variétés, 2 November 1813.

19. Van Aelbrouck, 181, quoting from the Brussels periodical, *L'Aristarque des spectacles*.

20. *Courrier des spectacles*, 10 June 1828.

21. *Léocadie*, lyric drama in three acts, music by Auber, libretto by Scribe and Mélesville, f.p. at the Opéra-Comique on 4 November 1824. Its plot was based on the novel, *La Fuerza de la sangre*, by Miguel de Cervantes.

22. *Courrier des théâtres*, 10 June 1828.

23. This was surely not Marie Gardel's father, who wrote the music for several of Gardel's ballets at the beginning of the century.

24. *Courrier des spectacles*, 31 October 1828.

25. Piccini's score for this ballet was not published, and has apparently not survived. The musical insertions in the play, *La Mansarde des artistes*, are identified in its scenario, but there seems to be no evidence as to whether any of them were used for the ballet (Scribe, *Oeuvres completes*, 2nd series, vol. 12, 135–86).

26. Etienne Laurençon (1803–83) was a character dancer who danced in Paris in 1829–30 and 1843. For a more detailed biography, see Van Aelbrouck, 160–2. His dancing career may have continued until 1862 if he was the Laurençon referred to in a news item in the *Entr'acte* of 26 June as having lost his left arm in an explosion of a property cannon while dancing in Saint-Etienne.

27. *Courrier des spectacles*, 1 August 1829.

11

The Turning Point

Towards midday on Monday, 26 July 1830, a rehearsal was in progress on the stage of the Opéra to polish a few details in the opera *Guillaume Tell*, which was billed for that evening. It was impossible not to feel tension in the air, for grave events were portending outside as a result of the repressive Ordinances published that morning in the Ministerial press. These royal decrees struck at the very root of the Charter, which Charles X had sworn in his Coronation oath to uphold. In the eyes of liberal-thinking people, therefore, they amounted to a conspiracy to impose a more reactionary order in defiance of the public will, and already the abolition of the liberty of the press, the dissolution of the Chambers and the repeal of the electoral laws had aroused an underswell of discontent that boded ill for the tranquillity of the capital.

On the surface that day's rehearsal seemed to be proceeding normally, when the moment came, in the famous trio of the second act, for Tell to fill his lungs and cry out: *'Ou l'indépendance, ou la mort!'* At the sound of those stirring words a sudden murmur arose, increasing in volume as those standing at the back of the stage – singers, musicians, supers, stage hands – took up the cry with a vehemence and precision that Halévy, who was sitting alone in the darkened auditorium, had never seen achieved by a producer. The rehearsal broke up in confusion as men snatched up the nearest implement to hand, even if only a wooden sword, to rush out to join the growing crowd on the boulevard and defend the cause of liberty.

That evening's performance was cancelled, and the Opéra did not reopen until 4 August. In the meantime the Revolution of the 'Three Glorious Days' had, not without some bloodshed, brought about the abdication of Charles X and the appointment, as Lieutenant General of the kingdom, of the Duc d'Orléans, who a few days later was proclaimed King of the French as Louis-Philippe. To outward appearances, the change in régime affected the Opéra very little, and for the time being Lubbert remained as Director. But a serious financial crisis was brewing. The abolition of the tax on the receipts of the minor theatres, which yielded more than 300,000 francs a year, was a grievous loss to the Opéra – and there was a general uncertainty about the future. Public opinion was against the Opéra remaining a department of the Court, and Louis-Philippe was too preoccupied with other matters to concern himself with the affairs of a theatre, however prestigious. So the responsibility for supervising the Opéra was merely transferred from the

Royal Household to the Ministry of the Interior, and a committee set up, under the chairmanship of the Duc de Choiseul, to advise the Minister how it should be administered in the future.

* * * * * * *

In the months preceding the July revolution, the authorities at the Opéra had become increasingly concerned by weaknesses that had become apparent in the male element of the ballet company. Paul was noticeably losing some of that youthful vigour and dash which had so thrilled the public in the early years of his career, and the need for a young virtuoso who could complement the innovative promise of Taglioni was becoming increasingly urgent. In addition, Ferdinand's health was giving cause for concern, and so a further priority was to find a younger dancer with a talent for mime who could be groomed to understudy and eventually succeed him in the leading male rôles of the repertory – but there seemed to be no appropriate candidate within the company. And thirdly, a replacement had to be found for the late Antoine Godefroy, whose character sketches of Farmer Thomas in *La Fille mal gardée* and tetchy old Gombault in *La Belle au bois dormant* had been the more recent of a series of memorable characterisations.

Finding a successor to Godefroy was the least of these problems, for the Opéra already possessed a very experienced and powerful mime in Simon Mérante,[1] who had been creating important rôles for upwards of twenty years. Although he was only three years short of his fiftieth birthday, he was giving no indication that his powers were waning. Mérante had made his début in 1808, partnering Bigottini in a *pas de deux*. He was then already a mature artiste of twenty-four, having earned his early laurels at the Ambigu-Comique and the Porte-Saint-Martin before being engaged at the Opéra, first as a dancer and then as a mime. Over the years he created a succession of notable character studies, including the scheming Julien in *Le Séducteur au village*, the Governor in *Nina*, the Danish chieftain in *Alfred le Grand*, the rascally recruiting sergeant in *Manon Lescaut*, and Vulcan in *Mars et Vénus*, to name but the more outstanding. Although he was already forty-seven, Mérante was offered a contract by the Opéra at 4000 francs a year from the beginning of 1831, but was to be retired in 1832.

To groom potential successors to Paul and Ferdinand, Lubbert made the bold decision, after discussions with Aumer and Albert, to look beyond the walls of the Opéra to dancers who had pursued their careers at the Porte-Saint-Martin and who, since the disbanding of that theatre's ballet company, were now available. To Lubbert, the most immediate problem was to seek an understudy for Ferdinand, whose health, it seemed, was 'visibly deteriorating day by day'. Here there was a ready candidate in the person of Joseph Mazilier, who was engaged as a *double* on a three-year contract from 1 January 1830 at 4000 francs a year, rising to 5000 francs for the third year; he made his début on 3 March as Colin in *La Fille mal gardée*.

In the longer term, much more depended on the choice of the dancer to understudy and eventually succeed Paul, and here the pool of dancers made available by the closure of the Porte-Saint-Martin provided a candidate of the most exciting promise, the nineteen-year-old prodigy Jules Perrot. With the backing of Aumer and Albert, an offer of a year's engagement at a salary of 2500 francs to commence at the beginning of April was made and accepted. As news came through that spring of the young dancer's triumph as principal dancer at the King's Theatre in London, it must have become clear that the Opéra had secured a good bargain.

Jules Perrot was truly a child of the theatre. When he was born in Lyons on 18 August 1810, his father was a stage carpenter employed at that city's Grand-Théâtre who would in time rise to the post of chief machinist. At the age of nine, young Jules began to study dancing and soon revealed not only a remarkable talent but also a precocious ambition. The arrival in Lyons of the celebrated comic dancer Charles Mazurier touched off the spark, and, thanks to his father's position in the theatre, Jules was able to attend several of Mazurier's performances. Being exceptionally observant, he assimilated Mazurier's technique so thoroughly that he was soon able to imitate his tricks, a gift that led to his first appearance on the stage, at the Théâtre des Célestins, in a piece called *Le Petit Carnaval de Venise.*

Encouraged by his success, he then ran away from home with just five francs in his pocket and took the diligence to Paris. At first he had to work long hours by day as a merchant's clerk to augment his casual earnings as a super at one of the boulevard theatres in the evening. It was not long, though, before his agility and his flair for comedy were recognised and he was engaged at the Gaîté at the princely salary, for a boy, of 1200 francs a year. And so, on the very evening at the end of 1823 when Bigottini was making her final appearance at the Opéra, Jules Perrot first came to the notice of the Parisian public in *Le Polichinel avalé par la baleine* – the Gaîté's answer to *Polichinel-vampire*, the popular farce then running at the Porte-Saint-Martin, with Mazurier. Next morning Mazurier learnt that he had a rival in a thirteen-year-old boy, while Jules had the satisfaction of reading in a leading newspaper that he 'already leaves Mazurier and the other contemporary jumpers and performers of *tours de force* far behind in bearing, suppleness and lightness'.[2] A year or so later, when the Porte-Saint-Martin presented the long-running *Jocko*, with Mazurier playing the rôle of the monkey, the Gaîté responded with *Sapajou,* in which Jules had a similar part that was no less sensational.

Although Jules Perrot followed Mazurier's example in visiting the Jardin des Plantes to study the movements and antics of monkeys, he was not content to remain a mere rival to the famous Polichinel. He was beginning to realise that the dance held more for him than a mere means of earning a living. Broader horizons began to beckon, and he was encouraged to make use of his spare time to complete his interrupted education, particularly by studying art and languages. It went without saying that the dance remained the central feature in this self-imposed period of improvement; seeking none but the finest of teachers that Paris had to offer, his steps led him to the studio of the legendary Auguste Vestris. Vestris, now an old man approaching three score years and ten, may have seen something of his younger self in this enthusiastic youngster who one day called on him; for the lad who stood before him was lissom and energetic, if somewhat on the short side and undeniably plain of feature. So it was that Jules found himself attending class with that revered master who had danced his first steps in public when Louis XV was still king.

Vestris was quick to perceive the potential of this new pupil, and to provide him with the formula of success. 'Never stay still,' the wise old teacher counselled him. 'Jump about, turn, move around, and above all, never give the public time to look at you closely.' This advice would be well heeded, for Perrot's fellow pupil, August Bournonville, remembered him as 'a zephyr with the wings of a bat, a divinity belonging not to mythology, but to cabalism, a restless being of indescribable lightness and suppleness, with an almost phosphorescent brilliance'.[3]

Indeed, it was all too apparent that Perrot was far from handsome, and it was perhaps one of his attractions that he had no illusions about his looks. Bournonville, in his memoirs, was to relate a revealing incident, which he must have had from Perrot himself. One day, as he was strolling on the boulevard, Perrot had come across the singers Duprez and Baroilhet, and found himself involved in friendly banter as to which of the three was the ugliest. Finally, to resolve the issue, Duprez proposed that they accost a passer-by and ask him to arbitrate. '*Ma foi!*' exclaimed the stranger, 'I would be very hard put to it to make a choice', and with that, continued on his way, his shoulders heaving with suppressed laughter.

It was probably around the time he began to take class with Vestris that Perrot left the Gaîté, where he was earning 1600 francs a year, and joined the ballet company at the Porte-Saint-Martin at a salary of 2000 francs. His career was now taking off. When the Opéra opened negotiations with him early in 1830, he was already committed to the Italian Opera in London for the first half of the season. This was his first visit to the English capital, and London was vastly impressed by his 'wonderful ease and agility'[4], which seemed to surpass anything that had been seen before. With this success behind him, he returned to Paris to prepare for his début at the Opéra, which took place on 23 June in a *pas de deux* with Pauline Montessu in Le Brun's opera, *Le Rossignol*. It was not exactly a propitious moment for a male dancer to appeal to the public, for, as a contemporary biographer recalled:

> when Perrot first appeared on the stage, male dancing was on the point of vanishing. People treated the most magnificent memories of the ballet as a joke: Vestris, Gardel and Duport had become no more than ridiculous heroes. Albert and the *danse noble* were consigned to oblivion, and Paul, of aerial memory, was almost forgotten. It needed courage to follow in the footsteps of those fallen, outmoded idols. But Perrot triumphed over the most formidable obstacles: he overcame the scorn – one might even say, repugnance – that was felt towards male dancing.[5]

* * * * * * *

In spite of financial difficulties and the uncertainty over his own position, Lubbert ably steered the Opéra through the last few months of his management. If any consolation were needed on his departure, he at least had the satisfaction of having presented Marie Taglioni in two rôles new to the Paris public at a time when she was most in need of them. For, in the summer of 1830, in spite of the extraordinary enthusiasm she had inspired on her first appearance in Paris three years before, a section of the public, of which the *Courrier des théâtres* was the mouthpiece, was grumbling at the lack of variety in the *pas* that her father would have her dance. For a time, Lise Noblet, whose reputation had been enhanced by her success in *La Muette de Portici*, seemed to be regaining lost ground. But Taglioni's hour was to come on 13 October 1830, with the first performance of the opera-ballet *Le Dieu et la Bayadère*, which Auber and Scribe had conceived with the express purpose of giving her a rôle of the same order as Fenella.

Unlike Noblet, however, Taglioni still had to prove herself as a mime, and the part of Zoloé had been carefully constructed not as a purely dramatic rôle, but as one that relied on both dance and mime. The wisdom of this was soon made clear, for Taglioni's miming was generally found disappointing, even though she surpassed herself in the danced passages. There was one unforgettable moment when Zoloé, whose love has been spurned by the god Brahma, dances before him with her hands clasped in a gesture of despair and with tears in her eyes. Another imaginative passage in her father's choreography was the *pas de schal*. This may have been an outworn formula, but seldom before had it been employed to such striking effect. The pink scarves of the dancing girls floated and hovered in the air in the most ingenious combinations, now streaming in undulating folds, now hanging loosely, and – at a most striking moment – stretched out fan-wise with their ends gathered beneath Taglioni's foot, making her appear like Venus emerging from the waves on her shell.

To many who saw her in this part, Taglioni appeared as the very image of perfection. An American visitor, Nathaniel Parker Willis, having heard her name 'constantly over the hum of the cafés and in the crowded resorts of fashion', was drawn to the Opéra to see *Le Dieu et la Bayadère* and was overwhelmed. Gathering his impressions after the performance, he endeavoured to analyse what set her apart from the generally accepted image of the ballerina:

> She takes the part of a dancing girl, of whom the Bramah and an Indian prince are both enamoured, the former in the disguise of a man of low rank at the court and the latter in search of someone whose love for him shall be disinterested. The disguised god succeeds in winning her affection, and, after testing her devotion by submitting for a while to the resentment of his rival, and by a pretended caprice in favour of a singing girl, who accompanies her, he marries her, and then saves her from the flames as she is about to be burned for marrying beneath her caste. Taglioni's part is all pantomime. She does not speak during the play but her motion is more than articulate. Her first appearance was in a troop of Indian dancing girls, who performed before the prince in the public square. At a signal from the vizier, a side pavilion opened, and thirty or forty bayadères glided out together, and commenced an intricate dance. They were received with a tremendous round of applause from the audience; but, with the exception of a little more elegance in the four who led the dance, they were dressed nearly alike; and as I saw no particularly conspicuous figure, I presumed that Taglioni had not yet appeared. The splendour of the spectacle bewildered me for the first moment or two, but I presently found my eyes rivetted to a childish creature floating about among the rest, and taking her for some beautiful young *élève* making her first essays in the chorus, I interpreted her extraordinary fascination as a triumph of nature over my unsophisticated taste; and wondered to myself whether, after all, I should be half so much captivated with the show of skill I expected presently to witness. *This was Taglioni!* She came forward directly, in a *pas seul*, and I then observed modesty both of fashion and ornament, and the unconstrained ease with which it adapted itself to her shape and motion. She looks not more than fifteen. Her figure is small, but rounded to the

very last degree of perfection; not a muscle swelled beyond the exquisite outline; and not an angle, not a fault. Her back and neck, those points so rarely beautiful in woman, are faultlessly formed; her feet and hands are in full proportion to her size, and the former play as freely and with as natural a yieldingness in her fairy slippers, as if they were accustomed only to the dainty uses of a drawing-room. Her face is most strangely interesting; not quite beautiful, but of that half-appealing, half-retiring sweetness that you sometimes see blended with the secluded reserve and unconscious refinement of a young girl just 'out' in the circle of high fashion. In her greatest exertions her features retain the same timid half smile, and she returns to the alternate by-play of her part without the slightest change of colour, or the slightest perceptible difference in her breathing, or in the ease of her look and posture. No language can describe her motion. She swims in your eye like a curl of smoke, or a flake of down. Her difficulty seems to be to keep to the floor. You have the feeling while you gaze upon her, that, if she were to rise and float away like Ariel, you would scarce be surprised. And yet all is done with such a childish unconsciousness of admiration, such a total absence of exertion or fatigue, that the delight with which she fills you is unmingled; and, assured as you are by the perfect purity of every look and attitude, that her hitherto spotless reputation is deserved beyond a breath of suspicion, you leave her with as much respect as admiration; and find with surprise that a dancing girl, who is exposed night after night to a profaning gaze of the world, has crept into one of the most sacred niches of your memory.[6]

Such was Taglioni's triumph at the first performance that when the *régisseur* stepped forward to announce the names of the composer and the librettist at the end of the performance, the audience would not allow him a hearing until they had given the ballerina a rousing ovation.

Lise Noblet played the smaller part of Néala. It was the first time she had danced to choreography by Filippo Taglioni, and one critic remarked how interesting it was to see a ballerina trained in the classical French school attempting 'the daring movements of the new manner'.[7]

That summer, another project was in the wind that would present Taglioni in a rôle that had not been conceived by her father – that of Flora in a revival of a ballet created at the Opéra nearly fifteen years before by a distinguished visiting choreographer, Charles Didelot. *Flore et Zéphire* had then created a sensation, not only for its flying effects, which were astonishingly novel for their time, but also, more poignantly, because it marked the last performances of the astonishing young virtuoso, Geneviève Gosselin. She was then revealing the potential of what would become a novel extension of the ballerina's technique, the skill known as *pointe* work. Tragically, she was already smitten by tuberculosis, and would appear only in the first six performances. She died little more than two years later, and memories of her had resurfaced when Taglioni had first appeared in Paris.[8]

Whether or not the idea of reviving *Flore et Zéphire* for Taglioni had been aired in Paris before she crossed the Channel for her first season in London, it was in that ballet that she made her English début early in June. Although it was produced by Arnaud Léon, a ballet-master of secondary status, it is probable that Taglioni's part was most carefully scrutinised by her father, if not arranged by him. Antoine Coulon, the son of her first teacher, partnered her in the part of Zephyr, and was not very impressed by Léon's staging, commenting in a letter to his friend Deshayes that 'without her, it would have given little pleasure'.[9]

According to a press report shortly after her return to Paris,[10] the Opéra had also been planning to revive *Flore et Zéphire* for her, but the preparations had been discontinued to concentrate on an important operatic revival, that of Spontini's *Fernand Cortès*, which was presented at the end of August. In it, Taglioni appeared in an interpolated *pas de deux*, partnered by Jules Perrot. To go by one account, they matched one another perfectly, giving a truly memorable performance. 'They responded to one another,' recalled a contemporary.

> They swayed as though filled with the same breath, rising and falling as if impelled by a single force. Perrot sprang about the sylphide while she reclined on the clouds, floated around her like a powerful balloonist, and immersed himself with her in the gentle mist. Then they both rose, she with her indescribable charm, he with his daring and audacity, and both in the most perfect harmony.[11]

When she returned to Paris in July, Marie Taglioni made known her desire that *Flore et Zéphire* be produced for her next rôle at the Opéra. There could, of course, be no question of inviting Charles Didelot to come to Paris to oversee the revival, but this posed no problem for Albert, the Zephyr of 1815. He had loyally kept the production fresh after Didelot's return to Russia shortly after the première, and was prepared to teach the principal dancers their rôles, leaving to Aumer the task of arranging the ensembles.

A prominent feature of the 1815 production had been the flying scenes, culminating in a sensational double flight – an effect never before attempted at the Opéra – for which Zephyr and Flora were portrayed by understudies. Didelot had brought the equipment for this effect with him from Russia, but it had been left in Paris when he returned to Russia early in 1816. For the 1831 revival, the flying effects fell within the province of the chief machinist,

Contant, with the principal characters being represented by understudies as before – in this case, Châtillon[12] and Jenny Sirot.

By 1830, mythological ballets were very much out of favour, but the attraction of Taglioni and Perrot was enough to assure the success of this work, the revival of which might have been too hazardous to contemplate without them. Not even the *Courrier des théâtres* could find fault with Taglioni, although it could not forbear recording that Perrot received the greater share of applause at the first two performances. Nor could it be concealed that the revival of a ballet that ran so counter to public taste could only be contemplated as a vehicle to present the two extraordinary virtuosi whom fortunate circumstances had brought together. Without one or the other, its impact would have been greatly diminished; without both, the revival would have been unthinkable. Never before had Taglioni appeared more seductive or more graceful; but judging from the applause, her twenty-year-old partner stirred the public's enthusiasm even more. This was not at all to Taglioni's liking, and she vowed never to allow it to happen again. The ballet was performed just nine times until July, when it was dropped. In future Taglioni was never again to accept a partner who might vie with her for the public's applause.

* * * * * * *

Early in 1831 the special committee appointed to consider the future structure of the Opéra presented its report to the Minister of the Interior. Its principal recommendation, that the Opéra should become a subsidised private enterprise, was accepted, and a crop of rumours began to circulate about the candidates for the post of Director and the chances of each. Among the names bandied about was that of the former dancer Louis Duport, who had been associated for some years with Domenico Barbaja in managing the Vienna Opera.

The choice finally rested on Dr Louis Véron, a larger-than-life character if ever there was one. He had begun life as a doctor, successfully launching a patent medicine, Pâte Regnault, for curing sore throats, before turning his hand to journalism, founding the *Revue de Paris*. For his age – and he was still only thirty-two – his achievements were remarkable; but, as his thick, ugly features and heavy frame suggested, he was one of those characters who seem to arrive early at full maturity and to acquire at once the confidence to face the world and their elders. He was admired and respected, but while he had a wide circle of associates and acquaintances, he did not inspire affection and had no really close friends. He was a bachelor and an epicure who was envied rather than loved, envied for the figure he cut in the world and for the good things in life he was able to enjoy. Neither a musician nor a man of the theatre, he had been chosen to direct the Opéra primarily because of his contacts with the literary, artistic and political milieux, and it was perhaps not an irrelevant factor in his success that the Minister of the Interior had been one of the contributors to the *Revue de Paris*.

Véron may have been flamboyant and vulgar, but his audacity and enterprise, his understanding of his artists – not to mention his skill in availing himself of their weaknesses – together with his appreciation of the value of the theatrical puff, eminently fitted him for managing the Opéra at this particular juncture. Better than most, he understood the social and political issues that lay behind the Revolution of 1830 and realised that the wealth and influence of the bourgeoisie, who had emerged as the real victors from the turmoil, would continue to increase with the years. This rising class, he foresaw, would crave to be amused, and where better than at the Opéra, which would also pander to their very human need for self-improvement. To quote his own words, the Opéra might well become their Versailles, and with proper handling they could be induced to flock there in their thousands, thus taking over the place of the Court and the privileged aristocracy of the former régime. Véron reasoned in this strain for a fortnight, before letting it be known that he was willing to undertake the task and ready to furnish the required security.

The *Cahier des charges*, the contract setting out the conditions of his management, was then drawn up. All was ready for its formal signing when a last-minute intervention by the Duc d'Orléans, pressing for the retention of Lubbert as Director, came near to dashing Véron's chances. Véron spent an agonising time kicking his heels in a waiting room at the Ministry of the Interior, able only to hear the buzz of a lively discussion in the room beyond, before he was at last called in and informed that his nomination had been decided upon. With the backing of the banker Alexandre Aguado, Marquis de Las Marismas del Guadalquivir, he was able to lodge the required security of 250,000 francs, and the *Cahier des charges* was signed. He was formally installed as Director on 2 March 1831, although his six-year term of management would not begin until 1 June, on which date the undertaking would be at his personal risk, lightened by a subsidy of 810,000 francs for the first year, 760,000 francs for the second and third years, and 710,000 francs[13] a year thereafter. The committee that had recommended him was to be kept in being to see that the conditions of the contract were observed, but Véron soon discovered that their vigilance could be distracted by more delicate tasks such as organising informal parties for ministers that would be attended by some of the more attractive dancers and singers of the company.

The first three months of Véron's management of the Opéra gave him time to take stock. He acquainted himself with the organisation of the theatre down to the last detail, something no Director had ever done before. He effected changes that he thought desirable, and he made himself known to everyone involved. The task held no fears for him, for a survey of his new empire filled him with confidence. As well as obtaining the subsidy, he had come into possession of an immense store of material, a company strong in talent and promise, including a ballerina idolised by the public and a male dancer to match her, an operatic repertory rich in works by Rossini, and a grand opera in preparation – Meyerbeer's *Robert le Diable* – which, by astute negotiation, he had taken over at the modest figure of 40,000 francs.

Before his term began, he had the auditorium completely redecorated, and installed Locatelli astro-lamps which, by means of their reflectors, not only threw a stronger light on the stage but spread it more evenly, giving a softer and more natural effect.[14] Before long, other reforms were introduced. Instead of the Friday performance being considered the only important one of the week, all three performances were now given equal prominence, with a corresponding rise in the receipts; the chorus was rejuvenated; and rôles that formerly had been the sole property of certain dancers and singers were now shared. Lise Noblet was one of the dancers who benefited from this last innovation. Pauline Montessu's monopoly of the rôle of Manon Lescaut was broken, and Noblet's success when she took it over on 28 September 1831 seemed a happy augury for the new Director.

* * * * * * *

Véron held decided views on what factors determined a ballet's success. 'I was sure,' he wrote in his memoirs,

> that ballets with a dramatic foundation could never count on a great success. I studied the box-office receipts of all the old works and observed that the two ballets that had been most successful were *Les Filets de Vulcain* [the subtitle of *Mars et Vénus*] and *Flore et Zéphire*. *Clari, Alfred le Grand, Manon Lescaut, La Somnambule* never made money... Dramas and comedies of manners do not come within the choreographer's ambit; in a ballet, what the public demands above all are a varied and striking score, new and unusual costumes, great variety, contrasting sets, surprises, transformation scenes, and a simple plot that is easy to follow and in which the dance develops naturally out of the situations. To all this must be added the charm of a young and beautiful dancer who dances better than and differently from those who have preceded her. If one is aiming neither at the intelligence nor at the heart, one must appeal to the senses and most particularly to the eyes.[15]

One of Véron's earliest concerns on becoming Director of the Opéra was to engage a new ballet-master to replace Aumer, the choreographer of *La Somnambule* and *Manon Lescaut*, who had submitted his resignation within a few weeks of the new Director's arrival. His choice had rested on Jean Coralli, who in his younger days had danced for several years at the Opéra – where in fact he had received his training – so that he could hardly be considered an outsider, even though his reputation as a choreographer rested on the ballets he had staged in Milan, Vienna and Lisbon before he came to the Porte-Saint-Martin. The ten ballets that he had produced there during the previous five years were still in the public's memory, and it was no doubt to that period of his career that he owed the two-year contract as *maître de ballet* that Véron offered him. The terms specified an annual salary of 4000 francs and a royalty of 30 francs for each performance of one of his ballets on the Opéra stage. His engagement would make him the junior of three *maîtres de ballet* on the Opéra's staff, but there were circumstances that would have made it especially attractive: for the more prominent of his two colleagues, Filippo Taglioni, while commanding a yearly salary of 10,000 francs, was unlikely to work for any other ballerina than his daughter, while Albert had not produced a ballet at the Opéra during the past eight years and, in fact, would retire from that post just a year after Coralli's appointment.

In the circumstances, therefore, the post held decided possibilities, and Coralli would find himself virtually in charge of the ballet. As an indication of his usefulness, he was soon given lodgings within the grounds of the Opéra. It was no doubt convenient to the Opéra to have one of its chiefs on the spot, and it would remain Coralli's home for several years. According to the memoirs of Gentil, the Controller of Material, who in time would occupy part of that building himself, it was spacious and well-heated and included a small terrace where Coralli grew flowers and green vegetables.

Coralli was to serve the Opéra as ballet-master for nearly twenty years, becoming chief of the ballet department when Filippo Taglioni left in 1836, and being generally respected as 'a good man who always took care not to offend anyone in the course of his duties'.

He had arrived at the Opéra at an appropriate moment, for no other new ballets were then contemplated and Meyerbeer's new opera, *Robert le Diable*, would not be ready until the end of the year. A straight revival of a ballet that had been seen already at the Porte-Saint-Martin was obviously out of the question, but Véron was in a position to be more pliable than his predecessors. Unlike them, he was not subject to the supervision of a superior court official, and so the rules could be stretched to allow a scenario based on the theme of a ballet that Coralli had produced at the Porte-Saint-Martin, *Léocadie*. For appearances' sake, three conditions were set: that it be given a new score and new choreography and presented under a different title.

In these discussions Coralli found a powerful ally in the man brought in to rewrite the action: none other than Eugène Scribe, several of whose plays and librettos the choreographer had already used as the basis for ballets produced at the Porte-Saint-Martin. Scribe's contribution had then been strictly off the record, but now that Coralli was working at the Opéra any misgivings he may have had vanished, and he agreed to be openly acknowledged as a co-author with Coralli. The resulting scenario possessed a number of new features; and while some similarities remained, the text was considered sufficiently original to allow the project to proceed under a different title, *L'Orgie.*

Auber's opera of that name, the ballet's original source, had been set in Portugal, but for the ballet this was now changed to Spain, no doubt with a view to giving Coralli the opportunity of inserting such colourful dances as *fandangos* and *boleros*, which could always be counted on to please the public. The ballet opened with a rowdy scene in a tavern on the outskirts of Seville, out of which developed a stirring *fandango.* Four young noblemen, headed by Don Carlos (Mazilier) and his friend Fernando (Coulon) arrive and begin to flirt with the local girls much to the annoyance of the regular clientele. Juanito (Desplaces), an old soldier, and his son Philippe (Simon) and daughter Marie (Legallois) then make their appearance. Philippe, who has been conscripted, is on the way to join his regiment. Before they leave, Philippe's father hands his son some papers that prove his noble birth. Meanwhile the young noblemen have been drinking hard, and Carlos calls for dances. Finding himself left without a partner, Carlos sees Juanito and Marie returning after bidding farewell to Philippe. Excited at the sight of a girl to make up the set, he runs out. In the struggle that follows, the old father draws his sword to defend his daughter, who swoons, and the scene ends with a tipsy Carlos picking up the girl and disappearing with her into the night.

The scene changes to Carlos's apartment in Seville. Carlos's uncle, Don Henriquez (Mérante), informs him that, with war now declared, the King has appointed him to command a regiment. Don Henriquez has plans for his nephew to marry his daughter Hermance (Julia), but Carlos declares that his only wish is to die at the head of his men. With an expression of shame, Carlos then goes into a darkened room in which Marie has been concealed. He kneels before her to beg forgiveness. She pushes him away, and in desperation seizes his sword. Disarming her, he begs her to trust him. He then leaves to ensure that their departure will not be observed. Left alone, Marie opens the shutters to let in the moonlight and carefully memorises her surroundings. Carlos then returns, blindfolds her and gently leads her away.

Five years have passed before the events of the second act take place. The setting is a village, which is awaiting the arrival of a company of soldiers. Marie enters to knock at the door of one of the cottages. A peasant appears with a four-year-old child, whom Marie embraces and tenderly watches at play. A fanfare announces the arrival of Carlos and his uncle, Don Henriquez, who are followed by Fernando and Hermance. Carlos does not recognise Marie, although touched by her sorrowful expression. Don Henriquez expresses concern at his nephew's delay in proposing to Hermance. The stage then empties except for Fernando and Hermance. Fernando has long loved her, but she tells him she regards herself as betrothed to Carlos. At this point the soldiers arrive, and Marie, recognising their officer to be her long-lost brother, throws herself into his arms. Philippe breaks the news that their father is dead, and declares that, now having found one another, they must never be separated again. Carlos is surprised at the attention Philippe is paying to Marie, but is appeased when told that he is her brother and of noble blood. Carlos is beside himself with joy, for he has long loved Marie but until now has assumed that their difference in status would make marriage impossible. Impulsively, he asks Philippe's permission to marry her, which Philippe is only too delighted to grant. But Marie declines, even though she has always loved him.

The hour has now come for the village fair to begin. Before Hermance can respond to her father's request to open the dancing, Fernando gives her his hand, thus leaving Carlos free to take Marie as his partner. The *divertissement* opens with a *bolero* for four couples, followed by a *pas de trois*, after which comes a firework display. Unhappily, a vagrant firework sets light to the thatch of the cottage. Marie runs to it terrified, climbs the outside staircase and reappears, surrounded by flames, holding the child in her arms. She throws it down onto a mattress, before descending to safety and collapsing at Carlos's feet. He carries her to the front of the stage, where she comes to her senses. She is fearful that her child might have perished, but all is well: the little girl is safe in Philippe's arms. Not realising that he is its father, Don Carlos is horrified at discovering that Marie has a child. Disillusioned, he declares his readiness to marry Hermance. Fernando is in despair, while Philippe is enraged at what he takes to be his sister's dishonour. Marie hides her face in her hands, as Don Henriquez extends his hands to bless his daughter and her fiancé.

The third act is set in Carlos's apartment, in the very room in which the final scene of the first act was played. Hermance is being dressed for the wedding. Fernando enters to bid her farewell, and reveals his love for her. After a *divertissement*, the wedding cortège forms. Philippe and Marie come to bid farewell. They now plan to settle in a distant land, and Philippe begs Carlos to give him his discharge from the army, which is willingly granted. When Carlos and Philippe leave to attend to the formalities, Marie suddenly recognises the room and realises that it was Carlos who had ravished her and is the father of her daughter. When the two men return, she confronts Carlos, who immediately acknowledges his guilt. As Philippe draws his sword, Marie runs out of the room, thrusting the child into Carlos's arms. At this point the doors at the back open to reveal the wedding party. Carlos now admits his secret and declares himself ready to marry Marie. A delighted Fernando takes Hermance in his arms, and Don Henriquez, after a brief hesitation, accepts the situation and blesses the union of his daughter with Fernando.

The rehearsal process had been remarkably free of complications, which in itself reflected upon both the skill and the tact shown by Coralli, who seems to have quickly won the respect of the dancers – not always an easy task for a newcomer at the Opéra. Nor had any untoward expense been incurred, the final figure for production costs coming out at the reasonable total of 10,175 francs. Nor could Coralli have had any complaint concerning the rehearsals: it was recorded that there were twenty-seven in all, ensuring a smooth performance when the ballet was first shown to the public on 18 July 1831.

It then met with a polite reception. The critic of the *Corsaire* had feared that under the new administration there might be a decline in the area of scenic splendour, but was agreeably surprised. 'We now have ostentation and authenticity,' he declared. 'This is a work of complete regeneration.' Maybe that was a little excessive, but the critics were being generally generous to the new administration. However, politely received though it was, *L'Orgie* was not to retain its place in the repertory for long. Véron had decided that the leading rôle should be given to Amélie Legallois, whom he felt had been passed over too often in favour of Lise Noblet; but neither she nor Julia, nor even Perrot, who danced in an inserted *pas de deux* with Pauline Montessu, could raise the ballet above the level of honourable mediocrity. It was all too patently a mimed play with inserted dances.

The score, however, was pleasing enough. Its composer, Michele Carafa, who was already known for several operas produced at the Opéra-Comique, had woven into it a number of borrowings. These included a song known as *El Caballo*, here played in a quicker tempo than usual and thereby losing some of its gypsy colouring; a chorus from Rossini's *Comte Ory* for the orgy scene of the first act; and the finale of Cherubini's *Les Deux Journées*, with an impressive crescendo that, as one critic put it, rose to a peak of sublimity and most effectively accompanied the moment when Marie recognises the scene of her seduction.

On balance, *L'Orgie* was a very competent début for the choreographer. It did not pass unnoticed that in his action scenes, notably the orgy of the first act that gave the ballet its title, Coralli had introduced a touch of realism – a feature that had distinguished several of his ballets produced at the Porte-Saint-Martin but was new to the Opéra stage. The firework display was effectively managed and the Spanish costumes were rich and colourful; but in spite of its merits, it was to suffer a misfortune that few could have foreseen. For it was produced on the eve of a turning point in the history of ballet. Little more than four months after its performance, Meyerbeer's *Robert le Diable* with its epochal Ballet of the Nuns was presented, and four months after that came *La Sylphide. L'Orgie* finally disappeared from the bills at the end of 1832. It had not been in the repertory long, but with thirty-one performances in less than two years, it had been a worthy beginning for a choreographer who would play a major part in the development of French ballet at the Opéra over the next two decades.

NOTES

1. The Mérante family was to provide the Opéra with dancers of three generations in the course of the century. Simon-Alexandre (born in 1783), who had become head of the family when his father died during the Revolution, had two younger brothers, François-Xavier (b. 1790) and Pierre-François. François-Xavier was the father of François Mérante, who was trained at the Opéra and danced there from 1834 to 1840, and can possibly be identified with the François-Pierre Mérante who was playing character parts and teaching at the Opéra in the early 1870s, Léo Staats being one of his pupils. François Mérante was also the father of Annette, Dorina and Elisa Mérante, who were soloists in the Opéra ballet in the 1870s. Simon Mérante's youngest brother Pierre-François was the father of Louis Mérante, ballet-master of the Opéra from 1869 until 1887.
2. *Journal de Paris*, 30 December 1823.
3. Bournonville, *Mit Theaterliv*, I, 75.
4. *Morning Post*, 22 March 1830.
5. Briffault, *Perrot (Galérie des artistes dramatiques, no.2)*, 4.
6. Quoted in *Dance Index*, July–August 1944, 118, as being taken from Willis's *Pencillings by the Way*. However, it is not to be found in the edition of 1835, and may have appeared only as a contribution to the New York periodical *The Mirror*.
7. *Courrier des théâtres*, 15 October 1830.
8. For a full account of the creation of *Flore et Zéphire*, see Guest, *Ballet under Napoleon*, chapter 28.
9. Bibl.-Mus. de l'Opéra, Fonds Deshayes, Coulon to Deshayes, 2 June 1830.
10. *Courrier des théâtres*, 16 July 1830.
11. Briffault, p. 2
12. Châtillon was the professional name of Lesueur de Petivil, who was later (1850–55) to hold the post of *régisseur de la danse*.
13. This was later reduced to 670,000 francs.

14. An advertisement in the *Corsaire*, 23 November 1832, described it as follows: 'The single wick, without the aid of a chimney, never carbonises and will remain alight for about 15 hours. It does not require snuffing, and emits neither smell nor smoke. With a single burner, a pound of oil gives 100 hours of illumination, which a reflector makes sufficiently strong for one person to work by'.
15. Véron, III, 225.

12

Conflict of Rôles: Temptress and Spirit

When Louis Véron became Director of the Opéra, Marie Taglioni was just one of several *premiers sujets femmes* who headed the ballet company; notwithstanding the extraordinary sensation she had aroused, she ranked no more prominently than her colleagues Lise Noblet, Amélie Legallois and Pauline Montessu. This profusion of *premiers sujets* resulted from the traditional division of the upper echelons of the company into the three genres of *noble, demi-caractère* and *comique*, each having one or, in the case of the *demi-caractère*, two *premiers sujets*.

On Véron's succession, this classification, which had increasingly become something of an anachronism, fell into disuse and was replaced by what a later age would call a star system. Ever alive to the over-riding importance of making his management financially successful, the new Director recognised the potential value of Marie Taglioni, whom he bound to the Opéra for a period of six years from 1 August 1831, on terms that would have staggered his predecessor – and were not likely to endear her to the other principal ballerinas. She was to receive no less than 30,000 francs a year, one third as a fixed salary payable monthly, one third in performance bonuses – or *feux*, as they were known – and the remaining third as a guaranteed benefit. It was further stipulated that the rôles she created were not to be given to another dancer unless the occasion was a début or she was unable to dance them herself; she was to have the right to insist on dancing in *pas* composed by her father and to compose them herself should he cease to be attached to the Opéra; and she was to be entitled to three months' leave of absence each year to enable her and her father to accept seasonal engagements elsewhere.[1] At the same time her father was engaged as ballet-master, but for a three-year term only, at a salary of 6000 francs plus 4000 francs in lieu of royalties.

When these contracts came into force, the Taglionis had just returned from a highly profitable season in London, where Marie had dazzled the fashionable audiences of the King's Theatre. For her it had been an exhausting three months, and she was in sore need of a rest on her return to France. So throughout August, she secluded herself in the leafy surroundings of Neuilly. From there, her father paid two visits to the composer Giacomo Meyerbeer to hear the music he had written for the ballets to be inserted in his new opera, *Robert le Diable*, which was then in active production. On the second of these visits, Meyerbeer played the music he had just finished composing for the seduction scene in the Ballet of the Nuns, and which Filippo Taglioni found 'charming'.

For both father and daughter this was a major commission, for no expense was being spared on the production, on which the hopes of the new administration depended. Véron had inherited the project from the previous administration, and had managed to negotiate a very favourable valuation of it as work-in-progress. Meyerbeer was not unknown in Paris, having come to the notice of its musical world some five years before through two of his early operas, *Il crociato in Egitto* and *Marguerite d'Anjou*.[2] On the strength of their reception, he had then proposed a new work for the Opéra-Comique. A wealthy man in his own right, Meyerbeer had already come to an arrangement with Scribe and another dramatist, Germain Delavigne, to write the libretto, and thus was *Robert le Diable* conceived. The composer began to write the music in the spring of 1827, but, as the work proceeded, came to realise that the project was developing into a work of a scale that would be much more suitable to the Opéra. Arranging the transfer posed no problem, and in the last days of 1829 Meyerbeer signed a formal contract with the Opéra for its production.

The July revolution and the reorganisation of the Opéra that followed called a halt to progress towards its production, and it was not until Véron was formally installed as Director that the production of such a major work could proceed. At that time no serious thought had been given to the ballets, particularly the one to be placed in the third act at the point where Robert is tempted to pluck a magic branch that will invest him with supernatural power. According to Véron's account, the original conception of this scene, which was to contain elements of pantomime as well as dance, was entirely neo-classical in flavour – or, as he graphically put it, 'an antiquated Olympus along with its quiver and arrows, gauzes and cupids'. However, Henri Duponchel, who had been placed in charge of the production with an extremely generous credit, scornfully rejected what seemed to him fusty and outdated nonsense, and proposed instead a scene with very much of a Romantic flavour, in which a band of ghostly nuns would be summoned from their tombs in a moonlit ruined cloister. Apparently, Véron failed to acquaint Meyerbeer of this change, preferring instead to invite him to a special rehearsal to be presented with the new concept in a finished state – confident that this would come as a most pleasant surprise. But his expectations that Meyerbeer would be carried away with delight were far from fulfilled. Alone among those present, the composer showed no emotion. 'All very beautiful,' he laconically remarked, 'but it seems, from your seeking a spectacular appeal, that you have no faith in the success of my music.'[3] In the final concept of the scene as described by the librettists, the action was skilfully woven into the opera's plot. In no way could it be seen as a mere interlude of dance with only a secondary relevance to the main action, for it was to serve as an integral part of the narrative. Robert, played by the charismatic tenor Adolphe Nourrit, is presented as a man born with evil in his soul, who has conceived a passion for the Princess Isabelle. In the preceding act, having been foiled in his attempt to abduct her, he is rescued by a mysterious knight, Bertram, a satanic figure who, unbeknown to Robert, is his own father. A tournament is in preparation, in which Robert sees an opportunity to win Isabelle's love. In the third act, Bertram leads him to a ruined cloister, the burial place of St Rosalie. Clutched in the hand of the reclining statue of the saint that surmounts her tomb is a talisman – a branch of evergreen – which, if he can secure it, will assure him of victory in the tournament. So, from their tombs in the cloister, Bertram summons the spirits of long-dead nuns who, in their lifetime, had broken their vows by indulging in licentious behaviour. As they emerge, their sinful passions revive, and led by their abbess Héléna (Taglioni), they throw themselves into an increasingly orgiastic bacchanal. At this point Robert makes his appearance. He finds himself surrounded by these mysterious wraiths, and Héléna interrupts her dance to hand him a goblet of wine. He recoils in horror, imagining he sees before him the features of his mother. The nuns then resume their dance; and after another solo by Héléna, Robert finally yields to her seductive graces, makes his way to the statue and seizes the talisman, which he triumphantly waves above his head as he leaves the stage.

Such was the scene, destined to make dance history, which now awaited Marie Taglioni at this critical point in her career, and would provide her with the rôle that would shape her future and mark her as one of the greatest dancers of all time. It came at a challenging moment. There can be no doubt that her elevation to a supreme rank in the company was deeply wounding to her senior colleagues – Noblet, Montessu and Legallois – who, unlike her, had grown up from childhood in the School of Dance and had remained at the Opéra ever since their débuts, enjoying loyalty from a broad segment of the public. So it was hardly surprising that a swell of discontent arose in support of these dedicated ballerinas who had given their working life to the Opéra. And in Charles Maurice, who owned and edited the leading theatrical journal, the *Courrier des théâtres*, they found a willing spokesman, who shortly after Taglioni's return launched a campaign to play down her talent and pour scorn on the pretensions of her father.

In the early days of October, when rehearsals for the ballet in *Robert le Diable* were about to begin, Maurice began insinuating in his journal that certain 'vile intrigues' were afoot, aimed at undermining those principal dancers who had virtually been demoted as a result of the exceptional favour granted to Marie Taglioni and her father – '*signor son papa*', as he scornfully called him. The latter, Maurice suggested, was merely using his daughter to secure a prominent position for himself in the company – an accusation not entirely devoid of truth, although when, a little later, that same critic accused Filippo Taglioni of striking a dancer at a rehearsal, he was going too far and Véron intervened to issue a stinging denial.[4]

At this moment in her life, Marie Taglioni was prey to another distraction. She was being assiduously courted by a young aristocrat, the Comte Gilbert de Voisins, and Maurice had no scruples in making use of his knowledge of this to add weight to his insinuating campaign. 'Malice and joking apart,' began one of his broadsides,

> there can be no denying that Mlle Taglioni's dancing is visibly on the decline. This is not just the natural result of satiety, which the eternal repetition of the same means must produce in a hardened audience hungry for novelty... The truth of the matter is that, whether the cause be physical or moral, Mlle Taglioni's talent has gone into ... a decline, as has been generally recognised. Might it be that in the hope of marrying, as a report would have it, this dancer is prey to preoccupations that are having a harmful effect on the exercise of her art? Or might she be trying to overcome her parents' reported opposition to this future match by arousing fears that she might lose her talent? A lover's ruse is always excusable. Be that as it may, what is certain is that on stage Mlle Taglioni is no longer what she was. She is losing her lightness and her strength; her attack savours of toil, and her back wilts with the efforts she makes; her knees have less power, her ankles less elasticity; her legs are becoming flabby; her aplomb, which has never been her strongest point, is not even that of a beginner; and finally, the grace of her *développements* is dry and her *jetés en arrière*, the boldness of which was once the key to her success, are now performed merely in a cold and off-hand manner as if prompted by necessity rather than inspiration.[5]

However, there may have been valid reasons for such criticism. Although Filippo Taglioni's own reputation and prosperity depended largely on his retaining control over his daughter's career, he and his wife might well have honestly felt that de Voisins did not have the makings of a suitable husband – a view that time would show to be well founded.

By the time this critical appraisal appeared, rehearsals of the Ballet of the Nuns were already well advanced. Filippo Taglioni had been working with the *corps de ballet* since 6 October, and on the 22nd the dancers appeared for the first time in costume. On that day he began working on the entrance of Robert with Adolphe Nourrit. It was not until the 31st that he started to rehearse the seduction scene with his daughter, who had no doubt been attending the earlier rehearsals. By 6 November the work was taking shape, but the effort of portraying a character that Marie found increasingly inimical to the conviction her father demanded, was proving more and more difficult and exhausting, and at the end of that day's rehearsal she broke down in a flood of tears. Nor was this her only worry, for de Voisins had made a proposal of marriage, which she had accepted, subject to her father giving his consent. And on 11 November de Voisins paid a call on her father to request her hand.

The first performance of *Robert le Diable*, just ten days later, was marked by a series of mishaps, any one of which might have had disastrous consequences. In the first scene of the third act, a gas-wing fell onto the stage, only narrowly missing Julie Dorus, the soprano playing the opera's heroine, Alice. At the end of that scene, a cloth painted to represent clouds was lowered to conceal the change to the complicated scene of the ruined cloister. When all was ready, it was then raised to reveal the moonlit scene for the Ballet of the Nuns, with Marie Taglioni reclining on one of the tombs. It was a blessing that she was then looking up into the flies, for she noticed the heavy cloth with its wooden bars breaking away from its ropes, and was able to leap to safety only just in time as it came crashing down on to the stage. Véron at once ordered the curtain to be lowered and for the stage to be cleared, so that Marie could recover her composure. An even more serious mishap was to follow at the end of the opera. As the trap opened to swallow up Bertram, Nourrit lost his balance and tumbled down too. Happily, he was not seriously injured, although sufficiently bruised and shocked for the next performance two days ahead to be cancelled.

Notwithstanding these mishaps, the opera was hailed as 'a complete success, a brilliant victory',[6] for which Marie Taglioni could justly claim a share for her spiritual performance as the Abbess. Meyerbeer, who had initially been troubled by the thought that his opera's success had depended more on the splendour of the production than on his music, was so disarmed by her dancing that he presented her with a fan on which he had had painted a scene from the Ballet of the Nuns.

The reason behind her distaste for the rôle was never publicly explained, but it must have been aggravated by the constant sniping at her father – and through him, at her – by Charles Maurice in his daily news-sheet, the *Courrier des théâtres*. This had already surfaced before the first performance, and at least to some extent may have reflected the discontent of those established ballerinas, Noblet, Legallois and Montessu. At the same time, the standing and the influence of the disaffected ballerinas had been further weakened by the retirement of the two senior ballet-masters, Aumer and

Albert – thus elevating Filippo Taglioni to the seemingly unassailable post of senior *maître de ballet* and *chorégraphe-servant* of his daughter.

Maurice launched his first broadside on 21 November, the very day of the première of *Robert le Diable*:

> The Opéra's new production has been confided to a man who is a foreigner twice over: firstly, by birth, and secondly, by his absolute ignorance – in short, to the Italian, Taglioni. This is what worries us. By assuming the task, this man has taken it upon himself alone to fill the places formerly held by Gardel, Aumer and Albert ... A man of merit would have quailed before such responsibility. But Signor Taglioni had to thrust himself forward.[7]

To give Maurice his due, he may honestly have disliked what he saw when the front-cloth rose to reveal the cloister scene at the first performance on the evening of 21 November, but the vitriol that poured from his pen was clearly intended to be wounding. 'Had it not been for M. Taglioni,' he wrote, 'the Opéra would have earned, alongside yesterday's crown, a sceptre. But that detestable producer has brought disorder, clutter and obscurity where the vast expenditure had given promise of order, design and clarity.'[8]

The following day Maurice confessed that he had been on the point of hissing a dozen times during the Ballet of the Nuns, but had refrained because 'the refined customs' of the august institution of the Opéra forbade it. 'Has nobody yet realised?' he went on.

> Is it for us to sound a warning note and speak out? ... Is any more convincing evidence needed to prove that M. Taglioni is unworthy of filling the place of *maître de ballet* at the Opéra? With all the means and resources at his disposal, together with such a novel idea, as well as scenery capable of producing the most singular effects, twenty highly talented *danseuses* and fifty picturesquely costumed supers, and a score so admirably suited to the librettists' conception, only a Taglioni could have produced such confusion, embarrassment and insupportable muddle with twisted lines, and runs *à la colin-maillard* reminiscent of the dance halls![9]

There may have been some justification for this critical onslaught, for the second performance, announced for the 23rd, was cancelled to enable revisions to be made to the Ballet of the Nuns. Rehearsals were hurriedly called in order to review the production, and the Ballet of the Nuns in particular. Time was too short for any radical reworking of the scene; but, as the *Courrier des théâtres* reported, 'while it was impossible in such a short time to replace the carnival scene that M. Taglioni has stuffed into the new opera by some beautiful and well-arranged dances, cuts have at least been made to the choreographic banalities by which this fine work was so impertinently dishonoured'.[10]

It was the best that could be done in the circumstances, without compromising the triumphant success of the opera itself. Maurice seems to have accepted that honour had been satisfied, but without altering his opinion of Filippo Taglioni. 'Now that the dances have been shortened, we can at least say of them that the audience has less time to suffer,' he observed,

> but the pity of it is that this feeble composition by the Italian, Taglioni, remains a problem for the Opéra, which is richer in this area than any similar institution in the world. When *Robert le Diable's* success has passed, if it ever will, the foreigner who spoilt this part of the work will have been responsible for the loss of 50 performances that it would have had if its ballets had been as they should have been. Then add to this the enormous salary of Mlle Taglioni as well as that of her father, and the damage he will cause to other works if he produces them, and calculate what each of the said ballerina's *ronds de jambe* is costing us.[11]

However, Marie Taglioni was never happy in the rôle; after dancing it only three times, she found a reason to be excused. At the opera's fourth performance, it was given without her, Amélie Legallois taking over at short notice for the following four performances.

One critic made no secret of his opinion that the injury to Taglioni's foot was just an excuse not to appear. 'Proof of the rare merit of the score of *Robert le Diable* is given in the increasing houses, even though Mlle Taglioni's name has disappeared from the bills,' he wrote. 'This dancer needs to dance in isolation to be appreciated, but in a crowd she does not stand out from her companions, and in any case one's eyes are too occupied with the double diorama of the third act to think of anything else.'[12] Once again, Véron had failed to inform Meyerbeer of this development, and the composer was not pleased. However, he was not a man to react without reflection, and he let two days pass before writing a pained letter to the Director, reminding him of his contractual rights:

> I have been surprised and, I must admit, at the same time grieved to learn from the playbill only the evening before last that Mlle Taglioni would not be dancing in *Robert*. If you had not considered it worth your while to inform me of that, you will be aware, Monsieur, that the regulations of the Opéra give authors the right not to have rôles played by understudies in the first six performances. Furthermore, apart from that, Mlle Taglioni's presence in my work is a right stipulated and granted by various specific

clauses in our contract, and if you will take another look at our contract, you will see that a breach of this clause falls into the same category as all other breaches.

I did not write this note the day before yesterday because I did not want to interfere with your performance, which had been announced. The same reason applied to today's. But how can one expect Mlle Taglioni to have recovered from her slight foot injury in time for Monday? I hope I can rely, Monsieur, on your kindness and your concern for authors, that as from Monday *Robert* will not be given again without Mlle Taglioni. Since I myself am quite sure that Mlle Taglioni is indispensable to the complete success of this work, I am deeply concerned and insist all the more strongly on this since it is formally required under the regulations and my contract.

But I hope that an appeal to your kindness will be all the more effective than insisting on my rights, and it is this that I am confidently doing by this letter.

After this I shall not insist on Mlle Taglioni remaining in my work from the moment your new ballet will be staged, because I know that her presence in it is indispensable, and that it would then be damaging to your interests for me to insist on the clause of my contract.[13]

Meanwhile, on 9 December, Taglioni had reappeared in the rôle of the Abbess to find Charles Maurice still on the warpath, describing in his review how

yesterday the audience laughed itself to tears during M. Taglioni's *divertissement*. Never was such a thing seen before – platitudes danced by so many talented souls and presented with more than effrontery by 'a choreographer lacking in imagination'. One might have thought oneself at the descent of the Courtille on an Ash Wednesday morning.[14]

By then she had completed the six performances for which she was bound, and a seventh for good measure, after which, on the 26th, the rôle of Héléna was taken over by Pauline Duvernay. Notwithstanding Meyerbeer's conviction that his opera depended on Taglioni's presence, it would stand firmly on its intrinsic merits. It was indeed much more than a vehicle for a star ballerina. The cause of its sensational impact went beyond the choreography of Filippo Taglioni, which some critics found confused in design, to the very conception of the scene itself. In the words of Castil-Blaze, it was 'the Witches' Sabbath of Victor Hugo and M. Boulanger's drawing set in motion'.[15] Here, in its eerie, spectral atmosphere, was all the mystery of Romanticism distilled with an artistry never achieved before on the operatic stage. Everything was subordinated to the general illusion – music, dance, stage design, and in particular the lighting. Specially for this scene, the footlights had been lowered and the auditorium chandelier extinguished, the moonlight being simulated by gas-jets suspended in boxes from the flies, an effect seen at the Opéra for the first time.

What was so novel was the air of mystery that pervaded the scene as the effigies of the shrouded nuns slowly rose and came to life under the gentle rays of the gas-lit moon. At the same time, as an eyewitness described,

> a crowd of mute shadows come gliding through the arcades. All these women then cast aside their nun's habits, shake off the cold dust of their tombs, and at once abandon themselves to the delights of their former life; they dance like bacchantes, they gamble like lords, they imbibe wine by the bottle. What a pleasure it is to see these light female figures in motion in this uncertain light.[16]

Few other works carried more potently the message of Romanticism than the Ballet of the Nuns, and the audiences of the time eagerly submitted to its magic. Typical was the reaction of a young American woman on her first visit to Europe – Fanny Appleton, the future wife of the poet Longfellow:

> It was magnificent and terrific and diabolical and enchanting and everything else fine. The music and the show and the dancing! The famous witches' dance (sic), in the freezing moonlight in the ruined abbey, was as impressive as I expected, though there was no Taglioni to lead the troupe. They drop in like flakes of snow and are certainly very charming witches with their jaunty Parisian figures and most refined pirouettes! The diabolical music and the dead rising from the tombs and the terrible darkness and the strange dance unite to form a stage effect almost unrivalled.[17]

So overwhelming was the impression made by the Ballet of the Nuns that the more conventional *divertissement* in the second act was completely overshadowed in the memories of those who saw it. Yet, even though it had no particular relevance to the action of the opera, it was an impressive display of dancing. It was probably set, not by Filippo Taglioni, but by Jean Coralli. Featuring three of the female *premiers sujets* – Noblet, Montessu and Julia – together with Noblet's sister Félicité (Mme Alexis Dupont), it also featured Jules Perrot, who aroused such enthusiasm that Castil-Blaze interrupted an essay on the music to insert an unusually detailed description:

> Mmes Julia, Noblet and Dupont advanced in a group like the Three Graces. My comparison is not a romantic one, but I make it because I can find

nothing in the Middle Ages that conveys my meaning more exactly. They form a charming trio, dancing with rare perfection, producing a multitude of graceful poses and arousing our delight by such variety. They are followed by Perrot, a vigorous and nimble dancer; he performs *tours de force* which would have no other merit than that of difficulties being overcome, had he not charmed us by the elegance of his steps and his attitudes. He does not confine himself to performing *demi-tours* to the right and to the left, but performs two or three turns in the air, landing firmly in a pose like that of Giovanni Bologna's Mercury as easily as if he had produced a simple *flic-flac* or even a *pas de bourrée*. He performs jumps *à cloche-pied* [18] and seems to flit about like a sylph. This admirable quintet is completed by Mme Montessu. Her three companions had twirled to a coruscation of notes and *arpeggi* and performed beats to the trills of the music; but now the orchestra, whose trills had become even more animated for Perrot's entrance, galloped along with Mme Montessu. The flute increases its tempo to match the speed of the dancer, who mounts an assault of agility that culminates in a marvellous sequence of *entrechats*. [19]

* * * * * * *

After reorganising the hierarchy of the ballet company by elevating Marie Taglioni to a pre-eminent pinnacle, Véron could hardly have hoped for a more suitable ballet to justify his policy than *La Sylphide*. Its scenario was brought to him during the rehearsal period of *Robert le Diable* by the tenor Adolphe Nourrit, who had conceived it specifically with Taglioni in mind. It had the obvious merits of a simple, straightforward narrative and a pathetic ending, and with its Scottish setting provided scope for the introduction of local colour. But what was important above all else was that it captured, with magical effect, that Romantic mood of mystery that had been so successfully created in *Robert le Diable*. Nourrit could not have been inspired by Taglioni's somewhat lacklustre performance in the Ballet of the Nuns, since his scenario had been read to the choreographer a week before she even began to rehearse her rôle. But preparations for that scene may have been sufficiently advanced for Nourrit to have perceived its mood. After *Robert le Diable* was produced, Véron fully realised the commercial value of exploiting the ethereal quality of Taglioni's talent, although no one could then have foreseen the full implication that Nourrit's conception was to have in the development of ballet.

The plot of the new ballet was inspired by a fantasy that Charles Nodier had written after a visit to Scotland some ten years before, called *Trilby, ou le Lutin de Argaïl*, but it was no less original because of this derivation. Instead of the goblin Trilby luring a peasant girl from her fisherman husband, the central character of the ballet was an aerial spirit, a sylphide (Taglioni), who at curtain-rise is discovered gazing lovingly at a handsome young Scot, James Reuben (Mazilier), as he lies asleep in a chair. James is engaged to marry Effie (Noblet), who is also loved by Gurn (Elie). Waking at the touch of the Sylphide's kiss, James catches just a glimpse of her before she vanishes up the chimney. This memory begins to haunt him, even in Effie's presence, and his secret is divined by Old Madge the witch (Mme Elie), who reveals to Effie that it is Gurn, not James, who truly loves her. When James is alone again, the Sylphide reappears on the window-ledge. Gurn observes their tender exchanges, but when he goes to the chair and pulls aside the plaid beneath which the Sylphide has hidden, it is empty. The wedding ceremony then begins, but just as James is about to place the ring on Effie's finger, the Sylphide glides out from the fireplace and snatches it from his hand. James follows her as she flies out of the cottage.

The second act opens as Madge and other members of her coven are casting an evil spell over a scarf. Dawn then breaks, and a forest glade comes into view. James enters in search of the Sylphide, whom he finds among her fellow spirits. While he is wondering whether he is chasing a chimera, Madge gives him the scarf, telling him that it will cause the Sylphide's wings to drop so that she will be his forever. Eagerly James places the scarf on the Sylphide's shoulders. Her wings do indeed drop to the ground, as Madge had promised, but to his horror her life-force vanishes too. And so the Sylphide dies, to be borne away through the treetops by her grieving companions. As James is left alone with his grief, the bridal procession of Gurn and Effie passes in the background.

Filippo Taglioni thought the story charming when Nourrit read it over to him on 23 October 1831, and within a fortnight was hard at work sketching out instructions for the composer. The musician selected for this task was the experienced Jean Schneitzhoeffer, who for once conquered his habitual indolence, setting to work so conscientiously that rehearsals began before the end of November. On 29 December, having relinquished her rôle in *Robert le Diable*, Marie Taglioni began studying the part of the Sylphide with Joseph Mazilier, who had been cast as James.

While rehearsals were in progress, Charles Maurice continued his campaign against the Taglionis in the *Courrier des théâtres*. Reporting that the scenario had been accepted, he uncharitably told his readers that Marie Taglioni would play the Sylphide 'notwithstanding her figure, which is completely lacking in etherealness'.[20] How he must have regretted that phrase later! Marie, however, was well able to hold her own against all the ill-will and intrigues that were being launched against her by hangers-on of dancers who felt themselves sacrificed by Véron's policy. For now she could count on a growing band of devotees, among the public as within the Opéra itself. Old Vestris, who certainly had no axe to grind, made a show of being present specifically to see her dance, to the disgust of a vocal section of the audience in the orchestra stalls, who made no secret of being in the opposite camp.

Filippo Taglioni set great store by the effects in the second act, and was bitterly frustrated at being unable to stage the witches' scene as he wished. Here the culprit was Duponchel, who was at the same time preparing the orgy scene for the forthcoming opera-ballet, *La Tentation*, and kept filching dancers from Taglioni to swell his own crowd of devils. Taglioni plagued Véron with tearful complaints about the miserly nature of his own '*diableries*', with so few witches placed at his disposal. If he received little satisfaction in this direction, he at least had the consolation of knowing that the flights being devised for the forest scene were far more complex than any that had been attempted before at the Opéra. Among these were a circling flight and, for the apotheosis, a magnificent multiple flight as the body of the Sylphide was borne aloft through the trees.

These effects caused Véron unbelievable anxiety, which was not lessened by the experience of the dress rehearsals. At the first of these, on 10 March 1832, nothing went well, and the next day there was nearly a disastrous accident when Marie Taglioni fell as she was vanishing up the chimney, fortunately without injury. Véron was also very concerned for the safety of the dozen or fifteen girls who were to make the flights, for which each was to be rewarded with a special bonus of 10 francs a performance. Throughout his management, he would make a personal inspection of the flying apparatus before every performance of *La Sylphide*, and not once did an accident occur.

Véron passed a sleepless night before the first performance on 12 March 1832, but its splendid triumph more than compensated him for all the anxiety he had suffered. The names of the authors – with the exception of Nourrit, who preferred to remain anonymous – were announced from the stage to loud applause; and when Marie Taglioni appeared to take her call, an enthusiastic burst of cheering broke out from every corner of the house.

La Sylphide sealed the triumph of Romanticism in the field of ballet, much as the first performance of *Hernani* at the Comédie-Française had determined the future of Romantic drama, although without the scrap that had broken out among the audience between the old guard and the new. The Ballet of the Nuns had already broken the ground, but *La Sylphide* was to set the tone for the future by providing a precedent that was to be followed in countless ballets even down to the present day. Its basic theme spoke to the imagination of the younger generation of artists – poets and painters as well as choreographers – and epitomised, with haunting effect, the quest of the Romantic artist for the infinite and the unattainable. It was this that made the first performance of *La Sylphide* a turning point of the greatest significance in the history of the choreographic art. That ballet was to usher in a golden age – one of moonlight and ethereal spirits – that retains its magic to the present day.

The importance of *La Sylphide*, however, lay not merely in the direction of a new formula, but in its inspired application. Although Marie Taglioni appeared as the interpreter of her father's choreographic design, stylistically her own part in the ballet was fundamental. Nor should the contribution of the scenarist, Adolphe Nourrit, be overlooked; for without his inspirational choice of theme, Filippo Taglioni might have been remembered very differently by posterity. The Sylphide, which Nourrit had conjured up in his scenario and which the Taglionis, father and daughter, had fashioned into an unforgettable vision, was the product of a three-fold inspiration of an intensity that wove its potent magic into the very fabric of ballet.

True to form, Charles Maurice remained difficult to please, and in a second notice pointed out a few faults in the production. The disappearance of the Sylphide in the arm-chair in the first act was effected in such a way as to suggest to him that she had vanished downwards into the ground – an action, he grumbled, more appropriate to a gnome than to a spirit of the air. And when one of the characters then had to pull off the cover to reveal that the chair was empty, this was done with the panache of a conjuror revealing a successful trick. Another moment that he cited as needing attention was the appearance of a stage-hand in full view of the audience to readjust the sliding step on which Taglioni had made her descent from the window-sill. These were details that were no doubt easily adjusted. A more serious comment, however, related to the aerial grouping and movements of the sylphides. Here Maurice suggested that the poses adopted in the air should not be uniform, but given variety, pointing out that leaving them in view of the audience for too long, destroyed the initial effect, for the initial sense of wonderment soon passed and the viewers then became concerned for the safety of the girls strapped aloft on wires.[21]

Marie Taglioni's triumph was complete, achieved not by startling feats of difficulty, but by an inner expressiveness that seemed to raise the dance to a different plane. The audience was left with the haunting memory of an impalpable vision, 'a shadow condensed into a mist', as one spectator remembered it long afterwards.[22] There was poetry in her dance, and nowhere was this more apparent than in the second act, when the Sylphide was shown dancing with her companions. 'Here there is a sequence of furtive, aerial steps,' wrote the critic of *L'Entr'acte*,

> something ravishing beyond description, in which painting, music and the dance all vie with one another. The irresolute flight of a butterfly and those spherical tufts that the mild April breezes pluck like down from the cups of flowers to hover in the air – these are the only comparisons one can make with the timid graces, the mocking abandon and the artful modesty of the Sylphide. In truth, Taglioni is no mortal. God could not have imagined the cherubim any better.[23]

By creating the Sylphide, Marie Taglioni had rendered more obsolete than ever the classical style that expressed itself in the *danse noble*, with its mannered poses, its stiffness, its stereotyped smiles, and above all its applause-catching tricks such as the *bouffante* – the conventional conclusion of a *pas noble* with a *pirouette sur la pointe* performed in such a way that the skirt flared out to the delight of the gentlemen seated near the stage. 'Imagine our joy one evening,' wrote Jules Janin, who held the *danse noble* in abhorrence,

> when, unsuspecting and by pure chance, like finding a pearl by the roadside, we were presented not with the *danse noble*, but with a simple, easy, naturally graceful Taglioni, with a figure of unheard-of elegance, arms of serpentine suppleness and legs to match, and feet like those of an ordinary woman, dancer though she is! When we saw her first, so much at ease and dancing so merrily – like a bird in full song – we just could not understand it. 'What has become of the *danse noble?*' asked the old men. The *danse noble* is as foreign to Taglioni's style as natural dancing is to that of her rivals. She uses her hands when she dances! See how she bends her body, how she walks, how she always keeps to the ground! Note the absence of *pirouettes, entrechats* and other technical difficulties! ... She has given us a new art, she has initiated us into a new pleasure, for she has completely reformed the ballet of her day. All the *danseuses nobles*, after seeing how she is applauded, have chipped off some of their nobility, just as their ancestors cast off their panniers. They have even begun to use their arms and legs like ordinary mortals, they have even risked splitting their satin corsets by bending their bodies more, and bending their arms much less, since Taglioni. The great Taglioni revolution has been specially felt in the arm movements; there has been a sensible improvement in the bust, and an improvement is now beginning to show in the legs. This is a step forward. While waiting for the revolution to be fully established, Taglioni continues her triumphs, every day learning to be more of a woman and less of a dancer than ever. Thanks be for that! But what must

have really astonished those ladies is that this newcomer ... does not permit herself a single *bouffante*. Not one poor little *bouffante* for the poor adoring public![24]

Marie Taglioni was uncompromising in her art: therein lay the secret of her greatness.

Her father's choreography was praised by Castil-Blaze for being as varied in conception as it was excellently performed. Its originality was most apparent in the second act, where it reflected the ethereal mood of the narrative to perfection. Nearly all the details have now been forgotten, but Castil-Blaze described one entrance as including 'an original effect' when the sylphides advanced from the back of the stage in groups of four to form a delightful group in the very front.[25]

Inevitably there would be some who, for one reason or another, refused to admit that Filippo Taglioni's success was deserved. Among these was Elise Henry, sister of the choreographer Louis Henry, who had himself produced a ballet called *La silfide* at La Scala, Milan, in 1828 for Therese Heberle. Taking up the cudgels on her brother's behalf, Mlle Henry wrote to the paper the *Renommée* in October 1832, accusing Filippo Taglioni of plagiarism.[26] Apparently unaware that Nourrit was the author of the scenario, she alleged that Taglioni received every ballet scenario that was published, and for *La Sylphide*, had stolen some of her brother's choreography. 'Let me mention,' she specified, 'the *pas de deux* that has been inserted, since his return to London, in the second act of *La Sylphide*, and in which [Marie Taglioni] makes a *tour en attitude sur la pointe* and Mazilier supports her so well. This movement is my brother's, and much of this *pas* is composed of movements from the same source.'[27] To this outburst Filippo Taglioni replied that his only knowledge of Henry's *La silfide* was that Heberle had once told him she had danced in it, and there seems no reason to doubt his word.

Elise Henry pointed out the following similarities with Taglioni's ballets:

1. The hero in each is discovered asleep.
2. The heroine expresses her love before he wakes.
3. The scene in Almanzor's cave has its counterpart in the witches' scene.
4. Spring comes during Act I of Henry's ballet, whereas day breaks during Act I of Taglioni's.

The superficiality of these similarities will be obvious to the reader. What Henry's ballet of course lacked was the Romanticism that Taglioni's ballet expressed to a sublime degree in all its parts.

Schneitzhoeffer's music met with a mixed reception. One critic considered it the weakest element in the work, lacking in descriptive power, particularly in the witches' scene, where something like the infernal music of *Robert le Diable* was called for, and again in the forest scene, for which more descriptively celestial music would have been appropriate for the aerial dances of the sylphides. However, Castil-Blaze found the score 'excellent' and 'an infinitely remarkable example of what might become a more important branch [of music] if only someone of talent and intelligence were to decide to take it up.'[28] He regretted that the composer had not made better use of borrowed melodies, of which he recognised no more than a fragment of the trio from Boïeldieu's opera, *Le Caliph de Bagdad*, and a little air by Pauline Duchambge, apart from the major interpolation in the witches' scene. This was a passage based on Paganini's variations *Le streghe*, the theme of which the great violinist had himself borrowed from an earlier ballet score: that of Süssmayer for Viganò's *Il noce di Benevento*.[29]

The scenery and costumes of *La Sylphide* played an essential part in evoking the local colour of the first act and the ethereal mood of the second. Ciceri's set for the first act might have seemed a little sombre to Parisian taste, and the colours of the costumes could, it was suggested, have been a little brighter; but thanks to Duponchel's supervision, the Scottish costumes were at least credible. The second act was to be considered one of Ciceri's masterpieces, and a murmur of appreciation ran through the audience when the gauze curtain rose after the witches' scene and the forest set was gradually touched by the light of day.

The costumes were, for the most part, designed by Eugène Lami. The assertion that he designed Taglioni's sylphide costume (which initiated the fashion of the bell-shaped skirt later to be popularly known as the Romantic tutu) rests, however, on a tradition that seems to be unsupported by any contemporary evidence.[30] It may even be that Lami did not himself design this costume. The absence of any sketch for it in the incomplete series of costume designs preserved by the Opéra might suggest that it was not truly designed at all in the way that the Scottish costumes were, but was made up by the costume department merely on instructions to produce a plain white costume with wings. Even the claim that it was the first bell-shaped skirt worn in ballet cannot be maintained. At the first performance in 1832 it was not very full, and certainly no more so than costumes that had been worn in some earlier ballets: a lithograph of Pauline Montessu in the sleepwalking scene from *La Somnambule* shows her in a costume of a very similar form, although a shade more elaborate, but with a fuller skirt. The sylphide costume caused no stir at the time, apparently because there was nothing unusual in its cut or its style. It was its absolute simplicity that was novel, and while this made it a model for the ethereal scenes that were to become so popular in ballet, its significance was not immediately apparent. The development of the bell-shaped skirt was gradual and followed the fashions of the day, its circumference continuing to grow until it reached its maximum under the Second Empire, in the heyday of the crinoline.

La Sylphide was to remain, on and off, a mainstay of the Opéra's balletic repertory for twenty-eight years, reaching a tally of 146 performances before it last appeared on the playbill in 1862. Perhaps no other major ballet has been so indelibly associated with the ballerina for whom it had been created. For Marie Taglioni, the title-rôle would remain her sole preserve until the end of 1838 – only after her connection with the Opéra had ceased did the rôle pass to another ballerina. For Fanny Elssler, who appeared in it a few times in 1838, it proved to be something of a poisoned chalice, even though she gave a rendering that some of her admirers found novel and valid. Lucile Grahn, Hermine Blangy and Flora Fabbri were seen in it briefly during the 1840s, but in that decade it was Adèle Dumilâtre who came closest to being an honourable successor to Taglioni, performing it seventeen times between 1841 and her retirement in 1848. Four years later, it was revived for Olimpia Priora, who was supported by Arthur Saint-Léon as James and Taglioni's niece, Louise Taglioni, as Effie. There was then to be a gap of six years before it was resurrected for the last time by the sixteen-year-old Emma Livry, whose extraordinary triumph enticed Taglioni back to Paris in 1858. 'I must have danced just like that,' she was heard to exclaim – and surely no greater compliment could have been paid to the young debutante. But Emma Livry was doomed to an early death from burns received during a rehearsal, and no one, it seems, could bear to awaken painful memories by reviving the two rôles that she had made so indelibly her own: that of her only creation, in the ballet *Le Papillon*, which Marie Taglioni had staged specially for her, and the impalpable Sylphide that had drawn the most fulsome praise from its legendary creator.

NOTES

1. The position of 'star' dancer was not yet dignified by any form of accolade. Not until many years later did terms such as *prima ballerina assoluta* and *première danseuse étoile* come into use. Marie Taglioni's contract with Véron was signed by her in London on 7 June 1831 (Arch. Nat., AJ[13] 129).
2. *Il crociato in Egitto*, created at the Théâtre-Italien on 22 September 1825; *Marguerite d'Anjou*, created at the Théâtre de l'Odéon on 11 March 1826.
3. Véron, III, 150.
4. *Courrier des théâtres*, 4 and 5 October 1831.
5. *Courrier des théâtres*, 24 October 1831.
6. Castil-Blaze, *Académie*, II, 229
7. *Courrier des théâtres*, 21 November 1831.
8. *Courrier des théâtres*, 22 November 1831.
9. *Courrier des théâtres*, 23 November 1831. The *colin-maillard* is the French equivalent of the game

of hide and seek.

10. *Courrier des théâtres*, 25 November 1831.

11. *Courrier des théâtres*, 26 November 1831.

12. *Corsaire*, 2 December 1831.

13. Harvard Theatre Collection. Meyerbeer to Véron, 2 December 1831.

14. *Courrier des théâtres*, 10 December 1831. This was one of the features of Carnival, which culminated in the procession of the *Bœuf Gras*, the prize ox, preceded by a band and accompanied by a numerous train of butchers in fantastic costumes, on Shrove Tuesday *(mardi gras)*.

15. *Moniteur*, 28 November 1831. Signed XXX.

16. *Revue des deux mondes*, 1831, II, 732–3.

17. Longfellow, *Selected Letters*, 27–8 (letter of 15 January 1836). In the rôle of the Abbess the writer would have seen Louise Fitzjames, who first played it on 31 December 1832 and danced it more frequently than any other ballerina throughout that opera's long history – a total of 245 performances. Louise Fitzjames was a pupil of Filippo Taglioni.

18. Littré, in his great *Dictionnaire*, described this as a gymnastic jump ending in a landing on one foot.

19. *Moniteur*, 4 December 1831. Signed XXX.

20 .*Courrier des théâtres*, 20 November 1831.

21. *Courrier des théâtres*, 15 March 1832.

22. *Vieil Abonné*, 140.

23. *Entr'acte*, 13 March 1832.

24. *Journal des débats*, 24 August 1832.

25. Castil-Blaze, *Académie* II, 234.

26. *La Silfide*, choreography by Louis Henry, music by Luigi Carlini, scenery by Alessandro Sanquirico, f.p. La Scala, Milan, 28 May 1828. Briefly, the plot was as follows. Ezelda, a sylphide, has fallen in love with a mortal, Azalide, whom she transports to her side. When he wakes and sees her, he falls in love with her. Ezelda's uncle, Almanzor, reveals that the fates have ordained that they must undergo the ordeal of the barrier of love. A garland of flowers is laid on the ground between the lovers. Ezelda tries to warn Azalide that he must keep to his side of it, but he leaps across and she is thereupon changed into a statue. Only Azalide himself can now break the spell, but at the expense of sacrificing himself. He does not hesitate to do so, but in the end Hymen and the amorets restore him to life again and the ballet ends happily with the lovers reunited.

27. The correspondence is to be found in *Courrier des théâtres*, 14, 17, 19, 21 and 24 October 1832.

28. Castil-Blaze, *Académie*, II, 234.

29. *Il noce di Benevento*, choreography by Salvatore Viganò, music by Süssmayer, f.p. La Scala, Milan, 25 April 1812.

30. Carlos Fischer was unable to obtain any corroboration from Lami's family. 'In his family,' he wrote, 'Eugène Lami – who used to talk freely of the past, his youth and the Opéra – never breathed a word, it appears, of his invention of the tutu, of which he had the right, however, to be proud and which he would not have dreamt of denying. None of his relations knows if he really designed and made with his own hands the first ballet skirt with several layers of gauze and tarlatan, but they agree, with a smile, that he was quite capable of it.' (*Les Costumes de l'Opéra*, 210.)

13

Of Temptation and Revolt

One of the doors of Véron's office communicated with a large room where the meetings of the Opéra's supervisory committee were held – and here Edmond Cavé, the secretary of the committee, had his desk. Véron found it politic to pass a few minutes' conversation each day with this watchdog, discussing the affairs of the Opéra, and in this way quickly took his measure. Cavé, who was at the same time Director of Fine Arts in the Ministry of the Interior, held the view that Véron's subsidy was not given to enable him to make a profit; if receipts were exceptionally good, as they usually were whenever *Robert le Diable* was billed, he would raise the subject of submitting a report to his Minister.

Véron soon decided that M. Cavé had to be tamed. Observing that Cavé had literary pretensions, Véron conceived a plan to put him in his debt. He was searching at that time for a work that would exploit the beauty and talent of the young Pauline Duvernay, and he approached Cavé with the suggestion that he might like to submit a scenario for a ballet. Cavé was duly flattered. His first proposal, a mythological subject entitled *Hercule et Omphale*, was plainly unacceptable, but he was more than satisfied when Véron suggested the grandiose project of a ballet-opera, to be produced under Duponchel's supervision with all the spectacular resources at the Opéra's disposal.

Pauline Duvernay, for whom this massive work was intended, had caught Véron's appreciative eye in the early months of his management. A true child of the Opéra, she had entered the School of Dance as a child and, in 1829, on her mother's insistence, had been admitted into Auguste Vestris's class. It was there that Véron had noticed her. Her mother, whose astuteness he readily acknowledged, was seldom far from her daughter's side, and on the rare occasions when the girl came to class unchaperoned, Vestris, ever anxious to please his new master, would obligingly seek him out to impart the glad news. Véron was amused by the old teacher – eyes shining with excitement, hair flying, feet always turned out, and pochette clasped firmly in his hand – while at the same time being no doubt secretly pleased by his thoughtfulness. For Véron had a weakness for Duvernay and her pretty air of melancholy, so different from Vestris's other favourite pupil, the bright and witty Pauline Leroux. One day, finding Duvernay in tears, and being told by her mother that she was upset because Lise Noblet, with whom she was to dance a *pas* that evening, had a caseful of jewels while she had none, Véron immediately sent to a jeweller's for 'the sovereign remedy for such great suffering and poignant sorrow'.[1] Vestris, too, was affected by the ease with which she dissolved into tears. He once took Véron aside and, pointing to some drops of water on the floor, which the Director knew very well had been sprinkled there by the watering-can, said in hushed tones, 'See, there are her tears'.

Pauline Duvernay passed the customary audition early in 1831 and on 13 April made her début in a *pas de deux* with Antoine Coulon in *Mars et Vénus*. Despite her nervousness, she met with an excellent reception. The *Courrier des théâtres* saw a resemblance to Bigottini in appearance and noted that

> her talent [was] a mixture of the two schools of Mlle Noblet and Mlle Taglioni, aiming at the former's correctness and the latter's simple, modern grace. With more strength, which would give her added assurance and elevation, Mlle Duvernay has the makings of an excellent dancer. She is already enchanting in *développements, posés* and *terre à terre* movements.[2]

Perrot partnered her in four of her six début performances. She was then formally engaged, and on 5 September appeared in her first rôle, Venus in *Mars et Vénus*. Uneasy at Véron's undisguised predilection for her, Filippo Taglioni turned a wary eye on her, but had to admit that she was 'not bad'.[3]

When a substitute had to be found for Taglioni in *Robert le Diable*, it was Duvernay whom Véron chose. 'Mlle Duvernay,' wrote the *Journal des débats* of her in this part, 'is very young and very pretty, she dances to perfection, and her miming is full of fascination. This young virtuoso is making rapid progress and is following in Mlle Taglioni's steps with a light foot.'[4] Marie Taglioni and her father did not take kindly to the boosting of this young dancer whom Véron hoped 'had the makings of another Taglioni, with the addition of beauty',[5] and during her visit to London in the summer of 1832, Marie Taglioni unwisely wrote to a friend begging him to ask Charles Maurice 'not to say too many good things of Mlle Duvernay'. Unfortunately, the friend indiscreetly let slip the source of this request, and the story found its way into print. Marie Taglioni was then rash enough to deny it, and Charles Maurice took a malicious pleasure in recounting the story again in the *Courrier des théâtres* and disclosing that he was the critic referred to.[6]

Many months of preparation preceded the first performance of *La Tentation*, as the new opera-ballet was entitled, on 20 June 1832. According to Castil-Blaze, Cavé based his scenario on an episode from an ambulatory ballet, *Lou Pichoun juè di Diable ou l'Armetta*, composed by King René of Anjou for the procession at Aix in 1462. It told of the struggle between the demon Astaroth (Montjoie) and the angel Mizaël (Mme Dabadie) for the soul of a hermit (Mazilier), who had been struck dead by lightning when on the point of yielding to his desire for the beautiful Marie (Leroux). They agree to settle their dispute by putting the hermit to the test of three temptations. Astaroth then creates Miranda (Duvernay), a being more alluring than any mortal woman, but whose infernal origin is revealed by a black spot over her heart. Brought back to life, the hermit arrives at a château on a snowy night. While being famished, he refuses to surrender his crucifix in exchange for food. Although unable to comprehend it, Miranda is touched by his faith and out of the goodness of her heart brings him provisions. At this charitable act, so contrary to her origin, the black spot vanishes, but she is snatched away by demons and the château bursts into flames. The hermit's next trial takes place in a harem, where he is tempted by jealousy to kill the Sultan (S. Mérante). But before the deed can be committed, Miranda snatches the dagger from his hand, and together she and the hermit leap into the sea and make their escape. For the final trial Miranda is commanded to seduce the hermit, but instead she hands him the crucifix that Marie had earlier given to her. In his fury at being thwarted, Astaroth plunges his sword into Miranda's heart. After a battle between the demons and the angels, good prevails over evil, and, in the apotheosis, the hermit is shown ascending the golden steps to the Heavenly kingdom.

The general opinion was that *La Tentation* was long, obscure, noisy and fatiguing. 'It is boring,' observed the Comte de Montalivet to his friend Romieu, 'and interminable, but even so the public will be fooled by it.'[7] The magnificence of the spectacle almost beggared description. It was 'superb, staggering, prodigious'.[8] No fewer than five distinguished artists had been called upon to design the scenery, which was given added realism by an unprecedented use of built pieces to achieve a realism greater than could be achieved by cloths – a departure that displeased Castil-Blaze, who grumbled that it 'took away all the Opéra's magic by no longer permitting the *changement à vue*'.[9] Edmond Bertin's design for the first set was conventional enough, but when the curtain rose for the second act, the product of Eugène Lami's imagination, the audience gasped with astonishment and admiration. A gigantic stairway, ablaze with flame and flanked by two enormous monsters, rose and disappeared into the darkness of the flies, and down it there rushed and tumbled a veritable army of demons to throw themselves into a wild orgy in honour of their lord and master, Astaroth. According to Castil-Blaze, seven hundred people took part in this scene – an exaggeration maybe, but nevertheless an indication of how exceptionally crowded was the stage. The third act, depicting a fantastic château standing in a snow-covered park and illumined by the meagre mist-bound rays of a winter sun, revealed the talent of Camille Roqueplan. Feuchères designed the harem of the fourth act, while the last act and the magnificent apotheosis showing the Temple of Heaven appearing in the sky – an effect of which the first-night audience had to be deprived when a stage-hand became caught in the ropes – was designed and painted by Paul Delaroche.

One celebrated name missing from this impressive roll of artists was that of Ciceri, whose monopoly Véron had resolved to break. Ciceri had been at the head of the Opéra's scenic department for some twenty years, receiving an annual fee of 6000 francs a year for touching up existing scenery stock; he charged additionally for new sets and enjoyed the profitable privilege of working rent-free in the Opéra's scenery store in the Menu-Plaisirs building in the rue Richer, where, on the side, he also produced scenery for other theatres. It was an arrangement that Véron considered incompatible with Ciceri's employment by the Opéra, and when the celebrated designer submitted preliminary sketches for *La Tentation*, Véron accepted only two, well knowing that this would bring matters to a head. Ciceri then claimed that he had an exclusive right to design scenery for the Opéra, and in the lawsuit that followed was awarded damages of 5000 francs and his costs.

Contrary to Montalivet's opinion, the public was not taken in by all the splendour of the new opera, and reserved its enthusiasm mainly for Pauline Duvernay, who played the rôle of Miranda 'like an experienced mime, her appearance perfectly suited to that fantastic being'.[10] She was, wrote *L'Entr'acte*,

> graceful and childlike in turn, and so modest, even when she accepts the mission which her creator and master, the demon, confides to her. Then, by degrees that are ably managed, she summons up the pathos, the devotion and the will of a martyr. She is a pretty woman and a talented one.[11]

Her first entrance, in the second act, was a memorable moment. Astaroth and his demons huddle around an enormous cauldron, into which ingredients are thrown, to the accompaniment of a magical incantation. Then, out of the cauldron, a monster emerges, misshapen, unformed, green of flesh, and frighteningly hideous.[12] At once this abortive creature is plunged back into the cauldron and the spell repeated. Soon, from the bubbling foam, there rises Miranda, young and lovely, her black hair loose on her shoulders, and clad all in white save only for the black spot on her breast. The remainder of the work was dominated by Duvernay's performance as this paradoxical being who has been formed by demons yet is free from vice, and who is destined to be instrumental in saving the hermit from damnation. Such was the conceit, wrote *Le Moniteur*, that 'alone introduced a few fleeting touches of interest' to the work.[13] Duvernay apart, *Le Tentation* was a muddled conglomeration of ideas that had been used before. Although it contained a few interesting passages – the dances for the demons in the second act, and, significantly, the voluptuous *Roméc* (a chain dance) in the harem scene – Coralli's choreography was not found particularly original.

After a number of performances, even Pauline Duvernay began to grow weary of it, and one day the entire Opéra was thrown into consternation when it was learnt that she had vanished from her home without a trace. The police were informed, and a visit was even made to the Morgue in the dreaded possibility that her body might have been dragged out of the Seine. The mystery was finally solved when Casimir Gide received an anonymous note telling him where she was to be found. Taking a cabriolet, he hastened to the address given. It was a convent, and there inside was the errant ballerina who, without being able to explain why, had been overcome by a sudden but passing urge to become a nun. More cynical observers, of course, saw in this only a ruse to obtain publicity.

Certainly Pauline Duvernay quickly recovered her poise on her return to the Opéra, where her admirers were waiting to welcome her. No other dancer was better at handling those rich flatterers who haunted the wings of the theatre, and another story was soon going round telling how she had given a salutary lesson to a certain wealthy old Russian.

'You tell me you love me,' she told him one day, 'but do you love me as much as 100,000 francs?'

The old gentleman took this remark as an invitation, and the next day she returned from class to find him comfortably installed in her salon with his feet on the sofa. By his side was a cash box.

'My dear,' he said casually as she entered, hardly troubling to stir, 'you asked me yesterday if I loved you as much as 100,000 francs, and here,' he continued, opening the cash box, which contained just that sum in gold pieces, 'is my answer.'

'To begin with,' Duvernay retorted, 'kindly do not soil my sofa with your feet, and then take away all that old metal. I was only joking. You know the song in *La Dame blanche* that says that hospitality among Scottish highlanders is given, never sold? Well, in matters of hospitality, my heart is Scottish, but completely Scottish.'

The news of the Russian's rebuff reawakened the hopes of another admirer, an impecunious diplomat, who lost no time in calling on her. After a few tactfully chosen remarks about his rival, he burst into his declaration.

'I am not offering you gold,' he cried, 'but my life, which I would gladly sacrifice for you.'

Duvernay laughed. 'Suppose I wanted your head, would you bring it to me

in person? You men are all the same. You always offer something that is
either impossible or not wanted.'

'But I swear –'

'Do not swear, or I shall take you at your word.'

'For mercy's sake, speak.'

'You really want me to?'

'Please do.'

'Very well, bring me one of your teeth – the middle one.'

He was gone in a flash, and an hour later was back, one hand clutching a
handkerchief to his mouth, the other holding a pillbox. Inside was the tooth,
and to prove it was his, the foolish young man opened wide his mouth and
displayed the cavity.

'Oh, you stupid fellow!' cried Duvernay. 'I asked for a lower tooth, and you
have brought me an upper one!'[14]

Well might the fears of the Taglionis have been allayed when they heard of
Duvernay's erratic private life. For she was a dancer destined, not for
greatness, but for notoriety.

* * * * * * *

Quietly, in the presence of her family and a few friends, Marie Taglioni was
married to Comte Gilbert de Voisins in St Pancras Church, London, on 14
July 1832. That the marriage would not last had been foretold by a lawyer
friend of the Comte, whose professional assistance had at one stage been
sought in overcoming his family's resistance to the match. 'I will gladly help
you in this matter, but on one condition,' he had cynically replied, 'namely,
that you will still give me your confidence when you seek a separation.' The
unhappiness that Taglioni was to suffer then lay hidden in the future, and for
some years Dr Véron welcomed the Comte's presence at the Opéra, finding
that he exerted a calming influence over his wife.

Radiantly happy, Marie Taglioni reappeared at the Opéra on 16 August in
Le Dieu et la Bayadère, and was billed to dance in *La Sylphide* on the following
Monday, the 20th. Few knew how closely this performance came to being
cancelled. Indeed, there would have been no alternative if Véron had not
been working in his office on the Sunday afternoon, when a note was
delivered telling him that Mazilier's father had just died. Since Mazilier was
the only dancer at the Opéra familiar with the part of James, Véron at once
sent a message to Filippo Taglioni that a change of programme was
inevitable. Taglioni, however, had a solution up his sleeve. His son Paul, who
happened just to have arrived in Paris, knew the part and was prepared to
take Mazilier's place at short notice if his wife, Amalia Taglioni, could play

Effie. This demand necessitated some delicate negotiation with Lise Noblet, who generously raised no objection, and the two visitors were well received on the Monday evening by an audience blissfully unaware of the crisis that had so nearly deprived them of their pleasure.

Before long, Filippo Taglioni was preparing another ballet for his daughter. He had chosen to revive *Nathalie, ou la Laitière suisse*, to a score by Gyrowetz, which he claimed to have paid for himself. He had first produced this ballet in Vienna in 1821,[15] and two years later it had been revived at the Porte-Saint-Martin, not by him, but by Antoine Titus, who had failed to acknowledge Taglioni's authorship. Accordingly, some Parisians now mistakenly believed that Taglioni was about to present another choreographer's work as his own. Louis Henry's sister Elise was only too happy to seize the opportunity of blackening Taglioni's reputation, alleging that it was filched from her brother's ballet, *I minatori valacchi.* She accused Taglioni of attempting to conceal his plagiarism by transporting the scene of the action to Switzerland, taking *pas*, groups and scenes from here, there and everywhere, and claiming the finished result as his own. Filippo Taglioni then freely acknowledged[16] that he had based his ballet on an episode from another ballet; but he had the pleasure of pointing out that it was not by Henry, but by Gaetano Gioja, the choreographer of the original version of *I minatori valacchi.*[17]

Filippo Taglioni had transposed the setting of the ballet from Wallachia to Switzerland. Nathalie (Taglioni), a farmer's daughter, is loved by Oswald (Mazilier), brother of the local lord. On his orders she is abducted and carried to the castle, where she recovers from her swoon to find herself in an elegant room containing a life-size statue of Oswald. When she realises it is only a statue, she loses her fear and dances before it. In the course of her dance, Oswald, who has sensed her feelings towards him, takes the statue's place and, to her astonishment, kneels at her feet and declares his love. At that moment the lord and his lady arrive, along with Nathalie's father and the villagers. Asked for an explanation of his conduct, Oswald finally makes amends by asking for Nathalie's hand in marriage.

This naive little work was given its first performance at the Opéra on 7 November 1832, and, on the whole, was favourably received. The meagreness of its plot was somewhat compensated for by a choreography that was fresh and original, particularly in the second act. This was devoted almost entirely to the statue scene, 'a sort of Harlequinade',[18] as one critic described it, presented with great delicacy and charm. Marie Taglioni admitted to a friend that she had agreed to take the part of the simple Swiss peasant girl 'not without some apprehension, because it seemed to be a new kind of rôle for me'.[19] However, she entered into the spirit of the light piece and portrayed the heroine with the simplicity and innocence that the part demanded. But, her presence apart, the ballet was found wanting by some critics: Jules Janin, for one, made the just comment that she had come to the rescue of a bad ballet.[20]

Another critic, who had taken the view that Lise Noblet or Pauline Montessu would have been better suited to the part of Nathalie, was able to judge for himself on 19 December 1832, when the latter appeared as the heroine. Discouraged by Véron's neglect of her talents and in particular by being left out of the cast of *Nathalie*, Mme Montessu had threatened to leave the Opéra unless given more opportunities. This had produced quick results. She had been promised a *pas* in Mozart's *Don Juan*, and, on 13 October 1832, had danced with Perrot in a *pas de deux* of his own composition. This was possibly his first essay in choreography, which created so little stir that no one could have then foreseen the brilliant career that lay before him as a choreographer. No doubt Pauline Montessu was much more satisfied by being allowed to play Nathalie, to which she brought many subtle individual touches, particularly in the statue scene – where she conveyed the conflict between the character's passionate feelings and shy modesty with clarity and conviction.

On 6 May 1833, a third dancer appeared as Nathalie – Véron's favourite, Pauline Duvernay, who was described by one critic as being 'as pretty as an angel and full of simple graces that are perfectly suited to this part.'[21]

* * * * * * *

Meanwhile, on 27 February 1833, the first performance had been given of a new opera by Auber, *Gustave, ou le Bal masqué*, a somewhat unbalanced work, which owed its triumphant reception almost entirely to its last act, the scene of the masked ball at which the Swedish king, Gustav III, was assassinated. Only in this scene, for which Filippo Taglioni had arranged the dances, did the work come to life – with an impact that swept the unsuspecting audience into unbridled enthusiasm. It was a scene of such colour as to satisfy even the most blasé of critics. Jules Janin declared:

> I do not think that a grander, more gorgeous, more fantastic, or more magnificent spectacle has ever been seen, even at the Opéra, than the fifth act of the masked ball. It is an unbelievable profusion of women, gauze, velvet, the grotesque and the elegant, good taste and bad, trifles, affectations, wit, folly, verve – in short, everything that went to make up the eighteenth century. As the curtain rises, you suddenly find yourself in an immense ballroom that takes up the entire Opéra stage, one of the vastest in Europe. This ballroom is completely surrounded by boxes, filled

with masked onlookers. Below them is an immense throng of disguises of every kind, dominoes of all colours, harlequins of every shape and form, clowns, merchants, and what have you. One is disguised as a barrel, another as a guitar; his neighbour is a bunch of asparagus; another has come as a mirror, another as a fish; there is one dressed as a cockerel and another got up as a clock: you would never have believed such utter confusion. Mme Elie and [Simon] are doubles: seen from one side as a peasant and his girl, from the other a marquis and marquise. It is impossible to take in all this verve, this rout, this endless fantasy. To see all these people revelling and dancing in their fancy costumes, you would think they were there for their own enjoyment, not ours. And among this motley crowd glide elegant and bejewelled women, very eighteenth-century, making a charming and fresh contrast with all the super-abundant folly that surrounds them. It is a sight for sore eyes! And above all this world of madmen and beautiful women ... imagine two thousand candles in large glass chandeliers, flooding the whole stage with a hundred thousand lights. All this takes place in a golden palace, without any confusion yet not without enthusiasm. I who, alas, am all too accustomed to seeing such scenes and not easily astonished, even I, as you see, am still dazzled by this spectacle.

Yet another admirable moment comes when everyone begins to dance a general galop. They all dance as one, coming and going, crossing, sweeping backwards and forwards, to the right and to the left, in every direction. It is wonderful. The galop takes possession of every one of these men and women body and soul... Its realism is beyond one's imagination![22]

Filippo Taglioni's dances in this scene included an *allemande* by Montjoie and Mlles Legallois, Perceval, Vagon, Fitzjames and Varin; a *pas des folies* by Lise Noblet and Mme Alexis Dupont and the *corps de ballet;* a *pas comique* by Mme Elie and Simon; and finally, the celebrated *galop général* in which a hundred and twenty-two demons took part. Marie Taglioni was happy to see her father's success. 'This time at least,' she wrote to a friend, 'the success cannot be attributed to me ... and they are forced to do justice to my father.'[23]

Now Louis Henry himself roundly accused Taglioni of plagiarism. He alleged that this scene was nothing more than a copy of *La Festa da ballo in maschera*, which he had produced at La Scala, Milan, during the Carnival season of 1830,[24] and to prove his point he had a Milanese engraving of his work republished in Paris.[25] 'It can be seen,' ran the caption,

how M. Taglioni has filched this work to insert it in the opera *Gustave*. He has not overlooked the *allemande*, the *folies*, nor the double masquerade of the minuet and the *savoyarde* that existed in L. Henry's ballet. M. Taglioni has called himself the author of this, as he has already done in the case of many other works by various choreographers. It is said that he is now preparing a new ballet that will comprise, first, part of *La Belle Arsène,* a ballet by L. Henry, performed in Naples in 1818 and in Vienna in 1823, when M. Taglioni himself danced in it and his daughter played the part of the Prude;[26] secondly, the revolt and the armed dances from *Les Amazones,* a ballet by L. Henry, performed in Vienna in 1823, in which Mlle Taglioni danced;[27] and thirdly, a rifle exercise, performed by women, which is a scene from the third act of the ballet of *Les Grecs* by M. Blache *fils,* performed in Bordeaux, and in which Mlle Taglioni danced at a special performance in 1829,[28] etc., etc., etc. Time will reveal many other thefts.

* * * * * *

This new ballet that Filippo Taglioni was preparing was in fact a second version of an earlier work of his entitled *Die Neue Amazon,* which he had staged in Berlin in 1830,[29] but with an entirely new score by the harpist Théodore Labarre. To yet another charge of plagiarism from Louis Henry's sister Elise, published in the *Courrier des théâtres* in October 1832, Taglioni responded to point out that his ballet was conceived in the faery style, whereas Henry's ballet *Die Amazonen* fell into the category of the heroic ballet. Elise Henry returned to the charge by asserting that this distinction was only due to the fact that Taglioni had also taken ideas from another of her brother's ballets, *Arsène.* Then it was Marie Taglioni's turn to join in the fray to deny ever having told Elise Henry that she preferred Louis Henry to any other choreographer. The acrimonious squabble finally closed with a letter from Elise Henry, putting on record that Marie had taken classes from Louis Henry at Baden and had been so grateful that, when dancing in *Die Amazonen* in Vienna in 1823, she had asked the *corps de ballet* to wear white and pink like her to add charm and variety to the *pas.*

The last word in this rather ridiculous squabble was spoken by the critic Jules Janin. Shortly after the first performance of Taglioni's new ballet, *La Révolte au sérail,* he received a visit from Elise Henry, who referred scornfully to Filippo Taglioni's pilfering and lack of ideas. If she hoped to find a sympathetic champion in the wily critic, she was to be disappointed.

'He has more than ideas, madame,' Janin told her. 'He also has more than genius, more even than Gardel had. While it may not be apparent, M. Taglioni is the greatest choreographer in the world because he has his daughter, whom he has stolen from no one.'[30]

Jules Janin, who had followed the preparation of *La Révolte au sérail* from its inception, invited a friend of his, a colonel in the Army, to watch one of the final rehearsals. They arrived at the moment the company was going through the military evolutions in the amazon scene of the third act. Catching sight of the visitor's uniform, Marie Taglioni gave the command, 'Halt!' Then she turned to the colonel, saluted him, and offered him her property sword with the words: 'General, please do us the honour of drilling us.' The rather embarrassed officer took it and began to give his commands – in as soft a voice as he could muster, but one that nevertheless echoed round the building. The discipline of the dancers astonished him; at the end he gallantly complimented them, and joined in the spirit of the occasion by giving Marie Taglioni an accolade. In later years Janin often looked back on this incident – for his friend, whose name was Bugeaud, later became a Marshal of France famed as the conqueror of Algeria.

La Révolte au sérail – the title was changed from *La Révolte des femmes* at the last minute, too late for the printed scenario to be corrected – had been in preparation since July, when a project to produce a ballet by Jean Coralli called *Le Zingaro* was abandoned to make way for it. That same month Montjoie, whom Filippo Taglioni envisaged for the rôle of the King, resumed his duties after serving four months' imprisonment. Stage rehearsals began at the end of September, and the ballet, expensively and spectacularly produced, was given its first performance on 4 December 1833. Its success was unprecedented, the receipts for its first twenty-five performances even surpassing those of *Robert le Diable*.[31] This triumph, however, was more a personal one for Marie Taglioni than an acclamation of her father's talent as a choreographer. 'With the exception of *La Sylphide*, which is hardly his,' wrote Charles de Boigne, 'Papa Taglioni's ballets are all alike: completely devoid of ideas, second-hand stuff, always the same... but the ballerina is there to rescue the choreographer, the daughter to rescue the father.'[32]

Set in Southern Spain during the Moorish domination, it opened in the audience-hall of the king, Mahomet (Montjoie). The Moors have defeated the Christian army in battle, and their victorious general, Ismaël (Mazilier), enters with his staff to lay the captured battle standards at the king's feet. After giving his report on the battle, Ismaël begs permission to withdraw to visit his betrothed, Zulma, but the king retains him to preside over a festival prepared in his honour. The women of the harem then enter. The king is surprised not to see his favourite among them, and gives orders for her to be fetched. Ismaël, to his horror, thus discovers that the king's favourite is none other than Zulma (Taglioni). The king, unaware of this complication, offers a diamond aigrette and a magnificent sword to his victorious general, who declines them and asks instead for the king's slaves to be granted their freedom. This the king at first refuses, but then, recalling the general's valour, changes his mind. However, after Ismaël has retired, the king summons Zulma to tell her of his decision, from which she alone is to be excepted – for his intention is to make her his wife. Zulma is this forced to confess that she loves another; and in his anger the king is on the point of giving the order for her execution when Ismaël returns, followed by a large crowd, to celebrate his great victory.

For the second act the scene changes to the bathing pool of the harem, where Zulma and her companions emerge from the water to be dressed. When refreshments are served, one of the slaves (Legallois) drops her vase and is saved from punishment only when Zulma takes the blame upon herself. In gratitude, the slave presents her with a talisman in the form of a posy of flowers that will protect her from danger. Ismaël is then brought in through a secret door by Zulma's devoted black servant (Mme Elie), and Zulma tells him how she had attempted to escape from the king's attentions, but was captured and placed in the harem. When the other women of the harem join her, it is learnt that the king has altered the wording of his edict to exclude Zulma, who incites them to revolt. The posy then drops from her girdle, and its flowers bloom afresh as a panel opens to reveal a stack of arms. They are then discovered by the chief eunuch, Myssouf (Simon). However, the weapons turn into lyres before he realises what is afoot; after allaying his suspicions with a graceful dance, the women seize him and bind him up. A curtain at the back then rises to reveal a golden gate, which opens at a touch of Zulma's lance. Their revolt has begun, and when the king comes running into the harem, they are already on their way to the shore to board boats.

The third act is set first in the mountainous region of the Alpuxaras, where the women's army is encamped. There they are reviewed by Zulma, whom they have recognised as their leader, and then settle down for the night. In the dark, Ismaël enters to beg Zulma to escape with him. She is reluctant to desert her followers, but he is so persistent that she is on the point of giving way when a trumpet call reminds her of her duty. She runs to rouse her companions, as Ismaël is escorted out of the camp. Soon an emissary arrives with a demand for surrender. This Zulma rejects, but is then told that the king desires to discuss peace terms. It is agreed to allow the king and his suite to be admitted to the camp. The king declares himself ready to free the women, but flies into a rage when Zulma insists on being free to marry Ismaël. Cunningly he feigns consent, and coffers full of jewels and other precious gifts are brought in. The women's attention being thus diverted, the men seize their weapons. Zulma feels for the magic posy, but it is no longer in her girdle. It seems that the revolt has failed. She is preparing herself for surrender, when Ismaël, who unknown to her has taken the posy as a keepsake, throws it at her feet in a fit of rage. With a cry of joy, she waves it aloft. There is a roll of thunder, and everyone kneels, as darkness covers the stage.

Slowly the scene brightens for the finale, set in the gardens of Generalife. At the back presides the Spirit of Womanhood (Legallois), whom Zulma recognises as the slave who had given her the posy. The king is ordered to desist from oppressing women, but to treat them with fairness: for by doing so he will find himself with two armies where before he had only one. A series of military manoeuvres then brings the ballet to a close.

To the audiences of its time, this plot appeared innocuous, but seen in a different perspective more than a century later, it would suggest a surprising concern on the part of its author in an issue that in his day had not yet begun to be taken seriously. Women's liberation, which featured prominently in Filippo Taglioni's scenario, could hardly be described as a serious political issue, and certainly none of the critics who commented on the ballet mentioned that aspect. Nevertheless, it was a subject that had dimly entered public consciousness as one of the objectives of the Saint-Simonians, a socialistic movement that had been in the news in the summer of 1831. At that time they were looked upon as little more than amusing cranks; but although the movement itself was shortly to disintegrate, its vision was to have an influence on the development of social ideology and the call for women's rights that would begin to be heard well before the century's end. However, none of this was to be foreseen in 1832, and as far as *La Révolte au sérail* was concerned, no one accused Filippo Taglioni of having eccentric political leanings, even though he was to produce another ballet on a somewhat similar theme, *Brézilia*, two years later.[33]

How innocuous the ballet appeared to the public of its time is revealed in an extract from a later review by Jules Janin, who saw it as no more than a harmless fantasy devised to display the ballerina in a different guise from that of the Abbess in *Robert* or the impalpable Sylphide:

There are some who say you need an idea to make a ballet. They are mistaken. To make a ballet you just need dancers – or rather *danseuses*, for we have ousted the male dancers. Therefore, the more *danseuses* and the less invention you have, the better your chances of creating a charming ballet. Take this worthy M. Taglioni. Generally speaking, he is the most naïve of men, and of choreographers in particular. No one could have a more composed imagination, a more restrained wit, a more innocent heart or more sober feelings than M. Taglioni; no one could be less of a poet, yet it is impossible to find anything prettier, fresher, more daring, more graceful, or more charming than his new ballet... You find me still dazzled by it.[34]

Such influences as might have been discerned in the plot were of little importance at that time. What the public came to see was the dancing of Marie Taglioni and Jules Perrot, who partnered her in a wonderful *pas de deux* in the first act. They bounded 'like balloons, skimming the ground ... and shooting into the air like those virtuosi that a painter's fancy has depicted on the walls of Pompeii, performing the most exacting and difficult feats with prodigious grace and agility.'[35] Taglioni was as incomparable as ever, and Perrot proved a match for her. 'One forgets he is a male dancer,' wrote Janin. 'I do not think that even the oldest and most rabid flatterers of Vestris ever saw Vestris dance like Perrot, and Perrot must have certainly danced superlatively well for me to speak of him thus.'[36]

Marie Taglioni viewed her partner's success with less enthusiasm. Overwrought at the end of the first performance, she flew into a tantrum.

'It's terrible,' she cried, 'that a male dancer should be given more applause than I! It's a scandal!'

Véron tried to pacify her. He summoned Auguste, the leader of the *claque*, and demanded an explanation, but the latter could only shrug his shoulders and say that he had been unable to restrain his men or prevent the public from applauding Perrot.

'Get out!' Véron shouted at him.

Duponchel and Filippo Taglioni did all they could to comfort the ballerina, but she wept inconsolably, crying, 'It's so hard to have made so great sacrifices for such a result'.[37]

Her *pas de deux* with Perrot was only the most remarkable moment among many in a ballet so packed with dancing that the thread of the plot was often in danger of being lost. Few tears were shed over that. If the scene showing the slave girls bathing failed to make the impact expected – 'well-bred people,' commented the *Moniteur*, 'will be grateful to M. Taglioni for not being more adventurous'[38] – the voluptuous dances and the contrasted warlike dances, and all 'the graceful poses, the little touches of coquetry, the artful affectations, the beguiling pouts'[39] and the military evolutions, so precisely performed by the amazon army, which brought the ballet to an end, provided a continuous succession of delights.

* * * * * * *

Marie Taglioni had conquered Paris by the expression in her dancing. Because she never sought to dazzle with *pirouettes, temps de batterie* and other feats of virtuosity, her style was recognised as being not only original but also artistically pure, and superior to the style that was in vogue at the Opéra when she first arrived there. Indeed, so controlled was her technique that it never obtruded on the poetry of her dancing; it was always the servant, and never the master, of her style.

This was not so with Amalia Brugnoli and Elise Vaque-Moulin, whose brief appearances in Paris caused little stir, despite the feats, wonderful enough in their day, that they could perform on their *pointes*. Brugnoli appeared fleetingly at the Théâtre des Bouffes in March 1832, partnered by her husband, Paolo Samengo. 'She is Mlle Gosselin made still more perfect,' wrote Charles Maurice, aiming a barb at Marie Taglioni. 'The cold public of the place received her politely. At the Opéra she would have brought the house down... Had Mme Brugnoli come first,' he concluded meaningfully, 'Paris would be mad about her.'[40]

Luck was also against Elise Vaque-Moulin, who had no greater success when she appeared at the Opéra. Not only did she have to contend with the nervousness natural on such an occasion, but she was not in perfect condition. Her début had to be postponed by a week, and when she did appear, on 27 May 1833, she had to face a discontented audience. She was partnered by Jules Perrot, whose right knee had been troubling him and mystifying the doctors for some weeks. The public was annoyed at his poor showing and voiced their disapproval. Deeply offended, Perrot stopped dancing and left the stage. He then realised that it was his duty to continue, and he reappeared and indicated that he was unwell. Thereafter all went happily, and Perrot danced as if he were at the top of his form. However, when Vaque-Moulin made her second appearance a week later, it was Louis Frémolle who stepped in to partner her. Although the precision, polish and lightness of her footwork were admired, she created little impression, and no one, not even Charles Maurice, spoke of her again as a possible rival to Taglioni.

Although Taglioni's style was considered revolutionary, it was nonetheless firmly founded on the traditions of the classical dance. This she proved on 27 September 1833, when she danced a new *pas de schal* in Cherubini's opera, *Ali Baba*. 'She dances like everyone else did in the days before her arrival, but have done so no longer since then,' wrote an astonished Janin before going on to imagine a scrap of conversation that might have been heard from an *habitué* in the stalls:

'I assure you, sir, she has actually performed an *entrechat*.'

'Not possible! An *entrechat*! Are you quite sure?'

'Two *entrechats*, three *entrechats*! Oh, the crazy creature! Look! She is even doing *bouffantes*!'

And indeed on that day she danced in such a manner that you would never have recognised her had it not been for her natural grace, her chaste beauty, and all the charm of her person. The pit was enchanted and applauded as never before, the old men because she was giving them the dancing of their youth, correct, charming and decent even in its most extended movements, and the young men because she was giving them proof that the *entrechat* was possible. I had the impression that day that I was seeing one of the leaders of the Romantic school writing about Theramenes... Mlle Taglioni is the General Monk of the Opéra: the old dance owes it restoration to her.[41]

NOTES

1. Véron, III, 279.
2. *Courrier des théâtres*, 15 April 1831.
3. Vaillet, 225. According to de Boigne, Duvernay abandoned Vestris to take lessons from Filippo Taglioni, and the former never forgave her and cursed her on his deathbed. However, Véron states categorically that Filippo Taglioni had only two pupils, his daughter and Louise Fitzjames. Contemporary biographers speak of Duvernay as being a pupil of Coulon, and it may have been for him that she abandoned Vestris.
4. *Journal des débats*, 14 February 1832.
5. De Boigne, 24.
6. *Courrier des théâtres*, 20 September 1832.
7. De Boigne, 25.
8. *Constitutionnel*, 23 June 1832.
9. Castil-Blaze, *Académie*, II, 235.
10. *Constitutionnel*, 23 June 1832.
11. *Entr'acte*, 21 June 1832.
12. This scene was cut after the first performance, but many English visitors objected to its removal and Véron was asked to announce that 'the monster scene would be restored as at the first performance' (III, 242.).
13. *Moniteur*, 25 June 1832.
14. De Boigne, 26–9.
15. *Das Schweizer Milchmädchen*, ballet in 2 scenes, choreography by Filippo Taglioni, music by Gyrowetz, f.p. Court Opera, Vienna, 8 October 1821.
16. *Courrier des théâtres*, 12 October 1832.
17. *I minatori valacchi*, ballet in 3 acts, choreography by Gioja, f.p. La Scala, Milan, 19 February 1814.
18. *Moniteur*, 9 November 1832.
19. Letter to Marquis de Maisonfort, quoted in Ifan Kyrle Fletcher's Catalogue No. 194 (London, 1960).
20. *Journal des débats*, 9 November 1832.
21. *Courrier des théâtres*, 7 May 1833.
22. *Journal des débats*, 1 March 1833.
23. Vaillat, 246. Letter from Taglioni to Marquis de Maisonfort, 14 March 1833.
24. *La Festa da ballo in maschera*, ballet by Henry, f.p. La Scala, Milan, 27 January 1829.
25. 'Quelques scènes du Bal masque,' lithograph by Delaunois, dated 1 November 1833.
26. *Arsene*, romantic ballet, choreography by Henry, music by various composers, f.p. San Carlo, Naples, summer season 1818, and revived at Court Opera, Vienna, 18 December 1822.

27. *Die Amazonen,* heroic ballet in 3 acts, choreography by Henry, music by Gallenberg, f.p. Court Opera, Vienna, 9 August 1823.

28. *Les Grecs,* ballet-pantomime in 2 acts, choreography by Alexis Blache, music by Hippolyte Sonnet, f.p. Grand-Théâtre, Bordeaux, 24 December 1827.

29. *Die Neue Amazon,* fairy ballet in 3 scenes, choreography by Filippo Taglioni, music by Kramer arranged by Henning, f.p. Royal Opera, Berlin, 4 May 1830. The title-rôle was apparently given the name of Arsène, which may suggest that the ballet was based on, or inspired by, the plot of Louis Henry's *Arsène* (see note 26 above), for in 1832 Taglioni was announced as playing the rôle of Arsene.

30. *Journal des débats,* 6 December 1833.

31. The average receipts over the first twenty-five performances of these two works were: *La Révolte au sérail,* 8922 francs; *Robert le Diable,* 8654 francs.

32. De Boigne, 48.

33. On this subject, see Joellen A. Meglin's article, 'Feminism or Fetishism: *La Révolte des femmes* and Women's Liberation in France in the 1830s' (Garafola (ed.), 69–90).

34. *Journal des débats,* 6 December 1833.

35. *Constitutionnel,* 6 December 1833.

36. *Journal des débats,* 6 December 1833.

37. *Ménestrel,* 2 February 1834.

38. *Moniteur,* 6 December 1833.

39. *Journal des débats,* 6 December 1833.

40. *Courrier des théâtres,* 28 March 1832.

41. *Journal des débats,* 30 September 1833. Theramenes, a moderate Athenean politician who was put to death by order of the tyrant Critias, c. 403 B.C., is here cited as a hero of the classical age of ancient Greece. General Monk was instrumental in restoring Charles II to the English throne in 1660, following the Civil War and the establishment of a republican Commonwealth, and bringing about a reconciliation between Parliament and the monarchy.

14

A New Star Rises

French ballet now fell under a new influence, which was precipitated, strangely enough, by a dynastic crisis in Spain that had followed the death of King Ferdinand VII in 1833. A dispute that had arisen over the succession between the dead king's infant daughter Isabella and her uncle Don Carlos not only threatened civil war, but brought in its wake a theatrical crisis in Madrid. The theatres of that city closed, salaries were halved and four of the country's leading dancers were, most exceptionally, authorised to accept an engagement in Paris, which had been offered, with his customary astuteness, by Dr Véron. Heading these visitors was Francisco Font, who was reported to have danced exclusively in the apartments of the sovereign. His three companions, Mariano Camprubì, Manuela Dubinon and Dolores Serral, came from the Teatro del Principe and the Teatro de la Cruz.

Véron had engaged these distinguished dancers primarily as an attraction for the masked balls that were to be given at the Opéra during Carnival, but they were also to appear in two performances of *La Muette de Portici*, on 15 and 24 January 1834. For many Parisians this first experience of authentic Spanish dancing was to come as a revelation. Castil-Blaze in the *Constitutionnel* could hardly find adjectives enough to describe their performance. It was 'brilliant, lively, poetic, strongly coloured, captivating, and full of charm, seduction, passion and fire'. Nothing like it had been seen in Paris before, not even the 'imitations' that had been thrust upon the public from time to time. These latest Spanish visitors seemed to dance with their entire bodies, with their arms as much as their legs, even with their eyes and their mouths. Their agility and suppleness were astonishing, and so too was the precision when all four were dancing together. 'Not a foot lags behind; there are none of those straggling volleys that throw a whole battalion of dancers into confusion. The scintillating chatter of castanets animates these virtuosi, imparting a thrilling brio to their performance, even causing their fingers to dance when they might perhaps be tempted to relax a moment amid the general hurricane.' They were received with wild enthusiasm. 'The Germans from the Stuttgart school,' concluded this critic, referring to the Taglionis, 'have brought about one revolution in French ballet, and now the Spaniards are following in their footsteps.'[1]

* * * * * * *

A more precise observation would have been that these Spaniards had pointed the way to a fuller exploitation of local colour in ballet. This aspect of Romanticism was now to be revealed with dramatic effect by the Austrian ballerina Fanny Elssler, whose engagement was the last great coup of Véron's stewardship. Although he had rearranged the hierarchy of the ballet company with Marie Taglioni at the top of the pyramid, Véron did not propose to leave her there unchallenged. Indeed, his encouragement of Pauline Duvernay had been partly aimed at lessening his dependence on Taglioni; and so, with more positive and lasting results, was his engagement of Fanny Elssler.

Véron had had his eye on Fanny Elssler and her sister Thérèse ever since his friend Alphonse Royer had recommended them after seeing them dance in their native Vienna in the winter of 1830. Almost certainly there had been negotiations with them before Véron's dramatic visit to London in the summer of 1834, when they signed their first contract with the Opéra. The *Courrier des théâtres*, which Véron used extensively for publicity, had reported rumours of their approaching début in Paris as early as January 1833.

Fanny Elssler was just twenty-four when she arrived in Paris in July 1834, and Thérèse, who accompanied her, was two years older. Their father had served as music copyist and manservant to the composer Haydn, who had bequeathed him a legacy of 6000 florins. Fanny was born in Vienna in 1810, a year after Haydn had died, and was brought up in an atmosphere impregnated with music. Having begun her professional career as a dancer when still a child, she was only fourteen when she left home to fulfil an engagement in Italy. On her return to Vienna a few years later, she came under an influence that was to bring her lasting benefit. Old Friedrich von Gentz, the celebrated political commentator, fell in love with her, and their friendship, which lasted until his death in 1832, would be of lasting benefit in raising her intellectually above the level of most of her professional colleagues. Her fame as a dancer soon began to spread. She was rapturously received in Berlin and London, and it was while dancing in the latter city in 1834 that Véron saw her for the first time.

He was quick to perceive that, while Fanny was by far the more gifted dancer of the two sisters, it was Thérèse whose decision would count in any business dealings. Fanny was very anxious to go to Paris, but for some time Thérèse hesitated to accept Véron's offer, fearing, as he imagined, that she herself might not please the Parisian public because of her above-average height. Véron then decided to adopt subtler tactics. He invited the sisters to a dinner party at the Clarendon hotel in Bond Street. As a committed gastronome, he made sure that the fare would be superb. His guests were therefore in a very mellow mood when, with skilful timing, he produced his surprise. During the dessert course, a large silver salver, heaped with jewellery, was passed round with the fruit for each lady to choose what took her fancy. To Véron's astonishment, Fanny, who considered this a rather vulgar compliment, was at first reluctant to take her pick, but, noticing his mortification, relented and selected the simplest bracelet. Véron then broached the subject of her coming to Paris to dance at the Opéra, in response to which she made it clear that her sister would have to be engaged as well. Véron must have expected this, for he at once agreed. Shortly afterwards, on the very day of his return to Paris, terms were agreed for a three-year engagement, determinable by either party at the end of fifteen months, and providing for a salary of 8000 francs for each sister, with bonuses of 125 francs for each performance.

When she arrived in Paris, Fanny might have imagined that she had already attained the summit of her art. She had mastered, she thought, every known difficulty and even devised several *tours de force* that she believed had never been successfully performed before. Her first sight of Taglioni, however, threw her into a state of great alarm. For it brutally revealed that standards at the Opéra were much higher than any she had experienced elsewhere, and that the test she was now to face would be the ultimate trial, in which failure would be irreparable. It was to be her good fortune that the eminent Auguste Vestris took an interest in her, and worked with her for several weeks before her début. To her relief and delight she made rapid progress, realising, as she freely admitted, that a dancer's education is never finished. 'It was not so much in elementary studies that I gained from Vestris,' she recalled afterwards, 'but rather in style and tone. He sought to give me grace and expression; in short, his finish to my poses and carriage.'[2]

Véron was determined to launch Fanny with the maximum of publicity, and from July until her début in September the *Courrier des théâtres* obligingly whetted the public's interest with a series of news items. Not the least effective of these was the tale that she had gladdened the last days of the Duc de Reichstadt, Napoleon's son, who since his father's fall had languished at the Court of Vienna before dying of tuberculosis in 1832. With the Napoleonic legend growing apace in French imaginations and Bonapartism coming to the fore as a political force, the very suggestion of such an association was bound to have an effective appeal. It mattered little to Véron that it lacked foundation. Indeed, it was such a telling press stunt that the myth of this romantic affair, later stimulated by Rostand's play *L'Aiglon*, still gains a modicum of credence to this day.

It was decided that Fanny would make her début in a new ballet, *La Tempête*, which Coralli had been preparing since the beginning of the year with Duvernay in the principal rôle. There could be no question, however, of depriving Duvernay of her part, and so a new scene had to be patched in for Elssler. In the middle of August it was announced that Fanny had begun to rehearse, and that after merely marking her *pas* for a few days – or, in the dancer's expression then in use, *répétant en robe de chambre*, rehearsing in a dressing-gown – she had danced full out, revealing the most remarkable qualities: vivacity, suppleness, astonishing strength and precision, a rich vocabulary of *pointe* work, and impressive *batterie*. Furthermore, her style was said to have a quality all its own; she would be the forerunner of a new school, and already the French dancers were showing interest in assimilating her style.[3]

It might have been assumed that the ballet of *La Tempête* would be based on Shakespeare's comedy; but apart from the similarity of a few of the characters' names – Prospero, Fernando, Caliban, not to mention Ariel, being slipped in from *A Midsummer Night's Dream* – Adolphe Nourrit's scenario bore no relation to the play. In fact it was so banal and lacking in interest that the *Moniteur* declared it an insult to the Immortal Bard.

The curtain rose on an introductory scene depicting the death of Thalès (Quériau) during a siege by the Turks. Mortally wounded herself, his wife embraces their baby child Léa. She is fearful at what the future might hold for it, but Oberon (Montjoie) hears her prayer and sends Ariel (Leroux), the spirit of the air, to bring the little girl to him.[4]

The first act was set on the Island of Genies. Léa (Duvernay) has now grown into a young woman, but is overcome with sadness. She is loved by Caliban (Simon), who watches over her, but she cannot help being revolted by his ugliness. Ariel tries to teach her the arts of coquetry, but with no success. He tells Oberon that she is seeking love, and, seeing a ship in the distance, suggests that his master should employ his magic powers to make it founder on the shores of the island. And so Fernando (Mazilier) manages to struggle ashore, to find Léa, in a state of terror at the might of the storm. They fall in love, but are surprised by Caliban and his companions. Only the timely appearance of Oberon saves Fernando, who declares his love for Léa and begs to be allowed to remain on the island. Oberon consents, but on one condition – that Fernando should prove his love by undergoing a series of trials.

In the second act the action shifts to another part of the island, to which Ariel has magically transported the lovers. Léa is embarrassed at finding herself alone with Fernando, whose passion has been aroused; she is not yet ready, and modestly enfolds herself in gauze. Caliban then summons the Daughters of Night to lull the couple to sleep and spirit them away to the enchanted palace of the fairy Alcine (F. Elssler). There Alcine leads Fernando to believe that an evil spirit has assumed Léa's form to seduce him, and, with feigned blushes, exerts her powers of fascination in an attempt to seduce him herself. She offers to share her power with him and gives him a talisman as proof of her sincerity. But Fernando is not to be tempted. Summoning up strength to thwart Alcine's influence, he calls out for Léa, swearing that his love for her is eternal. At this the fairy's influence is broken, and Fernando, having passed his test, is transported to the grotto of the ondines, where Oberon, Ariel and Léa await him. The lovers then enter a boat and row towards the ship, which has miraculously survived the battering of the storm.

At the general rehearsal of this ballet on the very eve of its first performance, a crisis arose, which Véron resolved in characteristic manner. It was discovered that some specially designed gas burners, ordered for the final grotto scene, had not been delivered; and at eleven o'clock that same evening Véron himself, accompanied by Duponchel and the designers Despléchin, Feuchères and Séchan, set out in a carriage.

'Albouy's, in the Rue Paradis, off the Rue Poissonnière!' cried Duponchel to the driver.

Albouy was in bed when they knocked on his door. Sleepily he explained that he did not make the burners himself, but had them manufactured in another part of Paris. So the five men set off again. It was past midnight when they reached their destination. Not knowing the name of the artisan or the number of his house, they roused almost the whole neighbourhood before discovering the man they were seeking.

Véron wasted no time making reproaches. 'There's an extra hundred francs for you,' he told him, 'if your burners are at the Opéra by ten o'clock this morning, ready to be fixed in position'. At nine o'clock that morning the burners were duly delivered, and an hour later a lighting rehearsal began with them already in place.[5]

So, in the evening of that very day, 15 September 1834, the curtain rose on time for the first performance of *La Tempête*. Happily, the ballet had merits that compensated for the emptiness of its plot. Coralli's choreography was found consistently fresh and graceful, the bacchanal of gnomes in the tempest scene being singled out as outstandingly original in its composition. For this passage, the composer Schneitzhoeffer had written some vigorous and descriptive music, which contained many pleasing melodies and original touches; among these was a martial bolero for Fernando's first entrance and, as was customary, a liberal sprinkling of borrowed melodies, *airs parlants*, to assist the audience to follow the subtleties of the pantomime action.[6]

Schneitzhoeffer's score received special attention from the anonymous critic of the *Gazette musicale*, who took the opportunity to recount some of the difficulties that the composer of a ballet score had to encounter during the rehearsal period:

> M. Schneitzhoeffer's music seemed to us remarkable wherever the composer was allowed to enjoy a little freedom. However, we have to criticise him for not introducing sufficient variety into the energetic passages that the plot so frequently demands. But do we really know whether he was allowed to do anything else? There is no task more irksome and at the same time unrewarding than having to compose music for a ballet. For once he has finished, he may be made to do a piece all over again. He may be satisfied with what he has skilfully composed and developed, when the choreographer appears and he is made to cut it here, expand it there, scrap a whole passage, or even rewrite the entire piece. Then the dancers turn up at rehearsal and demand a different orchestration – trombones here, the big drum there, in places where the composer had perhaps written for flutes against a pizzicato accompaniment. The poor composer! For a man of the calibre of those whom Italian choreographers carry in their baggage, this rôle of a slave is not a very difficult one, for that is the task he has been trained for; but where the musician is a distinguished composer such as M. Schneitzhoeffer, he is, in all sincerity, to be pitied for being landed in such a dreadful situation.[7]

Magnificent sets and exceptionally elegant costumes contributed further to the ballet's success. In the tempest scene, a novel effect was introduced to simulate the heaving of the waves, which was so realistic that the mere sight of it made the critic Charles de Boigne feel queasy: in his opinion it was not to be surpassed by the famous storm scene in *Le Corsaire*, twenty-two years later. The final curtain was brought down on a spectacular grotto scene with stalactites hanging from the roof, and, seen through an opening, a calm blue sea bathed 'in torrents of light'.[8]

Since Fanny Elssler appeared only in the second act, the public had to sit through the prologue and the first act before being given a glimpse of her. When she eventually appeared, there was so little show of enthusiasm that Fanny, who was always a prey to nerves before going on to the stage, clung anxiously to her sister and said a little prayer. She was inclined to be superstitious, and her fear had been aroused by the sight of a stage-hand giving the signal for the orchestra to strike up with three taps of his left foot instead of the right. When she remonstrated with him, he gallantly offered to do it again, but of course by then it was too late, for the music had already begun. In fact it was he, not Fanny, who was to be the unlucky one; for while her own success that evening could not have been greater, at the next performance, when the stage-hand remembered to give the signal with his right foot, he did so with such energy that he cracked a bone.

In fact, from the moment she had come into into sight, languidly reclining on a sofa, Fanny Elssler's triumph was never in doubt. Her face was covered in a veil, and as she rose, the audience was breathlessly silent, waiting for her to cast it aside and reveal her features. At that moment every opera-glass was levelled at her, and a roar of applause broke out from the whole house.

It was at once apparent that here was a remarkable dancer with an unusual style. 'It is only by seeing her,' wrote Charles Maurice,

> that a true idea can be formed of her, for no verbal description could be adequate. Those in the know describe her style as *tacquetée*; that is to say, consisting chiefly of small steps, rapid, correct, sharp, biting the boards, and always as vigorous and delicate as they are graceful and brilliant. *Pointes* play an important part in her dancing, gripping one's attention and arousing astonishment and admiration as she circles the stage with no apparent fatigue and without the charms they are supporting losing any of their incredible aplomb and seductive gentleness. There could be no more striking contrast with the justly appreciated talent of Mlle Taglioni, whose dancing is entirely *ballonnée* (to use another technical term).[9]

Echoing this description, Castil-Blaze lingered on the delicacy of 'a trill of *battements*, such as Paganini might play on his violin',[10] and later performances moved Charles Maurice to take up this theme again. After the second performance, he spoke of her 'lively and perfect *pointe* work and *batterie*, voluptuous poses and *développements* performed with such noble grace'.[11] Towards the end of the year, on 7 December, when she and Taglioni were dancing for the first time in the same programme, he observed that 'her poses, which are so replete with voluptuous modesty, and her astonishing *pointes*, which give the impression that Mlle Fanny is dancing on an invisible cloud, aroused an enthusiasm that a better-known talent of the capital', meaning of course Taglioni, 'was unable to inspire'.[12]

Indeed, Elssler's artistry went much further than being a mere display of technique, surprising though that was. This was duly recognised by the experienced critic Hippolyte Prévost, whose memories went back to Bigottini,[13] in a comment on the seduction scene with Mazilier:

> Her acting, which is natural, animated and expressive, reveals everything that is passing through her mind. She has no mannerisms nor the slightest touch of affectation; her talent is distinguished by sincerity, freshness, youth, and a welcome intelligence! That is how I would describe Mlle Elssler the actress.[14]

Taglioni's champions were quick to come forward in support of their idol. Some of them declared that Fanny Elssler's style was limited; others liked to see in 'its *terre à terre* movements, its *pas de bourrée*, its *petits pas jetés*, its *ailes de pigeon sur les pointes*'[15] a reversion to the style that had been in fashion thirty years before, although, of course, her command of *pointe* work was essentially modern. But not even the most fervent Taglionists could honestly deny her talent.

The Comtesse Dash admitted that the public was divided, describing Elssler's style as 'more voluptuous and more alluring. Unlike Taglioni, she was not a sylphide or a daughter of the skies. No, she came down to earth, and her looks inspired men with hopes which were much more positive and gave them pleasure even if they knew they would never be fulfilled.'[16]

Marie Taglioni herself had been present at the début, which she described in a letter to the Marquis de Maisonfort. She told him she had been practising hard,

> since it is necessary to maintain a reputation which people have been happy to cast somewhat into the shade so as to work up that of Fanny Elssler... The new ballet, *La Tempête*, is pitiful, and all its luxurious production and all M. Véron's power over the press will be needed to keep it going for some time. Mlle Elssler gave much pleasure. We recognised a certain perfection of timing with which she executes those rapid movements that characterise her style of dancing. However, hers is a style that deprives the body of grace. I do not think that her success will be a financial one. I find that M. Véron has forced it a little, this success, and I would even go so far as to say that it was his object to impose it on the public.[17]

Marie Taglioni returned in *La Sylphide* just a week after Fanny Elssler's début; but while the public was enthusiastic, the claque, no doubt acting on instructions, remained conspicuously silent. Véron, it seemed, was trying to create an artificial balance between Taglioni and his new star and, quick to seize on the budding rivalry between them, he was soon alternating the programmes with Taglioni in *La Sylphide* or *La Révolte au sérail* and Elssler in *La Tempête* or a *pas de deux* with her sister, inserted in some opera.

Thérèse Elssler made her first appearance at the Opéra *en travesti*, partnering her sister in a *pas de deux* of her own composition in Auber's opera *Gustave* on 1 October 1834. According to Castil-Blaze, she was 5 feet 6 inches tall, which in those days was well above average. Her height, however, did not tell against her so much as she had feared, and she was soon known as 'la Majestueuse'. Jules Janin described her as

> a tall and beautiful creature with an admirably shaped leg, who is on her

LES ARTISTES

CONTEMPORAINES.

1. Melle Taglioni.
2. Melle Noblet.
3. Melle Julia.

4. Mme Montessu.
5. Melle Legallois.
6. Mme Alexis.

30 The Ballerinas of the Opéra, 1832. Upper row: Lise Noblet, Marie Taglioni, Julia [de Varennes]. Lower row: Pauline Montessu, Amélie Legallois, Mme Alexis [Dupont]. Lithograph by Plantu.

31 *La Sylphide*, Act I. Madge reading Gurn's hand, as James, crossing his arms, walks away after refusing the old witch's offer.

32 *La Sylphide* James running after the Sylphide as she flies out of the house. From *Les Beautés de l'Opéra*.

33 *La Sylphide*, Act II. Marie Taglioni, as the Sylphide, at the tragic moment when James places the scarf around her waist.

34 The Sylphs depart as Madge gloats over James's distress.

35 *La Sylphide*, Act II. The Sylphide, feeling the onset of mortality as she clings to the scarf James has given her. From a print by Levasseur.

36 James realising to his horror the consequences of his gift. Lithograph by A. Didion from a drawing by Laederich.

37 Jules Perrot in *Nathalie*: engraving by König from a drawing by A.Lacouchie.

38 Marie Taglioni in *Nathalie*. Ink and water-colour drawing by Olivia de Roos.

39　Fanny Elssler in *L'Ile des pirates*. Oil painting by G. Lepaulle.

40   Mariano Camprubí and Dolores Serral in a bolero. From a lithograph by Delaunois, based on a drawing by A.Alophe.

41 Lise Noblet in a bolero.
Lithograph by Louis Lasalle.

42 *Le Diable boiteux.* Asmodeus enabling Cléofas to look down through the roof at Florina danc-ing the Cachucha.

43 Cléofas, now disguised as the régisseur, leading Florinda into her dressing room. From *Les Beautés de l'Opéra.*

44 Fanny Elssler dancing the Cachucha. An American lithograph.

45   *La Fille du Danube,* Act II, Scene I. Design for a lamp-shade.

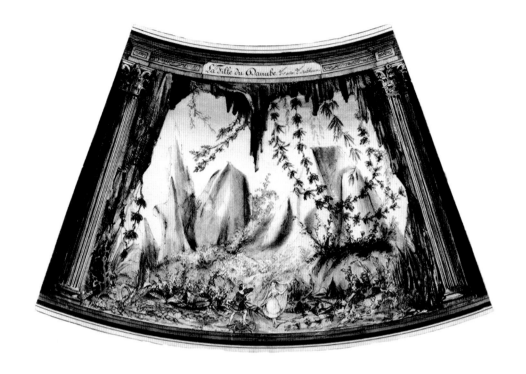

46 *La Fille du Danube* Act II, Scene II. Design for a lamp-shade

47 Marie Taglioni in *La Fille du Danube*.

48   Fanny Elssler as Kié-li in *La Chatte métamorphosée en femme.*

49 Pauline Leroux. Lithograph by M. Alophe.

50 Adèle Dumilâtre and Eugène Coralli in *La Gipsy*.

51 Louise Fitzjames in caricature

52 Sofia Fuoco in caricature

way to becoming the best male dancer at the Opera, without excepting Perrot, over whom Thérèse has the advantage of a very delicate figure and lovely features. As a *danseuse* Mlle Thérèse is a little on the tall side, particularly when compared to her sister who is so tiny... Without thought for herself, Thérèse has generously given Fanny the most beautiful poses and the liveliest pieces of music; she shows off her sister as much as she can, and dances herself only to give her time to recover her breath... The pit... applauded both of them rapturously, particularly at the conclusion of the *pas* when the two link arms back to back, a very novel and lively effect.[18]

The devotion with which her sister served her, both in the arrangement and in the execution of the *pas de deux* they danced together, was an important factor in Fanny Elssler's growing popularity. On 12 November, when they were seen in a *pas styrien*, new facets of Fanny's talent were revealed. 'Turning,' commented Charles Maurice,

is nothing to a dancer and generally is not a movement that is pleasing to the audience. But you have to see how Fanny Elssler does it in the pas *styrien*. It is like nothing we have seen before; here we have elegant rapidity, imperturbable aplomb, and a carefree spinning that electrifies the public. At other moments Mlle Fanny skilfully breaks away from the common mechanics of such *pas* by means of tricks of the body; and a tasteful play of the features adds drama and almost interest to the action. To justify such remarks in a simple *pas*, in which many other dancers would pass unnoticed, demands the combined gifts of a mime and a remarkable dancer.[19]

And also, it might have been added, of a choreographer at her service who understood her capabilities with a sisterly intuition.

* * * * * * *

Véron rightly claimed credit in his memoirs for strengthening the ballet at the Opéra by engaging Fanny Elssler, but he was understandably reticent about the departure of Jules Perrot.

Adice described Perrot as 'the very model of the *danseur de demi-caractère*, who instinctively dances *terre à terre* and *pas* requiring strength or *grand ballon* with equal perfection'.[20] Originally engaged at an annual salary of 2500 francs as a *double*, he had made such progress in his first year at the Opéra that his second contract entitled him to a salary of 10,000 francs for the year commencing on 1 April 1831, exclusive of bonuses of 30 francs a performance, eight of which were guaranteed to him each month. These terms were further increased from 1 April 1832 to a salary of 15,000 francs and a minimum of ten guaranteed bonuses of 45 francs a month. This last contract was due to expire on 31 March 1835, but, taking into account an unexpired period of leave, Perrot had in fact fulfilled all his obligations under it by the end of December 1834.

Around the turn of the year, he and Véron began to discuss terms for a new contract, and differences soon arose: Perrot considered his services to be worth at least 20,000 francs, while Véron was only willing to re-engage him at a reduced salary. This ungenerous attitude may have had its cause in the disappointing performances Perrot had been giving recently, the result of his recurring knee trouble. Probably another factor was the growing prejudice against male dancers, which may have led Véron to believe he could dispense with Perrot's services with impunity – particularly since he was only paying 8000 francs a year to Edouard Carey, an enormously strong dancer, if somewhat lacking in finish. But if he counted on Carey to replace Perrot at half the price, Véron was to be disappointed, for Carey too demanded an increase in salary and left the Opéra before the spring.[21]

Whatever Véron's motives, negotiations were soon broken off, and on 31 January 1835 Perrot left Paris, with engagements to appear in Bordeaux, London and Naples. The loss to the Opéra could only be assessed many years later, after Perrot's genius as a choreographer had flowered during the 1840s, not in Paris, but in London. Véron's subsequent silence on the subject suggests he had come to recognise his error.

* * * * * * *

Paris was then much too occupied with the rivalry between Taglioni and Fanny Elssler to shed many tears over the loss of Jules Perrot. Soon the prospect of Marie Taglioni's benefit, announced for 8 April 1835, was arousing intense interest, which was further stimulated by the announcement of the programme. Not only was a new ballet, *Brézilia*, to be performed, but in the masked-ball scene from *Gustave* the Elsslers were to present a new *pas de deux* and – as the climax of the evening – Taglioni had agreed to appear with Auguste Vestris in two dances from an earlier age, a Minuet and a Gavotte, *La Romanesca*.

At the age of seventy-five, Vestris was by now a legend, and his emergence from the wings that evening aroused many a nostalgic memory among the older spectators. To those of their juniors with a sense of tradition, it gave the last direct insight into the graces of the old régime. Wearing an elegant eighteenth-century costume, he stepped forward with measured elegance, touching hands with a charmingly demure Taglioni in *demi-paniers* and powdered wig. A murmur of appreciation swelled into applause as the couple moved into their dance. Even those who had never seen Vestris in his prime could not fail to appreciate the qualities that their grandparents had held so precious, even if his years no longer permitted him to indulge in very active movements. Jules Janin was lost in admiration. 'You can see he once rubbed shoulders with great nobles and retains something from that experience', he remarked.[22] While Vestris could summon up from his own experience the manners of the old régime, Marie Taglioni for her own part reproduced them so perfectly and with such an uncanny instinct that it seemed she was no less familiar with the manners of the Court of Versailles than he. All too soon, this unique display was over. As if conscious of the privilege just given to them, the audience broke into a frenzied ovation as a shower of floral tributes fell at the dancers' feet; and the public was left with a last memory of the young goddess of the ballet offering flowers to 'the old Saturn of the dance'[23] at her side.

Fanny Elssler told another story of this memorable evening. Taglioni's admirers had planned an extraordinary tribute. At the end of the minuet, and before the final *galop* that would bring the last excerpt from *Gustave* to a close, the plan was for the *corps de ballet* to enter, circling the stage in a dignified procession as Vestris placed a crown on Taglioni's head. There had been some opposition to this, but Véron had not intervened. So a plot was hatched, and when the moment came for Vestris to perform the crowning, the orchestra unexpectedly broke into the music for the *galop*. This galvanised the *corps de ballet* into action, forcing Vestris and Taglioni to make a hurried exit as best they could. Taglioni demanded an immediate inquiry. The conductor apologised for his mistake, insisting that he had received the signal to begin the *galop*, but no one was prepared to recall who gave it. A suspicion lingered, however, that Véron himself had instigated the incident in order to preserve the peace and prevent a demonstration on the stage.[24]

The *Courrier des théâtres* had got wind of the new ballet being prepared for Taglioni's benefit, and had passed on to its readers some weeks earlier the information that the ballerina would not be making 'any of those leaping strides (*sauts par enjambés*) with which she has for some time been arousing the admiration of the claque and which are not strictly dance steps'.[25] As to whether such steps were expunged by her father before the time came for the new ballet, *Brézilia*,[26] to be seen and judged, the critics remained silent in their reviews.

This 'newly hatched chick' from Filippo Taglioni's nest, wrote Jules Janin after seeing it for the first time,

is a work devoid of any idea, a piece of nonsense offered so coolly and composed with such seriousness that no one but her father has ever paid a more complete tribute to the genius of Mlle Taglioni by making her bear the brunt of a piece such as this! 'What need have I of ideas and inventiveness, or making it interesting or true to life? I have my daughter.' And no doubt, so long as he has his daughter, M. Taglioni must be right.[27]

This new piece contained just one male rôle, that of an American Indian called Zamore (Mazilier), who, while wandering in a forest, comes across a tribe of women asleep in hammocks. He cannot resist giving one of them, Brézilia (Taglioni), a kiss. She wakes, wondering if she has been dreaming, while he quickly hides in a rocky outcrop. The tribal queen (Legallois), who has sworn her followers to a hatred of the male sex, orders a search. Brézilia is left behind in the camp, and Zamore then emerges from his hiding place. The couple are immediately attracted to one another. Another member of the tribe, Méloé (Leroux), catches a glimpse of something moving by the rocks. The tribe then goes hunting, Brézilia being left behind. Aware of her love for Zamore, she realises she must somehow ensure his escape; but suspicions have been aroused and the couple are surprised by Méloé, who gives the alarm. Zamore is captured and condemned to death. There now arises a difference of opinion as to his fate, the Queen favouring death, while others, Méloé among them, argue for his being enslaved. A dispute arises as to who is to guard him. On the Queen's proposal, it is decided to settle the dispute by a contest of skill, agility and grace between four contenders. In this Brézilia is victorious; but another contest must follow, that of the dance, in which she again proves unsurpassed. Then, to everyone's surprise, she breaks Zamore's bonds and tells him to make his escape. But Zamore will not leave without her. She then discovers that she has supporters among her companions, and the couple are able to make their escape with their followers, leaving behind the Queen, still consumed by her hatred of the opposite sex, but now with but a handful of loyal adherents.

It was a measure of Marie Taglioni's genius that she managed to overcome the banal absurdity of the scenario that her father had concocted for her benefit, not to mention the forgettable music that the Count von Gallenberg had put together to accompany it. In other circumstances, this wretched piece would have been given short shrift, for there could be no doubt it was only saved from extinction by the one talent that could not be denied to Filippo Taglioni – that of having fathered a genius of a daughter and composing dances of beguiling freshness and stunning effect that revealed her extraordinary talent. But his talent stopped there, as the scenario of this ballet revealed all too clearly.

To Filippo Taglioni this absurd plot was merely a frame for dances displaying his daughter's genius, and in this area he could always be relied upon to demonstrate an inexhaustible reserve of ideas. The dances began with an introductory *pas de quatre* by Mme Alexis (Lise Noblet's younger sister, Félicité) and three of the Opéra's most promising dancers, Pauline Leroux, Pauline Duvernay and Louise Fitzjames. This led to the highlight of the ballet, a *pas seul* for Taglioni, who was featured again in the next dance, a *pas d'action,* enacting a contest of skill, agility and grace, entitled *La Lutte.* The *corps de ballet* seem to have been featured mainly in the action and as spectators of the dances, but their names were, as customary, listed in the printed scenario. Among them were several youngsters who, in one way or another, would come into prominence in future years: Albertine Coquillard, Maria Jacob and Nathalie Fitzjames.

A glance at the cast list in the printed scenario also reveals the curious fact that there was to be only one man in the entire cast of forty-five: an honour that fell to Joseph Mazilier, who in the rôle of Zamore was required to do no more than mime his part. Such was Filippo Taglioni's lack of interest in male dancing, and his daughter's reluctance to share her position with a male partner!

In an article inserted in *L'Entr'acte* on the very day of Taglioni's benefit, an anonymous writer reminded his readers how revolutionary Taglioni's style had been when she first appeared in Paris eight years before. 'Now that the revolution has been accomplished,' he continued,

> and Mlle Taglioni's style has been adopted by pupils and leading dancers alike, it is easy to recognise the ascendancy she has established over her rivals. This is because her dancing contains nothing that is not spontaneous; her training and her artistry have only served to correct a few little blemishes and to prevent them.

> The art of groups has necessarily declined in the presence of a dancer whose every movement is a grace. What lightness, what decency there is in such an uplifting manner of dancing! How precisely formed are her steps, how smooth her poses, how ladylike her abandon!

> After such a delightful vision, who can bear to see *pointe* work so painfully practised, or those spotted pirouettes, or those so-called voluptuous poses that consist of bending the waist and raising the legs one after the other, or finally those lascivious scenes *sur place* when it seemed that each foot in turn was about to drive itself into the floor?

> Mlle Taglioni has discarded that stilted, pretentious and overworked style. Since becoming aware of the daughter of the air, we have at last realised that a dancer is not an automaton whose hands and feet seem to be operated by wires and whose eyes are made to flutter by springs. Thanks to

her, automatons and tightrope walkers can no longer wear out or split the boards of the Opéra, and we are now aware that dancing is not a trade, nor even an art, but a gift of nature.[28]

Possessing a genius for a daughter, Filippo Taglioni had a unique advantage in being able to attach himself to her star and establish a monopoly in the ballets in which she was featured; but in the area of dramaturgical inspiration, his limitations were all too apparent. The eminent Hippolyte Prévost made this point clearly in his review:

Noverre, who almost raised choreography to the dignity of the first among the imitative arts, demanded that a ballet should present a lively and ingenious plot that is easy to follow, with situations containing dramatic meaning, skilfully drawn characters and fresh and varied scenes in which a touch of poetry can be sensed. A host of charming productions by Gardel, Aumer and Milon sparkled with those rare and precious qualities. But let no one seek the smallest trace of such qualities here, for that would be a waste of time. M. Taglioni does not proceed like the masters. He does not compose under the inspiration of a new and fertile idea, but is content to copy mediocre models. Take his *Révolte au serail*. Well, here is just another work of the same stamp...

There is really nothing to see in such a farrago of nonsense. All that can be done is for M. Taglioni is to pass over in silence his new composition, in which he seems to defy one to find a single situation, scene or idea, or even the smallest detail, that reveals artistic talent or even wit.

But these defects seemed irrelevant when Marie Taglioni was on the stage. 'You just have to see her,' he continued,

to realise what charm, vivacity and delicious skill she bestows on the rôle of Brézilia. How well she brings to life and illumines this inexpressive composition! Never have the smoothness and the sustained perfection of her steps, and the dignity of her execution, been more admired.[29]

Her presence was almost sufficient to make the ballet seem a minor masterpiece, but in the end she could not save it from oblivion after it had been performed just five times.

However, it nearly attained an unenviable notoriety. In the contest of skill, agility and grace, there was a moment when a salvo of arrows had to be shot into the wings. Pauline Duvernay was an uncertain markswoman with the bow, and on the opening night, to the consternation of the audience, her arrow flew into the auditorium and embedded itself in a column alongside one of the boxes, only a few feet from the head of the Duc d'Orléans. There was a curious sequel to this incident. A rumour began to spread that it was Amélie Legallois who, for certain personal reasons of her own, had shot the wayward arrow, and this gained such currency that it had to be denied in the *Courrier des théâtres*.

* * * * * * *

The following month, Pauline Duvernay's admirers were horrified to learn that she had attempted to commit suicide. But they would have been mistaken if they had attributed this near-tragedy to the shock at having almost assassinated the heir to the throne, albeit inadvertently. That incident was an insignificant factor compared with the emotional crisis that prompted her, for the second time, to contemplate putting an end to her days.

She had begun her career under the happiest auspices, being protected by 'Pasha' Véron himself. Her mother, an ambitious, scheming woman, believed she saw the opportunity of governing the Opéra through her daughter, but soon discovered her mistake – for the one thing Véron would share with no one was power. Though he indulged his passions quite freely, he never allowed himself to be ruled by them, and his weakness for Duvernay did not prevent him from teaching her mother a lesson. One day, when Mme Duvernay asked him for a seat for the evening's performance, she unwisely boasted that her daughter's talent had no need for anyone's protection. Véron made no answer; but after she had gone, he sent for Auguste, the leader of the claque, and gave instructions that his men were not to applaud Duvernay that evening. At the end of her *pas*, the unsuspecting dancer smiled gracefully to the audience and was on the point of acknowledging the expected ovation, when, to her dismay, she realised that complete silence reigned in the house. Mme Duvernay was beside herself with rage and told Véron that his conduct was outrageous. 'One swallow does not make a summer,' he reminded her. 'As you now see, your daughter's talent does have need of someone.'[30]

It was the final breach with Véron that was the cause of Pauline Duvernay's first suicide attempt. Happily, her neighbours heard her stifled groans and forced the door of her apartment, where she was found writhing in agony on her bed, having swallowed a concoction of vinegar in which copper coins had been soaked. The doctor was sent for, and the invalid quickly recovered.

Finding another lover presented no great problem, for a suitable candidate was already at hand in the person of the Marquis de La Valette, a well-known figure in the Foyer de la Danse and the *loge infernale*, who possessed all the advantages of youth, wealth and position. For some time past he had been tiring of Pauline Guichard, who had borne him a child. Feeling the need for a change and being strongly attracted to Duvernay, he had broken with his mistress – although in a kindly enough fashion, it must be said, for he continued to watch over her career, and in 1838 would use his influence to have her promoted to *coryphée*. Finding herself deserted, Pauline Guichard refused all offers of protection, and rumour had it that she was only saved from relative misery by the appearance of an altruistic Englishman who gave her 190,000 francs merely as a mark of his esteem!

There was much scandalous gossip about how the Marquis de La Valette eventually, and not without initial resistance from her, managed to persuade Pauline Duvernay to become his mistress. It was not a very savoury story. It appears that Pauline's mother was at that time being kept by a certain elderly gentleman who, finding himself temporarily short of ready cash, put forward a proposition to solve his own problem and also benefit her. They were both aware that La Valette was very much in love with Pauline and had been pressing her to become his mistress, which, out of propriety, and not wishing to enter into a relationship that might prove to be fleeting, she had rejected. He was thus ready to consider any means of breaking her resistance, and eagerly accepted an invitation from Mme Duvernay to an intimate supper. Unknown to Pauline, who was not in the plot, her wine had been laced with a sleeping draught, and the next thing she knew was waking the next morning to find herself in bed, clasped in La Valette's arms. Believing herself ruined beyond redemption, she sensibly decided to make the best of it and abandoned herself to enjoy the delights of illicit passion. The only loser in all this was Mme Duvernay. La Valette discreetly paid the price that had been agreed – rumoured to be 40,000 francs – to her elderly protector, who thereupon absconded, leaving her without a sou for the sale of her daughter's chastity.[31]

Her liaison with La Valette was not without its heartbreak. She discovered one day that he was contemplating marrying a young woman of high birth. The blow was all the crueller because Pauline was then carrying the Marquis's child. On a desperate impulse she made another attempt at suicide; but fortunately opium proved no more efficacious than pickled pennies, and she was dancing again within a month. Because of her condition, however, she soon had to make a discreet withdrawal from the public eye. As the *Courrier des théâtres* commented, 'pretty women are prone to more indispositions than others'.[32]

Early in 1836 she began taking class again. She had given up studying with Vestris, and had inveigled Filippo Taglioni into accepting her as a pupil. Her new teacher soon became exasperated with her and finally told her he would no longer admit her to his class. He sent her away several times, but she always returned and softened his determination with her tearful excuses.

With experience, Pauline Duvernay was finding she could now cope more easily with problems of the heart, and when a diplomatic appointment removed La Valette to Sweden, his absence did not provoke a third suicide attempt but merely opened the door to another lover. She had been admired by a wealthy Englishman called Stephens Lyne Stephens, and when she came to London to dance at the King's Theatre in the summer of 1837, he seized his opportunity. Undeterred by the constant refusals that his advances had met, he decided on a more circuitous tactic and entrusted his friend Count d'Orsay with the delicate mission of coming to terms with Mme Duvernay and her lover of the moment. They were offered £8000 in cash for themselves; while Pauline was to receive £2000 a year, which would be converted into a life annuity from 1 January 1840 should she prove faithful in the meantime. Soon after this settlement had been made, the unfortunate La Valette arrived in London to find himself refused admission to Pauline's dressing-room by order of Lyne Stephens. Only by the tactful intervention of the dancer herself was a duel averted, and La Valette returned crestfallen to Paris.

After that London season, Pauline Duvernay retired from the stage and for some eight years lived with her English protector in contented concubinage. Then, early in 1845, a problem arose that disturbed their harmony. Pauline had engaged a very superior lady's maid called Miss Temple, whose former employer, Lady Aldborough, had just died. A woman of intelligence and strict moral principles, Miss Temple seemed the ideal person to give tone to Pauline's establishment. But a few days after her engagement, just as guests were arriving for a dinner party, Pauline was nowhere to be seen. Eventually Lyne Stephens found her weeping on her bed. Between sobs she told him that Miss Temple had given notice because they were not legally married. 'I will not put up with such an insult,' she cried. 'We shall separate tomorrow if you do not respect me enough to put an end to such a situation.'[33] Lyne Stephens proved to be an honourable and devoted lover, and that summer led her to the altars of Putney Parish Church and the Catholic Chapel in Cadogan Square.

Thereafter the life of Mrs Lyne Stephens fitted into the respectable pattern of Victorian England. She was accepted in society and, according to a French paper in 1857, had become so conditioned to her new surroundings that when she went to the opera, the sight of the dancers' short skirts would cause her to lower her eyes and murmur, 'How shocking!' Her husband died in 1860, leaving her more than a million pounds sterling. Enormously wealthy and highly respected, her professional career forgotten by all save a very few ageing theatregoers, she lived on, devoting herself to good works. Among her many charitable benefactions, she paid for the building of the Catholic Church of Our Lady and the English Martyrs at Cambridge.[34] She was said to have given her jewels to the Church as an act of expiation. She was eighty-one when she died in 1894 at her country house, Lynford Hall in Norfolk, and among the beneficiaries under her will was the National Gallery in London, where a number of fine pictures are still held to testify to her taste and generosity.

NOTES

1. *Constitutionnel*, 18 January 1834.
2. *Letters and Journal of Fanny Elssler*, 11.
3. *Courrier des théâtres*, 19 August 1834.
4. This prologue was quickly recognised as superfluous, and was dropped after the first performance.
5. De Boigne, 79. It was apparently this scene that caused the ballet to be banned by the police in the summer of the following year, on the ground that the gas lighting was dangerous. Véron tried to circumvent the ban by announcing the ballet under the title of *Alcine*, but the police saw through the subterfuge and that night, 17 June 1835, the ballet had to be performed without the offending scenery. (Arch. Nat., AJ[13] 183).
6. Between them, Castil-Blaze (in the *Moniteur*, 20 September 1834) and the anonymous reviewer of the *Revue et Gazette musicale* (21 September 1834) recognised no fewer than eight such insertions: '*Je sens mon cœur qui bat, qui bat*' from Grétry's *Richard Cœur de Lion* for Léa's awakening; Cherubino's aria in Mozart's *Le nozze di Figaro*; '*Descends des cieux, doux Hyménée*' from Salieri's *Les Danaïdes* to accompany Oberon's agreement to the marriage; '*Les vents entre eux se font la guerre*' from Grétry's *Le Tableau parlant* to mark Oberon's agreement to the marriage; '*Je sens mon cœur qui palpite*' from Della Maria's *Le Prisonnier* and '*Sur cet autel sacré viens recevoir ma foi*' from Spontini's *La Vestale* for the scene when Fernando leads Léa to the bower where they fall in love; a popular song by Amédée de Beauplan, '*Dormez, chères amours*' for the moment when the lovers settle down to sleep; and '*Sur cet autel sacré viens recevoir ma foi*' from *La Vestale* for their marriage.
7. *Revue et Gazette musicale*, 21 September 1834.
8. *Moniteur*, 20 September 1834.
9. *Courrier des théâtres*, 16 September 1834.
10. Catil-Blaze, II, 244.
11. *Courrier des théâtres*, 18 September 1834.
12. *Courrier des théâtres*, 8 December 1834.
13. Interestingly, the comparison with Bigottini had been made two years earlier in Vienna by the critic of the *Bäuerles Theaterzeitung* (17 April 1832) after seeing Fanny Elssler as Fenella in *La Muette de Portici*.
14. *Moniteur*, 20 September 1834.
15. *Tribune*, 26 September 1834.
16. Dash, IV, 208.
17. Vaillat, 272–3.
18. *Journal des débats*, 6 October 1834.
19. *Courrier des théâtres*, 14 November 1834.
20. Adice, 108.
21. Chaffee's suggestion, in his 'epilegomena' to Slonimsky's *Perrot (Dance Index*, December 1945), that Perrot left the Opéra because Duponchel proposed a cut in his salary appears unfounded. The decision not to re-engage Perrot was made in January 1835. Duponchel did not become Director of

the Opéra until 1 September 1835. Nor is there any evidence to support the supposition that another reason for Perrot's departure was the refusal by the Opéra to allow him to exercise his talent as a choreographer.

22. *Journal des débats*, 13 April 1835.

23. *Constitutionnel*, 13 April 1835.

24. *Letters and Journals of Fanny Elssler*, 21–2.

25. *Courrier des théâtres*, 7 March 1835.

26. The title of the ballet was given as *Brézila* at its first performance, and was so entitled in the printed scenario. However, it was changed to *Brézilia* for the second and subsequent performances.

27. *Journal des débats*, 13 April 1835.

28. *Entr'acte*, 8 April 1835.

29. *Moniteur*, 27 April 1835.

30. Véron, III, 261–2.

31. *New Satirist*, 21 November 1841.

32. *Courrier des théâtres*, 23 October 1835.

33. Anon., *Ces Demoiselles de l'Opéra*, 118.

34. According to a tale of very dubious authenticity, this church was in its early days scornfully referred to in Protestant circles as the Eye-doll House, from the supposed provenance of the Lyne-Stephens fortune from the manufacture of dolls with movable eyes. I have been unable to trace this story to its source and am inclined to believe it to be a fabrication.

15

Louis Henry's Swansong

Dr Véron, whose relations with the government had been growing increasingly difficult, had now made up his mind to relinquish the management of the Opéra. The financial success of his enterprise was no secret and, when his intention became known, there was no shortage of candidates for the succession. The King had been giving serious thought to whether the Opéra should revert to being a state institution, but the scale of Véron's success made it politically unwise to envisage such a step without incurring the accusation that he was seeking profit for himself. It seemed likely that there would be a fortune awaiting the lucky contender, but it soon became clear that Véron intended to retire only on his own terms. Having successfully thwarted an intrigue to appoint François Crosnier, director of the Opéra-Comique, as his successor-designate during the last two years of his management, which in the normal course would come to an end in 1837, he proposed retiring immediately if he could nominate his successor. And so, after much manoeuvring, Henri Duponchel, with financial backing from the vastly wealthy Alexandre Aguado, Marquis de Las Marismas, was appointed Director of the Opéra from 1 September 1835, and Véron was at last able to strike his accounts to reveal a profit of some 900,000 francs.

Arranging for his retirement had absorbed most of Véron's time during the last few months of his management, and he had delegated the task of supervising the production of the next ballet to Duponchel. Destined as a vehicle for Fanny Elssler, it was to be staged by a choreographer who, although a Frenchman trained at the Opéra in Gardel's time, had spent the greater part of his creative career in Italy.

While considered to be a choreographer of the Italian school, in the tradition of Viganò and Gioja, Louis Henry was French both by birth and by his training as a dancer. He had not originally been intended for a theatrical career, for at the time of his birth, at Versailles in 1784, his father held an important post in the household of the Comte d'Artois, the future Charles X. But any plans for the young Henry to follow in his father's footsteps in the service of royalty had been dashed by the Revolution. His future career had been determined one day when he was sent to the Opéra by his father with a note for the chief machinist. Such were the uncertainties of those times that he might have remained a stage-hand all his life had not a lucky chance intervened. While waiting for a reply, the lad wandered off and found himself in the wings watching a group of children being rehearsed for the inferno scene in the ballet *Psyché* under the vigilant eye of Pierre Gardel. Noticing them hesitate when ordered to leap from a piece of scenery onto a mattress, the boy cried out to be given a chance. Much amused, Gardel let him have a try, and was so impressed by his fearlessness and his physique that he sent him home with an offer of a place in the School of Dance of the Opéra. There the lad came under two of the finest teachers of the time, Jacques-François Deshayes and Jean-François Coulon, and eventually, in 1803, made a successful début in a *pas de deux* with Mlle Clotilde. Both being tall, they made a striking and well-matched pair. Henry's qualities as a dancer were recognised by the public and the authorities alike, and at the end of 1806 his promise was recognised by promotion to the rank of *premier sujet* in the *genre sérieux* with a view to 'preserving the fine character of the *danse noble* and becoming its model'.[1]

He had then become fired by another ambition. In 1805, at the unusually early age of twenty-one, he managed to arouse the interest of the second most powerful man in France, the Arch-Chancellor of the Empire, Cambacérès, and to be authorised to produce a ballet of his own at the Opéra, *L'Amour à Cythère* [2]. Not surprisingly, this aroused the displeasure of Gardel and Milon, who took the matter so seriously as to make a formal complaint to Napoleon. In this way the two ballet-masters managed to prevent Henry from staging any further works at the Opéra. However, the ardent young man was not so easily tamed, and in 1807, in defiance of regulations, he produced a ballet at the Porte-Saint-Martin, *Les Sauvages de la Floride*.[3] Such an act of insubordination brought forth an order from the First Prefect of the Palace expelling him from the Opéra unless he withdrew his ballet. This caused him little concern, since he had already given notice to terminate his engagement, and he responded by producing another ballet at the Porte-Saint-Martin, *Les Deux petits Savoyards*.[4] His luck then turned, for almost immediately the Porte-Saint-Martin was closed by an Imperial decree that reduced the number of theatres in the capital, and Henry, foreseeing that the Opéra might make life difficult for him, secretly fled to Milan with a forged passport, describing himself as a wine salesman.

Paris being now closed to him, it was before Italian audiences in Milan and Naples that his choreographic style was to develop and mature. There, influenced by two of the most eminent Italian choreographers, Salvatore Viganò and Gaetano Gioja, he turned away from the lighter style accepted in Paris, to try his hand on more grandiose canvases that relied heavily on pantomime, brilliant production and skilfully arranged ensembles for large masses of dancers. As Bournonville recalled in his memoirs,

> Henry, a very ingenious Frenchman, had absorbed the Italian ballet style, but through his originality knew how to steer his own course. He used the

French style of pantomime for lyrical or idyllic subjects and the Italian for heroic and historical subjects. By this means he obtained a high degree of variety, and since he possessed a marked sense of the picturesque, his group formations were excellent. I have learned much from his works.[5]

Between his hasty flight from Paris in 1807 and his engagement at the Opéra in 1834, Paris had had three opportunities of seeing his work – at the Porte-Saint-Martin in 1816 and 1822, and more recently, in 1834, at the Théâtre Nautique. The Italian influence on his choreographic style was already apparent on the first of these visits, when Paris saw his three-act production of *Hamlet*[6] and *Samson*.[7] Six years later he gave further proof of his abilities with *Le Sacrifice indien*, a mimed version of Lemierre's tragedy, *La Veuve de Malabar*, which opened with a brilliantly staged battle scene. There was talk that year that Paris might see his *Romeo e Giulietta*,[8] but rumour had it that the Opéra prevented its production. Henry's choreographic approach was new to Paris and scorned in some quarters. 'If Gardel and Milon were hailed as the favourites of the Graces,' wrote the *Journal des théâtres* in 1822, 'Henry can well be called the choreographer of Romanticism', using that term to denote a deviation of his approach from the accepted norm of Paris.[9]

By 1834, however, Henry had become a senior figure in the European field of ballet; and the management of the newly opened Théâtre Nautique made the bold decision to capitalise on the vogue for ballet stimulated by Véron at the Opera by engaging him to present a daringly long season devoted entirely to ballet. With a long list of ballets to his credit, created largely in Italy but also in Vienna and Paris, Henry must have offered an infinitely better prospect of success than any other French choreographer whose services were not already retained by the Opéra. For his first production at the Nautique he had proposed *Guillaume Tell*, a ballet on a familiar theme which he had originally staged quarter of a century before in Naples.[10] This duly opened the season on June 10 with a large and motley collection of dancers in support, and drew a long and witty review by Jules Janin, who praised it as 'one of the most marvellous creations of that particular art which we call choreography and in which we have had no faith for a long time'.[11]

The scratch company served him better still in his next production, *Chao-Kang*,[12] the ballet that Véron took the two Elsslers to see – no doubt with an ulterior motive. The Chao-Kang of the title – the part the choreographer reserved for himself – is a Chinese emperor who has a habit of visiting his far-flung domains *incognito*. On one of these travels he finds himself at odds with an evil provincial governor, who abducts not only the bride of a mandarin, but the wedding guests too, including the disguised monarch. But all turns out well in the end: the villain gets his just deserts and the ballet concludes with a festival of dances in what, in Paris, passed as the Chinese style. From all accounts it was an impressive production, the critic of the musical journal *Le Ménestrel* praising it as 'an artistic creation, an act of defiance in the face of convention, a manifesto against the classical pirouette'.[13]

As the season drew to its close, Henry offered the public an unusual treat: a mimed sketch – for it was little more than that – created specially for Harriet Smithson, who had come to Paris with a company of English actors playing Shakespeare in the original. As a young tragedienne, who the year before had married the Romantic composer Hector Berlioz, she had doubly become a celebrity, and the directors of the Théâtre Nautique had boldly invited her to appear in a short pantomime sketch to be staged specially for her by Louis Henry. Entitled *La Dernière Heure d'un colonel*, it told of a wife's shock and despair at learning that her husband is about to be executed by order of a revolutionary committee. Left alone with her child, she is consumed with anger and, giving way to despair, tries to strangle herself with her hair before a kindly gaoler draws her attention to her baby. As she comes to her senses, her hair falls over her shoulders as she rocks the cradle, wailing bitterly until a lugubrious drum-roll announces that her husband's end has come. Coached by Henry, the young actress gave a highly charged performance to the accompaniment of a score specially composed by Cesare Pugni, who was then living in Paris. Despite her lack of experience in pantomime to a musical accompaniment, she gave an impressive performance that moved Jules Janin to prophesy that if she persevered in taking on pantomime rôles, she might soon be compared with Pauline Duvernay of the Opéra.[14] She was also rewarded by a two-page article in the *Revue et Gazette musicale,* which, although unsigned, perceptive readers may well have assumed had been written by her husband.[15]

Véron had set his sights on Henry as a choreographer who might be of use to the Opéra, and had made a conspicuous appearance in a box at the Paris première of *Chao-Kang* at the Théâtre Nautique in October 1834 in the company of the Elssler sisters. Little time was lost in coming to terms, and, in the middle of December, Henry's engagement at the Opéra was announced. However, the new ballet he was to stage there, *L'Ile des pirates* – his 127th according to report – failed to match up to the expectations that he and his friends must have held for it. The printed scenario attributed it to Henry himself and an unidentified collaborator, who was indicated on the title page by a row of stars denoting anonymity. However, it was no secret that this reluctant collaborator was Adolphe Nourrit, the author of *La Sylphide,* who was acquiring a reputation within the Opéra as something of a specialist in writing for the ballet. But on this count the main cause of complaint when the ballet was seen in its finished form was that the action was lacking in interest, primarily through being too frequently interrupted by over-long passages of dancing. As a consequence, opinions on the ballet's merits varied from lukewarm to dismissive.

The plot opens in the garden of an Italian villa near the sea. Preparations are in hand for the marriage of Mathilde, the younger daughter of a widowed Marquesa (Legallois). The bridegroom-to-be is not, however, the man to whom she had given her heart and who is believed to have been killed in a duel. An officer (Mazilier) then appears in the garden, and after enquiring of a gardener the object of the preparations, hands him a note for one of the two daughters of the house. At that moment the two girls, Rosalie (T. Elssler) and Mathilde (F. Elssler), enter, the latter of whom at once recognises the stranger as her lover, Ottavio, whom everyone has believed to be dead. She faints from the shock, and, on coming to her senses, declares her determination not to proceed with the wedding. The festivities, however, are already about to begin, and her mother, the Marquesa, enters with the intended bridegroom, Moncaldi (Montjoie). There follows a lengthy sequence of dances: a 'Greek *morro* as still performed by the countryfolk north of the Tiber'; a classical *pas de trois* by Albert, Lise Noblet and her sister, Mme Dupont; a minuet; some waltzes; and finally a *tarantella* and *pachiarelle* (again to quote the scenario). After this, Mathilde begs her mother to put off the marriage. Moncaldi, realizing that he has no chance of overcoming her resolution, leaves his seat to whisper a few words to a mysterious pilgrim who has appeared among the guests. A pistol shot is heard, and suddenly the stage is invaded by a band of armed pirates. Ottavio falls wounded, as Mathilde and her sister are carried away.

The action then moves to a pirate ship, which has reached its secret haven on a Greek island. The pirate chief, Akbar, turns out to be none other than Moncaldi himself; but Mathilde, whom he has made his slave, has so far managed to fend off his advances. However, she is distraught at the apparent hopelessness of her situation, and it is only her sister's encouragement that prevents her from throwing herself into the sea. A gleam of hope then appears when a sailor (Desplaces) hands her a note from Ottavio telling of his intention to destroy the pirates. When, a little later, Akbar distributes money to those who have served him well, this sailor refuses to accept it and is ordered to be flogged for his impertinence. Mathilde tries to intercede, but Akbar is unyielding. However, when the sailor's young son (Mlle Virginie) attacks Akbar with a knife and is disarmed, the latter is so impressed by the boy's bravery that he pardons the sailor. The pirates then settle down to their meal, being entertained by a series of wrestling bouts and a character dance by a Creole drummer and a black flute-player. At this point a quarrel breaks out between two pirates (Simon, Quériau), in which one is fatally stabbed. Akbar, without rising from his seat, delivers rough justice by shooting the assailant dead. Order is thus restored, and more dances follow. A stranger, whom Mathilde recognises as Ottavio, then makes his appearance, asking to be admitted to the band. After passing some tests, he is accepted, and the act closes with a 'general *branle*' around the main mast to a very noisy accompaniment of drums and cymbals.

The third act takes place in the women's garden. According to pirate law, Ottavio, as a newly admitted member, has the right to select two companions from the disposable slaves. He chooses the two sisters. Akbar is incensed at this unexpected turn of events, which is sealed, according to local custom, by an exchange of handkerchiefs and rings – explained in the scenario as 'a bizarre ceremony based on the customs of the Turks and the Christians'.

The fourth act is set in Akbar's tent, where the pirate chief, knowing he must abide by this local custom, offers Ottavio gold and a choice among the other women if he will relinquish the two sisters, or at least Mathilde alone. Ottavio remains adamant in his refusal, and Akbar, thus thwarted, demands that they settle their dispute by force of arms. However, the clash of their sabres brings some of the pirates into the tent, and Ottavio is arrested before being able to explain the cause of the dispute. Mathilde then appears, to beg Akbar to have pity on her – but this only enrages him further. However, more pirates are now brought in by Rosalie; on being told what has happened, they insist on the two sisters being restored to Ottavio. Akbar's fury at being thwarted knows no bounds. He is on the point of firing his pistol into a barrel of gunpowder to blow up the ship and all on board when the sound of cannon-fire is heard. The scene changes to the sea coast where a naval squadron is seen attacking the pirates' lair. Ottavio moves to arrest Akbar, but the pirate chief is not to be taken, and he dies by his own hand in the presence of Mathilde and the man she loves.

Henry had taken it as a great compliment to be asked to produce a ballet for the Elsslers, and had modestly assumed that Thérèse and Fanny would make it a requirement that the elder sister would take on the task of arranging any *pas de deux* that they would perform together. So when rehearsals began, he busied himself with the rest of the production – with the result that Therese eventually had to approach him herself to ask when he was going to start work on the *pas de deux*.[16]

In the course of the rehearsals, many of the dancers found the discipline and precision on which Louis Henry insisted in the ensembles unacceptably irksome, and began openly to grumble at the tyranny of the 'foreigner'. When the choreographer appeared for the final rehearsal, he could not ignore the groans that went up from the assembled company. 'Ladies and gentlemen,' he reminded them, 'although I have spent many years abroad, I still have French blood in my veins and I am not accustomed to being received in this manner.'[17] Under this rebuke, the dancers fell silent. But a feeling of discontent remained, giving rise to a lack of confidence which was felt even by the Elsslers, who, shortly before the first performance on 12 August 1835, made an appeal to Charles Maurice to show kindness to them in the pages of his journal. 'Please, we beg you,' they wrote, 'protect us as you have done in the past. You are so good. You make dancers so happy by your kindness. You will always find us two sisters your devoted friends.'[18]

However, there could be no doubt that in the days leading up to its first performance on 12 August 1835 *L'Ile des pirates* had been arousing considerable interest, not only because of the scale of the production, but also because it revealed the developing polarisation of the ballet between the rival charms of the Opéra's exotic ballerinas – exotic in the sense that neither Taglioni nor Elssler was, as the saying went, *un enfant de la maison*. 'Before the performance and during the intervals,' reported a critic on the first night, 'we became aware that there were two very distinct parties in the audience, the Taglionites and the Henryites... as well, I believe, as the Elsslerites, which only goes to prove the almost infinite shades of opinion that exist between the parties now in fashion.'[19] For there could be no doubt that Fanny Elssler was being groomed as a rival to Taglioni, and perhaps there was a lingering suspicion among Taglioni's supporters that Henry had been brought in to serve Elssler as a counterweight to the exclusive father-and-daughter partnership of the Taglionis. In the light of later events, it might not be reading too much into that revealing report to say that it would mark the first skirmish in a struggle for supremacy that would occupy Paris audiences in the months ahead.

Despite a glowing account in Maurice's *Courrier des théâtres*, the ballet received a somewhat muted reception from the press; but it was nevertheless to remain in the repertory for nearly three years, mainly because of the polished production and the skilfully designed groups and ensembles which, for invention and variety, were generally considered to surpass anything of their kind seen before on the Paris stage. But somewhat surprisingly, coming from a choreographer in whose adopted country pantomime was virtually an everyday means of expression, the action seemed to be only lightly sketched in, and none of the characters really came to life. Jules Janin even dismissed the plot as 'pitiable', although admitting that he had been greatly impressed by its crowd scenes, the brilliance of the principal dancers, and the spectacular scenic effects. [20]

It was, however, a work of considerable stature that deserved a more studied analysis, and this was to be supplied by one of the senior critics, Hippolyte Prévost of the *Moniteur*, whose theatrical experience went back longer than that of many of his contemporaries:

Not all choreographers view their art in the same way, but they do seek to achieve the same results even if by different means. Some, such as Dauberval, Gardel, Aumer and Milon, consider that a mimed piece, however light the subject, should nevertheless offer a basic conception that is skilfully developed with gripping true-to-life situations, a storyline clearly set out, and a form that may suggest drama or comedy, and in the final reckoning must appeal to the mind by arousing amusement or interest. In this way *Psyché* offers a fable set to action with marvelous artistry; there is nothing more beguiling to be found in mythology. *Nina*, a most graceful composition, speaks deliciously to the heart, and *La Fille mal gardée* might serve as a model for many comedies. It would only need a few mediocre words to emphasise Dauberval's indications to turn it into a charming opera. M. Henry, however, sees no need for such artistic combinations. He believes in an action that is only lightly sketched but yet develops in an active and rapid manner; not in situations reminiscent of a drama or comedy, but in skilfully scattered details; offering no startling contrasts nor a developed character, but here and there a few happy ideas and at all times a perfect understanding of theatrical effect. The ability to design and vary groups in a marvelous way is enough to ensure success for a choreographic composition like this – particularly when a ballet-master has had the good fortune to find a Fanny Elssler, who adds to the charm and delights of her expressive features and gestures a technique so correct and thrilling that one regrets not seeing her dance when she is 'speaking' and no longer hearing her 'speak' when she is dancing ... The public was of the same opinion, and this ballet will bring to an outstanding close the administration of Dr Véron, whose reign has been distinguished by so many popular successes and the appearance of a number of distinguished artistes.[21]

Fanny Elssler made as much of her part as she could, revealing herself as a ballerina of rare dramatic talent as well as a striking beauty. In that most precious quality, she had little to fear from Taglioni, and she capitalised on this advantage by entering to dance her *pas* in the third act wearing a deliciously fetching red velvet toque that caused a sensation among the ladies in the audience and would set a new fashion. Perhaps it might have been thought somewhat unwise to have Fanny partnered by her sister in the *pas de deux* that was the choreographic highlight of her rôle, but such was the public's lack of interest in male dancing that no such point seems to have come to mind. However, the critic of the *Artiste* could not refrain from a little good-natured banter at Thérèse's expense that came close to being facetious. 'Fanny,' he wrote, 'displayed all the coquettish, lively, provoking and rather mincing graces of her dancing. Thérèse's movements are broader, her immense strides making one think of Homer's gods. Fanny is able to pass under the legs of her sister, like a swan gliding through those of the Colossus of Rhodes.'[22]

To accompany the action, Henry had recourse to two composers: Luigi Carlini, who had served him before in Italy, and Casimir Gide, a French composer whose talents had already been recognised in *La Tentation*. Carlini's music for the first act contained 'a number of motifs that were fresh, well orchestrated and danceable – something not always to be found in ballet scores!' For his part, Gide made a strong impression in the second act with 'a charming andante for cellos accompanied in the upper register by horns, a most happy combination'. An unusual feature from the musical point of view was the introduction of a group of ten drummers, whose 'deafening' performance 'added a touch of excitement to a rousing *galop*'.[23]

L'Ile des pirates was to be one of Louis Henry's last ballets. It seems there was never any question of his being offered a longer engagement at the Opéra, as the Taglioni faction may have feared; for Naples had long been his adopted home and it was to that sun-drenched city that he returned to prepare for an engagement at the San Carlo the following summer. His imagination was afire with new projects, and in that season at the San Carlo he staged no fewer than three major ballets that were received with enthusiastic acclaim. But within days of the first performance of the last of those ballets, an epidemic of cholera swept mercilessly through the city. Henry's daughter was one of the early victims, and within a few days of her death Henry himself sickened and followed her to the grave. He was hastily buried, no doubt with little ceremony, on 4 November 1836. He was only fifty-two at his death, but he had already given to the world more ballets than perhaps any other choreographer dead or then living. The exact total still remains to be counted, but the *Courrier des théâtres* had reported that *L'Ile des pirates* was his 127th ballet, a statistic most probably received from the choreographer himself, and to this figure were still to be added the three last ballets he produced during his final season at the San Carlo.

NOTES

1. Arch. Nat., AJ[13] 83. Lucay to Bonet, 10 December 1806.
2. *L'Amour à Cythère*, ballet pantomime in 2 acts, choreography by Henry, music by Gaveaux, f.p. Opéra, 29 October 1805. See Guest, *Ballet under Napoleon*, 195–204.
3. *Les Sauvages de la Floride*, ballet pantomime in 3 acts, choreography by Henry, music by Darondeau, f.p. Th. de la Porte-Saint-Martin, 6 June 1807. See Guest, *Ballet under Napoleon*, 255–9.
4. *Les Deux petits Savoyards*, ballet-folie in 2 acts, choreography by Henry, music by Darondeau and Piccinni, f.p. Th. de la Porte-Saint-Martin, 27 July 1807. See Guest, *Ballet under Napoleon*, 260.
5. Bournonville, *Mit Theaterliv*, I, 32–3.
6. *Hamlet*, tragic pantomime in 3 acts, choreography by Henry, music by Gallenberg, f.p. Th. de la

Porte-Saint-Martin, 28 February 1816. Guest, *Ballet under Napoleon*, 417–22.

7. *Samson*, pantomime in 3 acts, choreography by Henry, music by Gallenberg, f.p. Th. de la Porte-Saint-Martin, 3 August 1816. Guest, *Ballet under Napoleon*, 255–9.

8. *Romeo e Giulietta*, ballet-pantomime in 3 acts, scenario and choreography by Henry, music by Gallenberg, f.p. Teatro del Fondo, Naples, spring season 1814.

9. *Journal des théâtres*, 25 July 1822.

10. *Guglielmo Tell*, music by Gallenberg, f.p. Teatro di San Carlo, Naples, 8 February 1809.

11. *Journal des débats*, 16 June 1834.

12. *Chao-Kang*, music by Carlini, f.p. Teatro San Carlo, Naples, 4 April 1820.

13. *Ménéstrel*, 26 October 1834.

14. *Journal des débats*, 1 December 1834.

15. *Revue et Gazette musicale*, 8 December 1834. The article immediately preceding the review was in fact signed by Berlioz.

16. *Ménéstrel*, 5 March 1840.

17. *Courrier des théâtres*, 7 August 1835.

18. Maurice, II, 124.

19. De Bernaville in *Monde Dramatique*, III, 15–16.

20. *Journal des débats*, 17 August 1835.

21. *Moniteur*, 24 August 1835. Pierre Gardel's *Psyché* (created in 1790 and performed 560 times until 1829), Milon's *Nina* (created in 1813 and performed 190 times until 1840) and Dauberval's *La Fille mal gardée* (created in Bordeaux in 1789 and, in a recreation by Aumer, still occasionally performed at the Opéra) were classics from pre-Romantic times still fondly remembered by older habitués of the Opéra.

22. *Artiste*, 1835, vol.10, 30.

23. *Revue et Gazette Musicale*, 16 March 1835.

16

The Eclipse of Marie Taglioni

The somewhat mixed reception accorded to *L'Ile des pirates* was not the most propitious beginning for a new management, and as 1835 drew to its close Duponchel found himself beset with another problem within the ballet department. In October the Elsslers had left for their contractual leave of absence, in the course of which they were to fulfil an engagement in Berlin. Plans had accordingly been made for Duvernay and Leroux to take over their rôles in *L'Ile des pirates*, and for the programmes over the next few months to be dominated by Taglioni to ensure good houses. But then, just as Paris was looking forward to a rich fare of *La Sylphide, Nathalie* and *La Révolte au sérail*, hopes were dashed by a message from Taglioni that she was laid low by an agonising nerve pain in one of her knees.

Apart from a few close friends and others who could be relied upon to hold their tongues, Paris would remain unaware of the true reason for her long absence from the stage that followed, for not until the following September would she resume her activity at the Opéra. It was, of course, no secret that she had married the Comte Gilbert de Voisins in London in 1832, and the assumption was generally made that the little daughter who was born to her on 30 March 1836 was a child of that union, for the dancer's wayward husband had unexpectedly and briefly reappeared in Paris in the middle of the previous May after an absence abroad of some six months.

The baby's arrival was not publicised, and many may have been under the impression that it had taken all that time for her knee to recover. Even the composer Adolphe Adam, no stranger to gossip, had remained in the dark; and when, some years later, he called on her during a visit to St Petersburg, he was surprised to be greeted by a three-year-old child and enquired who she was. Taglioni answered him with a twinkle in her eye: 'She's my injured knee, *mon mal au genou!*'[1]

Because of Taglioni's prolonged absence, the Opéra's programme schedule had to be hurriedly rearranged. Until the Elsslers returned in February, there was no alternative to making do with the talent at hand; and that winter a number of dancers benefited from opportunities that might not otherwise have come their way. The rôles of the Elssler sisters in *L'Ile des pirates* passed to Pauline Leroux, who took over Fanny's part, and Pauline Duvernay, who replaced Thérèse. There was also a single occasion when Fanny's rôle was played by a visiting dancer from the Rhineland, one Caroline Fuchs, who was presented under the stage-name of Mlle Augusta. According to one notice, she 'obtained a great success as a beauty, a middling success as a mime, and a mediocre success as a dancer',[2] but there was clearly no question of her being offered an engagement. Although she was to enjoy great success in America, in Paris her triumphs were limited to her amatory conquests. There she became the mistress of the Comte de Saint-James, whom she later married, and she also, so it was said, stirred the emotions of her teacher, Albert, while at the same time carrying on an affair with his son – a delicate situation indeed.

At a more serious level, the services of the Opéra's senior ballerina, Lise Noblet, were called upon to enhance a revival of Milon's *Nina*, which was indelibly associated with the great dancer-mime of the Napoleonic age, Emilia Bigottini. Notwithstanding the memory of her illustrious predecessor, Noblet gave the part an equally valid but somewhat less histrionic interpretation.

But perhaps the greatest pleasure offered in these rather barren months was the revival of the popular comedy ballet of *La Fille mal gardée* in the revised version that Aumer had produced seven years before. For this, Pauline Montessu was no longer considered suitable, and the rôle of Lise was given to a hitherto untried young dancer known simply as 'Mlle Maria'. Apart from a brief interlude when Fanny Elssler took possession of it, she was to play the part regularly until the end of her career, with a number of distinguished partners as Colas: Eugène Coralli, son of the ballet-master; Joseph Mazilier; and Lucien Petipa. Maria was to become one of the most popular dancers of the Opéra, both with the public and with her comrades; but gifted though she was, she was never to rise to supreme rank. In particular, her style was marked by an intrepid brio that never failed to thrill and enchant the public; she seemed always to be exerting herself to the limit of her strength – a daring that, one evening towards the end of her career, caused her to overshoot the footlights in a brilliant series of *jetés* and to land, miraculously without injury, among the musicians in the orchestra pit.

Her life was truly one of 'rags to riches'. The daughter of Jewish parents called Jacob, she first saw the light of day in a thickly populated slum on the Ile de la Cité, not far from the Morgue. When scarcely ten years old, she began to be hired at the Opéra as a *trottin*, taking part in processions at one franc a performance; but it was not long before she was inscribed as a pupil of Barrez. To attend class or take part in a performance, whatever the season, involved trudging in all weathers from her miserable home to the Opéra and back again on foot, encouraged only by her ambition, and alone save on those rare occasions when she was escorted by a stage-hand who lived in the same district. She often had to wait for him until two o'clock in the morning, for the following day's scenery had to be placed in position immediately the performance was over. And more than once, after sitting shivering on a bench in the pit for an hour or more, her escort failed to turn up and she had to walk home alone, poorly clad and half-starved, in the chill hours of the early morning. In those early years, when her earnings were no more than a single franc for each performance, she frequently went hungry, although Mme Crosnier, the concierge at the stage door, would occasionally take pity on the thin, pale girl and invite her into the warmth of her parlour to share her dinner.

Slowly, Maria's perseverance had its reward, but not before she had learnt the importance of discipline. Having been allotted the part of a demon in *La Tentation*, she had refused point-blank to mount astride a cannon until Coralli gave her a well-applied kick that sent her flying on to the gun. Wiser from the experience, she soon began to attract attention, being cast as a page in Halévy's opera *La Juive*, and a few months later being given the opportunity of playing Lise in *La Fille mal gardée*.

When she retired from the stage in 1849, Maria would be earning 5000 francs a year and was believed to be engaged to the Baron d'Henneville,[3] a man of considerable influence in the world of the Opéra, whose mistress she had been for some time. In those days, the temptation for a dancer to seek a wealthy and influential protector was heightened by the poverty that beset so many of them while they occupied a lowly place in the company. But unlike many of her contemporaries, Maria had the good sense and character to place her relationship with d'Henneville on a solid foundation. To him she was a devoted companion as well as a lover, and when the Baron died, it was reported that she had the tact to go into mourning.

* * * * * * *

For Hugo, Gautier and many other prominent writers of the Romantic school, Spain, with its vigorous and colourful folklore, held an irresistible appeal. But by stimulating the vogue for things Spanish, they were only responding to a widespread fascination, which purveyors of entertainment were not slow in exploiting. The appearance of Spanish dancers at the Opéra balls had been the sensation of the Carnival season of 1834, and now, two years later, Dolores Serral and Manuela Dubinon were brought back to exert their magic once more. They became the rage of Paris, and it was soon being reported that countless young people were studying their 'lascivious movements' and their *temps de cuisse* so as to introduce them in the unrestrained *cancans* and *chahuts* that were being increasingly featured at the popular dance halls.[4] Duponchel's choice of Spain as the setting for the new ballet for

Fanny Elssler – which was planned to follow the production of Meyerbeer's opera *Les Huguenots* – was thus to prove singularly appropriate.

It was Duponchel who had drawn Coralli's attention to Le Sage's novel *Le Diable boiteux* as a subject for a ballet, and who had recommended him to seek the assistance of Adolphe Nourrit, who was an adept hand at writing ballet scenarios. However, Coralli turned instead to a promising young writer who was yet to make his name, Edmond Burat de Gurgy. With the eagerness of one who recognises opportunity when it is offered, Burat set to work; but not surprisingly his first efforts betrayed his inexperience. Two draft scenarios were submitted to Duponchel and returned with suggestions for improvement. Duponchel, it seems, was seeking advice from Nourrit, but Burat was given no indication that his authorship would not be fully acknowledged. He was admitted to rehearsals, he was brought in on discussions, and once, when Duponchel suggested adding a scene in which the devil would be shown hissing at the heroine as she danced, he managed to argue successfully against its inclusion on the ground that the hissing might prove embarrassingly infectious. He was also invited to Duponchel's soirées, where, one evening, the Director introduced him to the stage designer Feuchères as the author of *Le Diable boiteux*.

So the shock was all the greater when Burat discovered, shortly before the first night on 1 June 1836, that his name would not be appearing on the bills or the printed scenario, and that he was to receive neither royalties nor the customary complimentary seats. Duponchel justified this by arguing that his contract was with Coralli alone, and that the only person the ballet-master had suggested as a collaborator was Nourrit. In the end Burat had to resort to litigation to establish his rights. At the hearing before the Tribunal de Commerce, he was partly successful, being awarded royalties as co-author but not the right to be named on the bills, on the ground that theatre managements were not obliged by law to do this. Both parties then appealed, and the Cour Royale de Paris not only confirmed the earlier judgment but ordered that Burat's name should figure on the bills.[5]

Fanny Elssler, who was to enjoy such a splendid triumph in *Le Diable boiteux*, found a devoted admirer in Burat, although their friendship was to be cut prematurely short when the young man died of consumption at the age of thirty-one in 1840. Many a time he would visit her in her dressing room when *Le Diable boiteux* was in the programme, and one evening was given the opportunity of doing her a real service. On entering, he found her complaining that the *corps de ballet* had stolen the chalk that she applied to the heels of her ballet slippers to prevent her from slipping. She had asked Nathalie Fitzjames, Noblet and Mme Alexis Dupont, but none of them had any to spare. It seemed that there was a conspiracy to prevent her from appearing. 'So now, Monsieur Burat, you will get me some chalk, won't you?'

'But, my dear lady, I don't know where to go for it,'

'Hurry,' she persisted. 'I will pay you whatever you like for it. You have a quarter of an hour before the curtain rises. I shall be waiting for you.'

It was a time when all the shops would be closed. But Burat was an enterprising man, and at last returned with twenty pieces of chalk and looking anything but cheerful.

'Ah!' cried Elssler greatly relieved. 'And how much do I owe you for all this?'

'Just ten glasses of wine,' he replied. 'I had to visit ten cafés and steal the chalk from the billiard tables.'[6]

Burat had shown no less ingenuity in working out his scenario. The ballet opened with a colourful scene in the foyer of the Teatro Real of Madrid, where a masked ball is being held and the penniless student Cleophas (Mazilier) has come in search of adventure. His gallant behaviour arouses the resentment of the escorts of two ladies whom he has approached, one after the other, with an offer of a verse in exchange for a little gift. One of the aggrieved escorts decides to order his servants to give the presumptuous young man a thrashing, a punishment that Cleophas evades by donning female attire. In this guise, he finds himself invited to join the two couples for supper, where he is unmasked, but, aided by the ladies, manages to make his escape. The scene then changes to an alchemist's laboratory. Cleophas appears at a window, and, after making sure he is not being followed, steps inside. Hearing a groan from a large bottle, he smashes it to release the crippled demon Asmodeus (Barrez), who, in gratitude, offers to serve him, and at a wave of his crutch conjures up the three women he met at the ball: a working girl, Paquita (Leroux), a young widow, Dorotea (Legallois), and the dancer Florinda (F. Elssler). Cleophas begs Asmodeus to use his powers to help him pursue Dorotea and Florinda, whom he prefers to the penniless Paquita. After Cleophas has begun to woo Dorotea, Florinda appears to arouse his passion. Delighted at what seems a double triumph, but then recalling that he is merely a penniless student, he seeks Asmodeus's help. The little devil waves his crutch, and Cleophas finds himself wealthy beyond his dreams and transported to the park of a magnificent mansion, where he is surrounded by servants and served with a splendid banquet while being entertained by musicians and dancers.

In the second act Cleophas, now besotted with Florinda, is introduced by Asmodeus into the Foyer de la Danse of the Opera House. By a stroke of magic, Asmodeus makes the ballet-master disappear, and takes his place. Paquita enters to seek employment as a dancer, but her simple country dance is received with derision. But suddenly, all interest shifts away from her as the glamorous Florinda makes her entrance. It is time for the evening's performance, and the scene changes to the stage, as seen from the viewpoint of the dancers, with the audience in the background. It was in this scene that Fanny Elssler, partnered by her sister Thérèse, was to dance the first of two authentic Spanish dances, the *Jaleo de Jerez*, in which the partner receives the lion's share of the applause to the mortification of the ballerina, who retires in a huff feigning a sprained ankle. The scene then moves to Florinda's dressing room, where Asmodeus and Cleophas enter through the wall, as if by magic, just as Florinda is being carried in. The departure of her lover, Don Gill, to fetch a doctor, enables Cleophas to make himself known. She warms to him, but they are interrupted, and Cleophas hides behind a screen. Don Gill then returns, and as he is expressing his love, Cleophas comes out of hiding and appears before him. Florinda coolly passes off Cleophas as being her maid's lover, upon which Asmodeus and Cleophas make a hurried departure.

Another scene change then reveals the most impressive scene in the ballet – a combination of the rooftops of Madrid and the salon in Florinda's mansion. By means of Asmodeus's magic, Cleophas is enabled to look down at Florinda as she dances the *Cachucha* at a supper party. But the sight of her flirting with her admirers so enrages him that he casts down at her feet the rose she had given him at the masked ball.

As the third act opens, Cleophas is found serenading Dorotea with a band of musicians, ignoring Asmodeus's warning that she is interested only in his wealth. But just as he is about to enter her house, he is accosted by a young officer – Florinda in disguise – who claims to be Dorotea's suitor, and challenges him to a duel. Paquita, whose declaration of love Cleophas has rejected, manages to separate the duellists; and after Cleophas has entered the house, she and Florinda make common cause, and discover they have an ally in Asmodeus. In the next scene they enter Dorotea's house together. The plot now takes another twist, when Cleophas loses his fortune at the gaming table and realises the truth of Asmodeus's warning.

The final scene of the ballet is set on the banks of the river Manzanares, where a festival is in progress. Asmodeus, now disguised as a gypsy, predicts happiness for Paquita, and now that Florinda has abandoned all thoughts of continuing her intrigue, Cleophas realises that Paquita is his true love.

The plot of the ballet could well be criticised for not capturing the flavour of Le Sage's novel. Asmodeus, for instance, far from being a malicious little devil who brings luxury and debauchery to the world, had, in Hippolyte Prévost's eyes, been transformed into 'a virtuous, moralising, sentimental devil – or, to put it bluntly, a boring little devil'. But whatever its faults as a literary adaptation, the ballet was a splendid spectacle, fast-moving in its action, and with a number of dances, varied in their flavour, skilfully woven into Coralli's choreography. Casimir Gide's score was composed with taste and a skilful understanding of the needs of the stage, and contained 'a host of very dramatic touches that reveal a talent destined for something more worthy than mere ballet music'.[7]

Above all else, the significance of *Le Diable boiteux* lay in the triumph of Fanny Elssler in the rôle of Florinda, which, with its wide range of expression, revealed to the full her remarkable gifts as an actress, while also making demands on her strength as a dancer that she met unflinchingly throughout three long acts. It was this ballet that finally established her as the rival to Taglioni, by presenting a most striking image of her as the prototype of the sensual facet of the Romantic ballet.

> *Le Diable boiteux* was the ballet *par excellence* for Fanny Elssler, that German maiden who has become transformed into a Spaniard; Fanny Elssler, the Cachucha incarnate, the Cachucha of Dolores raised to the state of a classical model; Fanny Elssler, the most spirited, precise and intelligent dancer who ever skimmed the boards with the tip of her steely toe.

So, with that marvellous flourish of which he was a master, wrote the poet and critic Théophile Gautier, who had joined the staff of the newly founded newspaper *La Presse* in that very summer of 1836, although he would not become its dramatic critic until the following year. 'Fanny Elssler,' he described,

> is tall, well-formed and well-shaped. Her legs are fashioned like those of Diana the Huntress, but with a strength that in no way deprives them of grace. Her head, which is small like that of an antique statue, sits with pure and noble lines on satiny shoulders that have no need of rice powder to give them their white complexion. Her eyes have a most poignant expression of mischievous voluptuousness, which is heightened by the half-ironical smile that plays at the corners of her finely curved lips. Finally, those features, which are as regular as if carved from marble, lend themselves to expressing every emotion, from the most tragic grief to the craziest gaiety. Very soft, silky and glossy brown hair, usually parted in *bandeaux*, frames her brows, which are as suited to bear the goddess's gold circlet as the courtesan's coronet of flowers. Although she is a woman in the full acceptance of the term, the slender elegance of her figure allows her to don male attire with great success. A moment ago she was the prettiest girl, and now she is the most charming lad in the world. She is Hermaphrodite, able to separate at will the two beauties that are blended within her.[8]

Fanny's first *pas* came in the second scene of the second act, with its ingeniously designed set depicting the stage of the Madrid Opera House as seen from the back-cloth, across the boards to the footlights and the orchestra pit, to the dimly seen audience in the background. Arranged by her sister, this *pas de deux* was full of 'effective moments, bold thrusts and graceful poses.'[9] And Thérèse partnered her, as always, with self-effacing devotion and tenderness.

But the most startling moment of all, which remained in the memory of everyone present that evening, was the *Cachucha*. According to Henry Wikoff, an American friend who would become her manager when she went to America, Fanny Elssler arranged this celebrated *pas de caractère* herself; but Louis Viardot recorded that she had learnt it from 'a Spaniard whom we once applauded at the Théâtre Italien'.[10] The sculptor Jean-Auguste Barre preserved an attitude from this dance in a 'ravishing statuette',[11] which was the talk of Paris in the winter of 1836, and Théophile Gautier recorded his impressions of it in one of his most brilliant descriptions:

> She comes forward in a basquine skirt of pink satin trimmed with wide flounces of black lace; her skirt, weighted at the hem, fits tightly about the hips; her wasp-like figure is boldly arched back, making the diamond brooch on her bodice sparkle; her leg, smooth as marble, gleams through the fine mesh of her silk stocking; and her small foot, now still, only awaits the signal from the orchestra to burst into action. How charming she is, with her high comb, the rose at her ear, the fire in her eyes and her sparkling smile. At the tips of her rosy fingers the ebony castanets are all a-quiver. And now she springs forward and the resonant chatter of her castanets breaks out; she seems to be shaking down clusters of rhythm with her hands. See how she twists and bends! What fire! What voluptuousness! What ardour! Her swooning arms flutter about her drooping head, then her body curves back, her white shoulders almost brush the floor. What a charming moment! Would you not say that in that hand, as it skims over the dazzling barrier of the footlights, she is gathering up all the desires and all the enthusiasm of the audience?
>
> We have seen Rosita Diaz, Lola, and the finest dancers of Madrid, Seville, Cadiz and Granada; we have seen the gitanas in Albaicín, but nothing approaches that Cachucha as danced by Elssler.[12]

Such a fiery exhibition was something quite new on the Opéra stage, and 'the public, the real public,' observed Charles de Boigne,

> needed several performances to become accustomed to the *Cachucha*.. The contortions, the movements of the hips, the provocative gestures, the arms that seem to be seeking and embracing an absent lover, the mouth crying out for a kiss, the thrilling, quivering, twisting body, the captivating music, the castanets, the strange costume, the shortened skirt, the low-

cut, half-open bodice and, above all, Elssler's sensual grace, lascivious abandon and plastic beauty were very much appreciated by the opera-glasses of the orchestra stalls and the side boxes. The public, the real public, found it more difficult to accept such choreographic audacities and exaggerated glances, and one might say that it was the *loges infernales* that forced the success on this occasion. The French *Cachucha* is not a natural, inborn taste; it is one that has to be acquired.[13]

The *Cachucha*, the performance of which was directed, quite intentionally, at the audience, and most particularly at the all-male section in the stalls and the side boxes abutting the stage, introduced a new element – that of sexual excitement. This was not too overtly explicit, such as would create a scandal, but in a measure that was to arouse unprecedented scenes of enthusiasm. To some, its manner of performance was even to suggest a relationship, albeit in a much more artistic form, with the cancan, an abandoned and largely improvised form of dance that was making its appearance in popular dancing halls and gardens, where some of its more daring exponents would indulge in the unrestrained and lascivious antics of a glorified gallop. In an anonymous booklet published a few years later, the relationship of the cancan to the *Cachucha* – along with another national dance to be adapted for the ballet stage, the *Cracovienne* – was amusingly touched upon:

> There are cancans and cancans, it is true, but the cancan is everywhere. For what does Mlle Elssler do at the Opéra but dance the cancan, and dance it in a manner more cancan-like than the cancan itself?
>
> The *Cachucha*, like a certain monarchist, can pride itself on being more royalist than the King. But just think of all the struggles the cancan, that poor victim of persecution, has to contend with every day to survive! And yet it is no more immoral than its two sisters, the *Cracovienne* and the *Cachucha*; indeed, one might even say it is less so, for the cancan only evokes dreams of pleasure, while the *Cracovienne* arouses visions of the boudoir, and the *Cachucha*, visions of the bedroom.
>
> It is true that some exponents of the cancan have strangely disfigured it, for its little coquettish and libertine swaying has been replaced by lascivious and coarse poses and a swaying that is trivial and improper. Several of its exponents have even danced it squatting on the floor! Shame on you heretics! You have ruined the cancan.
>
> Yet in spite of everything, in spite of being persecuted, in spite of heresy, it still remains all-powerful at the masked balls.

And now, dear public, do you know why the *Cachucha* and the *Cracovienne* are not in the doghouse like the cancan? It is because the police have a seat in the orchestra stalls and a good pair of binoculars. And do you know why the cancan has triumphed in spite of all this? It is because it has been forbidden.

That is the way of the world, my dear, that is the way of the world![14]

Such was the enthusiasm generated both by the ballet and by the extraordinary Spanish dance inserted in it, that few commentators noticed an unassuming figure in one of the boxes. It was Marie Taglioni, who had come, it was reported, 'to add a dancer's approval, a sylphide's gentle applause, which had more weight than those of the captive, spellbound multitude.'[15]

By August, the *Cachucha* was so much the rage of Paris that Fanny Elssler was summoned to dance it at the Trianon during the festivities for the visit of the King of Naples. On the afternoon of the previous day, no fewer than nine cabs were assembled in the courtyard of the Opéra to carry the dancers, musicians, dressers and costumes to the palace. Jean Coralli had had his white *favoris* dyed specially for the occasion, and before the convoy moved off, Duponchel went down the line of cabs exhorting their occupants not to indulge in too much revelry. Though court etiquette forbade applause at the performance, Fanny knew from the murmurs of satisfaction that her *Cachucha* had once again produced a sensation; and before she returned to Paris she was presented with a porcelain luncheon service in addition to the fee of 1000 fr. paid to her sister and herself. Three days later, on 14 August, a berlin drawn by four horses left Paris carrying the two sisters to Bordeaux, and Marie Taglioni found herself in sole command of the Opéra stage.

* * * * * * *

Marriage had brought more sorrow than happiness to Marie Taglioni, who all too soon had discovered that she could expect little affection or understanding from her husband; for the Comte Gilbert de Voisins had lost no time in revealing his true nature as an irresponsible young man who felt no scruples in taking money from his wife. He had even been known to wait in the wings while she was dancing in order to press his demands as she made her way, exhausted, to her dressing-room; and he thought nothing of deserting her to accompany his brother on a six-month journey to Constantinople. His return to his wife in May 1835 provoked a painful scene, but their reconciliation was as brief as it may have been passionate. Their relationship soon deteriorated, and they parted once again, this time finally.

Before long, Marie discovered she was pregnant, and in the middle of October she interrupted her career, feigning the injury to her knee, *un mal au genou*, which deceived almost everyone. Deprived of a husband's support when she needed it most, she had turned in her distress to a young writer, Eugène Desmares. Gossip had it that they first met at a masked ball at the Opéra, whither she had gone in the company of Louise Fitzjames, and that Desmares, taking her for some young woman of easy virtue, took her to a *maison de rendez-vous* in the Rue le Peletier. Only there, when she removed her mask, did he become aware of her identity. He proved an ardent and satisfying lover, and the following day Marie could not refrain from relating her good fortune to Louise Fitzjames. 'Ah! my dear Louise,' she sighed, 'if you only knew the difference between that young man and my scoundrel of a husband!'[16] When de Voisins learnt that his wife was living with Desmares, his only comment was: 'Upon my word, I cannot compliment him. He has not chosen a pretty mistress!'[17]

The incident at the masked ball, which was supposed to have taken place on 9 January 1836, was thus recorded by a chronicler of scandal within the Opéra; but in fact Desmares must have known Marie before then – and it is perhaps more likely that this was the occasion when they first became lovers. For, several months before this, Desmares had written the scenario of *La Fille du Danube*, the new ballet that Filippo Taglioni was planning while his daughter was expecting her child.[18]

Duponchel had little choice when Filippo Taglioni presented him with this scenario, for Marie Taglioni's contract stipulated that she should dance only in ballets composed by her father. So it was duly approved, and Adolphe Adam, who had been a school friend of Desmares, was commissioned to compose the score. Desmares kept the fact of his authorship so secret that, when the scenario was sent to Adam, the composer thought it was the work of Filippo Taglioni. 'Father Taglioni has sent me his ballet scenario,' he wrote to his brother on 7 April 1836. 'I can make absolutely nothing of it, but I am going to do the work very quickly, for they have to start rehearsing soon. As you know, I like to be hurried. For me it is a way to succeed.' And hurry he did. He first played the score through to Filippo Taglioni on 21 May, and on 1 June was able to tell his brother: 'I have nearly finished my ballet. Taglioni is satisfied with it, but rehearsals have not yet begun.'[19]

On 30 March Marie Taglioni had given birth to a daughter, whom she named – with a thought, perhaps, for her adoring new lover – Eugénie-Marie-Ludwige. During the early part of that summer, the final preparations for *Le Diable boiteux* were monopolising the time of everyone at the Opéra, and it was not until its first performance was over that Filippo Taglioni was able to begin work on *La Fille du Danube*. Marie's return to the stage was announced for 10 August, in *La Sylphide,* and everyone was curious to see whether she had retained all her purity of style and skill.

For her it must have been a nerve-wracking experience to reappear after such a long absence. But all went well, and the warm applause that greeted her on her first entrance gave way to absolute silence when she began to dance. A standing ovation awaited her at the end. Flowers fell in profusion at her feet, amid roars of applause, and Janin recorded an example of supreme enthusiasm. A young man in one of the upper tiers was so carried away that he snatched a bouquet from the hands of a girl in the adjoining box and hurled it on to the stage. As the girl started back in surprise, the crown of roses she wore in her hair slipped, and seizing this second opportunity, the zealous admirer plucked it off and sent it too flying through the air to land at the feet of the object of his devotion.

When *La Fille du Danube* was produced a few weeks later, on 21 September 1836, Marie Taglioni's magnetic attraction for the public was put to a severe test – for without her the work would doubtless have been a miserable failure. To anyone who had not studied the scenario beforehand, the action was almost totally incomprehensible. The Daughter of the Danube, played by Marie Taglioni, is a young foundling called Fleur-des-Champs who, after being discovered as a baby on the river-bank, has been brought up by mortals but watched over by the Nymph of the Danube (Legallois). She and Rudolph (Mazilier), the Baron's equerry, are in love, but to their dismay the Baron (Montjoie) summons the village maidens to his castle and chooses Fleur-des-Champs to be his bride. Rejecting him, Fleur-des-Champs throws her posy to Rudolph and jumps through the window into the Danube. Rudolph loses his reason and is about to plunge into the river himself when the spirit of Fleur-des-Champs makes her appearance. She vanishes at the approach of the Baron, who hopes to restore his equerry's reason with the help of a girl (Leroux) dressed to resemble Fleur-des-Champs. However, Rudolph sees through the ruse and leaps into the water himself. Here his love for Fleur-des-Champs is put to the test, and by means of Fleur-des-Champs's posy he is able to recognise her among the ondines. Finally, the Nymph of the Danube restores the lovers to life.

The blindly admiring Janin called this ballet 'the sequel to *La Sylphide*,'[20] but other critics were almost unanimous in dismissing it as a work of little merit. The *Moniteur* found it lacking in wit and invention, a lifeless nullity, 'boring and inconsequential nonsense, a jumble of worn-out, commonplace stuff.'[21] The dullness of the plot was only occasionally relieved by the choreography. 'M. Taglioni,' wrote Frédéric Soulié in the *Presse*, 'has never produced anything more commonplace... [He] is following the method of dressmakers and political and literary geniuses by applying the maxim that tells us that there is nothing new but what has been forgotten.'[22] In the *Siècle* Louis Viardot reproached the choreographer for being too miserly with his daughter's talent.[23] But here and there could be found some interesting passages: a *galop* in the first act that was, however, found wanting by comparison with a more animated and varied one of recent memory, that in *Gustave*; and in the final scene a skilfully arranged *pas d'ensemble*, in which Rudolph seeks Fleur-des-Champs among the ondines and which brought the ballet to a close with a ravishing tableau.

But all were agreed in acclaiming Marie Taglioni for carrying the whole weight of this ballet on her shoulders – even if, as one critic put it, no tears were shed when she threw herself into the river at the end of the first act. She was, in the words of the *Constitutionnel*, 'the only mortal creature able to portray a celestial apparition, an imponderable form, with endearing conviction... Never before has a choreographer relied so much on the inexhaustible resources of her strength and her grace. She never stops bounding and flying, and not one of her movements betrays a trace of fatigue.'[24] To Janin she had never appeared 'so light, so sad, so passionate, so calm'; but as an inveterate enemy of the male dancer, he could not help being a little offended by the sight of Mazilier. He recognised his ability as a mime and acknowledged that he did his best, but it was all too apparent that he was no longer slender enough to pursue the winged Taglioni. Janin thought the illusion would have been more complete had someone like Lise Noblet taken the part *en travesti*.[25]

Among the critics who had misgivings about the suitability of *La Fille du Danube* for a theatre of the Opéra's eminence was De Bernaville of the *Monde dramatique*, who posed a pertinent question that may have been in the minds of many:

> why her graceful talent was not being made available as a focal point for the fantasies of our own choreographers, and why a single ballet-master should have the exclusive right to submit the wondrous steps of the Sylphide to his own ideas... Do people really believe that in 1836, with a dancer so valuable as Taglioni, the public can be fobbed off with such provincial banality as that which the Opéra has just given us?'[26]

Marie Taglioni's performance aside, the only saving grace of *La Fille du Danube* was the contribution of Adolphe Adam, who had by then gained a certain reputation for his facility to produce tuneful scores for light operas and vaudevilles. Adam's important work still lay in the future, but he had already shown an aptitude for writing ballet music when his brother-in-law, Pierre Laporte, then manager of the King's Theatre in London, had asked him to compose the score for Deshayes's ballet *Faust* in 1833. This early work has now apparently disappeared, but Adam was later to incorporate several passages from it into *Giselle* and his comic opera *Le Chalet*. Few Parisians had heard his first essay in ballet composition, and for most of them *La Fille du Danube* was their introduction to his work as a composer for ballet. De Bernaville of the *Monde dramatique* described its texture as 'light, witty and graceful',[27] while Prévost in the *Moniteur* was struck by several successful melodies for the dances and a few strong dramatic touches, notably in Rudolph's mad scene.[28]

These were, of course, generalisations; but a more considered comment on the score appeared in the *Revue et Gazette musicale*, written by an experienced musician who, one senses, was somewhat puzzled to find himself being sent to the Opéra to review a new ballet. He comforted himself with the thought that, thanks to his presence, Adam would at least be able to read one assessment of his contribution by a critic whose qualifications he could respect. 'M. Adam's score was greatly appreciated,' he wrote.

It is full of freshness and grace. Not all its melodies are very novel, but generally they possess an elegant simplicity which the French prize as much as originality. The dramatic intention is always good, and the orchestration well chosen. Only one scene did not seem suitably treated – that in which Fleur des Champs's shade rises out of the Danube to console her lover. All the resources that the art possesses were needed there to produce a musical accompaniment that is misty and mellow, but the composer failed to achieve this, by using only the brass section! The sound was well toned down in performance, but nevertheless instruments of that kind always retain a somewhat lugubrious character, which was essentially not what the situation here required. To sum up, one might say that Adolphe Adam made too great a use of the brass, particularly the *cornets à piston*, which it is difficult to use conspicuously for long without to some extent vulgarising the orchestration. Among the numbers that appealed to us was a *pas* at the end of the last act. The melody that serves as its theme is given to the cellos, while an accompaniment of double crochets from the flutes and oboes harmoniously follows the lines of the melody by making it scintillate in a quite unusual manner. This is a very happy effect, which one does not come across every day.[29]

There was perhaps no more experienced observer than the Director of the Opéra, Henri Duponchel, who was in no way deceived by all the applause and bouquets at the end of the performance. Chancing to meet Véron the next day, he expressed his misgivings.

'The new ballet is pretty bad, is it not?' he asked gloomily.

'Do you really think so?' answered Véron, who merely saw it as a vehicle for Taglioni. 'I would have given it a hundred performances to packed houses.'[30]

****

Duponchel was now pondering a problem of the gravest import: whether or not to renew Marie Taglioni's contract, which would expire in April 1837. When his predecessor, Dr Véron, had negotiated the terms, it had been his intention to place her on a pinnacle as the supreme star of the company, and her salary was fixed accordingly. But now she was sharing the applause of the public with Fanny Elssler, particularly after the latter's triumph in *Le Diable boiteux*, and was no longer so indispensable. Another factor of which Duponchel no doubt took note was that Taglioni's character did not make her the easiest person to work with. She was not generally good-tempered, either on or off the stage; she gave the impression of being what the French call *'une pimbêche'*, an old miss. Véron, who was a loyal friend, was reticent about her character and would not be drawn into revelations. 'You know the French proverb, "You inherit nothing from those you kill,"' he said when pressed. 'Don't forget, she helped me make my fortune.'[31]

Duponchel had no such reason to bear with her, and now, as Director of the Opéra, he viewed her with very different eyes from those that had impelled him to throw her a bouquet at her first appearance in Paris ten years before. He was becoming increasingly exasperated by her interference in his own domain, and began to weigh up the advantages and disadvantages of dispensing with her services and saving the enormous salary she was receiving.

Meanwhile, Fanny Elssler, on whose continued support he was expecting to rely, had fallen seriously ill. She and her sister returned from Bordeaux towards the end of October, after being held up at Orleans where, early one morning, the axle of their carriage had broken. Fanny was running a high temperature when they reached Paris and was put to bed, where she hovered between life and death for ten days. She was bled, leeches were applied, and at long last the delirium passed and she began to improve. However, her illness had left her much weakened, and several weeks' rest were required before she was strong enough even to begin preparing for her return. Then, to her horror, she found she was unable to perform even the simplest feats. Day after day she worked under Vestris with desperate perseverance to make up the lost ground. The old teacher soothed and encouraged her, and at times even groaned and wept himself, such was his fear that all their endeavours might come to nought. At first, progress was disappointingly slow; but suddenly, one day, Elssler felt her strength return, almost as if by magic, and with a cry of delight she bounded in the air and danced before the delighted Vestris until she collapsed exhausted on to the floor.

Amid scenes of extraordinary enthusiasm, she made her reappearance in *Le Diable boiteux* on 3 April 1837. Even the dancers welcomed her back, and there was no cavilling when one of them spontaneously crowned her that evening on the stage. Duponchel must have felt he had made a correct decision in not re-engaging Taglioni, who had meanwhile decided to spread her wings and accept an offer from St Petersburg.

There was, of course, widespread regret at the imminent departure of Taglioni, whose final appearance in Paris was announced to take place on 22 April for her benefit. By many, Duponchel was held responsible for the damage that, as was forecast in some quarters, the Opéra ballet would surely suffer by her departure, and a small band of conspirators decided to organise a demonstration to express their discontent. The slogan 'The late Duponchel' appeared on the walls of Paris overnight, while invitations to his funeral were dispatched to a number of well-known people, and a firm of undertakers instructed to collect the corpse from the Opéra. Duponchel was as surprised to see the lugubrious faces of the mourners as they were to find him hale and hearty, but he accepted the joke in good humour, inviting the mourners to dinner and giving the undertaker's men a liberal tip. The only person to be disappointed was Maillot, the hosier of the Opéra, famous as the man who gave his name to tights. Grumbling that his day had been wasted, he swore to attend no more funerals until his own. Taglioni, whose opinion of Duponchel was that he was 'a gossip and not very serious', was sure he had engineered the whole incident himself in order to gain popularity.[32]

Another demonstration was planned to take place during the benefit performance itself. It was arranged that, at the moment when the bouquets were falling, the occupants of one of the *loges infernales* would throw a papier-mâché likeness of Duponchel's head on to the stage with the cry, 'Off with Duponchel's head! Long live Taglioni!' It was an amusing idea, but not in the best of taste when, at that very moment, Meunier, who had attempted to assassinate the King, was on trial for his life. Queen Marie-Amélie, who was to attend the performance, learnt what was being prepared and, horror-struck at the thought of seeing a head, albeit an imitation one, roll on the stage when Meunier's head might soon be dropping into the guillotine's basket, sent an aide-de-camp to beg the instigators not to carry out their plan. Her feelings were dutifully respected, and Paris was spared the sight of seeing both heads: for a few days later, Meunier was magnanimously reprieved by Louis-Philippe.

Marie Taglioni's benefit performance began at seven o'clock in the evening and continued until one o'clock on the morning of her thirty-third birthday.

She appeared both in *La Sylphide* and in *Le Dieu et la Bayadère*, in which a new *pas*, *La Diane chasseresse*, with music by Auber, had been inserted. It was an evening to be remembered, not only for the wealth of the programme, but also for an incident in the second act of *La Sylphide*, when two of the flying sylphides – Mlles Athalie and Perez – suddenly found themselves stuck in mid-air. At first the audience laughed at their plight, but soon, on realising that the girls were in distress, they began to voice concern. Finally, at considerable risk to life and limb, a stage-hand climbed on to a joist to restore the action of the counterweights and the two frightened dancers were lowered to the ground in the wings. Marie Taglioni begged Duponchel to announce that they were safe, but he refused and she took it upon herself to reassure the public.

'Ladies and gentlemen, there is no cause for alarm,' she told them. 'No one has been injured.'

These were the only words that the great ballerina ever uttered on the stage in public.

Now, richer by the record sum of 34,423 francs that her benefit had produced, she was about to depart, and many of her admirers felt aggrieved. Frédéric Soulié for one deplored the reluctance of the Opéra to retain her. 'We are losing Mlle Taglioni,' he wrote in a mood of near-despair.

> She is taking flight, bound for London, Edinburgh and St Petersburg. May the gods be kind and restore her to us, for we alone have a feeling for her and understand her as she deserves. We rather doubt whether that white floating shade who bears the name Taglioni will appear so clearly to the eyes of the English through their thick fogs. Alas, what will become of that white mist in all the smoke from common coal! And what fate lies in store for that beautiful butterfly in the icy wind of the Baltic! Taglioni belongs to us, and yet no one is raising an objection now that she is being snatched away! What has become of the France of July? How low indeed have the French fallen![33]

But there was to be no turning back. The decision had been made to let the Taglionis go, reached in all probability for reasons of expense, but also, one may suspect, because the Taglionis had never quite integrated themselves into the framework of the Opéra ballet. Apart from appearing in minor rôles in *La Belle au bois dormant* and *Manon Lescaut* early in her engagement, Marie Taglioni had been presented solely in ballets by her father. Certainly she owed an incalculable debt to him; but from the Opéra's point of view, to engage a ballet-master solely for the convenience of one particular ballerina was, on the very face of it, an unjustifiable extravagance.

NOTES

1. Vaillat, 294–300.

2. *Constitutionnel*, 10 November 1835.

3. Jean-Baptiste-Roger Fauchon, Baron d'Henneville (1780–1856) was a senior official at the Conservatoire de Musique, who had been appointed by Véron as one of the members of the Supervising Committee of the Opéra.

4. *Les Cancans de l'Opéra en 1836* (MS.), I, 9. Tamvaco, 105–6.

5. *Gazette des tribunaux*, 9 August 1837. According to the *Tam-tam* of 5 June 1836, the scenarios sold at the Opéra had their title pages torn out because Burat's name appeared on them. However, all the copies of the scenario that I have seen name Coralli as sole author until the third edition, published in 1838.

6. Léspès, 115–6.

7. *Moniteur*, 28 June 1836.

8. *Les Beautés de l'Opéra*. Notice of *Le Diable boiteux*, 4–5.

9. Castil-Blaze, II, 251.

10. *Siècle*, 12 August 1836. The dancer here referred to was Dolores Serral.

11. *Courrier des théâtres*, 5 December 1836. This was the first of Barre's four statuettes of dancers, the other three being of Taglioni (1837), Amani the Bayadère (1838) and Emma Livry (1862).

12. *Les Beautés de l'Opéra: Le Diable boiteux*, 20–21.

13. De Boigne, 132.

14. Anon., *Physiologie de l'Opéra, du Carnaval et de la Cachucha, par un Vilain Masqué*, Chapter XI. Paris, 1842,

15. *Revue et Gazette musicale*, 5 June 1836.

16. *Les Cancans de l'Opéra en 1836*, I, 243. Tamvaco, 200.
When de Voisins learnt that his wife was living with Desmares, his only comment was: 'Upon my word, I cannot compliment him. He has not chosen a pretty mistress!'

17. *Les Cancans de l'Opéra en 1836*, I, 156. Tamvaco, 165.

18. The *Courrier des théâtres* gave the first hint of this new work on 25 August 1835: 'We who ought not to be aware of what does not yet exist will merely say that a ballet, composed by a young writer, and the various scenes of which had been reproduced in several lithographs, will probably furnish the basic idea of this choreographic work. M. Taglioni will have the assistance of a scenarist, and glory will do the rest.'

19. Pougin, *Adolphe Adam*, 120.

20. *Journal des débats*, 23 September 1836.

21. *Moniteur*, 3 October 1836.

22. *Presse*, 26 September 1836.

23. *Siècle*, 23 September 1836.

24. *Constitutionnel*, 24 September 1836.

25. *Journal des débats*, 23 September 1836.

26. *Monde dramatique*, III, 268–70.

27. *Monde dramatique*, III, 268–70.

28. *Moniteur*, 3 October 1836.

29. *Revue et Gazette musicale de Paris*, 25 September 1836. Sadly, it is not possible to identify this critic, who signed himself 'A Stupid Old Man who has lost most of his teeth'.

30. Vaillat, 316.

31. *An Englishman in Paris*, I, 101.

32. The story of the mock funeral is recounted in de Boigne (168–73), and Taglioni's comments in Bord (72–3). Bord claimed to possess a copy of de Boigne's book with copious annotations in Taglioni's hand.

33. *Presse*, 27 February 1837. The reference to 'the France of July' in the penultimate sentence was to the revolution of 1830, when the people of Paris brought the Bourbon monarchy to an end.

17

The Supremacy of Fanny Elssler

In Henri Duponchel the Opéra had a very different master from the dominating and flamboyant Dr Véron. The new Director was by contrast a mild-tempered, even docile man, better suited to supervising the *mise en scène* of a new opera or ballet, for which he had an unfailing flair, than for coping with a situation that required firm handling. But while he could be criticised for a certain lack of authority, he had three admirable merits that were not always to be found in Directors of the Opéra. He could plan with initiative and foresight, he had no ambitions in the literary and musical fields, and he was never known to form an association with a principal artist under his command. His management was not, however, conducted entirely without regard to extraneous influences, and when he found himself faced with the imminent departure of Taglioni and the illness of Elssler, he was unable to resist the suggestion of his associate, Aguado, to launch a young dancer called Nathalie Fitzjames.

Duponchel relied heavily on the financial support of Aguado, who had underwritten half of the undertaking at the outset of his management, and was always ready to appear as a *deus ex machina* in moments of crisis. The two men worked together in close harmony. Aguado was a polished nobleman – unaffected, thoughtful and generous. He was often to be seen at the Opéra, and every year he distributed New Year gifts to its employees. His knowledge and love of the arts was considerable: he owned a fine collection of paintings, and he could count himself among the few close friends of Rossini, who composed part of his opera *Guillaume Tell* while staying at Aguado's country house.

Aguado's mistress was Alexandrine Fijan, whose elder sister Louise was a dancer of some importance at the Opéra, having adopted the aristocratic-sounding stage-name of Fitzjames. Louise Fitzjames had entered Romieu's class at the School of Dance in 1820 at the age of ten, and had proved a conscientious and willing pupil. Seven years later, she entered the class of Auguste Vestris, and had the distinction of being the last pupil of that legendary relic of a more graceful age. But it was not he but Filippo Taglioni who prepared her for her début, allowing her the unprecedented privilege of sharing his private class with his daughter.

Her first appearance on 1 October 1832, in *Les Pages du duc de Vendôme*, earned her an immediate engagement, but Taglioni was unimpressed, dismissing her with the laconic comment that she was '*pas grand'chose!*'. On the other hand, Pierre Gardel sent her a letter of congratulation with his portrait, and Véron asked her to take over the rôle of the Abbess in *Robert le Diable*. She agreed, but only after some hesitation, successfully passing this difficult test on the last day of 1832. The part was thereafter hers: she was to play it more than 230 times, and Meyerbeer commemorated her 200th performance by sending her a bust of himself in bronze. Later she appeared in two more of Taglioni's rôles, in *La Révolte au sérail* (15 April 1836) and *Le Dieu et la Bayadère* (24 November 1837). No one, however, considered her as anything other than an ordinarily gifted dancer. She was agile and had a correct technique, but she laboured under the disadvantage of being tall and excessively thin. A cruel caricature of the time depicted her 'in all her proverbial skinniness, performing her famous asparagus dance in a ballet of vegetables'.[1]

While no very brilliant future would be assured for Louise, the family still had hopes of fame, which became centred on the youngest of the three sisters. Nathalie Fitzjames had revealed an irresistible childish charm when studying under her first teacher, Guillet. In 1829, when she was barely ten years old, Aumer took a fancy to her and cast her as Cupid in *La Belle au bois dormant*. When her sister Alexandrine became Aguado's mistress, Nathalie gained a powerful guardian, who insisted that she should join her sister in taking lessons in reading, writing, and – what was so obviously required – elocution, so that they would become fit companions for a Spanish nobleman. Alexandrine saw her younger sister as a potential ballerina of the first order, but unfortunately none of the girl's teachers recognised anything beyond an ordinary talent. Filippo Taglioni had even given up teaching her in despair. But once Aguado had lent his persuasion to his mistress's whim, everyone suddenly discovered the most promising qualities in her, and clamoured to be allowed to cultivate them.

Aguado saw through this tardy and interested readiness, and he and Duponchel decided to entrust the task of producing the new ballet for Nathalie to Antonio Guerra, a young Italian dancer who had recently made his first appearance at the Opéra. Born in Naples of very poor parents on 30 December 1810, Guerra became a pupil at the Conservatoire attached to the Royal Theatres, where he studied dancing only because the singing and instrumental classes happened to be full at the time. His first teacher was Pietro Hus. He was soon taking part in crowd scenes at the Teatro di San Carlo, where he gained experience by observing at close quarters such dancers as Samengo, Albert and Paul. When only fifteen, he was selected by his teacher to play the rôle of Colas in a revival by Louis Duport of *La Fille mal gardée* at the Teatro de' Fiorentini. His success in this ballet had far-reaching results. The Duke of Salerno took an interest in 'little Duport', as the boy was affectionately referred to, and paid for him to have a good education in languages, history, music and the arts. This was to stand him in good stead when he began to devote himself to choreography. He staged his early ballets in Vienna and Naples, being strongly influenced by Gaetano Gioja, in many of whose productions he had danced at the San Carlo. From Gioja in particular he learnt how to arrange the action clearly and in strict accord with the music, how to give variety to his dances, and above all how to handle crowd scenes with the effective realism that was one of the hallmarks of Italian choreography at that time.

It was his great ambition to appear at the Opéra, and so, one day, he wound up his affairs in Naples and made his way to Paris to fulfil it. With intelligent determination he set about studying French taste, visiting the Opéra time and time again to observe the likes and dislikes and the reactions of the public. He had probably come provided with an introduction to the Taglionis from Salvatore Taglioni, Filippo's brother, who was in charge of the Naples Ballet School, for it was Filippo who prepared him for his Paris début in *La Sylphide* on 2 November 1836, when he was granted the enviable privilege of partnering Marie Taglioni herself. In Naples he had earned the reputation of being able to turn nine pirouettes, which feat he repeated with such exertion at his Paris début that Jules Janin was reminded of a whirling dervish. Fortunately he was intelligent enough not to repeat this error of taste, and when next seen, in a *pas* of his own composition in Mozart's opera *Don Juan*, his elegance and grace and his sound technique were much admired. 'Those who saw Vestris dance, when Vestris had legs,' wrote Janin, 'say that Guerra has legs exactly like those of Vestris.'[2]

In the spring of 1837, Duponchel and Aguado decided to commission Guerra to produce a new ballet for Nathalie Fitzjames. The prospective ballerina was placed in his charge, and he was offered a five-year engagement from May 1837 at 6000 francs a year, with ten bonuses of 50 francs guaranteed each month. However, power was reserved to the Opéra to terminate it at the end of the first eighteen months.

The scenario of the new ballet, *Les Mohicans*, had already been accepted, and Guerra had no option but to do his best with it. Its author was Léon Halévy, brother of the composer of *Manon Lescaut* and *La Juive* and father of the future author of *La Famille Cardinal*. It was rather carelessly based on James Fennimore Cooper's novel set in the backwoods of North America, *The Last of the Mohicans*. In the ballet, the Mohicans are not the noble savages of the book, but a cruel enemy, which attacks a camp of English soldiers after an advance party has been sent out under a Major (Mazilier), whose name was unaccountably corrupted from Heywood to Arwed in the transition from novel to ballet. The Colonel (Quériau) is wounded, and his daughter Alice (N.

Fitzjames) and the dancing-master Jonathas (Elie) are taken prisoner. The scout Hawk-eye (Simon) disguises himself as a Mohican conjurer to watch over Alice, whose beauty stirs the desires of the Indian chief (Guerra). To their dismay, Major Arwed, on whom their hopes of rescue depended, is brought in, a prisoner. He is bound to the stake, and the Indians are on the point of burning him there when Jonathas takes out his pocket violin. At the sound of such enchanting music the Mohicans throw themselves into an orgy of dancing. This leaves them so exhausted that the Indians find themselves in no state to resist when the rescuing troops arrive.

The ballet met with a rowdy enough reception after its first performance on 5 July 1837, but its second was even more tumultuous. Even some of the *abonnés* forgot their manners, and the occupants of the *loge infernale* had the dubious taste to hiss loudly, notwithstanding the presence of the Duc and Duchesse d'Orléans in the adjoining box. The critics were hardly any kinder. Jules Janin trusted that the first performance would indeed mark 'the last of the Mohicans',[3] while the *Moniteur*, after inveighing against the absurdity, vulgarity and poverty of the work, chided Duponchel for 'giving way to certain powerful considerations... He should not forget that it is a weakness to be accommodating.'[4]

Even the collaboration of Adolphe Adam failed to save the day. Louis Viardot described his score as 'facile, agreeable, popular and, above all, full of marches and repeated *pas*. Here and there are even some melodies that are almost savage and very suitable for inciting the Redskins to dance.'[5] Adam had written this music in no more than a week, and with prophetic foresight had arranged to receive a lump-sum payment equal to the royalties for forty performances.

Inevitably, no more was heard of *Les Mohicans* after its second performance. Malicious scandalmongers insinuated that Aguado had chosen the ballet for Nathalie Fitzjames's début, knowing full well that it would be a failure, in revenge for her having withheld her favours from him. Nathalie took several weeks to recover from the shock caused by this disaster; eventually a reconciliation was arranged with some of the more influential *abonnés*, who consented to tolerate her presence in the company so long as she appeared only in modest *pas* within her capabilities.

She was an attractive girl, with gentle blue eyes and delicate features set in a pale complexion that did not carry too well across the footlights. As a dancer, her outstanding quality was her lightness, which Jules Janin dismissed as 'a lightness without strength, that might be compared to that of a soap bubble'.[6] Théophile Gautier, however, was more perceptive, recognising qualities that offered promise for the future. To him she appeared 'very young, with pretty features and an air of distinction, and remarkably elegant. Although in appearance somewhat frail, she is agile and strong. She is destined to take her place among our finest dancers; her movements are designed with clarity and candour, she jumps well, and her *pointes* are strong and firm... She only needs a better part to be fully appreciated by the public.'[7]

She was not formally engaged until 1 October, when she was given a year's contract at the modest salary of 1500 francs, with bonuses of 10 francs a performance. After recovering from the disappointment of her début, she began to attract favourable notice in the New Year. 'Her attitudes are more elegant and better formed, her *pointes* are becoming stronger, and she is using her arms better,' reported Gautier in February 1838 after seeing her in the Tyrolienne in *Guillaume Tell* and as Zoloé in *Le Dieu et la Bayadère*. 'If she can give a little more play to her delicate, refined features without falling into the death's-head grin so often found among dancers, she will be quite above reproach.'[8]

Although she was never to attain the top rank at the Opéra, she became a useful member of the company. She excelled in *pas de caractère* such as the *Mauresca*, which she danced with Maria in de Ruolz's opera *La Vendetta*, and revealed a certain dramatic talent when she appeared as Thérèse in *La Somnambule* on 22 January 1840. Her progress was reflected in the increases of her salary, which was to rise to 5000 francs a year by the time she left the Opéra at the end of September 1842. Later she gained popularity in Italy, where she became the first ballerina to dance *Giselle* in Florence and Genoa; she visited the United States of America in 1850 and 1851; and she returned to dance in Paris again only at the end of her career, in 1853, when she took the principal part in Saint-Léon's *Le Danseur du roi* at the Théâtre Lyrique. She developed into a versatile artist who was almost equally gifted as a singer: on one occasion, before the Court at Versailles in 1842, she sang two acts of *Lucia di Lammermoor*, mimed two acts of *La Muette de Portici*, and danced in the peasant *pas de deux* from the first act of *Giselle*.

The prodigality with which she dispensed her talent was matched by the generosity she showed towards her friends. Shortly after her début, Charles de Boigne fell in love with her. A year later, his fortunes changed with uncomfortable suddenness, and, finding himself ruined as a result of a rash speculation, he hid himself from the world and from his mistress. But Nathalie loved him for himself with a steadfast and disinterested devotion. 'My dear Benoît,' she wrote to him,

I have learnt of your misfortune and am annoyed that I cannot put things right except by the sympathy of a tender and faithful friend. Should you have need of somewhere to live, do come to me. There you will find bed and board for so long as the 25,000 francs I owe you will last.'[9]

No woman ever had a more faithful cavalier: he left her only to go to work, and whenever she was dancing he would escort her to the theatre and devotedly wait for her in the wings or her dressing-room to accompany her home.

* * * * * * *

April 1837 was a month of farewells. The departure of Taglioni and Adolphe Nourrit deprived the Opéra, within the space of a few weeks, of its principal ballerina and its greatest tenor. But their places were not left vacant for long. On the 3rd, just two days after Nourrit's last performance, Fanny Elssler returned, fully recovered from her illness, and on the 17th a short and stocky tenor, Gilbert Duprez, conquered the public at a single stroke with a voice of tremendous power.

A new ballet was soon in preparation for Fanny Elssler, but first she was seen in three new rôles, all within a fortnight: Lise in *La Fille mal gardée* on 15 September, Fenella in *La Muette de Portici* on the 25th, and the title rôle of *Nina*, which she played before Louis-Philippe at Compiègne on the 28th. She had already revealed her exceptional talent as a mime in *Le Diable boiteux*, and this was now confirmed by her remarkable performance in the light rôle of Lise. In the words of Gautier,

> The voluptuous enchantress Alcina, the ardent Spaniard of the *Cachucha*, had turned into a dreamy young girl, scattering about her a sweet idyllic perfume. She was gentle and velvet-smooth like German moonlight. The very sight of her makes one think of Hermann and Dorothea. On this evening, decisive for her future, she showed herself to be as outstanding in mime as in the dance.[10]

But it was as Fenella, with Duprez as Masaniello, that she made the deepest impression. Berlioz had no hesitation in hailing her as the greatest mime since Bigottini:

> There could not have been a finer rendering – with gestures more natural or more implicit with simplicity, grace and warmth – of the poor girl's anguish at seeing her seducer lead her rival to the altar and being powerless to prevent it. And when, repulsed a second time by guards who bar her entry into the church, Fenella sat on the ground and dissolved into tears, just as a Fenella of real life would have done, the entire audience burst into applause at this revelation of a talent of the first order. Such expressiveness of features, movement and pose is hard to maintain for long, yet Mlle Elssler preserved it to the very end. Without excessive

gestures, and by her timing to the rhythm of the music in the Italian manner, she frequently displayed wit, but always the truest sensitivity.[11]

Such a performance stunned the audience, which was not accustomed to the naturalness and severe economy of means by which she brought the character so convincingly to life. The public, as the *Constitutionnel* observed, was still accustomed to 'gauze scarves and garlands of roses, and expected... a heroine to weep with a smile, suffer with coquetry, and raise her hands to implore the mercy of Heaven with the studied care of a pretty woman putting on her gloves for a ball'.[12] But in stark contrast, the depth and power of Elssler's acting was shatteringly novel.

After this revelation of her dramatic power, great things were expected of Jean Coralli's new ballet, *La Chatte métamorphosée en femme,* on which a fortune was being expended to provide sets and costumes of great magnificence and authenticity. Its subject was no mystery, for the title revealed the ballet to be an adaptation of a vaudeville that Scribe had written ten years before for the actress Jenny Vertpré.[13] The heroine is a Chinese princess Kié-li (F. Elssler), who is secretly in love with the student Oug-lou (Mazilier). To her consternation, Oug-lou is besotted with his cat, and Kié-li realises she must win his love by subterfuge. She begins by contriving an accident from which Oug-lou rescues her, and invites him to the palace. Here her tutor (Barrez), who is privy to her plan, announces that the dragon is about to consume the sun in anger because the princess is being asked to marry against her choice, and that when darkness falls over the earth she must leave her throne and become the bride of the first man she meets in the crowd. An eclipse duly takes place, and when daylight returns Kié-li is discovered in the arms of Oug-lou. But Oug-lou refuses to marry her, and the Emperor (Quériau) banishes him for his insolence. Kié-li persists in her determination to win Oug-lou, and in the second act her tutor gives Oug-lou a cap, which is supposed to have magic qualities, and, when placed on his head, will empower him to turn animals into humans. Delighted at the thought of being able to transform his beloved cat into a woman, Oug-lou returns to Pekin in disguise. In the meantime, however, his nurse (Florentine) has sold the cat to one of the Emperor's pages (Maria). But when Oug-lou goes to the cat's basket, it is the princess who emerges. Believing her to be his cat given human form, Oug-lou is overcome with joy until the page returns to announce that the cat has escaped. The police arrive and arrest Kié-li, who is delighted to observe Oug-lou's distress at the prospect of losing his pet. Oug-lou then makes his way to the pages' quarters in search of Kié-li, who torments him by accepting the flattery of the pages and taking no notice of him. At last, in desperation, Oug-lou waves his cap to turn her back into a cat, and at that same moment, by a happy coincidence, the cat itself emerges from the pages' dormitory. Kié-li explains all that has happened and reveals who she is, and Oug-lou is finally pardoned by the Emperor.

First performed on 16 October 1837, the ballet proved a bitter disappointment. Duveyrier's scenario was dismissed as stupid and trivial, and Coralli's choreography was judged to be below his usual standard: it was uneven in quality, its best passage – the finale to the festival in Act I – being compared unfavourably with the *ensembles* in Henry's Chinese ballet *Chao-Kang*, seen at the Théâtre Nautique three years before. Alexandre Montfort's music contained a fair number of borrowings – one being the introduction to Rossini's opera *Moïse*, to accompany the prayers of the people during the eclipse – but vivacity and colour were sadly lacking in the original part of his composition. The critic of the music journal *Le Ménestrel* commented that the score lacked any pretension to *couleur locale* in presenting a Chinese subject, and was 'perhaps too serious for such a crazy piece'.[14] 'One has the impression,' added the *Moniteur,* 'of always hearing the same tune, and what a tune!'[15] On the credit side, the sets and costumes could not have been more splendid – Elssler's cat costume was a ravishing confection of white feathers, and the audience's attention was caught by some imaginatively designed properties: in particular, a huge porcelain punch bowl, brilliantly painted and gilded, and two enormous pyramid-shaped lanterns on whose shades were projected shadows of moving mechanical figures in the manner of *ombres chinoises.*

About the ballet's only claim to be remembered was that it attracted a notice in the *Revue et Gazette musicale*, from the pen of Hector Berlioz. Berlioz was far from being qualified to pass serious critical judgment on an art that he considered little worthy of his attention, and he had even stubbornly refused to read the printed scenario beforehand. So it was hardly surprising that he was completely mystified by what was going on. The entrance of Fanny Elssler, however, suddenly awakened his interest; he was immediately captivated, and at the end of the evening was even able to write some amusing lines on his impressions of the ballet. 'You do not need to understand it,' he wrote,

> or, to put it another way, we understood it perfectly and were spellbound, enchanted. We did not seek permission to consider Fanny Elssler to be the greatest living dancer-mime, and so we applauded her to the limit of our strength. Having got going, we applauded a mass of kaleidoscopic combinations that were full of movement and brilliance; we applauded costumes that were admirable, dazzling and terrifying when we thought of all the imagination, erudition and money M. Duponchel must have lavished on them, and we applauded several charming passages in which

[the composer] Montfort gave proof of a fluent, elegant and graceful talent.[16]

However, Hippolyte Prévost, one of the most distinguished of critics, could hardly believe his eyes and ears as he sat through it. How could the Opéra have dared to stage such a mindless and trivial piece at a time when 'all the arts are burgeoning with imagination and progress?' The scenario, for the most part, was written in a style that was worse than negligent, a statement Berlioz might have taken as supporting his own contempt for ballet scenarios. Yet, Prévost argued, such stupidity had given birth to a magnificent spectacle with beautiful scenery, lively and original dances, a variety of wonderful costumes, and above all Fanny Elssler:

> a mime who speaks and a dancer who astonishes, whose every gesture and pose arouses sensual delight and whose every step is marked by an effortless vitality. All Paris will be flocking to see her as woman and cat – as a woman speaking such words of love, gaiety and sentiment in the manner of Mlle Mars, and as a cat so stunning in her playfulness and attitudes, leaping in a single bound to the top of a ladder, sliding her paw behind her ears, scratching, simpering, cuddlesome, yet shrewd and smart. And all this so effectively done that Duveyrier and Duponchel in their defence might argue that Mlle Fanny will be the making of the entire piece, its success and its vogue. All eyes will be on her alone, and the multitude will rush to see it. If this is what those gentlemen have calculated, the public will realise their forecast but not its repercussion. But as for the future, the Opéra should not pretend to be a branch of the minor theatres, for it has a very different function.[17]

As Berlioz had perceived, what small success the ballet achieved was almost entirely due to Fanny Elssler. Her rôle was not without possibilities, and, being a perfectionist, she had even gone to the length of trying to overcome her repugnance for cats by acquiring a white kitten and studying its movements and habits. As a result, in the passages where Kié-li pretends to be Oug-lou's cat in human form, she managed to add such mischievous wit and coquetry into her miming and to move with such supple elegance and lightness 'that the audience was carried away to the point where they might have imagined they were seeing a play, when in reality only a ravishing actress stood before them'.[18]

So carefree did Fanny appear that few spectators on the first night could have suspected the alarm that a seemingly small accident in the second act had caused her. At one moment, in the scene where she is pretending to be a cat, she had to leap on to a table, on which had been placed a bowl of milk. Misjudging her jump, she caused the table to overturn and the cold milk to spill over her foot, which was hot from exertion. Almost at once she began to shiver, but she concealed the fearful thought that the accident might bring on a recurrence of her illness of the year before, and played the scene through to the end.

Her sister Therese had only a small part in this ballet, appearing 'admirably dressed, her head aglitter, beautiful and calm as always'[19] in what the scenario referred to, rather bizarrely, as a *pas de un*.

Jules Janin prophesied that Fanny Elssler's presence would ensure the ballet a modest success that was unlikely to extend beyond mid-August – a forecast that was only very slightly inaccurate, for its fourteenth and last performance took place on 3 September 1838.

*　*　*　*　*　*　*

Despite the discouraging reception of *La Chatte métamorphosée en femme*, Fanny Elssler's popularity in the early months of 1838 remained as great as ever. Her *Cachucha* was still the rage: encored whenever she danced it at the Opéra, it inspired parodies in the more intimate theatres of the capital, and even spawned a horseback parody at the Cirque! It had also started quite a fashion for stylised Spanish dances at the Opéra. Lise Noblet and her sister, Mme Alexis Dupont, followed it with a bolero, *El Jaleo de Xérès*, and Auguste Mabille and Nathalie Fitzjames danced a *Jota aragonesa*, to music by Boisselot, that even met with the approval of the hispanophil Gautier.

The Noblets repeated their bolero in the long and curiously varied programme chosen for Fanny and Therese's benefit on 5 May 1838, inspiring a warm comment from Gautier:

> Just to see the fantastic, sparkling costumes glittering beneath their shower of sequins is enough to put anyone in a good mood. Mmes Alexis and Noblet danced with much fire and spirit, although far from the serpentine suppleness and intoxicating passion of Dolores Serral, whom the Opéra has had the signal clumsiness to let escape. How ravishing the *Jaleo* would have been if danced by her and Fanny Elssler! We applaud the invasion of Spanish dancing with all our might, for the Spaniards have always been, and always will be, the best dancers in the world.[20]

A brilliant audience, with the ladies in their new spring dresses, had assembled for the occasion, and Queen Marie-Amélie was in the Royal Box. The centre-piece of the programme was a new ballet by Therese Elssler, *La Volière*, but there was much else to enjoy or endure besides: the second act of Beaumarchais' *Le Mariage de Figaro*, with Mlle Mars, Rose Dupuis and Mme Cinti-Damoreau; an extract from *Lucia di Lammermoor*, with Duprez; and finally a rather tedious comic opera, *Le Concert à la cour*, which was memorable only for including a curious series of *tableaux vivants*. These were arranged by Clément Boulanger and Camille Roqueplan to represent some well-known paintings, including Winterhalter's *Le Décameron*, in which could be recognised Pauline Leroux, who was not dancing on account of an injury; Gérard's *Corinne au cap du Misène*, featuring Fanny Elssler; and Horace Vernet's *Judith et Holopherne* in which Therese Elssler appeared as a somewhat meagre Judith. According to the *Moniteur*, this form of entertainment had been included at the suggestion of the Elsslers. It apparently enjoyed considerable popularity in Germany, but found little favour in Paris, where the public expected dancers to dance. At the Opéra, however, the experiment was not repeated.

The new ballet, *La Volière*, did in fact seem to support the accusation, made by Charles Maurice against Duponchel, that by losing not only Taglioni but also Pauline Montessu and Legallois, who had retired, and failing to re-engage Perrot and Albert, he was bringing about 'the annihilation of the *ballet d'action*'.[21] The scenario, written by Eugène Scribe, who wisely decided to remain anonymous, was poor by any standard, and prompted Louis Viardot to sigh for the past. 'I do not know,' he wrote, 'what today's public would think of those famous ballets of the past – *Nina*, *Clari*, *Télémaque* – but it is truly difficult to believe they were as naïve as those we see today. *Les Mohicans*, *La Chatte*, *La Volière* all seem to be designed for children, like Perrault's fairy tales, but without the wit and the moral.'[22] Jules Janin was even more severe. 'If you only knew how many silly and insipid inventions it contains!' he exclaimed. '[*Nathalie*], the very model of the silly type of ballet... is a masterpiece when compared with *La Volière*, *La Chatte métamorphosée* a work of genius, and even the twice-performed *Les Mohicans* is a ballet to be admired. All the Opéra's ballets over the past ten years put together could not produce anything so silly, insipid and utterly boring as *La Volière*.'[23]

The action was set in a secluded garden on the island of San Domingo, where Théréza (T. Elssler), the victim of a deceiving lover, has managed to bring up her sister Zoé (F. Elssler) in total ignorance of the male sex. This unnatural existence is inevitably interrupted by the arrival of a young naval officer, Fernand (Mazilier), whom Zoé and the equally credulous slave-girls believe to be just another exotic bird, only much more wonderful than those kept in the big cage in the garden! Then Fernand's uncle, Don Alonzo (Dauty), arrives and is found to be none other than Théréza's former lover. He is now repentant, and after a number of little incidents the ballet ends with the couples happily united. To round off the story, Fernand's slave, Domingo

(Barrez), turns out to be the husband of Théréza's slave, Gunima (Roland), who in the final reconciliation forgives him for having sold her into slavery!

This plot was an inverted version of La Fontaine's fable, *Les Oies du Frère Philippe*, which itself was based on a tale by Boccaccio. As Janin suggested, it might have made more sense if the plot had been about a man mistaking a pretty girl for a bird, but Gautier would hear none of these carping criticisms. That *La Volière* did not enjoy much success, he attributed partly to the fact that the public were being spoilt by what he called 'aesthetic journalists'. 'A ballet can never have much meaning,' he maintained, 'and whatever the partisans of the old style might say, *La Fille mal gardée* and *Le Carnaval de Venise* had nothing very ingenious about them. The ballet of *La Volière* even has the advantage that men do not dance in it, while the Elssler sisters dance both often and for long.'[24] To Gautier, the absence of male dancing was a sign of the choreographer's good taste. 'Indeed there is nothing more abominable,' he declared, 'than a man displaying his red neck, thick muscular arms, and legs with calves like those of a parish beadle, while the whole of his heavy, virile frame shudders with his leaps and pirouettes'.[25]

Criticism of the ballet was levelled almost exclusively at the absurdity of the plot.[26] Casimir Gide was complimented on his score, and Therese Elssler's choreography, the highlights of which were an excellent *pas de huit* and an enchanting new *pas* for Fanny, *La Valaisienne*, received general praise. The various characters were skilfully drawn, the action was easy to follow and full of charming detail, and the whole production was highly finished. The highlight of the ballet was the *pas de deux* for the two sisters at the point at which Théréza tries to distract Zoé by making her dance with her. It was 'charmingly designed', wrote Gautier:

> There is one moment in particular, when the two sisters run forward from the back of the stage holding hands and shooting out their legs in unison, that for its harmony, correctness and precision surpasses the imagination. It is as if one were the shadow of the other, or there were only one dancer, advancing alongside a mirror that reflects her every movement. There could be no more delightful or harmonious sight than this dance, which was performed with great speed and precision. The audience's satisfaction was expressed by a storm of applause, accompanied by a chorus of canes and stamping of feet.

> Fanny, to whom her sister Therese had, as always, given the most prominent rôle, displayed a childlike grace, an artless rapidity, and a quite adorable sense of mischief. Her creole costume suited her to perfection – or, we should say, she suited her costume to perfection.

A well-supplied salvo of bouquets was aimed at the stage from every corner of the house. Flower sellers must love benefit performances! If this continues, camellias will become unobtainable and extinct.[27]

* * * * * * *

Neither Fanny Elssler's personal triumph nor Gautier's championship could prolong the life of *La Volière* beyond its fourth performance; and with three failures in succession, the Opéra found its ballet repertory sadly depleted. Revivals of *La Fille mal gardée* and *La Somnambule* caused little stir, and seeing no prospect of a creation for some months to come, Duponchel conceived the idea of reviving some of the ballets most closely associated with Taglioni. Realising that to present Fanny Elssler in *La Sylphide* was bound to arouse a strong reaction of some sort or another, he thought it wise to sound her out in advance. Not unexpectedly, whether through modesty or apprehension, Fanny at first demurred, but Duponchel's persistence eventually overcame her reluctance.

The revival of *La Sylphide* on 21 September 1838 aroused no storm of protest nor any turbulent enthusiasm, and most of the critics reviewed it warmly or at least kindly. Staged with care, it departed from the original version only in the substitution, for the *pas de deux* by Sylphide and James in the second act, of a dance for two sylphides performed by Fanny Elssler and her sister to music by Gide and choreography by Therese Elssler, said to be after Samengo.[28]

Fanny Elssler's interpretation was of course very different from that of Taglioni, as could have been foreseen. While Taglioni's was a more ethereal conception, relying principally for its effect on steps of elevation, and being more in keeping with the poetic aspect of the character, Elssler impressed with her heightened attack and her superior dramatic power. There had been moments when Taglioni's rendering appeared to lack expression, and Elssler made up for her more earthly style by giving a more deeply developed rendering; she was particularly moving in the ballet's final moments when the Sylphide loses her wings and her immortality.

Théophile Gautier was completely captivated, and wrote an enthusiastic article at Taglioni's expense. Her powers, he declared, had visibly declined as a result of her 'interminable travels'; she had lost much of her lightness and elevation, and had been showing signs of strain after a few bars. Fanny Elssler, on the other hand, he described as being still

in the full force of her talent. She can only vary her perfection, she cannot surpass it, because beyond the very good is the too good, which is closer to the bad than one thinks. She is a man's dancer, just as Mlle Taglioni was a woman's dancer. She has elegance, beauty, an intrepid and exuberant vigour, boldness to excess, a sparkling smile, and above all an air of Spanish vivacity tempered by a German simplicity, which makes her a very charming and adorable creature. When Fanny is dancing, a thousand happy thoughts enter your mind, your imagination strays into palaces of white marble flooded with sunlight and standing out against a deep blue sky, like the friezes of the Parthenon. You imagine yourself leaning on the balustrade of a terrace, with roses above your head, a cup of Syracuse wine in your hand, a white greyhound at your feet, and beside you a beautiful woman in a dress of flesh-coloured velvet, with feathers in her hair. And your ears are filled with the chatter of tambourines and the silvery tinkle of bells.

Mlle Taglioni made you think of cool and shaded valleys, whence a white vision suddenly materialised from the bark of an oak tree before the gaze of a surprised and blushing shepherd. She might have been taken for one of those Scottish fairies of whom Walter Scott writes, and who roam in the moonlight by a mysterious fountain, with a necklace of dewdrops and a thread of gold about her waist.

If I may express it thus, Mlle Taglioni is a Christian dancer, and Mlle Fanny Elssler is a pagan dancer...

So Mlle Elssler, while Mlle Taglioni's rôles may not be suited to her temperament, can replace her in anything without risk or peril, for she is sufficiently versatile and talented to adapt herself and assume the particular guise of the character...

The new Sylphide... displayed infinite delicacy, grace and lightness throughout her performance. She appeared and vanished like an impalpable vision... In the *pas* with her sister she excelled herself; you could not imagine anything more graceful. Her miming in the scene where her lover catches her in the folds of the enchanted scarf, expresses sorrow and forgiveness, and the sense of fall and irreparable error, with a rare feeling for poetry, and her last long look at her wings as they lie on the ground is a moment of great tragic beauty.[29]

Gautier's views were, on his own admission, coloured by the fact that he was writing about a 'man's dancer'. The other side of the question had, therefore, to be put by a woman, and Sophie Gay, the novelist, conveyed her opinion in a letter to Marie Taglioni, who was in St Petersburg at the time:

You would have smiled out of pity from the height of your cloud to learn that a simple mortal has dared to separate your name from that of the Sylphide. We are assured that her better judgment prompted [Elssler] to refuse, but I believe she was forced to yield to the despotism of the Director, who is short of new ballets and only has the remnants of your own to live on, for it was an act of voluntary self-immolation to appear where you had been seen. However, my admiration for you does not lead me to be unjust towards the pretty woman who has been so much harmed by exaggerated praise in the press. She has a charming talent, terrestrial and quite human, but the celestial and the divine only you have revealed; you alone have given the *danse de caractère* the chaste and noble poetry that sets it among the most distinguished arts. No longer is it a matter of mere posing. It is a language, in which passion and grace, voluptuousness and modesty speak to the soul and charm the eye. And that is the treasure of which we are deprived. I am for ever inconsolable.[30]

For some eighteen months *La Sylphide*, with Fanny Elssler in the title-rôle, pursued a fairly uneventful course, figuring occasionally in the programme without attracting very large receipts at the box office. In one of these performances, on 10 June 1839, a young dancer called Lucien Petipa made his début in the rôle of James. The son of the ballet-master Jean Petipa, he was to serve French ballet with great distinction for many years, while his younger brother Marius would be laying the foundations of an even greater reputation in St Petersburg. For Petipa's début, the Elsslers even condescended to transpose their *pas de deux* into a *pas de trois*. It was the first time they had allowed a man to share their laurels, and Petipa fully justified the honour they had paid him. His presentable appearance, his grace and his fine elevation were appreciated by public and management alike, and he was immediately engaged.

It might well have been expected that the staunch admirers of Taglioni would have reacted violently when Elssler appeared as the Sylphide, which of all Taglioni's rôles must have been considered sacrosanct; but they bided their time until 22 October 1838, when she appeared in another of the absent divinity's ballets, *La Fille du Danube*. Once again, Elssler rendered the part quite differently from Taglioni, giving it a greater range of expression, and dancing with all her usual boldness and precision. And again she inspired a fulsome eulogy from Gautier, who described her charms at length and concluded by boldly asserting that not only did she reveal a profound feeling for drama, which Taglioni lacked, but she danced just as well as her rival and acted better than her.

It could not have been easy to judge her impartially that evening. As she made her first entrance, two or three catcalls rent the air and were almost at once drowned by a wave of applause. Some minutes later, at the end of her *pas*, more whistling broke out, shriller than ever. During the interval between the acts, Auguste, the leader of the claque, left the theatre to seek reinforcements to counter the hostile demonstration, and during the second act his men set to with the utmost zeal. As soon as the demonstration recommenced, the claque went into action, mercilessly assaulting anyone they suspected of breaking the peace. The tumult mounted in intensity as the ballet continued; innocent and guilty suffered alike from the fury of the claque, suspected demonstrators were manhandled to the exits, and soon nearly everyone in the pit was on his feet. Fanny's appearance before the curtain at the end was a signal for a fresh salvo of whistling, which proved nothing except that the battle had ended with both sides in the field. In the final reckoning, the great Auguste discovered he had lost his watch-chain and eyeglass in the struggle.

NOTES

1. Second, 202.
2. *Journal des débats*, 11 November 1836.
3. *Journal des débats*, 10 July 1837.
4. *Moniteur*, 13 July 1837.
5. *Siècle*, 7 July 1837.
6. *Journal des débats*, 10 July 1837.
7. *Presse*, 11 July 1837. Guest, *Gautier*, 13–14; Fr. ed., 39–40.
8. *Presse*, 5 February 1838.
9. *Cancans de l'Opéra*, III, 165. Tamvaco, 449. De Boigne's first names were Charles-Benoît. While he used the name Charles professionally, it seems he was Benoît to his friends.
10. *Presse*, 18 September 1837. The allusion is to Goethe's poem *Hermann und Dorothea*.
11. *Journal des débats*, 27 September 1837.
12. *Constitutionnel*, 29 September 1837.
13. *La Chatte métamorphosée en femme*, folie-vaudeville in one act by Scribe and Mélesville, f.p. Théâtre de Madame, 3 March 1827.
14. *Ménestrel*, 22 October 1837.
15. *Moniteur*, 21 October 1837.
16. *Revue et Gazette musicale* (1836), 460.
17. *Moniteur*, 21 October 1837.
18. Charles Maurice in *Courrier des Théâtres*, 17 October 1837.
19. *Journal des débats*, 16 October 1837
20. *Presse*, 7 May 1838. Guest, *Gautier*, 36; Fr. ed., 61.
21. *Courrier des théâtres*, 12 April 1838.
22. *Siècle*, 7 May 1838.
23. *Journal des débats*, 7 May 1838.
24. *Presse*, 21 May 1838.
25. *Presse*, 7 May 1838. Guest, *Gautier*, 35; Fr. ed., 60.
26. The work was ridiculed in a parody entitled *La Volière des perroquets*, produced at the Théâtre de la Porte-Saint-Antoine, 28 May 1838.
27. *Presse*, 7 May 1838. Guest, *Gautier*, 35–6; Fr. ed., 60–1.

28. The sisters had danced in several ballets by Paolo Samengo in Naples in 1827 and in Vienna in 1831, and this *pas de deux* was probably originally arranged for one of these ballets.
29. *Presse*, 24 September 1838. Guest, *Gautier*, 53–4; Fr. ed., 78–9.
30. Vaillat, 398.

18

Elssler's Last Parisian Triumphs

To break the chain of ill luck that seemed to be dogging his efforts to reinvigorate the ballet, Duponchel decided to confide Fanny Elssler's next creation to a dramatist who had never before tried his hand at writing a ballet scenario. Jules-Henri Vernoy de Saint-Georges was a prolific writer of light plays and comic operas with the added experience of having briefly managed the Opéra-Comique. Without pretending to be a profound playwright, he was an acknowledged master of his craft. Charles de Boigne described him as the most elegant of French dramatists, an exquisite perfumed dandy who lived in an apartment that was almost feminine in its charm. Its soft carpeting, quilted door curtains and muslin hangings, and its profusion of *objets d'art* and coloured candles, reflected the fastidious tastes of a man who was said never to go bathing without first purifying the sea with the finest Eau de Cologne.

The association of Saint-Georges with an almost untried choreographer, Joseph Mazilier, fully justified Duponchel's bold decision, for their new ballet, *La Gipsy*, was unanimously acclaimed after its first performance on 28 January 1839. Perhaps its success was enhanced by the memory of preceding failures, but it was nonetheless real. Gautier saw it as 'a resounding success', and declared that the days of *Le Diable boiteux* had returned.[1] Such an assessment was a trifle excessive, for *La Gipsy* did not create quite such a stir as *Le Diable boiteux*, perhaps partly because the theatre-going public was still bedazzled by two sensational débuts, those of Rachel at the Comédie-Française and the tenor Mario at the Opéra.

Taking his inspiration from the *Novelas Exemplares* of Cervantes, Saint-Georges chose Edinburgh during the reign of Charles II as his setting. Stenio (Mazilier), a fugitive Roundhead who has thrown in his lot with a band of gypsies, saves the child Sarah (Guérinot) from a wild animal that has gored her arm. Stenio is warmly thanked by her father, Lord Campbell (Montjoie), but has to make a hurried disappearance after refusing to drink to the King's health. In the confusion, the gypsy chief (Simon) insults Campbell and is arrested, but that night makes his escape, taking the child with him. Thus Sarah (F. Elssler) is brought up as a gypsy, watched over by Stenio, who has fallen in love with her. Mab (T. Elssler), the gypsy queen, loves Stenio too; to rid herself of a potential rival, she maliciously gives Sarah a stolen miniature to wear at the fair. As she had intended, its owner recognises it and Sarah is brought before Lord Campbell and charged with theft. Found guilty, she tries to stab herself. But in the scuffle Lord Campbell's attention is caught by the scar on her arm, and he recognises her as his long-lost daughter. Restored to her stately home, Sarah soon begins to miss the carefree life of the gypsies. One evening Stenio finds his way to her, but Mab betrays his presence. Sarah then tells her father that Stenio and she are married, and Stenio in turn reveals that, though a rebel, he is of noble birth. But this scene of reconciliation is interrupted by the return of Mab, who orders a gypsy to shoot Stenio. Sarah, in a fury of grief at Stenio's death, rushes at Mab and stabs her in the heart as the final curtain falls.

With its strong dramatic interest, *La Gipsy* marked a return to the form of *ballet d'action* in that mime occupied as important a place as the dance. Its plot had 'as much action as a melodrama of the good old days', and the unexpected dénouement – 'too tragic perhaps for a ballet', as Gautier commented[2] – was fully exploited by Fanny Elssler. Joseph Mazilier was indeed fortunate to have such material to work on for his first ballet. He had already made a favourable impression with his *divertissement* for Halévy's opera, *Guido et Ginevra*, but it was *La Gipsy* that established his reputation as a choreographer. In the words of Prévost in the *Moniteur:*

> The new ballet is artistically conceived and skilfully developed. The action moves rapidly and is well held together... Add to this the quality of its choreography – scenes that are full of grace and elegance, a production that breathes variety, gaiety, ingenuity and in places originality, well-conceived ensembles and groups, an orderly design which is present throughout and an absence of confusion, and four delightful *pas* – and you will appreciate the talent of the choreographer.[3]

The only fault that Gautier could find was that the dances were all placed in the early scenes so that the later scenes depended exclusively on mime.

The first of Mazilier's dances was a *'saltarella* after the Scottish fashion', a *pas de caractère* of striking originality danced by Maria and Nathalie Fitzjames 'with unimaginable grace, precision and lightness'; but the most outstanding *pas* came in the fair scene in the second act. The setting was a public square in Edinburgh, 'a very fine set' in Gautier's view, 'full of open space, sunshine and light', with a bridge with massive arches revealing crevices of great depth, and the city rising above it in uneven layers like an enormous madrepore; in short, 'a view which people who have been there say is extremely realistic'. All is bustle and colour as a motley crowd of tumblers and pickpockets, rope-dancers and mountebanks, soldiers, peasants and passers-by, rich and poor, jostle one another in good-humoured mood. Suddenly the gypsies arrive, and almost at once two of them, Sarah and Mab, separate from their companions and begin to dance. This was one of the Elssler sisters' most charming displays, 'one of those ravishing *pas*,' to quote Gautier again, 'that suggest the fluttering of doves' wings by the way in which the two sisters shake and gently quiver in a cloud of white muslin'.[4] As with other *pas de deux* they had danced, it owed its effect largely to their perfect unison of movement.

Fanny Elssler then disappeared into the wings, returning some minutes later, having changed into a coquettish pseudo-military costume. Her trim figure was encased in a white tunic, sparkling with three rows of buttons and galloons of silver braid that set off the bright colours of her blue silk skirt and scarlet boots with metal heels and tiny golden spurs. Two long plaits tied with red ribbon escaped from a black military cap, decorated with a cockade and a white feather. It was in this colourful guise that she danced the vivacious *Cracovienne*, which was designed as a sequel to her famous *Cachucha*. 'Was it a woman, a youth, or a sprite?' wondered Jules Janin. 'No one could tell, for she danced at the same time like a coquettish young woman, a youth in love, and a sprite on a fine May morning. In this dance she displayed all her playful graces, her gentle frolicsome smile and her taking gestures.'[5] 'It is quite impossible to describe this dance,' added Gautier. 'It is a combination of rhythmical precision, charming abandon and an energetic and bouncy speed that surpasses one's imagination, and the metallic chatter of her spurs, like castanets worn on the heels, adds a marked accent to the steps and gives the dance a character of joyful vivacity that is quite irresistible'.[6]

The quick costume change between these two *pas* was a nerve-racking moment, for Fanny Elssler dreaded that the music might stop and destroy the illusion if she were just a few seconds late. At one or two performances the strain told on her so much that she fainted in the wings when the *Cracovienne* was over. Learning the reason for this, Duponchel, who was a man of feeling, ordered changes to be made in the ballet to give her more time – a decision that involved a more delicate touch than might ordinarily be imagined, for, as Elssler herself explained, 'right and left you touch the part of some indignant *coryphée* who stands or dances upon her rights'.[7]

The most striking factor in the success of *La Gipsy* was not so much Elssler's dancing as her acting. The *Moniteur* hailed her as 'an intelligent and winning actress, a new Bigottini, rich and prodigal of dramatic feeling, seizing the most fleeting nuances to impress them with profound meaning.'[8] In the scene in which she is wrongly accused of theft and her true identity is revealed, she rose to 'the most sublime peaks of tragic acting', wrote Gautier. Then came 'the noble pride of innocence, energy, tears, grief, love, intoxicating joy – she ran through the whole gamut of human emotions. Only Miss Smithson or Mlle Dorval could have produced such bursts of pathos, such forceful pantomime.'[9]

The English music critic H.F. Chorley was also full of enthusiasm, both for the production and for Fanny Elssler's performance:

> Much of the lovely music of Weber's *Preciosa* was used in it. The bolero that opens his overture was allotted to a scene where the gypsy girl compels her sulky mates to dance. When she appeared on the stage of Paris, the folk lay couched in fifties, huddled together in their wild and picturesque clothes as only the French stage-managers know how to group forms and colours. How she moved hither and thither, quick and bright as a torch, lighting up one sullen heap of tinder after another – gradually animating the scene with motion till at last the excited rout of vagabonds trooped after her with the wild vivacity of a chorus of Bacchanals – made a picture of many pictures, the brightness and spirit of which stand almost alone, in the gallery of similar ones. There have been Gitanas, Esmeraldas, Mignons by the score, but no Gipsy to approach Mlle Fanny Elssler.
>
> In the next act of the same ballet came the scene of the minuet danced by the heroine to gain time, and to distract attention from her lover in concealment hard by, whose life was imperilled. Lord Byron, when speaking of his own dramas, has subtly dwelt on the power of suppressed passion. Few things have been seen more fearful than the cold and measured grace of Mlle Fanny Elssler in this juncture – than the manner in which every step was watched, every gesture allowed its right time – so that neither flurry nor faltering might be detected – than the set smile – the vigilant ear – the quivering lip controlling itself. It is in moments like these that Genius rises above talent. It was by representations such as these that Mlle Fanny Elssler gradually established a fame among the few as well as the many, which could have been built up by no *pirouettes* nor *entrechats* but in right of which she is enrolled among the great dramatic artists of the century.[10]

As for her sister, she brought to the rôle of Mab what Gautier described as 'a suggestion of a Sybil of antiquity that was remarkably effective',[11] and which the sculptor Carle Elshoecht caught successfully in a statuette.

The ballet's weakest element was its musical accompaniment. This had been entrusted to three musicians, each working in isolation from the others. Unfortunately, but as could have been foreseen, their contributions turned out to be so varied in quality and style that the ballet was somewhat thrown off balance. For the first and last acts, Benoist and Marliani had respectively produced music that was no more than adequate, but for the second act the score was composed with unusual elegance and originality. This was an early work of a promising young musician who in his maturity was to become celebrated as a major figure of French opera, Ambroise Thomas.

By a coincidence, *La Gipsy* had a certain similarity with a ballet called *La Gitana*, in which Marie Taglioni had first appeared in St Petersburg a few weeks before.[12] Some of that ballerina's admirers were convinced there had been 'a dramatic pilfering',[13] as one of them, Sophie Gay, put it in a letter to Taglioni, written more than two months before the first night of *La Gipsy*. But the two plots were in fact quite different, the only real similarity being that the heroine of each was a girl of noble birth brought up by gypsies. Saint-Georges's scenario for Mazilier's ballet, it is true, had originally been approved under the title of *La Gitana*, but this had been changed, presumably to avoid confusion with Taglioni's ballet.

In the Russian capital, Marie Taglioni received coloured reports of *La Gipsy* from her partisans in Paris, and her lover Eugène Desmares wrote to Anténor Joly, editor of the theatrical paper *Vert-Vert*, to say:

> It appears that this *Gipsy* is a 'tear-jerker', a mimodrama, copied from our magnificent ballet, news of whose success is spreading all over Europe. The *Cracovienne* that Fanny Elssler dances in it is none other than the *pas*, and to the same music, that Mlle Taglioni danced in London with such success last summer.[14] She [Elssler] adds boots with ridiculous spurs that are not at all in the character of the dance, and she wears male costume [*sic*]. What price now the Opéra's claim to local colour? When you give a national dance, you should give it as such. All this smacks of the fairground and not the theatre, where art has a place; it is to place effect above merit, and when the effect misfires, what is there left? The French papers, which speak well of this *pas*, are a laughing-stock here; it is a pity, and vexing for us. You should try and say this. It would give Duponchel a rap over the knuckles.[15]

* * * * * * *

In the spring of 1839, Fanny Elssler had the misfortune to slip and fall down a flight of stairs. Shortly before this accident, Duponchel had returned to Paris from Milan, where he had gone to see a promising young ballerina who was rapidly making her name there, Fanny Cerrito. He had not been very impressed, but perhaps he had begun to doubt the wisdom of not engaging this young ballerina when he learnt of Fanny Elssler's plight. Happily, however, the injury did not prove serious and she was able to reappear at the Opéra about a month later. Very soon she was hard at work with Jean Coralli rehearsing a new ballet, which was ready only just in time to be presented before her departure for London.

La Tarentule was a very different kind of ballet from *La Gipsy*. It was a light and delicate piece, which more pompous critics thought somewhat trivial for the Opéra; but its vitality and its polished production earned it a complete success when it was first performed on 24 June 1839. Eugène Scribe's plot – once again he preferred to remain anonymous, although this time there was no cause for reticence – was centred on the adventures of Luidgi (Mazilier) and Lauretta (F. Elssler), whose love is not running smoothly because Lauretta's mother Mathea (Roland) considers the young man too poor to be a good match for her daughter. But she sees things in a different light when Clorinde (Forster) gives Luidgi a generous reward for rescuing her from brigands. Then, just before the wedding, Luidgi is bitten by a tarantula. A travelling quack, Dr Omeopatico (J.B. Barrez) consents to cure him, but only on being promised the hand of Lauretta. In despair, Lauretta pretends to be bitten by a tarantula herself on her wedding night. This time Omeopatico's remedy has no apparent effect, and the girl is borne away in a funeral procession. Meanwhile Luidgi has gone in search of his benefactress Clorinde, who fortuitously turns out to be Omeopatico's wife, whom he has believed to have been murdered by bandits. So, finding that Lauretta is not married to the old man after all, the lovers are happily reunited.

Duponchel had supervised the production with his usual fastidious care, taking great pains to get the smallest detail right, even down to spattering mud and muck on the post-chaise in which Omeopatico makes his first entrance. Scribe had also been present at many of the rehearsals, and one passage in the ballet had caused him particular anxiety. This was the funeral procession, which the *Moniteur* called 'a kind of burlesque parody of *Romeo and Juliet*'.[16] He was not concerned that Paris might consider it in bad taste, although when the ballet was to be revived in London a year later, the scene had to be prudently omitted so as not to offend the susceptibilities of the English! His qualms merely arose from an apprehension that it might throw a damper on the liveliness of the ballet, but Auguste, the leader of the claque, reassured him on that score.

'Worry not,' he said. 'I shall take the death gaily.'[17]

The *Cachucha* and the *Cracovienne* had caused such a furore that no new ballet for Fanny Elssler would now be complete without a *pas de caractère*, and Coralli duly followed this tradition by arranging a brilliant *tarantella* for Elssler to dance in the first act. With castanets purring, she came bounding in to the melody of *La Danza*, one of the many borrowings that Casimir Gide had skilfully woven into his pleasing score. 'The grace, lightness and precision that Lauretta puts into this *tarantella* is unimaginable,' declared Gautier. 'It is a mixture of ethereality and strength, of modesty and intoxication that defies description. Roguishness and passion are combined with unusual success, and the girl's reserve continually surfaces to temper the whole Mediterranean fire of this dance.' She was admirably partnered by

Lucien Petipa, who, as Gautier grudgingly had to admit, 'was not too repulsive for a man. He is young, good-looking enough, and has something of the proud elegance of the dancer who partners Dolores [Serral]. He performed his dangerous task very well.'[18]

There was no doubt that it was largely Fanny Elssler's spirited miming as Lauretta that carried the day. Her touch was light and graceful throughout, moving and wittily amusing in turn; her performance was a real object lesson in the art of mime. One of her most effective moments came when she entered with the news that her lover had been bitten by a tarantula. In Gautier's words, she 'attained the very height of sublime tragedy', and no words could have made the situation clearer when, 'awesome as the Pythia of ancient legend', she portrayed the mounting convulsions that held him in their grip. Then, in the bedroom scene, she displayed all the effervescent mischievousness of Colombine as she led the old bridegroom a dance by pretending to be bitten herself. 'She made a comedy out of the ballet,' wrote Gautier, 'and glossed over everything in the plot that was impossible or risky with admirable delicacy.'[19]

She was well supported by Mazilier, who brought grace and pathos to his part of Luidgi, and Barrez, who was very comical as Omeopatico without making the rôle at all unpleasant. 'He managed, most unusually, to avoid caricature,' wrote Gautier, 'never once overstepping the limit between exuberance and cynicism.'[20]

Clorinde was played by a dancer who was attracting considerable attention as a beauty. She made her first entrance on horseback, and Gautier was very impressed by this 'slim white figure in a straw hat and tight-sleeved muslin dress, with blonde ringlets falling on her shoulders, the very image of Clarissa and Pamela – one of those Romantic heroines who appear in the drawings of Angelica Kauffmann'.[21] Her name was Caroline Forster, and she possessed a quality that the novelist Taxile Delord thought so unusual for a dancer that he included the following dialogue in one of his stories, *La Lune de miel*:

'I prefer Forster. Do you know Forster?'

'What is Forster?'

'She is a *coryphée* at the Opéra, an Englishwoman who can dance. Extraordinary!'[22]

Casimir Gide's score included an unusual range of borrowings. The *Ménestrel* recognised snatches from the works of Grétry, Dalayrac, Meyerbeer, Boïeldieu, Auber and Halévy, and its critic coined the phrase 'musical marquetry' for the wealth of inserted *airs parlants*, which were provided to assist the listener in understanding what was happening on the stage.[23]

* * * * * * *

In the summer of 1834, August Bournonville had taken leave of absence from the Royal Theatre, Copenhagen, where he was leader of the ballet, and had spent a few weeks in Paris, seeing old friends and making a few guest appearances at the Opéra.[24] He had brought with him his favourite pupil, a pretty young Danish dancer called Lucile Grahn, whom he took to see Taglioni perform in *La Sylphide*. That evening the seed was sown in Bournonville's mind which, two years later, brought forth his own version of this ballet that he would stage in Copenhagen with Lucile Grahn in the title rôle.

The dance had claimed Lucile Grahn at an early age. She was born in Copenhagen on 30 June 1819, and shortly before her fourth birthday was taken by her father to the ballet for the first time. From that moment her one thought was to become a dancer, and she pestered her parents until they yielded and entered her for the Royal Ballet School. She was only seven when her teacher, Pierre Larcher, permitted her to face the public for the first time as Cupid, and in 1829 she was given a small part in the ballet, *Danina, or the Brazilian Ape*.[25] But these were just isolated appearances that broke the monotony of the rigorous training she was undergoing, first under Larcher, and then under Bournonville himself, who recognised her extraordinary promise and took her under his wing.

Her début at the Royal Theatre took place shortly after she and Bournonville returned from Paris. Success came very rapidly after that. In the following year, 1835, she created the leading rôle of Astrid in Bournonville's *Valdemar*,[26] in 1836 she became the first Danish Sylphide,[27] and in 1837 she appeared as Quitteria in the first performance of Bournonville's *Don Quixote*.[28] All Copenhagen was at her feet, yet she was becoming increasingly discontented at the Royal Theatre. Bournonville had conceived a passion for her, which she did not reciprocate; finding his advances rejected, he had turned against her. Feeling the need to escape from the cramping atmosphere that surrounded her in Copenhagen, she applied for a travel grant to go to Paris. Thanks to the intervention of Princess Wilhelmine, the King's aunt, her application was granted despite Bournonville's opposition, and, accompanied by her mother, she set out at last for France. She lost no time in taking class with Jean-Baptiste Barrez, and was looking forward to her début at the Opéra when, early in October 1837, she was recalled to Copenhagen to dance in a special performance in honour of the Queen.

This frustrating setback only added to her determination to dance at the Opéra, and the following summer she returned to Paris and made her début on 1 August in a *pas de deux* with Guillaume Coustou inserted in *Le Carnaval de Venise*. Her lightness and brilliance made an immediate impression on Gautier, who described her as 'tall, slender, loose-jointed and well proportioned', but criticised her for forcing her smile. 'A dancer's smile,' he reminded her, 'should play about her mouth like a bird hovering above a rose, unable to land without damaging it'. Despite this reservation, Gautier found her 'very charming' and thought she had the potential of becoming 'an excellent acquisition for the Opéra.'[29] Later in the month, after seeing her again, he told his readers that she 'has much charm and natural grace, but is still lacking in technique and firmness, and is a little troubled by her arms, but these faults, which will disappear of themselves, are more than compensated by her lightness, suppleness and charming features'.[30]

Lucile Grahn's contract with the Royal Theatre in Copenhagen made it impossible for her to accept the engagement that the Opéra offered as a result of her début appearances, but relations between her and the authoritative Bournonville deteriorated so rapidly on her return to Denmark that events shaped themselves in her favour. She managed to obtain a further leave of absence to dance in Hamburg, but when she applied for an extension of her leave to remain there a little longer, she received a peremptory order to return. The price of her disobedience was dismissal, which caused her little disappointment, for it left her free to sign a three-year engagement with the Opéra, commencing on 1 June 1839, at a salary of 4500 francs a year.

She reappeared before the Paris public on 12 July, in a performance of Mozart's *Don Juan*, dancing in a *pas de deux* that Coralli had arranged to music by Marliani. Her partner of the previous year, Coustou, was not available to support her on this occasion, for he had been stricken with the consumption to which he was to succumb just two months later; and it was Auguste Mabille who now had the privilege of squiring her. Her youthful good looks and her trim figure predisposed the audience in her favour from the moment she made her first entrance, dressed very simply in white and wearing her auburn hair loose about her shoulders. Jules Janin was captivated. 'Picture for yourself,' he wrote, 'an attractive, slender young girl, very pale of complexion, very pretty, very calm, very timid, who dances gently, noiselessly, effortlessly, without smiling – but with what composure!'[31] Her 'little foreign ways'[32] were found very taking, and, in the words of Théophile Gautier, 'she danced with much elevation and lightness',[33] although he found the *pas de deux* a little too vague in design to give full scope to 'her suave grace and her naïve coquetry'.[34] For Janin it was a delight to see 'a body that was supple by nature, legs that seemed to have passed through none of the tortures of the classroom, and feet undeformed by ballet-masters' – in short, 'a beauty who dances like the singing of a bird, and is born to be light. How soothing this is after raging capers, furious kicks and endless pirouettes!'[35]

Grahn's popularity soon began to alarm Fanny Elssler's staunchest partisans, those yellow-gloved young bloods who considered themselves all-powerful at the Opéra. Fanny Elssler had for some time been protected by the Marquis de La Valette, who was alleged to have become her lover so as to obtain the privilege and the status of being her business adviser. In this capacity he so persistently pestered Duponchel with demands on her behalf that the exasperated Director finally had to beg Aguado to use his influence to arrange a diplomatic posting for him. There were some who thought that Lucile Grahn was at a disadvantage in lacking that kind of support, but there was always the hope that this might be overcome. 'Endowed with a mediocre intelligence,' recorded a chronicler of backstage gossip, 'but shrewd and obstinate in getting her own way, she too will undoubtedly find a La Valette'.[36] Grahn's quiet and gentle manner, however, was deceptive. 'In spite of her fragile appearance,' wrote Albéric Second,

> Lucile Grahn has the strength and character to shake the world. She possesses a genius for diplomacy in its most subtle, intangible and ethereal form. She is Metternich and Talleyrand in one: she is the whole Congress of Vienna in petticoats... Alone and without any support, hardly able to speak our language, and endowed with a distinctly questionable talent and a spotless virtue, Lucile Grahn found ways and means to move heaven and earth. She interested everyone in her fortunes – journalists, *abonnés*, ambassadors, even ministers. Every day, at seven in the morning, whatever the weather, she set out to cross Paris from end to end, scattering on her way her most gracious looks and her sweetest smiles... If she were ever to enter the diplomatic service, successes even greater than those of Princess Lieven would surely await her.[37]

Among her staunchest champions were the former partisans of the Noblet sisters, who were the sworn enemies of the Elssler faction. They were soon prophesying that the day when Lucile Grahn appeared in *La Sylphide* would mark Elssler's dethronement; but to this Montguyon, La Valette and their friends retorted that, come what may, Fanny Elssler would remain in place 'like the Austrian Emperor'.[38]

Elssler would allow no other dancer to share the rôle of the Sylphide with her, but shortly before the performance of 6 November 1839 she fell ill and sent word to Duponchel that she would be unable to dance. Instead of changing the programme, as she had expected, Duponchel decided to present Lucile Grahn in the rôle. Grahn was in fact already familiar with the ballet, although not in Taglioni's version but in the later production that

Bournonville had produced for her in Copenhagen to different music. Learning Taglioni's choreography in such a short time must have been a daunting challenge, and it seems difficult to believe that some touches of Bournonville's production did not creep into her performance in Paris to Schneitzhoeffer's score. In the absence of any contemporary comment, this must remain an open question. What is certain, however, is that her effort was a remarkable achievement. It was the first time that she had taken the responsibility for a complete ballet at the Opéra, but there was no sign of inexperience in her performance. Almost at a single bound she became recognised as a rival to Elssler. The *Siècle* even suggested that, while Elssler should be left in possession of *pas de caractère* and the more terrestrial rôles, Grahn should remain supreme in the graces of the air. 'Why not do for these two dancers what is done for old masters – that is, place each of them in her proper light?'[39] The claque was conspicuously silent that evening, and it seemed from the reaction of the audience that Elssler would thenceforth have to share her sceptre with the young Danish ballerina.

Even Gautier, an ardent admirer of Elssler, praised Grahn's performance, although a little more coolly than his fellow critics. She was not, he noted,

> preoccupied with Mlle Taglioni or Mlle Elssler, making no effort to emulate the misty intangibility of the former or the profound sensitivity and poetry of the latter. She left much to that great guide, chance, and the whim of the moment, and consequently succeeded beyond every expectation. If she had had more time to prepare, she would have almost certainly been less successful. Although Mlle Grahn has already displayed a remarkable talent in a number of *pas*, it was doubtful whether she could yet sustain a rôle of this importance from beginning to end.[40]

There were some who acknowledged that her interpretation recaptured the essence of the rôle's conception, which had been somewhat lost sight of in Elssler's rendering. Elssler had replaced a *pas* in Act II with a display of *pointe* work, in which she excelled, and it did not pass unnoticed that Grahn restored the dance as it was originally arranged. Edmond Texier was so moved by her performance that he expressed his gratitude to her for restoring the poetic quality of the ballet in a sonnet:

Lorsque Taglioni, la fée aux blanches ailes,
Quittait la salle aimée où pleuvaient tant de fleurs,
L'insouciant Paris aux amours infidèles
Ne la vit pas partir sans répandre des pleurs.

Paris vit succéder aux grâces éternelles,

Aux pas aériens, aux célestes douleurs
La danse échevelée et les poses charnelles,
Et les élans lascifs aux bonds provocateurs.

Mais elle est revenue enfin l'enchanteresse,
Plus belle que jamais de grâce et de jeunesse:
De ses bravos encor Paris la saluera.

Ou Marie ou Lucile, ange à l'aile rapide.
Que m'importe son nom? C'est toujours la sylphide,
Dont la place est marquée au ciel de l'Opéra.[41]

The other critics were more generous than Gautier. The *Moniteur* was reminded of 'the intoxicating, voluptuous and modest poses' of Taglioni, and called Grahn's performance 'an essay that is already almost a master-stroke',[42] while the *Constitutionnel* was specially impressed by her interpretation. 'She was in love with her shepherd,' wrote its critic, 'with all the modesty, all the reserve, and all the timidity of a sylphide who will lose her wings at the first touch of a lover's lips, at her first kiss.'[43] Janin, for his part, was delighted by the surprise of going to the Opéra on an ordinary evening and finding *La Sylphide* resuscitated in all its freshness and charm. At her first appearance, he noticed Lucile Grahn to be trembling, but her fear wore off as she became aware of her success. Her final triumph was complete, and he ended his review with a plea to the Opéra to make the most of her talent.[44]

Throughout that performance old Vestris had been standing in the wings; and as she made her final exit, he clasped her in his arms and, kissing her on the forehead, murmured simply, 'You're an angel!'

Fanny Elssler was enraged to learn that Duponchel had allowed Grahn to dance the rôle, and was said to have returned her contract, torn into little pieces.[45] Not that he took her feelings very seriously, for it now seemed almost certain that she would leave the Opéra the following year to accept an engagement in New York, and Grahn's success had revealed that he had a ballerina who could step into her shoes. But in this he was to be doubly disappointed, for the Opéra was to lose both ballerinas. Shortly after Grahn had agreed to create the leading rôle in the next new ballet, *Le Diable amoureux*, she twisted her left knee during a rehearsal. The injury proved more serious than at first believed, and it would be nearly two years before she was fit enough to resume her career. In his review of her performance in *La Sylphide*, Janin had observed how ballerinas had a habit of making their reputations in Paris and then ungratefully deserting it to gather triumphs elsewhere.[46] And his forecast that this would in due course happen with Lucile Grahn was all too soon to be realised; for when at last she recovered, she turned her back on Paris, where she was to dance no more, to seek fresh laurels in St Petersburg.

* * * * * * *

Fanny Elssler's forthcoming American visit had been whetting the interest of the public all through the autumn and winter of 1839. The idea had been first mooted by the theatrical agent Seguin when Elssler was in London in 1838, but she had shown little interest in his proposal, and the matter was not pursued until the manager of the Park Theatre, New York, came himself to Paris the following summer. Negotiations then began in earnest, and early in October, after La Valette had given the proposal his blessing and Duponchel had granted her extended leave of absence, the contract was signed. The news that she would be away for some six months delighted those of the opposing camp, but caused dismay among her own admirers. The staunchest of these assured her that if she left Paris they would place an order for their tombstones and that the *loge infernale* would be hung with crepe, a protestation that she was shrewd enough not to take at its face value. Vestris, however, was quite heartbroken. He could not understand why she should choose to visit a country of savages at the very height of her career, but he nevertheless insisted on her devoting several hours each day to practice, in preparation for the ordeal that lay before her.

Everyone, it seemed, wanted to honour her by attending her benefit performance on 30 January 1840, and so great was the demand for seats that the benches of the pit had to be replaced by orchestra stalls. The occasion promised to be not only a great social event, but a severe test of endurance. In fact the programme lasted for more than six hours. It began, somewhat unpropitiously, with an indifferent performance of Molière's *Le Bourgeois Gentilhomme*, spun out by the insertion of a few arias and dances. These dances provided about the only moments of interest in the piece. In one of them, a *pas de châle*, Fanny Elssler and her sister – surely one of the most extraordinary dance partnerships in the history of ballet – danced together for the last time in their careers, and finally Fanny came on alone, wearing a charming velvet-trimmed costume, to perform a brilliant new *pas de caractère*, *La Smolenska*. It was a type of mazurka, not unlike the *Cracovienne*, but more refined and more varied, its moods ranging from romantic reverie to haughty pride. When, at the end, she threw back her head in a final defiant gesture, the applause continued so long that she had to signal to the conductor and dance it again.

Later in the evening, after sitting through an act of Rossini's opera *Otello*, the audience arrived at the final item, a revival of *Nina*. It soon became unmistakably apparent that tastes had radically changed during the twenty years since it had been created. Jules Janin found it 'deadly dull',[47] and Gautier confessed he was sickened by the surfeit of ridiculous sentiment, which had no doubt deeply moved his parents. Of those two critics, Janin's dislike was the greater; he declared he was so bored as to feel that Elssler could not have had her heart in the part. Gautier, on the other hand, found her interpretation supremely tragic:

> In her hands the mad girl of the *opéra-comique* has become Shakespearean, a worthy sister for Ophelia, a slender white vision whose eyes alone seemed to be alive, shining feverishly out of a marble-white face that is as pallid as a Greek statue in the moonlight. At the end of the ballet, when she realises that her lover is not dead, as she had believed, a shining radiance of sublime happiness comes over her features in luminous waves that formed, so to speak, a halo. It would have been difficult to give a better rendering of unexpected happiness and the outpouring of a heart that is overflowing with joy. As a mime, Mlle Elssler has no rival, and we can think of hardly anyone else other than Miss Smithson to compare with her.[48]

For those privileged to experience it, it was an evening rich in moments to be cherished in the memory long after the curtain had fallen. For many, no doubt, these would have included Fanny Elssler's heart-rending portrayal of Nina; for others, the stirring *Cracovienne*. But to one spectator of rare musical sensitivity it was the remarkable empathy that linked Fanny and her sister in their *pas de deux*, on this, the last occasion that they were to dance together in public:

> Fanny and Therese Elssler have invented a kind of danced harmony, the chords of which could almost be committed to paper. Above all, they revel in performing the same movements, nearly always dancing in thirds and sixths, thus producing visually the same effect as is created by two soprano voices, by two flutes, or even by a double chord of the violin. And this effect is perhaps even more suited to the dance than to music, for it is well known that the ear easily tires of a succession of thirds and sixths, and that [the rules of] counterpoint forbid the playing of more than three notes in the same movement, while the eyes, on the other hand, never tire of seeing this perfect mixture of graceful poses and steps that makes the dancing of the Elssler sisters so marvellously unique, and the like of which we shall perhaps never see again.[49]

After a few more appearances, Fanny Elssler left Paris in March, bound first for London, and from there, across the Atlantic for New York. The Opéra then began to lay plans for a new ballet to celebrate her return to Paris, a spectacular project entitled *La Vivandière*, with a historical theme having as its heroine the Empress Catherine I of Russia, in which Elssler would be cast as the peasant's daughter who became an Empress. During the summer, reports of extraordinary triumphs in the New World began to appear in the Paris papers, and the Opéra learnt that she wished to remain longer in America to take full advantage of her success. Her request for a two-months extension of her leave of absence was willingly granted, and shortly afterwards the Opéra gave her a further extension until the end of 1840. To obtain this second concession, however, the ballerina had accepted a condition that if she did not return by the due date, she would incur a penalty of 60,000 francs. When it became apparent that she had no intention of honouring her contract if it suited her not to, the Opéra reminded her of the penalty clause. To her threat that she would repudiate her contract if the penalty was claimed, the Opéra retorted by instituting legal proceedings for breach of contract. Fanny Elssler had a weak case, and the judgment given against her in the court of first instance was upheld on appeal. The Opéra had no wish to appear vindictive, for it was still hoped that she would return. For some time, therefore, no attempt was made to enforce the judgment; but she proved so unreasonably exacting in her demands that the Opéra finally lost patience and levied execution on the furniture in her Paris apartment and the receipts of her benefit performance, which unwisely she had failed to withdraw before leaving for America. It was hard to realise that the grasping ballerina was the same person as the young dancer who, seven or eight years before, had so reluctantly accepted a modest bracelet from Dr Véron.

NOTES

1. *Presse*, 4 February 1839.
2. *Presse*, 4 February 1839. Guest, *Gautier*, 59, 65.
3. *Moniteur*, 1 February 1839.
4. *Presse*, 4 February 1839. Guest, *Gautier*, 62.
5. *Journal des débats*, 30 January 1839.
6. *Presse*, 4 February 1839. Guest, *Gautier*, 63.
7. *Letters and Journals of Fanny Elssler*, 10.
8. *Moniteur*, 1 February 1839.
9. *Presse*, 4 February 1839. Guest, *Gautier*, 64. Harriet Smithson, the celebrated English tragedienne, had made a deep impression in Paris when she appeared in a Shakespearean season in 1827. She was now the wife of Berlioz. Marie Dorval was the star of many of the greatest Romantic dramas.

10. Chorley, I, 66–7.

11. *Presse*, 4 February 1839. Guest, *Gautier*, 65.

12. *La Gitana*, pantomime-ballet in 3 acts and prologue, choreography by Filippo Taglioni, music by Schmidt and Auber, f.p. Bolshoi Thatre, St Petersburg, 5 December 1838.

13. Vaillat, 408.

14. The reference is to the mazurka that Taglioni learnt when in Warsaw in March 1838. She had a national costume made for her in Cracow, which, as Eugène Desmares told Antenor Joly, was 'the town where the mazurka is danced best' (Vaillat, 395). She first danced it in public on 9 June 1838, at Her Majesty's Theatre, London. Such a dance was not new to London, however, for Angelica Saint-Romain had danced a *cracovienne* in the ballet *Beniowsky* at the same theatre in 1836.

15. Vaillat, 408.

16. *Moniteur*, 27 June 1839.

17. De Boigne, 90.

18 . *Presse*, 1 July 1839. Guest, *Gautier*, 70–1; Fr. ed., 95.

19 . *Presse*, 1 July 1839. Guest, *Gautier*, 71, 74, 75; Fr. ed., 96, 99.

20. *Presse*, 1 July 1839. Guest, *Gautier*, 74; Fr. ed., 99.

21. *Presse*, 1 July 1839. Guest, *Gautier*, 67; Fr. ed., 92.

22. *La Caricature provisoire*, 18 August 1839.

23. *Ménestrel*, 30 June 1839.

24. In *La Muette de Portici* on 2 July, and as Edmond in *La Somnambule* on the 4th.

25. *Danina*, or *Joko, den brasilianske Abe*, ballet in 3 acts, choreography by Larcher after F. Taglioni, music by Lindpaintner, f.p. Royal Theatre, Copenhagen, 1 May 1829. Original production first given at Stuttgart, 2 March 1826. Grahn danced the rôle of Zabi for the first time on 29 May 1829.

26. *Valdemar*, romantic ballet in 4 acts, choreography by Bournonville, music by Frøhlich, f.p. Royal Theatre, Copenhagen, 28 October 1835.

27. *Sylfiden*, romantic ballet in 2 acts, choreography by Bournonville, music by Lovenskjøld, f.p. Royal Theatre, Copenhagen, 28 November 1836.

28. *Don Quichote ved Camachos Bryllup*, idyllic ballet in one act, choreography by Bournonville, music arranged by Zinck, with extracts from Rossini, Méhul, Spontini, Schneitzhoeffer, etc., f.p. Royal Theatre, Copenhagen, 24 February 1837.

29. *Presse*, 7 August 1838. Guest, *Gautier*, 38.

30. *Presse*, 27 August 1838.

31. *Journal des débats*, 15 July 1839.

32. *Courrier des théâtres*, 13 July 1839.

33. *Presse*, 14 July 1839.

34 . *Presse*, 21 July 1839.

35. *Journal des débats*, 15 July 1839.

36. *Les Cancans de l'Opéra*. III. 205. Tamvaco, 515.

37. Second, 156–7.

38. *Les Cancans de l'Opéra en 1838*, III, 214. Tamvaco, 464.

39. *Siècle*, 19 November 1839.

40. *Presse*, 9 November 1839. Guest, *Gautier*, 78.

41. *Ces Demoiselles de l'Opéra*, 176–7. When the white-winged fairy, Taglioni,/ left the cherished arena showered with such a multitude of flowers,/ Paris, ever faithless in love/ did not view her departure without a show of tears. //Paris then saw her eternal graces,/ her aerial steps and her heavenly sorrow/ replaced with frenzied dances, carnal poses,/ and lascivious outbursts of provocative bounds. //But now at long last the enchantress has returned/ lovelier than ever in her grace and youth,/ and Paris will once again greet her with its bravos. //Whether it be Marie or Lucile, that fleet-footed angel,/ what matters the name? It is still the Sylphide,/ whose place is ever fixed in the firmament of the Opéra.

42. *Moniteur*, 14 November 1839.

43. *Constitutionnel*, 22 November 1839.

44. *Journal des débats*, 11 November 1839.

45. *Dancing Times*, June 1921. Unidentified press cutting from a London newspaper.

46. *Journal des débats*, 11 November 1839.
47. *Journal des débats*, 3 February 1840.
48. *Presse*, 3 February 1840. Guest, *Gautier*, 84–5.
49. A.M. writing in the *Revue et Gazette Musicale*, 2 February 1840.

19

Three Wayward Dancers

The summer of 1840 brought great changes to the Opéra. Leon Pillet was installed as Director, Duponchel being relegated to the position of Administrator that he was to hold until the summer of 1842, while Aguado withdrew half his capital from the enterprise. The suspicion that Pillet cared little for the ballet was to be strengthened by his infatuation for the soprano Rosina Stoltz, and the events of 1840 afforded little hope that there would be a revival in that department.

When he assumed his new duties, the state of the ballet had sunk very low. Three years had gone by since Taglioni had last danced in Paris; Elssler was already in America; and the Opéra could boast of no greater name than Pauline Leroux. At that moment, in fact, it was not art but scandal that held the stage, stimulated by the adventures of a mediocre younger dancer by the name of Albertine Coquillard.

Albertine and her two sisters, Fifine and Victorine, had passed from childhood to adolescence in the School of Dance during the 1830s, enduring the irksome routine of the classroom and now and again earning a few welcome sous by taking part in a performance as supers. Indolence was Albertine's besetting sin. Critics seldom paid serious attention to her, although Gautier did mention her once when her shoe ribbon came undone during a *pas de deux!* [1] But if she made little mark on the stage, her talents in other directions did not pass unnoticed. She was generous with her favours, and counted several distinguished men among her lovers: Paul Daru – whose influence was said to have gained her promotion to *coryphée* and the exceptional privilege of a dressing-room of her own (granted on condition that the furnishings supplied by her protector would revert to the Opéra) – and even, it was believed, Dr Véron himself. 'There is no girl who is more a *fille de l'Opéra* than Albertine,' wrote an observer of her extra-professional activity. 'It is a pity she has never been able to resist men in nicely cut trousers.' [2]

She found a kindred spirit in Pauline Montessu, who was notoriously promiscuous herself and whose surprised remark, made on discovering she was pregnant – 'If I only knew who was responsible!' – had become a classic saying among the *corps de ballet*. Mme Montessu was in the habit of attending lesbian orgies at the home of the dressmaker, Mme Leriche, and one day invited Albertine to accompany her. Albertine found the pleasures offered there not at all to her taste, and becoming aware of a pleasant male voice singing to the accompaniment of a guitar in the next room, quietly slipped away to investigate, oblivious to the disarray of her dress. To her delight she discovered that the source of the music was a most attractive young man. Returning to her hostess, she impulsively thrust her necklace and bracelet into her hands to obtain permission to pass the rest of the evening with the guitarist. The incident soon reached the ears of Daru, who was so concerned that he left his regiment and came post-haste to Paris to reclaim his faithless mistress. Somehow she managed to obtain his forgiveness, and in no time was to be seen driving proudly about Paris in a carriage and pair, with a liveried coachman and a footman in attendance

From there, in the early weeks of 1840, she moved up the social ladder by engaging the affections of the Duc de Nemours, one of the sons of Louis-Philippe, and causing a scandal of dynastic proportions. Nemours and his brother, the Prince de Joinville, found Albertine and her sister Victorine irresistible, and spent a passionate and dissolute week in their company before running short of money. Their eldest brother, the Duc d'Orléans, then came to their rescue with a loan, but unfortunately for them their absence from the palace had not escaped notice. Queen Marie-Amélie sent for Joinville and took him to task, but to no avail. The President of the Council, Marshal Soult, was no more successful. He burst upon the two couples when they were at breakfast, and instead of being listened to with the gravity which his age and position should have commanded, was whirled unceremoniously round the room in a wild *cancan*. It was then decided that Nemours must be safely married to an acceptable princess at the earliest possible moment. So, at the end of January 1840, a formal demand was made for the hand of Princess Victoria of Saxe-Coburg-Gotha, a first cousin of Queen Victoria, and a marriage settlement bill was presented to the Chamber of Deputies. This bill met with substantial opposition, for it was considered that the King was well able to provide for Nemours out of his private fortune. From the royal family's point of view, therefore, there was all the more reason why Nemours's escapade should not become public knowledge.

So the Director of the Opéra was requested to grant the two dancers leave of absence, and Albertine and her sister were persuaded to go into voluntary exile 'with a large amount of golden arguments, supplied,' it was said, 'by a very high source.'[3] According to gossip, Albertine cunningly let drop that she was pregnant and raised her demands, and when she left Paris for London, where an engagement at Her Majesty's Theatre had been arranged for her, 80,000 francs had been deposited on the understanding that the whole sum would be paid over to her if a child were born and she remained abroad for a year; and that half of it would be hers if there was no child and she remained out of the country for six months. But since she returned to Paris less than three months later, it is very doubtful that Louis-Philippe was so generous. Nemours was given no opportunity of bidding her a tender farewell, for when Albertine left Paris in the early hours of 19 February he was being spirited away to Compiègne in the charge of his elder brother, the Duc d'Orléans. On the following day the Chamber of Deputies threw out the marriage settlement bill, and Soult and his ministers resigned. It was a very embarrassing affair.

Albertine's banishment had the effect not only of convincing the public, rightly or wrongly, that the affections of the young Prince were serious, but also of enhancing her reputation. She was treated, commented Charles de Boigne, 'like a princess born out of wedlock, inscribed on the register of the national debt, and smothered with attentions and presents... During all the three months of her exile she was a real star: the English are always taken in by the romantic adventures of princes.'[4]

Her London début was, in fact, unremarkable, and after a few performances, she and her sister mysteriously disappeared from their lodgings. Some most extraordinary rumours then began to circulate. It was even suggested in print, by the scurrilous weekly the *Satirist*, that Nemours had given Albertine a note for Prince Albert, and that His Royal Highness was very much taken with her but could not escape the vigilance of Queen Victoria, who sent an emissary to pack the two girls back to France.[5] According to the *Irish Sporting Chronicle*, Albertine demanded £2000 as her price for breaking her double engagement, and so quickly was this agreed to that she was on her way to Dover the very next day.[6]

Whatever the true circumstances, her absence from Paris was short, and she was seen again on the stage of the Opéra in June, casting long glances at the empty proscenium box that Nemours and Joinville used to occupy. No one could be sure whether her expression betokened regret or disdain, although she certainly assumed an air of magnificent insolence. Gautier was shocked one evening to see her appear 'dressed and with her hair styled like the others, but wearing on her head a diadem of brilliants of which she seemed very proud'.[7]

Such pride was to precede a fall, which was occasioned by the return to the Opéra for a few performances of Edouard Carey, a muscular dancer of Swedish origin who was nicknamed 'the Hercules of the North'. One morning in May 1841, Albertine failed to appear at a rehearsal. On investigation it appeared that she had precipitously left Paris after selling all her worldly goods and abandoning a heart-broken protector who had lavished 150,000 francs on her over the past few months.

Carey, whose next engagement was to take him to Naples, was a pupil of

August Bournonville, who had arrived in Paris from Copenhagen and
proposed to accompany him to Italy. Shortly before their departure, the two
men were invited to a party at which, as Bournonville put it, 'a novel in the
modern manner' developed between the passionate Albertine and his
'phlegmatic young friend'. Carey was embarrassed by the pressing attentions
of Albertine and did all he could to keep the date of his departure a secret
from her. But when he and Bournonville boarded the steamer, they
discovered that Albertine was already on board. Carey, who was normally
very calm, became agitated and was torn between breaking his engagement
and returning to Paris, and behaving as a complete stranger to his
headstrong pursuer. Finally he decided to remain on board, and in a few
hours he discovered that he had underestimated the power of Albertine's
charms when allied with the Mediterranean moonlight. The couple were
reunited before the evening was out, and when the ship called at Genoa,
Albertine accompanied the two men wherever they went, clinging lovingly
to Carey's arm. 'We barely got rid of her,' recalled Bournonville, 'when we
wanted to take a swim in the salt waters of the Mediterranean.'[8] This early
rapture wore off not long after their arrival in Naples, and the conflict
between their temperaments erupted so frequently into stormy scenes that
the embarrassed Bournonville felt it wise to keep his distance. Albertine was
very bored, and in the end Carey yielded to her entreaties and negotiated an
engagement for her too at the San Carlo.

Meanwhile, the management of the Opéra had lost no time in instigating a
search for the wayward dancer, and kept a stern but amused eye on her
activities in Naples. In July, the administrator-general, La Baume, gave an
account of her latest escapade to Aguado:

> It appears that Albertine (the Duchesse de Nemours No. 2) has given up
> her ideas of grandeur and is swallowing bitter pills. This M. Carey of the
> pronounced figure whom she has gone to join in Naples does not at all
> appreciate the noble sacrifice of fortune that she has made for love. Far
> from it: his behaviour is said to be notoriously brutal. One may correct
> one's wife but not beat her, and gossip has it that this gentleman beats her.
> So far, however, this touching habit has only resulted in a redoubling of
> tenderness on the victim's part, as is sometimes the case in the district of
> the Lorettes.[9] But will it last? 'The girl is fickle. People tire of the best of
> things, even of being beaten. I shall not be surprised if we see her descend
> upon the Opéra like a bomb one of these days, and I am reserving for her
> welcome a little judgment which will be strictly enforced before any
> rehabilitation. For I wager you that she will want to return, and if I know
> the world, it will not surprise me if we are forced to take her back as a
> result of a very warm recommendation from a very exalted quarter.[10]

Albertine returned to Paris the following year; but when the Opéra carried out its threat and levied execution on her belongings, her apartment was found to be empty save for a frying pan, a water jug and a broken chamber pot. There remained the final remedy, attachment, and the Opéra eventually agreed to claim only half the debt, provided it was paid within three days. No 'warm recommendation' was forthcoming, and Albertine never danced again. The remainder of her life was a sad sequel to the passionate years that now lay behind her. Soon the first symptoms appeared of a cruel and painful malady, from which she was finally released on 20 February 1846, comforted from afar, it was reported, by the sympathy of the Duc de Nemours.

A small, sad procession to the Cemetery of Montmartre, where Victorine had purchased a tomb, a few pangs of regret in the Foyer de la Danse, and Albertine, who had loved so recklessly and had wilted to meet an early death in the Romantic manner of the Lady of the Camellias, was forgotten.

* * * * * * *

The authorities seem to have regarded the period of Fanny Elssler's absence, originally estimated to last not much longer than six months, as a kind of respite that could be adequately filled by a single new ballet production, *Le Diable amoureux*, and a series of revivals that could be inexpensively staged as testing pieces for budding young talent. A possible contender for the supreme rank of principal was then Nathalie Fitzjames, younger sister of Louise, and it was she who in January 1840 was launched in the principal rôle in a revival of *La Somnambule*, coached by its creator, Pauline Montessu.

It was in a performance of that ballet in the following spring that the regrettable incident occurred which brought to public notice that all was not well with company discipline. It was not the dancers who were at fault so much as the *marcheuses*, women who were casually engaged to fill out the crowd scenes. At a performance of *Robert le Diable* a few evenings before, some of these *marcheuses* had created an unseemly disturbance in the scene of the nuns; but that incident had passed virtually unnoticed and would have been forgotten but for a repetition of the offence a few evenings later during the second act of the ballet *La Somnambule*. The disturbance took place alongside one of the avant-scene boxes which abutted directly onto the stage behind the line of the footlights. They were occupied solely by men, among them some young bloods, collectively known as *les gants jaunes*, who were aroused more by the flesh than by the niceties of choreography. It was not difficult for some of the more brazen of the *marcheuses* to edge their way towards that box and engage in banter with the occupants, no doubt arranging rendezvous for later in the evening.

On this occasion they were more brazen than ever; the audience expressed its discontent in no uncertain terms, and a day or so later the critic who signed himself A.M. in the music weekly *Le Ménestrel* brought the scandal into the open in his review. What was intended to be a pretty village scene, he wrote, was presented to the audience more like a festive night at one of the city's notorious dancing gardens! 'Under the ballet-masters Gardel and Milon,' he went on, 'the women would have been summarily sacked, for in those days we had a *corps de ballet* that was respected because it was respectable, together with a *régisseur* who took notes every evening and made detailed reports to the first ballet-master, and the *figurants* were paid according to merit. As a result we had well-ordered *ballets d'action* and delightful groupings, with everyone doing their duty.'[11]

In the end the blame was placed on the *marcheuses*, although it is possible that some of the culprits may have been members of the *corps de ballet*, for in the next issue of his periodical,[12] A.M. called for a draconian reorganisation of the ballet company, suggesting that examinations should be held to prune out the inefficient and the trouble-makers. Edouard Monnais, who had been brought into the administration as a partner to Duponchel, was said to have been entrusted with the task of restoring stage discipline. Presumably an improvement resulted, for A.M. did not raise the subject again.

When summer came, however, matters had to be taken more seriously, for the attention of the public became focused on a return visit of Marie Taglioni, who had condescended to fit four appearances at the Opéra into her busy schedule. Four years had now gone by since she had abandoned Paris for St Petersburg, where she was benefiting from terms that no other opera house in Europe could hope to match. Her contract there gave her the right to an annual leave during the summer of sufficient length to enable her to keep her fame alive in the Western European cities. Well might Paris have expected her to return to the fold where, more than anywhere else, her extraordinary talent had been nurtured; but it had been first London, then Vienna and finally Berlin that had monopolised her services during the first three years. It was only now, in 1840, that Pillet, as Director of the Opéra, was moved to send his friend Charles de Boigne to London, where Taglioni was appearing, to negotiate a flying visit to Paris. And a flying visit it would be, giving time for only four appearances.

Whether, even then, Pillet really had his heart in engaging her might be doubted, for that summer a new star had appeared in the balletic firmament – Fanny Cerrito, the toast of London's opera-goers, who had been carried away by her thrillingly youthful talent. Hearing of the extraordinary sensation she was causing, Pillet dispatched another emissary across the Channel to negotiate terms with her. The younger dancer's demands, however, proved too high to be acceptable, and de Boigne thereupon concluded an agreement with Taglioni for four guest appearances during July.

The announcement of Taglioni's return created such excitement in Paris that additional staff had to be employed in the box office to cope with the demand for seats. When the evening of her first appearance arrived on 17 July 1840, the audience seemed strangely restrained, as if they feared that the magic of her art might have paled with the passing of time. She had chosen to return in *La Sylphide,* her greatest rôle, which, since the departure of Elssler and Grahn's accident, had been danced by Hermine Blangy, a young and somewhat inexperienced dancer. Very soon all doubts were laid to rest. A new *pas de trois* had been inserted in the first act, in which the Sylphide appeared to her Scottish lover while remaining invisible to his fiancée Effie. Here, for all to see, was the Taglioni of old, with what Berlioz described as 'that unknown dance, that sweet melancholy joy, that chaste passion, that swallow's flight over the surface of a lake, those gazelle-like leaps, that rapid and unexpected run, like an arrow shot across a clearing in a wood'.[13]

Gérard de Nerval informed his readers that this *pas* was supposedly taken from Filippo Taglioni's ballet *L'Ombre*,[14] but it had in fact been danced by Taglioni in Vienna six months before the first performance of that ballet.[15] 'The newly inserted *pas*,' Gautier now wrote,

> is very graceful. The Sylphide comes to mingle in the dances of the mountain folk, visible only to her lover, which somewhat contradicts the effect of the previous scene [when Gurn has seen the Sylphide with James]. Mlle Taglioni is sublime at every step, just as Racine is on every page; this is tiresome from a critic's point of view, but it is acknowledged and true. If pressed to go further, we would go on to say that hers is a dance that is entirely her own and in which she is incomparable, and that if that style were the only one to exist, one would have to declare ballet to be impossible after her or without her, just as is tragedy after Racine. But happily [Gautier went on, his thoughts now turning to Elssler] there is a form of dancing more facile, more human, less graceful and less artistic perhaps, but eternal like love and nature, and which is the dancing not of goddesses but of women. For that form, we still have hopes of finding satisfactory performers when the Opéra deigns to give the matter thought. In the meantime one must complain in such a way as not to clip the wings of Taglioni or shroud them with a heavy golden dust, which will probably amount to the same thing.[16]

Three days later, on the 20th, Marie Taglioni appeared in *Le Dieu et la Bayadère*, in which the Spanish *pas*, *La Gitana*, was inserted; on the 22nd she danced again in *La Sylphide;* and finally, on the 26th, she took her benefit, leaving her admirers with nostalgic memories of both aspects of her talent – her ethereal mood in the second act of *La Fille du Danube*, and the vivacity she summoned up in her Spanish dance, which she was made to repeat.

* * * * * * *

Two new reputations in French ballet had emerged from the success of *La Gipsy*. Saint-Georges's scenario had revealed his professional understanding of the medium, and this had been matched by the ability with which his collaborator, Joseph Mazilier, handled his first major assignment as choreographer. Not to encourage these two talents would have been folly on the part of the Opéra, and Saint-Georges was soon at work on another scenario. Delivered in the summer of 1839 with the title of *Le Diable amoureux*, it was accepted at the end of September and handed to Mazilier to be produced for the stage. Duponchel, who was then still Director, envisaged the work as a spectacular production in which the most brilliant dancers on his payroll would be deployed. Unfortunately his plans did not work out entirely as he wished, and the first rehearsal, called for 2 December, had to be postponed at short notice.

'The dancer who is to play the principal rôle has not yet been given it,' reported the *Courrier des théâtres*, 'and yet the theatre has no one else but her to play it. Rumour has it that there is some secret arrangement between the highest authority in this affair and a certain lady who is no longer in a position to take the part in question.'[17] This was a roundabout way of disclosing that Duponchel had been trying to buy back part of Fanny Elssler's holiday so that she could create the part before leaving for America. Those negotiations, however, proved abortive, and before the end of the year it was reported that Pauline Leroux, Lucile Grahn and Nathalie Fitzjames would head the cast.

Then Lucile Grahn had second thoughts, objecting that the rôle would overtax her strength. M. Metternich,[18] who was supposed to have some influence with her, was then implored to intercede, and she finally condescended to accept the part, only to relinquish it shortly afterwards when she injured herself during a rehearsal.

Pauline Leroux, who had been offered the part of Urielle, must have seen it as a compensation for the ill luck that had dogged her over the last few years. When Pauline Duvernay left the Opera, Duponchel wanted Leroux to double Taglioni's rôles, but in this she was frustrated by an untimely attack of rheumatism. In the summer of 1837 Leroux met with a further misfortune, tearing a ligament in her right leg during a rehearsal of *La Fille du Danube*. For many months she could barely stir from her sofa. The most learned medical authorities in Paris feared she might never dance again, and had it not been for old Vestris, who scornfully dismissed these pessimistic prognostications, she might well have abandoned her career in despair. But her teacher gave her such courage and hope that eventually, by sheer force of willpower, she began to recover her strength. There was much leeway to make up; for apart from appearing in the *tableaux vivants* at the Elsslers' benefit in May 1838, she had not set foot on the stage for more than two years.

As if she had not been tried enough, she was made to endure several anxious moments during the rehearsals of *Le Diable amoureux*. One day a serious accident was only narrowly averted when she caught her foot in a trap, and a few weeks later she fell ill just before the ballet's first performance. But the Fates were not excessively cruel. The first performance was only postponed by two days, to 23 September 1840, when, for all the heartbreak and effort of the past few months, she was rewarded with a splendid triumph.

The critic Hippolyte Lucas described *Le Diable amoureux* as 'one of the prettiest ballets produced on the Opéra stage',[19] and Berlioz thought it was varied and quite entertaining, if not particularly original.[20] Saint-Georges had taken his idea from Cazotte's story of the same name, but the details of the plot were quite original.[21]

The curtain rose on the park surrounding Phoebe's villa. Phoebe (Lise Noblet) is being courted by Frédéric (Mazilier), whose roving eye is caught by Lilia (N. Fitzjames), one of the peasant girls engaged to entertain the guests with dances. Lilia reminds him that her mother had been his nurse and that they had played together as children. Phoebe interrupts this exchange, telling him to send the peasant girl packing with a gift of money, but instead he gives her a ring. To show her displeasure, Phoebe then delights in the compliments being paid to her by the male guests. Now it is Frédéric's turn to show displeasure, trying his luck at the gaming table and, not knowing when to stop, losing his entire fortune. The kind-hearted Lilia returns his ring and gives him a gold cross. Frédéric is convinced he has been cheated by one of the gamblers; swords are drawn, and a duel averted only by Phoebe's intervention.

The scene changes to a library in Frédéric's castle, where, displayed over the fireplace, is a painting depicting an ancient family legend about an ancestor who had sold his soul to Beelzebub and was given a devil as a page. Frédéric enters with his tutor (Barrez). Facing ruin, he can think of only one solution – to seek the aid of Beelzebub. In a book of black magic he finds the required incantation, and Beelzebub duly appears, accompanied by a female demon, Urielle (Leroux). Transformed into a page, Urielle is commanded to do Frédéric's bidding. After Beelzebub has vanished, Frédéric falls asleep after a splendid supper, and Urielle appears in his dream as an alluring dancer who vanishes the moment he wakes. At that point a crowd of creditors arrive, demanding payment, but Urielle strikes them motionless. Bags of gold then mysteriously materialise; but when the creditors open them, they are found to contain only puffs of smoke. Urielle, however, has obtained receipts from them, and they are left bemoaning their losses.

The second act opens with a wild orgy in Frédéric's palace. Frédéric is now rich. Urielle, still dressed as a page, invites Phoebe to join her in a dance that so enraptures her that she swoons in the page's arms. At this, Frédéric dismisses the page, and growing ardent towards Phoebe, is distracted by the momentary apparition of Lilia. At that very moment, Lilia herself appears with her mother. Mad with jealousy, Phoebe draws a knife to stab Frédéric, but Lilia darts forward and averts the blow. In the ensuing confusion, Frédéric is arrested, but the page spirits him away through a wall.

The scene changes to a fisherman's hut by the seashore, with a hill behind it surmounted by a chapel. Lilia and her mother emerge from the hut just as Frédéric comes running in to ask Lilia to be his wife. But then Phoebe arrives, to be enraged at finding him with Lilia. At this point a band of pirates appear. Phoebe bribes them to kidnap Lilia, but Urielle, who has witnessed this little scene, offers the pirate chief a larger bribe to carry off Phoebe instead. Frédéric, who has not witnessed the incident of the pirates, comes across Urielle and asks for her blessing on the occasion of his marriage. Urielle becomes more and more agitated as the wedding procession forms. The chapel door then opens to reveal the candlelit altar, but a sudden flash of lightning strikes the bride. Horrified, Frédéric lifts her veil to discover the victim to be, not Lilia, as he had feared, but Urielle. Realising that Lilia has been abducted by the pirates, Frédéric and his friends leave in pursuit. As Lilia's mother and the other women kneel in prayer, the body of Urielle bursts into flames and disappears into the earth.

The third act contained no less than four scenes. In the first, Beelzebub is discovered in his grotto with Urielle lying unconscious at his feet. Furious that she has failed in her mission to seduce Frédéric, he commands Urielle to make sure that Frédéric signs away his soul. The scene then changes to the slave-market in Ispahan, where the pirates bring their captives for sale. Then, from another ship, Frédéric disembarks. Lilia begs him to bid for her, but the Grand Vizier (Elie) outbids him. Frédéric is furious, and Urielle offers to help him if he will sign away his soul. Such is his desperation that he unthinkingly complies. Urielle then transforms herself into a bayadère. The Vizier is spellbound by her dancing. She tells him that Frédéric is her master, and when Frédéric is asked what he will take for her, he demands Lilia in exchange. At first the Vizier refuses, but Urielle only dances more seductively before him and he eventually yields. The Vizier is in despair at losing Lilia, but the pirate chief then appears with Phoebe, whom the Vizier is happy to accept instead. Another scene change then takes the audience back to the castle of the first act, where Frédéric and Lilia have now taken refuge. When Frédéric is alone, Urielle appears to him, ordering him to follow her. Enraged at discovering that he is about to marry, Urielle is inflexible. But then Lilia returns, and Frédéric declares that he would rather kill himself than submit. He is on the point of making good this threat when Urielle restrains him. Her better nature has been aroused; she tears up the contract and, begging Frédéric to place his hand on her heart, expires. In the apotheosis – set before a lake of fire overlooked by a monstrous flaming rock – Urielle's body is laid at Beelzebub's feet when, suddenly, an angel appears on the rock and restores her to life. Holding Lilia's cross and rosary before her, she mounts the steps towards a waiting angel, who takes her in his arms as the curtain falls.

The part of Urielle in this extraordinarily complex plot was a severe test of endurance for Pauline Leroux, who was on the stage throughout most of the ballet's action, which lasted a full three hours, yet she betrayed no sign of fatigue. Far from being damaging, her long absence from the stage seemed to have developed qualities of airiness and poise, and emphasised 'the precious traditions of the noble school, of which she has always been one of the most graceful exponents'.[22] To Hippolyte Lucas she was 'the dancer who can console us most for the loss of Mlle Taglioni'.[23] But what made her performances so memorable was her interpretation, her acting, which Berlioz praised as 'elegant and noble, with always the right expression marvellously enhanced by her large eyes and mobile features.'[24]

'In turn page and woman, lover and bayadère,' wrote another critic,

she managed to give each scene its appropriate character, while losing nothing of her delicate prettiness, and conceiving each disguise with incomparable aptness and nicety. In a sense Mlle Pauline Leroux is the entire ballet, the *deus intersit* of the plot; it is she who gives the work momentum, entering by one trap and disappearing down another, changing in a split second from man to woman, now descending to Hell and now rising up to Heaven, spreading her beauty and wit wherever and whenever she appears. Here at last we have a French dancer miming with our native wit, lively, petulant, with countless enticing little ways and mischief, but full, above all, of despair and love. Now she is the Cherubino of Beaumarchais, teasing and hiding; a little later she has turned into a hot-blooded Andalusian giving full rein to her feelings in a passionate *cachucha;* and then, before the cupolas of Ispahan set against a blue sky and the superb minarets reflected in the golden waters of the Bosphorus, she has become a gold-belted bayadère in gauze tunic and silver spangles losing herself in a dazzling *saltarella.* Nor must I forget to mention that touching love scene, when she sees her lover for the first time and is smitten to the heart, or the effect produced by that diabolical *pas de deux* when she fascinates the courtesan.[25]

This last was the *pas de diable* in the orgy scene of the second act, which she danced with Lise Noblet, an astonishing *pas d'action* in which Phoebe is fascinated by the page and, after trying vainly to come to her senses, finally abandons herself in a delirious frenzy under Urielle's spell – 'a strange scene that is truly fantastic, like Faust's waltz,' wrote Hippolyte Lucas.[26] As another experienced observer, Hippolyte Prévost, described:

> both dancers seemed to kindle an interpretative flame that had long remained dormant. Fascinated by the page, Phoebe becomes disconcerted, shudders, and then, all of a sudden, shakes off her wild expression to yield to the convulsions of a satanic delirium. It is a truly astonishing scene, without parallel on the stage, and in which the two dancers are wonderfully, dangerously and surprisingly true to life.[27]

No less striking was the *pas de bayadère* in the last act, a *pas seul* that Urielle dances before the Grand Vizier. In this dance, Prévost was carried away by the skill with which 'she mingled with the most charming perfection all the styles, from the ideal grace of Taglioni to the impassioned grace of Elssler, reproducing, one after another, their poses and their most delicate and most characteristic steps'.[28]

Nathalie Fitzjames was excellently cast as Lilia, whom she portrayed with a natural simplicity that contrasted with Pauline Leroux's strong characterisation. She was warmly applauded in a *pas de trois,* and again in a *mazourka* that she danced with Auguste Mabille. One pose from this *mazourka* was preserved for posterity by Emile Thomas in a statuette, which Gautier praised as 'a *tour de force,* like the *pas* itself. The male dancer,' he went on to describe, 'is seen balanced on the tip of one foot, the ballerina being high in the air in a pose full of grace and boldness. The sweet, pretty features of Mlle Nathalie are reproduced in their most charming details; the small hands done with perfect delicacy, and the feet extremely lifelike.'[29]

It was in dances such as these and the *pas de trois* in the first act for Lucien Petipa, Hermine Blangy and Sophie Dumilâtre that Mazilier excelled. With more than a few dancers to handle he was somewhat less successful, his *pas d'ensemble* in the first act, while tastefully arranged, being found a little lacking in originality.

The music was written by two composers. François Benoist, who had composed the first act of *La Gipsy*, provided a score for the first and last acts, the second act being supplied by Henri Reber. Benoist's contribution earned the praise of no less an authority than Hector Berlioz, who appreciated its careful treatment and the composer's understanding of the stage action. He noted that nearly the whole of Benoist's contribution was original. 'We only recognised,' he wrote,

> a few fragments interpolated from Spohr's *Faust*. The rest is well orchestrated, perhaps a little too constantly noisy, particularly in the third act, but the series of infernal scenes contained in the ballet made it difficult to avoid being strident. The second act, by Reber, is written with much more reserve. Trombones and percussion are rarely used, and then always appropriately. The melodies for the dances are fresh and very well developed, outstanding among them being a charming waltz and the *pas de pirates*, which was a piece conducted in masterly fashion. Again, in the music for this act only a few concessions were made to the custom that permits ballet composers to insert well-known fragments in their scores, and M. Reber has taken these from his own works. Thus we met the pirate song[30] again and, if I am not mistaken, some extracts from his symphonies. In conclusion we express the hope that the Director of the Opéra will before long give M. Reber a better opportunity of displaying all the resources of his delicate and original talent. In truth he well deserves it.[31]

The production was a feast for the eyes. No less than seven new sets were mounted during the course of the performance. The opening scene in the garden of Phoebe's villa struck a fresh, colourful note the very moment the curtain rose, and this was followed by other, no less picturesque stage pictures – the chapel with its great flight of steps hewn out of rock, the slave market of Ispahan, and the final scene of the burning lake of Hell. Disappearances, instant costume changes and trick effects added depth and detail, as well as excitement, to the spectacle.

Little wonder, then, that *Le Diable amoureux* became a popular work in the repertory. In it, on 18 November 1840, Marie Guy-Stéphan made her début at the Opéra in a *pas de deux* with Lucien Petipa; this was not to be followed by an engagement, but the following summer she was to play the rôle of Urielle when the ballet was revived in London. However, the fortunes of *Le Diable amoureux* were to vary with the uncertain health of Pauline Leroux, whose engagement was renewed for four years from the beginning of 1841 at a

salary of 10,000 francs a year plus nine guaranteed bonuses of 60 francs
each month. Her pale features and somewhat fatigued air seemed to set her
apart from her companions. 'That,' explained a friend who was initiating
Albéric Second into the mysteries of the Opéra,

> is Mlle Pauline Leroux, a dancer of good schooling who has the misfortune
> to possess less good health than talent. Alas, how often has an audience,
> attracted by the announcement of *Le Diable amoureux* with her in the
> leading rôle, had to be content with seeing her play the *'diable boiteux'* to
> the life. Of all the dancers of the Opéra. Mlle Pauline Leroux is the most
> courageous and the most determined in facing the tortures of
> choreography. Hardly a day passes when she does not submit to the ordeal
> with a conscientiousness that would break your heart if you were allowed
> to witness the mysteries of M. Mazilier's class.[32]

It was not long before her weakness began to take its toll. Early in February
1841 her left leg began to trouble her, and Maria took over the rôle of Urielle
at short notice on the 3rd. On the 25th, Leroux was suddenly stricken with
cramp during the first act, and again Maria had to step into her shoes. She
was ordered to rest, and was unable to return until 14 June.

But for this weakness, Leroux's success in *Le Diable amoureux* might well
have earned her the leading rôle in *La Jolie Fille de Gand,* which Pillet was now
debating whether to give to his new star, Carlotta Grisi. As compensation,
Leroux was allowed to treat with foreign theatres as she pleased, without
prejudice to her rights under her contract with the Opéra. There was talk of a
new ballet, *Le Chevalier d'Eon,* which Mazilier was to produce for her, but that
project came to nothing. She had to wait several years before another
creation came her way. As events turned out, her ill luck continued and she
would have the mortification of ending her career with a failure.

* * * * * * *

In the summer of 1839 a newcomer appeared among the pupils in Jean
Coralli's class, a child of fourteen called Augusta Maywood, who had come to
Paris with her mother and her stepfather to finish her dance education. In
her homeland in America she had already been acclaimed as a child prodigy;
but successes in Philadelphia and New York counted for nothing in Paris in
those days, and even in the mind of the young girl they must have paled into
insignificance before the prospect of the glittering rewards to be won in
Europe. Spurred by ambition, Augusta worked hard at her daily class and by
November was considered ready to make her début on the stage of the Opéra.

On the 11th of that month she was billed to dance a *pas de deux* with Charles Mabille in the first act of *Le Diable boiteux.*

There had been no advance publicity, but the distance the child had travelled – 'from the virgin forests of America,' as Janin put it[33] – was enough to arouse interest, and it was clear from the first step she took that an unusual talent had arrived. The *Constitutionnel* described her as 'a bustling, turbulent, bounding young dancer... darting impetuously right and left, bouncing from the stage with all the resilience of a rubber ball, and leaping with body and soul so that the spectator wants to join in her dance'.[34] 'She possesses,' added Charles Maurice, 'an extraordinary strength, particularly for one so young, plenty of elevation, vivacity, and a childlike grace that embraces those happy gifts. She crosses the stage in leaps and bounds like a hunted doe. To crown so many qualities, her features are very interesting, and her expression very spiritual.'[35] Another critic, Charles Merruau, described her style as 'mad-cap and frenzied', with prodigious leaps, *entrechats* and *pirouettes* that would do credit to Perrot, *'battements horizontaux'* such as Paul used to perform, tremendous verve, incredible brio, and a miraculous assurance.[36]

Her success was sealed by a long appreciation by Théophile Gautier:

> Mlle Maywood has a very distinctive type of talent. There is nothing of the melancholy grace, the dreamy abandon and the carefree lightness of Mlle Grahn, whose eyes reflect Norway's clear blue sky, and who is like a valkyrie dancing in the snow; and there is still less of the matchless perfection, the sparkling assurance and the allure of Diana of antiquity, and the sculptural purity of Mlle Fanny Elssler. She has something brusque, unexpected and fantastic that sets her utterly apart... For a prodigy, Mlle Maywood really is very good.

> She is of medium height, supple-jointed, very young (eighteen according to the scandalmongers) with dark eyes and a bright wild little face that comes very near to being pretty. Add to that sinews of steel, legs of a jaguar, and an agility not unlike that of a circus performer. And to cap it all, no one could have been less overawed by such a formidable test. She faced the footlights and opera-glasses that terrify the strongest hearts, with the calm of an experienced ballerina. You would have thought she was simply dealing with a pit full of Yankees. She covered that great stage from the backcloth to the prompter's box in two or three bounds, performing those almost horizontal *vols penchés* for which Perrot was famous, and then began to gambol, revolve in the air, and perform *tours de reins* with a suppleness and strength worthy of Lawrence and Redisha.[37] She was like a rubber ball bouncing on a racquet. She has excellent

elevation and attack, and her small legs, like those of a wild doe, make strides as long as those of Mlle Taglioni.

The costume she wore on the day of her first début in *Le Diable boiteux* was very much in the American taste. Imagine a pink bodice with a pink skirt without any white petticoats underneath, and pink tights, the over-all effect being enhanced by lace frippery and tinsel of various colours. A costume to delight a rope dancer! (This is not a term of scorn – we adore rope dancers.) For her second appearance, in *La Tarentule*, she was dressed as a peasant, with that eternal black bodice and no less eternal petticoat, so hackneyed in ballets with rustic pretensions. If the first costume was too barbaric, this was too civilised... Mlle Augusta Maywood will be a fine acquisition for the Opéra. She has a style of her own, a very remarkable touch of originality. Connoisseurs who have been to the Coronation festivities in Milan assert that Mlle Maywood has a style that is very similar to that of Mlle Cerrito.[38]

As a result of this successful début she was engaged for a year from 1 December 1839, at a salary of 3000 francs with bonuses of 15 francs for each appearance. Although she occupied only a modest position in the company, her progress during the following months was followed with great interest. When she danced in *Nina* at Fanny Elssler's benefit early in 1840, it was observed that she had been 'profitably studying the customs of Paris'.[39] She also attracted notice in a *pas de trois* in *Le Diable amoureux*, which she danced with Nathalie Fitzjames and Mme Alexis Dupont, and greater opportunities seemed in store when, without any warning, she disappeared from Paris and the Opéra.

She and the young dancer who had partnered her at her début, Charles Mabille, had fallen passionately in love. But there had been one obstacle to their happiness: Augusta was very vigilantly chaperoned. Whether at class or rehearsal, or in the town, her mother was always close at hand, and young Mabille soon realised that only by stratagem could he win the prize that was almost within his grasp. So, one rainy day in November he disguised himself as a young woman and, waiting until Mrs Maywood had gone out, presented himself to the concierge of their apartment at 2[bis] Rue de la Victoire, inquiring whether Mrs or Miss Maywood was at home. The concierge, who had received strict instructions to see that Miss Maywood did not go out, replied that Mrs Maywood was out but that her daughter was in.

'Mademoiselle is the principal person concerned. I have brought the velvet hat she left to be remodelled,' he replied, pointing to the hat-box he was carrying.

'Very well, leave it with me,' said the concierge. 'Her mother will take it up when she returns.'

'But Mademoiselle has to try it on,' insisted Mabille. 'If she should be dissatisfied, I shall be in trouble.'

Any suspicions the concierge may have had were thus allayed, and the young man was allowed to go upstairs. There, after the lovers had embraced, Mabille disclosed his plan. Then he returned to the concierge's lodge and engaged her in conversation so that she would not notice Augusta tiptoeing past. That evening the couple left for Boulogne, where they planned to cross the Channel to England to marry.

Mrs Maywood soon discovered their destination. She laid a formal complaint with the American Consul that her daughter, who was a minor, had been abducted. At the Consul's request, a message was sent to Boulogne by the semaphore telegraph. Soon Paris was buzzing with strange rumours, for it was reasoned that the telegraph would only be used in an extraordinary emergency. It was even rumoured that the young couple who had been arrested in the principal hotel and conveyed to the Sub-Prefecture were the Duc de Bordeaux, the Legitimist pretender to the throne, and his sister. Charles Mabille was duly charged with abducting a minor, but as a result of the mediation of friends and an affecting interview between Mrs Maywood and the young man's father – owner of the celebrated dancing garden, the Bal Mabille – she not only withdrew her complaint but consented to the marriage.[40]

That this was done more to save appearances and to prevent further scandal, Léon Pillet realised when he received a letter from the indignant lady. 'My profound sorrow resulting from the bad conduct of my unfortunate child,' she told him in a letter written on 15 November,

> has prevented me from writing to you sooner. You yourself are a father, monsieur, and can understand a parent's sorrow in such circumstances. The double dealing and lying of the young man who abducted her from her home allows of no apology, and yet to save him from a severe punishment, I signed a consent to their marriage and he is not satisfied. He still persecutes me so that a child of fifteen can become his wife at once. The letter she has written to you was a pretext, for I have always treated her with care and affection, as all who know me are very aware. This letter is due to you as an explanation, and also to express my thanks for the kindness you have always shown towards this ungrateful girl, to ask you to treat her contract as at an end, and to pay her salary for last month. I would not ask for this money if I did not find myself without means as a result of annoying circumstances, and consequently a little would be received with gratitude by your obedient servant, Louisa Maywood.[41]

Having obtained Mrs Maywood's reluctant blessing, the young couple went to Dublin, to return early in the New Year, having, according to the *Courrier des théâtres*, gone through a ceremony of marriage. Augusta Maywood was never to dance at the Opéra again. She and her husband were engaged at Marseilles in 1841, and in the early months of 1842 she was dancing in *Giselle* and *La Sylphide* at Lyons. Later that year they went to Lisbon, to appear at the São Carlos for the 1843–44 season. This engagement was renewed for the following season; but before its terms had run out, the marriage, which had begun in such romantic circumstances, foundered.

The blow fell when Mabille returned to their home in the Pateo do Pimenta, No. 15, on 5 February 1845, to find that his wife had fled but half an hour before, leaving their three-year-old daughter behind. She had left a note for him:

> You know that we have had no conjugal relations for nearly a year. Well, I now find myself in a situation that makes it impossible for me to live in your house any longer. Our characters, as you know, are not compatible, and my affection has for a long time been bestowed on someone else, so I consider it best for our mutual happiness that I should leave. I am therefore leaving, I do not say to be happier, but at least to escape your reproaches. I accuse you of nothing. Ever since we have been married you have always acted like a good husband, but unfortunately your character has not been able to suit me, and with another less highly strung woman than myself, I doubt not that you would be very happy. Forgive me for not bringing you happiness. I know how much you love our little girl, so I have no need to recommend her to you. Only never tell her of her mother's wrongdoing.[42]

There was no hope of a reconciliation, and in April Mabille went to Paris, to be granted a judicial separation on the evidence of a certificate by the French Consul in Lisbon that Augusta had deserted him. Although the management of the São Carlos had suspected that a French hairdresser by the name of Henri Gavand was the man responsible and even obtained a warrant for his arrest, Augusta's lover was apparently a Portuguese actor. Their child was born on the high seas, aboard the English steam-packet *Pasha*, four hours after leaving Lisbon for Cadiz on 3 July, and, according to information received by the Ministry of Foreign Affairs in Paris, was left by Augusta in Cadiz, presumably with foster-parents.

That autumn Augusta resumed her career. Turning her back on Paris, which never saw her again, she danced for many years in Vienna and Italy, becoming the first American ballerina to win major renown in Europe.

Meanwhile expectations still ran high that Fanny Elssler would be returning in accordance with the terms of her contract before the end of the year. News of her extraordinary reception wherever she appeared on her American tour – in New York, Philadelphia, Washington, where she was received by President Van Buren, Baltimore, Boston – filtered through to the pages of the European press, and as 1841 dawned, it was becoming increasingly clear that she had little intention of returning to Europe in the immediate future. The Marquis de La Valette, whose mistress Fanny had been, had pressed Pillet to extend her leave of absence until the end of 1840, and even offered to go to America himself to bring her back. But then came news that she was on her way, bound not for Europe but for Havana. Clearly she had no intention of returning.

The Opéra then served formal notice that failure to return by the end of the year would amount to a clear breach of their contract, and a penalty of 60,000 francs would become payable; but even this threat went unheeded. For such were her dollar earnings that she could afford to snap her fingers at the Opéra and prolong her American visit for as long as it suited her. In February 1841 the Opéra was driven to issue proceedings and was awarded damages of 60,000 francs for breach of contract, a verdict that was upheld on appeal in August of the following year. A month before that final resolution of the dispute she had landed in Liverpool, but by then the Opéra was no longer interested in pressing the errant ballerina to return, for she had been replaced at the head of the ballet company and in the hearts of the Parisians by a younger star – Carlotta Grisi.

NOTES

1. *Presse*, 3 March 1838.
2. *Les Cancans de l'Opéra en 1838*, I, 65. Tamvaco, 138.
3. *Court Journal*, 25 May 1840.
4. De Boigne, 209.
5. *Satirist*, 29 March 1840.
6. *Irish Sporting Chronicle*, 30 May 1840.
7. *Presse*, 23 January 1841.
8. Bournonville, *Reiseminder*, 43–52.
9. 'Lorette' was a term applied to prostitutes, deriving from the district in Paris where many of them were to be found, in the vicinity of the church of Notre Dame de Lorette.
10. Montmorency, 57–8.
11. *Ménestrel*, 29 March 1840.
12. *Ménestrel*, 5 April 1840.
13. *Journal des débats*, 19 July 1840.
14. *Courrier des théâtres*, 26 April 1839.
15. *L'Ombre*, grand ballet in 3 acts, choreography by F. Taglioni, music by Maurer. f.p. Bolshoi Theatre, St Petersburg, 4 December 1839.
16. *Presse*, 21 July 1840.

17. *Courrier des théâtres*, 3 December 1839.

18. Presumably Richard Metternich, son of the celebrated Austrian chancellor, and future Austrian ambassador to the court of Napoleon III.

19. *Siècle*, 28 September 1840.

20. *Journal des débats*, 26 September 1840.

21. Saint-Georges used the plot again in 1853 for the light opera *Les Amours du Diable*. The ballet also inspired a parody, similarly called *Le Diable amoureux*, produced at the Théâtre Saint-Antoine in 1840, with music by Eugène Déjazet (son of Virginie Déjazet) who also played the leading rôle.

22. *Sylphide*, 26 September 1840. Review by G. Guénot-Lecointe.

23. *Siècle*, 28 September 1840.

24. *Journal des débats*, 26 September 1840.

25. *Sylphide*, 26 September 1840.

26. *Siècle*, 28 September 1840. The reference to *Faust* is to Spohr's opera.

27. *Moniteur*, 28 September 1840.

28. *Siècle*, 28 September 1840.

29. *Presse*, 15 June 1840.

30. *Chant des pirates*, a song by Reber to words by Victor Hugo.

31. *Journal des débats*, 26 September 1840.

32. Second, 245.

33. *Journal des débats*, 11 November 1839.

34. *Constitutionnel*, 22 November 1839.

35. *Courrier des théâtres*, 12 November 1839.

36. *Revue et Gazette Musicale*, 14 November 1839.

37. Lawrence and Redisha were two English contortionists who had first appeared in Paris, at the Cirque Olympique, in January 1838.

38. *Presse*, 25 November 1839. Guest, *Gautier*, 79–80.

39. *Courrier des théâtres*, 12 November 1839.

40. *Gazette des tribunaux*, 9/10 November 1840.

41. Arch. Nat., AJ[13] 195.

42. Archives of Ministry of Foreign Affairs, 1845, dossier 1371.

20

Giselle: *Gestation of a Masterpiece*

In spite of the success of *Le Diable amoureux*, the ballet of the Opéra had suffered a noticeable decline in its appeal when compared with its brilliance a few years earlier. With Taglioni now in St Petersburg, Fanny Elssler in New York and Lucile Grahn injured, the Opéra found itself, as one observer put it, in a state of so-called widowhood: 'its *première danseuse* was Pauline Leroux, but the post itself was vacant.'[1] To some it may have seemed that Léon Pillet, the new Director, had become so besotted with the singer Rosina Stoltz, who was to exercise a dire influence throughout the years of his direction, that he gave little of his attention to the ballet. However, this was not entirely fair, for in the last weeks of 1840 his attention was drawn to a young dancer who was to revive the fortunes of the ballet in a most glorious fashion.

This young dancer, a protégée of Jules Perrot, was to become famous under the name of Carlotta Grisi. She was born in romantic surroundings on 28 June 1819, entering this world, very appropriately for a future queen of the ballet, in a modest palace built by the Austrian Emperor Franz I in the Istrian village of Visinida, not far from Mantua, and reputedly in the very bed in which His Majesty had slept. It was a wild place, where mice would come scuttling onto the tables in search of food, and bears sometimes prowled in the streets outside. Carlotta did not remain there long, for by the time she was ten she had become a star pupil of the ballet school of the Scala, Milan, and was already a favourite with the public, who affectionately called her 'the little Heberle' after a popular ballerina of the time.

Then, yielding to the persuasive arguments of an impresario, Alessandro Lanari, she left Milan to tour the principal cities of Italy with a travelling opera company, achieving easy triumphs but lacking the discipline of working regularly with the same teacher. By a most happy chance, her path crossed that of Jules Perrot in Naples. Perrot was greatly taken with her. Not only was he captivated by her youth and beauty, but he saw her at once as a dancer of exciting promise who needed only a dedicated master such as himself to develop her budding talent to the full. For her part, she was no less aware of the benefits of such an arrangement, and so, when Perrot declared his love, she willingly joined her fortunes to his own and assumed his name.

Perrot's ambition was stronger than his love, and he set to work with a burning determination to transform the still immature young dancer into a ballerina, making her practise at all hours of the day and night. She willingly accepted his stern training, dreaming of glory, fortune, and above all, it was said, freedom. 'The most ardent caress,' she confided to Alexandre Dumas in later years, 'was when Jules stood on my hips like the Colossus of Rhodes while I was lying face-downwards on the floor. This was to strengthen my hips.'[2]

The worthy Perrot did not begrudge Carlotta the singing lessons with which she occupied her active mind when not practising or busy at her needlework. She possessed an excellent, if small, voice, which was hardly surprising in one who was first cousin to one of the greatest sopranos of the day, Giulia Grisi. When Carlotta was a child, Giuditta Pasta, the great diva who created the leading soprano rôles in Bellini's operas *La sonnambula* and *Norma*, had predicted a brilliant future for her as a singer and had even offered to take the child to London.

'Give up dancing,' Maria Malibran, another great singer, had urged her. 'Work at your singing. You have a voice and talent, and you will take my place.'

Had Carlotta been a whit less dedicated to the dance, she might easily have been persuaded to devote her talents to opera, but if she had not made up her mind when she met Perrot, his faith in her must have finally settled the matter. 'Dance, Carlotta, dance,' he exhorted her. 'You are too pretty to be a singer. Besides, there are already two Grisis who are singers, and you will be stifled by being compared with them and later by the memories they will leave behind them.[3] So dance, my child. Taglioni is flying on only one wing, and Fanny Elssler is growing old.'[4]

Carlotta's first appearance in Paris caused little stir. She and Perrot passed through the city on their way from London to Vienna in the summer of 1836, pausing to make a single appearance at Mme Paradol's benefit at the Théâtre Français on 30 August. Handicapped by her costumes – 'poor satin, wretched ribbons, a dress of sad whiteness', as Janin described them[5] – Carlotta was appreciated for what she was, 'still very young to possess any real skill, but displaying little Italian graces that have great charm.'[6] In their first *pas de deux*, an unremarkable piece of choreography by Perrot, she displayed her *pointe* work and revealed a remarkable lightness; while in the tarantella that they danced later on, she displayed a true Neapolitan dash as 'she circled and turned and stopped in her tracks and hopped around in a wondrous way'.[7]

When they made their next appearance in Paris – at another benefit performance, this time at the Opéra-Comique on 5 September 1837 – they enjoyed greater success, but once again it was only an isolated occasion. It was believed at the time that one of Perrot's motives in devoting so much attention to Carlotta was to negotiate a triumphant return to Paris for himself and avenge the slight of having been unable, some years previously, to remain at the Opéra on terms that he considered acceptable. According to an unconfirmed report in July 1837, the Opéra had been prepared to re-engage him, but his insistence that Carlotta should be engaged as well was more than Duponchel was prepared to accept.

Not for some years did another opportunity of dancing in Paris arise, and it was then a much more mature Carlotta who appeared alongside Perrot in the light opera *Zingaro*, at the Théâtre de la Renaissance on 29 February 1840. This time they were dressed in the best of taste, in colourful costumes designed by Gavarni, and performed a series of character dances: *La Bohémischka*, a *pas de deux*; *La Valse saxonne*; *La Forlana*; and *La Ziguerrerinna*.

To many critics of that time, male dancers were anathema, but even Janin conceded that Perrot was 'the only bearable male dancer in the world',[8] and Gautier hailed him as 'Perrot the aerial, Perrot the sylph, the male Taglioni'. His success was complete, both as performer and choreographer, and greater perhaps than Carlotta's, although the public took her too to their hearts. Gautier noted not only her features, which he found particularly pleasing for not being too markedly Italian, but also her lovely complexion and her slender, well-formed figure. The only fault he could find was with her feet, which he described as Italian or English, but on this subject he was later to change his mind. As for her dancing, it revealed 'fire, but not enough originality. She lacks a personal cachet,' he thought. 'She is good, but no more than that.' Perhaps it made little difference that she sang with such a pronounced accent that it was almost impossible to distinguish whether the words were French or Italian. Her singing voice was 'agile, clear, a little shrill, weak in the middle register, but she employs it,' Gautier noted, 'with skill and method. For a dancer it is a pretty voice.'[9] Seeking analogies with bird-life, he went on to describe her as a warbler, while his less generous colleague, Janin, saw 'a rather hoarse nightingale that has fallen too early out of the harmonious nest of the Grisis'.[10]

The couple spent the summer dancing at Lyon, and Paris missed them. The time was now ripe for the Opéra to make overtures to the young ballerina, and a pressing letter of recommendation arrived on Pillet's desk from, strangely enough, a namesake of her master – Louis Perrot, chief of the Theatre Section of the Department of Fine Arts. 'I am taking the liberty,' he wrote on 30 November 1840,

> to introduce you to Mme Carlotta Grisi, concerning whom Monnais[11] has already had a word with you. He has told you of the 'influence' that is interested in her being engaged by you. So far as I am concerned, I assure you that she deserves to be, and is, a charming dancer, that her talent and her name are good recommendations to the public, and I believe I may say

that in more than one respect your interest will be served by this. After the recommendations I mention to you, my own accounts for little.[12]

The veiled allusion to perhaps a royal, or at least a ministerial, wish allowed of no refusal. Negotiations were immediately opened between the Opéra and Louis Perrot, who was acting on Carlotta's behalf, and on 10 December a contract was signed by which she was engaged for one year from 1 January 1841 at a salary of 5000 francs without bonuses. If Jules Perrot was disappointed at not being re-engaged as well, he was given some consolation in being asked to arrange the *pas* that his *protégée* would dance at her début, and was given hope that, later on, he might be commissioned to produce a ballet.

Carlotta's first appearance at the Opéra took place in a performance of Donizetti's opera *La Favorite* on 12 February 1841. It was the first time for many years that she had danced without Perrot, with whom she was so perfectly matched that Jacques Arago had said that people did not throw flowers to them but held them out from the boxes until they rose together to take them. Her partner was now Lucien Petipa. She was rewarded with an ovation so thunderous, as one critic remarked, as surely to have given Mme Stoltz a sleepless night. To critical eyes, however, her technique might still appear a little immature; but she had certainly made great progress since her appearance on the stage of the Renaissance.

'She is young, she is pretty, she is elegant, and she dances like a worthy pupil of her devoted teacher,' wrote Janin.

> In her manner of bounding in the air and softly alighting, there is an indefinable gentleness. But, poor girl, there is still something lacking, she is not complete: even when in the air, she is worried and looks up to see whether someone is at her side. This absent figure is Perrot, her lord and master, that light male sylphide and fine dancer for whom we have made a great concession in allowing him, a man, to be a dancer.[13]

Perrot was not to fulfil his long-cherished ambition of being re-engaged at the Opéra until many years later, but his usefulness to Carlotta was by no means over. For that very summer he was to present her – discreetly, for his contribution would not be officially acknowledged – with the greatest rôle of her career, Giselle.

* * * * * *

For the first few weeks of her engagement, Carlotta danced only in operas, her *pas* always being arranged by Perrot,[14] but it soon became apparent that her increasing success could not be ignored, and the question of presenting her in an important rôle in the ballet repertory now began to be considered. The first suggestion was to revive *La Sylphide* for her, and preparations to this end advanced to the point where Perrot was coaching her in a new *pas de trois* for the scene in the first act where the Sylphide appears to James while remaining invisible to Effie. But these plans met with an obstacle when Adèle Dumilâtre reminded Pillet that the rôle had been promised to her; and since she enjoyed the support of an influential protector, the Director was forced to concede the justice of her claim.[15] Carlotta was then offered the leading part in the projected ballet *La Rosière de Gand,* which Albert was to produce to music by Adolphe Adam, but now it was her turn to object – on the grounds that the ballet was too long and that its theme did not readily lend itself to dancing. It was at this point, in the early spring of 1841, that Adolphe Adam providentially showed Pillet a scenario entitled *Giselle, ou les Wilis,* which had been written by Saint-Georges in collaboration with Théophile Gautier.

Gautier had not been particularly impressed by Carlotta's performance in *Zingaro* at the Renaissance, but when she made her début at the Opéra a year later, he was at once captivated. 'Now she sings no longer,' he wrote,

> but dances marvellously. Her strength, lightness, suppleness and originality of style place her at a single bound between Elssler and Taglioni. Perrot's teaching is there for all to see. Her success is complete and lasting. She has beauty, youth and talent – an admirable trinity.[16]

Not long after writing these words, he was reading Heinrich Heine's *De l'Allemagne* when his attention was caught by a passage telling of the Slavonic tradition of the wilis, a species of nocturnal sprites that lure young men to their death by enticing them to join in their pitiless round. In a burst of enthusiasm he seized a sheet of paper and on it, in his finest hand, wrote the words: '*Les Wilis,* a ballet'. Then cold reason took over, and convincing himself that such poetic fantasy was incapable of being adequately conveyed on the stage, he threw the paper into the basket.

But the idea was not to be so easily discarded, and that evening, at the Opéra, he could not resist telling his friend Saint-Georges about his inspiration. Saint-Georges was at once fired with enthusiasm, and in three days produced a scenario. It bore little similarity to Gautier's original idea. 'Being unversed in the requirements of the theatre,' the poet was later to admit,

> I had been thinking of quite simply setting to action, for the first act, Victor Hugo's charming *Orientale.*[17] The scene was to be set in a beautiful ballroom belonging to some prince. The chandeliers would be lit, the flowers arranged in the vases, the tables laid, but the guests not yet arrived. The wilis would appear momentarily, attracted by the pleasure of

dancing in a room ablaze with crystal and gilding, in the hope of attracting a new recruit. The Queen of the Wilis would touch the floor with her magic wand to inspire the dancers with an insatiable desire for *contredanses*, waltzes, *galops* and *mazurkas*. The entrance of the ladies and gentlemen would make them fly away like insubstantial shadows. Then Giselle, having danced the night through, exhilarated by the enchanted floor and the desire to keep her lover from inviting other women to dance with him, would be surprised by the chill of morning just like the young Spanish girl [of Hugo's poem], for the Queen of the Wilis, invisible to everyone, would place her icy hand on her heart.'

But then, he conceded, after reading Saint-Georges's first act, 'we should not have had such a touching and well-acted scene that concludes the first act in its present form, Giselle herself would have been less interesting, and the second act would have lost its element of surprise.'[18]

Gautier's original conception of the second act was closer to that of the finished scenario, but had contained an abundance of colour, which Saint-Georges discarded. 'At a certain time of year,' continued Gautier, revealing his earlier vision,

the wilis gather in a forest glade by the shore of a lake, where large water lilies spread their disc-like leaves over the viscous water that closes in on the drowned dancers. Moonbeams glitter between those black, carved hearts that seem to float like long-dead loves. Midnight chimes, and from every point of the horizon, led by will-o'-the-wisps, come shades of girls who have died at a ball or as a result of dancing. First, with a purring of castanets and a swarming of white butterflies, with a large comb cut out like the interior of a Gothic cathedral, and silhouetted against the moon, comes a cachucha dancer from Seville, a gitana, twisting her hips and wearing finery with cabalistic signs on her skirt – then a Hungarian dancer in a fur bonnet, making the spurs on her boots clatter, as teeth do in the cold – then a *bibiaderi* in a costume like Amani's,[19] a bodice with a sandal-wood satchel, gold lamé trousers, belt and necklace of mirror-bright mail, bizarre jewellery, rings through her nostrils and bells on her ankles – and then, last of all, timidly coming forward, a *petit rat* of the Opéra in her practice dress, with a kerchief around her neck and her hands thrust into a little muff. All these costumes, exotic and commonplace, are discoloured and take on a sort of spectral uniformity. The solemn assembly takes place and ends with the scene of the dead girl emerging from her tomb and seeming to come to life again in the passionate embrace of her lover, who is convinced that he can feel her heart beating alongside his.[20]

Although Gautier later included the scenario of *Giselle* in his published dramatic works, he was always careful to acknowledge Saint-Georges's contribution. The original idea was indeed his, but it was Saint-Georges, with his professional expertise in writing for the stage, who gave it shape as a ballet scenario. When, shortly before the first performance, the question arose of whose names were to appear as its authors, Adolphe Adam advised Gautier against putting his name to it on the ground that it was inappropriate for the first dramatic work of a writer of his eminence to be only a fractional share of a whole. Gautier seemed convinced, but the next day changed his mind and insisted on his name appearing alongside Saint-Georges's both on the title page of the scenario and on the bills.

The new work was intended specifically for Carlotta from the outset, for it was shown first of all to Jules Perrot, who considered it a more suitable work for his pupil than *La Rosière de Gand* and at once took it to Adolphe Adam. With Adam, Gautier and Saint-Georges all in agreement, Léon Pillet was persuaded to postpone *La Rosière de Gand* in favour of the more modest *Giselle* on the ground that the former would surely gain by Carlotta's success in the latter. It was necessary to indemnify Saint-Georges and Adam, who were respectively librettist and composer of *La Rosière de Gand*, for agreeing to give *Giselle* priority, but that posed no problem, suitable indemnities being agreed.[21] Having undertaken to deliver the score as quickly as possible, Adam now attacked his task with vigour and delight, his imagination stimulated by the need for speed. He re-used some pages from an earlier ballet score, *Faust*,[22] which had been performed in London some years before, but otherwise the manuscript he delivered to Pillet was almost wholly original.[23] The composer's collaboration was a close one throughout: being on terms of friendship with Perrot and Carlotta, the ballet was virtually produced in the privacy of his drawing-room.

Adam set to work with an almost feverish intensity, and the structure of the ballet and in particular the central rôle that Carlotta was to play soon began to take shape. In his memoirs Adam recalled that the composition of the score took him only three weeks, but in fact the orchestration took considerably longer, as is revealed by the dates he inserted in the manuscript orchestral score. As this record reveals, Act I was completed by the end of April, but Act II took longer: the beginning was finished towards the end of April, the final *pas de deux* on 30 May, and the overture and the remainder of Act II and the finale not until the early part of June.[24]

In the *Courrier des théâtres* of 5 April 1841, it was announced that *La Rosière de Gand* was being delayed as a result of Pauline Leroux's indisposition – an event that presented a convenient excuse – and that *Giselle* would be going into rehearsal under Coralli with a view to its being presented in May. Five days later, Mme de Girardin gave further details in the *Presse*. The ballet, it was reported, would be quite novel in its style, there was to be hardly any male dancing (which was not entirely true), and the leading rôles were to be danced by Carlotta ('because she is the Opéra's lightest sylphide') and Adèle Dumilâtre ('because she is the prettiest actress in Paris'). 'Only Gautier could have ideas like that', observed Mme de Girardin.[25]

Any hopes Perrot may have had of being solely responsible for producing *Giselle* proved illusory, for Pillet was clearly not prepared to risk offending his first ballet-master, Jean Coralli, more than was necessary. Coralli was therefore to be nominally in charge, and he alone would be announced from the stage as choreographer at the end of the first performance, even though by then it was becoming common knowledge that Perrot had arranged the whole of Carlotta's part. The two men seemed to have worked together comfortably enough, with Perrot apparently accepting that there would be no formal acknowledgment of his contribution. As for Coralli, the quality of his share of the choreography came as a pleasant surprise to Pillet, who a few days before the first performance wrote to Aguado: '*Giselle* seems destined to be a great success. Coralli has recaptured, for this ballet, a freshness of ideas of which I no longer thought him capable.'[26]

Although Coralli was nominally in charge of the rehearsals, Jules Perrot was at all times very much in evidence, 'giving advice to Carlotta', as the *Courrier des théâtres* reported on 30 April. In fact his collaboration went much further, for it was common knowledge that he would be arranging all Carlotta's *pas* and mime scenes. Bournonville, who visited Paris that summer, attended a rehearsal of this ballet, in which, as he put it, 'Théophile Gautier and the ballet-master Coralli shared the idea and the arrangement with the dancer Perrot.'[27] 'I have seen for myself,' he continued, 'how, for *Giselle*, Perrot taught Carlotta Grisi fragments from the main part of another ballet.'[28] Adam put it succinctly when he wrote, in a letter to Saint-Georges, that 'Perrot had a large finger in the pie'.[29] It was probably an indication of Pillet's opinion of Coralli that Perrot should have been allowed to arrange Carlotta's part, particularly since he had choreographed all the *pas* she had danced at the Opéra from her début. However, Perrot's contribution was to be acknowledged neither on the title page of the scenario nor on the playbills, no doubt because to do so would have recognised him as one of the authors of the work and so entitled him to a share in the royalties. Clearly this was the arrangement that had been agreed, for Perrot gave no indication that he felt aggrieved. His reward had to lie in Carlotta's triumph.

As the ballet took shape in rehearsal, Gautier was lost in admiration at the power of Perrot's choreographic invention, but there were times when he feared for Carlotta's safety. Perrot's apprenticeship in the boulevard theatres had given him a predilection for spectacular choreographic effects, and he had devised some rapid aerial swoops for Carlotta in the second act. Quaking with apprehension, the ballerina was about to embark on one of these perilous flights during a rehearsal when Pillet ordered it to be tried out first with a stagehand. The wisdom of this intervention was shown a minute later when the unfortunate fellow crashed face first into a wing. The proposed effect was at once cut.

Hopes that the ballet would be ready by May were soon found to be premature. Progress, however, was steady, and all the dancers, from Carlotta to the humblest member of the *corps de ballet*, were filled with unusual enthusiasm. A slight indisposition resulted in Carlotta being absent for a few days, arousing fears that too early a resumption of activity might overtax her strength and bring about a relapse after the first few performances. But there was another reason why the ballet was delayed. All was not ready. Duponchel went to great pains to give the second act the appropriate atmosphere of spectral mystery, but he could not make the chief machinist, Clément Contant – known behind his back as 'Contant-de-lui-même' – understand what he wanted. At one rehearsal, after he had complained that the lighting was too dim, the stage was suddenly flooded with light. At another rehearsal a day or two later everything – scene changes, traps, flights – seemed to go wrong, and to enable matters to be put right, the first night, which had been arranged for 25 June, had to be postponed to the 28th, which happened to be Carlotta's twenty-second birthday.

A few final touches were applied, one of the most important being suggested by Adam himself. He was not satisfied with Giselle's return to her tomb at the end, which seemed to lack a poetic touch that would crystallise the romantic mood built up during the second act, and he proposed that Giselle should be carried by Albrecht to a bed of flowers and slowly sink into the ground. This was at once agreed. Also, a few cuts were made in the part of Giselle to spare Carlotta.

The plot had now reached its final form. The first act was set in the country, with Giselle's cottage at the left and, seen in the distance, painted on the back-cloth, a castle perched on the crown of a hill, beyond a stretch of vineyards. Giselle (Grisi), a young peasant girl, the only child of her widowed mother, is unaware that the handsome stranger (L. Petipa) who has been courting her, and whom she knows only as Loys, is Prince Albrecht in disguise. However, the suspicions of the woodsman Hilarion (Simon), who has come across Albrecht's sword and cape in a nearby hut, have been aroused. A hunting party then arrives. Recognising his fiancée Bathilde (Forster) with her father, the Duke of Courland (Quériau), Albrecht discreetly withdraws. Bathilde is enchanted by Giselle, who blushingly confesses that she is in love and that she adores dancing, an obsession that frightens her mother (Roland), who intervenes to relate, with great dread, the local legend of the wilis. When Hilarion reveals Albrecht's duplicity, Giselle loses her reason and in a final, faltering dance, snatches her lover's sword and plunges it into her breast.

The second act takes place in a forest glade, by a lake. Here, at the hour of midnight, the wilis are summoned by their Queen (A. Dumilâtre), and Giselle is raised from her tomb and admitted to their band. After Hilarion has been ensnared by them and sent to his destruction in the lake, Albrecht is lured into their round, but Giselle, who still retains a vestige of her love for him, manages to protect him from the wilis' vengeance until the break of dawn, when their power must dissipate. Albrecht then finds himself alone with the shade of Giselle, whom he gently lays on a bed of flowers that rise and cover her, before Bathilde arrives to comfort him and bring him back to reality.[30]

The only person who predicted failure for this new ballet appears to have been Saint-Georges's eccentric housekeeper, Marguerite, who was always given a seat at first performances of her master's work. If the public verdict did not agree with her own – especially if Saint-Georges had not adopted her suggestions and the work proved a success – she would become angry and vent her wrath when preparing dinner, with embarrassing consequences to all concerned. *Giselle* was a most decided success at its first performance on 28 June 1841, and when Saint-Georges entertained some friends for dinner shortly afterwards, the cooking was execrable!

Saint-Georges had not been present at the première, and heard the good news of the ballet's success from Adolphe Adam:

> We enjoyed a roaring success. The first act, which is the less strong, had already achieved success, thanks to Carlotta, who was enchanting in it, when the second act came... and transformed the success into a triumph. The fact is that I believe there has never been anything in choreography so pretty as the groups of girls that Coralli has designed in a most talented manner. The second act has no other connection with *La Sylphide* than in presenting naked [*sic*] women in the middle of a forest... but here the effects are more varied and more distinguished. It was Perrot who arranged all his wife's *pas*, a task he has performed with real talent. Petipa was charming both as dancer and as actor, and at this performance rehabilitated male dancing, which had been so well and truly buried by the dancing of the ladies. Dumilâtre, in spite of her coldness, deserved the success she obtained by the correctness and the 'mythological' quality of her poses: perhaps this word may seem a little pretentious, but I can think of no other to express such cold and noble dancing as would suit Minerva in a merry mood, and in this respect Mlle Dumilâtre seems to bear a strong

resemblance to that goddess... Ciceri's first set is not good; his backcloth represents one of those rocks surmounted by a strong castle and having at the foot numerous vineyards such as one finds in Germany, but it is all weak and pale. On the other hand, his second act is a delight, a dark humid forest filled with bulrushes and wild flowers, and ending with a sunrise, seen first through the trees at the end of the piece and quite magical in its effect.[31]

It was the second act much more than the first that impressed the audiences of the 1840s. It was 'a delight,' wrote the *Constitutionnel*, 'and its originality and poetic effects largely compensate for the old-fashioned rusticity of the first act'.[32] The sunrise was commented upon by several of the critics, who were so enchanted by the act's Romantic atmosphere that they were hardly aware of the orders of the harassed chief machinist that were audible to everyone in the audience on the first night. At the next performance the mood was shattered again, when the machinery for Giselle's flight across the stage stuck; but when the ballet was next given, this had been rearranged further back so that not only was there no repetition of the mishap, but the wires were no longer visible.

Carlotta and Lucien Petipa made 'a real poem, a choreographic elegy full of charm and tenderness' out of this second act. 'More than one eye that thought it was seeing only *ronds de jambe* and *pointes*', wrote Gautier, 'was surprised to find its vision obscured by a tear – something that does not often happen in a ballet.'[33] Giselle proved an ideal rôle for Carlotta. 'Giselle is Carlotta Grisi,' added Gautier,

a charming girl with blue eyes, a delicate, artless smile, and a lively step, an Italian with the allure of a German, just as the German Fanny had the allure of an Andalusian from Seville... [She] danced with a perfection, a lightness, a boldness, a chaste and refined seductiveness that place her in the foremost rank between Elssler and Taglioni. In her miming she surpassed every expectation – there was not a conventional gesture, nor a false movement – she is nature and artlessness personified.[34]

Her dancing seemed to betray no sign of fatigue or effort.

She... seems to dance for her own pleasure, like a young girl at her first ball, and whatever the difficulty of what she is doing, she performs it as though it were the merest trifle, which is as it should be, because in art nothing is so disagreeable as a difficulty that is all too obviously being overcome.[35]

With *Giselle* began Gautier's life-long friendship with Carlotta. It was a true idyll: in later years he was to spend happy weeks under her roof in her château at Saint-Jean, near Geneva, and whenever he saw *Giselle*, his mind would hark back to the halcyon early days of their friendship. 'I think of the fine years that are gone,' he wrote nostalgically more than twenty years later,

> and I return in thought to those performances when I leant against your canvas tomb, waiting to catch a little smile as you passed, a friendly word, holding your cloak to put it around your shoulders when you came into the wings. It was I who took you back, after the curtains fell, after the applause, to the door of your room. Yesterday, more than once, I felt the tears come to my eyes at certain phrases in the music which brought back little forgotten things to my mind: and these came to life again so tenderly, so sadly, that my heart swelled in my breast and stifled me. It seemed to me that as I went from the auditorium to the stage I was going to find you with Mamma and Annette behind the folding screen where you put on your powder and rearranged your hair in the looking-glass.[36]

The vision of Carlotta in *Giselle* remained imprinted on Gautier's memory to his dying day, and in his vivid description she can still be seen through the poet's eyes. Neither petite nor tall, she was well-proportioned for her size and had none of 'that anatomical skinniness' that made dancers look like race-horses, all bone and muscle.[37] Her feet would have 'driven an Andalusian maja to despair' and her strong yet elegantly shaped legs would not have disgraced the Goddess Diana.[38] She was fair-haired – 'blonde, or at least chestnut'[39] – and her eyes were blue with a very limpid and gentle expression. Her mouth was 'small, dainty and childlike',[40] and forever breaking into a fresh and natural smile. All in all, there was a 'childlike artlessness, a happy and infectious gaiety, and sometimes a little pouting melancholy'[41] about her features; but what truly made her beauty glow was her complexion. It was so fresh and delicate that she never needed to apply any make-up, and her small jar of rouge, the only one that stood upon her dressing-room table, was resorted to only to heighten the colour of her shoes if they were too pale. This texture of her skin Gautier likened on one occasion to a tea rose that has just opened, and again to the softest Chinese rice-paper or the inner petals of a freshly bloomed camellia.

Unable to find another journalist to write his article for the *Presse* and a little embarrassed in having to speak of himself, Gautier delivered a copy of a letter he had written to Heinrich Heine, who was taking the waters at Cauterets. Early the following year, Heine visited Paris and saw for himself the ballet that his writings had inspired. Like everyone else, he was captivated by Carlotta, who stood out from all other dancers, as he put it, 'rather like an orange in a sack of potatoes,' and to his mind had captured something of the elusive magic of the wilis.[42]

Carlotta's miming was also praised by the *Moniteur,* but of all the many appreciations, few were more vivid than that of J. Chaudes-Aigues, which appeared in the *Moniteur des théâtres:*

> But the real Queen of the festival was, beyond comparison, Carlotta Grisi. What a charming creature! And how she dances! We already knew, from the *pas* she has danced from time to time since her arrival at the Opéra, that she was graceful, light, supple and charming, but what we did not guess was the strength she displayed in this new ballet. So slender, so fragile, and yet so indefatigable! It is truly incredible. Just remember that from one end of *Giselle* to the other the poor child is perpetually in the air or on her *pointes.* In the first act she runs, flies and bounds across the stage like a gazelle in love, so much so that the peace of the tomb does not seem too profound for such racing and expenditure of effort. And yet this is nothing compared to what is in store for her in the second act. Here she must not only dance as she did just before, but must be a thousand times lighter and more intangible, for now she is a shade. No longer is the earth beneath her feet, no longer has she any support! She cleaves the air like a swallow, she balances on rushes, she leans from the treetops – this is actual fact – to throw flowers to her lover. Do you remember the Sylphide's swift and sudden appearances? Giselle is a Sylphide given not a moment's rest. Decidedly Mlle Taglioni has found a successor... Of course Carlotta Grisi does not yet have the skill of Mlle Taglioni, nor such a long experience on the stage, which is simply because Carlotta is only twenty; but the qualities of Mlle Taglioni, her most precious qualities – precision of movement, graceful bearing, lightness and suppleness – all these Carlotta possesses to the highest degree. And more, she has an indefinable provocativeness, but a modest provocativeness withal, if I can so put it, which was the secret of Mlle Fanny Elssler's success. Yes, for myself, I have no hesitation in proclaiming that the diverse qualities of Taglioni and Fanny Elssler are combined in Carlotta Grisi.[43]

Ostensibly the greater share of the triumph belonged to Carlotta, and through her, to Perrot, but Coralli's contribution, as choreographer responsible for the overall production, also received general praise. The peasants' *pas de deux* in the first act was as enchanting choreographically as it was musically. If it was somewhat conventional, Nathalie Fitzjames and Auguste Mabille gave it style and expression, and included at least one *fromage* to delight the *abonnés,* but a *fromage* that was suitably 'calm, grand, noble and imposing'.[44] For this, a suite by Burgmüller had been inserted in

Adam's score, concluding with a lilting waltz that was already well known under its original title of *Souvenirs de Ratisbonne*. Coralli's dances for the wilis were also praised as being skilfully planned and arranged, and, in the words of Gautier, were distinguished by their 'exquisite elegance and novelty'.[45] One element in this approval may well have been the selection of the prettiest girls in the *corps de ballet* to play the peasants and the wilis, which was apparently due to Gautier's own suggestion. 'The almost pretty were pitilessly turned away,' reported Mme de Girardin. 'It was done with great severity.'[46]

Over the years that have passed since *Giselle* was created, the ballet has undergone a number of changes. Omitted nowadays is a mime passage between Giselle and Albrecht at the beginning, in which Giselle tells of a disturbing dream that he loved another. Much of the long pas de deux in the first act has also now been cut, as has a variation of later date inserted in place of the sparkling solo, with its 'infinity of intricate footwork',[47] which Carlotta danced to Perrot's choreography. The entrance of the hunting party, too, has suffered: originally several of the party were mounted, including the heavily bearded Duke of Courland and his daughter Bathilde, who made an imposing figure on a white steed. In later productions the Duke and Bathilde were made to leave the stage before the mad scene, but in 1841 they both remained to witness Giselle's death in her mother's arms.

The second act gave greater scope for effects, and advantage was taken of this, even if Perrot's most daring ideas had to be discarded and Gautier's suggestion, that small pieces of mirror be fixed to the backcloth to produce the effect of moonlit reflections in the water, was ignored. But the entrance of the Queen of the Wilis and the appearance of the wilis from reeds, flowers and tree trunks was achieved with magical illusion. Giselle made her entrance in this act, rising on a trap before the tombstone, her head covered with a light shroud which vanished at Myrtha's bidding as wings sprouted from her shoulders. Before Giselle was admitted to the wili band, Myrtha placed on her head a circlet of flowers with a star in the centre. After this came a scene, now long since omitted, in which several villagers pass through the glade and are pursued by the wilis. Giselle and Albrecht's *pas de deux* in this act contained a number of novel effects, which Gautier described as 'the transverse flight, the bending branch, and her sudden disappearance when Albrecht wishes to fold her in his arms'.[48] This bending-branch effect was obtained by means of a kind of see-saw contraption, which enabled her to appear in a tree, as if floating, to drop flowers at her lover's feet.

The score was Adam's third for the Opéra, and to many people's surprise it was Habeneck, the chief conductor, who entered the orchestra pit to conduct the ballet at the first performance. Normally it was his assistant, Battu, who took over for the ballet, but Habeneck had been so impressed by Adam's score that he told the composer it was too important a work to be consigned to Battu. If Adam was at first flattered by such a compliment, he took a different view after the performance. Habeneck had 'conducted stupidly', he complained in his letter to Saint-Georges:

> The rehearsals had earned me much applause from the musicians, who played with all possible zeal, and everything went well in spite of the bad conducting. I know of no reputation for ability that is less deserved than Habeneck's. There are two conductors in Paris who are much superior to him – Valentino and Girard of the Opéra-Comique. Nevertheless, my music created a great impression.[49]

Apart from being an early example of the use of *leitmotiv* in ballet music, Adam's score was appreciated on its own merits and given the unique distinction, at that time, of a serious analysis in *La France musicale*. The writer was its editor, Marie Escudier, who must have discussed the music at length with Adam beforehand, since the composer, who was himself a contributor to the review, had given the gist of this analysis in his letter to Saint-Georges, written some days before the article appeared in print. Indeed the only passage he mentioned on which Escudier did not comment was a quartet for two *cors anglais* and two bassoons, which accompanied the summoning of the wilis in the second act.

Escudier praised the score as 'a real *tour de force*', distinguished by the elegance, freshness and variety of its melodies, its vigorous and novel harmonic combinations, and the momentum that it preserved from beginning to end. Unlike many ballet scores of that time, it was almost entirely original, the only borrowings that the critic could recognise being eight bars from a song by Luise Puget and three from the Huntsmen's Chorus in Weber's opera *Euryanthe*. Wrote Escudier:

> As the curtain rises we have a delightful introduction, in which we take note of an orchestration quite in the manner of Cherubini. This introduction perhaps has one fault, that of not being long enough. The first scene between Giselle and Loys contains some very attractive passages. Then comes an enchanting waltz, quite in the Germanic spirit of the subject, which may well become as popular as the finest of Strauss's waltzes. This waltz is interrupted by Giselle's mother warning her daughter of the dangers of abandoning herself too much to dancing, and expressing her dread of one day seeing her transformed into a wili. The music for this scene contains several entirely novel modulations. Hunting calls follow this number. Here the use of brass is very felicitous, and we have rarely heard this kind of instrument written for in such a favourable

compass: it has power and sonority without a trace of stridency. The little *andante* that accompanies the scene between Giselle and her sweetheart's fiancée is delightful in its naïvety and stylishness. The *divertissement* opens with the *Marche des vignerons*, which has an original and powerful rhythm. In it the progression of a third from G to B flat, followed always by the chord of D major, produces a most unusual effect. The *pas de deux* by Giselle and Loys ends with a *louré* movement, which was found very pleasing. The *galop* that concludes the *divertissement* is less distinguished than the numbers that precede it, but its rhythm is infectious and it is all that a *galop* should be. The finale of the first act, in which the mad scene is enacted, is complete in itself with all its developments, and we know of no better finale in all [of Adam's] operas.

All the pleasure aroused by the music of the first act is small by comparison with what the musician has kept back for the second. It would be too difficult to analyse each number in this act, but we must mention the orchestral effect that accompanies the entrance of the Queen of the Wilis: to *arpeggi* on the harps, four muted first violins play in their highest register a four-part melody, the effect of which is truly magical. It really makes one feel transported to fairyland. This combination of instruments is absolutely new, and its effect is excellent. There then follow, linked together in succession, several dance tunes whose rhythm is constantly varying without the fantastical colouring for a moment ceasing to dominate all these ethereal melodies. From a musical point of view, this part of the ballet is the most remarkable. It is the first time we have seen the fantastic treated with due regard to grace and charm, and perhaps this will never be more happily achieved. Giselle's last *pas* is accompanied by a viola solo that is very well played by M. Urhan. There is nothing sweeter to the ear or more melancholy than the qualities of the viola, which is so seldom used as a solo instrument

The phrase to which Giselle disappears into the bed of flowers, played by a solo flute against the harmonic notes of the harps, is full of charm and sadness. With this phrase, the score, which may well achieve both a fashionable and a popular success, is brought to a close in a ravishing manner.

There are some who talk of a score that is heavy and boring. 'It's highbrow music,' they will say. But, Good Heavens, there may indeed be a prodigious amount of skill contained in the score of the new ballet, but it is skill merely employed in the service of melody. It never becomes a pretext for doing without ideas.

A very original idea in M. Adam's ballet is to be found in a fugue in which the four voices of the subject are reflected in successive entrances of the *corps de ballet*. 'A fugue in music,' said Régnault, 'is a very powerful piece.' What then would he have thought of a fugue in dance? This is a novel problem that M. Coralli has just triumphantly resolved. However, we have strong suspicions that M. Adam, who may not enjoy a very high reputation as a choreographer, has exercised a little influence in the production of this ballet.[50]

Adam sold his score to the music publisher Meissonnier for 3000 francs, but this did not of course include the interpolated pas *de deux*, the music of which was Burgmüller's property, and had been sold by that composer to another publisher, Colombier, for 1000 francs. Naturally Colombier wished to make capital out of the ballet's success, and he reissued the waltz from this pas *de deux*, which had previously been sold under its original title of *Souvenirs de Ratisbonne*, with a new title page bearing the subtitle, 'danced by Mlle Nathalie Fitzjames and Mabille in *Giselle*', with the name of the ballet printed in large capitals. In the legal proceedings that followed, Colombier was ordered to print the composer's name, the title of the work, and the word 'interpolated' in characters as large as the word 'Giselle'. But Colombier then appealed, and the First Chamber of the Cour Royal allowed his appeal on the ground that, as the success of *Giselle* was due partly to Burgmüller's waltz which had been included in the music for the ballet, Colombier was within his rights in printing the name of the ballet in large characters, and that the small changes he had made in the design of the title page had satisfied Meissonnier's original objection.

The immediate success of *Giselle* was reflected in the box-office receipts, which were unaffected by the seasonal exodus of the Parisians in July.[51] Prints of Carlotta Grisi were eagerly snapped up, and the sculptor Emile Thomas made a charming statuette of her in her costume for the second act. Quadrilles and arrangements of the music proliferated. In October a parody called *Les Wilis* made its appearance at the Théâtre du Palais-Royal. A silk material came on the market with the name of *'façonné Giselle'*, and the milliner Mme Lainné introduced an artificial flower called 'Giselle'.

Carlotta's own astonishing triumph did not go unrewarded, and within a few weeks she was given a new contract, under which her salary was increased to 12,000 francs a year and seven guaranteed bonuses of 43 francs each month during 1842, rising to 15,000 francs and 72 francs respectively for 1843. This was a clear recognition of her supremacy at the Opéra, given that Pauline Leroux, her nearest rival, was receiving only 10,000 francs a year with bonuses of 60 francs.

The rôle of Giselle became regarded so much as Carlotta's property that during the next eight years, until her departure from the Opéra in 1849, only one other dancer played it there. This was Elisa Bellon, who performed it just twice, on 12 and 19 September 1842. Mlle Bellon, who had just been engaged at the Opéra for three years, had played the rôle in Bordeaux on 1 December 1841, in the first production of the ballet to be staged outside Paris. In Paris she gave a creditable performance, and was adjudged a very musical dancer with a good technique, although lacking Carlotta's prowess on the *pointes*. Some, however, thought her miming to be superior, and her mad scene was warmly applauded.

So long as Carlotta remained at the Opéra, few changes were made in the casting of *Giselle*. Lucien Petipa retained the part of Albrecht, in which he had revealed an unsuspected talent as a mime. Adèle Dumilâtre remained the principal interpreter of the Queen of the Wilis, although this rôle was also played by Hermine Blangy for a few performances in 1841, by Louise Fleury, a pupil of Albert, who made a majestic début in the part on 27 February 1843, and by Célestine Emarot, who first played it in 1845. The role of Bathilde was played by the English dancer who had created it, Caroline Forster, until her retirement in 1844, when she was succeeded by Delphine Marquet.[52] Théophile Gautier was one of Forster's ardent admirers and wrote a charming poem in praise of her ear:

> *Oui, Forster, j'admirais ton oreille divine;*
> *Tu m'avais bien compris, l'éloge se devine:*
> *Qu'elle est charmante à voir sur les bandeaux moirés*
> *De tes cheveux anglais si richement dorés...*[53]

Giselle, born of a poet's fancy, given music that reflected so faithfully the moods of its strange tale, and danced with lyrical sweetness by an entrancing ballerina whose steps had been dictated by a true poet of choreography, was to be recognised as the greatest and most lasting masterwork of the Romantic ballet. Of all the productions staged at the Paris Opéra during this period, it alone has survived with a proportion of its choreography intact. As representative of its time as Berlioz's *Symphonie fantastique*, Géricault's *Raft of the 'Medusa'*, or the poems of Victor Hugo, it contains the very quintessence of the Romantic ballet – the local colour of the rustic first act, and in contrast, revealing that duality to be found in so much of Romantic art, the mystery of the forest scene; the fragility of the heroine, her mind balanced between reason and madness; the hero's love that outlives his passion and stretches out to seek his beloved beyond the tomb; the hopelessness of their love in this life, and finally the purification that it brings to his soul. *La Sylphide* had been its precursor, the prototype of a more lyrical form of ballet, expressing Romantic fantasy set in a mood of mystery; *Giselle* was created to the same formula, but penetrated more deeply. It elevated the art of ballet to a more exalted level. The greatest achievement of the Romantic ballet, it was a true masterpiece that can justly aspire to be hailed as a poem in dance.

NOTES

1. De Boigne, 251.
2. Unidentified newspaper cutting, dated shortly after Grisi's death in 1899. Article entitled 'Carlotta Grisi' by An Old Stager.
3. Giuditta and Giulia Grisi were cousins of Carlotta Grisi. The former, a mezzo-soprano, was a star in her own right, but overshadowed by her sister, a soprano who created the rôles of Adalgisa in *Norma*, Elvira in *I Puritani* and Norina in *Don Pasquale*.
4. De Boigne, 249.
5. *Journal des débats*, 5 September 1836.
6. *Courrier des théâtres*, 31 August 1836.
7. *Journal des débats*, 5 September 1836.
8. *Journal des débats*, 27 April 1840.
9. *Presse*, 2 March 1840.
10. *Journal des débats*, 2 March 1840.
11. Edouard Monnais, the Royal Commissioner, the government official appointed to see that the subsidy was properly spent.
12. Arch. Nat., AJ^{13} 194.
13. *Journal des débats*, 15 February 1841.
14. In *La Juive* (4 April) and *Don Juan* (30 April).
15. The revival was presented on 22 March. Mazilier, not Perrot, was given credit for arranging the new *pas de trois*, presumably for the same reason that Coralli would be solely credited as the choreographer of *Giselle*.
16. *Presse*, 7 March 1841; Fr. ed., 120-1.
17. *Les Orientales* was a series of poems by Victor Hugo. The part that inspired Gautier was entitled *Fantômes*. It told of a young Spanish girl who loves dancing to excess and dies at daybreak after a ball.
18. *Presse*, 5 July 1841. Guest, *Gautier*, 98.
19. Amani was an Indian dancer who appeared in Paris with a troupe of Bayadères in 1838.
20. Preface to *Giselle*, published by Gautier in *Théâtre, Mystère, Comédies et Ballets*, 366.
21. Arch. Nat., F^{21} 1069. Indemnities between Pillet and Saint-Georges and Adam respectively.
22. *Faust*, choreography by Deshayes, music by Adam, f.p. King's Theatre, London, 16 February 1833.
23. The *Moniteur des théâtres* of 12 May 1841 reported that the music for the first act had been completed and a satisfactory rehearsal had taken place. This does not necessarily contradict Gautier's statement about the speed with which Adam wrote the score. Adam may well have wanted to do some final polishing, and the orchestral parts had to be copied.
24. Bibl. Nat. (Musique), MS 2644. Adolphe Adam, manuscript orchestral score of *Giselle*.
25. *Presse*, 10 April 1841.
26. Montmorency, 144.
27. Bournonville, *Reiseminder*, 42.
28. Bournonville, *Mit Theaterliv*, I, 30.
29. Lifar, *La Danse*, 284.
30. Bathilde's reappearance at the end of the ballet was cut when the Diaghilev Ballet brought *Giselle* back to Paris in 1910.
31. Lifar, *La Danse*, 281–2.

32. *Constitutionnel*, 1 July 1841.

33. *Beautés de l'Opéra. Giselle*, 23.

34. *Presse*, 5 July 1841. Guest, *Gautier*,

35. *Galérie des artistes dramatiques. Carlotta Grisi*, 4.

36. Richardson, 190.

37. *Galérie des artistes dramatiques. Carlotta Grisi*, 4.

38. *Beautés de l'Opéra, Giselle*, 5, 6.

39. *Galérie des artistes dramatiques. Carlotta Grisi*, 4.

40. *Galérie des artistes dramatiques. Carlotta Grisi*, 4.

41. *Beautés de l'Opéra, Giselle*, 5, 6.

42. Lifar, *Carlotta Grisi*, 60.

43. *Moniteur des théâtres*, 30 June 1841.

44. *Musée Philipon*, 67. Littré's Dictionary defines the term *'faire des fromages'* as, familiarly, a game played by little girls who, after turning rapidly, sink suddenly to the ground so that their skirts puff out and present a circular form like that of a cheese.

45. *Presse*, 5 July 1841.

46. *Presse*, 17 May 1841.

47. *Musée Philipon*, 67.

48. *Presse*, 5 July 1841.

49. Lifar, *Danse*, 282–3.

50. *France Musicale*, 4 July 1841.

51. In 1839 the average receipts for July, August and September had been between 3000 and 4000 francs. Performances that included *Giselle* between that ballet's première and the end of September 1841 brought in an average of over 6500 francs.

52. During the nineteenth century the leading rôles in *Giselle* were taken by the following dancers at the Paris Opéra, the dates in parentheses being their first appearance in the particular rôle:

GISELLE: Carlotta Grisi (28.6.41), Elisa Bellon (12.9.42), Regina Forli (11.8.52), Martha Muravieva (8.5.63), Zina Mérante (30.9.63), Nadezhda Bogdanova (13.11.65), Adèle Grantzow (11.5.66).

ALBRECHT: Lucien Petipa (28.6.41), Eugène Coralli (12.9.42), G. Léopold Adice (7.11.42), Jean Ragaine (15.9.43).

BATHILDE: Caroline Forster (28.6.41), Delphine Marquet (6.5.44), Zélie Pierson (28.8.46), Caroline Lassiat (2.12.46), Pauline Laurent (7.9.49), Louise Marquet (8.5.63), Blanche Montaubry (2.10.68).

BERTHE: Elina Roland (28.6.41), Aline (6.5.44).

MYRTHA: Adèle Dumilâtre (28.6.41), Hermine Blangy (20.8.41), Louise Fleury (27.2.43), Célestine Emarot (25.7.45), Laure Fonta (8.5.63), Elise Parent (26.6.63).

PEASANT *PAS DE DEUX* (Man): Auguste Mabille (28.6.41), Hippolyte Barrez (29.5.43), Théodore [Chion] (7.11.45), Henri Desplaces (2.10.46), Jules Toussaint (13.11.46), Louis Mérante (11.8.52), Alfred Chapuy (8.5.63), Magloire Beauchet (11.9.63), Félix Rémond (1.5.68).

PEASANT *PAS DE DEUX* (Woman): Nathalie Fitzjames (28.6.41), Sophie Dumilâtre (10.12.41), Julie Dabas (12.4.43), Maria (29.5.43), Elisabeth Robert (7.11.45), Sofia Fuoco (8.10.47), Nadezhda Bogdanova (11.8.52), Zina Mérante (8.5.63), Adèle Villiers (30.9.63), Léontine Beaugrand (28.10.63), Angelina Fioretti (11.5.66).

53. Gautier, *Poésies complètes*, 299. Yes, Forster, I was lost in admiration of your divine ear;/ You had read my thoughts, my praise was there to be divined;/ How charming was the sight of it resting on the shimmering coils/ of your English tresses so richly golden in hue.

21

More Laurels for Carlotta

In the event, no one could criticise Pillet's handling of the switch of priority between *La Rosière de Gand* and *Giselle*, and in the years to come, so far as the ballet was concerned, he was to show himself to be an understanding and active administrator. In the field of opera, however, his record was to prove much less praiseworthy, because he fell under the influence of a singer, Rosina Stoltz, whose every whim became law. This association had already become a scandal by the summer of 1842, and Escudier, the eminent music critic, prefaced his article on the ballet *La Jolie Fille de Gand* (formerly known as *La Rosière de Gand*), the second of Carlotta Grisi's creations at the Opéra, with a powerful condemnation of Mme Stoltz's malign influence.

Fortunately, however, this had little effect on the ballet, which was to flourish throughout the term of Pillet's directorship under the benevolent star of Carlotta Grisi, one of the most charming and popular ballerinas ever to appear on the Opéra's stage. *Giselle* had launched her into fame at a single bound, and by the end of 1841 had been performed twenty-six times in little more than six months – a record that not even *La Sylphide* could match.[1] A decision on another creation for her could not now be long delayed, and it was Pillet's good fortune that a solution lay to hand. The Opéra had already accepted Saint-Georges's scenario of *La Rosière de Gand*, which had been offered to Carlotta early on in her engagement and rejected. Pauline Leroux had then been selected for the leading rôle, which required a dancer with considerable dramatic powers. That requirement Leroux certainly filled, but there was now a growing concern over whether she would be fit enough to carry the ballet through what was hoped would be a long and successful run. This was a cause of particular worry owing to the scale and financial outlay of the proposed work, and to the effect on the takings that an interruption of performances would entail. By the end of 1841, Pillet was becoming seriously concerned at the prospect of launching such a major work with a dancer whose fitness could not be relied upon. Another consideration, of course, was that a new creation had to be found for Carlotta in order to build upon her triumph in *Giselle*.

The banker Aguado, who ever since Véron's time had provided financial backing to the Opéra, was kept informed of the delicate negotiations by the Opéra's general administrator, La Baume. 'At this very moment, we are beginning to give serious consideration to the new ballet,' he wrote early in 1842.

On this subject, an important question has arisen as to whether we should leave the principal rôle with Pauline Leroux, or modify the character with a view to giving it to Carlotta. Pauline has recently had trouble with her feet again, and, since we shall be spending 60,000 to perhaps 80,000 francs, would it be wise to run the risk of an interruption just at the moment when everything has been finally arranged and all that should be left is to gather in the harvest? M. Pillet seems determined not to risk it. Carlotta is popular and in favour; with her we are almost certain to attract all Paris. But with Pauline – even discounting accidents – rightly or wrongly, there can be no such certainty. So I think that the change will take place.[2]

The critical day was 10 January, when two discussions took place, one in the morning and the other in the late afternoon. On the following day La Baume reported to Aguado:

Yesterday we were present at the decisive discussion that [M. Pillet] had to have with Mlle Pauline Leroux, who is at present in possession of the rôle and is far from giving it up willingly. In spite of the insistence of this lady and her champion, M. Lafont, the Director did not give way. Fundamentally he is a hundred times in the right, and for the sake of form he was prepared to offer every possible compensation – but who can soothe an artist's pride? Be that as it may, the decision has now been made: there will be no going back, and we are pressing ahead.[3]

Carlotta was genuinely concerned by the thought that she might be accused by friends and supporters of Leroux of complicity in a decision that would deprive a comrade of the prospect of a major triumph, and these misgivings were compounded by the off-hand manner in which she was called to a rehearsal of *La Jolie Fille de Gand*. The next day she wrote to the Director to make her position absolutely clear:

A call-boy came to me yesterday to tell me to be at the theatre today to begin rehearsals for the ballet *La Rosière de Gand*. Without dwelling on the casual nature of this request, allow me to protest against the responsibility and the legitimate reproaches that I shall incur by accepting. Although it is not for me to judge the motives behind your decision concerning the rôle in question, I must nevertheless inform you that so long as the difference between you and my comrade Pauline Leroux exists, I shall persist with all my strength in the opposition I have shown.[4]

As to how Carlotta was persuaded to forgo her resistance to Pillet's decision, the record is silent; but before her departure for London in the latter half of February she was already working with Albert on the rôle of the ballet's heroine, Béatrix. At this early stage of her career she may have realised it would have been foolish to have refused it, particularly if Saint-Georges and Gautier had added their weight, as they may well have done, to the pressure on her to accept. In her hands the rôle would inevitably take on a different colour to that which Leroux would have given it, and Carlotta's assumption of it at such an early stage in the ballet's preparation would render any comparison academic.

So a compromise was eventually reached, and Carlotta accepted the part. In less than a month she would be on her way to London during her two months' leave, but there was time enough for Albert to give her a good idea of her rôle so that she could profit from the advice of Perrot, whom she would find in England. Before leaving Paris, she attended a three-hour rehearsal, after which Elina Roland would stand in for her so that Albert could continue setting the action during her absence. In the meantime, Carlotta was to gather fresh laurels in London, where Perrot's production of *Giselle* provided a triumph for them both. When her two months' engagement there drew to its close, Lumley, the manager of Her Majesty's Theatre, pressed her to extend her stay so as to build upon her triumph; but Pillet was adamant that she should return on the due date for the final preparations of Albert's ballet.

During Carlotta's absence in London, the wisdom of giving her the principal rôle was all too clearly revealed, for Pauline Leroux, who had reappeared in *Le Diable amoureux*, suffered a serious fall, not during a performance but while practising in the Foyer de la Danse. More than seven months were to pass before she was fit enough to resume her career, by which time *La Jolie Fille de Gand* (as it was to be finally called) had been triumphantly launched.

That spring, a misfortune of a different kind had befallen Lise Noblet, now the Opéra's senior ballerina, who had recently celebrated her fortieth birthday. Somewhat unwisely, she ventured to appear in Taglioni's most celebrated rôle, the Sylphide, expecting no doubt to be received with the respect due to one of her reputation. But here she gravely miscalculated, as Aguado's correspondent La Baume informed him in one of his gossipy letters:

The other week Mlle Noblet was given a bitter taste of public favour. She was appearing in *La Sylphide*. The orchestra stalls and the lions [in the stage box] somewhat ungallantly found her little to their taste. On several occasions her ears were assailed by mournful sounds. Feeling entitled to answer back, she ironically thanked Maître Boucher[5] in the wings for the goodwill of himself and his friends. The joke was felt to be in poor taste by his colleagues in the lions' box, who gave vent to their anger. The over-sensitive dancer did not dare face danger again, and has given up the rôle. It was Sophie Dumilâtre (she of the broken nose) who played it yesterday.[6]

Meanwhile, the final rehearsals of *La Jolie Fille de Gand* were passing without complications. Albert had raised no objection to taking on a scenario that he had not himself written, and was no doubt pleased to be working for the celebrity of the moment. How much he had worked with Pauline Leroux is not known; but as soon as Carlotta returned from London, he was able to concentrate on her interpretation, adjusting the part as necessary to suit a talent that was less histrionic than Leroux's. To Carlotta it would certainly present a very considerable challenge: for whereas in *Giselle* the drama to be mimed was mainly concentrated in the first act, in *La Jolie Fille de Gand* she would have to develop her character through three acts lasting, in performance time alone, not far short of two-and-a-half hours.

Saint-Georges's scenario was inspired by an idea that had been successfully employed ten years or so before in a play at the Porte-Saint-Martin entitled *Victorine*,[7], in which the heroine is smitten with a series of disasters before waking up to realise with relief that it had all been a horrible nightmare. In the ballet, Victorine was transformed into Béatrix (Grisi), who is engaged to be married to Bénédict (L. Petipa), but has had the misfortune of catching the eye of the philandering Marquis de San Lucar (Albert). Unsure whether she is really in love with Bénédict, she innocently gives the key of her chamber to her cousin Julia (Maria), to whom she wishes to confide her anxiety over the Marquis's advances. However, the Marquis manages to gain possession of that key, and that night enters Béatrix's room with the intention of seducing her. Interrupted by the timely arrival of Béatrix's sister Agnès (A. Dumilâtre), he makes his escape through the window.

When the second act opens, Béatrix has become the Marquis's mistress and is installed in a splendid palace in Venice. There she is refused nothing, but his attentiveness to the prima ballerina of the Fenice Theatre (L. Fitzjames) is giving her grounds for concern. However, her sadness is soon forgotten at a masked ball, where, dressed as Diana, she is the centre of attraction. Suddenly a man confronts her, removing his mask. It is her father (Mazilier), who has come to chide her for her loose behaviour and bid her sternly to choose between the Marquis and her duty to himself. When she hesitates, he curses her.

In the third act, the Marquis loses heavily at the gaming table to his friend Bustamente (Elie). He is then invited to wager his mistress against all he has lost. He loses again, and Bustamente, masked like the Marquis, goes to claim Béatrix, who is unaware of what has happened. When she discovers his identity, she struggles to free herself from his embrace. But at that moment the Marquis bursts in and kills Bustamente in a fit of jealousy. Horror-struck, Béatrix makes her escape and returns to her native town of Ghent, where she learns that her sister is about to marry her former sweetheart, Bénédict. Still not recognised, she then discovers that her old father is dead. Overcome with remorse, she runs wildly up a rocky slope and throws herself over a precipice. This is the moment when she wakes to find herself in her old room and realises that it has all been a nightmare. Her father and Bénédict come for her, and, her doubts of the previous evening being now removed, she prepares for the wedding procession, ignoring the presence of the Marquis at the window.

La Jolie Fille de Gand was first given on 22 June 1842, and quite overshadowed Ambroise Thomas's new opera, *Le Guerillero*, with which it shared the programme. No expense had been spared on its production. It was one of the most costly ballets to have been mounted at the Opéra, its production costs amounting to 51,993.70 francs. Its three acts and nine scenes required no less than seven different sets, including a Kermess in Ghent, a brilliant ballroom ablaze with light, and a lush park.

Not only was this plot interesting, but it had a point and a moral; and for some, a story of real life was a welcome change from escapist themes of sylphides and wilis. Hippolyte Prévost complimented Saint-Georges and Albert for producing 'such a harmonious combination of dance, mime, painting and music'.[8] The ballet may have dragged in a few places, but there were many arresting passages. The ballroom scene contained several strikingly original dances, including a *cracovienne* danced by Sophie Dumilâtre and Auguste Mabille, and a comic dance for a three-legged man; but generally the emphasis lay on the dramatic action. One of its highlights was a realistically staged duel between the Marquis and Bustamente, which was enacted by Albert and Elie with great realism, and which Gautier praised as 'one of the best produced and most energetic ever to have been seen on the stage'.[9]

Adolphe Adam's music was deemed worthy of the composer of *Giselle*, even if it did not attain the spiritual depth of that earlier work. It was fresh and lively, and excellently orchestrated. Gautier found in it enough motifs for three comic operas, and commented that Adam's prodigality was all the more praiseworthy in that ballet music generally attracted little recognition for the work that its composition entailed. One of the score's loveliest passages accompanied the *pas de deux* by Carlotta Grisi and Lucien Petipa in the Kermess scene – the *pas de deux de carillon*, as it was known. It was danced to a rippling melody rung out by little bells that broke through the orchestration like 'a scale of silver filigree', reminding Gautier of those

Flemish clocks that had inspired one of Victor Hugo's most charming poems.[10]

Carlotta had at first been apprehensive when the rôle of Béatrix was offered to her. She felt she might be miscast in such a dramatic part, and for a time resisted on the grounds that the plot was not suitable for a ballet. But although, purely from a dramatic standpoint, Leroux might have seemed better qualified for the part, Carlotta enjoyed a great triumph. Gautier lovingly described the highlights of her performance. In the Kermess scene, he recounted how in her *pas de deux* with Petipa she seemed hardly to touch the ground, finishing as fresh as she had been at the outset. When the curtain rose on the second act, she was seen reclining on a sofa, a vision in a beautiful satin gown embroidered in gold, with fair ringlets falling about her shoulders and framing a complexion as delicate as a Bengal rose. When she rose, her gazelle-like step left the audience in no doubt as to her identity, and after an initial hesitation they broke into an enthusiastic ovation. But her great moment came during the ballroom scene, when she danced the *pas de Diane chasseresse*. 'She leaves the stage for a moment,' Gautier described,

> and soon afterwards reappears as Diana, wearing a tunic bespattered with silver stars, a crescent of precious stones in her hair, quiver slung over her shoulder and bow in hand. Shouts of admiration greet this graceful mythological vision. Béatrix imitates the poses of Diana of antiquity, pricking up her ears and conveying the impression of a frightened deer fleeing from her over leaves dampened with the dew. Then, curving her arm, smooth as alabaster, she draws a deadly arrow from her quiver, places it to her bow, and looses the string with a vibrating twang. Having killed the deer, she throws down her arms. No longer is she the huntress Diana, the cruel virgin running in the depths of great woods, followed by her white hounds; she has become the Diana of moonlight, the silvered smile of fine spring nights, the bearer of a divine kiss that finds its way, through leaves disturbed by passion, to the transparent brow of the sleeping Endymion...

No one had any doubt that Carlotta would dance her *pas* to perfection, for she is now the leading dancer in Europe. But there might have been fears that the dramatic and violent scenes of the narrative, conceived entirely in pantomime, would not suit her simple, poetic nature. She surpassed every expectation. Her demure shock at the sight of all the orgies and quarrels, her keen sensitivity, her energetic reaction in the duel scene, her horror, depicted with such realism and pathos, at her father's curse, left nothing to be desired.[11]

At one stage during the rehearsals, Albert had thought of confiding the part of the Marquis to Lucien Petipa, but he changed his mind because of Petipa's youth and took the rôle for himself, leaving Petipa to play Bénédict. His decision was justified, for the character of the haughty roué was much more suited to a man of Albert's mature years. Petipa's turn was to come, however, for he was to take over the part of the Marquis with considerable success when Albert retired. In 1843, during Carlotta's absence in London, another ballerina was seen in the rôle of Béatrix, Adèle Dumilâtre, who first played it on 4 October. Her interpretation was, throughout, somewhat gentler than that of Grisi, who danced with an indefatigable vigour and was found to mime somewhat in the Italian manner.

La Jolie Fille de Gand remained in the repertory for some six years. For its combination of spectacle, drama and brilliant dancing, it was a remarkable work which, by the very scale of its production, emphasised the prestige that the ballet in Paris had acquired in the wake of *Giselle*.

* * * * * * *

Auguste Vestris had now become very old. In the summer of 1842 he lost his wife, and as the year drew towards its close, on 5 December, his own life ebbed away in his home in the Rue des Trois Frères, on the slopes of Montmartre. A few days later a requiem mass was said for his soul at Notre Dame de Lorette, after which the funeral procession set off on its final journey to the Cemetery of Montmartre – perhaps a little too hurriedly, for the time-table was tight, there being a rich wedding to follow. Louise Fitzjames was one of the few ladies present, and at the graveside Jules Perrot stepped forward to give the funeral oration over the remains of his former teacher. Vestris, who had made his début under Louis XV, had been the last link with the Old Régime, but his death would not break the chain of tradition; for his art would now endure in his pupils, notably in Perrot and – no less important for the future – in Bournonville, who in Copenhagen was upholding the dignity of the male dancer at a time when the ballerina reigned too often alone in her supremacy.

* * * * * * *

In the soaring imagination of Théophile Gautier, the triumph of *Giselle* prompted ideas for a further collaboration, but this time he alone would be the progenitor. The germ from which the poet's new scenario emerged was a novel called *La Mille et deuxième Nuit*, which he had written around the beginning of 1840, although it would not see print until August 1842. This novel had existed only in manuscript when Gautier, with Saint-Georges, wrote the scenario for *Giselle,* and, inspired by the triumph of that ballet and its ballerina, Carlotta Grisi, conceived the idea of following it with another ballet, this time with a theme in the genre of the Arabian Nights. By then his relations with Carlotta and Jules Perrot had become very close, and in the months following the triumph of *Giselle* he placed his proposal before them.

Early in 1842, Jules Perrot left Paris for London, where he was engaged for the opera season at Her Majesty's Theatre as second *maître de ballet* to the ageing Deshayes. His first task there was to stage *Giselle* for Carlotta, who was contracted for the first few weeks of the season. Gautier could not resist the opportunity of crossing the Channel himself to attend the revival of the ballet that he looked upon as his brainchild. And there was a further inducement, for it would also provide him with the opportunity to share with Perrot an idea for another ballet that was taking shape in his mind. In fact he had already committed to paper a few ideas, which were eventually to be developed into the scenario of *La Péri.*[12]

Returning to Paris, he immersed himself in this new task, apparently expecting it to be produced as speedily as was *Giselle* and shown to the public during the course of 1842. But such hopes were to prove sanguine. This time the Opéra was not to be hurried, for two other projects, neither of which would be realised, then intervened. The first of these was a proposal to present a major *ballet d'action* by Mazilier, entitled *La Chevalière d'Eon* and based on the life of the celebrated eighteenth-century adventurer, secret agent and transvestite, for Pauline Leroux. However, this project was to be stillborn, not so much on account of that dancer's uncertain fitness, as through a dispute between its author, Leuven, and a certain Bernard Lopez, who claimed the plot to be based on one of his own works.[13]

Then another distraction surfaced, resulting from the return that summer of Fanny Elssler from her two-year-long American triumph. Notwith-standing the litigation that had resulted from the breach of her contract, the Opéra was still hoping to let bygones be bygones, and had been in negotiation with a person purporting to be acting on her behalf – probably her sister Thérèse – that culminated in a proposal for her to make a series of appearances at the Opéra in November and December. But Fanny Elssler then dropped a bombshell, refusing to acknowledge the authority of the person purporting to be her agent, and making it abundantly clear that she was not disposed to dance in Paris ever again. The litigation that ensued in the French courts, to which the Opéra had successfully resorted to recover damages and costs for breach of contract, had left too bitter a taste. It was probably little consolation to her that the Opéra too had suffered, Pillet now finding himself with no novelties to offer for the rest of the winter, since Halévy's new opera

Charles VI would not be ready until March and there was no possibility of staging a new ballet until May at the very earliest.

Gautier had thus been forced to accept a much longer period of gestation than he had originally counted on, and it was not until December 1842 that he finished work on preparing a draft scenario in a form that would enable rehearsals to begin. He was clearly affronted by the delay, but now at last there was some movement towards realising the project on stage. He must have long since abandoned any hope, if ever hope there had been, of inviting Jules Perrot to stage the work, and philosophically accepted that the task of producing it must now devolve on Jean Coralli, who, while not a creative genius of Perrot's stature, had nonetheless made a real contribution in fashioning *Giselle* into such a seamless production

The first specific mention of *La Péri* appeared in the *Coureur des spectacles* on 7 December 1842. The following month, in the *Presse* of 16 January 1843, Gautier revealed that he was the author and that its subject was 'taken from the legends of the Orient'. Later, when he came to write his notice on the ballet, he recalled how the idea had first come to him on a grey, wet, blustery day, when he found himself daydreaming of the romanticised East that he liked to imagine was his spiritual home, and began to compose some verses. Then, reflecting that poetry was the language of the Gods and, to the despair of publishers, seemed to be read by the Gods alone, he threw the stanzas he had written into the waste-paper basket and started afresh, this time shaping his idea as a ballet scenario, dedicated to the feet of his beloved Carlotta. It had then passed through several stages of revision from his first very rough draft to a longer version he had discussed with Perrot, and eventually to the final version on which rehearsals had begun, not to mention the few perfecting touches added at the last minute.

In its final form, the ballet opened in the luxuriously appointed harem belonging to the hero, Achmet, whose women are discovered, on curtain-rise, beautifying themselves under the eye of the chief eunuch Roucem (Barrez). A slave-dealer (E. Coralli) comes to offer for sale four European women of great beauty. After the price has been bargained over and agreed, Achmet (Petipa) enters in a mood of utter boredom. Roucem presents the newly purchased slaves, who hail from Spain, Germany, Scotland and France, and each of them performs a dance from her own country. But Achmet, who has a poetic soul and yearns for celestial rather than terrestrial love, is unmoved. He dismisses the women, and, reclining on a divan, takes up his opium pipe. In his dream he finds himself by a radiant oasis, where those fairy-like creatures, the peris, are gathered about their queen (Grisi). Achmet sleeps on until he is awakened by a kiss and, to his utter delight, finds himself in the presence of the ideal beauty of his dreams. He pursues her, and she gives him, as a talisman, the star that shines on her forehead, by which, on kissing it, he can summon her at will. The peris then vanish and Achmet falls into a deep trance, from which Roucem awakens him. He begins to tell Roucem of his vision, but, on observing Roucem's look of disbelief, begins to wonder whether it was no more than a dream. His favourite among his harem, Nourmahal (D. Marquet), then tries to arouse his passion, and he seems about to yield when the Peri appears before him again, snatching from his hand the handkerchief Nourmahal has just given him, and replacing it with a magic bouquet. His memory of the Peri then returns, and he places the star she has given him to his lips. The Peri reappears, but chides him for being unworthy of her love and vanishes, taking the bouquet with her. Nourmahal, who has observed this scene, gives way to tears, but Achmet repulses her. Delighting in her triumph, the Peri then returns to restore the bouquet to him, while Nourmahal leaves, swearing to be avenged.

The second act opens in Achmet's palace, overlooking the domes, turrets and minarets of Cairo, with the pyramids of Giza in the far distance. The peris flutter about the palace, while their queen peers through a window as if seeking Achmet. She is urged by one of her companions to renounce her foolish love for a mortal who is merely fascinated by her magic powers. At that moment a white-clad figure, a fugitive slave-girl, Leila, is seen being hotly pursued by a band of armed men. She reaches the terrace only to be felled by a gunshot. The Peri now decides to enter the dead slave's body to test Achmet's love. When Achmet and Roucem find her, she explains that her error lay in not returning the love of her master, the Pasha, and begs Achmet to take her under his protection. Fearful of the Peri's jealousy, Achmet treats Leila (as he believes her to be) with reserve, but gradually warms to her and is finally captivated when, at a festival in his honour, she performs the renowned dance of the bee. Nourmahal, consumed with jealousy, vows to be avenged, but her attempts to stab first Achmet and then Leila are parried. News is then brought that the Pasha is on his way with his guards to reclaim his fugitive slave and put her to death; and amid the general confusion, Roucem is seen conducting Leila to an underground passage.

The scene changes to a simple prison cell, where Achmet is languishing as a prisoner of the Pasha. In the background is a plain wall with a single barred window. As he mournfully contemplates his future, the wall opens to reveal the Peri. She asks him to give up Leila and share eternal happiness with her. He refuses, and she vanishes in a feigned show of pique. The Pasha then enters to give Achmet one last chance to surrender Leila to him; on Achmet's refusal, he orders his men to cast him from the window to be impaled on the sharp hooks attached to the wall outside.

As Achmet disappears, the walls vanish to reveal a sky of soft clouds on which the peris are gathered. The clouds then part to reveal Paradise, towards which Achmet is seen ascending, hand in hand with the Peri.

At the end of 1842, when the decision to produce *La Péri* was made, Carlotta had been passing through a difficult period and attracting a few unfavourable notices, which some cynics might have suspected had been planted to strengthen the Opéra's bargaining power in the discussions that were shortly to open to agree terms for the renewal of her engagement. Charles Maurice of the *Coureur des spectacles*, who had taken the side of Pauline Leroux when the rôle of Béatrix in *La Jolie Fille de Gand* was given to Carlotta, may not have been above suspicion; for while Gautier, who was admittedly partial, was lyrically praising 'the boldness of her *pointes renversées* and dangerous steps which no other dancer performs as she does',[14] Maurice was chiding her for a certain negligence that he claimed had crept into her style and technique. 'Her head is no longer well placed,' he wrote, 'it moves about in every direction with no regard to the tempo... Mlle Grisi is at present dancing with her shoulders, she is making very ungraceful efforts with her hips, her insteps are weak, and the whole of the upper part of her body tends to be bent towards the footlights'.[15] In addition, he found cause for criticism in her miming, and said that her interpretation in *La Jolie Fille de Gand* had lacked interest.

A day or two after these strictures were published, it was announced that Carlotta was indisposed; but a notice of *Giselle* that found its way into a London theatrical paper, the *Era*, spoke in much the same strain:

> The public begin to show that they have had enough of this ballet, which, after all, contains but one or two pretty *pas*. These steps Carlotta Grisi danced far better some time since than now, although she does not give them amiss. Far from improving as a mime, La Carlotta is losing that little air of ingenuity [*sic*] which was once so attractive. She plays at present on the stage as if she were playing in her own apartment before her private friends, chattering and laughing aloud, oftentimes in the most pathetic moments. The public is very indulgent; for if Carlotta is applauded, it is simply because she is classed *la première danseuse* of the Opéra. In the country of the blind (says the proverb), one-eyed women are queens.[16]

The Opéra, however, thought highly enough of Carlotta to engage her for a further three years from 1 January 1844, increasing her salary to 20,000 francs a year, with seven guaranteed bonuses of 142 francs each month. The negotiations leading up to this new contract were not without difficulty, and may have had a hampering effect on the rehearsals of *La Péri*. But once Carlotta's new contract was signed at the end of May, all went smoothly, and on 17 July 1843, the bills outside the Opéra announced that the first performance would be given that evening.

The title of the new ballet had been finally settled only at the last minute; indeed, most of that morning's papers referred to it as *Léila, ou la Péri*. When the suggestion had been first made that it should simply be called *La Péri*, M. de Kératry, who chaired the Committee for the Royal Theatres, objected. It then appeared that he had been under the misunderstanding that the title was *La Pairie*, and had been shocked at the thought of the peerage being ridiculed in a ballet. When Pillet pointed out his error, Kératry persisted in his objection, now suggesting that the public might be misled by the similarity in the pronunciation of the two words. Several other committee members supported him, fearing that it would inspire a crop of frivolous puns in the opposition press, and it required a strong protest from Gautier to restore what he considered was the right title.

Whether or not Carlotta's powers had really been waning, she appeared in this new ballet at the very peak of her form. Indeed, Théophile Gautier and the choreographer, Jean Coralli, had provided her with a rôle that suited her to perfection and contained two striking *pas*: the *pas du songe* of the first act, and in the second, the *pas de l'abeille*. The *pas du songe*, in which the Peri appears to Achmet in his opium dream, was, in Gautier's words,

> a real triumph for Carlotta. When she appeared in that luminous glow with her childlike smile, her eyes shining with astonishment and delight, posing like a bird trying to alight but carried away by its wings, the whole house broke into unanimous cheering. And what a wonderful dance it is! How I should love to see it danced by real peris and fairies! You just have to see her skimming the ground without touching it; she is like a rose petal wafted by the breeze, and yet what nerves of steel are enclosed in her frail legs, what strength there is in her feet, which are so small that they would be the envy of the most daintily shod lady of Seville! And you have to see her alighting on the tip of her slender toe like an arrow piercing the ground with its barb.
>
> Carlotta Grisi's dancing is both correct and daring; it has a very special character, resembling neither Taglioni's nor Elssler's. Every pose and movement is stamped with the seal of originality. It is wonderful to be novel in an art that is so limited! In this *pas* there is a certain fall that will soon become as famous as those of Niagara. The audience waits for it with bated breath. At the moment when the vision is about to end, the Peri lets herself fall from a cloud into the arms of her lover. If it were no more than an acrobatic feat, we would not mention it, but this dangerous flight forms a group that is full of grace and charm, giving the impression of a dove's

53 Therese Elssler as Mab in *La Gipsy*.

54 Fanny and Therese Elssler in their *pas de deux* in *La Gipsy*.

55   Georges Elie and Pauline Leroux in the seduction scene in Act III of *Le Diable amoureux*.

56 Pauline Leroux in *Le Diable amoureux*.

57   Pauline Leroux as Miranda in *La Tentation*. Black-and-white engraving from a portrait, the present whereabouts of which is unknown.

58   The ballet company of the Opéra, c. 1841, a section of a longer panoramic sequence of caricatures by Benjamin, depicting actors, singers and dancers of that time and entitled *Chemin de la Postérité*. Taglioni (cruelly named "Taglionifini") is seen departing for St Petersburg while, immediately to her left, Fanny Elssler is shown escaping in another direction, her leg pointing to New York on the globe. Carlotta Grisi, left in possession of the vacant throne, is shown holding a couple of money bags over her head. The Dumilâtre sisters also appear: Sophie, faintly in the rear, and Adèle to her right. The unidentified dancer to their left may be Pauline Leroux. The male dancer leading the battalion of *petits rats* is Lucien Petipa, wearing his costume as Albrecht in *Giselle*.

59 Carlotta Grisi as Giselle. Engraving from a portrait by A.E.Chalon.

60 *Giselle*, Act I: Carlotta Grisi and Lucien Petipa in the first *pas de deux* of the lovers.

61 Giselle crowned as queen of the vintage.

62 *Giselle*, Act I: The entrance of the hunting party (note the road by which the party enters to the left).

63 The death of Giselle.

64 *Giselle,* Act II: Giselle, now a wili, appears to Albrecht in the forest.

65 Albrecht is left bereft before Giselle's tomb.

66 *Giselle*, Act I. Caricatures by Lorentz, from the *Musée Philipon*, 9th issue.

67 *Giselle*, Act II. Caricatures by Lorentz, from the *Musée Philipon*, 9th issue.

68 Nathalie Fitzjames and Auguste Mabille in the inserted *pas de deux* in *Giselle*, Act I.

69 Carlotta Grisi in the *pas de l'abeille* in *La Péri*, Act II, Scene I.

70 *La Péri*, scene from Act I: the Peri (Grisi) appearing to Achmet (Petipa), with Nourmahal (D.Marquet) and Roucem (Elie). Lithograph from a drawing by Victor Dollet.

71 *La Péri*, scene from Act II: Nourmahal (D.Marquet) surprising Achmet (Petipa) and Leila (Grisi). Lithograph from a drawing by A.Mouilleron.

72 *Lady Henriette*, Act II. Henri Desplaces and Adèle Dumilâtre in a *pas de deux*, with Lyonnel
(Petipa) about to interrupt. Lithograph from a drawing by C. Deshays.

73 *Paquita*, two scenes from Act II, Scene I, with the gypsy chief (Georges Elie), Paquita (Carlotta Grisi) and Lucien (Petipa). Lithograph by Henry Em.

74 *Le Diable à quatre*.

75 *Le Diable à quatre*. Act II, Scene II, the
dancing lesson with Lucien Petipa, Eugène
Coralli and Carlotta Grisi.

76 Act II, Scene I: Mazourki (Mazilier)
ordering his supposed wife (Maria) to kiss
the cheek which she has struck.

77 *Ozaï*. Act I, Ozaï (Plunkett) dancing on the island before French sailors and Bougainville (Elie). Engraving from a drawing by Victor Coindre.

78 *Ozaï*, Act II, Scene I, showing Ozaï on board the ship taking her to France, with Bougainville (Elie) and Surville (Desplaces).

feather drifting down in the air rather than a human body hurtling from a platform.[17]

Hippolyte Prévost was a little more precise in his description of this *pas*. In it, he recorded,

> Carlotta attempted some novel poses and some novel *pirouettes sur les pointes*, balancings, *jetés*, *enlacements*, and groups that were most wonderfully effective. But the unexpected, astonishing, extraordinary thing that crowns this *pas*, which is so striking from every point of view, is when Carlotta hurls herself from a six-feet-high platform, on which are seated the celestial court of the Queen of the Peris, and pirouetting on herself, falls into Petipa's arms without allowing this *tour de force*... in any way to disturb the calculated resolution and the purity of line of the few bars of dancing that complete this... dangerous jump.[18]

The Parisian public soon showed themselves to be very exacting with regard to the performance of Carlotta's famous leap into Petipa's arms. Once, when she failed to perform it properly, they insisted on her repeating it three times before they would condescend to applaud her. Compare this with the reaction of a London audience, who begged her not to risk repeating it after a similar mistiming at Drury Lane in the autumn, and gave her three hearty cheers when she fearlessly did it again. Not that the English were always so considerate: one of Queen Victoria's subjects was convinced that the ballet would eventually prove fatal to her, and on that premise did not miss a performance at the Opéra so as to be present at her end![19]

The *pas de l'abeille* was no less original. This was the dance that the slave girl Leila performs before Achmet in the second act. The idea behind it originated with Gautier, who claimed to have heard of such a dance being performed in Egypt.[20] It opened with the Peri plucking a rose and disturbing a bee. She tries in vain to shake it off with her handkerchief, but the angry insect buzzes around her and eventually seeks refuge in her dress. In her struggle to rid herself of the intruder, the Peri casts off first her embroidered tunic, then her scarf, and finally her skirt, before seeking refuge beneath her master's cloak.

Carlotta's femininity could not have been better displayed than in this brilliantly original dance. As Gautier wrote,

> I wish you could see for yourself the embarrassed modesty with which Carlotta removes her long white veil; the way in which she poses as she kneels beneath its transparent folds, like the Venus of antiquity smiling from her pearly shell; the childlike fright that seizes her when the angry bee emerges from the flower, and all the hope and the anguish, and the

changing fortunes of the struggle that she conveys as tunic and scarf, and the skirt which the bee has tried to penetrate, are rapidly discarded right and left and vanish in the whirl of the dance, before she drops at Achmet's feet, breathless, exhausted, smiling through her fear, and desiring a kiss far more than the golden sequins that her master's hand places on the brow and the breast of his slave-girl.[21]

Fundamentally, it was a sensual dance, but the delicacy with which Carlotta performed it stilled any protests. 'That,' wrote Janin admiringly, 'is how one should undress in the middle of the stage – not in an unpleasant and unseemly way, with fat red hands like the pretty wenches of the Théâtre des Variétés (what insect is biting them?), but cleverly and vivaciously, and with such grace in that luminous distance.'[22] If there was a flaw in the performance of this dance, it lay in Carlotta's lack of dramatic ability – a shortcoming that she seemed to acknowledge when shortly afterwards she substituted for this *pas* a sort of Spanish dance.

The ballet, with its charming score by Burgmüller, was designed specifically as a vehicle for Carlotta and would remain one of her favourite works. Later, from March 1846, it was to be given, more often than not, in a shortened version with the second act completely cut; but as the interest of the ballet was mainly concentrated in the first act, this did not much matter. The best of the choreography was preserved, including the delightful use of pupils from the School of Dance in the scene in the kingdom of the peris, an innovation that Pillet himself was said to have proposed. And no one mourned the cutting of the scene where the fugitive slave girl is shot, which had caused Janin to exclaim in horror: 'What! A murder in the middle of a ballet! A poor girl shot in the heart! Blood, murder, pure blood at the Opera! What would you have thought of that, Vestris!'[23]

NOTES

1. Both ballets were performed twenty-six times in the year of their creation, but *Giselle* achieved this in 6 months and 2 days, whereas *La Sylphide* took 9 months and 20 days to reach that mark.
2. Montmorency, 102–03. Letter dated 5 January 1842.
3. Montmorency, 106–07. Letter dated 11 January 1842.
4. Arch. Nat., AJ[13] 194. Grisi to Pillet, 21 January 1842.
5. Achille Boucher, the wealthy *abonné* of one of the ground-floor boxes, features in that wonderful collection of Opéra gossip, *Les Cancans de l'Opéra*. The identification by the editor of La Baume's letters as a reference to the singer Lucien Bouché is incorrect.
6. Montmorency, 127. La Baume to Aguado, 3 April 1842.
7. *Victorine, ou la Nuit porte conseil*, drama in 5 acts by Dumersan, Gabriel and Dupeuty, f.p. Th. de la Porte-Saint-Martin, 21 April 1831.
8. *Moniteur*, 29 June 1842.
9. *Presse*, 2 July 1842.

10. No. XVIII in *Les Rayons et les Ombres*, in which the poet imagines the carillon as a Spanish dancer. This poem was written in August 1837, when Fanny Elssler's *Cachucha* was still a novelty and the rage of Paris.

11. *Presse*, 2 July 1842. Guest, *Gautier*, 108, 111.

12. Gautier, *Correspondence général*, I; Fr. ed., 130, 133.

13. *Courrier des théâtres*, 18 and 23 February and 2 March 1842. The dispute was reported to have been settled in Leuven's favour by the Committee of Authors, but the uncertainty surrounding Leroux's fitness was probably the final straw.

14. *Presse*, 16 January 1843.

15. *Coureur des spectacles*, 1 February 1843.

16. *Era*, 11 June 1843.

17. *Presse*, 25 July 1843. Guest, *Gautier*, 118–9; Fr. ed., 140–1.

18. *Moniteur*, 24 July 1843.

19. A similar leap was incorporated in Bernardo Vestris's *Elda* (f.p. La Scala, Milan, 26 December 1843) and performed by Lucile Grahn. *(Coureur des spectacles*, 12 January 1844.)

20. This dance, which was performed by courtesans for the erotic edification of their clients, was said to have been banned by Mohammed Ali.

21. *Presse*. 25 July 1843. Guest, *Gautier*, 119–20.

22. *Journal des débats*, 19 July 1843.

23. *Journal des débats*, 19 July 1843.

22

Coping with the Absence of Carlotta

Looking forward to 1844, Léon Pillet now found himself in a quandary. Under the *Cahier des Charges* that set out the conditions of his management, he was obliged to replenish the repertory with a specified number of new works each year.[1] There was now little prospect of his being able to present his star ballerina, Carlotta Grisi, in a new ballet before the autumn; for, being contracted to dance in London during the first half of its opera season, she would be away until May. In the meantime, therefore, he would be left with three ballerinas, all very talented but, in the eyes of the public, of considerably lesser magnitude – Pauline Leroux, whose fitness was now much in doubt; Maria; and the still inexperienced Adèle Dumilâtre.

By far the most aspiring of these three, as well as being the youngest, was the twenty-one-year-old Adèle Dumilâtre, who was not only very ambitious but possessed the indisputable advantage of enjoying influential protection. Her father, an actor of the Comédie-Française, had wanted her to become a tragedienne, but her dance teacher, Charles Petit, persuaded him that her gifts were too promising to be wasted. So, in due time, she followed in the footsteps of her elder sister Sophie and, from the School of Dance, entered the ranks of the Opéra, becoming something of a white hope. She soon began to make her mark. After being noticed in a number of minor parts, she advanced to the fore with surprising rapidity. In 1841, when still only eighteen, she was allowed to dance the title-rôle of *La Sylphide*; a few weeks later she created the part of the Queen of the Wilis in *Giselle*, and the following year was understudying Grisi in the part of Béatrix in *La Jolie Fille de Gand*. Such early success and the adulation that accompanied it may have gone to her head, to judge from an observation by Jacques Arago in his *Mémoires d'un petit banc de l'Opéra*:

> If I knew [he wrote] why the Mlles Dumilâtre, who used to be so good-natured, now barely nod to their saddened comrades, I would willingly pass it on, for pride does not sit well with merit. I am told that they owe this unworthy kind of pride to their relationship with the ruler of the place. This is not only wrong of them, but ridiculous, and their father, who so warmly applauds them evening after evening, ought to be hissing them for such a show of bad taste.[2]

When Saint-Georges submitted a scenario for a new three-act ballet, probably some time in the late summer of 1843, Pillet's first thought was to cast Adèle Dumilâtre in the leading rôle; but after a while he began to have doubts as to whether she was yet ready to develop a character in pantomime throughout the course of three acts. Learning of these doubts, Edouard Monnais, the Royal Commissioner, whose duty it was to supervise the expenditure of the subsidy, summoned Pillet to his office. Pillet explained that he was becoming reluctant to incur the heavy outlay that the production of this new ballet would entail with a dancer of Dumilâtre's standing in the leading rôle. Monnais did not insist, but a few days later a gentleman was shown into Pillet's office, where he offered the sum of 100,000 francs conditional on the ballet being produced for Dumilâtre with all possible speed.

Saint-Georges had found the idea for this new ballet in a play, produced some years before at the Théâtre des Variétés, entitled *La Comtesse d'Egmont*[3] – sensing perhaps an opportunity that it might arouse sentimental memories of the popular actress Jenny Colon, who had given such a delightful performance as its heroine, and had not long since died at the height of her career. However, in the process of converting the book into a ballet libretto, and being something of an Anglophile, he changed the setting from the Versailles of Louis XV's regency to Windsor under Queen Anne. This would entail a change of title, and up to a few days before the ballet's first performance there was some confusion as to what it was to be called. An early manuscript of the scenario bore the title *Un Caprice de Lady Henriette*; three weeks before the première it was being announced simply as *Un Caprice*; a fortnight later it was being referred to as *Le Marché aux servants*; but when it was finally offered to the public, it had become, quite simply, *Lady Henriette*.

The heroine of the ballet, Lady Henriette (A. Dumilâtre), is a lady-in-waiting at the court of Queen Anne, and the ballet opens in her boudoir in Windsor Castle, where she is being courted by her dull but worthy beau Sir Tristan Crakfort (Elie). She is bored to distraction, but the sound of a procession outside reminds her that it is the day of the servants' market in Greenwich, and on an impulse she invites some of the marchers into her apartment to entertain her with their dances. After they have left, on a sudden whim she decides to go to the market herself, taking as companion her friend Nancy (Maria) and with Sir Tristan as their escort. The scene then moves to Greenwich, where they arrive to find the festivities in full swing and a group of young women gathering for the market at which they hope to find employment. Among those seeking servants are Lyonnel (Petipa) and his farmer friend John (Barrez), who have come with their respective fiancées, Mina (S. Dumilâtre) and Alison (Emarot). As the women form in line to be inspected, Henriette and Nancy attract the attention of the two men, who assume they are seeking employment and make bids for them. To Sir Tristan's horror, Henriette and Nancy accept the offers without a thought for the consequences. But the joke has gone too far, for when they attempt to leave, the crowd will not permit it and the two ladies are forced to go with their new masters, leaving the horrified Sir Tristan behind. The scene then moves to Lyonnel's farm, where the two men discover that the women whom they thought they had engaged as servants are hopelessly inept and inexperienced. But happily for the two ladies, help is at hand, and in the middle of the night they hear a tap on their window. It is Sir Tristan come to rescue them. When Lyonnel, who has fallen in love with Henriette, discovers they have fled, he is plunged into despair; he tears up his marriage contract with Mina and decides to take up a new life as a soldier.

The second act opens in Windsor Park. There enters a company of soldiers, among whom is Lyonnel, who has been followed by his friends, John and Alison. The Queen's hunting party then rides by. Among them is Henriette, who, feeling tired, begs to be excused. She lies down to rest on a grassy bank, where she is discovered by Sir Tristan, who declares his love and is rejected. She then falls asleep, and wakes to find, to her astonishment, Lyonnel at her side. She pretends not to recognise him, but cannot maintain her pretence when John and Alison appear too. Henriette and Nancy make a hurried departure. Shots are then heard, and the Queen's horse appears, galloping out of control, with Her Majesty helpless in the saddle. Lyonnel manages to stop and calm the animal, and the grateful monarch appoints him a captain on the spot and gives him a ring by which he can summon her if ever he is in need of help. Lyonnel, who is desperate to find Henriette, then begs the Queen to ask her ladies to unmask. But Henriette is not among them. The scene now changes to a room in the Castle, where preparations are in progress for a mythological ballet. Tristan, in his costume as Jupiter, is mocked by the maids of honour, who blindfold and mercilessly tease him. The act then closes with the ballet, in which the Queen appears as Juno. Among the dances is a love scene between Venus, played by Lady Henriette, and a pursuing shepherd, at which point Lyonnel, who has been appointed captain of the Queen's guard, comes running on to the stage and takes Henriette in his arms. As she faints from the shock, he is seized and led away under arrest.

The third act opens in Henriette's boudoir, where she is bitterly regretting her imprudence in going to the fair. Lionel, having evaded his guards, then bursts in to beseech her to have pity on him. She is touched, but her pride gets the better of her feelings and she summons the guards to arrest him. At this point Lyonnel's mind gives way, and he rushes to the window with the intention of throwing himself out, but is restrained. The action then moves to Bedlam, where he is to be confined as a lunatic. Here Sir Tristan arrives to announce a royal visit; but being left on his own, finds himself set upon by some of the inmates, who deprive him of his uniform, wig and sword before he is rescued. The Queen then arrives, accompanied by her ladies. Among them is Henriette, who, at the sight of Lionel, is consumed with guilt and admits to being the cause of his unhappy condition. The asylum's doctor then intervenes to propose a plan that might restore the hero's sanity, and in the final scene Lyonnel has been taken back to his farm, where the clock is put back to the time of the dinner on the evening of the fair. Here, the entrance of a smiling Henriette wearing her simple peasant dress restores his memory; and on the lovers being united, the cottage walls vanish to lead into a grand apotheosis in which they receive the blessing of their sovereign.

The plot may have appeared more suited to a drama than to a ballet, but Saint-Georges was a writer of considerable experience of the theatre and not above stretching the dramatic powers of the performers. And in the character of Lady Henriette this seems to have been his intention, for he presented the young ballerina who was to play her with a real challenge – to display a personality far from that of the conventionally sweet heroine: a character who is irresponsibly headstrong and whose sympathy for the hero is only belatedly awakened by a sense of guilt.

Adèle Dumilâtre's success in creating the character was to be fully appreciated by one of the most experienced of theatre critics, Hippolyte Lucas, who described her performance appreciatively, although not uncritically, in the *Moniteur*:

Thanks to her intelligence and in particular her feminine instinct, Mlle Dumilâtre has understood full well the flaw in Henriette's character that up to the very end makes her remain utterly indifferent to Lyonnel's devotion... In some of her scenes with Lyonnel she tries to soften this with a few gestures of pity and interest, but – contrary to the intention of the scenario – those fleeting expressions of sensitivity and sympathy generally passed unnoticed, particularly at the first performance, and since those feelings were only lightly stressed, they did little to relieve the unfortunate impression produced by the persistent hardness of a young girl of twenty.

Mlle Adèle Dumilâtre, whom we have so often applauded, even alongside Carlotta Grisi, has for the first time created the principal rôle in a ballet. That of Lady Henriette does her the greatest honour. A few imperfections were observed in her miming on the first night, particularly when she was expressing spite, pride and disdain, and her movements had perhaps not become fully integrated. But she was more appreciated on the second night.[4]

For Adèle Dumilâtre the ballet was her first important creation, and while it was evident that she found the complex nature of the heroine's character daunting at the first performance, she soon took its measure. Of the many tributes she received from the critics, the one she no doubt appreciated most must have been that of Théophile Gautier. Her classic profile and limpid blue eyes worked their charm on him, and his thoughts strayed from Saint-Georges's prosaic plot to dreams of Northern myths, seeing her in his imagination as an elf in the Harz mountains or a valkyrie in Odin's Valhalla. But jolting himself back to reality, he noted her 'remarkable elegance and distinction', her 'charming coquetry and affected artlessness' when she was masquerading as a servant girl, and 'the nobility of attitude, the aerial lightness and the modest grace' which characterised her dancing throughout.[5]

She could hardly have been better supported in this exhausting three-act piece, which incidentally required the services of nearly a hundred dancers and supernumeraries, than by those two experienced performers, Lucien Petipa and Maria, who brought their acting skills to bear respectively on the rôles of Lyonnel and Henriette's companion, Nancy. The former had no peer as a male dancer, with his impeccable classical technique allied to a strong power of expression as a mime. His only fault, in the eyes of some, was an inclination to overact, which was noticed by one critic in the passage when Lyonnel loses his reason. As for Maria, she gave a sparkling portrayal, finding a powerful foil in Jean-Baptiste Barrez, who portrayed John Plumkett as a ruddy-faced, muscular farmer whose cheeks, in the words of Lucas, 'seemed made to be slapped by the back of [her] pretty little hand.'

The Bedlam scene offered an opportunity to another dancer with a talent for comedy, Eugène Coralli, the ballet-master's son, who had the audience in fits of laughter at his portrayal of a 'dansomane' in the entertaining *divertissement* at the point when the unfortunate Sir Tristan finds himself surrounded by the inmates of the asylum. This dance, which was apparently largely improvised, was one of the ballet's highlights. Young Coralli, wrote Lucas, had 'found himself at last. Such was the vivacity of his steps and his pantomime that the rôle of the dansomane is an object lesson for scenarists in what can be extracted from the unexpected.'[6]

Pillet's decision to commission three composers to provide the music, each given responsibility for a single act, was fundamentally flawed, but according to one critic[7] had been prompted by the last-minute rush to present the public with a new ballet. This may explain why P.S. of the *Revue et Gazette musicale* found that Burgmüller's orchestration for the second act 'left much to be desired'[8]. Generally, however, the three contributions were well received. Apart from Burgmüller, who was known for his delightful waltz inserted into the first act of *Giselle* and his more recently acclaimed score for *La Péri*, neither of the other two musicians had had their music played before at the Opéra.

For the sensitive Deldevez, who had been allotted the last act, the opportunity was particularly daunting, so conscious was he that his entire musical future might depend on it. Probably because of the last-minute rush to get the work on stage, the tradition of honouring a composer with the opportunity of playing his score to the renowned Opéra orchestra was, in his case, omitted – an oversight for which he never forgave the conductor, Habeneck, who seems to have been under the weather with a cold, for he was absent at the first performance a few days later. However, taking this oversight as a reflection on his music, Deldevez so lost his confidence that he could not face the ordeal of attending the first performance. Instead, he spent several hours moodily pacing the boulevard, returning to the Opéra only when the public was coming out. But having gloomily feared a failure, he was now to find relief in hearing several people humming his melodies. In fact, he had no need to worry: in future years this sensitive musician was to be offered the opportunity to compose the music for three more ballets at the Opéra: *Eucharis, Paquita* and *Vert-Vert*.

Friedrich von Flotow, on the other hand, was made of sterner stuff. Undeterred by the small stir created by his own contribution – and to the disgust of Deldevez, who thought his action unethical – he shortly afterwards collaborated with Saint-Georges in composing an opera based on the plot of the ballet that was to achieve widespread renown. This was *Martha*,[9] and in his later days he was amused to reflect that it might never have been conceived but for the ambition of Adèle Dumilâtre.

* * * * * * *

Experiment, it seemed, was now Pillet's watchword, and a few weeks later, on 25 March 1844, Maria was given the distinction of dancing the polka on the stage of the Opéra for the first time. Her partner was the dansomane of *Lady Henriette*, Eugène Coralli. That season the polka had burst upon Paris, where it had rapidly become the rage in the ballrooms and the public dance halls and gardens; and after its first showing at the Opéra, for which Burgmüller wrote a lively accompaniment, it was quickly to be adopted by musicians and choreographers in their ballets.

Maria was an ideal choice for this lively new dance. Over the years, she had developed into a popular and useful member of the company, with the ability and the personality to sustain principal rôles. After her success as Lise in *La Fille mal gardée*, she had played leading parts in *La Somnambule, Le Diable amoureux* and *La Tarentule*. When Milon's *Les Noces de Gamache*[10] was revived on 20 January 1841, it was she who was cast in Chevigny's old rôle of Quitterie. She had also danced as guest artist in Vienna with some success in 1839, and only recently had returned from a triumphant visit to Hamburg. She had travelled there by sea from Le Havre, suffering so much from seasickness that, in disembarking, she missed her footing on the gangplank and fell into the water. She was happily rescued with no ill effects, and proceeded to dance magnificently in Bournonville's *Napoli*[11] and *The Toreador*.[12] One evening the audience continued to call for her so long after she had returned to her dressing-room to change that she had to come before the curtain for a final call in her travelling dress. Her unusually deep curtsey delighted the public, who saw it as a mark of becoming humility, little realising that she was merely trying to conceal the fact that her dress had shrunk to an embarrassing degree after its soaking! Another of her experiences in Germany, which she recounted afterwards with relish, took place at a dinner party, at which a learned German doctor, soberly dressed in black, delivered no fewer than two hundred verses in her honour, not one word of which she understood.

* * * * * * *

Two days after the polka had been introduced to the Opéra stage, Pillet launched another experiment. Lola Montez had been recommended to him by two literary giants, Alexandre Dumas and Méry, and when the all-powerful Mme Stoltz added her approval, the matter was as good as sealed. So, on 27 March 1844, the bills announced that on that evening she would perform two Spanish dances, *L'Ollia* and *Las Boleras de Cadiz*, in the ball scene of Mozart's *Don Juan*.

Spanish dancing had been popular in Paris for a number of years, but Pillet was soon to discover his error in engaging Lola Montez. She had been tolerably well received when she made a single appearance at Her Majesty's Theatre in London the summer before, but her engagement there had been cancelled for fear of scandal when she was accused of being an impostor. It was true that she was born in the army barracks at Limerick, where her father was serving as a junior officer, and that she had somehow and somewhere acquired a fair knowledge of Spanish dancing could not be denied. Her early years were veiled in mystery, and her recent past had earned her a measure of notoriety, which was little compared with what the future held in store for her, but still enough to sow doubt as to her worth as an artist.

Before facing the Paris public, she prudently took a few lessons from

Barrez, but these proved to be of little value in the scandalous circumstances of her début. Eyewitnesses differed in describing the object that she suddenly flung at the audience; many thought she had accompanied this action with a gesture of contempt, and so hissed her for such a breach of good manners. Was it a shoe, or a garter, or an even more intimate item of attire? Was it an unforgivable show of temper, or did she impulsively cast off a shoe that had come untied or a garter that had slipped? It seems, in fact, to have been a shoe, for one of her biographers recorded that a young man of fashion, Comte Alfred de Bellemont, one of the occupants of the stage box known as the *loge infernale*, seized it and kept it as a trophy.

Whatever it was, the Opéra could not tolerate such a scandal, and two days later, when she was to have made her second appearance, slips of paper were pasted over her name on the bills. This was no great loss to lovers of the dance. For once, even the usually kind-hearted Gautier was severe. Spain and all things Spanish were especially close to his heart, but he was sufficiently knowledgeable to see through Lola Montez. 'There is nothing Andalusian about Mlle Lola Montez,' he wrote of her,

> except a pair of magnificent dark eyes. She '*habla*' very mediocre Spanish, and speaks hardly any French and only passable English. So from what country does she really come? That is the question. We can say that Mlle Lola has tiny feet and pretty legs, but as for the way she uses them, that is quite another matter... Mlle Lola Montez is much inferior to Dolores Serral, who at least has the advantage of being authentic, and who makes up for her imperfections as a dancer by a sensual abandon, a passion, a fire, and a rhythmical precision that command admiration.[13]

It could hardly be said that Lola Montez lacked passion. During her brief passage at the Opéra she became infatuated with Lucien Petipa's younger brother, Jean-Claude, who was also a dancer but one of minimal achievement. In fact, in the course of his career, it was a single incident involving Lola that brought him very briefly to public notice in the columns of the *Coureur des spectacles*. Since there is no other evidence to suggest an association with the fiery Lola, the report can only be given without comment:

> Let the terrible whip of Mlle Lola Montez do what it will to prevent us performing out duty, we are going to reveal what recently took place at the dance studio where that young woman is working to recover her form so as to appear again before the public. The dancers were at class when there appeared M. Jean Petipa, the brother of our dancer. Seized with an indescribable outburst of rage, Mlle Lola Montez threw herself at the young man, delivering an attack that he at first countered with only a

meek defence. His very gentleness, however, only egged his attacker on, and he was forced to change his tactics. M. Jean Petipa managed to reconcile what was necessary for his safety with the respect due to a lady. The others present managed to separate the combatants and order was restored in the class. This outburst of temper results from personal causes between the parties.[14]

Presumably his idyll with Lola Montez was short-lived; and when he announced his intention of leaving her, she told him that her ring contained a deadly poison and that she would kill them both if he deceived her. One day he managed to obtain possession of the ring. On sending it to a chemist to analyse the grey powder it contained, he was very relieved to be told it was nothing more dangerous than ashes.

Following the fiasco of her début, Lola Montez could never appear again at the Opéra, but she had the courage to return to Paris the following year and dance at the Porte-Saint-Martin. The Jockey Club and the *jeunesse dorée* turned up in force to have their fun by encouraging her, but her notoriety proved too much even for that theatre. She was dismissed before she could appear in the faery spectacle, *La Biche au bois*, for which she had been engaged. The death of her lover in a duel was the talk of Paris, but the Porte-Saint-Martin was not worried by that sort of scandal. The real reason for her dismissal, it was said, was her refusal to wear tights beneath her skirt.

Lola Montez was soon to earn a place in history, not as a dancer but as a royal mistress who by her brazen arrogance rocked the throne of Bavaria. These later exploits, however, have no place in the annals of the Paris Opéra, where she made but a single unhappy appearance and was found wanting both in art and in manners.

* * * * * * *

Leon Pillet had not renounced the more serious side of his duties. While the public was being beguiled with the polka and the fleeting appearance of Lola Montez, he was negotiating with Marie Taglioni for a series of performances in the summer. Although she was then contemplating retiring from the stage to live in a peaceful retreat on the shores of Lake Como, the thought of giving a farewell season in Paris appealed to her, and in May a contract was signed for seven performances at the Opéra during June, the last of which would be given for her benefit.

It was a disillusioned woman who arrived in Paris. Her marriage had been a failure, and she was on the point of obtaining a judicial separation.[15] A.D. Vandam, who derived little pleasure from her dancing and was clearly unsympathetic, was even more disappointed when he met her socially. 'I had been able to determine for myself before then,' he wrote,

> that Marie Taglioni was by no means a good-looking woman, but I did not expect her to be so plain as she was. That, after all, was not her fault, but she might have tried to made amends for her lack of personal charms by her amiability. She rarely attempted to do so, and never with Frenchmen. Her reception of them was freezing to a degree, and on the occasions – few and far between – when she thawed, it was with Russians, Englishmen or Viennese. Any male of the Latin races she held metaphorically as well as literally at arms' length. Of the gracefulness, so apparent on the stage, even in her decline, there was not a trace to be found in her private life. One of her shoulders was higher than the other; she limped slightly, and, moreover, waddled like a duck. The pinched mouth was firmly set; there was no smile on the colourless lips, and she replied to one's remarks in monosyllables. Truly she had suffered a cruel wrong at the hands of men – of one man, *bien entendu*; nevertheless, the wonder to most people who knew her was not that Comte Gilbert de Voisins should have left her but that he should have married her at all. 'The fact was,' said someone with whom I discussed the marriage one day, 'that de Voisins considered himself in honour bound to make that reparation, but I cannot conceive what possessed him to commit the error that made the reparation necessary'.[16]

Her presence in Paris aroused great curiosity, which mounted when her father joined her a few days later, having come post-haste from Warsaw to supervise her performances. On 24 May she was recognised in a box at the Opéra, applauding Carlotta Grisi in *La Péri*. By then the house was completely sold out for her first appearance on 1 June.

Gautier admitted that he was apprehensive as he sat waiting for the curtain to rise on *La Sylphide*. For Paris, as he knew, was the most forgetful of cities. Let a singer or a dancer leave who had built up her reputation there, and the public would harbour a grudge and at once transfer its loyalty to a new favourite. Apart from this peculiar failing of the Paris public, there was a natural tendency to form an idealised image of a long-absent artist, which could so easily lead to disillusionment. And Marie Taglioni was now forty. But all Gautier's fears were dispelled when she stepped on to the stage. 'The four years that have passed since her departure,' he was pleased to note, 'have left her untouched. Happy woman! There is the same elegant, slender form, the same gentle, spiritual, modest expression. Not a feather has fallen from her wig, nor a hair faded beneath her coronet of flowers.'[17]

Gautier imagined he could see no change in the great dancer, but there were others who found Taglioni's lightness and strength much diminished, although her dancing was as correct, graceful and chaste as ever. Perhaps a balanced judgment lay somewhere between these two views. 'Paris has regained its Sylphide,' wrote the *Constitutionnel*,

> perhaps a little more careful, perhaps a little less impalpable, but what does that matter? Is it such a crime that wisdom should come with age even to sylphides, and temper their leaps towards the stars? When a sylphide rises no higher than the treetops, is she less of a sylphide for that? Must one proclaim her downfall? Nonsense! We earthly mortals believe ourselves to be zephyrs and eagles for very much less... For me, art does not reside entirely in *tours de force*. I gladly leave that to tumblers and equilibrists. True art, delicate art, accomplished art, Marie Taglioni possesses it still and has brought it all back to us. Here still is the modesty of her gestures, the exquisite grace of her movements, the harmony of her poses, her purity of line, of which Phidias or Canova would not have been ashamed; here still is the divine interplay of charm and reserve, modesty and voluptuousness – rare gifts which have made Marie Taglioni a great artist among all those famous bounding spirits who are, after all, only dancers.[18]

For her next performance she chose *Le Dieu et la Bayadère*. In this rather unsatisfactory opera-ballet, Gautier found difficulty in keeping his mind on her. His thoughts wandered to the troupe of Indian Bayadères who had visited Paris six years before and virtually swept him off his feet. The beautiful Amani and her comrades had been appreciated by a very limited public when they had appeared at the Variétés, but Gautier had been assiduous in paying homage to her in the house in the Allée des Veuves where the company was lodged. He used to come with presents of tobacco, which she smoked in her clay and reed pipe, and carry on a conversation that was restricted to saying goodbye to her in Hindustani and listening to her counting in French. How interesting it would be, he mused as these memories came crowding back, if *Le Dieu et la Bayadère* were played by Indian dancers, with the brown-skinned Amani in the rôle of the fair Taglioni. Then, recalling having been told that she had hanged herself in London – "no doubt, on one of those days when the yellow fog is so thick that you cannot see the candle in your hand" – he came back to earth, realising that his dream must forever remain a dream.

For Taglioni's admirers, June passed all too quickly, and the evening of the 29th arrived, when her final performance was billed. On that last evening she displayed her genius before a packed house. Groups of men stood in great discomfort for four hours at the entrances to the orchestra stalls, while those less fortunate were content to peer through the peep-holes of the box doors for just a glimpse of the performance. The galleries seemed to be as full of bouquets as of people, and everywhere people had brought opera glasses and even field glasses in their concern to fix in their memories every moment of this historic performance.

The second act of *La Sylphide* recalled earlier triumphs, but the two *pas* from *L'Ombre*,[19] a ballet that Filippo Taglioni had produced in St Petersburg, would be new to Paris. For the first of these, part of the Wolf's Glen set from *Le Freichütz* had been used to represent a moonlit forest, in which Taglioni came on in a shadow dance, trying in vain to seize her shadow while her lover competed for her attention. Then followed a *pas des fleurs* from the same ballet, a feature of which were the stout property flowers on which Taglioni posed without appearing to bend their stems. Though lacking the poetry and wit of the shadow dance, it was full of variety, at first displaying her noble style, and then developing into 'a very lively *stretta* composed entirely of delicate, coquettish, capricious little steps'.[20] Finally, she danced the *pas de Diane* from *Le Dieu et la Bayadère*, which she had performed first at an earlier farewell at the Opéra in 1837, before setting out for St Petersburg.

At the end of the performance, Louise Fitzjames came out from the wings and presented Taglioni with a golden apple. Meanwhile, bouquets were being showered at the stage, not all of which reached their objective. One, indeed, landed on Gautier's head. Another only just cleared the footlights, and when one of the *petits rats* darted forward to pick it up, the curtain came down and separated her from the rest of the company. The sight of the child scurrying confusedly into the wings brought the evening to a close, for the curtain did not rise again.

* * * * * * *

In a very small measure, Taglioni's farewell was compensated for by two interesting débuts that took place that same summer. Both dancers had established themselves elsewhere before coming to Paris. The first, Flora Fabbri, was one of the finest pupils of Carlo Blasis and had won many laurels in Italy, while the second, Tatiana Smirnova, came from distant St Petersburg.

Flora Fabbri's first appearance took place on 12 May 1844, in a *pas de deux* with her husband, Louis Bretin, inserted in *Lady Henriette*, and her success earned her a remunerative engagement. In September she was featured in Rossini's opera *Othello*, captivating the audience with her exceptional lightness – a lightness, Janin wrote, such as Taglioni had possessed fifteen years before[21] – and her astonishing speed. The particular qualities of her style obviously marked her out for Taglioni's rôles. On 6 November 1844 she danced *La Sylphide* for the first time, inserting a *pas de deux* in the second act that she had performed in Italy but was new to Paris, and the following year she assumed the rôles of the Abbess in *Robert le Diable* (30 March) and Zoloé in *Le Dieu et la Bayadère* (14 April). In all of these parts she was very well received, although her miming was found to be less distinguished than her dancing. The effect of *Robert le Diable,* however, was unfortunately marred by the ungainly posturing of the tenor, Duprez, who sent the *corps de ballet* into such fits of giggling that Pillet had to fine every one of them on the spot.

Fabbri had come to Paris with the hope of securing an engagement, but Tatiana Smirnova was only on a passing visit between two St Petersburg seasons. Smirnova, who had studied under Charles Didelot, thus had the privilege of being the first Russian ballerina to appear before a Paris public.[22] In St Petersburg she had modelled her style on that of Taglioni, which did not go unperceived when she made her début at the Opéra on 12 July 1844, in a *pas* from *La Sylphide* interpolated in a performance of *La Jolie Fille de Gand.*

The future triumphs of Russian dancers, however, could hardly be foreseen in her reception. The Paris audience applauded her sympathetically but politely, and the general impression was that her 'simple success ... [was of] no significance'.[23] She was small, with a technique that the French found to be incorrect, and a rather affected manner. Gautier observed that she had 'one dreadful fault for the Parisians – she was provincial!'[24] And Janin also found something strange about her. 'She is quite unlike the beauties we love,' he wrote. 'She is not a woman, but a child who has suffered from cold and hunger.' But, he continued, 'the skilful dancer soon revealed herself. Mlle Smirnova successfully copies the great models; she has in the highest degree the quality that Russian artists possess – imitation. But what effort, what punishment, what misery must she have undergone before arriving at dancing Mlle Taglioni's most difficult *pas.*'[25]

From Paris she moved on to Brussels, to dance the title-rôles in *La Sylphide* and *Giselle* at the Monnaie. Here the public was easier to please, and she returned to her native Russia with some warm tributes from the Belgian critics. 'Mlle Smirnova,' wrote the *Independance Belge,*

> is as light as a bird, and in her case this lightness in no way detracts from her strength. Her steps, which are always perfectly marked, are full of elegance; she jumps with a rare strength, and constantly alights with assurance and without making the slightest movement of her body. She is a distinguished dancer in the full force of the term, and will soon be classed among the dance celebrities of Europe.[26]

The success of this first Russian ballerina to dance on the boards of the Opéra was relatively modest, but she could return to her country with the signal honour of an achievement that no one could take from her. As the next two decades were to show, she was to be the forerunner of three ballerinas of the next generation – Bogdanova, Marie S. Petipa and Muravieva – who would reveal the growing prestige of the mightily endowed ballet of Imperial St Petersburg.

NOTES

1. Under Article 24, two ballets of at least two acts each had to be produced in the year, one of which, however, could be replaced by two one-act ballets or one one-act ballet and one one-act opera.
2. Arago, 279.
3. *La Comtesse d'Egmont*, comedy in 3 acts by Ancelot and de Camberouse, f.p. Th. des Variétés.
4. *Moniteur*, 27 February 1844.
5. *Presse*, 26 February 1844.
6. *Moniteur*, 27 February 1844.
7. *Ménestrel*, 25 February 1844.
8. *Revue et Gazette Musicale de Paris*, 25 February 1844.
9. *Martha oder Der Markt zu Richmond*, opera in 4 acts, libretto by Saint-Georges, translated into German by W. Friedrich, music by Flotow, f.p. Court Opera, Vienna, 25 November 1847.
10. *Les Noces de Gamache*, ballet-pantomime-folie in 2 acts, based on Cervantes' *Don Quixote*. choreography by Milon, music by Lefebvre, f.p. Paris Opéra. 18 January 1801.
11. *Napoli eller Fiskeren og hans Brud*, romantic ballet in 3 acts, choreography by Bournonville, music by Paulli, Ed. Helsted and Gade, f.p. Royal Theatre, Copenhagen, 29 March 1842.
12. *Toreadoren*, idyllic ballet in 2 acts, choreography by Bournonville, music by Ed. Helsted, f.p. Royal Theatre, Copenhagen, 27 November 1840.
13. *Presse*, 1 April 1844. Guest, *Gautier*, 130; Fr. ed., 152.
14. *Coureur des spectacles*, 12 September 1844. Van Aelbrouck gives Jean-Claude Petipa an entry (198–9), from which it appears that he danced briefly in Brussels as a teenager in 1830-1, and in 1847 went with his brother to St Petersburg, where he died in 1873.
15. Taglioni's judicial separation was pronounced by the Tribunal Civil de la Seine (First Chamber) on 21 August 1844. Her grounds were that differences between her husband and herself arose when she continued her career against his wishes, and that when she returned to France from Russia, hoping to find he had changed his mind, she was refused access to the matrimonial home. Comte Gilbert de Voisins defended the suit on the ground that his refusal was justified because she had lived apart from him for ten years. He had in fact left her at the end of 1834 to go on a six-month journey to Constantinople, and they had not lived together since, except for a brief reconciliation in the summer of 1835. Marie Taglioni had two children: a daughter, Marie, born on 30 March 1836, and a son, Georges, born on 5 October 1843, who could not have been the son of her husband, although he took his title.
16. [Vandam], i, 100–01.
17. *Presse*, 3 June 1844.
18. *Constitutionnel*, 3 June 1844.
19. See Note 15 to Chapter 19.
20. *Moniteur*, 1 July 1844.
21. *Journal des débats*, 16 September 1844.
22. Félicité Hullin-Sor used to bring some of her Russian pupils to Paris, but they appeared at private recitals, not in public. Consequently, only a few Parisians would have seen Tatiana Karpakova (mother of Nadezhda Bogdanova, who was to dance at the Paris Opéra between 1851 and 1855,

and again in 1865) in 1827, and Ekaterina Sankovskaya (who was the first to dance *La Sylphide* in Moscow, in 1837, and was known there as 'the Russian Taglioni') in 1836.

23. *Coureur des spectacles.* 13 July 1844.
24. *Presse,* 15 July 1844.
25. *Journal des débats,* 15 July 1844.
26. *Indépendance Belge,* 29 August 1844.

23

A Sad Farewell and Some New Faces

When Carlotta returned from London still exhilarated by the triumph of Perrot's new ballet, *Esmeralda,* she was undoubtedly in need of a rest. For the third year running, she had taken advantage of her entitlement to leave by accepting an invitation to dance in the English capital, this time returning to Her Majesty's Theatre for the first two months of the season. Two years before, she had given London its first taste of *Giselle,* and this she had now followed with a no less sensational creation, the gypsy girl Esmeralda. Her last appearance of the London season on May 2 had been given for her benefit, and that same evening she had begun her journey back to Paris. Three days later, the *Coureur des spectacles* reported her return in glowing detail:

> Mlle C. Grisi has returned, which is excellent news. Here are the details. Having come off the stage after dancing Esmeralda for the last time, she had hardly time for a meal, as a considerable crowd gathered at her front door. She was greeted with cheers as she made her way through them to a four-horse chaise, which, with a courier riding on ahead, took her like the wind to Dover. There the *Magicienne,* a fine steamship, welcomed our dancer aboard and an hour and three quarters later the artiste disembarked at Boulogne... And yesterday, having arrived [in Paris] at midnight the evening before, Mlle Carlotta presented herself to the Director, who was delighted by her punctuality. It was at Lumley's expense that this rapid journey was made: it cost 600 francs.[1]

Carlotta had returned to Paris exhausted, and before May was out was ordered by her doctor to take a rest. She danced one more time – in *La Péri*, a performance attended by Taglioni – before retiring for a month's sick leave. Her fatigue then turned out to be more serious than was thought, and it was only towards the end of August that she was strong enough to resume her activity.

As events turned out, she must have been greatly relieved to be spared from having to appear in a new ballet, *Eucharis*, which proved an abject failure when it was presented to the public on 7 August 1844. It was presented under the sole authorship of the choreographer Jean Coralli, but the scenario had, it appeared, been written by the Director himself, a fact that had not escaped the notice of the critic and historian of the Opéra, Castil-

Blaze, who was to put the record straight in his two-volume history of the Opéra:

> Among the comic touches with which *Monsieur le Directeur* adorned his ballet, I must mention the scene of striking novelty that showed Calypso, the inconsolable nymph, walking in her grottos in a nightdress with a candle in her hand. But let it be noted that the drama was serious and in no sense intended to be funny.[2]

In defiance of the increasing indifference to classical themes, Pillet had conceived the idea of a mythological ballet. No one seemed to have advised him – or if they did, their warning was not heeded – that his scenario was hardly a credit to his imagination, and that the work would inevitably arouse memories of two earlier ballets on the same subject: Pierre Gardel's *Télémaque*,[3] one of the most popular works of the pre-Romantic repertory with over 400 performances to its credit, and Dauberval's ballet of the same name.[4] As matters turned out, the dismal failure of *Eucharis* was to stand as an object lesson to any Director with literary ambitions.

The action of *Eucharis* took place on the island of the goddess Calypso (Leroux). Many years before, Calypso had been abandoned by her lover, Ulysses, a slight she has never forgotten. Not even her favourite nymph, Eucharis (A. Dumilâtre), can assuage her sorrow. Indeed, her lover's desertion has left so deep a wound that she has determined that no man shall ever set foot on her island. But when Ulysses' son Telemachus (L. Petipa) and his tutor, Mentor (Elie), are shipwrecked off the shore, she relents and spares them because of Telemachus's resemblance to his father. However, Venus (D. Marquet) disapproves of Calypso's attitude and conspires with Cupid (Maria) to make Calypso fall in love with Telemachus. Cupid arrives in the disguise of a sailor, and carries out his task so successfully that Calypso cannot bear the thought of Telemachus leaving her and sets fire to his ship. That evening Calypso sleepwalks to the grotto that had formerly sheltered Ulysses, and where now Telemachus is lodged. In her dream she relives her passion for Ulysses. But when she wakes, she discovers her handmaiden Eucharis there, and orders her to be taken away. Mentor too is worried by Telemachus's infatuation for Eucharis. He passes his hands before the young man's eyes and induces him to dream that his father is in danger. Telemachus resolves to leave the island, but weakens at the sight of Eucharis chained to a rock by Calypso. Failing to loosen her bonds, he begs Calypso to release her. The goddess relents, but just as the lovers are about to be united, Mentor recalls Telemachus to his filial duties by leaping into the sea. Ashamed at his weakness, Telemachus dives in after him. The ballet closed with an epilogue, showing the two men saving Ulysses from his enemies, and finally, Mentor revealing himself as Minerva in disguise.

The rôle of Calypso was given to Pauline Leroux, whose better judgment might have told her that it was too feebly sketched for her to make much out of it. However, her loyalty to the Opéra overrode her objections and she consented to play it, even though it was purely a mime part. The prospect of having no opportunity of dancing, however, distressed her greatly, and at one of the final rehearsals she made a bitter complaint to Pillet. She sensed that she was meeting with no sympathy. Her voice became choked with sobs, and finally she broke down completely. But her tears were in vain, and she had to do her best with her part, such as it was.

The ballet was a lost cause before the curtain went up on the first performance on 7 August 1844. 'Take away the dances,' wrote the critic of the *Era*,

> and all that remains will be three or four colourless scenes, destitute of dramatic power, incapable of moving a public now grown indifferent to the mythological school of ancients, having being won away by the grace and poetical illusions of *La Sylphide, Giselle* and *La Péri*. The authors who in our days seek inspiration from heathen mythology should endeavour to paint it in its native originality, in its romanticism (if we may so call it), rather than in the conventional aspect, the classic mantle in which it has been enveloped until now.[5]

Théophile Gautier thought that the subject could only have been rejuvenated by a more careful study of local colour and a better production. The poverty of the *mise en scène* was apparent from the very first. The storm passage and the burning of the ship were particularly ineffective, while the cloud on which Venus made her descent was disgracefully cumbersome, with Venus herself reclining on what appeared to be a Louis XV sofa. But these defects were as nothing compared with the ridiculous effect of Calypso's sleepwalking scene in the second act. Her appearance with a lamp in her hand reminded Gautier of Lady Macbeth, but others were far less charitable, and the passage was greeted with titters of laughter, to the acute discomfiture of Pauline Leroux. Coralli, the choreographer, had done his best with the wretched scenario, and arranged several delightful *pas*, including a *pas de deux* for Adèle Dumilâtre and Petipa in the first act which, while containing nothing strikingly novel, was redolent of grace and charm, and a *pas de trois* for Sophie Dumilâtre, Auguste Mabille and Hoguet-Vestris as a dryad and two fauns. Deldevez, the composer of the music, who was an inveterate grumbler, did not consider Coralli an ideal choice as choreographer. 'His musical knowledge,' he remarked, 'was such as to admit no motifs that were not supported by a strong tempo... Otherwise he blamed his wig, which he tormented on his head until he found the rhythm, which he then embellished with charming steps.'⁶

Perhaps the fault had not lain entirely with Coralli, for Deldevez's music, while carefully written and orchestrated, was criticised as being lacking in both melody and rhythm. The most successful number was the finale to the first act, the *bacchanale aux flambeaux*, which many years afterwards was resurrected at a concert at the Trocadero during the 1878 Exhibition. Its one claim to be remembered, it seems, was that it was the first ballet score to contain an important solo for the *cornet à piston*.

This was small consolation to those who had to sit through it. Jules Janin left the theatre in a very bad mood. 'What a concoction!' he declared. 'What a story! What a lot of nonsense there is in this so-called mythological ballet! And whose idea was it to throw those faded flowers at our heads, fill us with that sour milk, and make us eat those insipid fruits picked from the ancient trees of Pagan Olympus?'⁷

After the sorry reception of the first performance, it was announced that revisions were in hand, and indeed the epilogue was cut completely so as to end the ballet with Telemachus leaping into the water. But much more was needed to turn an abject failure into even a passable success, and after six performances *Eucharis* was dropped from the repertory and forgotten.

Pauline Leroux's ill luck dogged her to the end. A few months later, in November 1844, she suffered another leg injury. This accident hastened her decision to retire, and, in recognition of her long and faithful service, she was offered a benefit performance. A mixed programme was planned that promised to attract a full house. Rossini's *Stabat Mater* might have seemed rather a strange item to include in a ballerina's benefit, but it was to be balanced by a piece featuring the celebrated comic actor Benoît Arnal, who was to take part in the ever popular *bal masqué* from *Gustave* with Carlotta Grisi as his partner in a rumbustious *galop*. Then Pauline Leroux decided that she could risk dancing in the *galop*, and it was announced that she also would be partnered by a famous comedian, Bouffé. Unhappily these plans had to be scrapped when the Minister of the Interior, who held strong views on the propriety of mixing sacred music with profanities, ordered a change of programme. All would have been well if it had been the *Stabat Mater* that had been dropped, but inexplicably it was the other items that were sacrificed, and the ballerina's bewildered admirers who had bought tickets were confronted with bills announcing nothing more than an orchestral and choral concert and adding, by way of small comfort, that they could have their money back if they were not satisfied.

The austerity of Pauline Leroux's benefit, which had been postponed from the Friday to the following Sunday, 25 January 1845, would have been worthy of comment even in Holy Week, as one commentator put it; but to present such a programme for a ballerina's benefit during Carnival seemed an act of the purest folly, not to say base ingratitude. Certainly Pauline Leroux deserved more of the Opéra than the receipts of this lugubrious evening, which amounted to no more than 6205 francs[8] – only a third of what the takings might have been had the programme been as originally announced. Pauline Leroux retired to live a life of calm domesticity with her husband, the actor Pierre Lafont. Paul Mahalin suggested that the Roman matron's epitaph – *Domum mansit, lanam fecit* (she stays at home with her distaff) – might have been written specially for her. In her peaceful retreat she grew old gracefully away from the public gaze. In 1883 a friend described her as 'a very lively and pleasant old lady'[9]. Her death in 1891 passed almost unnoticed: she left the world as modestly as she had lived.

* * * * * * *

Putting aside the disappointment of this failure, Pillet was soon occupied with new plans. Tales of the wonderful qualities of a troupe of child performers known as the Danseuses Viennoises had been reaching him from abroad. This company had been formed not long before, when Frau Josephine Weiss, then ballet-mistress of the Josephstadt Theatre in Vienna, gathered about twenty little girls from poor families in the city and drilled them into a *corps de ballet* that quickly became famous for its discipline and precision. Before long their success led more well-to-do parents to confide their children to Frau Weiss's charge, and the company embarked on a foreign tour, starting in Paris, where Pillet had engaged them for a series of performances at the Opéra. On their arrival in the French capital, accompanied by Frau Weiss and a doctor, the children numbered thirty-six, aged between five and twelve. Only twelve of them were in fact Viennese.[10]

Their first appearance at the Opéra was on 15 January 1845, when three of their dances were inserted in a performance of *La Jolie Fille de Gand*. As they came on stage to perform a *pas allemande* in the kermess scene, the audience found them quite irresistible. 'First roused by a lively instrumentation,' described the correspondent of the *Era*, whose English text appears to have been translated rather awkwardly from the French,

[the audience] perceived four little fairy rosy sylphides making their appearance from an angle of the scenes, smiling, and with their hands intertwined in each other, advancing with a captivating grace and *légèreté*, then four a little taller, then four more, until the stage was covered with a troop of young girls, whose charming poses and delicious beauty could only be retraced by the pencil of Watteau or Correggio. Their costume is the most ravishing the eye can behold. Tufts of ribbon in their hair, a small hat in the corner of their ears, and garments of pink satin, whose reflections changing in the light play before the eye like the wings of a butterfly.[11]

But there was more to their success than their innocent charm. Such precise and well-drilled ensemble work had never been seen on the Opéra stage before, and yet there was no evidence that this had been obtained by ruthless training. Their *pas allemand*, in Gautier's description, was

> composed of a number of figures, rounds and waltzes that intertwined and unwound with extraordinary facility and precision. There were moments when a charming confusion reigned in the fresh bevy of girls and everything was tangled up and jumbled together beyond belief – like a heap of rose petals scattered by some mischievous zephyr with the tip of his wing. Skirts, tresses and ribbons fluttered in the whirlwind. Then, at a given measure, everything fell into place with dazzling rapidity and clockwork precision. In particular, there was a delightful moment when the whole troupe, forming a single line stretching from one wing to the other, advanced from the back of the stage to the footlights balancing on one leg. Not one of those microscopic feet was behind by a thousandth of a second. They alighted as if moved by a single mind.

Their next dance was a *pas hongrois*, in the ball scene of Act II. 'Half the troupe,' continued Gautier,

> dressed in male costume, served as partners to the others. You cannot imagine the rapidity and daring of these little Hungarians, the majesty with which they clicked the silver spurs on boots that might have been made for pussy-cats, the determination with which they slapped thighs that were decorated with rich trimmings, and the swagger with which they wore their Uhlan bonnets on the sides of their heads. You know full well that a feeling for tempo, an energetic and free rhythm and a calculated allure are indispensable qualities for these national and popular dances. Every beat must be stressed with heel-taps or the clatter of spurs, so that the slightest error would be noticed at once. Well, in this turmoil, in this circular flight, not once did a spur click or a foot touch the ground out of time. The two *coryphées* – who are taller than their companions – showed, in addition to their skill in ensemble work, a real talent in the *pas* that they performed on their own.

Finally, they appeared in the orgy scene of the last act, when their *pas des fleurs* roused the audience's enthusiasm to its highest pitch. 'Everything that Mme Josephine Weiss's young pupils do with their garlands,' noted Gautier,

> is truly beyond belief. They turn them into double, triple and intertwining cat's cradles, baskets, networks and arabesques, through which all these pocket Taglionis, Elsslers and Carlotta Grisis, as fresh as the paper flowers they use in their evolutions, circulate with the rapidity of hummingbirds. The concentration and application that must be needed to know one's place in such a variety of passes and figures is something quite amazing, as we believe it would be difficult to make the Opéra *corps de ballet* perform a similar *pas*. We have to admit that our stage is deficient in the area that demands teamwork and the sacrifice of pride in the interest of an overall effect... The *pas seul* is the dream of the ballet-girl, who apathetically performs the choreographic ensembles that could be so charmingly effective and form such a pleasing contrast to the *pas* of the leading artistes. The success of the Viennese children has shown what an advantage a skilful choreographer could obtain from a *corps* that is well drilled and motivated with their own outlook; but for such a thing to happen, the girls of the *corps de ballet* must somehow be regimented and submitted to a unified training in a Conservatoire. But what can be done with children is no longer possible with young adults, and moreover one can only afford to devote time to dancing when one is earning 60 francs a month.[12]

The children's success surpassed all Pillet's hopes. The Opéra was packed whenever they appeared. At later performances they gave other numbers from their repertory – a *pas des amours*, a polka, a small *divertissement* called *Les Moissonneurs;* and on 15 February, at their benefit performance, the audience was presented with a real feast of dances of a quite extraordinary range: *Hornpipe, Pas suisse, Tarantella, Tyrolienne, Cracovienne, Linzer Tanz, Pas polonais, Polka, Hongroise, Jaleo de Xérès*, and a *Coda finale* by the whole company.

'In the midst of all these dances,' recorded the *Morning Post*, 'thirty-six boxes of comfits and sugar-plums were thrown to them from the omnibus box of the ruling lions of the Opéra, and all at once the little goddesses of the ballet resumed their human feelings and ran about the stage after the comfits with all the eagerness of children who have never figured in the painted sky of mythology'.[13]

The children had few enough luxuries; for while Frau Weiss tended them with admirable care, there was little money to spare after their food and lodging had been accounted for and a percentage of their earnings paid over to their parents. One of the members of the Committee for the Royal Theatres was upset to see the children shivering with cold as they passed him one evening in a corridor of the theatre, on their way home. The next day each child received a present of a thick, warm shawl.

The *corps de ballet* viewed the success of the children with mixed feelings. One of them suggested that Pillet might just as well have engaged the young Risleys from the circus; others encouraged their protectors to complain that the appearance of the Danseuses Viennoises lowered the dignity of the Opéra. The astonishing discipline of the children, however, did not go unnoticed, and for a while the Opéra dancers became much more assiduous in their attendance at class. For some weeks Desplaces, the *régisseur de la danse*, had no cause to impose a single fine, and Coralli and Albert were besieged with demands to give more frequent classes. In fact, by August, the standard of the *corps de ballet* had noticeably improved. Pillet hoped for something more than this, and offered engagements to ten of these young dancers[14] to form the nucleus of a separate group attached to the *corps de ballet* of which Frau Weiss would have special charge. The terms were accepted and the contracts signed, but circumstances were to prevent this interesting plan from being realised.

Even before arriving in Paris, Frau Weiss had had to contend with opposition, which mysteriously seemed to originate in official quarters, but this was nothing to the hostility that began to emanate from the Austrian Embassy from the moment she set foot in the French capital. She was informed that some of the parents were demanding their children's return because they were not being taken regularly to Mass, and was ordered to take them back to Vienna. When she ignored the order, the Embassy denounced her to the Prefecture of Police for abducting minors. However, the Prefect was not easily deceived: being satisfied that she held valid contracts signed by the parents with two years still to run, and that the children were being well cared for, he refused to recommend that the Minister of the Interior should make an expulsion order.

This was perhaps just as well, for the Minister was not well disposed towards them. This was the same high-principled gentleman who was responsible for turning Pauline Leroux's benefit into such a fiasco. He disapproved strongly of the Viennese children, and when his approval was sought for them to appear in a performance of *La Muette de Portici* at the Tuileries, he suddenly had scruples on the ground that they had not taken their first Communion. 'How many grown-ups are in the same condition, yet are not on that account barred from showing their legs at the Opéra!' commented Charles de Boigne.[15]

Shortly afterwards, Frau Weiss entered into a contract to present the children at Her Majesty's Theatre in London. This provided the Austrian

Embassy in Paris with another weapon. She was told that her departure would be opposed by every possible means, because several of the parents had made complaints and it was feared that the children might be converted to Protestantism. A few days later, two of the parents arrived in Paris, bearing powers of attorney signed by several others. Frau Weiss had to go again to the Prefecture of Police, where it was recognised that out of the twelve children claimed, seven were firmly under contract. The other five were duly delivered to the two parents, but only an hour later Frau Weiss was asked to take them back. The parents were now satisfied, and all seemed settled. But the Austrian ambassador persisted in his refusal to grant the necessary visas. The affair had assumed quite extraordinary proportions, and even the Austrian Empress and the Queen of the French had become involved in this strange, quixotic campaign to save the children's souls from the heretic English. In the end, after the British ambassador in Paris had intervened and Benjamin Lumley, the manager of Her Majesty's Theatre, had complained to the Austrian ambassador in London, the difficulties were smoothed over and the little troupe reached London safely early in April.

Frau Weiss's troubles were not over yet. To her dismay she discovered that her agent had so committed her to Lumley that she would not be free to return to Paris in time to fulfil her contract with Pillet. Pillet had been counting on her return, and had granted a number of his dancers leave of absence. So when Frau Weiss failed to appear in Paris in accordance with her obligations, he found himself in a very difficult situation. But there was nothing to be done beyond obtaining a court order rescinding the contracts.

* * * * * * *

Faced with a growing deficit, Pillet was always glad of a little financial help, and so he listened very attentively when a rich young Englishman, Henry Baring, called and proposed that he should engage his mistress. The girl had an English-sounding name, Adeline Plunkett, but she was in reality Belgian, although partly of Irish extraction.

Much had happened to her in the four years that had passed since she made a hazardous journey over the Alps by carriage in the depth of winter to make her début in Trieste. The director of the theatre there had discovered her in Paris, where he had picked her out from the pupils of Barrez's class and engaged her on the spot. From Trieste, where in February 1841 she enjoyed an extraordinary success for one so young, she was on the point of leaving for Venice to fulfil another engagement, when she was suddenly stricken with a mysterious illness. Whether it was cholera, typhus or catalepsy – the doctors were not only divided but nonplussed – the symptoms were so alarming that after three days her family gave her up for lost. She was lying in bed, unconscious and desperately weak, her breathing hardly perceptible, when the inventor of a new cure turned up. He was probably admitted to the house only because all hope had been abandoned, and no one objected when he carried the girl from her bed and placed her in a tub of ice-cold water. No harm appeared to be done, and the same procedure was repeated the next day. By slow degrees the alarming symptoms wore off, and after three weeks of this regime of daily cold baths, Adeline Plunkett was pronounced out of danger.

After a long convalescence, she returned to Paris to resume her classes with Barrez. There she was noticed by Jules Perrot, whose recommendation obtained her an engagement at Her Majesty's Theatre in London, where he was *maître de ballet*. For two seasons she attracted considerable attention, as much by her love affairs, however, as by her dancing. Fashionable London was agog at the struggle that raged between her and her comrade Elisa Scheffer for the affections of the Earl of Pembroke, a struggle that they were quite unable to prevent erupting onto the stage. After two disgraceful incidents during performances, Lumley dismissed both dancers. While Elisa Scheffer abandoned her career to live with her lord, Adeline Plunkett consoled herself with Henry Baring and the Comte de Biron, and in the winter of 1844 accepted an engagement to dance at Drury Lane.

Here she enjoyed the position of prima ballerina, dancing in *The Revolt of the Harem*. During one of the performances of this ballet, the costume of a promising young English dancer, Clara Webster, caught fire and she was so horribly burnt that she died after little more than two days' agony. Oblivious of the danger to herself, Adeline Plunkett had made a vain but valiant attempt to catch hold of the burning girl. Her own costume even began to burn, but with great presence of mind she sat down on the stage and stifled the flames herself.

Baring's intervention with Pillet on her behalf was no secret. One report said that he had paid over the sum of 8000 francs. His possession of her, however, was apparently none too secure, for the scurrilous but knowledgeable *Satirist* reported in April: 'On dit that Plunkett receives in Paris just half as many lovers as she wears petticoats. The latter are more than a dozen in number. Such a damsel, one would think, requires a little more than she experiences of the *Baring rein*.'[16] Adeline Plunkett's presence in Paris was noticed long before she was seen on the stage of the Opéra. Charles Maurice observed her at the ball of the Ecole Lyrique, and described her 'very long *anglaises* without curls, straight as if the hair had come out of the water. Only a very pretty face,' he added, 'could have risked such a coiffure.'[17] Her début was deferred until after the Danseuses Viennoises had completed their tally of performances, leaving one balletomane fretting impatiently at the delay. This was Prince Piotr Tiufiakin, an elderly Russian who had been Director of the Imperial Theatres under the Tsar Alexander I, and was now one of the most extravagant characters of Paris with his crinkled boots and his strange, old-fashioned carriage, manned by coachman and footman wearing Russian infantry colonel's uniforms. His interest in ballet never waned, and it was reported that as he lay dying, his last words were, 'And Plunkett... is she dancing tonight?'[18] Alas, the old prince died a few days before she made her début on 17 March 1845.

She chose for that occasion, perhaps a little unwisely, *La Péri*, and made a sensational first entrance sparkling all over with diamonds. Charles de Boigne considered the début too insignificant to write about, but she was vociferously supported by a band of about two hundred *claqueurs* packed in the pit. This did not deceive Jules Janin, who merely saw a pretty but rather ordinary girl, with long and somewhat sluggish arms, who danced gracefully although none too confidently, and was not much of an actress. 'Her miming,' he remarked, 'consists of half a dozen pretty gestures, a few pretty little smiles and a million mincing ways which she directs to herself, since she seems highly satisfied with her own attractions, as well she might be'. He was shocked that she should replace Carlotta's *pas de l'abeille* with 'an Anglo-Spanish bolero of a somewhat languorous kind', and concluded that in spite of all her jewellery, the most she could hope for would be a place below the Dumilâtres and between Louise Fitzjames and Maria.[19]

Gautier, the champion of Carlotta, was the most charitable of the critics, perhaps because the new dancer's appearance as the Péri had merely satisfied him that she would be no rival to his own special favourite. 'Mlle Plunkett is young and pretty,' he wrote,

> well formed, with dainty feet, slender legs and features that are charming though a little delicate for the stage and not easily distinguishable from afar. She has, in short, everything that is needed to make a ballerina. Many people say that she is one already, but that is a little premature. That she will become a ballerina, there can be no doubt, nor shall we be surprised. The rôle of the Péri was chosen by Mlle Plunkett. To dance the Péri after Carlotta is boldness itself, but the boldness was not misplaced. Mlle Plunkett was applauded very frequently for her pretty face, and at times for her talent. The hazardous leap in the dream scene, which Carlotta performs with the lightness of a dove's feather wafted on the breeze, seemed to terrify the *débutante*, who clung to Petipa's neck in a rather earthly way with her two little fists very visibly clenched. She has *ballon* and travels well, but her *pointes* are still a little soft. Her arms are not lacking in grace, her body is supple, but she still has to acquire the

precision, perfection of detail and firmness that distinguish dancers of the top rank.

As for the insertion of the Spanish dance, Gautier noted that she was only following the example of Carlotta. Plunkett's Spanish dance, a *pas de deux*, was

> a very lively and exaggerated sort of *bolero*, which was applauded to the echo for reasons that were not always associated with the dancing… For its violence of expression, Mlle Plunkett's *bolero* surpasses anything that Elssler, Noblet, Alexis Dupont and Dolores [Serral] ever dared to do. By performing many frenetic and fantastic things that the dancers of Seville, Granada and Cadiz would never have permitted themselves to attempt, she displayed qualities of flexibility and suppleness which, had they been more controlled, could have created a great impression.[20]

No one now seriously considered her as a rival to Carlotta, and Pillet began to have doubts about the terms of her contract. Happily for him, he had the power to terminate it at the end of the first year, and so he was able to insist on a variation, reducing her salary for the second year by about a quarter. She did not seem to take this too much amiss, for at the end of the year she appeared as Zoloé in *Le Dieu et la Bayadère* (24 November) and as Héléna in *Robert le Diable* (5 December), making in the latter part, Gautier said, 'a very pretty ghost to meet by moonlight'. Always observant in such matters, Gautier noted that she did not make proper use of her beautiful feet, the 'small feet of an Andalusian marquesa'.[21]

Perhaps success came a little too easily with her Spanish dances, which the pit adored, even if the occupants of the boxes seemed less enthusiastic. At any rate, she persevered with these exhibitions, and in time she would plane away those rough surfaces that had shocked Gautier, who, by 1847, was praising her *Manola* as the finest *pas de caractère* since Fanny Elssler's *Cachucha*.[22]

NOTES

1. *Courrier des spectacles*, 5 May 1844.
2. Castil-Blaze, *Académie*, ii, 267.
3. *Télémaque dans l'île de Calypso*, heroic ballet in 3 acts, choreography by P. Gardel, music by Miller, f.p. Paris Opéra, 23 February 1790. See Guest, *Ballet under the Enlightenment*, chapter 16.
4. *Telemachus in the Island of Calypso*, pantomime ballet in 3 acts, choreography by Dauberval, f.p. Pantheon Theatre, London, 19 March 1791.
5. *Era*, 18 August 1844.
6. Deldevez, 33.
7. *Journal des débats*, 12 August 1844.
8. Compare this figure with the receipts at the benefits of Taglioni on 29 June 1844 (21,193 francs)

and of the Danseuses Viennoises on 15 February 1845 (18,404 francs).

9. 'The Foyer of the Opera'. *The Theatre*, 1 January 1883.

10. The Paris press and the Archives of the Opéra speak of the children collectively as *'danseuses'*, but when they were in London, the *Satirist* (11 May 1845) reported that they included one boy. The advertisement of their benefit performance at Her Majesty's Theatre lists a Franz Weiss among their number. In the short biography of Léon Espinosa in Edouard Espinosa's *Technical Vade Mecum* (London, n.d.) it is stated that Espinosa joined the company to replace the boy who partnered the *première danseuse*, Katti Lanner. However, no evidence of Espinosa's participation is to be found either in the Paris press or in the Opéra archives, nor was Katti Lanner herself ever a member of the company, although it is not impossible that Espinosa may have replaced Franz Weiss at one or more performances.

11. *Era*, 26 January 1845.

12. *Presse*, 20 January 1845. Guest, *Gautier*, 156–8; Fr. ed., 177–9.

13. *Morning Post*, 22 February 1845.

14. Wilhelmina Weber (said to be a niece of the composer), Leopoldine Koch, Marie Florianschütz, Mina Waldberger (called Werner), Charlotte Pyrok – each engaged at 800 francs; Marie Rozarius, Helene Sperle – engaged at 700 francs; Marie Henke, Fanny Bracher, Barbara Maszka – engaged at 600 francs.

15. De Boigne, 34. According to him, Frau Weiss and the children were all Jewish, which, if it was true, is not consistent with the concern shown in official Catholic quarters.

16. *Satirist*, 6 April 1845.

17. *Courrier des spectacles*, 17 January 1845.

18. *Dance Index*, VI, 213.

19. *Journal des débats*, 31 March 1845.

20. *Presse*, 31 March 1845. Guest, *Gautier*, 161–2; Fr. ed., 182-3.

21. *Presse*, 8 December 1845.

22. *Presse*, 8 March 1847.

24

Carlotta Takes to Comedy

The Opéra was now in sore need of a success. Pillet's blind compliance with every whim and caprice of Rosina Stoltz had brought the fortunes of the theatre to a low ebb. When Rossini's opera *Othello* was produced in 1844, the most brilliant passages in Desdemona's rôle were omitted because they were beyond the powers of Madame Stoltz. Many lost the habit of going to the Opéra, and box-office receipts dropped to a low level, to be raised only momentarily by the highly successful appearances of the Danseuses Viennoises. Bitter tongues said that Madame Stoltz viewed their departure with satisfaction, but for the public it only marked, in the words of Castil-Blaze, the return of pestilence and famine.[1]

Success in good measure eventually came, not with an opera but with a ballet, *Le Diable à quatre,* which harked back in spirit, as had *Eucharis,* to an earlier age. Before the Romantic ballet reached its full flowering in the days of Taglioni and Elssler, light opera had provided choreographers with many themes, and now Adolphe de Leuven, the new ballet's scenarist, had turned to such a source with the happiest of results. Both the title and the plot were familiar to many Parisian theatre-goers, for its history on the French stage went back nearly a hundred years to 1756, when Sedaine adapted an English comedy called *The Devil to Pay* into a successful light opera with a musical arrangement by Philidor; and half a century later in 1809, Solié had composed another opera to the same plot.[2]

For the ballet scenario, De Leuven had transposed the setting of the action to Poland, on the estate of Count Polinski (Petipa). The curtain rises to reveal the castle and a little summer house on one side, and on the other the hut of the simple basket-maker Mazourki (Mazilier). The sound of a horn summons the gamekeepers to receive the Count's orders for a hunting party. Two of his servants, Yvan and Yelva (Desplaces and Emarot), are engaged to be married, and the good-hearted Count gives them permission to celebrate their betrothal. The hunting party is gathering for the day's sport when Yelva returns in great alarm to announce that the Countess, who has been woken up by the fanfares, is in a furious temper and demanding that the hunt be abandoned. The Countess (Maria) herself then appears and berates her husband for thinking of nothing but hunting. Failing to calm her down, the Count asserts his authority: not only will the hunt proceed, but festivities will be held the next day over which the Countess will preside to atone for her ill humour. The hunting party sets off, leaving the Countess to return to the castle in tears.

Mazourka (Grisi), the wife of the basket-weaver, now enters, carrying a basket of provisions. Seeing no sign of her husband, she begins to dance; but he soon appears with a bottle in his hand to chide her for leaving him so long and wasting her time dancing. In return, she accuses him of being overfond of the bottle, but the quarrel that follows soon subsides, and they make their peace, agreeing to forgo their particular pleasures. But Mazourki is quite unable control his urge to imbibe, and, seeing him at the bottle again, Mazourka retaliates by beginning to dance. Yelva now arrives to invite the couple to the planned festivities, for which a mysterious old blind man, whom nobody seems to have seen in the vicinity before, has been brought in to accompany the dancing on his violin.

The hunting party returns, and the village festival begins. But the dancing is interrupted by the Countess, who is in an uncontrollable temper at being disturbed when she is feeling sad. She snatches the fiddler's violin and stamps on it. The festivities break up in confusion, and the kind-hearted Mazourka gives the old musician a few coins to compensate him for the damage to his instrument. In thanking her, he secretly reveals that he is a magician, and persuades her to allow him teach the Countess a lesson by casting a spell that will cause Mazourka and the Countess to change places for a day.

The second act opens with a scene in the basket-weaver's hut. Day is about to break. Waking up in a somewhat drunken stupor, Mazourki is surprised to find that he is not in bed, having drunk himself to sleep in his clothes. He does not, of course, realise that the occupant in the family bed is not his own Mazourka, but the Countess who has taken her form. She is naturally filled with alarm when she wakes, and is on the brink of returning to the castle when Mazourki prevents her from doing so by locking the door. Yvan and Yelva then arrive to invite them to their wedding. Now, in a furious temper, the Countess orders them to tell Mazourki who she is, but to them she is only the basket-maker's wife, and they laugh in her face. At this the Countess loses her temper, and when Mazourki takes up his stick to chastise her, she gives him a smart slap on the cheek. To assert his authority he orders her to dance, and grudgingly she performs a few steps of the minuet. But he will have none of that, and demands a more rustic dance. Finally, by distracting his attention and then tipping a large basket over his head, she makes her escape.

The scene then changes to the Countess's boudoir, where the magician is watching over Mazourka, who is lying luxuriantly on the bed. Yelva enters, to be quite astonished at the change in her mistress's character. The Count then appears, to be no less delighted at the transformation that seems to have come over his difficult wife. He tells her that a ball is to be held the next day, and she chooses the costume she will wear for it. Then the dancing master (E. Coralli) comes to teach her a new dance, and cannot understand why she suddenly seems to have lost all her ladylike elegance. But the timely arrival of the old magician rescues her from an awkward situation, for at a gesture from him she finds herself able to perform the dance to perfection, and is so carried away by the experience that she waltzes out of the room, followed by the delighted Count.

For the last scene, the stage opens up to reveal a vast gallery filled with exotic flowers. The ball begins, soon to be interrupted by the arrival of the Countess, still in the guise of Mazourka. Her rage is intensified by the sight of Mazourka wearing one of her own dresses. At that moment, Mazourki enters in search of his wife. The Countess instinctively seeks her husband's protection, but her protestations that she is the Countess meet with general derision. Mazourka then intervenes to make Mazourki solemnly promise never again to beat his wife, and implores the Countess to turn over a new leaf and be kind and considerate of others. The Countess goes down on her knees to beg the Count to forgive her, at which point the magician fortuitously reappears. The Countess pathetically begs the Count to grant her a kiss, at which Mazourki makes a strong objection until Mazourka tells him that if the Count kisses his wife, she will allow him to give her a kiss. At this point, the magician waves his stick and the two women find themselves suddenly restored to their respective selves, and the ballet ends with a scene of general rejoicing.

This scenario was accepted in the summer of 1844 to be at once reserved for Carlotta Grisi's next creation. Originally it was Albert who was envisaged as the choreographer, but in the end that honour passed to Mazilier, while at Carlotta's special request Adolphe Adam was commissioned to compose the music. The ballet went into rehearsal at the end of the year, but a number of delays intervened before the work was ready. Maria, who was chosen to play the Countess, went to dance in London in the early months of 1845, and a proposal to cast Delphine Marquet in her part so as not to prolong the rehearsals was wisely abandoned. Then Carlotta was engaged at Her Majesty's in the summer, which caused further delay.

Le Diable à quatre was finally given its first performance on 11 August 1845, to be immediately acclaimed as an unqualified success. Hippolyte Lucas even saw it as representing a new era in ballet. 'It is a good thing,' he remarked,

> for a ballet... to be based on a popular idea. A folk tale, a tradition or some old farce that everybody knows has a greater chance of success than the

most original flights of fancy. What is needed is visual appeal added to a
very clear plot. It does not matter if the plot is known in advance, for no
great effort is needed by the audience to follow every detail. The
mythological ballet had the advantage, when it was in vogue, that the
loves of Mars and Venus and the annoyance of Vulcan still had a wide
appeal. But now mythology has gone out of fashion. The fantastic ballet
succeeded it and enjoyed its day, when sylphides glided in the air, wilis
lightly brushed the ground, and romantic apparitions displaced the
nymphs and gods. Ballet then became more obscure, but acquired a
certain nebulous and aerial quality. But now, at this present moment, it
seems desirous of coming to the aid of man's understanding. *Le Diable à
quatre* aims at illustrating a proverb.[3] This comedy, which was already old
in Sedaine's day and was intended to make shrews see reason, is not a bad
choice to open a new era of ballet with works that are instructive and have
a moral. And, joking apart, it is not a bad thing for ballet to be led back,
from time to time, to the simple rules of good sense.[4]

The absence of far-fetched or tortuous complications in the plot was
certainly a happy feature, for the result was, as one spectator put it, a ballet
with 'not a moment of boredom' and packed with 'scenes of genuine
comedy'.[5]

Carlotta had returned from London with her reputation wondrously
enhanced after dancing in the great *Pas de Quatre* with Taglioni, Cerrito and
Grahn.[6] Now, as Mazourka, she revealed a new and unsuspected side to her
talent, both as a dancer and as an actress. *La France musicale* called it
'indisputably her finest rôle'.[7] With this, Gérard de Nerval agreed. 'In her
own language,' he wrote,

> she played this amusing comedy as it might have been played at the
> Théâtre Français in the good old days... In her other rôles she proved that
> she possessed all the poetry of the dance... Today she has proved that she
> also possesses its wit, and to the highest degree. One might say she has
> almost reinvented it, for in our time the *ballet bouffe* has had to give way to
> the *ballet mélancolique*, no doubt for want of worthy interpreters.[8]

The *Constitutionnel* described the character of Mazourka as

> a complete dramatic part. It calls for wit, gaiety and strong expression.
> Mlle Grisi revealed herself to be a charming and skilful actress. When she
> takes the form of a great lady, nothing could be funnier than her little
> awkwardnesses and her inability to manage the train of her dress. This
> scene made the whole audience laugh, a rare occurrence at the Opéra.
> Mlle Grisi also gave proof of great taste, for even in this comic situation she

remained elegant and graceful. Mlle Grisi's dancing lesson was, for her, a veritable *tour de force*. All Paris will want to see her dancing badly![9]

Jules Janin was no less enthusiastic. 'Carlotta Grisi,' he wrote,

in her dual rôle of great lady and roguish little charmer, is in all truth a delightful dancer. She could not possibly be livelier or gayer. You can see that she loves to dance with a happy enjoyment that the exercise even of the art one knows best can so rarely give. In her little short dress, and so long as she is the little Mazourka, the young village girl comes up with all sorts of steps, whims, fantasies and roguish little graces that are personal to her alone. In particular there is a moment when Mlle Grisi is inimitable – when Mazourka's husband wants to force her to weave his baskets. Her hands are busy with her work, but her feet are skipping. There is dancing in her attitude, in her repose, her look, her impatience... She summons her entire soul into her eyes, which is what speaking is all about. And finally, when her inner demon gets the better of her, there she is, bursting out like a spring that has too long been compressed in its steel casing. The dance is the very life-blood of Mille Grisi; she has been created just to dance. But also, when at last she offers you a ballet, she does not rest unless she appears in every scene. She wants to be everywhere at once, to dance in every corner of the stage. She accepts every step she is given and, if necessary, invents new ones, and then, when she has danced all evening long, see how fresh and serene she is. She is like a pretty child awakening after sleeping soundly the whole night through.[10]

There was no dearth of dancing opportunities in her part. She had several *pas* which were 'very well arranged and included a number of passages of great novelty'.[11] The credit for this may not have been entirely Mazilier's; for according to one report, she had been allowed to introduce into her variations two borrowings from *La Esmeralda*, the great dramatic ballet that Perrot had produced for her in London the year before.[12] 'No ballerina surpasses Carlotta in strength,' was the opinion of Hippolyte Lucas:

Her vigorous, assured dancing places her in a class apart. The air may be Taglioni's element, but the earth belongs to Carlotta. Her satin ballet slipper seems to end in a blade of steel. Never has anyone dug into the stage... more firmly. She stays poised on her *pointe* with the immobility of a marble statue. Her high, bold jumps have also shown a prodigious improvement.[13]

It was a little unfortunate that Maria, who played the part of the Countess, did not look more like Carlotta, for this rather spoilt the illusion of the transformation. Nevertheless she was most happily cast in another sense, for her brilliant portrayal strengthened the ballet and gave it balance. 'Maria,' wrote the *Era*, 'was absolutely fascinating, such was the malice, the finesse and the humour in her acting... Can you cite many actresses like her? Who, in speaking, could speak better than she has done without uttering a word?'[14] Janin found her arrogance perfect in the scene in which the Countess wakes up to find herself in the drunken Mazourki's hut:

> She defended herself tooth and nail, striking her borrowed husband, showing her claws, and then becoming feline when the old bully demands she play her part. In fact... this is no rose-water ballet; far from it. On the contrary, people fight with their feet and their fists, a slap here and a buffet there! More is not given and taken at Deburau's.[15]

The male dancer's lot in this ballet was meagre, for the men merely fitted into the background as peasants, lords and ambassadors, while the principal ensemble dance, the mazurka of the first act, was arranged for twenty-two women with no male partners. Lucien Petipa, however, earned praise for his portrayal of the Count, although at the first performance he was suffering so severely from ear-ache that he fainted in the wings after dancing his *pas*.

Mazilier, who himself played the basket-maker, paid more attention than usual in his choreography to the *pas d'ensemble*. There had at one time been a question of featuring the Danseuses Viennoises in this ballet; although in the end they did not appear, several of the *pas* clearly revealed their influence. The *corps de ballet* had been very sternly warned that they were expected to make the public forget the Viennese children. 'And our grown-up ladies of the ballet,' reported the *Moniteur*, 'proved remarkable for their precision.'[16] For many of the *abonnés* it was a novel sight to see their favourites so attentive to their duty for once, and having no eyes for anyone save the hero of the ballet!

Adolphe Adam's score for *Le Diable à quatre*, the third he had written for Carlotta, was, in the fullest sense of the word, inspired. It was the perfect accompaniment for a ballet that displayed a side of her talent hitherto unrevealed – her flair for comedy. Marie Escudier, the eminent music critic, devoted the greater part of his review in *La France musicale* to Adam's contribution, a review that was both an extraordinary tribute to the composer and a revealing account of the use of *airs parlants* to aid the understanding of mime scenes:

> The music of *Le Diable à quatre* is at least as good as that of *Giselle*, even though possessing quite different qualities. While in *Giselle* the source of inspiration was the grace, the gentleness and the mist-laden poetry of the German gods, in *Le Diable à quatre*, vivacity, gaiety, wit and lively rhythms predominate. Only a composer with as long an experience of writing for

the theatre as M. Adam... could have given the music for the pantomime scenes such clarity and insight into the situations that dominate the action of this charming piece.

The introduction that serves as an overture is extremely simple. A simple country tune, played by the oboes and bassoons, is taken up by the woodwind quartet, with imitative entrances and delightful harmonic progressions between flute, oboe and clarinet. A brilliant fanfare by the horns follows to announce the hunt as the curtain rises. Here we find a modulation from D major to C natural that is extremely novel and unexpected and would be unplayable without the use of a valve horn by the second horn player... such as has been adopted at the Opéra and ought to form part of every orchestra in France, as has long been the case with all those in Germany...

The use of *'musique parlante'* is a major resource to enable the audience to understand a ballet, and it is here that the composer can take full advantage of his musical knowledge, for the use of popular motifs removes the rigidity found all too often in theoretical compositions. The charming opening scene between Carlotta Grisi and Mazilier is a most happy example of this kind of composition. The young woman makes her first entrance to a light and graceful motif; she is returning from a visit to the town, and has hardly reached her home when she realises that her husband's brutality is awaiting her. But she tells herself, 'My husband is not there, so I can indulge in my favourite pastime' (this to the refrain from *La Lettre de change*).[17] And so she begins to dance. But soon the *ritournelle* from those delightful couplets from the *Fête du village voisin*,[18] – 'Amuse yourself, yes, that I recommend' – announces the return of her husband, who has taken advantage of her absence to go drinking... After a spat when the two spouses accuse one another of their respective failings, they end by making it up. After allowing her husband to have a drink on condition that he allows her to dance, she starts to dance again: here the motif, 'Gregory and I think alike', has been very skilfully woven in without interrupting the 6/8 measure of the melody. The entrance of the Countess, the *Diable à quatre*, is announced by the opening bars of Méhul's *Irato (The Angry One)*.[19]

The *divertissement* includes several very successful orchestral effects, in particular a galop that will surely become popular... and a passage for Carlotta Grisi in which we were impressed by a very happy effect when the piccolos and the clarinets were playing notes that were two octaves apart without anything in between, and a trumpet solo (Saxe system) in which flutes and clarinets weave a design that is both whimsical and original.

And as for the *mazurka* which concludes the *divertissement*, it is a triumph of animation that needs no explanation. The *mazurka* in *Diable à quatre* will soon be heard played on every piano and by every orchestra throughout France. The entire spectacular scene that brings the act to its close is accompanied by a solo violin supported by the harps, and the substitution of the two women is explained to perfection by that delightful motif of Beethoven, first used at the Gymnase in *La Chatte métamorphosée en femme* to the words 'Change, oh change me, Brahma'.

The first scene of the second act, between Mlle Maria and Mazilier, offers music of a quite different order, contrasting the rough good-heartedness of the basket-maker with the wounded dignity of the Countess. A solo for the four bassoons of the orchestra echoes, in a most comical fashion, the scene when the basket-maker is obliging the Countess to carry on with her toilette. In the next scene, that of the dancing lesson, in which it is so strange to see Carlotta Grisi managing to 'dance badly', as the *Constitutionnel* has put it, she has never been more misunderstood by the composer! Finally, in the last scene, which opens with a motif from the charming chorus of *Cagliostro*,[20] the dance melodies, while more brilliant than those of the first act, have just as much charm and vigour. This is revealed first in the *pas* by M. Hoguet-Vestris and Mlle Dumilâtre, a delicious polka full of spirit and gaiety, then in Carlotta's *pas*, to a solo on the French horn superlatively played by M. Forestier, and finally in M. Leudet's violin solo that accompanies the entire *pas des sylphides*. In that final section is a waltz that is truly novel and full of originality...

Violin solos form a large part of the music in this ballet, such repeated use of the same instrument arising from the very nature of the subject. From the moment when the Sorcerer makes his first appearance as a blind violinist, the composer could not have resorted too much to this instrument, and so the fairy scene, the Countess's dance, that of the basket-maker, etc., all provided opportunities for numerous violin solos which aroused well-deserved applause for the player's skill.[21]

Le Diable à quatre was not, however, to everyone's taste, and one who was not entirely satisfied was a correspondent of the *Morning Post*. 'When *Le Diable à quatre* was brought out,' he wrote,

we heard nothing on all sides but *'exquis! superbe! magnifique! mirobilant!'* It was with the utmost astonishment that we beheld this *ridiculus mus* coming out of the mountain of newspaper adulation. Far from being another *Giselle*, with a good plot and original music, this ballet is a mere pasticcio of reminiscences, both of the librettist and of the composer. The only clever bit of music is a Scotch air, well instrumented for wind instruments. There is a good mazurka and polka, and a good sort of *ballabile*, imitated from the Viennese children. All the rest depends upon the grace and talent of the charming Carlotta Grisi. Her dancing was found to be more picturesque than ever, in spite of a *faux pas* that she made, which left her sitting in the least picturesque and romantic position imaginable. Her pantomime is likewise excellent, particularly in a scene taken from the *Paysanne Grand Dame*, brought out at Her Majesty's Theatre two years since.[22] As for the scenery, it looks as if it had belonged to some ballet of the days of the Grand Monarque, and had been discovered by M. Pillet in a broker's shop. Besides the incomparable Carlotta, we saw but two dancers that were not detestable – Mlle Robert, who is second-rate, but both graceful and handsome, and Mlle Sophie Dumilâtre, sister of the absent Adèle, who, if she were not so ugly, would rank with the first dancers in Europe.[23]

The success of *Le Diable à quatre* continued unabated, but on 2 February 1846 the ballet had to be shelved, though happily only for a few weeks, when Carlotta injured herself during a performance. The Opéra stage was notoriously dangerous. 'Sometimes a scene comes toppling down,' explained the *Era*, 'or an abyss is gaping beneath your feet, or jagged nails are left unnoticed. What a hairbreadth escape had Carlotta, for the whole weight of her body fell on an upright nail, which, after having pierced through the *chaussure*, had its point bent in her foot, and was not extracted without a word of pain; the blood flowed in abundance.'[24]

On the evening of this accident, Adeline Plunkett had been playing the rôle of the Countess, but a year later, on 26 May 1847, she was given the privilege of taking the part of Mazourka. 'Mlle Plunkett,' wrote Janin, 'felt the need to simper through Carlotta Grisi's best rôle, and the public, which is not very particular, allowed Mlle Plunkett to indulge in her whim. It is a great pity to waste a good ballet, as if good ballets were not as plentiful as good operas.'[25]

* * * * * *

In the late summer of 1845, Yelena Ivanova Andreanova arrived in Paris from Russia to face the test that her compatriot Tatiana Smirnova had failed to pass the year before. She and Smirnova had emerged from the St Petersburg Ballet School in the same year and were now the principal Russian-born dancers in the company of the Bolshoi Theatre. There they had both been featured in the first Russian production of *Giselle*, Andreanova as Giselle and Smirnova as the Queen of the Wilis. Andreanova, however, enjoyed one indisputable advantage over Smirnova: she was the mistress of

Alexandre Guedeonov, Director of the Imperial Theatres, and it is possible that some of the publicity that preceded her Paris début was officially inspired. The public was informed beforehand, for instance, that she was no cold daughter of the Northern snows. 'Under this apparent calm, this virgin fairness,' it was explained,

> are concealed volcanic ardours and an Andalusian verve and abandon which nothing hitherto seen can equal. We have heard of a certain *Saltarello,* which made such inroads, even among the most virtuous boyars, that a deputation composed of some of the principal ladies of the Court, solicited the Emperor in person to forbid the scandal of this incendiary dance. The Emperor resolved on deciding after a personal view, and it resulted that His Majesty, instead of being satisfied with one encore, ordered the *pas* to be repeated three times.[26]

Paris had its first opportunity of judging this Russian star in a performance of *Robert le Diable* on 5 December 1845. She was trembling like a birch leaf when she made her entrance – a simile used by both Gautier and Janin in their reviews – but the applause of the audience quickly banished her nervousness. The critics took note of her qualities. She held herself well and preserved an excellent line. Also, she was strong and steady, she turned well, she was light in her movements, and her manner, unlike Smirnova's, was found pleasing and charming.

It was at her third performance that she danced the famous *Saltarello,* in which in St Petersburg, it was reported, she was accompanied by eight other *danseuses.* The audience loved it. 'The music of this Neapolitan *pas* is delicious,' wrote one critic.

> No description can give an idea of the impetuosity, rapidity and ardour displayed by the young Russian [dancer]; neither the *Cachucha* of Elssler, nor *El Jaleo,* nor the *Mazurka* of Cerrito, nor any other Spanish dance is to be compared with this *pas diabolique,* for either voluptuousness or abandon. Never have we witnessed so much grace, united to so much vigour. Loud and wild applause... never ceased resounding through the house from the beginning to the very end of this dazzling, bewitching *Saltarello.* The whole pas was encored, and it was re-demanded a third time, but Desplaces [her partner], who was quite exhausted, was unequal to the task. It may be well called a pure-blooded *pas espagnol.* As to Mlle Andreanova, she is indefatigable. The enthusiasm she excites in Russia is a wonder no more, nor is the concern of the Emperor Nicholas not to part with her.[27]

It was left to Janin to pronounce the final verdict and pay her the ultimate compliment. 'She was applauded,' he wrote, 'as a Parisienne'.[28] She was accepted, and was a provincial no longer! Unfortunately, her stay in Paris could not be extended, for she was engaged at La Scala, Milan, for the Carnival season. She never danced in Paris again; but after her retirement in 1855, she returned to France to settle in Auteuil. However, there could be no question of her resuming her career, for she was suffering from an incurable malady, to which she was to succumb in October of 1857 at the age of only thirty-seven. She was laid to rest, quietly, in the cemetery of Père-Lachaise.

NOTES

1. Castil-Blaze, II, 268.
2. The original source was the comedy *The Devil of a Wife, or A Comical Transformation*, attributed to Thomas Jevon but possibly written by T. Shadwell, and first performed at the Dorset Gardens Theatre, London, in 1686. Charles Coffey, in collaboration with J. Mottley, based a ballad opera, *The Devil to Pay, or The Wives Metamorphos'd*, on it: this was produced at Drury Lane Theatre on 17 August 1731. The opera *Le Diable à quatre, ou le Double Métamorphose*, with libretto by Sedaine and music arranged by Philidor, was produced at the Foire Saint-Laurent, Paris, on 19 August 1756. The libretto of Solié's opera, *Le Diable à quatre, ou la Femme acariâtre*, was a new version of Sedaine's book. This was first given at the Opéra-Comique on 30 November 1809. Adolphe Adam, who composed the score of the ballet in 1845, was to rescore Solié's music for a revival of the opera at the Théâtre Lyrique in 1853.
3. *'Faire le diable à quatre'* is a colloquial phrase meaning 'to make a great fuss over very little'.
4. *Siècle*, 18 August 1845.
5. *Era*, 24 August 1845.
6. *Pas de Quatre*, divertissement by Perrot, music by Pugni, f.p. Her Majesty's Theatre, London, 12 July 1845. One of the greatest dance events of the Romantic ballet, this work displayed four of the leading ballerinas of the time dancing together: Taglioni, Cerrito, Grisi and Grahn. It was revived in 1847 with Carolina Rosati replacing Grahn.
7. *France Musicale*, 17 August 1845.
8. *Presse*, 18 August 1845.
9. *Constitutionnel*, 14 August 1845.
10. *Journal des débats*, 8 September 1845.
11. *Constitutionnel*, 14 August 1845.
12. *Coureur des spectacles*, 13 August 1845. *La Esmeralda*, ballet in 5 scenes, based on Hugo's novel, *Notre Dame de Paris*, choreography by Perrot, music by Pugni, f.p. Her Majesty's Theatre, 9 March 1844.
13. *Siècle*, 18 August l845.
14. *Era*, 24 August 1845.
15. *Journal des débats*, 8 September 1845. 'Deburau's' was the Théâtre des Funambules , where the celebrated mime, Jean-Gaspard Deburau, was to be seen.
16. *Moniteur*, 18 August 1845.
17. *La Lettre de change*, opéra-comique in one act by Bochsa to a libretto by de Planard, f.p. Opéra-Comique, 11 December 1815.
18. *Le Fête du village voisin*, opera-comique in 3 acts by Boïeldieu to a libretto by Sewrin, f.p. Opéra-Comique, 5 March 1816.
19. *Irato*, opéra-comique in one act by Méhul to a libretto by Marsollier, first performed at the Opéra-Comique, 17 February 1801.
20. *Cagliostro*, opéra-comique in 3 acts by Adam, to a libretto by Scribe and Saint-Georges, f.p. Opéra-Comique, 10 February 1844.

21. *La France musicale*, 17 August 1845.
22. *La Paysanne Grand Dame, divertissement* by Perrot, f.p. Her Majesty's Theatre, 25 July 1844, not two years but one before *Le Diable à quatre* was produced. However, Carlotta Grisi could not have seen this soon-to-be-forgotten piece, for she was then preparing for her return after her illness.
23. *Morning Post*, 13 October 1845.
24. *Era*, 22 February 1846.
25. *Journal des débats*, 31 May 1847.
26. *Era*, 14 September 1845.
27. *Era*, 21 December 1845.
28. *Journal des débats*, 15 December 1845.

25

The End of the Pillet Regime

One of Deldevez's shortcomings was that he could not take a joke, and his fellow musicians took full advantage of this failing. So when they heard he had been asked to compose the music for the next new ballet, *Paquita*, they teased him unmercifully, finding endless amusement by ruffling his temper with gloomy predictions of failure. His touchiness was perhaps understandable in this case, for he may have seen the commission, at least in part, as an act of contrition by the Director, Léon Pillet, who, as scenarist of the unfortunate *Eucharis*, had felt indebted to him for that ballet's failure.

This time, however, there was less risk involved in the ballet's plot, which was both straightforward and easy to follow, and enlivened with a generous dose of *couleur locale*, its action being set in Spain during the French occupation at the time of Napoleon. Its author was Paul Foucher, who had early come to notice collaborating with his brother-in-law, Victor Hugo, in writing the successful drama *Amy Robsart*, produced at the Odéon in 1829. *Paquita*, which would be his first venture in the field of ballet, certainly showed promise, in that its plot was straightforward and the chosen setting not only gave scope for a brilliant display of local colour, but also, daringly, set out to recreate the period of 1810 that to many might have seemed a little too recent to have acquired historical charm.

After the overture, the curtain was to rise to reveal a colourful scene in the Valley of the Bulls, near Saragossa. A tablet is to be dedicated to the memory of the French General d'Hervilly's brother, who had been assassinated there by bandits seventeen years before. The General (Monet) has plans to marry his son Lucien (Petipa) to the Spanish Governor's daughter Seraphina (Z. Pierson). To this, the Governor seems unenthusiastic, without, however, openly objecting. A band of gypsies, led by their chief, Inigo (Elie), arrives to enliven the festivity with their dances. Among them is Paquita (Grisi), whose blonde beauty is in sharp contrast to the swarthy complexions of her gypsy companions. She knows little of her origin, beyond a belief that a miniature portrait in her possession depicts her soldier father whom she has never known. After the dancing, Inigo orders her to hand round her tambourine to collect the bystanders' contributions. Displeased with the sum collected, he then orders her to repeat her dance. When she refuses, Lucien intervenes to protect her from being struck by the gypsy. He finds it difficult to believe that this fair-haired creature is a gypsy; she looks for her miniature to show it to him, only to discover that it has been stolen – clearly by Inigo, whom she accuses of the theft. Lucien wants him arrested, but the Spanish Governor intervenes. Paquita is happy to dance again for the handsome Lucien, and this dance brings the entertainment to a close. The Governor then invites the General and his party to dine with him that evening, explaining that he will follow them after attending to certain duties that he has to perform as mayor. The others having departed, the Governor gives the gypsy instructions to dispose of Lucien, whom he has no wish to see married to his daughter, and suggests using Paquita as bait. Inigo arranges for a posy to be delivered to Lucien, as if coming from Paquita, with a note giving instructions to find her dwelling.

The second act opens in the gypsy dwelling that is Paquita's lodging. Hearing a noise, she sees someone approaching, and hides. Inigo then enters with a masked individual, whom Paquita is surprised to recognise as the Governor. In this way Paquita learns of the plot to murder Lucien, the deed to be carried out by two men who will enter through the fireplace, which is so constructed as to swivel on itself to provide a secret entrance. The Governor and Inigo become aware of Paquita's presence, but she assures them that she has only that moment come in. The Governor then leaves. To Paquita's surprise, Lucien now enters and produces the posy. Inigo, who is, of course, expecting him, invites him to share their meal, but Paquita, now aware of Inigo's evil intentions, changes the wine glasses when he is not looking so that it is he, not Lucien, who drinks the drugged wine. As Inigo loses consciousness, the stolen miniature drops from his hand onto the table. Paquita and Lucien then make their escape through the revolving fireplace.

The stage opens up for the final act to reveal a magnificent ballroom in the French General's residence, where the great ball is to take place. To everyone's surprise, while the dancing is at its height, Lucien appears with Paquita and recounts how she has just saved his life. Seeing the Governor among the guests, Paquita boldly denounces him as the instigator of the plot to murder Lucien, and he is arrested. Paquita then prepares to leave, for she feels awkward among such grand company, but her eye is caught by a portrait on the wall that is identical to that of her miniature. She is thus recognised as the daughter of Lucien's assassinated uncle, and on this happy note the ballet concludes with a brilliant display of dances in vogue at the time of the First Empire.

As the critic Fiorentino observed, it was 'a mimodrama in all its primitive naïveté'; but Carlotta Grisi's performance as Paquita and the lavishness of the production – 30,000 francs had been spent on the final ball scene alone – assured the ballet of a satisfactory success when it was first presented on 1 April 1846.[1]

If any risk had been taken, it lay in the choice of period for the ballet's setting. Fifteen years before, the ballet of *Manon Lescaut* had shown how the fashions of the not very distant past – in that instance, the eighteenth century – might appear ridiculously outdated two or three generations later. *Paquita* evoked a somewhat later period, the First Empire, which proved hardly more acceptable to the tastes of 1846 than did the *ancien régime* to those of 1830. 'The most deplorable slush then reigned in architecture, furniture and women's fashions,' commented Fiorentino, 'and all the efforts of Vernet, Gros, Charlet and their like could not instil poetry into those heavy, curtailed, graceless uniforms, which are still associated with so many great and noble memories.'[2] However, this view was not held by everyone – Janin, for one, finding 'this Empire in silk, satin and velvet, and the glitter of helmets and breast-plates ... not so ridiculous as some make out'.[3]

Carlotta's first entrance was carefully planned as a moment to remember. It certainly made a strong impression on the audience, and in particular on the anonymous critic of *La France musicale*, who wrote an ecstatic description of those opening minutes:

Fair-skinned and with the pride of a lily in a bed of buttercups, Paquita, whom fate has cast among these gypsies of the Peninsula, reveals her noble origin by a dignity that in its attitude is very patrician. While obeying Inigo's orders like a slave, she scornfully repels his coarse advances. For an instinct, supported by a medallion that Inigo has managed to steal from her, has led her to believe that she was not born for the shameful calling that she has been forced to follow. But being young, beautiful and carefree, yearning for a happier future does not trouble her for long, for dancing in the open air and the grace she scatters around her by the roadside are for Paquita more a pleasure than a profession. So the festival begins, and our pretty little gypsy, dazzled by the encouragement of her audience and a military splendour to which she is unaccustomed, darts through the air like a deer, seeming hardly to touch the ground with her quick little feet and their ankles of steel! Breathless but smiling, she obeys Inigo's order to solicit the generosity of her admiring audience, holding out her little tambourine. But like Esmeralda in the presence of Phoebe de Châteaupers, Paquita cannot look at Lucien without her heart fluttering with an emotion that is as gentle as it is violent. For his part, the young officer is greatly taken with the gypsy girl's grace. He rises to his feet, following her with his eyes and gestures, and when the brutal Inigo, discontented with the collection, attempts to strike the trembling girl, he separates them and, with an imperious gesture, grasps the arm that was about to strike her.[4]

Deldevez was very relieved that it was Mazilier, not Coralli, who was entrusted with the choreography. For Mazilier, he found, was very sensitive to his music, listening to it with great care and taking note of the composer's intentions before beginning to construct his choreography. As a result, changes and cuts during the period of rehearsal were reduced to a minimum.

The choreography did not, however, meet with unanimous acclaim. Charles Maurice, for example, had reservations. 'It is a pity,' he wrote,

> that his use of such brilliant resources smacks so much of the old school of choreography. More imagination in the art of distributing the *corps de ballet* and organising their movements on the stage would have made the *ensembles* more satisfying. Mazilier is lacking in new ideas. His own are clever but hackneyed, orthodox but not very prolific. One becomes aware that he has not been brought up in the old school and that his praiseworthy gifts were first exercised in the boulevard theatres. His real talent, such as it is, was displayed in the design of several *pas* in which he reveals that he was once a dancer, and is conversant with the tricks of the trade – a merit not to be scorned.[5]

The opening scene of the second act was entirely devoted to pantomime, giving Carlotta the opportunity to act out the story of how Paquita outwitted the gypsies who have come with intent to murder Lucien, by switching the glasses so that it is Inigo who drinks the drugged wine – thus enabling the lovers to make their escape in the nick of time before the would-be murderers appear to carry out their nefarious instructions. For Carlotta, this short scene was followed by a brief but very necessary respite, in which to recover her breath for the awesome demands of her final variation.

Immediately after her exit, the stage opened up to reveal the vast ballroom for the final scene, which began with three dances that gave Carlotta about ten minutes to recover her breath: a classical *contredanse* with, in the words of one observer, 'its *en avant deux* and its *ailes de pigeon*',[6] then a waltz with couples 'pirouetting like German tops', and, to 'crown this retrospective tableau of the gallantries of our parents' day', a gavotte.

It was at this point that Carlotta reappeared in the company of Lucien. Paquita is still resisting Lucien's pressure to marry him, for she is painfully aware of the difference in station that exists between the two of them. But just as she is slipping away to make her escape, her eye is caught by a portrait on the wall that is identical with that of her miniature. It shows Lucien's assassinated uncle, whom she now realises must be her father. Thus all obstacles are removed to her marrying Lucien, and the ballet concluded with an astonishing variation that electrified the audience by its technical daring.

This *pas*, in the words of Théophile Gautier, was 'daring and difficult beyond belief. There were some hops on the tip of the toe combined with a dazzlingly vivacious spin that caused both alarm and delight, for they seemed impossible to perform, even though repeated eight or ten times.'[7] Fiorentino was equally dazzled: for him it alone was 'worth all the rest of the ballet put together. It is but a variation lasting at most ten minutes [*sic*], but we have never seen anything more aerial, more vaporous or more rapid. It is a jumble of *ronds de jambe* and *emboîtés sur la pointe* which even the most experienced eye could not follow without becoming dazzled and dizzy.'[8] It sent the public into a paroxysm of delight, and at the first performance the applause continued undiminished for so long that she had to return twice before the footlights to acknowledge the ovation before the ballet was allowed to continue. Such was the complexity and difficulty of the *pointe* work which Mazilier had devised for her in this *pas* that when the moment came for her to disappear into the wings, she was heard to complain as she passed him: 'Oh *maître*, this *pointe* work is so painful!'[9] It only seemed unfortunate that the ballet did not end with this sensational display, for the temperature of the audience's response then noticeably diminished, because the waltz that brought the ballet to its conclusion, well-known in its day as *La Reine de Prusse*, was neither specially remarkable nor, to one observer, improved by Lucien Petipa, who was criticised for 'waltzing like a dancer, which is to say, very badly and awkwardly'.[10]

Quite apart from Carlotta's part, there was much to enjoy in *Paquita*. In the first act, which was full of Spanish and gypsy dancing, local colour abounded. The dances were full of character, particularly the *pas des manteaux*, a sort of *cachucha*, performed in the manner of the Viennese Children by dancers of the *corps de ballet*, half of them dressed in male attire and brandishing voluminous red cloaks with which they enveloped themselves and their partners. To Fiorentino this was the highlight of Mazilier's choreography. The *pas des éventails* was also skilfully arranged, although some thought that Mazilier had somewhat spoilt its effect by making the dancers hold their fans in one hand while playing castanets with the other, a combination that was all too obviously awkward.

The pastiche of a French ball under the Empire that occupied the final scene also included a *pas de deux* in which Adèle Dumilâtre's elegance was set off by the supple and vigorous movements of her partner, Adeline Plunkett. This had been inserted to celebrate Dumilâtre's return from Milan, where she had been dancing at the Scala. It had been originally planned that Carlotta would partner her, but the ballerina had had second thoughts. Since the proposed *pas* was to come at the end of the ballet, Carlotta wisely foresaw that she might find herself at a disadvantage, being exhausted by the exigencies of a most demanding rôle while her younger partner would still be quite fresh.

But in the final result the honours of the ballet were entirely hers. She looked ravishing in the gypsy costume she wore for the first act. 'See her,' exclaimed Fiorentino,

> skimming, like a bird in flight, over the enormous rock in the middle of the stage, and alighting, proud and breathless, in the midst of her companions. See her happily casting aside her striped mantilla and replying to Inigo's volcanic sighs with leaps and bounds, frantic pirouettes and disdainful *entrechats*. In the *pas des tambourines*, Mlle Grisi performed prodigies of lightness, elevation and *parcours;* in her last *écot* especially, she performs *temps de pointe* which bring forth thunders of applause.[11]

The theme for the *Queen of Prussia* waltz was only one of a number of popular contredanses and waltzes of the Empire period that Deldevez had introduced into the ball scene. His score was full of tripping melodies, but was generally found lacking in fire and originality. He was given the satisfaction, however, not only of seeing it tolerably well received, but of taking part in the actual performance. The ball scene reached its final climax with the chiming of midnight, and Mazilier, who was very anxious that this effect should not be spoilt, asked Deldevez if he would strike the hour himself. The composer agreed, but discovered that it was none too easy to keep in time. He went through an agony of nerves, fearing that inadvertently he might strike thirteen, but happily no such ill portent materialised and he was mightily relieved to find that the dismal prognostications of his fellow musicians were not realised.

In spite of its spectacle, *Paquita's* initial success was not maintained in the longer term. At the Opéra it achieved no more than forty performances before being dropped from the repertory five years later. Then, in the usual course of events, it would no doubt have disappeared; but as chance would have it, it was to be transplanted in a foreign city many hundreds of miles away and, with revisions made down the years, would survive – not in exactly the same form as that in which Carlotta had danced, but certainly with much of its original texture still intact. Its rescue was due to Lucien Petipa's younger brother, Marius, who was to dominate Russian ballet throughout one of its most glorious periods. On the occasion of his début in St Petersburg in 1847, he chose to appear in his brother's rôle in *Paquita*, which was revived for the occasion, no doubt with Mazilier's consent, by Frédéric Malavergne. Thereafter it would be regularly performed both in St Petersburg and Moscow, occasionally undergoing revisions by Marius

Petipa, the most notable being the addition, in 1881, of the now celebrated *grand pas* to music by Minkus.

* * * * * * *

On the very day of *Paquita's* first performance, the *Coureur des spectacles* reported that Sofia Fuoco was on her way to Paris. Not long before, Pillet had gone to Milan in search of a tenor, and had been so taken with this young ballerina one evening at the Scala that he forgot the purpose of his visit and engaged her instead. Shortly after her arrival in Paris, she began to prepare for her audition under the guidance of Mazilier. Then, after she had shown her capabilities in the intimacy of the Foyer de la Danse, the news began to seep through to the outside world that she possessed an astonishing and original talent. 'All the dancers are agreed,' Charles Maurice told his readers,

> on her brilliant use of what are called the *pointes*. Rumour has it that it will be in this area that the young dancer will make her mark. There is talk of three turns in this position, which have not been accomplished before now. It is one of the movements of which Mlle Fuoco alone possesses the secret. And, Good God! in Paris, however gracelessly she performs it, and however unattractive her features, nothing more will be needed than that.[12]

Sofia Fuoco was born in Milan, where her father earned his living as a painter. There she entered the ballet school of the Scala as a child of seven, well below the minimum age of admission laid down in the regulations. She had not even attained her tenth birthday when she made her first stage appearance, discarding her family name of Maria Brambilla in favour of that of Sofia Fuoco. She continued to make rapid progress, and after successfully taking over the part of a ballerina who had fallen ill, she was engaged as *prima ballerina assoluta* in 1843, when still only thirteen. Shortly before leaving for Paris in the summer of 1846, she had been given the signal honour of taking part in the only performance of the *Pas de Quatre* to be given outside London during Romantic times. Revived at the Scala by Marie Taglioni during the Carnival season of 1846, it was interpolated in a performance of *Le Diable à quatre* and danced by Fuoco, Carolina Galletti (later to be better known as Rosati), Carolina Vente and Taglioni herself.

For Fuoco's début in Paris a new ballet was quickly prepared. It was to be a balletic version of a comedy by Alexandre Duval, *La Jeunesse d'Henri V*,[13] but with the action transposed to the England of Charles I. Mazilier and Ambroise Thomas were entrusted with the choreography and the music respectively, and the services of no fewer than seven artists were called upon to design the scenery.

When the critics first saw this new ballet, presented under the title of *Betty*, on 10 July 1846, they were mostly of one mind in dismissing it as too heavily weighted by its action and difficult to follow without continual reference to the printed scenario. Briefly, the ballet was concerned with a scheme by the Duke of Rochester (E. Coralli), in connivance with the princess Catherine (Emarot), aimed at curing Prince Charles (L. Petipa) of a propensity for seeking amusement in low haunts. Rochester's suggestion that the Prince should accompany him on a visit to the Grand Admiral tavern is welcomed, and the two men set off in disguise. Betty (Fuoco) is the daughter of the landlord (Mazilier), and the Prince's page Edward (Maria), who is in love with her, is in the habit of visiting her in the disguise of a dancing master. After drinking and carousing with the sailors and their women, the Prince is presented with the bill. But Rochester has meanwhile slipped away, and the Prince, having no money on him, offers his watch as security. Seeing the royal arms engraved on it, the landlord takes the Prince to be a common thief and locks him up while he goes to fetch the patrol. However, with the aid of Betty and Edward, the Prince makes his escape and returns to the palace. Soon Betty and her father arrive to return the watch, the plot is disclosed and the ballet ends with the Prince having learnt his lesson and everyone implicated being forgiven.

In spite of the lavish production, and in particular a glittering set for the final ball scene, which was lit by eleven enormous crystal chandeliers and peopled by a host of richly costumed dancers and supers, each of whom might have stepped out of a canvas by Van Dyck, the ballet was not a success. Ambroise Thomas's score, which had been somewhat hurriedly composed, was adequate enough. The critic of *La France musicale* gave it a favourable mention, singling out for praise an English jig, a charming polka and the grand waltz at the end which had 'crowned Mlle Fuoco's triumph',[14] but Mazilier's choreography was generally considered somewhat uninspired.

As a result, the entire interest of the evening centred on Fuoco, and the fact that the audience received the ballet politely was a measure of her success. Gautier called it one of the most brilliant dance débuts he had seen for a long time. However, much of the ovation originated from the claque, whose behaviour disgusted Fiorentino and deceived Fuoco herself, to judge from her confused bows, with hand on heart, at the end of the ballet. '*Son tanto buoni!*' she was heard to murmur afterwards, blissfully unaware that many of the more vociferous section of the audience had been paid to applaud her.

Although in no way pretty, Fuoco's features were animated and piquant, and she smiled happily as she danced. The way she wore her hair, drawn back severely from her face in a sort of Chinese style, seemed to emphasise her naive and childlike air. Her body, too, was a little unformed, and her legs so unnaturally thin that it almost seemed that she had no calves. In Gautier's judgment, a little French coquetry would not have come amiss. While she may have been a little short of that, there could be no question that she had developed her skill on the *pointes* to a quite phenomenal degree, albeit at the expense of style in the broader sense. An interesting comment on her style was proffered by a correspondent of the London *Morning Post*, who recorded that 'though very far behind both, she occasionally, but only occasionally, reminds us of two dancers differing much in style – poor Fanny Bias and Flora Fabbri, but without the exquisite neatness of the first or the vigour and irresistible enthusiasm of the other.'[15]

However, the most perceptive assessment of her technique came from Théophile Gautier, who was also struck by her over-reliance on *pointe*-work. Regarding her as something of a passing phenomenon, he limited himself in his review to discussing just that particular aspect. 'Her *pointes* are particularly astonishing,' he recorded:

> She performs a complete *écot* without once lowering her heel to the ground. Her feet are like two steel arrows rebounding on a marble pavement. There is not a moment of softness, nor a quiver or tremor. That inflexible toe never betrays the light body it supports. It has been said of other dancers that they had wings and flew through the air in clouds of gauze. Mlle Fuoco flies too, but by skimming the ground on the tips of her toes, lively, nimble, and dazzlingly quick. Dancing, it will be said, does not consist exclusively of *pointes* and *tacquetés*. True, but since in everything that Mlle Fuoco did, we observed cleanness, polish and precision, which in dancing are what style is in poetry, we believe she also possesses the other qualities, no doubt to a lesser degree, but in sufficient measure.[16]

Although her personal success was not in doubt, it was clear that she still had much to learn. Perhaps in four or five years' time, thought Fiorentino, she might achieve true distinction, but at the moment her excessive reliance on *pointe* work would soon blunt the audience's initial astonishment. Indeed, it was solely as a technician that she was to be remembered in Paris, nicknamed there for her special prowess as '*la pointue*'. Much more had been expected of her, and the disappointment of the public was echoed in a verse sung in one of the New Year revues:

> *Cette Betty, vaille que vaille,*
> *Croit faire à l'Opéra grand feu;*
> *Mais j'ai peur que Fuoco ou feu,*
> *Ce ne soit qu'un fuoco de paille.*[17]

* * * * * * *

Carlotta's engagement was due to terminate at the end of 1846, and Pillet, not wishing to risk losing her, had wisely opened negotiations with her advisers for a new contract as early as the previous spring. Since she was already contracted to dance at the Apollo Theatre in Rome throughout January 1847, she required that her new engagement should commence on 1 February. She also stipulated that she should have three months' leave of absence in each year: a period between 15 April and 15 June which in no circumstances was to be denied her, and an additional month in the summer, at Pillet's choice. This new engagement was for two years, at an annual salary of 24,000 francs and seven guaranteed bonuses of 190 francs each month.

Towards the end of 1846, all energies of the Opéra were being concentrated on the production of a new opera by Rossini, *Robert Bruce*, and Carlotta, assuming a little too readily that her services would not be required before the end of the year, booked a place in the Marseilles diligence leaving Paris on 20 December. Unfortunately, Rosina Stoltz fell ill at the last moment, and, faced with the task of rearranging the programmes, Pillet asked Carlotta to defer her departure so as to give one more performance.

Her compliance with this request was the beginning of her misfortunes. Because her departure was postponed, she did not reach Marseilles until 3 January, only to discover that the next packet would not be leaving for another four days. Then the ship developed engine trouble and had to call at several ports on the way before finally arriving at its destination. Consequently, it was 17 January before Carlotta reached Rome, to be faced with the almost insoluble problem of how to honour her contract, which was for twelve performances, and be back in Paris by 1 February. To make matters worse, the manager of the Apollo refused to agree to her dancing on successive evenings. She then rather rashly threatened to leave Rome before she had danced the stipulated number of performances, to which he retaliated by complaining to the police department, which withheld her passport until her contract was honoured to the letter.

Only on 18 February was she permitted to leave Rome. After a terrible voyage, she disembarked at Marseilles in a state of utter exhaustion. Determined nonetheless to be in Paris as soon as possible, she purchased a carriage and sent a messenger on ahead to prepare the relays. Even then she did not arrive in the capital until the 26th, and so worn out that she needed several days' rest before she could reappear at the Opéra.

As a result of her delayed return and her neglect in not writing to inform Pillet of her misfortunes, the Opéra found itself in a serious difficulty, for it had planned to present her in a new ballet within a few weeks of her return. Rehearsals of this work, provisionally called *La Taïtienne,* were already in progress when she left for Rome, and during her absence they were continued, with Elina Roland standing in for her.

Carlotta assumed that Pillet would take an understanding view and overlook her breach of contract as a misfortune over which she had no control, and this he might well have done had she not claimed her salary for February. This was too much for Pillet, who refused to pay her for a month during which he had been unable to make use of her services. A law suit was commenced, which resulted in Carlotta being ordered to pay Pillet 10,000 francs damages, and Pillet's counterclaim that she should give up a month of her summer leave period being dismissed.

These proceedings had already been instituted when Carlotta told Pillet that she could not attend the rehearsals of the new ballet because of a knee injury, a fact that was confirmed when a doctor saw her on 17 April. Pillet, however, was convinced that this indisposition was just a caprice. He informed her that the rôle would be given to Adeline Plunkett, and refused to go back on his decision when she recovered.

As events turned out, Carlotta could congratulate herself on not being associated with *Ozaï,* as the ballet was to be finally called. The public was informed of this change of cast on the 20th, and just six days later, on 26 April 1847, the ballet had its first performance. For what was to be his last ballet, Jean Coralli had sought his inspiration in a novel called *La Jeune Indienne* by one Chamfort. The plot was a variation on a theme that was much in vogue in the latter half of the eighteenth century, that of the 'noble savage' – in this case set on the island of Tahiti and introducing the celebrated admiral and explorer, Bougainville. The ballet opens with a scene in Tahiti looking out over the sea. A shipwrecked naval officer, Surville (Desplaces), is here being tended in a concealed grotto by a native girl called Ozaï (Plunkett). He is, in fact, the nephew of the admiral, to whose daughter he had been engaged before being lost. But now, convinced that he will never see France and his fiancée again, he gives Ozaï a ring and swears fidelity to her. Surville, however, has returned to his grotto when a French man-of-war appears on the horizon, and a dinghy containing Bougainville (Elie) himself and an advance party of French sailors lands on the shore to take possession of the island in the name of the King of France. The sailors depart to make a reconnaissance, leaving the admiral dozing on the beach. Ozaï enters, and in her innocent curiosity at the sight of this picturesque visitor, picks up a rifle that is lying by his side. Inadvertently she presses the trigger; the admiral awakes, and his men come running in. Their alarm vanishes at finding their Admiral unharmed and in the presence of such a pretty girl; they begin to dance, and are soon instructing Ozaï in the steps of the hornpipe. But the time comes when they must return to the ship, and they entice Ozaï to accompany them. Surville, who has meanwhile been asleep in his cave, wakes to see the dinghy being rowed away with Ozaï on board, and, without a moment's hesitation, he plunges into the water to swim out to the ship.

The scene changes to on board the ship. Placed in a cabin to rest, Ozaï wakes to find herself surrounded by nautical instruments that excite her wonderment and curiosity. Here she soon finds a friend in the Admiral's Negro servant (E. Coralli). Surville is then spotted swimming towards the ship, but in a state of utter exhaustion. He is carried on board, and from his pocket there drops a miniature, which the Admiral is at first mystified to recognise as a portrait of his daughter.

In the second act, Surville has returned to France, where he is torn between his love for Mlle de Bougainville (Emarot) and the promise that he gave to Ozaï when there seemed no hope of his ever returning to his native land. In the final scene, a year has passed. Ozaï has come to realise that Surville is still deeply in love with the admiral's daughter, and when Bougainville, who has been ordered by the King to return to the South Seas, is on the point of setting sail, she puts on her native dress and – to the melody of a well-known song, *'Rendez-moi ma patrie'* – begs him to take her back to her native island, generously and sadly releasing Surville from his vow.

There was something naïve about this innocent, sentimental little ballet that Janin, for one, found rather pleasing, but the lamentable thinness of the plot could not be concealed. The second act was found to drag interminably,[18] relieved only by the brilliant backcloth for the final scene, showing a panorama of the waterfront of Marseille. In writing his review, Gautier was reminded of the fate of an earlier ballet on a savage subject, *Les Mohicans*, and summed up the production as an unfortunate idea that had not been very well realised.[19] His colleague Fiorentino was of much the same opinion; to him it seemed to have been composed on one of Coralli's off-days, for it was 'lacking in wit, imagination and taste'.[20]

The most interesting feature of *Ozaï* was the music, which was composed by Casimir Gide, a musician with a reputation that rested firmly on his scores for four of Fanny Elssler's most glittering successes. In his score Gide had inserted several borrowings to provide *airs parlants* that highlighted some of the mime passages. Among these, designed to accompany a scene on board ship in which Ozaï playfully encourages the young cabin boy, who was black, to put on the captain's tunic, was a song by Auguste-Mathieu Panseron, *'Petit blanc, mon bon frère'*. Another telling borrowing occurred at the dramatic moment in the final scene, when Ozaï presents herself in Tahitian costume as Bougainville is about to set sail from Marseille, and the melody of the well-known *Rendez-vous ma patrie, ou laissez-moi mourir* alerts the audience to the pathos of her sacrifice. Gide was also a practised hand in writing danceable music, as he displayed most effectively in the brilliant ball scene in the second act, in which he had inserted a veritable *pot-pourri* of waltzes, galops and polkas, which one critic foretold would quickly pass from the orchestra of the Opéra to those of the Château Rouge and the Bal Mabille.[21]

Adeline Plunkett had had to learn the part of Ozaï, her first creation, in less than a week, and had little enough time to absorb the character as fully as she would have wished; Janin noticed that she seemed ill at ease in those passages in which she had to portray the heroine's ingenuous surprise at the fruits of civilisation. Gautier, however, found that she played 'very intelligently, displaying much naivety and grace'. Her miming, he went on, 'is simple, expressive and intelligible. In the mirror scene she revealed a childish coquetry that was charming without seeming affected. She missed none of the effects of her rôle, and her dancing was, as always, crisp, supple and lively. Mlle Plunkett has greatly improved in elevation and her ability to cover the stage.'[22]

Although the absence of Carlotta Grisi was certainly felt, the failure of *Ozaï* was not the fault of Adeline Plunkett, who was rewarded a few weeks later by being allowed to appear in Carlotta's rôle in *Le Diable à quatre*. After ten performances, *Ozaï* was dropped from the repertory and forgotten.

* * * * * * *

Ozaï was to close a chapter in the history of the ballet in Paris from more than one perspective. It would be the last ballet to be set on stage by Jean Coralli, and also the last to be credited to that great master of Romantic stage design, Pierre Ciceri. And it was to prove the last ballet to be presented during the directorship of Léon Pillet, which was now approaching its end.

The retirement of Rosina Stoltz, on whom the devoted Pillet had misguidedly lavished too many of his projects, foreshadowed the premature termination of his management. In the summer of 1847, a year before his term was due to expire, he proposed – perhaps as a last resort – a partnership with Henry Duponchel and Nestor Roqueplan to manage the Opéra until 1 January 1858. In the event, differences arose and Pillet withdrew, leaving the other two to shoulder the responsibility for the Opéra and the deficit that had accumulated during the years of his management.

The prospect of a change in management at once gave rise to hopes of better things to come. 'It is probable,' hazarded Gautier, 'that the new management will be inaugurated by some spectacular ballet, the success of which will give them time to look round for a *prima donna* and an opera.'[23] Rumours began to spread that the new Directors were shortly to engage another choreographer. Albert's name was mentioned, then that of Jules Perrot, who for the past six years had produced a series of exceptionally brilliant ballets in London. The new Directors were clearly very conscious of the importance of improving the quality of the ballet, and one day in August Duponchel and Desplaces *père*, the *régisseur de la danse*, surveyed the *corps de ballet* in the Foyer de la Danse with a view to cutting out the dead wood. Of far more interest to the public, however, was the news that Fanny Cerrito and her husband, Arthur Saint-Léon, had been engaged to dance at the Opéra.

* * * * * * *

A change of direction and the engagement of the renowned Cerrito, one of the greatest luminaries in the firmament of the Romantic ballet, were enough to arouse the expectations of ballet-goers in those calm summer days of 1847. On the wider front, no one could then foresee the turbulence that within half a year was to overturn the monarchy of Louis-Philippe, which would be replaced by a short-lived republic and, not long afterwards, by the establishment of the second Napoleonic empire. However, the great vessel of the Opéra would weather these political storms virtually unscathed, and, for many years to come, the supremacy of its ballet would remain unchallenged.

In the historical perspective the term Romanticism was to be increasingly ascribed to those heady two decades that followed the celebrated 'battle of *Hernani*', when, in 1830, a band of committed young Romantics rowdily imposed a triumph at the Comédie-Française for Victor Hugo's drama against the stubborn opposition of the old-guard Classicists. In the artistic revolution that followed in its wake, ballet was to reveal itself a most potent force when touched by the wand of Romanticism. And now, in the summer of 1847, while it was not for man to foresee what the future held, there was certainly ground for confidence that the ballet, considered as a sister-art of opera in providing the repertory of Paris's most illustrious musical theatre, rested on the firmest of foundations.

NOTES

1. An indication of the ballet's success was the appearance of a parody at the Théâtre Beaumarchais in September, a ballet-vaudeville with the same title.
2. *Constitutionnel,* 7 April 1846.
3. *Journal des débats,* 6 April 1846.
4. *La France musicale,* 5 April 1846. The article is signed, rather tantalisingly, with the initials O.P.R.A. The reference to Esmeralda is to Hugo's classic novel, *Notre Dame de Paris.*
5. *Coureur des spectacles,* 3 April 1846.
6. *Ailes de pigeon* (literally, pigeon wings), known also as *'le pistolet'*, is defined by G.B.L. Wilson in his *Dictionary of Ballet* as 'a difficult step in which the dancer leaps off one leg, throwing the other forward. The legs beat, change and beat again, and the dancer lands on the leg he jumped from.' *En avant-deux* denotes two persons advancing, as in quadrilles. For a more technical definition of *ailes de pigeon*, see Charles d'Albert, *The Encyclopædia of Dancing* (London, 1913).
7. *Presse,* 6 April 1846. Guest, *Gautier,* 169.
8. *Constitutionnel,* 7 April 1846.
9. Deldevez, 35.
10. *Constitutionnel,* 7 April 1846.
11. *Constitutionnel,* 7 April 1846.
12. *Coureur des spectacles,* 24 June 1846.
13. *La Jeunesse d'Henri V,* comedy in 3 acts by Alexandre Duval, f.p. Théâtre Français, 9 June 1806.
14. *La France musicale,* 12 July 1846.
15. *Morning Post,* 20 July 1846.
16. *Presse,* 20 July 1846. Guest, *Gautier,* 176–7; Fr. ed., 195–7.
17. *Un veil abonné,* 178. This Betty, after a fashion, / thinks she can make a great stir at the Opéra; / but whether it be Fuoco or fire, I fear / it may be no more than a flash in the pan.
18. *Journal des débats,* 3 May 1847.
19. *Presse,* 3 May 1847.
20. *Constitutionnel,* 2 May 1847.
21. These were two of the most frequented centres of popular dancing in Paris at that time. The latter, run by the Mabille family, was an open-air dancing garden in the Allée des Veuves (now the Avenue Montaigne) and one of the places to go to see the *cancan.*
22. *Presse,* 3 May 1847. Guest, *Gautier,* 181; Fr. ed., 202.
23. *Presse,* 5 July 1847.

26

An Afterword

It should not be assumed that the point selected to bring the narrative of this volume to a close marks the end of what can justifiably be termed as the Romantic ballet in Paris. Periods in art history do not have clear-cut beginnings, nor do they end like reigns of monarchs on a precise and ascertainable date. They acquire their labels when historians survey them with hindsight, and a personal one at that, in an endeavour to distinguish them from what has gone before and to highlight certain aspects to explain those novel characteristics that bring a new vitality to the art under review. Romanticism, as it affected the ballet, is very much a case in point. Certainly, one can date its flowering with some degree of precision, to the creation by Marie Taglioni of those two truly seminal rôles, the Abbess in *Robert le Diable* and the Sylphide, respectively in 1831 and 1832. But when ballet should cease to be termed 'Romantic' is a different question, and indeed one to which it would be rash to hazard a hard and fast opinion. For movements in art do not vanish; they live on to inspire later generations of artists even if the heady enthusiasm that they originally generated has given way to a gentler attachment.

The years covered in this volume are those of Romanticism's initial and spectacular flowering at the Paris Opéra, where the productions of *La Sylphide* and *Giselle*, so indelibly associated with their original interpreters, Marie Taglioni and Carlotta Grisi, have ever since been unanimously hailed as seminal works in the choreographic art, and where Fanny Elssler revealed another aspect of Romanticism in her dazzling *Cachucha* that initiated the injection of a veritable stream of regional dances.

The account given in the pages of the present volume has reached its conclusion in the summer of 1847, but it must not be inferred that the ballet had reached a point when it was no longer 'Romantic'. The careers of some of its first exponents may have been coming to an end – Marie Taglioni, for example, retired from the stage in 1847, Fanny Elssler in 1851, Carlotta Grisi in 1853 – but the influence of Romanticism on the ballet was to endure, and indeed endures still to a certain extent, embedded knowingly or unknowingly in the psyche of everyone with a feeling for the arts.

Looking forward from the cutting-off date of this volume, there are dancers still to make their appearance at the Opéra who are to be counted among the generation that produced Taglioni, Elssler and Grisi. Most notable of these is Fanny Cerrito, one of the greatest ballerinas of the golden age, who danced more regularly than any other under the auspices of Jules Perrot in London and was featured in every one of the performances there of his legendary *Pas de Quatre*. Her Paris début is anxiously awaited at the point where this volume closes. Then there are those two slightly younger stars who would also appear in Paris in the 1850s: Carolina Rosati, who took over Lucile Grahn's part in the *Pas de Quatre* and was to create the rôle of Medora in Mazilier's *Le Corsaire*, and Amalia Ferraris, for whom in the same year, 1856, Mazilier staged *Les Elfes*. These two ballets taken together summed up the very spirit of Romantic ballet, with its emphases on *couleur locale* and the supernatural.

And we must surely count among ballerinas nurtured in the spirit of Romanticism the tragic figure of Emma Livry, who in 1858 made a sensational début in *La Sylphide*, no less. Marie Taglioni was tempted out of her retirement virtually to adopt the sixteen-year-old prodigy in that epoch-making role and singularly to honour her by producing a ballet for her, *Le Papillon*, to music by Offenbach, as well as settling in Paris to take charge of the perfection class at the Opéra throughout the 1860s. The 1850s – a decade that was to see the establishment of the Second Napoleonic Empire and the beginning of the modernisation of Paris under Haussmann – would continue to be distinguished by the brilliance of its ballet, following in the tradition set in the previous two decades, and guided still by such figures as Mazilier, Adolphe Adam, and Marie Taglioni. Another figure, who appeared briefly in the early years of the 1850s, was Arthur Saint-Léon, who produced several ballets before assuming the post of ballet-master to the Russian imperial theatres.

Still the links with the golden age continued. In 1860 Lucien Petipa, the first Albrecht in *Giselle*, was appointed first ballet-master in succession to Mazilier, and in 1863 Saint-Léon was to make the first of annual summer visits to Paris during which he staged a series of ballets culminating with *Néméa*, *La Source* and *Coppélia*. The last of these, which was to become by far the most frequently performed ballet on the Opéra stage, was produced only weeks before the outbreak of the Franco-German War of 1870–1. By then Romanticism as a movement was generally considered to be in decline, and the impetus it had given to the art of ballet had certainly begun to slacken. Not one of the ballets from its golden age then survived in Paris: even *Giselle* was dropped from the repertory in 1868, not to be revived until fifty-six years later almost fortuitously, thanks only to its having been retained in the repertory in distant St Petersburg.

By 1847 the brilliant flush of Romanticism that had burst forth so dramatically to give life and colour to the art of ballet for nearly two decades might to some have seemed at the point of waning. Taglioni and Elssler were approaching the end of their careers, and while Carlotta Grisi was still on the payroll of the Opéra, she too would leave the fold two years later to seek new laurels in distant St Petersburg. With the short-lived *Ozaï*, the veteran Jean Coralli had produced his last ballet. He would remain as titular first ballet-master for a few more years yet, but his creative output now lay behind him. For some years he had in fact been giving ground to his younger colleague, Joseph Mazilier, on whom the main burden of renewing the ballet repertory of the Opéra had fallen.

So when the Pillet regime crumbled in the summer of 1847, there was no cause for alarm that the tradition of the Paris ballet was under threat. Indeed, there were well-founded hopes that a reinvigoration might take place in the ballet with the engagement of Fanny Cerrito, the one great Romantic ballerina whom Paris was yet to see, and her husband, the multi-talented Arthur Saint-Léon. As the future would ultimately reveal, ballet would retain its vitality on the Opéra stage for many years yet. In fact, only after the disastrous war of 1870 did its standing alongside its sister-art of opera begin noticeably to diminish as the balance between opera and ballet began to swing in favour of opera. But in the summer of 1847, the point at which its story has been taken in these pages, ballet was energetically holding its own in Paris hardly less vigorously than it had in the golden years that were not long past.

The Romantic Ballet in Paris

Appendices A to E

Bibliography

Appendix A Ballets created at the Paris Opéra, June 1820 – September 18-

Abbreviations: B = Ballet; BF = Ballet faery; BFt = Ballet fantastique; BP = Ballet pantomime;
D = Divertissement; a = act(s); s = scene(s)

Date of first performance	Title of ballet	Description	Scenarist	Choreographer	Composer
19 June 1820	Clari, ou la Promesse de mariage	BP, 3a 5s		Milon	Kreutzer
18 Oct. 1820	Les Pages du duc de Vendôme	B, 1a		Aumer	Gyrowetz
15 June 1821	La Fête hongroise	D, 1 a		Aumer	Gyrowetz
18 Sept. 1822	Alfred le Grand	BP, 3a 5s		Aumer	Gallenberg,
3 Mar. 1823	Cendrillon	BF, 3 a 4s		Albert	Sor
1 Oct. 1823	Aline, reine de Golconde	BP, 3a 4s		Aumer	Dugazon
18 Dec. 1823	Le Page inconstant	BA, 3a 6s		Aumer, after Dauberval	Habeneck
20 Oct. 1824	Zémire et Azor	BF, 3a 6s		Deshayes	Schneitzhoeffer
29 May 1826	Mars et Vénus, ou les Filets de Vulcain	B, 4a 5s		J.B. Blache	Schneitzhoeffer
29 Jan. 1827	Astolphe et Joconde, ou les Coureurs d'aventures	BP, 2a		Aumer	Hérold
11 June 1827	Le Sicilien, ou l'Amour peintre	BP, 1a 2s		Anatole [Petit][1]	Sor, Schneitzhoeffe
19 Sept. 1827	La Somnambule, ou l'Arrivée d'un nouveau seigneur	BP 3a	[Scribe]	Aumer	Hérold
2 July 1828	Lydie	BP 1a		Aumer	Hérold
17 Nov. 1828	La Fille mal gardée	BP 2a 3s		Aumer, after Dauberval	Hérold
27 Apr. 1829	La Belle au bois dormant	BF 4a 6s	Scribe	Aumer	Hérold
3 May 1831	Manon Lescaut	BP 3a 5s	Scribe	Aumer[5]	Halévy
18 July 1831	L'Orgie	BP 3a 4s	Scribe	J. Coralli	Carafa
12 Mar. 1832	La Sylphide	BP 2a	[Nourrit]	F. Taglioni	Schneitzhoeffer
7 Nov. 1832	Nathalie, ou la Laitière suisse			F. Taglioni	Gyrowetz, Carafa
4 Dec. 1833	La Révolte au sérail	BF, 3a 4s		F.Taglioni	Labarre
15 Sept. 1834	La Tempête, ou l'Ile des génies	BF 2a 4s + Intro.	[Nourrit]	J. Coralli	Schneitzhoeffer
8 Apr. 1835	Brezilia, ou la Tribu des femmes	B 1a		F. Taglioni	Gallenberg

Scene designer	Costume designer	Principal dancers	A: Performance tally	B: Years in repertory
			A	B
Ciceri	Garneray	Bigottini; Albert	94	1820–31
Garneray	Garneray	Bigottini, Bias; Aumer	126	1820–33
		Anatole; Aumer, Paul	1	1821
Ciceri	Garneray?	Bigottini, Anatole; Albert	29	1822–26
Ciceri	Albert	Bigottini; Albert	111	1823–31
Ciceri		Bigottini, Noblet; Montjoie	45	1823–26
		Bigottini, Marinette; Ferdinand	44	1823–27
Ciceri,	A.E. Fragonard	Legallois; Montjoie	22	1824–27
Ciceri	Lecomte	Anatole, Noblet; Albert	138	1826–37
Ciceri	Lecomte	Anatole, Noblet, Montessu; Albert, Paul	52	1827–31
		Noblet; Albert, Ferdinand	6	1827
Ciceri	Lecomte	Montessu, Legallois; Ferdinand	120	1827–59
		Taglioni; Albert	5	1828
		Montessu; Marinette	75	1828–54
Ciceri, mechanical effects by Contant		Noblet, Montessu, Taglioni; Ferdinand	77	1829–40
Lecomte, Lami, Duponchel	Ferdinand	Montessu, Taglioni;	47	1830–32
Ciceri	Lami	Legallois, Julia; Mazilier	31	1831–32
Ciceri	Lami	Taglioni, Noblet; Mazilier	146	1832–60
Ciceri		Taglioni, Leroux; Mazilier	47	1832–40
Ciceri, Léger, Feuchères, Despléchin	Lormier, Duponchel	Taglioni, Leroux; Mazilier	81	1833–40
Ciceri, Séchan, Despléchin, Diéterle, Feuchères/C.	Boulanger	F. Elssler, Duvernay, Leroux; Mazilier	30	1834–38
Philastre, Cambon		Taglioni, Legallois, Leroux; Mazilier	5	1835

Date of first performance	Title of ballet	Description	Scenarist	Choreographer	Composer
12 Aug. 1835	L'Ile des pirates	BP 4a	[Nourrit]	Henry	Carlini, Gide
1 June 1836	Le Diable boiteux	BP 3a 10s	[Burat de Gurgy, Nourrit]	J. Coralli	Gide
21 Sept. 1836	La Fille du Danube	BP 2a 4s	[Desmares]	F. Taglioni	Adam
5 July 1837	Les Mohicans	B 2a	[Léon Halévy]	Guerra	Adam
16 Oct. 1837	La Chatte métamorphosée en femme	B 3a 7s	Duveyrier	J. Coralli	Montfort
5 May 1838	La Volière, ou les Oiseaux de Boccace	BP la	[Scribe]	T. Elssler	Gide
28 Jan. 1839	La Gipsy	BP 3a 5s	Saint-Georges	Mazilier	Benoist, Thomas, Marliani
24 June 1839	La Tarentule	BP 2a	[Scribe]	J. Coralli	Gide
23 Sept. 1840	Le Diable amoureux	BP 3a 8s	Saint-Georges	Mazilier	Benoist, Reber
28 June 1841	Giselle, ou les Wilis	BFt 2a	Gautier, Saint-Georges	J. Coralli, [Perrot]	Adam, Burgmüller
22 June 1842	La Jolie Fille de Gand	BP 3a 9s	Saint-Georges	Albert	Adam
17 July 1843	La Péri		Gautier	J. Coralli	Burgmüller
21 Feb. 1844	Lady Henriette, ou la Servante de Greenwich	BP 3a	Saint-Georges	Mazilier	Flotow, Burgmüller, Deldevez
7 Aug. 1844	Eucharis	BP 2a 3s	[Pillet]	J. Coralli	Deldevez
11 Aug. 1845	Le Diable à quatre	BP 2a 4s	de Leuven	Mazilier	Adam
1 Apr. 1846	Paquita	BP 2a 3 s	Foucher	Mazilier	Deldevez
10 July 1846	Betty	BP 2a		Mazilier	Thomas
26 Apr. 1847	Ozaï, ou l'Insulaire	BP 2a 6s		J. Coralli	Gide

Notes
1 One pas choreographed by Albert.
2 Choreography of pas danced by Marie Taglioni was by her father, Filippo Taglioni.

Scene designer	Costume designer	Principal dancers	A: Performance tally B: Years in repertory	
			A	B
Feuchères, Despléchin, Séchan, Philastre, Cambon	Lami	F. & T. Elssler, Mazilier, Montjoie	24	1835–38
Feuchères, Séchan, Diéterle; Philastre, Cambon		F. Elssler, Legallois, Leroux; Mazilier, Barrez	67	1836–40
Ciceri, Diéterle, Feuchères, Despléchin, Séchan		Taglioni, Legallois, Leroux; Mazilier	36	1836–44
Devoir, Pourchet Mazilier, Elie		N. Fitzjames; Guerra,	2	1837
Pourchet, Devoir, Philastre, Cambon		F. Elssler, Mazilier	16	1837–38
	Lormier	F. & T. Elssler; Mazilier, Dauty	4	1838
Philastre & Cambon	Lormier	F. & T. Elssler; Mazilier	42	1839–44
Séchan & Feuchères, Diéterle, Despléchin	Lormier	F. Elssler; Mazilier, Barrez	28	1839–46
Philastre & Cambon	Lormier	Leroux, N. Fitzjames, A. Dumilâtre, Noblet; Mazilier	52	1840–45
Ciceri	Lormier	Grisi, A. Dumilâtre; L. Petipa	465 to 2000	1841–
Ciceri, Philastre & Cambon	Lormier	Grisi, L. Fitzjames; L. Petipa	57	1842–48
Séchan, Diéterle, Philastre & Cambon	Lormier, d'Orschwiller	Grisi; L. Petipa	76	1843–53
Ciceri, Rubé	Lormier	A. Dumilâtre, Maria; L. Petipa	39	1844–47
Ciceri (act I), Séchan, Diéterle, Despléchin (act II)	Lormier	A. Dumilâtre, Maria; L. Petipa	6	1844
Ciceri, Séchan Diéterle	Lormier	Grisi, Maria; L. Petipa	105	1845–63
Philastre & Cambon, Diéterle, Séchan, Despléchin	Lormier, d'Orschwiller	Grisi; L. Petipa	40	1846–51
Ciceri, Rubé, Despléchin, Diéterle, Séchan, Philastre, Cambon	Lormier	Fuoco; L. Petipa	21	1846–47
Ciceri	Lormier	Plunkett; Desplaces	10	1847

Appendix B

Opera divertissements *produced at the Paris Opéra, July 1820 – September 1847*

Date of first performance	Title of opera	Composer
17 July 1820	*Aspasie et Périclès*	Daussoigne[-Méhul]
7 Feb. 1821	*La Mort du Tasse*	Manuel Garcia
3 May 1821	*Blanche de Provence*	Berton, Boïeldieu, Cherubini, Kreutzer, Paër
6 Feb. 1822	*Aladin*	Isouard, Benoncini
26 June 1822	*Florestan*	Manuel Garcia
16 Dec. 1822	*Sapho*	Reicha
11 June 1823	*Virginie*	Berton
5 Dec. 1823	*Vendôme en Espagne*	Auber, Boïeldieu, Hérold
31 Mar. 1824	*Ipsiboé*	Kreutzer
12 July 1824	*Les Deux Salem*	Daussoigne[-Méhul]
2 Mar. 1825	*La Belle au bois dormant*	Carafa
10 June 1825	*Pharamond*[1]	Boïeldieu, Berton, Kreutzer, Le Sueur
7 Dec. 1825	*Armide* (revival)	Gluck
27 Feb. 1826	*Olympie* (revival)	Spontini
9 Oct. 1826	*Le Siège de Corinthe*	Rossini
26 Mar. 1827	*Moïse*	Rossini
29 June 1827	*Macbeth*	Chélard
29 Feb. 1828	*La Muette de Portici*	Auber
3 Aug. 1829	*Guillaume Tell*	Rossini
15 Mar. 1830	*François Ier à Chambord*	de Gineste
13 Oct 1830	*Le Dieu et la Bayadère*	Auber
21 Nov. 1831	*Robert le Diable*	Meyerbeer
20 June 1832	*La Tentation*	Gide (ballet music), Halévy
27 Feb. 1833	*Gustave*	Auber
22 July 1833	*Ali Baba*	Cherubini[3]
10 Mar. 1834	*Don Juan*	Mozart
23 Feb. 1835	*La Juive*	Halévy
29 Feb. 1836	*Les Huguenots*	Meyerbeer
3 Mar. 1837	*Stradella*	Niedermeyer
5 Mar. 1838	*Guido et Ginevra*	Halévy
1 Apr. 1839	*Le Lac des fées*	Auber
6 Jan. 1840	*Le Drapier*	Halévy
10 Apr. 1840	*Les Martyrs*	Donizetti
2 Dec. 1840	*La Favorite*	Donizetti
7 June 1841	*Le Freischütz*	Weber[4]
22 Dec. 1841	*La Reine de Chypre*	Halévy
15 Mar. 1843	*Charles VI*	Halévy
13 Nov. 1843	*Dom Sébastien de Portugal*	Donizetti
2 Sep. 1844	*Othello*	Rossini[5]
6 Dec. 1844	*Marie Stuart*	Niedermeyer
17 Dec. 1845	*L'Etoile de Séville*	Balfe
20 Feb. 1846	*Lucia de Lammermoor*	Donizetti
3 June 1846	*David*	Mermet
29 June 1846	*L'Ame en* peine	Flotow
30 Dec. 1846	*Robert Bruce*	Rossini, arr. Niedermeyer

Notes
1 For the coronation of Charles X.
2 One *pas* choreographed by Albert.
3 Music for two *pas* in the ballet composed by Halévy.
4 Ballet music included *Invitation à la valse* and extracts from *Preciosa*.
5 Ballet music arranged by Benoist.

Choreographer	Principal dancers
P. Gardel	Bias, Anatole, Noblet, Paul; Paul
Milon	Bias, Anatole, Noblet, Paul; Albert, Paul, Ferdinand
P. Gardel, Milon	Bias, V. Hullin, Anatole; Paul, Coulon, Ferdinand
P. Gardel	Bigottini, Bias, Noblet; Paul, Ferdinand
P. Gardel, Milon	Bigottini, Bias, Montessu; Albert, Ferdinand
P. Gardel	Bias, Noblet, Montessu; Albert, Paul, Coulon
P. Gardel	Bias, Noblet, Montessu; Albert, Paul, Ferdinand
P. Gardel	Anatole, Noblet, Montessu; Albert, Paul, Coulon, Ferdinand
P. Gardel	Noblet, Montessu, Lacroix; Paul
P. Gardel	Anatole, Legallois, Lacroix; Albert
P. Gardel	Anatole, Noblet, Montessu; Albert, Paul, Coulon
P. Gardel	Legallois, Montessu; Paul, Coulon, Ferdinand
P. Gardel, Milon	Noblet, Montessu; Paul, Coulon
P. Gardel	Noblet, Legallois, Montessu; Albert, Paul, Ferdinand
P. Gardel	Noblet, Anatole, Montessu; Albert, Paul, Coulon
P. Gardel	Noblet, Legallois, Anatole, Montessu, Leroux; Albert, Coulon, Bournonville
P. Gardel	Noblet, Anatole, Montessu, Leroux; Albert, Paul, Ferdinand
Aumer	Legallois, Dupont, Dupuis, Leroux; Albert, Paul, Ferdinand (Noblet as Fenella)
Aumer[2]	Taglioni, Noblet, Legallois, Montessu; Albert, Paul
Aug. Vestris	Taglioni, Noblet; Paul
F. Taglioni	Taglioni, Noblet
F. Taglioni	Taglioni, Noblet, Legallois, Montessu, Leroux; Perrot
J. Coralli	Leroux, Duvernay; Mazilier, Montjoie, S. Mérante
F. Taglioni	Noblet, Montessu, Julia; Mazilier, Simon
J. Coralli	Noblet, Dupont, Legallois, Leroux; Perrot
J. Coralli	Noblet, Legallois, Julia; Montjoie, Simon
F. Taglioni	Noblet; Montessu
F. Taglioni	Montessu; Mazilier
J. Coralli	Dupont, L. Fitzjames, Leroux
Mazilier	Dupont, N. Fitzjames; Mazilier
J. Coralli	Noblet, Dupont, S. & A. Dumilâtre, Barrez
	L. & N. Fitzjames; E. Coralli
J. Coralli	Dupont, L. & N. Fitzjames, Blangy, Forster, S. Dumilâtre
Albert	Maria, Noblet, Dupont, Blangy, A. Dumilâtre
Mazilier	A. Dumilâtre, Maria; L. Petipa, A. Mabille
J. Coralli	A. & S. Dumilâtre, Maria; L. Petipa, A. Mabille
Mazilier	Leroux, S.Dumilâtre, Maria; A. Mabille
Albert	A. & S. Dumilâtre, Maria, Fleury; A. Mabille
Mazilier	Fabbri, S.Dumilâtre, A. Dumilâtre, A. Mabille, Hoguet-Vestris
J. Coralli	Maria, A. & S. Dumilâtre, Robert
J. Coralli	Maria, Plunkett, Robert
	Plunkett, Robert; L. Petipa; Hilariot
J. Coralli	Plunkett, Robert, A. Dumilâtre
J. Coralli	A. Dumilâtre, Plunkett; L. Petipa, Desplaces
Mazilier	A. Dumilâtre, Maria; L. Petipa, Desplaces

Appendix C

Principal dancers at the Paris Opéra, 1820 to October 1847

Female

Albert-Bellon, Elisa 1829, 1842–43
    d. Paris, 8 February 1892
Anatole, Mme (*née* Constance Gosselin) 1812–29
    b. 5 January 1794
Andreanova, Elena 1845
    b. 13 July 1816 (?); d. Auteuil, 26 October 1857
Augusta (Caroline Fuchs) 1835
    b. Munich, 17 September 1806; d. New York City, 17 February 1901
Aumer, Julie 1820–23
Bias, Fanny 1807–25
    b. 3 June 1789; d. 6 September 1825
Bigottini, Emilie 1801–23
    b. Toulouse, 16 April 1784; d. Paris, 28 April 1858
Blangy, Hermine 1835–42
    d. New York, before 1870
Brocard, Caroline 1818–29
Dumilâtre, Adèle 1840–48
    b. Paris, 30 June 1822; d. Paris, 4 May 1909
Dumilâtre, Sophie 1838–45
    b. Paris, 18 July 1819
Dupont, Mme Alexis (*née* Félicité Noblet) 1826–41
    b. Paris, 1 November 1807; d. Paris, 3 April 1877
Duvernay, Pauline 1831–36
    b. Paris, 1813; d. Mundford, Norfolk, 2 September 1894
Elie, Mme (*née* Louise Launer) 1810–35
Elssler, Fanny 1834–40
    b. Vienna, 23 June 1810; d. Vienna, 27 November 1884
Elssler, Therese 1834–40
    b. Vienna, 5 April 1808; d. Merano, 19 November 1878
Fabbri, Flora 1844–51
    b. Florence, 12 August 1820
Fitzjames, Louise 1832–46
    b. Paris, 10 December 1809
Fitzjames, Nathalie 1837–42
    b. 1819
Fjeldsted, Caroline 1843
    b. Copenhagen, 26 February 1821; d. Frederiksburg, nr. Copenhagen, 20 May 1881
Fleury, Louise (*née* Laurént) 1843–48
Forster, Caroline 1834–44
Fuoco, Sofia 1846–50
    b. Milan, 16 January 1830; d. Carate Lano, 4 June 1916
Gaillet, Marie 1805–26
    b. Toulouse, 1787
Grahn, Lucile 1839–40
    b. Copenhagen, 30 June 1819; d. Munich, 4 April 1907
Grisi, Carlotta 1841–49
    b. Visinida, 28 June 1819; d. nr. Geneva, 20 May 1899
Hullin, Joséphine 1828–29
    b. c. 1818; d. Paris, July 1838
Julia [de Varennes] 1823–38
    b. 25 March 1805; d. Paris, September 1849
Launer, Marinette (*née* Boissière) 1809–28
    b. Paris, 23 October 1789
Legallois, Amélie 1822–37
    b. Paris, 1 July 1801
Leroux, Pauline 1826–37, 1840–44
    b. Paris, 19 August 1809; d. 1891
Maria [Jacob] 1837–49
    b. c. 1818

Marquet, Delphine 1842–46
  b. Tours, 1824; d. Neuilly, 23 May 1878
Maywood, Augusta 1839–40
  b. 1825; d. Leopoldville (Lvov), 3 November 1876
Mercandotti, Maria 1821–22
Montessu, Pauline *(née* Paul) 1820–36
  b. 6 June 1803; d. Amiens, 1 August 1877
Nielsen, Augusta 1842
  b. Copenhagen, 20 February 1822; d. Copenhagen, 29 March 1902
Noblet, Lise 1818–41
  b. Paris, 24 November 1801; d. September 1852
Plunkett, Adeline 1845–52, 1855–57
  b. Brussels, 31 March 1824; d. Paris, 8 November 1910
Saint-Romain, Angelica 1829
Smirnova, Tatiana 1844
  b. 1821; d. 1871
Taglioni, Amalia *(née* Galster)1832, 1834
  b. 1801; d. Berlin, 23 December 1881
Taglioni, Marie 1827–37, 1840, 1844
  b. Stockholm, 23 April 1804; d. Marseille, 22 April 1884
Turczynowicz, Konstancja 1842
  b. 5 March 1818; d. 9 November 1880
Vaque-Moulin, Elise 1833
  b. Paris

Male
Albert (François Decombe) 1808–31, 1842–43
  b. Bordeaux, 4 April 1787; d. Fontainebleau, 19 July 1865
Aumer, Jean 1798–1809, 1820–31
  b. Strasbourg, 21 April 1774; d. Saint-Martin-en-Bosc, July 1833
Barrez, Jean-Baptiste 1821–41
  b. Paris, 28 November 1792; d. 27 November 1868
Bournonville, August 1826–28, 1834
  b. Copenhagen, 21 August 1805; d. Copenhagen, 30 November 1879
Carey, Edouard 1834–35, 1841
  b. c. 1816; d. after 1879
Coralli, Eugene 1834–70
Coulon, Antoine 1816–32
  b. 19 July 1796; d. 3 September 1849
Coustou, Guillaume 1836–39
  b. 1813; d. September 1839
Dauty, François 1838–70
  b. Toulon, 1808; d. Paris, 11 May 1871
Desplaces, Henri 1841–47
Elie, Georges 1817–48
  b. Paris, 15 October 1800; d. c. 1883
Ferdinand 1813–33
  b. Bordeaux, 3 November 1791; d. Bordeaux, 1837
Godefroy, Antoine
  b. 2 August 1775, d. 10 September 1829
Gosselin, Louis 1820–26
  b. Paris, 24 February 1800; d. 5 February 1860
Guerra, Antonio 1836–38
  b. Naples, 30 December 1810; d. Neuwaldegg bei Wien, 20 July 1846
Mabille, Auguste 1835–45
  b. Paris, 10 January 1815
Mabille, Charles 1839–40
  b. Paris, 16 May 1816; d. Paris, 18 February 1858
Mazilier, Joseph 1839–48
  b. Marseilles, 13 March 1801; d. Paris, 19 May 1868
Mérante, Simon 1808–32
  b. Paris, 8 March 1783
Milon, Louis 1790–1826
  b. Gravenchon, 18 April 1766; d. Neuilly, 26 November 1849
Montjoie, Louis 1808–42
  b. La Chaux-de-Fonds, Switzerland, 15 December 1790; d. Saint-Germain-en-Laye, May 1865

Paul, Antoine 1813–31
    b. Marseille, 7 December 1795; d. Anet, November 1871
Perrot, Jules 1830–35, 1849
    b. Lyon, 18 August 1810; d. Paramé, 18 August 1892
Petipa, Lucien 1839–62
    b. Marseille, 22 December 1815; d. Versailles, 7 July 1898
Simon, François[1] 1822–42
    b. Paris, 3 April 1800; d. Crécy-sur-Morin, December 1877
Taglioni, Paul 1827, 1832, 1834
    b. Vienna, 12 January 1808; d. Berlin, 6 January 1884

[1] Simon was nominated a member of the Legion of Honour on 10 June 1837. He seems to have been the first dancer to be admitted to the order. It was not, however, for his services to the dance that he was decorated, but as a Grenadier in the National Guard of Paris, 'for services rendered as a soldier preserving order'.

Appendix D

Ballets performed at the Théâtre de la Porte-Saint-Martin, 1820 – September 1847

First perf.	Title	Notes	Years in repertory	Number of perfs.
15 Sept. 1821	*L'Amour au village*	Ballet by J.B. Blache, revived by F.A. Blache. Cast included Alexis; Mlles Juliette, Pauline	1821	32
3 Feb. 1822	*Une Nuit de carnaval*	Masquerade in 2 acts by Télémaque, said to be 'after Taglioni'	1822	2
9 July 1822	*Le Sacrifice indien*	Pantomime in 3 acts by Louis Henry, music by Raimondi, Carafa, Carlini; settings by Ciceri. Cast included Mme Henry-Quériau, Louis Henry, Dufresne	1822	29
22 July 1822	*Agnès et Fitz-Henri*	Pantomime in 2 acts by Louis Henry. Cast included Louis Henry, Mme Henry-Quériau	1822	21
10 Sept. 1822	*La Fortune vient en dormant*	Pantomime in 3 acts by Louis Henry. Cast included Louis Henry, Mme Henry-Quériau	1822	30
27 May 1823	*Polichinel-Vampire*	Divertissement by F.A. Blache. For début of Charles Mazurier	1822–47	165
25 Sept. 1823	*La Laitière Suisse*	Ballet-pantomime in 2 acts arranged by Titus, music by Gyrowetz, settings by Ciceri. Cast included Pierre Aniel, Louise Pierson. Based on Filippo Taglioni's ballet of the same name	1823–24	44
12 Aug. 1824	*Jean-Jean*	Ballet-pantomime in 2 acts by F.A. Blache and Mazurier. Cast included Mazurier and Louise Pierson	1824–26	5
30 Dec. 1824	*Milon de Crotone*	Pantomime historique in 2 acts by F.A. Blache. Cast included Zélie Molard, Mathevet	1824–25	27
20 Jan. 1825	*Les Marchandes de modes*	Ballet-pantomime in 2 acts by Aniel. Revival of a work originally given at the Foire-Saint-Laurent in 1778. Cast included Mazurier	1825	16
16 Mar. 1825	*Jocko*	Melodrama, with choreography by F.A. Blache. Cast included Mazurier, Mazilier		over 100
8 Sept. 1825	*Lisbell*	Ballet in 2 acts by J. Coralli, music by Grossoni. Cast included Mazurier, Mazilier; Mimi Dupuis	1825	18
29 Oct. 1825		J.B. Hullin's pupils appear in *La Fille mal gardée*. Principal rôles by Mélanie Duval and Angelina, aged 6 and 5 respectively	1825	
24 Nov. 1825	*Les Ruses espagnoles*	Ballet comique in 2 acts by J. Coralli, music by Pâris. Cast included Mazilier; Florentine Dufour	1825	16

First perf.	Title	Notes	Years in repertory	Number of perfs.
28 Jan. 1826	*Monsieur de Pourceaugnac*	Ballet comique in 2 acts arranged after the piece by Molière, choreography by J. Coralli, music by A. Piccini with *intermèdes* by Lully. Cast included Mazurier, Mazilier; Mimi Dupuis	1826	30
9 May 1826	*Gulliver*	Ballet-pantomime in 2 scenes by J. Coralli, music by A. Piccini. Cast included Mazurier, Mazilier; Mimi Dupuis	1826–27	33
19 Aug. 1826	*Scaramouche*	Pantomime in 2 acts by Aniel, music by Chautagne. Cast included Parsloe; Mimi Dupuis	1826–27	33
19 Sept. 1826	*La Visite à Bedlam*	Ballet-pantomime in 2 scenes by J. Coralli, music by A. Piccini. Cast included Mazurier, Mazilier; Zélie Paul (formerly Molard)	1826–27	23
3 Feb. 1827	*Le Mariage de raison*	Ballet-pantomime in 3 scenes by J. Coralli, music by A. Piccini. Cast included Mazurier, Mazilier; Zélie Paul	1827	43
6 Oct. 1827	*La Neige*	Ballet-pantomime in 3 acts by J. Coralli, music by Chautagne and Ferrand. Cast included Mazurier, Mazilier; Mimi Dupuis, Zélie Paul	1827–28	47
18 Feb. 1828	*Les Hussards et les jeunes filles*	Ballet-pantomime in one act by J. Coralli. Cast included Mazilier	1828	20
9 June 1828	*Léocadie*	Ballet in 4 scenes by J. Coralli, music by Béancourt and Miller. Cast included Mazilier	1828–29	18
30 July 1828	*Les Artistes*	Ballet-pantomime in 2 acts by J. Coralli, music arranged by A. Piccini. Cast included Mazilier, Perrot; Aimée Gautier	1828-29	16
2 June 1835	*Les Amours de Faublas*	Ballet-pantomime in 3 acts and 4 scenes by Léon, music by A. Piccini and Darondeau. Cast included Martin, Isaac, Edouard and Gustave Carey, Rose Fourcisy, Mme Carey	1835	44
1 June 1838	*Capsali*	Ballet-pantomime in 3 acts	1838	3
9 Feb. 1841	*Les Jours gras aux enfers*	Divertissement by Marin. Cast included Laurençon; Mme Laurençon, Pauline Guichard, Mélanie Duval, Mlle Féli	1841	26
4 Apr. 1841	*La Nuit aux aventures*	Comic ballet by Gabriel Ravel	1841	16
8 May 1841	*Les Farfadets*	Ballet-fantastique in 3 acts, scenario by Cogniard brothers, choreography by Laurençon, music by Pilati	1841–45	78

First perf.	Title	Notes	Years in repertory	Number of perfs.
11 Sept. 1841	*La Foire de Beaucaire*	Comic ballet in 2 acts, scenario by Cogniard brothers, choreography by Laurençon, music arranged by Pilati, settings by Ciceri. Cast included Ratel, Léon Espinosa (*'le petit Espinosa Auriol-en-herbe'*, as the *Courrier des théâtres* called him), Laurençon; Mlles Féli, Mélanie Noblet, Louise Ropiquet, Mme Laurençon	1841–43	71
5 Dec. 1841	*Les Aragonais*	Divertissement by Laurençon	1841	3
17 Dec. 1841	*La Fête vénitienne*	Divertissement by Laurençon	1841	7
18 Dec. 1841	*Le Songe de Pygmalion*	Ballet in one act, scenario by Cogniard brothers, choreography by Laurençon, music by Pilati. Cast included Louise Ropiquet	1841–42	7
1 June 1842	*Le Fils mal gardé!*	Cast included Berthier, Grédelue; Mmes Laurençon, Richard, Mélanie Noblet, Adèle Pailliet, Clément, E. Nehr, Héloïse	1842–47	105
25 Nov.1843	*L'Ombre*	Ballet-pantomime in 2 acts, scenario by Cogniard brothers, choreography by Berthier, music by Pilati. Cast included Berthier, Grédelue; Mlles Camille, Mélanie Noblet	1843–47	50
17 Mar. 1844	*La Polka*	Divertissement in one act and 2 scenes by Cogniard brothers and Simonnin, music by Pilati	1844	17
15 June 1844	*Le Songe d'un nuit d'été*	Divertissement-ballet by Cogniard brothers and Simonnin, with Risley and his sons	1844-45	25
5 Aug. 1845	*Les Jeux d'Ilus*	Divertissement-ballet, with Risley and his sons	1845–46	36
20 Sept. 1845	*Les Moresques, ou la Chasse aux jeunes filles*	Divertissement-pantomime in 1 act by Ragaine	1845–47	49
10 Jan. 1846	*Trilby, ou le Lutin de la Chaumière*	Ballet in 2 acts and 5 scenes, scenario by Cogniard brothers, choreography by Ragaine, music by Pilati. Cast included Mlles Richard and Nehr	1846	44
14 Feb. 1847	*Le Carnaval du Diable*	Ballet-pantomime in one act by Ragaine	1847	26
19 Apr. 1847	*Le Démon de la forêt*	Ballet in 2 acts by Fenzl	1847	9

Appendix E

Dance activities at other Paris theatres, 1822 – 1847

Théâtre de L'Ambigu Comique
F.A. Blache was ballet-master at this theatre in 1827. James Sylvain made his Paris début here in July 1828.
20 Dec. 1828: *La Landwer*, pantomime in 1 act by F.A. Blache, music by Adrien.
7 Nov. 1829: *Cocambo*, divertissement-pantomime in 2 acts by F.A. Blache, music by Amédée after Lecomte. Cast included Gabriel Ravel and Anatole [Petit].

Théâtre des Bouffes-Parisiens
26 or 27 Mar. 1822: Amalia Brugnoli and Paolo Samengo dance a *pas* while passing through Paris on their way to London.

Cirque National
18 Sept. 1845: Moorish dancers and musicians.

Théâtre Français
30 Aug. 1836: Carlotta Grisi, making her first appearance on the Paris stage, and Jules Perrot dance in Mme Paradol's benefit performance.

Théâtre de la Gaîté
4 June 1822: *Le Petit Matelot*, ballet in 1 act by Lefebvre, based on the comic opera by Pigault-Lebrun.
29 Dec. 1823: Jules Perrot makes his Paris début in *Polichinelle avalé par la baleine*, for which Lefebvre arranged the mime scenes.
13 Aug. 1836: *Les Tribulations d'un barbier*, ballet-pantomime by Girel.

Théâtre Nautique
10 June 1834: *Les Ondines*, ballet-pantomime by Louis Henry, music by Struntz.
10 June 1834: *Guillaume Tell*, ballet-pantomime in 4 acts by Louis Henry, music by Struntz with extracts from the works of Pugni, Weigl, Gyrowetz, Gallenberg, Carlini. Cast included Louis and Achille Henry, Mlles Sismann, Bettoni, Petit, Lesage and Mme Mazilier. This was a revised version of the ballet of the same title, but with music by Gallenberg, f.p. San Carlo, Naples, 8 February 1809.
12 Aug. 1834: *Le Nouveau Robinson*, tableau comique in 1 act by F.A. Blache, music by Hanssens.
16 Oct. 1834: *Chao-Kang*, ballet-pantomime in 3 acts and an epilogue by Louis Henry, music by Carlini. Cast included Louis and Achille Henry, Gosselin; Mme Mazilier.
22 Nov. 1834: *La Dernière Heure d'un colonel*, tragic mime scene by Louis Henry. With Louis Henry and Harriet Smithson.

Théâtre du Palais-Royal
6 Mar. 1838: *L'Ile d'ébène*, divertissement-pantomime danced by Castelli troupe of child dancers.
16 Mar. 1838: *Les Sylphides*, ballet danced by Castelli troupe of child dancers.

Le Panorama-Dramatique
28 Sept. 1822: *Le Coq du village*, ballet-pantomime, scenario by Favart, choreography by Achille Renouzy, *dit* Ranuzzi, music by Darondeau. Cast included Mlle Chéza.
26 Dec. 1822: *L'Amour mendiant*, ballet-pantomime in 1 act, scenario by Cuvelier, choreography by Ranuzzi, music by Amédée. Cast included Mlle Chéza.

Théâtre de la Renaissance
23 Aug. 1839: *El Marco bomba, ou le Sergent fanfaron*, comic interlude interspersed with Spanish dances. Dancers: Maria Goze, Maria Fabiani and Señor Piatoli.
29 Feb. 1840: *Zingaro*, opera in 2 acts and 4 scenes, with dances arranged by Jules Perrot. Cast included Perrot and Carlotta Grisi.

Théâtre des Variétés
22 Aug. 1838: The Bayadères (Amani, Tilly, Soundiroun, Rhangoun, Veydoun).
4 July 1843: Dolores Serral, Mariano and Juan Camprubi, Manuela Garcia.

Théâtre du Vaudeville
20 Oct. 1841: Dolores Serral and Mariano Camprubi
16 Jan. 1847: Dolores Serral and Mariano Camprubi

Bibliography

Adam, Adolphe, *Souvenirs d'un musicien* (Paris, 1868)

Adice, G.Léopold, *Théorie de la gymnastique de la danse théâtrale* (Paris, 1859)

Anon., *Les Adieux à Mlle Taglioni* (Paris, 1837)

Anon., *Biographie des acteurs de Paris* (Paris, 1837)

Anon., *Galérie biographique des artistes dramatiques des théâtres royaux de Paris* (Paris, 1826)

Anon., *Galérie de la presse, de la litterature et des beaux arts* (Paris, 1841)

Anon., *Galérie des artistes dramatiques de Paris* (Paris, 1842)

Anon., *Galérie théâtrale,* (Paris, 1873)

Anon., *Grande Biographie dramatique* (Paris, 1824; supplement, (Paris, 1825)

Anon., *The Letters and Journal of Fanny Elssler* (New York, 1845)

Anon., *Petite Biographie dramatique* (Paris, 1821)

Allevy, M.A. *La Mise-en-scène en France dans le première moitié du dix-neuvième siècle* (Paris, 1938)

Apponyi, Count Rudolf, *Vingt-cinq ans à Paris* (Paris, 1913-26)

Arago, Jacques, *Mémoires d'un petit banc de l'Opéra* (Paris, 1844)

Augustin-Thierry, A. *Lola Montès* (Paris, 1936)

Bapst, Germain, *Essai sur l'histoire du théâtre* (Paris, 1893)

Barbier, Patrick, *A l'Opéra au temps de Rossini et de Balzac* (Paris, 1987)

Beaumont, Cyril, *The Ballet called 'Giselle'* (London, 1944)

— *Complete Book of Ballets* (London, 1937)

— *A Miscellany for Dancers* (London, 1934)

Binney, Edwin, *Les Ballets de Théophile Gautier* (Paris, 1965)

Blasis, Carlo, *The Code of Terpsichore* (London, 1830)

— *Manuel complet de la danse* (Paris, 1820)

Blessington, Lady, *The Idler in France* (London, 1841)

Boigne, Charles de, *Petits Mémoires de l'Opéra* (Paris, 1857)

Bord, Gustave, *Rosina Stoltz de l'Académie royale de musique* (Paris, 1909)

Borisoglevskii, M., *Materiali po istorii russkova baleta* (Leningrad, 1938-9)

Bournonville, August, *Lettres à la maison de son enfance*, edited by Nils Schiørring and Svend Kragh Jacobsen (Copenhagen, 1969-78)

— *Mit Theaterliv* (Copenhagen, 1848, 1865, 1877)

— *Reiseminder, Reflexioner og biographiske Skizzer* (Copenhagen, 1878)

Briffault, Eugène, *L'Opéra* (Paris, 1834)

Buguet, Henry and Heylli, Georges d', *Foyers et coulisses – Opéra* (Paris, 1875)

Castil-Blaze, *L'Académie impériale de musique* (Paris, 1855)

— *La Danse et les ballets depuis Bacchus jusqu'à Mlle Taglioni* (Paris, 1832)

Chaffee, George. *Three or Four Graces. Dance Index* (New York), III, 9-11, Sept.-Nov. 1944

Challamel (editor), *Album de l'Opéra*, (Paris, n.d.)

Chapman, John, *Jules Janin, Romantic Critic* (in *Rethinking the Sylph*, ed. Lynn Garafola, Hanover, NY 1997, 197-241)

— Silent Drama to Silent Dream. *Dance Chronicle* (New York), 11, 365-80

Chorley, H.F., *Thirty Years' Musical Recollections* (London, 1862)

Claqueur patenté, *Un Nouvelle biographie théâtrale* (Paris, 1826)

Claudin, G., *Mes Souvenirs* (Paris, 1884)

Dash, Comtesse, *Mémoires des autres* (Paris, 1896-97)

Delaforest, M.A., *Théâtre moderne: cours de littérature dramatique* (Paris, 1836)

Delarue, Alison, *Impresario 1840* (manuscript)

Deldevez, E.M.E., *Mes Mémoires* (Le Puy, 1890)

Deshayes, A.J.J., *Idées générales sur l'Académie de musique* (Paris, 1822)

Du Fayl, Ezvar, *Académie nationale de musique, 1671-1877* (Paris, 1878)

Duprez, Gilbert, *Souvenirs d'un chanteur* (Paris, 1880)

Ehrhard, Auguste, *Une Vie de danseuse: Fanny Elssler* (Paris, 1909)

Escudier, Léon, *Mes Souvenirs* (Paris, 1863)

Félix-Bouvier, *Une Danseuse de l'Opéra: la Bigottini* (Paris, 1909)

Fétis, *Biographie universelle des musiciens* (Paris, 1860-65)

Fischer, Carlos, *Les Costumes de l'Opéra* (Paris, 1931)

Fontenay, Adolphe Bréant de & Champeaux, Etienne de, *Annuaire dramatique* (Paris, 1845)

Gann, A., *La Genèse de la Péri* (in *Théophile Gautier: l'art et l'artiste* (Montpelier, 1983), 207-220)

Gautier, Théophile, *Gautier on Dance*, edited and translated by Ivor Guest (London, 1986); French edition, *Ecrits sur la danse* (Avignon, 1995)

— *Histoire du romanticisme* (Paris, 1874)

— *Peau de tigre* (Paris, 1866)

— *Poésies complètes* (Paris, 1845)

— *The Romantic Ballet in Paris as seen by Théophile Gautier* (trans. Cyril Beaumont (London, 1932)

— *Théâtre* (Paris, 1872)

Gautier, Théophile; Janin, Jules; Chasles, Philarète, *Les Beautés de l'Opéra* (Paris, 1845)

Géréon, Léonard de, *La Rampe et les coulisses* (Paris, 1922)

Ginisty, Paul, *Le Théâtre romantique* (Paris, 1922)

Gourret, Jean, *Ces Hommes qui ont fait l'Opéra* (Paris, 1984)

Guest, Ivor, *Ballet under Napoleon* (Alton, 2002)

— Dandies and Dancers. *Dance Perspectives*, 37 (New York, 1969)

— *Fanny Elssler* (London, 1970)

— *La Fille mal gardée* (London, 1960)

— *Gautier on Dance* (London, 1986), French edition, *Ecrits sur la danse* (Arles, 1995)

— *Jules Perrot, Master of the Romantic Ballet* (London, 1984)

— Pioneers of the Pointes. *Dance Gazette*, 201, 5-7

— *The Romantic Ballet in England* (London, 1954)

Hadamovsky, Franz, *Die Wiener Hoftheater (Stattstheater)*, vol. 2 *Die Wiener Hofoper (Staatsoper), 1811-1974* (Vienna, 1975)

Halévy, François, *Derniers souvenirs et portraits* (Paris, 1863)

Hammond, Sandra Noll. Clues to Ballet's Technical History from the Early Nineteenth Century Ballet Lesson. *Dance Research*, London, III, 1 (Autumn 1984), 53-66

— Searching for the Sylph. *Dance Research Journal*, New York, 19/2 (Winter 1987-8), 27-31

— *Windows into Romantic Ballet*, Proceedings of Society of Dance History Scholars (New York and Eugene, Oregon, 1997-98), 137-143 and 47-53

Heine, Heinrich, *Lutèce* (Paris, 1853)

— *Sämtliche Werke* (Munich, 1975)

Henry, Stuart, *French Essays and Profiles* (London & Toronto, 1922)

Hervey, Charles, *The Theatres of Paris* (Paris & London, 1846)

Jahrmärker, Manuela, *Die Balletpantomimen von Eugène Scribe* (*Meyerbeer-Studien*, 3, Paderborn, 1999)

Joinville, Prince de, *Vieux Souvenirs, 1818-1848* (Paris, 1894)

Joliment, T. de, *De la Nouvelle Salle de l'Opéra* (Paris, 1821)

Jouvin, B., *Hérold, sa vie et ses œuvres* (Paris, 1868)

Kahane, Martine, *Robert le Diable*: catalogue de l'exposition au Théâtre National de l'Opéra de Paris, 20 juin – 20 septembre 1985 (Paris, 1985)

Karsavina, Tamara, *Theatre Street* (London, 1930)

Kochno, *Le Ballet* (Paris, 1954)

Kragh-Jacobson, Svend and Krogh, Torben, *Den Kongelige Danske Ballet* (Copenhagen, 1953)

Krasovskaya, Vera, *Ruskii baletnii teatr ot vozniknovenia do seredni XIX goda* (Leningrad and Moscow, 1958)

Lajarte, Théodore de, *Bibliothèque musicale de l'Opéra* (Paris, 1878)

Lanchbery, John, and Guest, Ivor. The Scores of *La Fille mal gardée*. *Theatre Research*, vol. 3, 32-42, 121-34, 191-204

Lecomte, Louis-Henry. *Histoire des théâtres de Paris: le Panorama-Dramatique* (Paris, 1900)

— *Histoire des théâtres de Paris: La Renaissance* (Paris, 1905)

Léspès, Léo, *Les Mystères du Grand Opéra* (Paris, 1843)

Levinson, André, *Ballet romantique* (Paris, 1929)

— *Marie Taglioni* (Paris, 1929)
— *Meister des Balletts* (Berlin, 1923)
Lewinsky, Josef, *Vor den Koulissen* (Berlin, 1882)
Lifar, Serge, *Carlotta Grisi* (Paris, 1941)
— *La Danse* (Paris, 1938)
— *Giselle, apothéose du ballet romantique* (Paris, 1942)
— *Histoire du ballet russe* (Paris, 1950)
Louis, Maurice A.-L., *Danses populaires et ballets d'opéra* (Paris, 1965)
Louvenjoul, Vicomte de Spoelberch de, *Histoire des œuvres de Théophile Gautier* (Paris, 1887)
Lyonnet, Henry, *Dictionnaire des comédiens français* (Paris, 1904)
Maurice, Charles, *Histoire anecdotique du théâtre* (Paris, 1856)
Meglin, Joellen A. Behind the Veil of Terpsichore: an interesting reading of the *ballet fantastique* in France, 1831–41. *Dance Chronicle*, 27 (2004), 67–135, 313–408; 28 (2005), 67–142
— 'Sauvages'. Sex Roles, and Semiotics. *Dance Chronicle*, 23 (2000), 87–132, 275–320
Migel, Parmenia, *The Ballerinas: from the court of Louis XIV to Pavlova* (New York, 1972)
Mirecourt, Eugène, *Auber* (Paris, 1857)
Montmorency, Duc de, *Lettres sur l'Opéra (1840-42)* (Paris, 1921)
Moore, Lillian, *Artists of the Dance* (New York, 1938)
Neiiendam, Robert, *Lucile Grahn: en Skœbne i Dansen* (Copenhagen, 1963)
Noverre, Jean-Georges, *Lettres sur les arts imitateurs en general et sur la danse en particulier* (Paris & The Hague, 1807)
Oberzaucher-Schüller, Gunhild & Moeller, Hans, *Meyerbeer und der Tanz* (*Meyerbeer-Studien 2*, 215-49, Paderborn, 1998)
Pirchan, Emil: *Fanny Elssler* (Vienna, 1940)
Pitou, Spire, *The Paris Opéra: an encyclopedia of operas, ballets, composers and performers* (New York and Westport, CN, 1983-90)
Pougin, A., *Adolphe Adam* (Paris, 1877)
— *Hérold* (Paris, 1906)
Prod'homme, J.-G., *L'Opéra (1669-1925)* (Paris, 1925)
Q [Charles G. Rosenberg], *You Have Heard of Them* (New York, 1854)
Quicherat, L., *Théophile Gautier: His Life and Time* (London, 1948)
Raab, Riki, *Fanny Elssler: ein Weltfaszination* (Vienna, 1962)
Rivalta, Camillo, *Il Tramonto di una Diva: Sofia Fuoco* (Faenza, 1916)
Roberts, Jenifer, *Glass: The Strange History of the Lyne Stephens Fortune* (Chippenham, 2003)
Roqueplan, Nestor, *Les Coulisses de l'Opéra* (Paris, 1855)
Royer, Alphonse, *Histoire de l'Opéra* (Paris, 1875)

Saint-Léon, Arthur, *De l'Etat actuel de la danse* (Lisbon, 1856)

— *La Sténochorégraphie* (Paris, 1852)

Séchan Charles, *Souvenirs d'un homme de théâtre* (Paris, 1883)

Second, Albéric, *Les Petits Mystères de l'Opéra* (Paris, 1844)

Seymour, Bruce, *Lola Montez: a Life* (New Haven and London, 1996)

Scribe, Eugène, *Oeuvres complètes* (Paris,

Slonimsky, Yuri, *Giselle* (Leningrad, 1926)

— *Mastera baleta* (Leningrad, 1937)

— *Sylfida* (Leningrad, 1927)

— *Teatralnii Parizh 30-kh. godov,* in *Utrachennie illyuznii* (Leningrad, 1936)

Smith, Marian, *Ballet and Opera in the Age of 'Giselle'* (Princeton, NJ, 2000)

Soler, Andrés, *Biografia de la Terpsicore milanese Sofia Fuoco* (Madrid, 1850)

Soloviev, N.V.,Soloviev, N.V. *Maria Taglioni.* St Petersburg, 1912.

Tamvaco, Jean-Louis (editor), *Les Cancans de l'Opéra* (Paris, 2000)

Touchard-Lafosse, G., *Chroniques secrètes et galantes de l'Opéra* (Paris, 1846)

Travers, Seymour, *Catalogue of Nineteenth-Century French Parodies* (New York, 1941)

Vaillat, Léandre, *La Taglioni, ou la vie d'une danseuse* (Paris, 1942)

Van Aelbrouck, Jean-Philippe, *Dictionnaire des danseurs à Bruxelles de 1660 à 1830* (Liège, 1994)

[Vandam, A.D.], *An Englishman in Paris* (London, 1892)

Véron, Louis, *Mémoires d'un bourgeois de Paris* (Paris, 1853-5)

Vieil abonné, Un [Paul Mahalin], *Ces Demoiselles de l'Opéra* (Paris, 1887)

Vilain masque, Un, *Physiologie de l'Opéra, du Carnaval, du Cancan et de la Cachucha* (Paris, 1842)

Wagen, Edward (ed.), *Mrs Longfellow: Selected Letters and Journals* (London and Toronto, 1956)

Willis, Nathaniel Parker, *Pencillings by the Way* (London, 1835)

Winter, Marian Hannah, *Augusta Maywood, First American Ballerina* (New York, 1962)

— *Le Théâtre du merveilleux* (Paris, 1962)

— *The Pre-Romantic Ballet* (London, 1974)

XYX, *Almanach des spectacles* (Paris, 1819-24)

PERIODICALS AND NEWSPAPERS

PARIS
Actes Parlementaires de 1787 à 1860
La Caricature
La Caricature provisoire

Le Charivari
Le Constitutionnel
Le Corsaire
Coureur des spectacles
Courrier des théâtres
Le Diable boiteux
L'Entr'acte
Le Fanal
Le Figaro
La France musicale
Le Frondeur
Gazette des tribunaux
Gazette musicale de Paris
L'Incorruptible
Journal de Paris
Journal des débats
Journal des théâtres
Le Ménestrel
Le Mentor
La Mode
Le Monde dramatique
Le Monde universel
Musée Philipon
Le Pandore
La Presse

La Réunion
Revue de Paris
Revue et Gazette musicale de Paris
Le Siècle
La Silhouette
Le Tam-tam
La Sylphide

LYON
Le Lyonnais

LONDON
Le Courrier de l'Europe
Court Journal
Maestro
Morning Herald
Morning Post
New Satirist
Sunday Times
The Theatre
The Times
World of Fashion

BRUSSELS
L'Indépendance belge

Index